APPLICATION SOFTWARE WITH WordPerfect®, The TWIN™/1-2-3®, and dBase III Plus®

Dennis P. Curtin

IMPORTANT NOTICE: READ APPENDIX A BEFORE USING SOFTWARE THAT ACCOM-
PANIES THIS TEXT.

PRENTICE HALL
Englewood Cliffs, New Jersey, 07632

Library of Congress Cataloging-in-Publication Data

Curtin, Dennis, (date)
   Application software with WordPerfect, The TWIN/1,
2, 3 and dBase III Plus.

Includes index.
   1. Computer software. 2. WordPerfect (Computer
Program) 3. Twin (Computer Program) 4. MS-DOS
(Computer operating system) 5. Microcomputers.
I. Title.
QA76.754.C87 1988   005.36'5   87-36119
ISBN 0-13-039595-1
ISBN 0-13-039587-0 (pbk.)

 © 1988 by Prentice-Hall, Inc.
A Division of Simon & Schuster
Englewood Cliffs, New Jersey

Printed in the United States of America

10 9 8 7 6 5 4 3

ISBN 0-13-039587-0 {BK ONLY}
ISBN 0-13-039595-1 {BK/DSK PKG}

Prentice-Hall International (UK) Limited, *London*
Prentice-Hall of Australia Pty Limited, *Sydney*
Prentice Hall Canada Inc., *Toronto*
Prentice-Hall Hispanoamericana, S.A., *Mexico City*
Prentice-Hall of India Private Limited, *New Delhi*
Prentice-Hall of Japan, Inc., *Tokyo*
Simon & Schuster of Southeast Asia Pte. Ltd., *Singapore*
Editora Prentice-Hall do Brasil, Ltda., *Rio de Janeiro*

Contents

Preface   *vii*
Acknowledgments   *xv*
Roadmap   *xvii*

PART ONE   MICROCOMPUTER SYSTEMS   1

	Introduction *2*	
Topic 1-1	Information Processing and Applications Programs	*3*
Topic 1-2	The Microcomputer *7*	
Topic 1-3	Input Devices *17*	
Topic 1-4	Output Devices *23*	
Topic 1-5	External Storage Devices *34*	
Topic 1-6	Distribution Devices *44*	
Topic 1-7	Applications Software *51*	
Topic 1-8	Microcomputer Issues *63*	

PART TWO   THE OPERATING SYSTEM   71

	Introduction *72*
Topic 2-1	Getting Ready *78*
Topic 2-2	Loading DOS *80*
Topic 2-3	Changing Default Drives *83*
Topic 2-4	Listing Files on Disks *86*
Topic 2-5	Using Wildcards *93*
Topic 2-6	Formatting Data Disks *97*
Topic 2-7	Formatting System Disks *100*
Topic 2-8	Copying Files *102*
Topic 2-9	Duplicating Disks *105*
Topic 2-10	Comparing Disks *107*
Topic 2-11	Renaming Files *108*
Topic 2-12	Erasing Files *111*
Topic 2-13	Checking Disks *114*
Topic 2-14	Using Directories *116*
Topic 2-15	Creating Batch Files *123*
Topic 2-16	Displaying and Printing ASCII Text Files *127*

PART THREE   WORD PROCESSING APPLICATIONS   129

	Introduction *130*
Topic 3-1	Getting Loading the Program *132*
Topic 3-2	Entering, Saving, and Printing Documents *140*
Topic 3-3	Retrieving and Editing Documents *149*
Topic 3-4	Working with Blocks of Text *160*
Topic 3-5	Searching and Replacing *168*
Topic 3-6	Using the Spell Checker and Thesaurus *175*
Topic 3-7	Aligning and Hyphenating Text *182*

Topic 3-8   Emphasizing Text   *187*
Topic 3-9   Changing Page Layout   *194*
Topic 3-10   Tab Stops and Indents   *202*
Topic 3-11   Page Breaks, Page Numbers,
             and Headers and Footers   *210*
Topic 3-12   Merge Printing Form Letters   *217*
Topic 3-13   Merge Printing Labels and Envelopes   *227*
Topic 3-14   Drawing Lines   *232*
Topic 3-15   Entering Special Characters   *237*
Topic 3-16   Creating Newspaper-Style Columns   *240*
Topic 3-17   Entering Parallel-Style Columns   *245*
Topic 3-18   Creating and Using Macros   *249*
Topic 3-19   Using Math Functions   *254*
Topic 3-20   Creating Automatically Generated Lists   *263*
Topic 3-21   Entering Footnotes   *270*
Topic 3-22   Sorting Data   *275*
Topic 3-23   Creating an Outline   *283*
Topic 3-24   Superscripts and Subscripts   *288*
Topic 3-25   Changing Default Settings   *291*

PART FOUR   SPREADSHEET APPLICATIONS   297

Introduction   *298*
Topic 4-1   Getting Acquainted with Your Program   *306*
Topic 4-2   Entering Labels and Values and Saving Files   *319*
Topic 4-3   Entering Formulas and Functions   *327*
Topic 4-4   Retrieving and Editing Models   *343*
Topic 4-5   Printing Models   *349*
Topic 4-6   Changing a Model's Appearance   *355*
Topic 4-7   Copying and Moving Data   *368*
Topic 4-8   Using Absolute and Relative Cell References   *379*
Topic 4-9   Using Windows and Fixed Titles   *387*
Topic 4-10   Using Recalculation Methods   *393*
Topic 4-11   Using Lookup Tables   *398*
Topic 4-12   Using Data Tables   *404*
Topic 4-13   Using Date and Time Functions   *411*
Topic 4-14   Using Protection and Security   *415*
Topic 4-15   Combining and Extracting Files   *418*
Topic 4-16   Creating and Printing Graphs   *422*
Topic 4-17   Creating and Using Macros   *437*
Topic 4-18   Creating Menus   *444*
Topic 4-19   Using Data Management   *449*

PART FIVE   DATABASE MANAGEMENT APPLICATIONS   463

Introduction   *464*
Topic 5-1   Getting to Know Your Program   *470*
Topic 5-2   Defining a Database File   *480*
Topic 5-3   Entering Records   *492*
Topic 5-4   Displaying Records   *498*

Topic 5-5   Using Criteria to Display Records   *504*
Topic 5-6   Adding, Editing, and Deleting Records   *510*
Topic 5-7   Joining Database File   *520*
Topic 5-8   Sorting Records   *523*
Topic 5-9   Indexing Records   *526*
Topic 5-10   Making Calculations   *532*
Topic 5-11   Printing Reports   *534*
Topic 5-12   Restructuring the Database   *541*
Topic 5-13   Writing Programs   *543*

Appendix A   Software License Agreements   *549*
Appendix B   WordPerfect Quick Reference   *557*
Appendix C   The TWIN Quick Reference   *559*
Appendix D   dBase III Plus Quick Reference   *563*

Index   *575*

Preface

INTRODUCTION

An exciting revolution is going on in today's businesses and you are going to play an important role. Not too many years ago, most information in the office was processed on machines that were primarily mechanical in nature. Words were processed on manual or electric typewriters, numbers were processed on adding machines, lists were processed on index cards, and graphics were prepared on drafting tables. The revolution is the increasing computerization of these manual tasks.

When computers first became available in the early 1950's they were purchased only by large companies. The cost of operating these large, expensive, and complicated computers, called "main- frames," was too great to use them to solve problems and increase productivity at the individual employee or departmental levels. These companies used their computers for only the most important corporate-level tasks, like processing the payroll. All of this is changing now with the growing popularity of the smaller and less expensive microcomputer and a large variety of easy-to-use applications programs. Low-cost computers are now accessible to almost everyone in large corporations, small businesses, professional offices, and wherever else people think, create, organize or plan.

The microcomputer, also called personal or desktop computer, is rapidly becoming the standard word and information processing component in businesses large and small. The microcomputer is gaining in popularity, not only because of its low cost but also because of its flexibility. You can use a microcomputer to prepare a financial analysis; then to write, edit, and illustrate a report on the results of that analysis; and finally to send the final document over the telephone lines to an office half-way around the world. Because of this power and flexibility, the microcomputer will someday be as familiar to everyone in business as the telephone, typewriter, or calculator are today.

What does this revolution mean for you, one of the people who will be using this new breed of computer? For one thing, it means you will be able to do certain tasks faster and better—for instance, preparing business reports, and sending out hundreds, or even thousands of individually personalized form letters. It also means you can do work now that you could not have done before the arrival of microcomputers. For example, you can now create and print documents at your desk that rival the high- quality results obtained by professional printing services.

In many companies, the microcomputer is frequently used for word processing, financial analysis, and record keeping. This text presents an introduction to these subjects. The goal of this text is to introduce you to all of the possibilities of your computer regardless of the actual programs you are using. Once you have gained an understanding of the systems and procedures discussed in this text you will be able to stay up-to-date with new and changing technology and move easily from one program or computer to another.

HOW THIS TEXT IS ORGANIZED

This text is organized into five parts.

Part One, Systems, introduces you to microcomputer systems and is divided into eight topics. The first topic introduces you to information processing in the modern business office. The next five topics introduce you to the microcomputer and its input, output, storage and distribution devices. The final two topics introduce you to applications software and microcomputer issues.

Part Two, The Operating System, introduces you to operating systems and procedures for the PC- and MS-DOS operating system commands that you use to manage your files and applications program disks. If you complete all of the exercises in this part in the order in which they are presented, you will have a duplicate set of program disks (so you can put the originals in a safe place) and formatted data disks on which to store your own work.

Part Three, Word Processing Applications introduces you to the principles of word processing and the procedures you use with WordPerfect.

Part Four, Spreadsheet Applications introduces you to the principles of spreadsheets and the procedures you use with The Twin and Lotus 1-2-3.

Part Five, Database Management Applications introduces you to the principles of database management programs and the procedures you use with dBase III Plus.

All five parts of this text are organized into topics, each of which is a self-contained unit of study. Some exercises are based on the documents, spreadsheet models, or databases that you created in an earlier exercise. To complete the later exercise, you must first complete the exercise it is based on. A complete list of the exercises and the exercises on which they are based is given in the *Roadmap* below. Each Topic has the following elements:

- **Objectives** tell you what you should be able to accomplish when you have finished the topic.
- **Background** discusses the principles behind the procedures presented in the topic. You can either read these background sections before you go into the computer lab to practice the procedures or afterwards.
- **Exercises** are provided for each topic to show you how to use the procedures discussed in the topic on the program you are using. All together, the text contains 141 exercises. All topics (with the exception of Part One) have a step-by- step exercise that leads you keystroke by keystroke through the procedures. Many topics (with the exception of Part One) also additional exercises that introduce you to other procedures. Some of these additional exercises are step-by-step, and others only provide you with the basic commands and suggest an exercise that you can complete on your own.
- **Questions** at the end of each topic test your understanding of the principles and procedures that you just learned.

A NOTE TO THE STUDENT

This text is designed to help you understand how to use applications software on microcomputers. Using a microcomputer and applications software may seem complicated at first but it really is not. You can learn the basic skills you need to use an applications program in a few hours. As you begin to feel comfortable with the computer and your programs, you can build on these basic skills.

The best way to learn an applications program is to combine reading with hands-on learning. Begin by reading enough about the program to become familiar with its principles, then get some hands-on experience, and then read some more. Continue this cycle of reading and hands-on experience until you have mastered the program.

If you are anxious about this course, do not worry. Anxiety is a common feeling among people when they are first introduced to computers. This anxiety will pass after a very short time, and you will then be wondering why you ever experienced it in the first place. When beginning, avoid worrying about the large number of unfamiliar details you have to learn. Just keep in mind that all of these details really boil down to a few basic steps:

- How to insert a program disk into a disk drive. (This is rather like learning to put a record onto your turntable.)
- How to turn on the computer. In a few moments a display appears on your screen.
- How to move the cursor (a small bright "pointer" on the screen) so you can enter and edit information.
- How to make choices from a list of commands. This list, called a menu, displays choices you select to operate the program. For example, you can select commands that save or print your work.

After you grasp these basic procedures, you can increase your understanding through further study and practice.

COMPUTERS AND THE ENGLISH LANGUAGE

As you are introduced to applications programs and microcomputers, you will have occasion to talk to experienced users and read magazine articles and books on the subject. You will soon discover that a microcomputer's performance is far ahead of its language. There are two reasons for this, the variety of terms used to describe the same "thing," and the jargon that is widely used.

VARIETY

The basic computer terminology has not been used long enough to become standardized. Computer language is evolving almost daily, and as a result the same "thing" is frequently known under a variety of names. For example, the term "return key" is a carryover from typewriters, where it is primarily used to end lines of text, and return the print element to the left margin of the paper so you can type another line. When word processing on a microcomputer, this is frequently done for you automatically so IBM renamed the key the "**Enter** key" on their computers because it is also used to enter commands. As a result, the two expressions "**Return** key" and "**Enter** key" are both widely used to describe the same key. In this book we call this the **Return** key, not because its more descriptive, but because it is still the most widely used name for the key.

There are a number of other items that are described with more than one term. Table 1 lists just a few of the synonyms you will encounter most frequently.

TABLE 1
Computer Terminology

First	Second	Third	Fourth
Microcomputer	Personal computer	Desktop computer	
Display screen	Terminal	Monitor	Video Display
Internal memory	Main memory	User memory	Working storage
Software	Programs	Software programs	Software packages
Hard disk	Fixed disk	Rigid disk	Winchester drive
Return key	Enter key	Carriage return key	
Documentation	Manuals	Books	
Spreadsheet	Worksheet		

JARGON

Much of the language used to describe computers has its roots in the past when only scientists and engineers had to understand it. Now that we users have direct access to computers, we are also asked to understand some of this jargon. Why, you may wonder, are you asked to "boot" the computer instead of switch it on? At the moment, we are forced to deal with this jargon because it is widely used in books, manuals and magazines. For example, in computer jargon this textbook is the "documentation" for the course you are taking.

As in any other course, you should ask questions if you are confused or unsure about computer terms. Asking questions—lots of them—is still the best way to become familiar with, even excited about, computers. Never hesitate to ask "What do you mean?", or "What is that?"

WHAT YOU NEED TO USE THIS TEXT

To complete all of the exercises in this text, you need the following hardware, operating system, applications programs, and supplies. You will learn about each of these items in the following pages.

Hardware

[ ] *Computer*. An IBM PC, XT, AT, PS/2 or compatible computers with 2 floppy disk drives and at least 256K of memory for WordPerfect and dBase III Plus and 320K for The Twin.

[ ] *Display screen*. Any display screen will suffice for the exercise except for the graphics tutorials in Part Four. To display graphs with the Twin or Lotus 1-2-3, you need a graphics display.

[ ] *Printer*. Any printer will suffice for the exercises except for the graphics tutorials in Part Four. To print graphs with the Twin or Lotus 1-2-3, you need a dot-matrix printer capable of printing graphics.

Disks and Supplies

To complete the exercises in this text you need the disks and other supplies listed in the Checklist below. The underlined program disks are limited versions supplied by the publisher and are either enclosed in a disk folder at the back of the text or are available from your instructor. Before proceeding with the exercises in this text, use this checklist to determine the program and data disks that you need for each part. The disks shown in boldface type are available from the publisher of this text.

CHECKLIST
Disks and Supplies Needed for this Text

Part Two The Operating System
    [ ]   MS-DOS® 2.0 or later
    [ ]   PC-DOS® 2.0 or later.
    [ ]   Blank disks for backup copy of DOS.
    [ ]   Blank disks for backup copies of program disks used in Parts Three through Five.
    [ ]   Blank disks for your data files. One is needed for an original copy and one for a backup copy.
    [ ]   Labels for each disk (same number as disks).
    [ ]   Tape to cover the write-protect notches on each of the DOS and program disks.

Part Three Word Processing Applications Programs
[ ] **WordPerfect® 4.2 Educational Version program disk**.
[ ] WordPerfect® 4.2 full-featured Program, Speller, and Thesaurus disks.

Part Four Spreadsheet Applications Programs
[ ] **The TWIN Introductory version program disk.**
[ ] **The TWIN™ Educational version System Disks 1 and 2.**
[ ] The TWIN™ full-featured System Disks 1 and 2.
[ ] Lotus® 1-2-3® full-featured version System and PrintGraph^R disks.
[ ] Lotus® 1-2-3® Student Edition.

Part Five Database Applications Programs
[ ] **dBase III Plus® Educational Version System Disks #1 and #2.**
[ ] dBase III Plus® full-featured version.

NOTES ON THE SUPPLIED APPLICATIONS DISKS

The applications program disks supplied for use with this text are limited versions of popular business programs. To make them available at such low cost, they have been limited by their publishers so they do not include all features included with the versions you would actually use in business. Here are the major requirements to run these programs and the differences between the educational versions and the full-featured versions as they affect their use with this text.

WordPerfect

WordPerfect 4.2 is available in two versions, the full-featured version and the 50K educational version. (A more limited but fully compatible version, referred to as the 4K version, is also available from the publisher). The differences between the educational and full-featured versions are described in Table 2. These differences do affect the use of these versions with this text. For example, some print formats may not print correctly when using the educational version with some printers. Also, you cannot see the results of superscripting and subscripting characters. The exercises that you cannot complete with the educational version are indicated in the Roadmap.

TABLE 2
The WordPerfect Full-featured and Educational Versions

- Saved documents are limited to about 50,000 characters on the 50K version and 4,000 on the 4K version.
- Printed documents contain the notice *WPC at the end of every paragraph or every fifth line (50K) or randomly (4K). n
- Advanced printing features like superscripts and subscripts are not available.
- You can only print on a printer connected to LPT1.
- Files that you create on the 4K version are compatible with files created on the full-featured version. Files created on the 50K version cannot be retrieved on the full-featured version and vice versa.
- The dictionary and thesaurus contain only a few words.

The Twin

The Twin is available in three version, the regular full-featured version, and the introductory and educational versions. The only difference between the full-featured version and the educational version is the size of the spreadsheet. The educational version is limited to 64 columns and 256 rows and is otherwise fully compatible with the full-featured version.

Lotus 1-2-3

The Lotus 1-2-3 program is available in three versions, the full- featured Release 1A, Release 2, and the student edition. None of the differences between these versions affect their use with this text however, files created on the Student Edition are not compatible with the full-featured version.

dBase III Plus

dBase III is available in two versions, the full-featured version and the educational version (also called a sampler). The educational version is supplied on two disks and the only major difference between it and the full-featured version is that it is limited to twenty records. This difference does not affect their use with this text.

CONVENTIONS

This text uses the following conventions for keys (see Table 1), prompts, and commands.

TABLE 3
Key Conventions

Name	IBM Keyboard	This Text
Return or Enter	↵	**Return**
Caps lock	Caps Lock	**Caps Lock**
Control	Ctrl	**Ctrl**
Escape	Esc	**Esc**
Function keys	F1 through F10	**F1** through **F10**
Home	Home	**Home**
End	End	**End**
Page up	PgUp	**PgUp**
Page down	PgDn	**PgDn**
Delete	Del	**Del**
Backspace	←	**Backspace**
Insert	Ins	**Ins**
Print screen	PrtSc	**PrtSc**
Number lock	Num Lock	**Num Lock**
Scroll lock	Scroll Lock	**Scroll Lock**
Shift	⇧	**Shift**
Space bar	None	**Spacebar**
Alt	Alt	**Alt**
Left arrow	←	←
Right arrow	→	→
Down arrow	↓	↓
Up arrow	↑	↑
Tab	↦	**Tab**
Backtab	↤	**Backtab**
Hyphen or Minus sign	-	**Hyphen**
Underscore	–	**Underscore**
Gray+	+[a]	**Gray+**
Gray–	–[a]	**Gray–**

a The **Gray+** and **Gray** keys are the keys labeled + and – to the right of the numeric keypad.

Commands

■ Keys you press in sequence are separated by commas. For example, if you are to press **F8**, release it, and then press **Return**, the instructions read—**F8**, **Return**.

■ Keys you press simultaneously are separated by dashes. For example, if you are to hold down the **Ctrl** key while you press **F8**, the instructions read—**Ctrl-F8**.

Prompts

All prompts that appear on the screen are shown in italics. When a prompt appears, you have two choices; press a key to make a selection from a menu, or type a response and press **Return**. All keys you press, and all answers you type in response to prompts are shown in **boldface**.

Summary

Now that you have read about how keys and commands are presented, see if you can understand the following instructions.

To Delete a Word

1. Move cursor to beginning of word to be deleted.
2. Press **Ctrl-Backspace**.

To delete a word, the instructions tell you to move the cursor to the beginning of the word. You then hold down the **Ctrl** key while you press the **Backspace** key.

To Save the Document

1. Press **F10** to display the prompt *Document to be Saved:*.
2. Type **MEMO** and press **Return**.

To save the document you press **F10** and a prompt appears asking you for the name of the file you want to save. You type the file name and then press **Return** to complete the command.

Acknowledgments

No book is ever the result of the efforts of a single individual. Although the author accepts responsibility for the final results, he was greatly assisted during the development of this text by a number of others, all of whom have made contributions that are reflected in the final work. Dennis Hogan not only suggested to the author that he write this text, he also sketched the broad outline and goals for the project. Without this guidance, the author would not have attempted the project. Robert Fiske not only edited the manuscript but acted as a coauthor in many respects. He made significant improvements in both the manuscripts style and accuracy. Daphne Swabey made numerous comments that were incorporated into the manuscript and tested all tutorials for accuracy and completeness. Nancy Benjamin oversaw the production aspects of the books and performed miracles in getting it published in such a short time. Peggy Curtin handled all picture research and communications with computer companies. Michael Morin tested the spreadsheet part and made suggestions for improvements in accuracy that everyone else had missed.

The Roadmap

PART TWO The Operating System

Exercise	Title	Program	Prerequisite Exercises
1	Getting Acquainted with DOS	DOS 2.0 thru 3.3	None
2	Specifying Drives	DOS 2.0 thru 3.3	None
3	Listing Files	DOS 2.0 thru 3.3	None
4	Printing File Directories of Other Program Disks	DOS 2.0 thru 3.3	None
5	Using Wildcards	DOS 2.0 thru 3.3	None
6	Using Wildcards to Display Additional Filenames	DOS 2.0 thru 3.3	None
7	Formatting a Data Disk	DOS 2.0 thru 3.3	None
8	Formatting Additional Data Disks	DOS 2.0 thru 3.3	7
9	Formatting a System Disk	DOS 2.0 thru 3.3	None
10	Formatting Additional System Disks	DOS 2.0 thru 3.3	9
11	Copying Files	DOS 2.0 thru 3.3	7
12	Copying Other Program Disk Files	DOS 2.0 thru 3.3	7, 11
13	Duplicating Disks	DOS 2.0 thru 3.3	7
14	Duplicating The Twin Introductory Version Disk	DOS 2.0 thru 3.3	None
15	Comparing Disks	DOS 2.0 thru 3.3	13
16	Comparing The Twin Original and Working Copy Disks	DOS 2.0 thru 3.3	14
17	Renaming Files	DOS 2.0 thru 3.3	13
18	Review of Renaming Files	DOS 2.0 thru 3.3	13
19	Erasing Files	DOS 2.0 thru 3.3	None
20	Review of Erasing Files	DOS 2.0 thru 3.3	13
21	Checking Disks	DOS 2.0 thru 3.3	None
22	Review of Checking Disks	DOS 2.0 thru 3.3	13
23	Using Directories	DOS 2.0 thru 3.3	7
24	Review of Using Directories	DOS 2.0 thru 3.3	None
25	Creating Batch Files	DOS 2.0 thru 3.3	11
26	Creating AUTOEXEC Batch Files for Other Program Disks	DOS 2.0 thru 3.3	12, 14
27	Displaying and Printing ASCII Text Files	DOS 2.0 thru 3.3	25

PART THREE Word Processing Application Programs

Exercise	Title	Program	Prerequisite Exercises
28	Getting Acquainted with WordPerfect	All versions	None
29	Displaying the Tab Ruler	All versions	None
30	Using Windows	All versions	None
31	Entering Text	All versions	None
32	Printing Files on the Disk	All versions	31
33	Using the Type-thru Mode	All versions	None
34	Retrieving and Editing Text	All versions	31
35	Using the Go To Command	All versions	31
36	Using the List Files Menu	All versions	31
37	Working with Blocks	All versions	None
38	Working with Predefined Blocks	All versions	None
39	Copying or Moving Blocks to their Own Files	All versions	None
40	Searching and Replacing	All versions	None
41	Using Wildcards	All versions	None
42	Searching for Formatting Codes	All versions	None
43	Checking Spelling	All versions	None
44	Looking up Synonyms	All versions	None
45	Counting Words	All versions	None
46	Aligning Text with Margins	All versions	None
47	Hyphenating Text	All versions	None (or 46)
48	Centering text in columns and aligning existing blocks of text	All versions	None
49	Using Boldfacing and Underlining	All versions	None
50	Editing and Deleting Formatting Codes	All versions	49
51	Using Redlining and Strikeout	All versions	None

Exercise	Title	Program	Prerequisite Exercises
52	Changing Page Layout	All versions	None
53	Changing Pitch	Full-featured version only	None
54	Entering Text to the Left of the Left Margin	All versions	None
55	Using Tab Stops	All versions	None
56	Indenting Paragraphs	All versions	None
57	Entering and Editing Headers and Footers	All versions	46 or 52
58	Previewing a Document	All versions	None
59	Printing Headers and Footers on Bound Documents	All versions	None
60	Merge Printing a Form Letter	All versions	Any 2 documents
61	Assembling Documents on the Screen	All versions	60
62	Merge Printing Labels	All versions	60
63	Merge Printing Envelopes	All versions	None
64	Drawing Lines	All versions	None
65	Using the Repeat Command	All versions	None
66	Entering Special Characters	All versions	None
67	Using ASCII Codes to Enter Special Characters	All versions	None
68	Creating Newspaper-Style Columns	All versions	None
69	Creating Parallel-Style Columns	All versions	None
70	Creating and Using Macros	All versions	None
71	Pausing a Macro for Keyboard Input	All versions	None
72	Using Math Functions	All versions	None
73	Creating a Table of Contents	All versions	None
74	Creating an Index	All versions	None
75	Creating a List	All versions	None
76	Entering Footnotes	All versions	None
77	Changing Footnote Options	All versions	76
78	Sorting Data	All versions	None
79	Sorting a Secondary File	All versions	60
80	Creating an Outline	All versions	None
81	Numbering Paragraphs	All versions	None
82	Entering Superscripts and Subscripts	Full-featured version only	None
83	Changing Your Display	All versions	None
84	Changing Default Settings	All versions	None

PART FOUR   Spreadsheet Application Programs

Exercise	Title	Program	Prerequisite Exercises
85	Loading and Setting Up The Twin	The TWIN, all versions	None
86	Loading Lotus 1-2-3	Lotus 1-2-3, all versions	None
87	Getting to Know Your Program	All Versions	None
88	Entering a College Budget	All Versions	None
89	Entering a Series of Numbers	Not The TWIN Intro. version	None
90	Using Ruled Lines and Borders	All Versions	None
91	Adding Formulas and Functions to the Budget Model	All Versions	88
92	Creating an Auto Loan Model	All Versions	None
93	Using Strings	Not Lotus 1-2-3 Release 2	None
94	Retrieving and Editing the Auto Loan Model	All Versions	92
95	Safely Inserting and Deleting Rows and Columns	All Versions	None
96	Printing a Model	All Versions	92, 94
97	Formatting the Auto Loan Model	All Versions	92, 94
98	Exploring Formats	All Versions	None
99	Using Data and Label Entry Spaces	Not Lotus 1-2-3 Release 2	None
100	Checking a Spreadsheet's Status	All Versions	None
101	Calculating Grade Point Averages	All Versions	None
102	Copying Formulas and Creating a Simple Graph	All Versions	None
103	Creating a Five-Year Plan	All Versions	None
104	Exploring Absolute and Relative Cell References	All Versions	None

Exercise	Title	Program	Prerequisite Exercises
105	Using Windows and Fixed Titles	All Versions	103
106	Formatting Cells Differently in Each Windows	Not The TWIN[1]	103
107	Changing Recalculation	All Versions[1]	None
108	Using a Lookup Table for Taxes	Not The TWIN Intro. version	None
109	Using Data Table 1	Not The TWIN Intro. version	92
110	Using Data Table 2	Not The TWIN Intro. version	92
111	Calculating Dates and Times	All Versions	None
112	Protecting Your Work	All Versions	103
113	Combining and Extracting Files	All Versions	103
114	Creating and Printing Graphs on The Twin	All Twin Versions	103
115	Creating Graphs on Lotus 1-2-3	All Lotus Versions	103
116	Printing Graphs on Lotus 1-2-3; Release 1A	Lotus 1-2-3 Release 1A	103, 115
117	Printing Graphs on Lotus 1-2-3; Release 2	Lotus 1-2-3 Release 2	103, 115
118	Creating a Macro that Enters a Label	Not The TWIN Intro. version	None
119	Creating a Macro that Widens Columns	Not The TWIN Intro. version	None
120	Printing a Model with a Macro	Not The TWIN Intro. version	Any Model
121	Creating a Macro that Automates the Five-year Plan Model	Not The TWIN Intro. version	103, 115 or 116
122	Exploring Data Management	Not The TWIN Intro. version	None
123	Creating a Database	Not The TWIN Intro. version	None

PART FIVE Database Management Application Programs

Exercise	Title	Program	Prerequisite Exercises
124	Getting Acquainted with dBASE III Plus	All Versions	None
125	Defining a Data File for Names and Addresses	All Versions	None
126	Defining a Data File for Amounts	All Versions	None
127	Entering Records in the NAMELIST File	All Versions	125
128	Entering Records in the AMOUNTS File	All Versions	126
129	Displaying Records in the NAMELIST File	All Versions	125
130	Displaying Records in the AMOUNTS File	All Versions	126
131	Using Criteria to Display Records in the NAMELIST File	All Versions	125
132	Using Criteria to Display Records in the AMOUNTS File	All Versions	126
133	Updating the NAMELIST File	All Versions	125
134	Updating the AMOUNTS File	All Versions	126
135	Joining Files	All Versions	125, 126, 133, 134
136	Sorting the NEWFILE1	All Versions	125, 126, 133, 134, 135
137	Indexing the NEWFILE1	All Versions	125, 126, 133, 134, 135
138	Calculating with Functions	All Versions	125, 126, 133, 134, 135
139	Printing Reports	All Versions	125, 126, 133, 134, 135
140	Modifying the Zip Code Field in the NAMELIST File	All Versions	125
141	Writing a Screen Display Program	All Versions	125, 126

[1]On The TWIN, natural recalculation does not calculate forward references.

MICROCOMPUTER SYSTEMS

PART

ONE

Topic 1-1   Information Processing and Application Programs

Topic 1-2   The Microcomputer

Topic 1-3   Input Devices

Topic 1-4   Output Devices

Topic 1-5   External Storage Devices

Topic 1-6   Distribution Devices

Topic 1-7   Application Software

Topic 1-8   Microcomputer Issues

This text is about applications software. In it, we describe several applications software programs and how you use them. But to use applications software, you must know a little about the microcomputer system of which they are only one part. Thus in Part 1, we introduce you to microcomputer systems, which consist of hardware and software.

HARDWARE

Hardware is the physical equipment you use, the parts you can touch, drop, and break. A **microcomputer** is the hardware component at the center of the system; it processes all the information you enter. Other hardware components connect to the microcomputer so that you can enter information and get the results back out of the computer. Typical components of this kind are the **keyboard, display screen**, and **printer**.

SOFTWARE

Microcomputers are general-purpose machines with many capabilities. The software programs you use determine their specific applications. This is what distinguishes microcomputers from single-purpose machines like typewriters or calculators. **Software** is the set of instructions, called a **program**, that is distributed on magnetic disks, much like movies are distributed on magnetic tapes. To use the program, you insert the disk into the computer, and then transfer the program from the disk into the computer's memory. The program tells the computer what to do and when to do it.

The computer is like an actor, and the program is like a script. When the actor changes scripts, he or she can perform a different role. By changing programs, you can make your computer perform different functions. For example, if you want to use your computer for word processing, you load a word processing program. If you want to use your computer for financial analysis, you load a spreadsheet or accounting program. If you want to file and manipulate information, you load a file or database management program. You need not learn programming to make the computer a valuable tool. Instead, you learn how to effectively use these applications programs.

SYSTEMS

A **system** is a set of related parts that operate together as a whole. You encounter systems every day. For example, your circulatory system moves blood through your body. This system contains your heart, lungs, blood vessels, and so on. These parts are all related and work together to distribute energy throughout your body. Your stereo is also a system. Its parts, like the turntable, amplifier, and speakers, work together so that you can hear music. A microcomputer system, like these other systems, is also composed of several interacting parts. The central element in the system is the **computer** itself. Connected to the computer are several related parts, or **peripherals**, that you use to get data into and out of the computer and to store data and programs. Finally, the element of the system that lets you use it is the software that you load. In Part 1, we introduce you to the parts of the computer system shown in Figure 1-1.

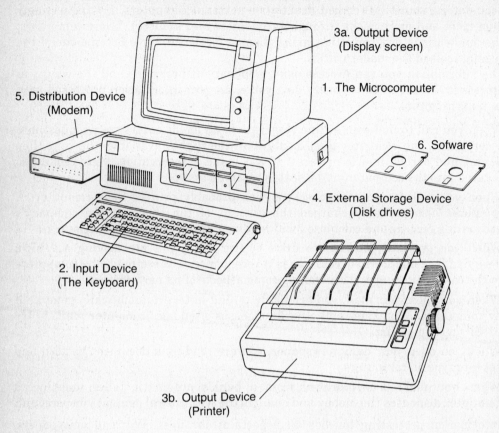

FIGURE 1-1
A typical computer system has the following elements:

1. The **microcomputer** performs all calculations and processes all data.

2. **Input devices**, like a keyboard, enter data into the computer.

3. **Output devices**, like (a) a display screen or (b) printer, get data out of the computer so that you can examine, analyze, edit, file, or distribute it to others.

4. **External storage devices**, like disk drives, store programs and data that you are not currently processing with the computer.

5. **Distribution devices**, like networks and modems, let you exchange information with other computers and users.

6. **Application software** are the instructions you load into the computer's memory to enable the computer to perform specific applications like word processing, financial analysis, or record keeping.

3a. Output Device (Display screen)

1. The Microcomputer

5. Distribution Device (Modem)

6. Sofware

4. External Storage Device (Disk drives)

2. Input Device (The Keyboard)

3b. Output Device (Printer)

TOPIC 1-1
Information Processing and Application Programs

In this topic, we introduce you to the use of application programs to process information. After finishing this topic, you will be able to

- Understand the concept of information processing
- Distinguish between the terms *word processing, number processing, data processing,* and *graphics processing*
- Name the applications programs used in each area of information processing

Information is the lifeblood of the modern office, factory, farm, professional office, and home. Without large amounts of information being distributed and consumed, our economy would quickly grind to a halt. Until the development of the computer in the 1950s, most information was processed by hand. Words were written by hand or typed on typewriters, numbers were written into large ledger books, and records were stored on forms and filed in cabinets. The development of the computer made it possible to automate many of these tasks and in the process eliminated many repetitive tasks from the daily workload. The development of the microcomputer in the 1970s and 1980s (Figures 1-2 and 1-3) has sped the automation of information processing. Microcomputers, sometimes called desktop or personal computers, are increasingly found on more and more desks throughout business and industry. These computers, and the applications programs that make them so powerful, have become one of the most useful tools in the modern office.

The information you can process using applications programs and the ways you can process it are vast. Almost every day, you encounter information processed with applications programs.

- When you call to make an airline reservation, an agent enters your request into a computer. The computer then displays all the flights available, the time they depart and arrive, and their fares. If you make a reservation, your request is entered into the computer, and a seat is reserved for you.

- When you pick up your paycheck, it was probably printed by a computer. A computer also probably charged the amount of the check to the company's accounting records and calculated withholding taxes and other deductions.

- When you get into your car to drive to the store, you are driving a vehicle designed by computers. If your car is a recent model, there might be computers in the car monitoring and controlling some aspects of its performance.

- When you open your mail, you are likely to find letters automatically generated by computers. Magazines and other businesses often use "computer mail" to try to sell you something.

- When you open your daily newspaper, you are reading a document written and set into type on computers.

- When you make a withdrawal from a bank's automatic teller machine, a computer dispenses the money and charges the withdrawal against your account.

Information processing touches all aspects of our lives. We read newspapers, magazines, and books created with the help of computers. The schools we attend maintain all of our records on computers. Computerized dating services help us find a mate. Employers pay us and promote us based on computer-processed information. In our retirement years, the government sends us social security checks processed on computers. If you were to list all of your activities in two columns, those influenced by information processing and those not, the activities not influenced by information processing would be the shorter column. This influence has happened within a very short period. In 1946, there was only one operational computer in the United States. Since then, the growth has been explosive. In 1980, there was 1 computer for every 160 Americans. By 1985, there was 1 for every 10.

As the field of information processing matured, specialty areas emerged. All information processed on computers falls into four broad classes: **words**, **numbers**, **data**, and **graphics**. The terms *words, numbers, data,* and *graphics* can be somewhat misleading because they overlap. Let us look a little more closely at what these terms mean.

FIGURE 1-2
The Apple II changed all of our lives by making an easy-to-use microcomputer widely available. Its success led to the introduction of many other microcomputers by many manufacturers. Apple's latest model, the Macintosh II, is shown here. (Courtesy of Apple Computer, Inc.)

FIGURE 1-3
The IBM PC was introduced in 1981 and was soon adopted by businesses as the industry standard. The standards it set are now followed by almost all other computer manufacturers. In 1987, IBM announced a new family of microcomputers, the Personal System 2, or PS/2™. The PS/2 Model 30 is shown here. (Courtesy of International Business Machines Corporation)

WORD PROCESSING

Words are the tools we use to communicate facts and ideas. The development of **word processing** applications programs made it possible to write, edit, and format text so that the appearance of documents could be controlled. Using these programs, you can enter any kind of data in almost any form. Word processing programs are **interactive**—that is, you can see data on the screen and easily copy it, move it, or change its appearance. A **document** prepared on a word processing program can include the body of the text (words), the date or other numbers, and even graphic symbols like bullets (• and ■) and lines.

NUMBER PROCESSING

Numbers are the tools of those who do analysis. Accountants, financial planners, engineers, sales managers, and many others analyze numbers every day. Deciding whether to buy or sell a stock, what job to take to earn tuition money, or whether to buy a new home or car is based on the analysis of numbers. The development of **spreadsheet** applications programs made the analysis of numbers faster and easier. By entering numbers and formulas into a spreadsheet, you can determine the monthly payment on a loan, the cost of a product, or your grade point average. Because spreadsheets are dynamic, you can change one or more of the numbers, and the spreadsheet program instantly displays a new result.

DATA PROCESSING

Data is the information used by people who need to discuss or decide something. For example, if you were running a small store, you could carefully record all items as they arrive from your suppliers and then record each item as it is sold. You could use these records to determine when to reorder more items and how many you should order.

When first developed, computers were primarily used to process data like this. Large computers and company **data processing** departments are still largely used for this purpose. They process payrolls, keep track of inventory and sales, and solve scientific and engineering problems. All these tasks require the computer to calculate numbers, sort entries into a designated order, and find a specific record when needed. **Database management** applications programs have been developed to perform these tasks on microcomputers. Often these programs display a form on the screen that you fill in to feed information, in the form of words, numbers, and even graphic images, into the computer.

GRAPHICS PROCESSING

Images are used to clarify ideas, illustrate points, design products, and entertain. Recently, it has become possible to create and manipulate images with the computer. Graphics applications programs have been developed that read images into the computer or that let you "paint" images on the screen. These images can then be manipulated, stored, printed, and distributed just like data and words. A graphic image prepared with one of these programs can include graphic symbols, numbers, and words. For example, you can create an outline map of the United States, label each location where your company has a branch office, and show the sales achieved by each office.

INFORMATION PROCESSING

As we have seen, words, numbers, data, and graphics processed on a computer can include words, numbers, and graphics. For this reason, word processing, number processing, data processing, and graphics processing refer less to the content than they do to the way the data is handled by the computer and the intent of the operator.

- People who process words focus on conveying ideas or preparing documents that can be read by others.
- People who process numbers are most interested in analyzing the quantitative aspects of issues or problems.
- People who process data focus on compiling and organizing data so that it can be analyzed and used for decision-making purposes.
- People who process graphics are most interested in obtaining images that illustrate ideas.

Since words, numbers, data, and graphics refer to distinct types of processing, the field needed a new term when computers became powerful enough to blur the distinctions among these four tasks. The term *information processing* includes not only word, number, data, and graphic processing but also all other forms of creating, recording, storing, retrieving, distributing, and analyzing information with computers.

Until recently, each area of information processing was a specialty, requiring training and expensive equipment. The development of the microcomputer and easy-to-use applications programs now make it possible for a single **user** to create, process, print, store, and distribute all this information.

QUESTIONS

1. List and describe the four types of information that need to be processed.
2. List the types of applications programs used to process each of the four types of information.
3. Describe information processing. How is it different from word, number, data, or graphics processing? How is it the same?
4. Briefly describe the difference between hardware and software.

TOPIC 1-2
The Microcomputer

In this topic, we introduce you to the microcomputer, the central component in a microcomputer system. After finishing this topic, you will be able to

- Explain the concepts behind the term *digital*
- Describe how information is stored and processed in a computer
- Explain how peripheral equipment, like printers, is attached to the computer
- Describe how accessory boards can be plugged into the computer to improve its performance
- List things to do and to avoid doing with your computer

A single concept, called digital processing, makes the computer possible. You may have heard this term used in connection with the music industry, where music is stored on compact discs in digital form. **Digital processing** simply refers to a way information, be it music, numbers, words, or images, is stored so that it can be processed and used. Before looking at the parts of the computer in detail, let us look at this basic concept.

Digital is derived from the word *digit*, which means a single number. When you write a check or count your change, you use the digits 0 through 9 either alone or, to convey larger numbers, in combination. For example, the digits 1 and 9 can convey $1 or $9, or they can be combined to convey $19, $91, $19.19, and so on. This numbering system, which uses the ten digits from 0 to 9, is called the **decimal system**. You use this system when you dial the phone, look up pages in the index of a book, or address a letter to a specific street address.

The decimal system is complicated. To master the system in grade school, you had to memorize tables. For example, to add 2 + 2, you do not calculate, you recall the answer 4 from memory. To multiply 3 x 2, you recall the answer 6 from memory. If you never learned the tables, or forgot them, you find it hard, or even impossible, to calculate with the decimal system.

Computers and other digital equipment use a simpler numbering system, the **binary system**. The binary system uses only two numbers, 0 and 1, to convey all numbers. As Table 1-1 shows, any number can be conveyed with these two digits.

TABLE 1-1
Decimal and Binary Equivalents

Decimal Number	Binary Equivalent
0	0
1	1
2	10
3	11
4	100
5	101
6	110
7	111
8	1000
9	1001
10	1010
11	1011

Because binary numbers are conveyed in a form unfamiliar to most of us, they look especially complicated, but they look more complicated than they are. Since binary numbers comprise only 0's and 1's, their major advantage is they can be processed in several ways with a variety of devices.

■ If you have a device that can be turned on and off, you can have on represent 1 and off represent 0.

■ If you have a device that can emit high or low voltages, you can have the high voltage represent 1 and the low voltage represent 0.

■ If you can align magnetic particles on a surface so that they point in opposite directions, you can have one direction represent 1 and the other direction represent 0.

■ If you can have dots on a display screen be either illuminated or dark, you can have a 1 tell the screen to illuminate a dot and a 0 tell the screen to leave a dot dark.

■ If you can have a printer print black spots onto a white sheet of paper, you can have a 1 tell the printer to print a black dot and a 0 tell the printer to leave a dot white.

All these techniques are used in microcomputers to store and process information. To take it one step further, you can convey information with these numbers if you have an agreed-on code. Let's now see how various devices and codes can be used to convey information.

PAUL REVERE'S RIDE—THE FIRST DIGITAL REVOLUTION?

You may have heard or read Longfellow's poem, *Paul Revere's Ride.* Here are a few stanzas of the poem.

> Listen, my children, and you shall hear
> Of the midnight ride of Paul Revere,
> On the eighteenth of April, in Seventy-five;
> Hardly a man is now alive
> Who remembers that famous day and year.
>
> He said to his friend, "If the British march
> By land or sea from the town tonight,
> Hang a lantern aloft in the belfry arch
> Of the North Church as a signal light,—
> One, if by land, and two, if by sea;
> And I on the opposite shore will be,
> Ready to ride and spread the alarm
> Through every Middlesex village and farm,
> For the country folk to be up and to arm."

This was a digital message. In case you have forgotten the story, Paul Revere was assigned the job of notifying the Minutemen who lived in the countryside if the British left Boston to attack them. He and his friend Robert Newman, the sexton of Old North Church, decided that Revere would wait on the other side of the harbor so that he had a head start should the British troops begin to move. Newman would remain in Boston to watch for any troop movements. Since Revere would be miles away, they needed a way for Newman to let him know the route the British were taking if they left Boston to attack. They decided Newman would light one lantern in the belfry of Old North Church if the British were leaving Boston by land and two lanterns if they were going by sea. This simple digital signal sent Paul Revere on his famous ride that resulted in "the shot heard round the world" at the bridge in Concord.

THE TELEGRAPH—THE FIRST DIGITAL CODE

Lanterns have their limits when it comes to sending information. It is hard to spell out messages. For example, if the British had been able to fly or take any other unexpected route, Paul Revere's prearranged code would not have been able to convey the message. This problem was solved by Samuel Morse who coincidentally lived on the same shore where Paul Revere stood when he saw the lantern's light in the Old North Church. Morse invented the telegraph in the early 1800s.

To send a telegraph message, a person taps on a key to transmit pulses of electricity down a wire to a distant listener. At the listener's end, a device called a sounder clicks when each pulse arrives. Like the lanterns in the belfry, this is a digital process. However, random clicks do not convey information, so Morse had to develop a code. He based the code on the pauses between the clicks, using a long pause and a short pause. When printed, these were represented as dots and dashes. An experimental telegraph line was constructed between Baltimore and Washington, and on May 24, 1844, a series of long and short pauses between clicks sent the historic message "What hath God wrought" down this first telegraph line.

THE TRANSISTOR—THE COMPUTER'S DIGITAL DEVICE

Like these early message systems, computers need a device that can send, process, or store information and a code to give the information meaning. Instead of lanterns or a key to send electrical pulses down a wire, a computer uses transistors. Like lanterns, transistors have only two possible states: on and off.

Recent advances have made it possible to pack thousands, even millions, of transistors on a single silicon chip (Figure 1-4). These chips store and process large amounts of information.

BITS AND BYTES—THE DIGITAL CODE

Instead of using a code of long and short pauses, as Morse did, a microcomputer uses the transistor's on and off states. The code is based on bits and groups of bits called bytes.

Bits

A transistor that is on is assigned the value 1, and a transistor that is off is assigned the value 0. These values are called **binary digits**, or **bits**.

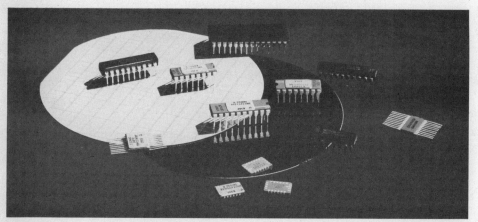

FIGURE 1-4
An integrated circuit is created on a wafer of silicon cut apart and mounted in a chip. The chip contains thousands of transistors. (Courtesy of The Computer Museum and Inmos Corporation)

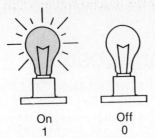

On
1

Off
0

To visualize a bit, imagine a light bulb (Figure 1-5). When the light bulb is on, it represents the number 1. When it is off, it represents the number 0. You could send a message to a nearby recipient by turning the bulb on and off, but to send even a short message would take a long time.

Bytes

Since bits are small units and can convey only two possible states, they are organized into larger units to convey more information. This larger unit is a **byte**, and it usually contains 8 bits.

To understand a byte, imagine using eight light bulbs instead of one. Each letter in the alphabet could easily be assigned a pattern of lights. For example, the pattern in Figure 1-6 could represent the letter *A*. By flashing agreed-on combinations one after another, you could quickly spell out a message.

Characters

By themselves, bytes are meaningless. Bytes must be assigned definitions. To have meaning, these definitions form a code. With 8 bits that can be either on (meaning 1) or off (meaning 0), there are 256 possible combinations. If all the bits are off, the byte reads 00000000. If all are on, the byte reads 11111111. These two numbers, and any in between like 10000000 or 11000000, can stand for anything the computer's designer wants them to stand for. They can represent characters, numbers, symbols, or commands to the computer

Usually, you see these numbers converted into **characters** like letters, numbers, and symbols displayed on the screen. To standardize the meaning of these number combinations, the computer industry has agreed on a code, the **A**merican **S**tandard **C**ode for **I**nformation **I**nterchange, or **ASCII** (pronounced AS-KEY).

Pressing any key on the keyboard generates a byte that is sent to the computer's central processing unit, which then interprets it as a character and displays that character on the screen. For example, if you press the letter *A*, the byte 01000001 is sent to the computer, and the letter *A* is displayed on the screen. Table 1-2 lists some typical characters and their ASCII numbers.

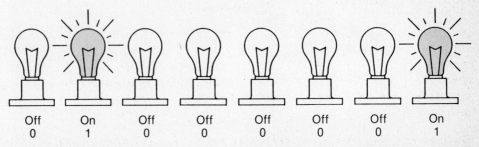

Off
0

On
1

Off
0

Off
0

Off
0

Off
0

Off
0

On
1

TABLE 1-2
ASCII Characters

Letters				Numbers and Symbols			
A	01000001	a	01100001	0	00110000	!	00100001
B	01000010	b	01100010	1	00110001	%	00100101
C	01000011	c	01100011	2	00110010	&	00100110
D	01000100	d	01100100	.	.		
E	01000101	e	01100101	.	.		
.	.	.		9	00111001	+	00101011
.	.	.					
.	.	.					
Z	01011010	z	01111010				

TABLE 1-3
Bytes, Kilobytes, and Megabytes

Bytes	Kilobytes	Megabytes
1		
1,000	1	
10,000	10	
100,000	100	
1,000,000	1,000	1
10,000,000	10,000	10

Kilobytes and Megabytes

Most references to a computer's memory, processing power, and storage capacity use the byte as a standard unit of measurement. But because the number of bytes can be quite large, they are usually expressed in shorthand (Table 1-3).

For example, you can say a computer's internal memory is 128,000 bytes or 128 kilobytes. **Kilobytes (KB)** indicate a magnitude of approximately 1,000 (actually 1,024). A computer with 512KB of memory can store 512,000 bytes. As memory increases, kilobytes are replaced by **megabytes (MB)**, which indicate a magnitude of approximately 1,000,000. For example, you can say a computer's memory is 1,000,000 bytes, 1,000 kilobytes, or 1 megabyte. As computer capacity expands, you will begin to encounter the next levels of magnitude, the **gigabyte (GB)**, or 1 billion bytes, and the **terabyte**, or 1 trillion bytes.

THE CENTRAL PROCESSING UNIT

The heart of a computer is the central processing unit (CPU). The CPU is a microprocessor—the device that made microcomputers possible in the first place. Though powerful, microprocessors are extremely small. They are similar to the silicon chips that store data but have advanced capabilities allowing them to process the information that flows through them. The microprocessor performs three key functions.

■ It coordinates all the computer's activities. For example, it retrieves files from the disk, interprets data and commands entered from the keyboard, and sends data to a printer.

- It performs arithmetic calculations like addition and subtraction. For example, if you enter a list of numbers in a spreadsheet and ask for the total, the microprocessor performs the addition.
- It performs logical operations using equal to, greater than, and less than comparisons. For example, it can determine if your grades are higher or lower than other students in the same course, and it can print a list ranking everyone in descending order of the grades they received.

One of the differences among microprocessors is the number of bits of information they can process at one time. A bit, as we have seen, is the basic unit of computer information. At the moment, microprocessors are available in 8-bit, 16-bit, and 32- bit versions. Generally, the more bits a microprocessor can process at one time, the faster and more powerful it is. Faster, more powerful microprocessors make it possible to run faster, more powerful programs.

MEMORY

When you load a program into the computer or enter data from the keyboard, it must be stored where the microprocessor can quickly find it. The computer stores the program or data in its internal memory. The two types of internal memory are read-only memory (ROM) and random-access memory (RAM). However, software makes it possible to create a third type, virtual memory.

Read-Only Memory (ROM)

Read-only memory (ROM) is static, unchanging memory. Your computer can read data stored in ROM, but you cannot enter data into ROM or change the data already there. The data in ROM is permanently recorded on memory chips by the computer's manufacturer. Neither turning the computer off nor electrical failure affects it; the data will still be there when you resume. ROM is generally used to store programs and instructions that the computer frequently needs. For example, it contains the instructions your computer follows to start up when you first turn it on.

Random-Access Memory (RAM)

Random-access memory (RAM) is also called **main, primary,** or **user memory**. When you load a program into the computer or create a document with an applications program, the program you load and the data you enter from the keyboard are temporarily stored in RAM. Usually, if you turn off the computer, any programs or data stored in this memory are lost; thus RAM is said to be **volatile memory**. The term *volatile* comes from the way the data in memory can be located, or accessed, by the computer.

One way to understand random access is to think of the differences between a tape player and a turntable. If you want to play the third song on a tape, you must advance the tape past the first two songs. This is called sequential access because you access each song sequentially. On a turntable, you can lower the needle onto the track where the third song begins without having to play the first two songs. This is called random access because you can access songs randomly.

Virtual Memory

Very large programs and very large files of data can strain the capacity of computers' memories. To solve this problem, many software designers store parts of their programs or data files outside RAM until needed. This type of storage, which is usually stored on a hard disk (see Topic 1-5), is called virtual memory. Although the programs or data are not actually stored in memory, they are treated as if they were. When the computer needs them, it moves something in memory that it does not then need to the disk to make memory available. It then moves the program or data from the disk into memory.

Buffers

While we are talking about memory, one other important aspect should be understood. Some programs allocate a small portion of the computer's random-access memory as a buffer. Buffers have several applications.

- Most users do not type on a typewriter fast enough to outrun it. However, these same people can occasionally type faster than a computer can process the input, especially when the CPU is busy performing other tasks. To keep you from having to stop typing, keyboards have **buffers**, small areas of memory where keystrokes are saved until the CPU is ready to accept them. If the buffer becomes full, the computer beeps, and any keys you press are not stored, so you must reenter them when the CPU empties the buffer.

- A **buffer** can temporarily save a record of the most recently used commands and deleted text so that the commands or deletions can be undone if you discover you made a mistake.

- A buffer, sometimes called a clipboard, is used as a storage area when you cut or copy text so that you can later retrieve it to insert elsewhere in your file.

- A print buffer, can store a file so that you can work on a new file while the previous one is being printed.

PORTS

A computer system is like a component stereo system where you use cables to connect a tape deck, turntable, and speakers to the main amplifier. The amplifier does not care what model turntable or tape deck is being connected as long as the right cables are used and they are plugged into the right sockets. The same is true of computers. The computer's external components, or peripherals, may include a printer, display screen, modem, keyboard, digitizing tablet, and mouse. You connect these peripherals to the computer with cables that plug into ports, sockets mounted on the computer's cabinet. Like a stereo system, if you use the right cable and connect it to the right socket, the peripheral will work with the computer. These sockets are called *ports* because, like seaports where ships enter and leave a country and airports where airplanes enter and leave a city, they are where information enters and leaves the computer. Generally, ports are on the back of the computer and are either serial or parallel.

Serial Ports

Serial ports (sometimes called **RS-232-C ports**) are where you attach **modems**, devices used to communicate with other computers (see Topic 1-6) and some types of printers.

When data is sent out a serial port, it is sent 1 bit at a time (Figure 1-7). Since the data is processed inside the computer 8, 16, or even 32 bits at a time, a serial port is like a narrowing on a highway at a construction site. Data slows down, just as the highway traffic does, so that it can funnel out of the computer in single file.

FIGURE 1-7
Serial ports are like
a single-lane tunnel.
Information fed to it
has to squeeze
through the port a
single bit at a time.
Here, the ASCII code
for the letter *A* is sent
1 bit at a time
through the port.

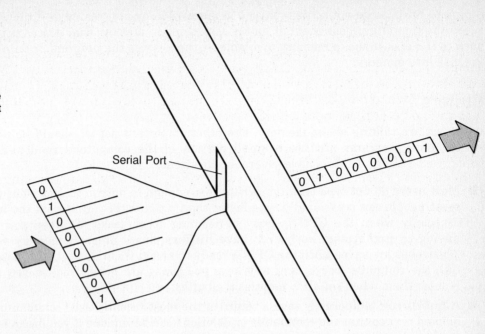

Serial Port

Parallel Ports

Parallel ports (sometimes called **centronics interfaces**) carry data 8 bits at a time on parallel paths (Figure 1-8). Because they can transmit data 8 bits, or 1 byte, at a time, they are a faster way for the computer to communicate with input and output devices. There is less narrowing than on a serial port, so traffic moves faster. Parallel ports are usually used to plug in certain types of printers.

EXPANSION SLOTS AND BOARDS

Many users like to customize their computers to better serve their needs. To make this possible, most computers have expansion slots into which you can plug boards

FIGURE 1-8
Parallel ports are
like tunnels with
almost the same
number of lanes as
the highway that
feeds them.
Information flows
through faster since
there is little or no
constriction.

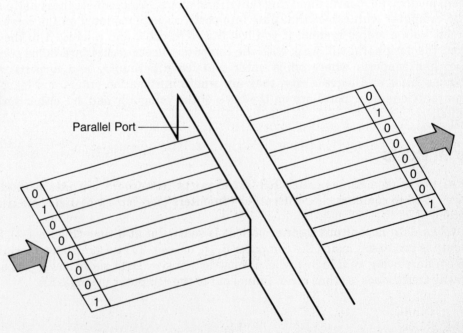

Parallel Port

that contain electronic components. These boards can serve several functions. Some boards expand the computer's memory, others allow the computer to display colors or graphics, and still others connect peripherals or are the peripherals themselves. For example, you can plug in a board that controls a hard disk drive (see Topic 1-5) located elsewhere in the system, or you can plug in a board that contains the hard disk drive itself. Computers that have these slots are said to have an open architecture, whereas those that do not have a closed architecture.

CARING FOR YOUR COMPUTER

Computers are rugged and will provide good service with minimal maintenance if you treat them properly. Here are a few important dos and don'ts that will ensure you get the maximum life out of your equipment.

DO turn down the screen intensity if you will not be working on the computer for a while so that an image is not burned into its phosphor surface.

DO use a surge protector, a device that you plug into an outlet and then plug the computer into. This device protects the computer from any surges of electricity that might come down the power line. Surges occur when the power company restores service after it has been lost or when a nearby line is struck by lightning. A surge temporarily increases the current in the line, much like a wave of water is created when you suddenly remove a dam from a river. This surge, or wave of current, can damage a computer.

DON'T get it wet.

DON'T use it during lightning storms. If fact, to be completely safe, unplug it when there is lightning.

DON'T drop it.

DON'T smoke around it.

DON'T leave it where it is exposed to direct sunlight.

DON'T turn the computer off more than is necessary. Computers, like other electronic equipment, are harmed more by the surge of power that runs through them when you first turn them on than they are by being left on all the time. Many users never turn their computers off; others turn them off only at the end of the day or on weekends.

DON'T use an ultrasonic humidifier without a mineral filter nearby the computer. These units break the water and minerals into small particles that are then distributed throughout the room. When the particles land on a computer, the water evaporates, leaving behind a powder that can damage sensitive equipment.

QUESTIONS

1. List the four components in a microcomputer. Briefly describe each.
2. What is the difference between a bit and a byte?
3. What is the name of the code used to assign characters to numbers or bytes in the computer?
4. Memory is measured in bytes, kilobytes, and megabytes. On the chart below, convert the bytes in column A into their equivalent kilobytes in column B and their equivalent megabytes in column C.

A	B	C
Bytes	Kilobytes	Megabytes
1,000	____KB	
10,000	____KB	
100,000	____KB	
1,000,000	____KB	____MB

5. Match the items in column A with their description in column B.

A

__ Central processing unit (CPU)
__ Expansion slots and boards
__ Memory
__ Ports

B

A. Storage for documents and programs
B. Used to attach peripherals like printers
C. Processes data and controls computer operations
D. Used to expand the computer's capabilities

6. List three functions performed by the computer's central processing unit (CPU).

7. Describe the differences between RAM and ROM.

8. Describe the function of a buffer. Briefly describe three applications for buffers.

9. What is the function of a port? List the two kinds of ports on a computer, and describe the basic difference between them.

10. What is the purpose of a computer's expansion slots? What can they be used for?

11. List four things you should never do with your computer.

12. List two things you should always do with your computer.

13. What is the name of the digital device used inside a computer to store and process information? When thousands of these are put together, what is the device called?

14. When you press a key on the keyboard, what does it send to the computer?

ACTIVITIES

1. Sketch one of the computers in the lab and label the ports that the peripherals are attached to. They probably are not labeled on the computer, so you may have to ask. Try to identify the following ports, and list what is attached to them:

   A. Parallel port
   B. Serial port
   C. Keyboard port
   D. Other ports

2. Find an advertisement for a computer that describes the computer in some detail. List the features it mentions the computer having, and briefly describe what each means.

3. List the kinds of computers in your lab. Who is the manufacturer of each? How much memory does each computer have?

4. List the kinds of printers in your lab. Are they parallel or serial printers?

TOPIC 1-3
Input Devices

In this topic, we introduce you to input devices, the devices you use to enter data into a computer. After finishing this topic, you will be able to

- Describe the keys on the computer's keyboard
- Explain how scanners work
- List the differences between scanners that read text and those that read images
- Explain why voice input to the computer has not yet been fully developed

All computers come with a keyboard, but there are also several other input devices available to enter data into your computer for processing. For example, you can scan text or images into your computer, or you can give it verbal instructions in special applications.

TEXT INPUT DEVICES

You usually enter data that you want to process by typing it on the computer's keyboard or scanning it in with a text scanner that can recognize characters. As you type or scan a document, the information is fed to the central processing unit and then either executed (if a command) or stored in memory (if data).

Keyboards

Keyboards vary in design and layout from computer to computer, but all have essentially the same types of keys. Figure 1-9 shows a typical computer keyboard although the names of the keys and their location vary somewhat from keyboard to keyboard. Many keys have an **autorepeat** feature; that is, if you hold down the key, it continues entering its character or repeating its function until you release the key.

The most common layout of the **alphabetic keys** is identical to the layout of the keys on a typewriter. There are also several other arrangements, such as the **Dvorak keyboard**, named after its developer, Dr. August Dvorak. Many people claim, and research studies support, that designs like Dvorak's are more efficient. These claims make sense. An accomplished pianist can hit as many as two thousand keys a minute, the equivalent of typing almost four hundred words a minute. Compare this to a typist who can rarely attain speeds of more than a hundred words a minute on a much smaller, easier-to-reach keyboard. The difference in speed is not caused by a difference in talent but by the inefficiency of the keyboard's design. However, despite its limitations, most people are familiar with the standard **QWERTY keyboard**, so called because those are the first six keys on the top row of letter keys. Other keyboards have not gained wide acceptance.

A person writing a software program (called a programmer) can assign any function he or she chooses to each of the keys on the keyboard. Therefore, the actual functions that each key performs vary from program to program. In general, here is what each of the keys does.

- Alphabetic keys are arranged on the keyboard just as they are on a typewriter. When you press them, they enter lowercase letters. If you hold down the **Shift** key when you press the letter keys, or if you engage the **Caps Lock** key, they enter uppercase (capital) letters.

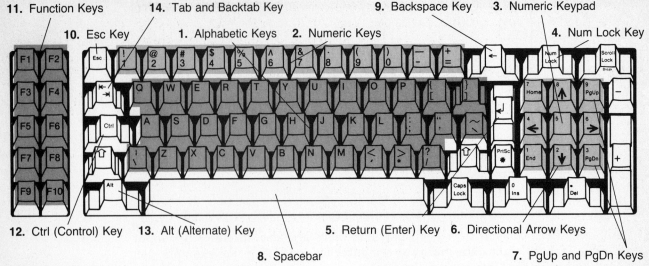

FIGURE 1-9
The typical microcomputer keyboard has several different types of keys.

1. Alphabetic keys	3. Numeric keypad	7. PgUp and PgDn keys	11. Function keys
2. Numeric keys	4. Num Lock key	8. Spacebar	12. Ctrl (Control) key
	5. Return (Enter) key	9. Backspace key	13. Alt (Alternate) key
	6. Directional arrow keys	10. Esc (Escape) key	14. Tab and Backtab key

■ Numeric keys are above the alphabetic keys and are labeled with both numbers and symbols. When you press these keys, you enter either the indicated numbers or, if you hold down the **Shift** key, the indicated symbols.

■ Many keyboards have a separate set of number keys arranged like those on a calculator. With this **numeric keypad**, you can enter numbers more quickly. But on some computers, the numeric keypad serves a second purpose. It also contains the **directional arrow keys**, which move the cursor around the screen, and the **PgUp** and **PgDn** keys, which move the cursor a screen or page at a time. If the numeric keypad serves this dual purpose, the **Num Lock** key must be engaged to enter numbers. When it is not engaged, the keys on the numeric keypad move the cursor.

■ The **Return** key (also called the **Enter** key) is often pressed as the final keystroke. For example, when sending commands to the computer, you often must type, or otherwise indicate, a command and then press **Return** to send the command to the CPU. And when ending paragraphs or lines of text before they reach the right margin, you must press **Return**. But unlike a typewriter, you need not press **Return** to end lines within a paragraph.

■ Cursor movement keys move the **cursor**, a reverse video (dark against a light background) or underline character, around the screen. You use the cursor to point to where you want to enter or edit data on the screen. Generally, the directional arrow keys move the cursor one line or character at a time. However, since keyboard designs vary, so do the other keys that move the cursor.

■ The **Spacebar** enters spaces. On some programs, it is also used to move a highlight to choices listed on a menu. These menus list commands you can choose from by highlighting them and then pressing **Return**.

■ The **Backspace** key is used to move the cursor backward. If the program assigns this key the ability to delete characters you back it over, it is called a **destructive backspace**. This lets you quickly back over and delete characters when you discover a mistake while entering text.

■ The **Esc** (Escape) key (or other designated key) is frequently used to cancel a command in progress if you change your mind before completing the command.

■ Computer manufacturers recognize the need for special keys that software designers can assign frequently used tasks to. For that reason, they have added

function keys that perform functions assigned to them by the programmer. For example, on a word processing program, function keys are often assigned to select, copy, move, or delete text. On some keyboards, the function keys are at the left side of the keyboard. On other computers, they are the top row of keys.

■ Many keys are assigned more than one function. For instance, pressing the right directional arrow key may move the cursor one column or character at a time, but pressing the right directional arrow key while holding down the **Ctrl** (Control) key might move the cursor several columns or characters at a time. Pressing the letter *b* enters the letter alone, but pressing *b* while holding down the **Alt** (Alternate) key might enter a code that tells the printer to begin boldfacing text. Neither the **Ctrl** key nor the **Alt** key sends characters to the computer; they change what is sent when you press other keys. Combining keys in this way lets software designers assign many more functions to the keyboard than there are keys available. This is much like the standard typewriter, which uses the **Shift** key to type uppercase letters. Using this approach, fifty-two characters (twenty-six uppercase and twenty-six lowercase letters) can be generated with only twenty-six keys.

■ The **Tab** key moves the cursor to the next tab stop. The **Backtab** key, which is usually the same key as **Tab** but is pressed along with the **Shift** key, does the same thing but moves the cursor in the opposite direction.

Text Scanning Devices

When you type text into a computer and then print it out on a printer, you are actually converting the text from a digital form (the form used by the computer) into a printed form.

This conversion process has been like a one-way street. Until recently, it was not possible to easily convert printed copy into an electronic form that could be processed by a computer. For example, if a document has already been typed and printed, rekeying it back into the computer is time consuming. To more efficiently convert printed text into electronic text, **scanners** have been developed. Scanners convert printed text into digital form using **optical character recognition** (OCR).

The scanner reads the pattern of dark characters against a light background and converts each character into its digital ASCII number. This ASCII number is then stored in the computer's memory or on a disk. Since the text is converted into its ASCII numbers, it can be stored, displayed, printed, and otherwise manipulated just as if it had been entered into the computer through the keyboard. Text you enter with a scanner can be edited by word processors and processed by other programs that accept ASCII input.

Although these text scanners are ideal for converting text documents into electronic form, they cannot convert graphs and other illustrations. They also cannot read corrections and notes made with a pencil or pen. These must be manually entered into the computer after the main body of the document has been scanned.

GRAPHICS INPUT DEVICES

Besides scanning text to convert it from printed into electronic form, input devices allow you to scan graphic images into the computer or create them directly on the screen. Until recently, charts, graphs, and illustrations were prepared separately and inserted into a document after it was printed. But today it is possible to create these images on a microcomputer and insert them directly into the document while you are working on it. With desktop publishing becoming more widespread, the use of graphics in documents is increasing.

Image Digitizers

To scan graphic images like photographs, line drawings, charts, and maps into the computer, **image digitizers** (also called graphics scanners) are used. Instead of converting the image into characters, these scanners take a digital picture of it, much as a copy machine does. The difference, of course, is that the copy is stored in the computer in electronic form.

Unlike text scanners, image digitizers do not assign ASCII codes to any text that appears in the image. Thus text scanned into the computer with one of these digitizers cannot be edited with a word processing program. To convert these images, parts of which are either dark or light, into digital form, the scanner divides the printed image into a grid of small dots, or **pixels**. As the image is scanned, the image digitizer determines if each of these pixels is light or dark. If dark, the scanner assigns it the value 0. If light, it assigns it the value 1. These values are fed into the computer and stored in memory. When displayed on the screen, the digitizing process is reversed—the numeric value of each pixel in the original image is used to control the brightness of its corresponding pixel on the display screen (Figure 1-10). Once the image has been stored in the computer's memory and displayed on the screen, it can be manipulated by a program designed to work with images of this kind.

Digitizing Tablets

One of the most interesting devices for creating graphics on the screen is a **digitizing tablet**, or **graphics pad**. These devices also come with a penlike stylus. You move the stylus across the surface of the pad to trace existing drawings laid on top of the pad or to create new ones. The pad always knows the position of the stylus because the pad is broken up into a grid of individual pixels. The screen is also divided into pixels, so if you press on a given pixel on the pad, the corresponding pixel on the screen is illuminated. To draw a line, you press on one pixel after another, and the corresponding pixels on the screen are illuminated to display a line.

FIGURE 1-10
There is a one-to-one correspondence between pixels on a document and pixels on the screen. If the pixel on the document is light, the scanner sends the value 1 to the computer, which then illuminates the corresponding pixel on the screen. If the pixel on the document is dark, the scanner sends the value 0 to the computer, and the corresponding pixel on the screen is left dark.

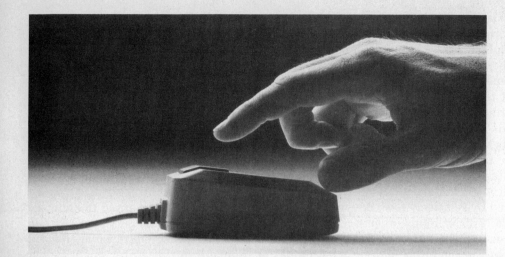

FIGURE 1-11
A mouse is a device you move across a smooth surface. As you do so, the cursor moves on the screen so that you can draw lines and make selections from menus by pressing the buttons on the mouse. (Courtesy of Apple Computer, Inc.)

Light Pens

Light pens let you draw directly on the screen. No tablet is between the pen and the screen as with a digitizing tablet. You simply hold the pen against the display screen and the image is "painted" on the screen by a beam of electrons that sweeps across and down the screen a line at a time. When you hold a light pen against the screen, it senses the electron beam as it sweeps by. The computer, knowing where the electron beam is at any time, calculates the pen's position and places a dot at that point on the screen on the next scan.

Mice

One of the most common input devices is the **mouse**, which contains a rolling ball and one or more buttons that you press to execute commands (Figure 1-11). As you move the mouse around on a flat, smooth surface, the ball rolls and feeds electrical signals to the computer to move the cursor on the screen. Another type, optical mice, use a mirrorlike pad to reflect a tiny beam of light.

VOICE INPUT DEVICES

Despite the incredibly fast processing speed of the computer, it is slowed by its slowest element, namely, the keyboard. To process information, you must first enter it into the computer, and people can type only so fast. It is not yet possible to converse with your computer, but **voice input devices** have been developed that, though limited, do convert the human voice into a signal the computer can understand. This is not a simple task. The following two sentences from a recent article in *The Economist*[1] illustrate the difficulty:

> This new display can recognize speech.
> This nudist play can wreck a nice beach.

To tell the difference between these two sentences requires very good hearing. Even then you probably could not tell the difference unless the words were pronounced very carefully. Imagine how difficult it is to program a computer so that it can tell the difference!

Advances are slowly being made, and systems have been developed that can understand as many as ten thousand words. To use one of these systems, you must first

[1] *The Economist*, November 15, 1986, p. 109.

familiarize the computer with the way you pronounce each word. To do so, each word in the program's vocabulary is displayed on the screen, and you speak each aloud into a microphone. The computer then stores your pronunciation along with the matching word displayed on the screen. This computerized match is a **voice template**. The next time you speak to the computer, it quickly matches the pattern of your voice against the voice templates stored in its memory. If it finds a match, it can display the word or execute the command.

This approach limits the computer to a small vocabulary. As you add words, training the computer takes longer. More words require more computer memory, and it then takes the computer longer to search though the larger number of voice templates for a match. Despite these limitations, the approach is useful when there are a limited number of commands or when larger amounts of information can be conveyed by relatively few code words. For example, what if you wanted to know all the details about items in your company's inventory. These details might include the price, size, quantity in stock, and color. The details for each product could then be stored in the computer and assigned names or numbers. A typewriter might be assigned the stock number 100, and a copy machine the number 200. To display the details about an item, you would only have to say "DISPLAY." The computer might then ask "DISPLAY WHAT?" and you would respond "ONE," pause for a moment, and then say "HUNDRED" to display details about the typewriter. You could also say "TWO," pause, and then say "HUNDRED" to display details about the copy machine. In this way, a great deal of information can be manipulated with a limited vocabulary.

QUESTIONS

1. List three different input devices, and briefly describe each.
2. What is the **Return** key on the computer keyboard used for?
3. What are function keys, and what are they used for?
4. What is the cursor, and what does it do?
5. What is the difference between text and graphics scanners? List two input devices from each category.
6. What is a Dvorak keyboard? How does it differ from the QWERTY keyboard?
7. What is a pixel?
8. What is the first step you must complete when using most voice processing systems?

ACTIVITIES

1. Sketch one of the computer keyboards in the lab, and then label each of the major keys.
2. Find an ad for a scanner in a magazine or newspaper. From the ad copy, try to determine if you can use the scanner to input text or graphics.
3. List all the input devices available in the lab.

TOPIC 1-4
Output Devices

In this topic, we introduce you to output devices, the devices you use to get information out of a computer. After finishing this topic, you will be able to

- Distinguish between the various types of computer display screens
- Explain how images are displayed on the screen
- List the differences between character-based and graphics- based screens
- Describe the types of color monitors available
- Explain how printers form images on paper
- Discuss the different types of printers
- List and describe common printer accessories

When working on a computer, you want to be able to see what you are working on and to print it out to take with you, share with others, or file for future reference. Output can be generated either as **soft copy**, what you see on the display screen, or as **hard copy**, what you print out on paper.

DISPLAY SCREENS

The display screen of your microcomputer gives you instant feedback while you are working. The display screen is like a window into your computer's memory. As you type text on the keyboard, it is entered into memory and echoed to the screen so that you can see it. Since you spend most of your time looking at the display screen, its quality and capabilities are important. For example, some screens display only text characters, whereas others also display graphics. Some display an image in a single color, and others in several colors.

Inside a Display Screen

Display screens fall into two main classes: **cathode ray tubes (CRTs)** and **flat-panel displays**.

Cathode Ray Tubes (CRTs)
Most microcomputers are equipped with a cathode ray tube because these displays create the best image. A CRT contains an **electron gun**, a device that fires a stream of electrons at the screen. As the beam sweeps across the screen, it is turned on and off, illuminating some parts of the screen and leaving other parts dark. Most CRTs display twenty-four or twenty-five lines of eighty characters each, but some display as many as sixty-six lines, enough to show a full page of text. Displays capable of showing the full page are highly desirable but at the moment, are still quite expensive. With the increasing popularity of desktop publishing, these full-page displays will inevitably become more popular and less expensive.

Flat-Panel Displays
CRTs are bulky, so portable computers use flat-panel displays. On these, the image is created using a variety of technologies, all of which offer advantages and disadvantages, with the tradeoffs usually being made between readability, battery life, and cost. Since these screens are most often used in portable computers, power consumption is a major concern. If a display requires too much power, the battery life between

recharges is very short, perhaps as short as one hour. Lower power consumption can increase a battery's life as many as six or more hours. Table 1-4 lists the four basic types of flat-panel displays and their advantages and disadvantages.

Liquid crystal displays (**LCDs**) create an image by changing the reflectance of areas of the screen so that light is either reflected or absorbed. Characters appear as black against a silver background. In some lighting, these displays are hard to read, and in the dark, they cannot be read at all. To reduce this problem, some LCDs are now backlit or use other technologies to increase their contrast.

Light-emitting diode (LED) displays have many very small light-emitting diodes arranged in a grid on the screen. By lighting the appropriate diodes, an image of light characters appears against a dark background.

Gas plasma displays sandwich small bubbles of gas between two glass plates. When charged, these dotlike bubbles light up, and when lit in specified patterns, they form characters on the screen.

Electroluminescent displays create characters by illuminating small diodes on the screen's surface. Characters appear light against a dark background.

Monochrome and Color Screens

Display screens are classified as either monochrome or color.

Monochrome Displays

Monochrome screens display a single color, usually white, green, or amber characters against a black background. On some of these screens, you can reverse the display so that dark characters are displayed against a light background.

Color Displays

Color displays have become increasingly popular. The two basic types are composite monitors and RGB (red, green, blue) monitors.

Composite color displays are just like color television sets. The signals for the three primary colors, red, green, and blue, are combined into a single composite signal when fed from the computer to the display. Though generally inexpensive, composite color displays give relatively poor quality.

RGB color displays are fed three separate video inputs from the computer. A separate input is used for red, green, and blue. The image is sharper, and the cost is higher, than that of a composite color display.

To generate colors, three dots or thin stripes of phosphor (red, green, and blue) must be illuminated to create a single dot that characters are created from. The size, or pitch, of the dots (or stripes) determines the sharpness of the character displayed on the screen. High-quality monitors have a pitch of 0.31 mm (about 1/3 of a millimeter) or less. Not long ago, even the best color monitors could not provide the resolution—that is, sharpness of characters—that monochrome monitors could. With the introduction of expansion boards called **color graphics cards** and **enhanced color graphics adapters**, or with new graphics chips built into the computer itself, much higher resolutions can be sent to the screen.

TABLE 1-4
Flat-Panel Technologies

Type	Readability	Battery Life	Cost
Liquid crystal displays (LCDs)	Lowest	Longest	Lowest
Light-emitting diodes (LEDs)	Low	Long	Low
Gas plasma	High	Shortest	High
Electroluminescent	Highest	Short	Highest

How Images Are Displayed

Besides categorizing display monitors as either black and white or color, they can also be categorized by how the image is created on the screen. Two approaches are used: **graphic** and **character.** Both the hardware and software of the computer system determine which approach is used. To understand the differences between graphic and character displays, you first must understand how images are created on the screen.

Picture Elements

All images displayed on a screen are created with dots or small squares. To do this, the screen is divided into a grid (Figure 1-12). The grid divides the screen into dots (or small squares) called picture elements, or pixels. A typical screen may have as many as 250,000 pixels.

When an image is painted on the screen, the appropriate pixels are illuminated. The pixels are illuminated in patterns that form characters and other images on the screen. The number of pixels, and hence the resolution, is determined by how many rows and columns the screen is divided into (Figure 1-13). Table 1-5 shows the number of pixels displayed on typical IBM computers when equipped with the appropriate hardware.

Although all screens display characters that are composed of pixels, these characters are generated either as graphics or as characters. The difference between these two approaches is important because it determines what you can display on the screen.

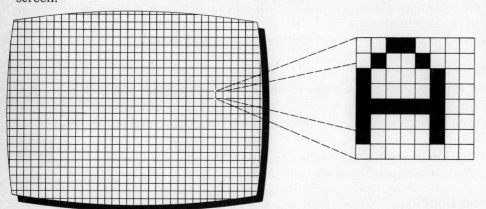

FIGURE 1-12
Picture elements, or pixels, are small dots the screen is divided into. By illuminating selected pixels, the computer can display text and other images.

TABLE 1-5
Typical IBM Computer Displays

Type of Display Adapter	Number of Pixels	Number of Colors
Monochrome	Text only	1
Color graphics card	320 x 200	4
	640 x 200	2
Enhanced graphics adapter	320 x 200	4
	640 x 200	2
	640 x 350	16
	640 x 350	1
IBM Personal System/2	720 x 400 (text)	
Color Display 8512	640 x 480 (graphics)	256
IBM Personal System/2		
Color Display 8514	1,024 x 768	256

FIGURE 1-13
A high-resolution display divides the screen into more pixels than a low-resolution display. Because each character is formed from more dots, the result is a sharper image.

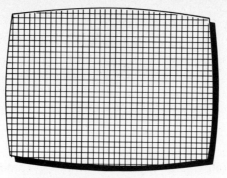

High Resolution

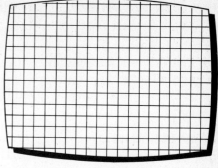

Low Resolution

Graphics Displays

If you are using a graphics display, some programs display the image on the screen using a technique called **bit mapping**, **memory mapping**, or **all points addressable (APA)**. A bit-mapped display stores each of the screen's pixels in one or more bits of memory. Thus a one-to-one relation exists between pixels on the screen and pixels stored in memory. If the bit in memory is a 1, the corresponding pixel on the screen is illuminated. If the bit in memory is a 0, the pixel is not illuminated. By approximately setting the values in memory, any kind of image can be displayed on the screen.

To use a program that has bit mapping, you must have a graphics display screen. If your computer does not have graphics built in, you also must insert a graphics card into one of the expansion slots.

Advantages and disadvantages of graphics displays include

- They require a lot of memory.
- They operate relatively slowly, so there are delays when you scroll though a document or spreadsheet.
- A graphics display can display different fonts, type sizes, and enhancements like italics.
- Both text and graphics can be displayed on the screen at the same time, which is especially important in desktop publishing applications (Figure 1-14).

Character Displays

When text is displayed on some screens such as the IBM monochrome monitor, bit mapping is not used. Instead, the computer stores the ASCII value of each character in memory. A **character generator** (a special ROM chip) then converts these values into the dot pattern needed to create characters on the screen.

FIGURE 1-14
A graphics display is more versatile than a character display. For example, a character can be displayed in more than one size or type style, and both text and graphics can be displayed on a graphics display.

A.
This text has been formatted with the Palatino Italic typeface and appears on the screen much like it will appear in the printout.

B.
This text has been formatted with the Times Roman Condensed typeface and appears on the screen much like it will appear in the printout.

C.
This text has been formatted with the Helvetica Bold typeface and appears on the screen much like it will appear in the printout.

Figure 1-15 shows the characters in the IBM PC character set. Each of these characters, and no other, is stored in ROM; they are the only characters that can be displayed on the screen.

Advantages and disadvantages of character displays include

- They require little memory.
- They operate very quickly, so you can scroll through a document or spreadsheet quickly.
- They can display only the characters in the computer's character set.
- They can display only simple graphics using the graphics characters in the character set. For example, the IBM character set (Figure 1-15) has ruled lines and corners so that you can create boxes. You cannot create circles because these are not stored in the character set.
- Programmers and users cannot create their own characters and graphics; they must use those included in the character set.
- Characters must occupy a fixed position on the screen; they cannot be offset half a line or half a column. This prevents you from seeing on the screen the effects of proportional spacing, different type sizes, and subscripts and superscripts.
- A character display cannot display italic type.

PRINTERS

The second most widely used output device is the printer. Having a printer is essential if you want a hard copy of the data you process with your computer. Until recently, you had to choose between an expensive printer that printed **letter-quality** characters and an inexpensive printer that created each character from a pattern of dots. Today, these differences have narrowed, and you have a wide variety of printers and prices to choose from. The quality of all types of printers has improved dramatically.

Hundreds of printers are available, and nearly all of them have unique features. Two ways of categorizing printers are by how they form characters and by how they transfer characters to paper.

FIGURE 1-15
The IBM character set contains letters, numbers, symbols, and graphics characters. A character display can display only the characters in its ROM character set. Although the computer identifies them with eight-digit ASCII codes, you can access them on many applications programs with three-digit decimal codes. To find the three-digit code for any character, read the first two digits from the left column and the last digit from the column numbers. For example, 5 is 053, a is 097, and « is 174.

How Printers Form Characters

Printers use one of two approaches when they form letters. Either characters are printed as fully formed characters (referred to as letter-quality), similar to the characters a typewriter prints, or they are created by arranging a series of dots on the paper, much as characters are displayed on the screen.

Fully Formed Character Printers
Fully formed character printers print solid characters using a type element with raised characters like those on a typewriter. The two basic type elements of these printers are print wheels and thimbles.

Printers that use print wheels are commonly called **daisy-wheel printers**. The term *daisy wheel* comes from the way individual characters are arranged on flexible "petals" radiating from the center of the type element. Thimbles also have raised characters, but they are arranged on an inverted thimble.

Advantages and disadvantages of fully formed character printers include

- They transfer sharp, crisp characters onto the paper.
- They are relatively slow.
- They cannot print graphics.
- Typefaces and sizes can be changed only by changing the type element. To do this, you must stop the printer. This is so time consuming that most users use the same type style and size for the entire document.

Dot-Matrix Printers
Dot-matrix printers form characters using an array of dots. Because the spacing of the dots affects the resolution and **density**, or quality, of the characters, the closer the dots, the closer to letter quality the characters will appear (Figure 1-16).

Advantages and disadvantages of dot-matrix printers include

- They can print any image on the paper. The image need not be available on a print element, as it does on a fully formed character printer. Any image that can be created in memory or displayed on the screen can be printed on a dot-matrix printer.
- You can use a wide range of type styles and sizes within the same document. The ease with which you can do this depends on the program you are using.
- They can print graphics (Figure 1-17). Since the print head scans the entire page, dots can be printed anywhere. If the dots are close enough, solid, dark areas can be printed. This ability to print dots anywhere on the page is called all points addressable.
- The less expensive models do not print characters as clearly as fully formed character printers.

FIGURE 1-16
The quality of the character is determined by the spacing of the dots. This enlargement of a dot-matrix character shows the closer the dots are, the more like letter quality the character is.

FIGURE 1-17
Graphics can be printed on a dot-matrix printer. By varying the spacing between the dots, an illusion of brightness can be created. Here an enlargement of a small area of the illustration clearly shows how the image is formed from dots. (Courtesy of Xerox Ventura Publisher)

How Printers Transfer Characters to Paper

Printers can also be categorized by how they transfer the characters to paper. The two methods of transfer are impact and nonimpact.

Impact Printers

Impact printers create an image on the paper using a mechanical print head that strikes an inked ribbon against the surface of the paper. As you have seen, all fully formed character printers use impact to form characters.

Dot-matrix impact printers use a **print head** containing pins, or wires, arranged in a column to print characters. As the print head passes across the paper, the computer tells it which pins are to be fired to form a particular character. As the pins are fired, they strike an inked ribbon against the paper. The printed dots are arranged in an invisible matrix—frequently seven columns across and nine lines deep.

The number of wires and dots determines the character's resolution. Older, less expensive printers usually use nine pins to create characters. The latest printers have eighteen or twenty-four wires in their print head.

Nonimpact Printers

Nonimpact printers do not use an inked ribbon. Characters are transferred to the paper using, for example, spraying ink, electrostatic charges and toner, or heat. However, all nonimpact printers use dot patterns, much like those in a dot-matrix impact printer, to form characters. Great advances are being made in this area. Many industry observers predict that over the next few years these printers will replace impact printers as the most popular printer type. Nonimpact printers offer many advantages, including their speed and quietness. Their one drawback is they cannot print multipart forms that require impact to print the image through the carbon paper. Ink-jet, thermal, laser, LED, and electrostatic printers are all nonimpact printers.

Ink-jet printers use moving nozzles to focus a stream of ink onto the paper. The number of nozzles determines the printer's resolution. Color ink-jet printers use three separate jets, one for each of the primary colors (red, green, and blue). When printing in color, all ink jets can work simultaneously, thus speeding up the printing, since the printer need not make successive passes for each color. Ink-jet printers are also very quiet.

Thermal printers use a dot-matrix print head and heat-sensitive paper to create images; however, recent models no longer require heat-sensitive paper. The print head of a thermal printer is composed of a grid of wires. When an electric current is applied to any pair of wires, heat is generated where they intersect, leaving a dot on the paper.

Laser printers, an increasingly popular type of printer, also form characters using dots. They are very fast, usually printing eight or more pages per minute, and their cost has fallen to where they are now competitive with other types of printers.

The resolution of laser printers is greater than most other dot- matrix printers because of the much higher number of dots and their greater density. Most laser printers can print 300 dots per inch although 400 or more dots per inch are available. Despite the great number of dots, laser printers are fast because the dots are not transferred to the paper with mechanical devices that strike a ribbon. Laser printers provide extremely high quality. Figure 1-18 shows a sample (text and graphics) of laser printing.

The technology of laser printers is similar to that of office copiers. They print images in two steps. First, a laser beam is focused onto a moving drum by a mirror. The moving drum is charged with electricity. As the drum revolves, it is scanned by the laser, and the image is "painted" onto the drum. The intensity of the laser beam is varied, and at selected points, the beam removes the electrical charge from the drum to form invisible characters with a neutral charge. Charged toner is then electrostatically attracted to these characters. This toner is transferred to the paper and fused to it by heat and pressure as it is pressed against the revolving drum. Current laser printers can print in only one color.

LED printers have many of the same performance characteristics as laser printers, but instead of using a laser to create the image, they use an array of light-emitting diodes (LEDs).

Electrostatic printers use a dot-matrix print head to apply electrostatic charges to the surface of the paper. When the paper is passed through toner, the toner ad-

FIGURE 1-18
Laser printers can print both text and graphics and are very close to letter quality. The dots making up the image are so closely spaced that they look like characters typed on a typewriter. (Courtesy of Software Publishing Corporation)

MICROCOMPUTER SYSTEMS

heres to the charged areas, making the image visible. This process is similar to that used in copy machines.

Printer Speed

The speed of a printer is generally given in **characters per second** (**CPS**). Printers do not often print at their advertised CPS because these speeds are usually for straight text only. If you use boldfacing, underlining, or any other character enhancements, the printer will print at a slower speed because the print head must make more than one pass over the material.

Density is controlled on a fully formed character printer by striking the same character in the same position one or more times. On an impact printer that forms characters with dots, density is controlled by slightly offsetting the print head to create overlapping dots.

Many dot-matrix impact printers offer at least two modes. In **draft** mode, they print quickly, but since the density is light (fewer dots are used to increase the speed), the characters are light and obviously formed from a series of dots. In **near-letter-quality** (**NLQ**) mode, either they make more than one pass over each character, slightly offsetting the print head on each pass, or they use more pins in the matrix to form the characters. These techniques increase the characters' density and make them look more like fully formed characters. NLQ, however, slows down the printer because of the number of dots transferred for each character.

The Printer's Controls

When you want to send a document to the printer, you first load the printer with paper, align the paper, and turn the printer on. The way you load paper varies, depending on the type of printer and paper you are using. If you are using single sheets, you usually stack them in a paper tray or bin. If you are using continuous form paper (also called fan-fold paper), you feed it into the printer as shown in Figure 1-19.

The settings you can make on the printer vary. Many have some or all of the following switches:

On/Off turns the power to the printer on and off. Knowing when to use this switch is important.

■ If you turn the printer off while it is operating, all data in its buffer will be lost. When you turn the printer back on, your document may resume printing but a large block will have been missed.

■ If you have canceled a print job and want to start over, turning the computer off and back on is a good way to ensure that text from the previous job does not remain in the buffer.

■ If after you turn the printer off, you turn it back on, it resets the top of the form so that the printer considers the line that the print element is resting on the top line of the sheet of paper. It uses this line as the starting point when calculating top margins and page length. This is useful, since you can adjust your paper in the printer, and just turn it off and then back on to set the top of the form.

Off-Line/On-Line connects the printer to and disconnects it from the computer. The printer must be on-line to print documents, but it must be off-line to use some of the other switches on the printer like Form Feed and Line Feed.

Form Feed advances a sheet of paper out of the printer. If the printer has an automatic sheet feeder or tractor feed, it inserts a new sheet. For this switch to work, the printer must be off- line.

Line Feed advances paper in the printer by one line. This is useful when making fine adjustments to the paper's position in the printer. For this switch to work, the printer must be off- line.

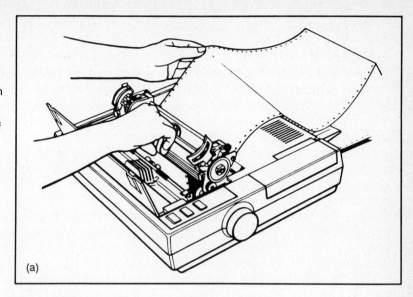

FIGURE 1-19
To load continuous form paper into a printer, you feed it through a slot, around the platen, and back out of the printer (a). In the process, you engage the holes in the perforated, tear-off margins with the tractor or pin feed mechanism (b). (Courtesy of Epson)

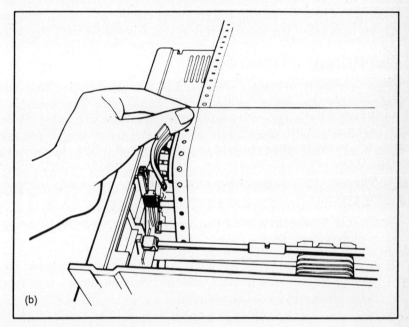

Letter Quality/Draft Quality switches the printer between its high quality but slower letter-quality mode and its lower quality but faster draft-quality mode.

Font changes the default font so that the entire document is printed in that font unless you specified otherwise by entering font change codes within the document.

Printer Accessories

Printers require supplies and accessories for specific purposes.

Paper

Most printers accept both single sheets of paper and **continuous form paper**, which has perforated margins with holes. These holes are engaged by a tractor or pin feeder to pull the paper through the printer one sheet after another and keep it aligned. After the printout is completed, the holes can be used to hold the paper in special binders, or they can be torn off. Continuous form paper is available in single sheets, as multipart carbon forms, or preprinted with specially designed forms or company letterheads on each sheet.

Changing from continuous form paper to single sheets can be a nuisance. Many printers now come with a separate slot that single sheets or envelopes can be inserted into without having to remove the continuous form paper.

Ribbons or Toner

Inked **ribbons** or other supplies like **toner** are needed to transfer the characters to the paper. Supplies depend on the type of printer being used. Cloth and film ribbons are available. Cloth ribbons are more economical, but film ribbons produce sharper characters on the paper.

Fonts

Many newer printers can print type in a variety of styles, or **fonts** (Figure 1-20). Some fonts may be permanently stored in the printer's memory (ROM). Others are available on cartridges or stored on disks. Font cartridges are plugged into the printer when you want access to the fonts they contain. Printers using this system can print only the fonts stored in ROM or on the plugged-in cartridge. Fonts stored on disks, called **software fonts** or **down-loadable fonts** are more flexible. You can choose from the fonts on the disk and load them into the printer's RAM when you need them. This way the printer has access to any fonts you want to use.

Sheet Feeders

When using single sheets of paper or envelopes, **bins**, or **sheet feeders**, are needed. These bins hold as many as five hundred sheets of stationery and feed it to the printer one sheet at a time. When printing letterhead, you need two bins: One holds the letterhead used for the first sheet, and the other holds the nonletterhead paper used for subsequent sheets. On many printers, bins are accessories, but on laser printers, they are built in because laser printers do not accept continuous form paper.

Tractor Feeds

Tractor feeds are used with continuous form paper to move it smoothly through the printer. When long printouts are made without a tractor drive, the paper can easily become skewed in the printer. Tractor feeds built into the printer are called **pin feeds**.

Soundproof Enclosures

Soundproof enclosures are insulated covers that are placed over a printer. They are often used with impact printers to reduce the noise level and usually have a hinged door so that you can gain access to the printer.

Switches

Switches can be used to connect two or more printers to the same port on a computer. These allow you to switch quickly between a fast, dot-matrix impact printer used for draft copies and a fully formed character or laser printer used for a final copy.

This is 10pt Times Roman

This is 12pt Times Roman

This is 10pt Helvetica

This is 12pt Helvetica

This is 10pt Times Roman bold

This is 12pt Times Roman bold

This is 10pt Helvetica bold

This is 12pt Helvetica bold

This is 10pt Times Roman italic

This is 12pt Times Roman italic

This is 10pt Helvetica italic

This is 12pt Helvetica italic

FIGURE 1-20
Fonts are different type styles and sizes. The fonts shown here were all printed on the same printer.

QUESTIONS

1. Describe the two basic types of display screens.
2. Name two kinds of color screens. What are their advantages and disadvantages?
3. What is the difference between a soft copy and a hard copy?
4. What is the difference between a graphics display and a character display? What are their advantages and disadvantages?
5. What are the two methods used by printers to form images?
6. What are the two methods used by printers to transfer characters to paper?
7. What are printer bins used for?
8. On printers that form characters from dots, what determines the sharpness, or resolution, of the characters?
9. What are fonts?

ACTIVITIES

1. Sketch and label the controls on one of the printers in the lab. Describe the function of each control.
2. Sketch and label the controls on one of the display screens in the lab. Briefly describe the purpose of each control.
3. Look at current issues of computer magazines for advertisements of display screens. List the features each display screen offers, and decide whether you would pay extra for these "new" features if you were (a) writing college papers or (b) composing a graphics layout.
4. How many dot-matrix printers does the lab have? What type are they? How many fully formed character printers?

TOPIC 1-5
External Storage Devices

In this topic, we introduce you to external storage devices, the devices you use to store programs and information that you are not currently processing in the computer. After finishing this topic, you will be able to

- List and describe the main features of floppy disks
- Describe how data is stored on magnetic media
- Explain how floppy and hard disk drives work
- List and describe ways to protect and secure your data
- Describe optical disks
- Care for your disks

The memory in your computer is a limited resource, yet it must serve many uses. For example, you load different programs for different applications. The files you create with applications programs vary, and there can be a lot of them. The computer's memory is not large enough to store all the programs, documents, and other computer-generated files you work on. Moreover, most memory will lose its data when you turn off the computer.

For these reasons, another form of more permanent storage is provided. This **external storage** (also called **auxiliary storage** or **secondary storage**) has seen several improvements, and new approaches are still being introduced.

Today's computers usually use magnetic disks or tape to store documents and programs. But new storage devices are being introduced that use lasers and light to store even more data. External storage media, and the devices used to store and retrieve data on them, fall into four major classes.

- Floppy disks and **floppy disk drives** are the most common external storage media and devices.
- Hard disk drives with built-in or removable metal platters have become increasingly popular because of their storage capacity and speed.
- **Magnetic tape**, once a major storage medium, is now used along with tape drives primarily as a backup device.
- **Optical disks** and disk drives that store and retrieve data with lasers are the latest external storage and media devices.

Regardless of the technique, once data is stored on these storage media, you can reload it into the computer's memory without having to rekey it. All these media, except the optical disk, can be erased and reused.

FLOPPY DISKS AND DISK DRIVES

Floppy disks are available in three sizes: 8, 5 1/4, and 3 1/2 inches (Figure 1-21). Each size works only with drives specifically designed to accept it.

The Outside of a Floppy Disk

Although floppy disks come in a variety of sizes and styles, they all have certain features in common (Figure 1-22).

- A *storage envelope* protects 5 1/4- and 8-inch disks from scratches, dust, and fingerprints. Some envelopes are treated to eliminate the static buildup that attracts abrasive grit. These envelopes are not used on the better protected 3 1/2-inch disks.
- A *plastic outer covering* protects the disk itself while allowing it to spin smoothly inside the jacket. 5 1/4- and 8-inch disks are protected by flexible plastic jackets, whereas 3 1/2-inch disks are mounted in a rigid plastic housing. The jacket or housing is permanently sealed and contains lubricants and cleaning agents that prolong the life of the disk.

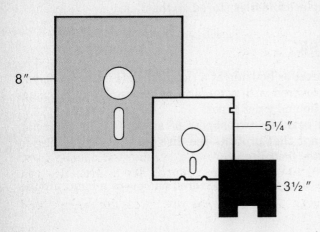

FIGURE 1-21
Floppy disks come in three different sizes. Disk drives are designed to accept one of the sizes.

8″

5¼″

3½″

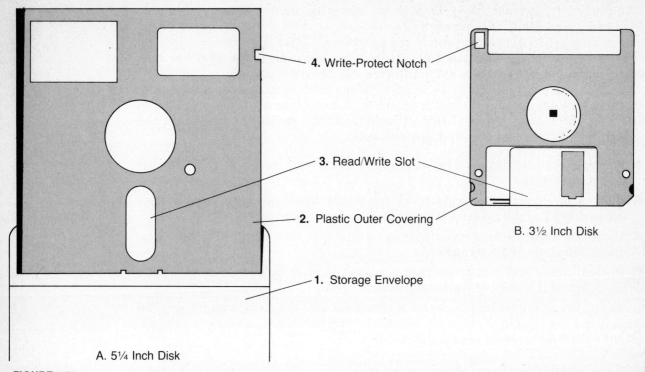

4. Write-Protect Notch

3. Read/Write Slot

2. Plastic Outer Covering

B. 3½ Inch Disk

1. Storage Envelope

A. 5¼ Inch Disk

FIGURE 1-22
The outside appearance of 5 1/4-inch and 3 1/2-inch disks varies, but both have many features in common. Both have plastic outer coverings, read/write slots, and write-protect notches.

■ The **read/write slot** in the jacket is where the disk drive's read/write head contacts the surface of the disk. This read/write head stores data on (writes) and retrieves data from (reads) the surface of the disk as the disk spins inside the drive. On 3 1/2-inch disks, the read/write slot is protected by a sliding metal cover called the shutter. When you insert the disk into the drive, this shutter is automatically pushed aside so that the read/write slot is exposed, and the drive can come in contact with the floppy disk within.

■ The **write-protect notch** allows you to write on a disk when it is uncovered and prevents you from writing on the disk when it is covered. To write-protect a 5 1/2- or 8-inch disk, you cover the write-protect notch with tape. On 3 1/2-inch disks, you press a sliding tab to cover the write-protect hole. A switch, or photoelectric circuit, inside the disk drive determines if the write-protect notch is uncovered. If it finds it is covered, the switch disables the drive's ability to write information onto the disk. Permanently write-protected disks, like those some applications programs are distributed on, have no notch. This is to prevent you from inadvertently erasing irreplaceable files stored on the disk.

The Inside of a Floppy Disk

If you were to remove the plastic jacket or housing of a floppy disk (Figure 1-23), you would find a round piece of plastic covered with a metallic oxide similar to the magnetic recording material used on audio and video tapes.

The round disk is sandwiched between two sheets of a soft feltlike material, which is impregnated with a lubricant that protects the disk when it is spinning in the drive. The blank disk has three key features.

■ The magnetic recording surface that the data is stored on covers a band around the disk.

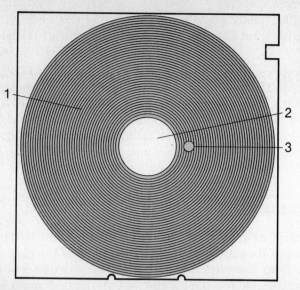

FIGURE 1-23
The inside of a floppy
disk is a plastic disk
coated with magnetic
material similar to
that used on cassette
and video tapes.

1

2

3

■ The large hole in the center of the disk is used by the drive to align and spin the disk. This hole is sometimes reinforced with a plastic hub and, on 3 1/2-inch disks, is covered by a metal hub.

■ The **sector hole,** which is punched through the disk, is used by the computer to know where to store data to and retrieve data from the disk. A light and photoelectric cell inside the disk drive, much like those that automatically open doors for you at the supermarket, are positioned on either side of the sector hole in a 5 1/4-inch disk's plastic cover and at the top of the read/write slot on a 3 1/2-inch disk. As the disk spins inside its outer cover, the hole in the disk aligns once each revolution with one of these openings. When the holes are aligned, light shines through them, and the photoelectric cell signals the computer so that it can keep itself oriented to the disk's position, much as a ship can orient itself from a lighthouse beacon.

The Floppy Disk Drive

The floppy disk drive is the device that the floppy disk is inserted into so that you can store data to and retrieve data from it. The floppy disk drive has two parts you should be familiar with: the slot and the light (Figure 1-24).

■ The slot is where you insert a floppy disk into the drive. On 5 1/4-inch drives, the slot has a door that you must open before inserting or removing a disk. To insert a disk, you open the door, insert the disk into the slot, and then close the door. If the door is not fully closed, you may have problems. On 3 1/2-inch drives, the slot

FIGURE 1-24
A floppy disk drive has a
slot that is opened and
closed with a handle. It
also has a light that tells
you when it is operating
so that you do not open
the door until the drive
stops spinning.
(Courtesy of
International Business
Machines Corporation)

does not have a door. You just firmly press the disk into the slot until it locks into place. To remove the disk from the slot, you press a lever that releases it from the drive.

■ The light on the front of the drive goes on when the drive is operating. When the light is on, you should not open the door or eject a disk. Doing so can damage the disk and cause you to lose data. If you make a mistake and the drive spins when the door is open or without a disk inserted, do not close the door or insert a disk. In a few moments, a message will usually appear telling you the drive's door is open or no disk is in the drive. When the light goes out, close the door or insert a disk, and follow the instructions displayed on the screen.

Floppy Disk Storage Capacity

The size of a disk does not determine how much data you can store on it. This is determined by the processes used in its manufacture and the ability of the disk drive to pack more data on the disk. Over the past few years, steady progress has been made in storing data on disks so that today's floppy disk can store much more information than its predecessors. A few years ago, most disk drives could store data on only one side of the disk, but almost all new disk drives store data on both sides. This simple improvement doubled the storage capacity of the disk.

The disks you buy must be compatible with the system you use them on. There are several terms on the floppy disk box and disk labels that you should be familiar with. You must know the number of sides and the density used by your system to use the correct disks.

Sides
Disks are either single sided or double sided. **Single-sided disks** can store data on only one side of the disk. **Double-sided disks** can store data on both sides of the disk if your system's disk drive is capable of doing so.

Density
Data is stored on a disk in concentric tracks. The closer these tracks are, the more data the disk can store. The spacing of tracks is measured in tracks per inch (TPI). **Single-density disks** can store data on twenty-four tracks per inch. **Double- density disks** can store data on forty-eight tracks per inch on both sides of the disk, or as many as 360KB. **Quad-density** or **high-capacity disks** can store data on ninety-six tracks per inch, or as many as 1.2MB. The newer 3 1/2-inch disks can store as many as 720KB per side, so on a double-sided disk, you can store 1.44MB. These smaller disks can store more data than the larger 5 1/4-inch disks because data is stored on them in 135 TPI.

When using 5 1/4-inch disks with different TPI ratings, keep the following points in mind:

■ If you format a 96 TPI disk on a system that can read and write only 48 TPI disks, it is formatted as a 48 TPI disk. You cannot use the additional storage capacity.

■ To use a 48 TPI disk on a system designed for 96 TPI disks, you must format it as a 48 TPI disk before you store data on it.

■ You cannot retrieve files stored on a 96 TPI disk using a disk drive that can read and write only 48 TPI disks. Even if the disk is formatted with 48 TPI and the file is saved onto it, you cannot always retrieve the file. This makes it very difficult to exchange files created on a computer with a high-density disk drive with other users who use double- density or 48 TPI disk drives.

Floppy Disk Storage

When you first start working on a microcomputer, the number of disks you work with is manageable. But before long, keeping disks filed in an orderly way can present quite a problem. Several disk filing systems have been developed. They include plastic sleeves that can be filed in three-ring binders, plastic cases, and sophisticated filing cabinets for large collections.

HARD DISK DRIVES

Hard disk drives (also called fixed disks or **Winchester disk drives** after their code name while being developed at IBM) were not commonly used with microcomputers until recently because of their high cost.

Over the past few years, however, their cost has dropped dramatically. Their lower cost and superior performance has made them the first choice of serious computer users. Moreover, their storage capacity greatly reduces the number of disk "swaps" that must be made when working with floppy disk drives. Since many programs come on several floppy disks, this can save a great deal of time.

Instead of a floppy disk, hard disk drives use rigid metal platters to store data. This allows them to store data more densely. This increased density plus the number of platters greatly increases their storage capacity. Hard disk drives generally provide 5, 10, 20, 40 or more megabytes of storage capacity. They can store much more information than a floppy disk. Two factors determine how fast you can store data on and retrieve data from a hard disk drive: access time and data transfer rate.

Access Time

When you execute a command that requires the computer to find information stored externally, it takes time to find it. The time it takes to do this is the **access time**.

Data Transfer Rate

Once the computer has located the data in the external storage device, it must transfer it to memory. The rate at which data can be transferred is the **data transfer rate**. Hard disk drives generally have the fastest data transfer rates, and tapes the slowest; floppy disk drives are somewhere in between.

A hard disk drive spins at 3600 rpm, about ten times faster than a floppy disk drive, allowing data to be stored and retrieved faster. For example, an IBM PC with a hard disk drive transfers data twenty times faster than an IBM PC with a floppy disk drive.

In a floppy disk drive, the read/write heads are in contact with the disk. In a hard disk drive, they fly over its surface on a cushion of air with a space smaller than a piece of dust separating the head from the rapidly spinning disk. To prevent objects from damaging the drive or affecting its performance, hard disks are hermetically sealed in a case. But even a small particle can cause the read/write head to come into contact with the disk's surface, creating a **head crash**, which, with the disk spinning at almost 60 miles per hour, can cause a lot of damage to the disk and the data stored on it. Figure 1-25 shows the distance between the disk and the head compared to some typical items that can cause damage.

Even hard disks eventually become full. When there is no room for additional files, you must either delete files (after copying those that you want to save onto floppy disks) or add a larger disk drive. A few hard disk drives now come with removable disks that make deleting files or adding a larger drive unnecessary since you can insert a new disk just as you do on a floppy disk system.

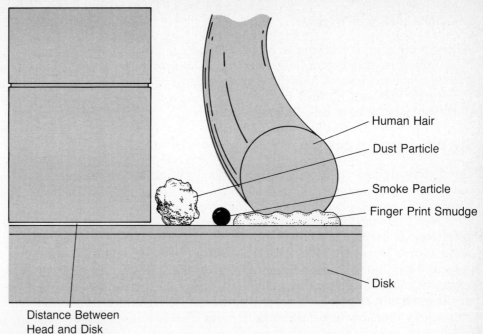

FIGURE 1-25
Hard disks have very small tolerances. When the read/write head is flying over the surface of the disk, the two are so close that smoke, a dust particle, a hair, or even a fingerprint could cause the head to crash.

Human Hair

Dust Particle

Smoke Particle

Finger Print Smudge

Disk

Distance Between
Head and Disk

MAGNETIC TAPE

Magnetic tape was once a major storage medium for microcomputers. But the problem with magnetic tape is its slow speed. For data to be retrieved, the tape first must be advanced to where it is stored; the data cannot be accessed randomly as on a disk. This is much like the difference between a song recorded on a cassette tape and a record. On the record, you can lower the needle directly onto any song, whereas on a cassette tape, you first must advance the tape to the song you want to hear. Because of this delay, playing a specific song on a tape takes longer than it does on a record. Moreover, when the desired data is located on a computer tape, it is then transferred into the computer's memory more slowly than it is from a disk. For these reasons, magnetic tape is now used mostly as a backup medium for hard disk files.

OPTICAL DISKS

One of the most recent and far-reaching developments in the microcomputer field is the new technology of optical disks. These disks currently come in two forms: CD-ROM disks and WORM disks.

CD-ROM Disks

CD-ROM disks (Figure 1-26), which are similar in concept to the compact disks (CDs) now popular in the music recording industry, can store so much information that it is measured in gigabytes. A small 4 3/4-inch CD-ROM can store as many as 550MB of data, or more than 1/2GB. This is equivalent to more than 1,500 floppy disks. Larger CD-ROMs can store as many as 20GB, and that limit will be exceeded long before you read this text.

Combined with search and retrieve software, these disks are changing the way information is stored, distributed, and accessed. One of the first optical disks to be published is *Microsoft's Bookshelf CD-ROM Reference Library*. This CD-ROM disk contains ten of the most widely used reference works, including *The World Almanac and Book of Facts, Bartlett's Familiar Quotations, The Chicago Manual of Style,* and the *U.S. ZIP Code Directory*. It also includes search and retrieve software, which makes it possible to look for information while working on another program. With

FIGURE 1-26
Optical disks and disk drives will become popular in offices that need to quickly access large amounts of data. Parts catalogs, reference files, and listings of all kinds will be stored on optical disks. (Courtesy of Laser Products)

only a few keystrokes, you can find information in any of these references and insert it into a document on the screen.

Another CD-ROM disk contains all forty-seven of the U.S. Postal Service ZIP+4 Code information on a single disk (Figure 1-26). These nine-digit ZIP codes identify areas of cities but also apartment buildings, office suites, and floor numbers in commercial buildings. Software with the disk can check a new address as it is being entered and display the full address and ZIP code for approval.

The possibilities for CD-ROM are limitless. Parts catalogs, stock market reports, reference books, library card index files, and telephone directories are just some of the items that can be distributed and used more effectively with this new technology.

WORM Disks

Unlike a magnetic medium, where the information can be recorded and then erased when not needed, optical disks currently cannot be erased. CD-ROM disks are prerecorded, and you cannot save your own data on them. However, another type of optical disk, **write- once, read-many (WORM) disks**, is making it possible for you to store data. To record data on WORM disks, a laser actually burns microscopic pits into their surface. The storage area on these disks is so vast that you can afford to record the same file in different places on the disk each time you make changes. The old version is not erased, it is just ignored. Eventually the disk will be filled, but even the early versions of these disks store 200MB of data. With this much space, they will not be filled quickly. When refined, the optical disk will seriously challenge the hard disk drive as an external storage device for large amounts of data.

PROTECTING YOUR FILES

When you enter data into the computer, it is not permanently stored until you save it onto disks. But even then the data is not protected from loss, damage, or scrutiny by unauthorized persons.

Security

If you work on a computer with floppy disk drives, you can secure your work by removing the floppy disks and taking them with you. On a hard disk system, this is not possible. Protecting sensitive data on hard disks from other users who have access to the computer is difficult. One way to provide security is to **encrypt**, or code, files using an encryption program. Then, only users who know an assigned password can gain access to the files.

Another way to provide security is by using hard disk drives with removable media. The media can be removed and stored separately from the computer.

Backup Copies

It is also wise to make a **backup copy** (a duplicate) of the files on a hard disk so that they are not lost in the event of a head crash or other problem. The least expensive, but most time-consuming, way is to back them up on floppy disks.

More expensive hard disks have a built-in backup system that copies files from the hard disk onto a tape using a tape drive. These tapes can then be removed for safekeeping. It is also possible to use a video tape cassette player to back up a hard disk provided that you have the hardware and software needed to connect them.

CARING FOR YOUR DISKS

Although disks, both hard and floppy, are very reliable storage media, the data they contain can be lost or damaged if you do not take a few precautions. For example, floppy disks have a useful life of about forty hours' spinning time but that life can be shortened or abruptly ended by improper handling.

Care of hard disk drives

DON'T drop or jar them. They are very sensitive.

DO use a park program to move the drive's read/write head to a section of the disk that has no data. This prevents the head from damaging data on the disk should it move.

Care of floppy disk drives

DON'T use commercial cleaning kits too frequently. Overuse can cause problems with the drive.

DO insert the cardboard protectors that came with the computer into the disk drives and close the doors when moving the computer.

Care of floppy disks

DO keep disks in their protective storage envelopes. These envelopes reduce static buildup, which can attract dust that might scratch the disk.

DO keep disks dry, away from sneezes, coffee, or anything wet. A wet disk is a ruined disk.

DO prevent disks from getting too hot or too cold. They should be stored at temperatures of $50°–150°F$ ($10°–52°C$). Extreme temperatures can destroy a disk's sensitivity, so treat them the same way you treat photographic film: Keep them out of direct sunlight, do not leave them in a car exposed to temperature extremes, and so forth.

DO keep disks at least 2 feet away from magnets. The magnets found in copy stands, telephones, radios or stereo speakers, vacuum cleaners, televisions, air conditioners, novelty items, electric motors, or even some cabinet latches can ruin a disk's sensitivity.

DO always make backup copies of your important disks, and save them a safe distance from your working area. Make sure the same accident cannot happen to both the disk and its backup copy. The information on the disk is usually worth much more than the disk itself, so do not take chances.

DO load disks into the drive gently; otherwise, they may bend, center improperly, or rotate in an elliptical orbit that misses data.

DON'T touch a disk's recording surface. Handle them by their protective covers only.

DON'T use a hard-tipped pen to write on a disk label while it is on the disk. This can crease the disk inside the protective cover and cause you to lose data. Write on the label before putting it on the disk, or use a felt-tip pen with very light pressure.

DON'T leave a disk in a nonoperating disk drive with the door closed for more than an hour. Open the drive door to lift the read/write head from the surface of the disk.

DON'T insert or remove a disk from the drive when the disk drive is running (that is, when the red light is on).

DON'T bend, fold, or crimp disks.

DON'T use paper clips to attach a floppy disk to a file folder or printout. Special folders are available that allow you to keep disks and printed documents together.

DON'T expose disks to static electricity. In dry climates or in heated buildings, static builds up when you walk on carpeted and some other kinds of floors. If you experience shocks when you touch metal objects, you are discharging the static that has built up. If you touch a disk when still charged with this static, you can damage the data. To prevent this, increase the humidity in the air, use static-proof carpets, or touch something like a typewriter to discharge the static before you pick up a disk.

Even with the best of care, floppy disks can last only so long. Close to the end of their useful life, they show their own form of senility by losing information or giving invalid commands. These are signs that it is time to replace the disk, which ideally, you have already made another backup copy of.

QUESTIONS

1. List and briefly describe the four main types of external storage media.
2. What two factors determine the amount of information that can be stored on a disk?
3. What is the purpose of the write-protect notch on a floppy disk, and how do you use it?
4. Describe the purpose of the red light on the front of a disk drive.
5. What should you always do before you move a hard disk drive?
6. Why should you make backup copies of files on a hard disk drive?
7. What is the major advantage of optical disks over other types of storage media?
8. What two factors determine how fast a drive can store data to and retrieve data from a disk?
9. If you are working on sensitive documents, what are two ways to protect them from being seen by unauthorized users?
10. List three things you should do to protect floppy disks. List three things you should not do.

ACTIVITIES

1. Sketch a floppy disk, and then label each of its parts.

2. Using a manual that accompanies one of the computer systems in the lab, specify the following information about the disks that you use with the system:

Number of sides: _____

Density (TPI): _____

Sectors (hard or soft): _____

3. What kinds of storage devices are available in the lab?

TOPIC 1-6
Distribution Devices

In this topic, we introduce you to distribution devices, the devices you use to exchange information between computers and people. After finishing this topic, you will be able to

- Describe how computers can be connected into networks
- Explain the difference between a computer connected into a network and a multiuser computer system
- Explain the function of a modem
- Describe the different types of modems
- Explain how you send documents to facsimile machines from your microcomputer

When computers were first introduced into businesses in the early 1970s, they were expensive and hard to operate. This led to their being installed in a centralized place called the data processing department. Most employees in the company had only limited access to the computer through **dumb terminals**, that is, terminals lacking the ability to process data on their own. To work, a dumb terminal must be connected to a central computer that can process data for it. The terminal is used only to send information to the computer and receive information from it.

With the development of low-cost microcomputers, computers became more decentralized. When microcomputers are used, the user sits at a **workstation**. If you were to walk through a modern office, you would see computer workstations throughout the building. Each workstation is either an intelligent computer or a dumb terminal, and you cannot tell the difference just by looking at it. The significant differences are inside the cabinet. Dumb terminals cannot function unless connected to the central computer, whereas **intelligent computers** can process information when disconnected from the system.

Each workstation has a display screen and a keyboard. The way these workstations are organized, and the other equipment they have, depends on the technology the company is using. The basic approaches are standalone microcomputers, networks, or multiuser computer systems.

STANDALONE MICROCOMPUTERS

Standalone microcomputers are not tied together into a larger system. Each standalone microcomputer is a complete system that includes a computer, keyboard, dis-

FIGURE 1-27
**A standalone
workstation** has
everything a user needs
to do information
processing. The
workstation is not
connected to other
computers. (Courtesy of
International Business
Machines Corporation)

play screen, and printer (Figure 1-27). A standalone system like this is used by a single person or shared by several people who use it at different times. Users generally process information for themselves, another person, or a small group. Although standalone units are not operated by a specialized staff, they may be supervised by a manager from the company's **management information systems (MIS) department**. This manager approves the purchase of hardware and software and provides training and support to the users.

NETWORKS AND MULTIUSER COMPUTER SYSTEMS

With recent advances in technology, it has become possible to connect computers together so that users can share data, programs, and peripherals. Workstations in these systems are often organized into two types of systems: networks and multiuser computer systems.

A **network** (Figure 1-28) is a group of computers that are connected so that users can exchange messages, share files, and share resources like printers. Networks are popular because they allow users to exchange electronic mail and data and

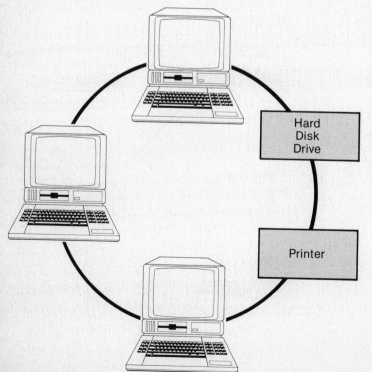

FIGURE 1-28
**A computer
network** combines
the best features
of centralized and
standalone
systems. Users
can work
individually or
share documents
and resources like
printers with other
users on the
network.

Hard
Disk
Drive

Printer

to access expensive peripherals like laser printers.

This arrangement means each workstation is an intelligent computer and has the ability to process data even if disconnected from the network. Systems organized into a network are usually supervised by a **network manager**. This person can be a member of either the department the network is located in or the company's MIS department. The network manager is responsible for supervising the use of the system and authorizes or denies users access to specific files. An **authorized user**, for example, may be authorized access to correspondence files but denied access to financial analysis files.

A **multiuser computer system** has a central computer that does the processing for the other workstations connected to it (Figure 1-29). These workstations can be either intelligent computers or dumb terminals.

MODEMS

A **modem** is a communications device that links computers by using telephone lines. With a modem, you can send data from your computer to another computer equipped with a modem anywhere you can reach by phone (Figure 1-30). This process in called **telecommunication**.

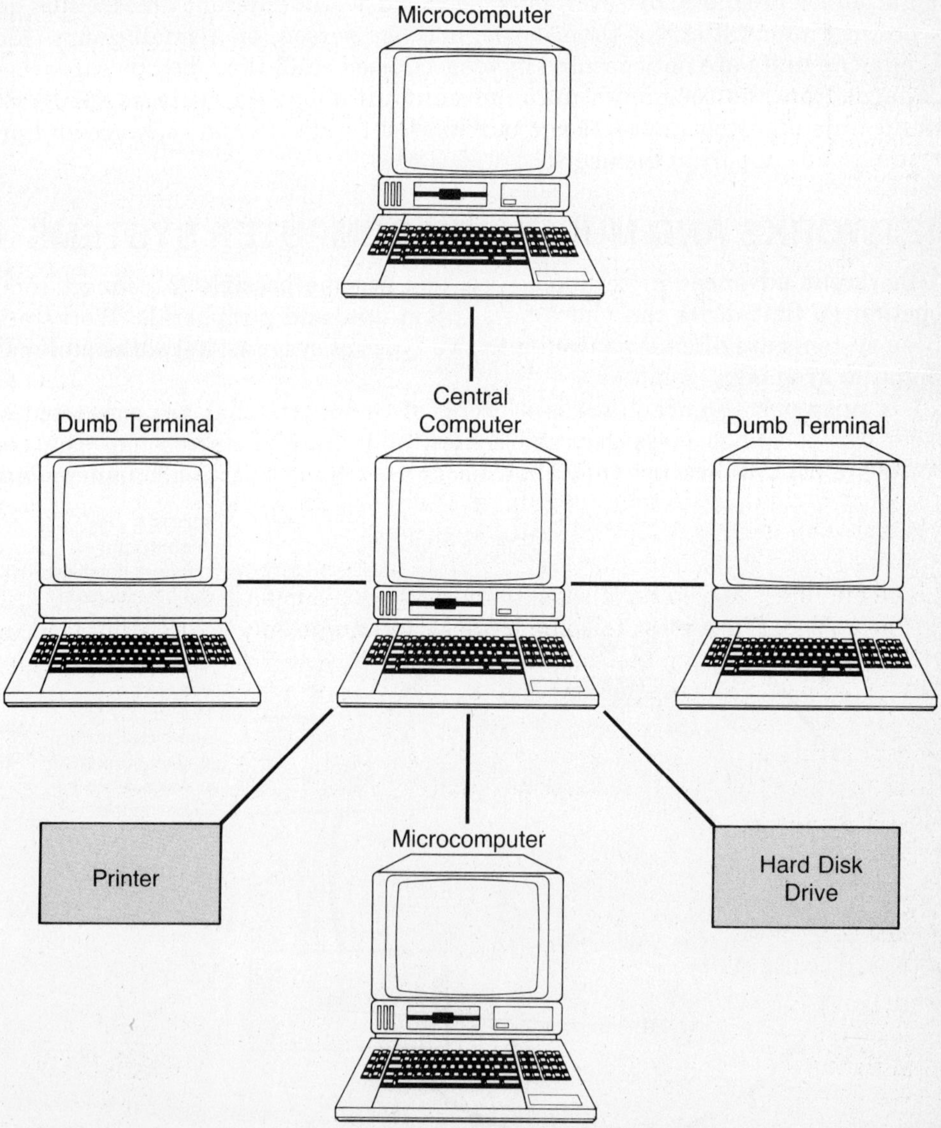

FIGURE 1-29
A multiuser computer system is similar to a network, but all processing is done by a central computer that the workstations are connected to. The workstations can be dumb terminals or intelligent computers.

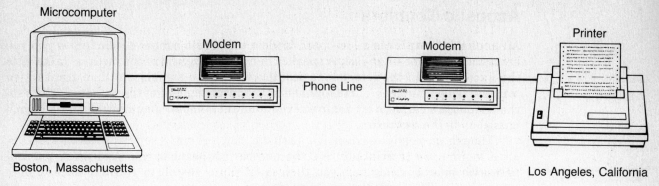

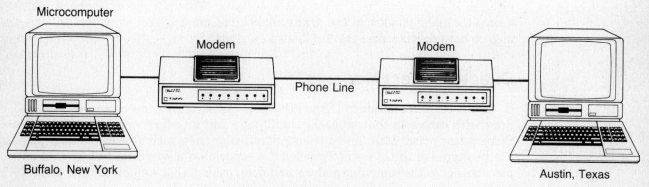

FIGURE 1-30
Modems must be used at both ends of the telephone circuit. The sender can then transmit data over the telephone lines to the modem at the other end. The receiving modem can be connected either to another computer or to a printer.

You need a modem to telecommunicate because computers generate **digital signals**, whereas telephone lines carry **analog signals**. When you transmit a message, the modem at the sending end converts the computer's digital signals into analog signals (**modulation**) so that they can be transmitted effectively over telephone lines (Figure 1-31). The modem at the receiving end then converts the analog signals back into digital signals (**demodulation**) so that they can be used by the computer. The name *modem* derives from *modulate-demodulate*.

The type of modem determines how it is connected to the computer and telephone lines. As you have seen, data inside the computer is processed 8, 16, or 32 bits at a time. Since most telephone lines can handle only a single bit at a time, the data must be sent from the computer to the modem serially, one bit at a time. To do this, you need to connect your modem to a serial port on your computer. A serial port converts the parallel signal used by the computer into a serial signal suitable for transmission over telephone wires. The two basic types of modems are acoustic couplers and direct-connect modems. Both types of modems require a communications program.

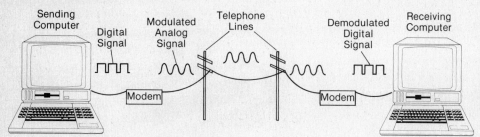

FIGURE 1-31
Modems are simply conversion devices. A modem at the sending end converts the digital signal from the computer into an analog signal that can be transmitted over the telephone wires. The modem at the receiving end converts the analog signal back into a digital signal.

Acoustic Couplers

An **acoustic coupler** is a low-speed modem that has a rubber cradle into which you press the telephone's handset. A speaker in the sending end of the modem "talks" into the microphone in the telephone's mouthpiece. These signals are then transmitted over the telephone lines. A microphone in the receiving end of the modem "listens" to the telephone's earpiece for data received from the remote computer. The data is then passed on to the computer.

Though generally inexpensive, acoustic couplers have several drawbacks. They often require you to manually dial the number you want to call. And when you connect with another computer, you then must flip a switch to go from voice to data transmission. These modems have fairly high error rates because the modem picks up any background noise in the room, and this can garble the data transmission. Moreover, a telephone always feeds some of the transmitted signal back into the earpiece so that you can hear what you are saying. This telephone feedback confuses acoustic coupler modems. The transmit volume must be set very low so that the modem does not interpret this feedback as a signal.

Direct-Connect Modems

A **direct-connect modem** (Figure 1-32) is connected to the computer and phone lines with cables so that no background noise can interfere with the data. Because there is less noise, data can be transmitted faster than with acoustic couplers. There are two types of direct-connect modems: a modem on a board that plugs into an expansion slot in the computer and a standalone modem that connects to the computer's

**FIGURE 1-32
Direct-connect modems** plug directly into the phone line so that you do not need a phone to use them. They come in two basic versions: (a) a modem on a board plugs into an expansion slot in the computer, and (b) a standalone modem connects to the computer's serial port. (Courtesy of U.S. Robotics)

MICROLINK 1200

serial port with a cable. Both types plug into the telephone's wall jack with a standard phone cable.

Communications Programs

To communicate with other computers, your computer and the computers you want to communicate with must be connected to a telephone line. A communications program is then used so that the computers can call one another and exchange data. These programs store the phone numbers you use to call another computer. Once installed, you can also specify the filenames to be sent or received.

FACSIMILE

Until recently, you could distribute the documents you created on your computer in only two ways: as electronic digital signals or as printed copy. Today, you can distribute them electronically over a network, or you can use a modem to connect to a remote computer. You can distribute printed copy through the mail, or you can use a facsimile (fax) machine (Table 1-6).

A **facsimile machine** is like a copy machine where you insert the original document into your machine, and a copy comes out on another facsimile machine anywhere in the world.

Since the cost of fax machines has dropped, they have become widespread. To send a document on a fax machine, you insert the document into the fax's document tray, and then dial the phone number of another fax machine. When the other fax answers the call, your fax automatically feeds the document through its scanner. This scanner converts the document into digital signals. These signals are sent over the phone line to the recipient's fax machine, which reverses the process. It converts the digital signals back into an image, which it prints out. When the transmission is completed, both machines hang up.

With an expansion board, it is possible for you to send a document to someone's fax machine directly from your computer (Figure 1-33) or for someone with a fax machine to send a document directly to your computer. This speeds the process since you do not have to first make a printout and then walk to a fax machine. These expansion boards are installed in one of the slots in your computer and then connected to the telephone jack on the wall.

TABLE 1-6
Methods of Document Distribution

Sender	Recipient	Method of Distribution
Printout	Printout	Facsimile to facsimile
Digital	Digital	Computer to computer
Digital	Printout	Computer to facsimile
Printout	Digital	Facsimile to computer

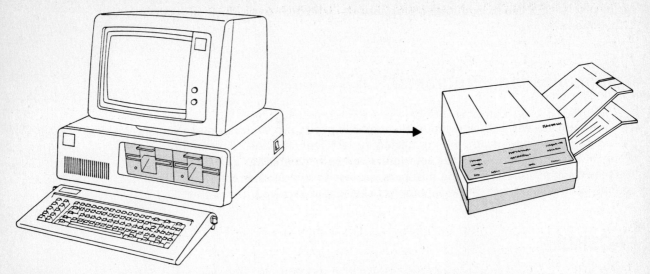

FIGURE 1-33
Microcomputer-based facsimile is now possible by inserting an expansion board into one of your computer's ports. With this board you can send documents directly from your files to another fax. You dial the number of another fax, and the document is drawn through the scanner and converted into digital signals. These signals are sent over the telephone lines. The receiving fax then reverses the process and converts the signals back into a printed image.

QUESTIONS

1. Computers are connected together on networks or as multiuser systems. What is the basic difference between these two arrangements?

2. What is the difference between a dumb terminal and an intelligent computer?

3. What is the function of a modem?

4. List two types of modems, and describe the differences between them.

5. What is the purpose of a communications program?

6. What is the purpose of a facsimile machine?

7. Assume you want to send a document to a recipient in another state and want to send it over the telephone lines. Describe four ways you could send it.

ACTIVITIES

1. Find an article on telecommunications in a magazine in the library that describes the services you can subscribe to if your computer is equipped with a modem. List some of these available services and describe the possible benefits of subscribing to them.

2. Find out if the computers in the lab are standalone units or are connected into a network. If connected into a network, describe the type of network.

TOPIC 1-7
Application Software

In this topic, we introduce you to application software and the data files you create with these programs. After finishing this topic, you will be able to

- Describe the most common types of application programs, and explain what they are used for
- Explain the difference between disk-based and memory-based programs and data files
- Describe the various types of data files and how they differ from one another
- Describe how to save and retrieve data files and assign names to them
- Describe how to assign filenames on IBM PC and compatible computers
- Explain why you must install programs
- Describe a driver, and explain why it is important

As you know, application programs are designed to convert a general-purpose computer into a working tool for a specific task. Examples of application programs include word processing programs and spreadsheet programs. You load a word processing program into the computer when you want to write a letter, and you load a spreadsheet program when you want to prepare a budget. In many jobs, you are expected to become familiar with several application programs so that you can process all the company's information.

Let us now briefly look at some popular types of application programs that are not discussed in Parts 3, 4, and 5.

GRAPHICS PROGRAMS

The old saying "a picture is worth a thousand words" appropriately applies to computer graphics. In a single glance, graphics can convey information that would be difficult to put into words. You can easily use your microcomputer to generate graphics. Two kinds of **graphics programs** are those used to create business charts and graphs and those used to create illustrations.

Business graphics programs (frequently integrated into spreadsheet programs) create charts and graphs that represent numeric data (Figure 1-34). Interactive graphics programs generate original, free-form art and designs (Figure 1-35). These programs are called interactive because you create, edit, and manipulate the images directly on the screen. Business and interactive graphics programs are being used more and more to create images that are then included in word-processed documents.

INTEGRATED PROGRAMS

Most programs do one task and thus are called standalone programs. But several programs are available that combine two or more of the five basic types of applications programs—word processing, database management, spreadsheets, graphics, and communications. These **integrated programs** try to meet the following standards:

- Use common commands or command structures in all functions
- Allow data to be shared by all functions
- Have sufficiently powerful functions so that standalone programs are not needed

**FIGURE 1-34
A business graph** can convey a great deal of information in a single picture. There are many types of graphs, including those shown in this illustration. (Courtesy of Microsoft Corporation)

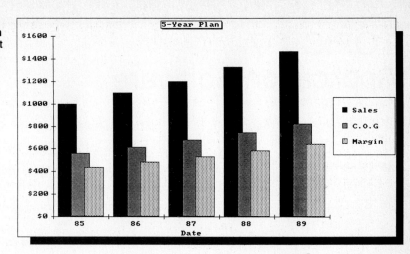

**FIGURE 1-35
Interactive graphics programs** let you draw and manipulate an illustration on the screen. (Courtesy of Xerox Corporation)

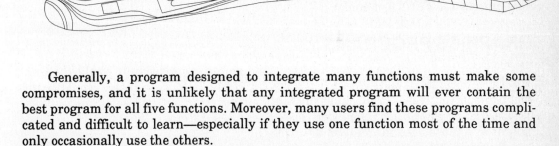

Generally, a program designed to integrate many functions must make some compromises, and it is unlikely that any integrated program will ever contain the best program for all five functions. Moreover, many users find these programs complicated and difficult to learn—especially if they use one function most of the time and only occasionally use the others.

The most successful integrated programs combine only two or three functions. Many word processing programs have built-in record management programs so that you can maintain and use mailing lists to send out form letters. Spreadsheet programs commonly have built-in graphics programs so that numbers can be displayed or printed as graphs.

DESKTOP PUBLISHING PROGRAMS

Desktop publishing programs (also called page makeup, page composition, or page processing programs) are used to design documents. These programs, which offer a wide selection of type styles, make it easy to organize type into columns, add ruled lines, and combine text with graphics on the same page. Desktop publishing programs are among the newest software available and are still being refined. Generally, first you enter and edit a document on a word processing program, and then you transfer it to a desktop publishing program, where you lay out and design the final document. Word processing programs are better at editing than at formatting, and desktop publishing programs are better at formatting than at editing. Increasingly, however, the features offered by desktop publishing programs are being incorporated into word processing programs.

UTILITY PROGRAMS

Utility programs are small, generally inexpensive programs that perform a single task. They are designed to make you or your computer faster and more efficient. There are many types of utility programs.

Memory resident programs (also called terminate and stay resident or TSR programs) let you use more than one program at the same time. You load these programs into the computer's memory before you load an applications program. Memory resident programs are always in memory when you are working on your applications. You can switch back and forth between the two programs in memory by pressing two or three designated keys. When you display the memory resident program, the other program is suspended. When you press another key, the memory resident program disappears from the screen (but is still available in memory), and the applications program you were working on returns.

Outline programs were initially designed as utility programs but are increasingly being integrated into word processing programs. These programs let you enter headings much as you do when manually preparing an outline. But outline programs automatically number headings and indent subheadings to indicate their level. If you insert or delete an entry, the program automatically renumbers all headings that follow the revision. Many of these programs also let you enter text linked to a specific heading. If you copy, move, or delete a heading, all text associated with it is also copied, moved, or deleted.

These programs let you look at your document in two ways. You can view the entire document, or you can close it up so that you see just the outline's headings (Figure 1-36). Not only does this let you see both the overall structure of the document and the details in each section, it also lets you move quickly through a long document. You display the document in outline view, highlight the heading of the section you want to move to, and open that section to see the text it contains.

File recovery programs let you recover files when you inadvertently delete a needed file from a disk. When you delete a file, you delete only its name from the disk's directory; the file itself remains intact. You can recover the file provided you do not store any other files on the disk since these would overwrite the file. A file recovery program restores the name of the file to the directory. You can then retrieve the file with the program you used to create it.

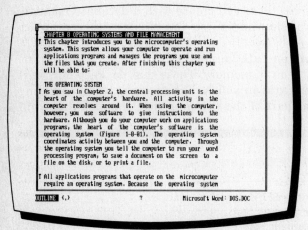

A. Document View   B. Outline View

FIGURE 1-36

An outline program lets you view your document in two ways: (a) you can look at it in document view to see and work with details, or (b) you can look at it in outline view to look at the overall structure and organization.

PROGRAM FILES

The computer's memory is a valuable, but limited, resource. For this reason, the way applications programs and data files are stored in memory is a key feature of how a program operates.

Applications programs operate in memory and store data files in two basic ways: They are either memory based or disk based.

Memory-based applications programs are loaded entirely into memory when you load the program. There are both advantages and disadvantages to memory-based programs. Since the entire program is loaded into memory, it can perform its functions quickly because everything the program needs is accessible. And since the entire program is in memory, the program disk can be removed from the disk drive, making it available for another disk. The main disadvantage is that these programs can take up a lot of the computer's available memory, leaving little for your own files.

Disk-based applications programs are so large that loading them entirely into memory would leave little memory available for the files you are working on. Thus disk-based programs load only part of the program into memory; the rest of the program, using the technique of virtual memory, remains on the disk until needed. This lets a large program run on a small amount of memory. Programs of this kind have two parts. The core, or kernel, is that part of the program always in memory. It executes the most often used commands and calls other parts of the program, the overlay files, into memory when they are needed. When you execute a command, the disk drive often operates because the command you are executing is not in memory, so the core goes to the disk to load the overlay file. You can sometimes identify these files in your disk directory because they often have the extension .OVR.

There are advantages and disadvantages to disk-based programs as well. Since a disk-based program must go to the disk occasionally for those parts of the program or data files it needs, these programs are slower than memory-based programs. Retrieving overlay files from a disk slows down the execution of commands. Moreover, since the program leaves part of its own files on the disk, the disk must be left in the drive so that the program can find these files when it needs them.

DATA FILES

When you use an applications program to create a document, spreadsheet model, or database, you store your work on a disk in a data file so that you can retrieve it later. Each type of application creates its own type of data file. For example, files you create with a word processing program are called document files; those you create with a spreadsheet program are worksheet files; those you create with a database management program are record or database files; and those you create with a graphics program are picture files (Table 1-7).

Some programs use virtual memory for data files and other do not. Those that do not, keep the entire file you are working on in memory. Those that do, keep only part of long files in memory and store other parts on a disk. For example, when operating a word processing program that stores part of the file on a disk, the disk drive will

---

TABLE 1-7
Applications Programs and Their Files

Type of Applications Program	Type of Files
Word processing	Document files
Spreadsheet	Worksheet files
Database management	Record or database files
Graphics	Picture files

operate when you are working on a long file and move the cursor to a distant part of the file. The program has to retrieve from the disk the part of the file you are moving to because it is not in memory at that moment.

Both approaches have advantages and disadvantages. The size of files created on programs that keep the entire file in memory is limited by the available memory, but you can get around large files more quickly. The size of files created on programs that store part of the file on a disk is limited only by the amount of storage space on the disk, but may be slower to move around, since the program may have to retrieve sections of the file from the disk.

SAVING AND RETRIEVING FILES

One of the primary functions of all applications programs is file management, saving and retrieving files. Most programs let you specify the drive a file is to be saved on, and if you are using a hard disk drive, you can also specify the directory. Later, when retrieving the files, you must specify the same drive and directory.

When you save a data file, the program copies it from the computer's memory onto a disk (Figure 1-37).

Each file saved onto a disk must have a unique name. You can assign the same name only under the following circumstances:

■ When you save the files onto different disks

■ When you save files on a hard disk drive that has been divided into directories (as is described in Part 2)

The name you give a file is generally determined by the **operating system**--the master set of programs that manages the computer (see Part 2). PC-DOS, MS-DOS, and OS/2, the operating systems used by IBM and IBM-compatible computers, have the following rules for naming files. First of all, filenames generally have two parts, a filename and an extension (Figure 1-38).

■ The filename can have from one to eight characters. The following characters are legal for a filename:

Letters   A–Z
Numbers   0–9
Symbols $ # & @ ! % ( ) - _ {} ' ' ~ ^

All other characters are illegal. You can use either uppercase or lowercase letters. The program automatically converts all lowercase letters into uppercase letters.

FIGURE 1-37
When you save a file, the computer copies the version currently on the screen and stored in the computer's memory to a file on the disk so that you can retrieve it later when you need it. Retrieving a file from the disk copies it from the disk into the computer's memory. The copy of the file on the disk remains unchanged.

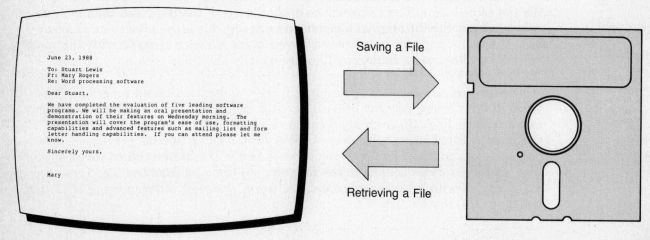

June 23, 1988

To: Stuart Lewis
Fr: Mary Rogers
Re: Word processing software

Dear Stuart,

We have completed the evaluation of five leading software programs. We will be making an oral presentation and demonstration of their features on Wednesday morning. The presentation will cover the program's ease of use, formatting capabilities and advanced features such as mailing list and form letter handling capabilities. If you can attend please let me know.

Sincerely yours,

Mary

Saving a File

Retrieving a File

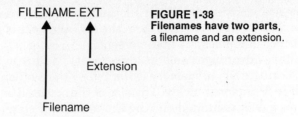

FILENAME.EXT

↑   ↑

Extension

Filename

FIGURE 1-38
Filenames have two parts,
a filename and an extension.

If you specify an illegal filename, the program normally does not accept it and prompts you to enter a correct filename.

If you enter a filename with more than eight characters, the program normally accepts it but uses only the first eight characters. For example, if you save a file named FILENAME1 and later create and save another file named FILENAME2, the program overwrites and erases the first file. It assumes they are the same file because the first eight characters are identical.

■ The extension can have from one to three characters (the characters that are legal for a filename are also legal for an extension), but it must be separated from the filename by a period. Often, the extension is automatically added to identify the program that generated it.

TYPES OF DATA FILES

Applications programs are frequently capable of saving files in various formats. In many cases, the program automatically adds an extension to the filename to differentiate one type of file from another.

Binary files are the files you create with an applications program. Binary files contain formatting codes specific to the program used to create the file. For example, when you underline words, add page numbers, change margins or line spacing, or add headers and footers, you are actually entering codes into the document. These format codes are specific to the program you are using; there is no established standard. Thus these codes cannot be interpreted by other programs, which have their own codes. To use binary files with another program, the program-specific codes must be either removed or converted into codes the program will understand. This is generally done by saving them with a command designed for this purpose or by using a separate program to convert them.

Binary files are usually saved with an extension specific to the program you are working on. Some programs automatically add an extension, for example, .DOC (for document) to every file you save. Other programs do not automatically add an extension, but you can add one. Different extensions let you distinguish among files created with different programs.

Back copy files are automatically generated by some programs when you save a file the second time. They rename the original copy of the disk, and then store the new version under the original filename. A back copy file is the previously saved version of the file and can be retrieved if you make a major mistake with the most recently saved version. Back copy files are usually identified with an extension like .BAK (for back).

ASCII files are saved in a standard format understood by all programs. When saved in this format, they can be used by other programs or transmitted by a modem over telephone lines. Since binary files can rarely be interpreted by other programs or telecommunicated using a modem without first making special provisions, many programs let you save files for these purposes as ASCII text files. When saved in this way, all format codes specific to the program are removed from the file. These files are identified with a variety of extensions, two of the most common being .TXT (for text) and .ASC (for ASCII).

Print files are like ASCII files, but all format codes are interpreted. A print file is created just like a printout on the printer. The only difference is that the output is sent to a file on a disk instead of to the printer. For example, headers, footers, page numbers, top and bottom margins, and other formats that would appear on a printout also appear in the print file on the disk. Print files are created so that you can preview the results of format codes before actually printing the file on paper. They can also be printed directly from the operating system and, in some cases, can be used (as ASCII files can be) by other programs. For example, using print files, you can exchange formatted text between programs. You can create a financial model using The TWIN or Lotus 1-2-3, and then print it to the disk. You can then load a word processing program and insert this print file into a document. Print files are usually identified with an extension like .PRT or .PRN (for print).

Temporary files are created on the disk by some programs when you use them. For example, many word processing programs print a file to the disk before sending it to the printer. It then automatically erases the files from the disk when they are no longer needed. The only time you see these files is if you display a directory of the disk they are stored on before they are deleted or if the computer shuts down for some reason before it erases them. You should always use the program's commands to exit from a program so that it can erase any temporary files it has created. If you simply turn off the computer, these files will remain on the disk, and the regular document files on the disk may not reflect any of the changes stored in these temporary files.

EXECUTING COMMANDS

One of the main differences among programs is the number of commands they have and the way you execute them. It is not necessary for you to know all the commands to use a program because many of them are for advanced features that you learn if and when you need them.

Most programs come with a quick reference card that lists all the program's commands and briefly describes how you execute them. These cards are useful when you cannot remember a specific command. You should always keep one handy when working on the computer.

Using On-line Help

One function key on the keyboard is usually designated by the program as the help key. If you need help at any time, pressing this key displays text that describes the program's commands and how to use them.

If the help screens are **context sensitive**, the help displayed may be directly related to what you are trying to do at the moment. For example, if you have begun the sequence of commands to save a file and cannot remember how to complete the sequence, pressing the help key displays help on saving files.

Most help screens also have a table of contents or menu that allows you to display help on various topics. This lets you look up information on any topic at any time.

When you have finished with help, you press the key specified, or select Quit from the Help menu to return to where you were in your document, or procedure, before you asked for help.

Using Function Keys and Typing Commands

One way to execute commands is to press function keys, or other designated keys, and then type the commands. Typing commands is fast, especially for touch-typists. For example, if the program's command to save a file is to hold down the **Ctrl** key while you press the letters **K** and **S**, you can execute the command without looking at the keyboard or screen. The problem is remembering the commands.

Computer keyboards have several function keys whose sole purpose is to perform tasks assigned to them by the program's author. For example, on a database program, the function key **F10** may be assigned the task of adding a record, whereas on a word processing program, **F10** may be assigned the task of saving a document.

Many keys are assigned more than one task; for example, pressing the right arrow key may move the cursor one column or character at a time, but pressing the right arrow key while holding down **Ctrl** may move the cursor several columns or characters at a time. The **Ctrl** key does not send characters to the computer; rather, it changes what is sent when other keys are pressed. Using combinations of keys in this way allows software designers to assign many more tasks to the keyboard than there are keys.

When you use these control keys, usually the **Ctrl, Alt,** and **Shift** keys, the sequence you press them in is important. For example, to use the **Ctrl** and right arrow keys together (usually specified in manuals as Ctrl-right arrow or ^right arrow), you press the **Ctrl** key and hold it down while you quickly press the right arrow key. On many commands, if you hold down both keys, the computer keeps repeating the command, causing unexpected results.

Programs that assign specific task to keys often supply a plastic or cardboard keyboard template that fits over some of the keys (usually the function keys). These templates briefly describe the tasks assigned to each key so that you need not memorize them.

Using Menus

Another way to execute commands is to use menus (Figure 1-39).

Choosing commands from a menu is easy because you do not have to memorize commands. Menus are like those you get in a restaurant--they list available choices. To execute commands on a menu-driven program, you usually have two options.

- Use designated keys to highlight a selection with a menu pointer. You then press **Return** to execute the highlighted command. On some systems, you can also make the selection from the menu with a mouse or by pointing to a choice on a touch sensitive screen.

- Type the number preceding the command or the first character in the command's name. On some programs, you must press **Return** after doing this.

Many menu-driven programs use more than one level of menus. These multilevel menus allow numerous commands to be listed on a relatively narrow screen. Choosing many of the commands listed on the menu just displays another menu on the

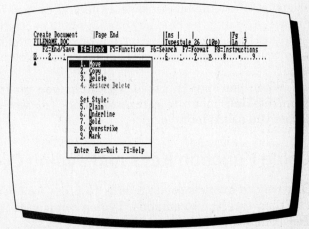

FIGURE 1-39
On programs with pull-down menus, when you select a choice from a menu bar at the top of the screen, a list of related commands descends from the choice. This pull-down menu lists specific commands that you can choose by highlighting them and then pressing **Return.**

screen. Getting to the actual command you want to execute occasionally means you must select a series of commands from the displayed submenus.

As you make selections from multilevel menus, you are actually working your way through a menu tree (as in Figure 1-40), which, like a family tree, is simply an arrangement of menu commands.

As you work your way through the commands shown on the menu tree, you may find you are on the wrong branch or decide not to continue for some other reason. Usually, **Esc** is designated as the key that returns you to your starting point. Some programs designate **Esc**, or another key, as the key you can retrace, a command at a time, your steps to back out of the menu. Sometimes you retrace your steps only part way so that you can continue the command down a different branch of the tree.

Often, the menu disappears when you complete a command, and you are returned to where you were before you began executing the command. In some cases, you must select a Quit or Exit choice on the menu or press a designated key to remove the menu. These sticky menus stay on the screen, anticipating that you want to use more than one of the listed choices. For example, you might want to boldface, italicize, or underline the same phrase in a document. If the menu were to automatically disappear when you make a selection, you would have to repeat the entire sequence of commands to make another selection from the same menu. Since the menu remains on the screen, you can make several choices and remove the menu only when you are finished.

When you are first learning a program, ease of use is of primary importance. But as you gain experience with the program, ease becomes secondary to the speed you can execute commands with. If you point to a choice on a menu to execute a command, you may have to press keys ten or more times to call up the menu and select the choice. At this point, you will want to type the least possible number of keys to execute commands. Thus many programs combine the two approaches. They provide

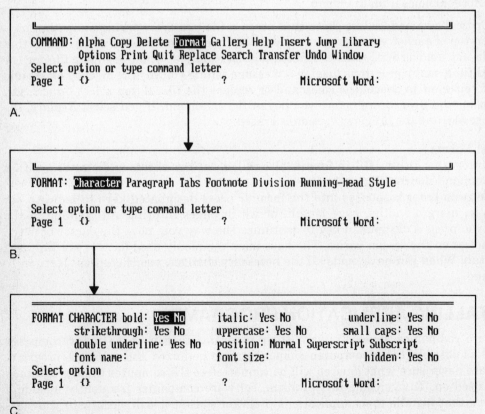

FIGURE 1-40
A menu tree shows how commands are organized in multilevel menus. (a) When you press **Esc** on Microsoft Word, the menu at the bottom of the screen is activated. (b) When you move the highlight over the choice *Format*, and then press **Return**, a submenu listing format commands is displayed. (c) When you move the highlight over the choice *Character*, and then press **Return**, a list of format options is displayed.

full menus that you make choices from when you are first learning the program. However, the menus are designed so that as you gain experience with the program, you can execute the commands by typing only the first letter in the name of the command listed on the menu. Since fewer keystrokes are required, this speeds up the execution of commands.

Responding to Prompts and Fill-in Forms

When executing commands, programs occasionally ask you to enter information they need to complete the command, for example, a page number to print, the name of a file to save or retrieve, or a word to be searched for. The text that appears on the screen asking you to supply this information generally appears as either a prompt or a fill-in form.

Prompts

Many commands display **prompts**, lines of text at the top or bottom of the screen that ask you to enter the information the computer needs. You answer prompts in one of three ways.

- You type information from the keyboard, and then press **Return**. You can type information in lowercase letters, uppercase letters, or both. For example, filename, FILENAME, and FileName are all the same.
- You make a choice from a menu.
- You press **Return** to accept the default response. Default responses either are entered by the program's designer or are remembered by the program as your previous responses to the same prompts. If the program displays default responses, you can type over them to enter a new response, or you can make another choice from the menu.

Critical commands, like those that erase a file you are working on or that save files on top of earlier versions, generally prompt you to confirm the command so that you do not inadvertently make a mistake. For example, when saving a file for the second time, many programs display a message telling you the file already exists and ask if you want to cancel the command or replace the file. If you select *Cancel*, you return to where you were before you began the command. If you select *Replace*, the file is saved, and the previous version is erased.

Fill-in Forms

Some programs display **fill-in forms** (also called settings sheets or dialog boxes) that list command choices (Figure 1-41).

You can enter responses into the form or press designated keys to indicate, for example, margin widths, page length, or which pages to print. After filling in the form, you press a designated key to continue. The way you move the cursor between the choices on the screen varies. The keys most commonly used for this are **Tab** and **Backtab**. When you have made all the necessary changes, you then press **Return** to continue.

INSTALLING APPLICATION PROGRAMS

Software companies obviously want their programs to run on as many computer setups as possible. Since computer components can be mixed and matched, programmers are never sure what devices will be connected to the computer their program is being used on. To overcome this problem, software companies frequently include a program that installs their applications program so that it will work with your display monitor, printer, disk drives, and other equipment.

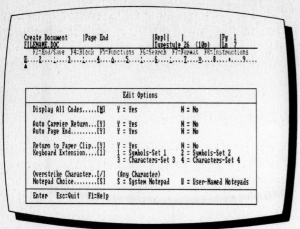

A. DisplayWrite 4

Installing a program is usually a one-time task unless you change equipment, for example, when you add a new printer. The program may then have to be reinstalled. The specific installation procedures vary from program to program, but the principles are the same. When you first use a program, you run the installation (sometimes called the setup) program that comes with it. When you run this program, it displays prompts or lists of choices on the screen. You answer the prompts or choose items from the lists to tell the program what type of display monitor, printer, and other peripherals you are using.

Drivers

Based on the information you supply, the program then knows what drivers to use. **Drivers** are small programs that translate the programmer's generic instructions into instructions for a specific piece of hardware. Programs using drivers do not have to be revised by the software companies when new devices become available because the program addresses only the drivers, not the device itself. As new components become available, software companies just add new drivers.

Applications programs generally have a library of drivers, one for each specific piece of hardware (Figure 1-42). For example, there may be a driver for a specific model of a dot-matrix impact printer and another driver for a specific model of laser printer. If you tell the installation program what printer you are using, it knows what driver to use.

For a program to run on your system, it must contain drivers that communicate between the program (which can run on a wide variety of systems) and your equipment. If you have a piece of hardware that the program does not include a driver for, you may be unable to use it with the program (Figure 1-43). Using a printer without the correct driver can give totally unexpected results. Type that you expected to be small may be large, headers and footers may not print, or margins may be incorrect. When buying applications programs, always be sure they contain the drivers you need to have them work with your equipment.

Emulation

As you have seen, many different types of printers are available. Unfortunately, there are no agreed-on standards for the way a printer works. Each manufacturer has its own way of doing things; thus you may not be able to print a document that prints on your printer on another printer. To help solve this problem, many printers can emulate, or act like, other printers. When installing a program, if drivers are not supplied for your printer, you can specify a different printer if your printer is able to emulate it.

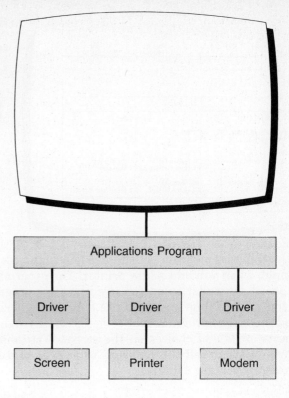

FIGURE 1-42
Drivers translate your program's commands into commands that peripheral devices can understand. For example, if you boldface a word on the screen, the driver translates that command into one the printer needs to boldface the word.

Applications Program

Driver · Driver · Driver

Screen · Printer · Modem

QUESTIONS

1. Why must you give a file a name?

2. What two kinds of graphics programs are widely used in business?

3. What is an integrated program?

4. What is a desktop publishing program?

5. What is the purpose of a utility program? List four typical utility programs, and describe the function of each.

6. What is the difference between a disk-based program and a memory-based program? List one advantage and one disadvantage of each.

7. What is a data file? List four types of data files.

8. What is the difference between programs that create disk-based and memory-based data files? List one advantage and one disadvantage of each.

FIGURE 1-43
Reprinted from INFOSYSTEMS, May 1985, (C) Hitchcock Publishing Company

"Your hardware doesn't like your software and they both despise your printer!"

9. Indicate whether the filenames listed below are legal or illegal on a PC-DOS or MS-DOS system.

FILENAME.DOC	____ Legal	____ Illegal
FILE/DOC	____ Legal	____ Illegal
LETTER.DOCUMENT	____ Legal	____ Illegal
DOCUMENTS.DOC	____ Legal	____ Illegal
MEMOJOHN.DOC	____ Legal	____ Illegal
MEMO^5.DOC	____ Legal	____ Illegal
99999.999	____ Legal	____ Illegal
2	____ Legal	____ Illegal
2-2	____ Legal	____ Illegal

10. What is a binary file?

11. What is an ASCII text file? How does it differ from a binary file?

12. What is a print file? How does it differ from an ASCII file?

13. Why do you install a program the first time you use it? When do you have to reinstall the program?

14. What is the purpose of a driver? What happens when you use a program that does not have a driver for your printer?

ACTIVITIES

1. Ask the person in charge of the lab to show you the manual for one of the programs you will be using. Find the section in the manual on installing the program, and list the steps you have to follow.

2. Assume you are writing three term papers for each of your classes on a computer. List the filename you would assign to each paper so that you could later identify the courses and the papers from them.

TOPIC 1-8
Microcomputer Issues

In this topic, we introduce you to many of the issues involved with using microcomputers and application software. After finishing this topic, you will be able to

■ Describe the causes behind most complaints from people who work long hours on computers

■ Arrange your work at a computer to reduce or eliminate any health problems

■ Explain some of the major issues that arise for users of applications software

■ Explain some of the issues that make programs and computers compatible

The introduction of microcomputers into businesses has raised several issues that affect both users and employers.

HEALTH ISSUES

The medical and physical effects of working long hours on video displays are not fully known. It is suspected that some problems can result. Complaints generally concern vision and muscle strain. However, you can avoid most, if not all, of these problems.

Your eyes were made for most efficient seeing at a far distance. Working on video display equipment calls for intense concentration on a task close at hand, usually no more than a couple of feet away. When your eyes change focus from far, their natural state, to near, several different muscles are called into action. A muscle inside the eye changes the shape of the eye's lens to focus sharply and clearly on the display screen. Other muscles turn both eyes inward, pointing them together at the same character on the screen, and still other muscles move the eyes quickly from one character or word to another. [2]

Users complain most often of headaches, blurred vision at both near- and far-viewing distances, itching and burning eyes, eye fatigue, flickering sensations, and double vision.

Ergonomics, the study of the relationship of human to machine, has developed the following suggestions to reduce or eliminate any potential problems:

- Use an adjustable chair, which can be an aid to better vision by enabling you to sit at a proper angle to the display screen (Figure 1-44). Generally, the top of the display screen should be 10 degrees above, and the center of the screen 20 degrees below, your straight-ahead seeing position. The distance from your eyes to the screen should be 14 to 20 inches.

- Place your reference materials as close to the display screen as possible to avoid frequent large eye and head movements. A copy stand is very useful in this situation.

- Place your reference materials the same distance from your eyes as the display screen to avoid having to change focus when you look from one to the other. Every time your eyes change focus, it requires muscles to work inside the eye. Frequent changes may cause you to feel tired.

Lighting and glare control can also make a difference. The following recommendations are designed to maximize comfort, accuracy, and productivity and minimize eye fatigue and other complaints:

- Although lighting needs vary among people, check that the overall illumination for video display equipment is between 30 and 50 foot-candles, which is less than the customary office lighting level. Display screen brightness should be three or four times greater than room light. A lower level of room lighting can be achieved by using fewer bulbs or fluorescent tubes and by replacing cool white tubes with cool white deluxe tubes, which provide less light but a more comfortable and pleasing atmosphere.

- Adjust the characters on the display screen to contrast well with the screen background.

- Minimize reflected glare on display screens by placing the screens so that windows and other sources of light are behind you. Do not sit facing an unshaded window or other bright source of light. Make use of drapes and shades to reduce glare. Small hoods can be attached to extend above the screen to shield it from overhead light if necessary. You can also use nonreflective surfaces or buy antiglare filters that fit over the screen.

- Use localized lighting like flexible lamps for other desk work as required. They are shielded and must be placed to avoid glare on the display screen.

- Avoid white or light-colored clothing if it causes a reflection on the screen.

Taking breaks can often solve many problems. Because information processing generally requires intense concentration on the document and screen, rest is important. The National Institute of Occupational Safety and Health (NIOSH) recommends a fifteen minute break after two hours of continuous work for users having moderate visual demands or moderate workloads (less than 60 percent of your time looking at the screen) and a fifteen minute break every hour for users having high visual demands, high workloads, or repetitive work tasks.

Computer Users' Checklist

Your workspace and vision habits: Do they measure up?

- ❐ Correct angle and distance from screen to eyes (see Figure 1-44)
- ❐ Reference material placed near the screen
- ❐ Reference material and screen same distance from eyes
- ❐ Screen brightness properly adjusted
- ❐ Proper overall room lighting
- ❐ Shielded windows and other sources of bright light
- ❐ Proper lamps for reference material
- ❐ Sources of screen reflection eliminated
- ❐ Fifteen minute break every two hours for moderate users
- ❐ Fifteen minute break every hour for frequent users

APPLICATION PROGRAMS ISSUES

When you use microcomputers and application programs, you should be aware of several issues, including your legal responsibilities and training.

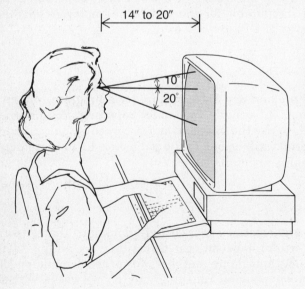

14" to 20"

10°
20°

FIGURE 1-44
Correctly positioning your display screen can reduce the strain of working at a microcomputer and make your work healthier and more enjoyable.

[2] *Vision and the VDT Operator,* American Optometric Association, 243 N. Lindbergh Blvd., St. Louis, Missouri 63141, 1984.

Copy Protection

Software publishers have done an outstanding job at producing and providing useful, powerful, easy-to-use software. Users generally appreciate this and pay well for the privilege of using it. But one issue deeply divides users and publishers: **copy protection**. Most software publishers feel the investment they have made and the risks they have taken justify their charging a high price for their products. Most people who understand the principles of business agree with them. But some publishers, rightly or wrongly, do not trust users. They feel users would copy unprotected disks and freely distribute them to friends and co-workers. To prevent this theft, many software publishers copy-protect their program disks so that users cannot copy them.

Copy protection presents serious difficulties for users. The first problem occurs when an important disk containing a program is lost or damaged, especially if the firm that produced it is no longer in business. Generally, publishers provide a backup copy along with the original disk, but this disk could also be lost or damaged, leaving the user unable to work with valuable files. The second problem occurs when computers are connected into networks. Some publishers code their program disks with "keys" that must be checked by the computer when the program is first loaded. This means a copy of the disk must be provided for every computer in the network. The program disk that contains a key must be inserted into the disk drive when the program is loaded even when the program is already stored on the hard disk drive.

Piracy

Several firms have produced special programs designed to copy disks that have been copy protected. The rationale for these programs is that users need backup copies in case something goes wrong with the primary disk. But some users and almost all software companies feel a different rationale predominates--that these programs are used to copy programs so that they can be distributed to others. This costs the software company lost revenues, and they are increasingly taking legal action to prevent the distribution, sale, and use of these disks, especially in large corporations. Corporations are even being held accountable for the actions of employees who use these programs to copy disks.

Licensing

When you walk into a computer store and pay $100 or more for a program, you may think you have bought the program, but usually you would be wrong. You have actually bought the **license**, or right, to use the program and documentation contained in the package. The physical materials still belong to the publisher. Read these licenses carefully; they spell out your rights in detail.

Site-Licensing

As corporations and other large organizations increasingly dominate the software market, they have become more forceful in setting the terms they are willing to accept when they buy applications programs. More and more firms are demanding site licenses. A **site license** allows a company to run programs on networks without having a copy for each workstation or making only a limited number of copies for use within a single department or location. Site licenses reduce the company's total software costs, lessen the likelihood of violating the publisher's legal rights, and make it easier on all network users since they need not have individual copies of the program.

Documentation

Computer and software manuals, or **documentation**, are the computer industry's Achilles heel. Much of what you are expected to read and understand has been written by programmers for programmers. The reason we point this out is simple: You are not nearly as dumb as some of this material will make you feel.

We all need patience and help to overcome the shortcomings of documentation. Most users do not rely entirely on the documentation that comes with their hardware and software. They take courses, use on-screen tutorials, read books, talk to other users, and join users groups. Not only does this make them more knowledgeable, but it also gives them a better sense of the excitement of being in a new field.

Support

Many leading software publishers offer support for their programs. This support usually consists of a technical representative you can call if you have a problem. Some of these support services charge a fee.

Training

When new employees are hired or new programs introduced into a company, users must be trained. The responsibility for this training is usually assigned to the MIS department or to a special training division. The high cost of this training makes companies reluctant to introduce new programs and has led to the standardization of programs within each company. Most companies specify that you can use no more than one or two programs in each of the main applications categories. If you use an unauthorized program, the company may not supply training, and the files you create may be unusable by other employees.

Program Updates

Companies that publish programs generally update them every one or two years. **Updates** (also called upgrades) generally include old features that have been corrected and new features that improve the program.

When new versions are prepared that contain only corrections, users who have registered with the company are often informed of their availability. Most programs come with a card that you fill out and return to the company to become a registered user.

New versions generally build on the previous version so that you have to learn only the new features. Generally, new versions of a program can work on any files created with earlier versions. But files created with the new version may not be usable with earlier versions.

Updates are not free, but publishers usually offer attractive discounts to get previous users to buy the update. This process of releasing new versions is occasionally misused. Publishers know it is easier to sell updates to their existing customers than it is to attract new customers. The fact that files created on the new version usually cannot be used by earlier versions forces users who exchange files to buy the new update. If only a few users buy the update and others do not, the files created by those using the new version cannot be shared by those who chose not to upgrade. When faced with a new version, you should be an informed consumer. Find out what features the new program has. If it does not have any that you need, you probably should not buy the new version.

COMPATIBILITY ISSUES

In the early days of microcomputers, several conflicting standards prevented programs from being run on a variety of computers. The dominance of IBM and Apple has reduced the variety of standards, but all programs still do not run on all computers. To run a program on a particular computer, the program must be designed for, or compatible with, that computer. Compatibility is a major issue in the microcomputer field. Let's look at two aspects of this problem that have arisen with the introduction of the new IBM Personal System/2 (PS/2) computers. Compatibility problems arise because some of the computers in these new machines use different operating systems and different microprocessor chips.

Operating Systems

The original line of IBM PCs and compatible computers use an operating system called MS-DOS and PC-DOS. One of the limitations of this operating system is its ability to address only 640KB of memory. Since the operating system takes up part of this memory, and applications programs take up a lot more of it, the memory available for data files and other programs is limited. To correct this deficiency, several schemes have been developed that allow you to add additional memory to your computer and use it to store data or run programs. These schemes let DOS use part of the 640KB that it can address, called lower memory, to address additional memory over and above 640KB, called upper memory.

The first expanded memory scheme, Expanded Memory Specification Version 3.2, was introduced by Lotus, Intel, and Microsoft (LIM) in 1985. EMS 3.2 allowed programs to store as much as 8MB of data files in memory above 640KB. An improved version, EMS 4.0, was introduced in 1987 and incorporated the best features of both EMS 3.2 and Enhanced Expanded Memory Specification (EEMS), a competing scheme previously introduced by AST, Quadram, and Ashton-Tate. EMS 4.0 allows multitasking when used with programs designed to handle it and increases the amount of addressable memory to 32MB.

CPU Chips

More than 9 million IBM PCs or compatible computers are installed in businesses. All these computers use the 8086 or 8088 microprocessor chips made by Intel. The more powerful models in the new PS/2 line use new chips, the Intel 80286 or 80236 (usually called the 286 or 386). When the Intel 286 and 386 chips were being developed, one of the goals was to make them compatible with previous chips, specifically the 8086 and 8088 chips used in IBM PCs. This compatibility allows the newer chips to run all software developed for the earlier, slower chips. To do this, the 286 and 386 chips have three modes, real, Virtual, and protected, that you can switch between by pressing designated keys.

Real mode is used to run applications programs written for earlier chips. The term *real* comes from the chips acting as if they were a real 8086 or 8088 chip. Real mode has the following features:

- It is essentially a much faster 8086 or 8088 chip.
- It addresses as much as 1MB of memory.
- It does not use the advanced features of the 286 and 386 chips.
- It cannot do multitasking, that is, run more than one program at a time. (But this shortcoming can be overcome by using EMS.)

Virtual 86 mode is an extension of real mode that you can use to run existing applications with the following differences:

- You can run multiple existing applications simultaneously as if they were running on different computers.
- It makes it relatively easy to use EMS to address as much as 8MB of RAM per application.

Protected mode refers to the way the chip prevents programs running at the same time (multitasking) from interfering with one another by trying to use one anothers' memory space. This is important because if two programs try to store data in the same area of memory, one or both of the programs will crash. Protected mode has the following features:

- It will not run existing 8086 or 8088 applications programs.
- It can do multitasking.
- When used on a 286 chip, it addresses as much as 16MB of physical memory and uses as much as 1GB of virtual memory (memory on the hard disk treated as if it were memory inside the computer's chips).
- When used on a 386 chip, it addresses as much as 4GB of physical memory and uses as much as 64 terabytes (a trillion bytes, or the equivalent of more than 3 million 20MB hard disk drives) of virtual memory.

QUESTIONS

1. What is ergonomics? Why is it important?
2. List three things you can do to avoid vision and muscle strain problems when working at a microcomputer.
3. Using a ruler, and Figure 1-44 as a guide, organize a workstation in the lab so that you are properly positioned in relation to the equipment.
4. What does it mean when a disk is copy protected?
5. What is the difference between real mode and protected mode?
6. What is expanded memory, and what purpose does it serve?

ACTIVITIES

1. Ask the person in charge of the computer lab to show you a license agreement that covers a software program. Read the agreement, list the rights it gives you, and list the things it prohibits.
2. Sit at one of the computers in the lab, and compare the computer users' checklist in this topic with the computer's setup. How could the setup be improved if you had to work there for many hours at a stretch?
3. Look at three examples of documentation in the lab. Which manual is easiest to understand? Which do you prefer and why?

THE OPERATING SYSTEM

PART

TWO

Topic 2-1   Getting Ready

Topic 2-2   Loading DOS

Topic 2-3   Changing Default Drives

Topic 2-4   Listing Files on Disks

Topic 2-5   Using Wildcards

Topic 2-6   Formatting Data Disks

Topic 2-7   Formatting System Disks

Topic 2-8   Copying Files

Topic 2-9   Duplicating Disks

Topic 2-10 Comparing Disks

Topic 2-11 Renaming Files

Topic 2-12 Erasing Files

Topic 2-13 Checking Disks

Topic 2-14 Using Directories

Topic 2-15 Creating Batch Files

Topic 2-16 Displaying and Printing ASCII Text Files

As you saw in Part 1, the central processing unit is the heart of the computer's hardware. All activity in the computer revolves around it. But you use software to give instructions to the hardware. Although you do your computer work on applications programs, the heart of the computer's software is the **disk operating system (DOS)**. The operating system coordinates activity between you and the computer. Through the operating system, you tell the computer to run your word processing, spreadsheet, or database applications program, save your work into a file on the disk, print a file, and so forth.

All applications programs that operate on a microcomputer require an operating system. Because the operating system coordinates activity between any applications program you run and the computer hardware, you must load the operating system into the computer's memory before you load an applications program. Most applications programs that you buy from the publisher do not contain the operating system. To use these programs, you must first load the operating system from another disk, or copy the appropriate operating system program files to the applications program disk. This is necessary because the operating system may have been written by one company and the applications program by another. Even if the same company publishes both, they are not sure which version of their operating system you may be using, so they cannot anticipate which version to put on the disk.

THE FUNCTIONS OF AN OPERATING SYSTEM

The primary function of the operating system is to coordinate, or supervise, the activities of the computer. The operating system controls your computer without your involvement or awareness. In this respect, it is like your body's respiratory system, which keeps you breathing and your heart beating even though you are hardly aware of it. The operating system decides where programs and data are stored in the computer's memory and handles communications among the computer's components, the applications software, and you, the user.

Input/Output Management

The **input/output (I/O) manager** coordinates the computer's communications with all peripheral devices. For example, it coordinates the flow of data to the display screen and to other output devices like printers and modems. It also controls the flow of data to and from the disk drives.

Command Processing

The **command processor** interprets what you enter from the keyboard or other input devices. In this respect, it is rather like an interpreter. If you spoke only English and tried to carry on a discussion with someone who spoke only French, you both would need an interpreter to translate what was being said so that you could understand each other. The same is true of a computer. You control computer hardware using an applications program. Many of the program's commands are interpreted by the operating system for the hardware. For example, on one program, you might save a file you are working on by holding down the **Ctrl** key while you press the letters **K** and **D**; on another, you might press the **F10** function key, and then press **Return**. The operating system interprets these commands and instructs the disk drive to spin while it copies the file to the disk from the computer's internal memory.

TYPICAL OPERATING SYSTEMS

All computers use an operating system, but not all use the same one. Over the years, a variety of operating systems have been developed.

CP/M was the first operating system for microcomputers. It was widely used until the IBM PC began to dominate the microcomputer market. The main advantage of CP/M is that it can be easily adapted to run on a wide variety of computers.

MS-DOS and **PC-DOS** were developed as the operating system for IBM PCs and compatible computers. The PC-DOS version usually runs on IBM PC computers, and the MS-DOS version usually runs on compatibles made by manufacturers other than IBM. These two versions of the operating system are essentially identical in the way they work and the commands you use to operate them; usually they are interchangeable.

Since the IBM PC set the standard for microcomputers, these two operating systems are currently the most widely used, but they are being replaced on the new IBM Personal System/2 computers.

IBM Operating System/2^{TM} was developed to overcome the built-in limitations of PC-DOS and MS-DOS. These operating systems are not user friendly, they run only one applications program at a time, and they can address only 640KB of memory. They also make it difficult for microcomputers to exchange information with mainframe computers, which are used by many corporations. In an attempt to solve these problems, IBM and Microsoft introduced the IBM Operating System/2 (OS/2) when IBM introduced their IBM Personal System/2 computers. This new operating system is available in two basic versions: the standard edition and the extended edition.

The standard edition makes it possible to address as many as 16MB of memory instead of the 640KB addressable by PC-DOS and MS-DOS. This makes running larger programs and creating larger files possible. The standard edition also incorporates a graphics display and features a built-in Presentation Manager^{TM} based on Microsoft's Windows program. This Presentation Manager allows you to divide the screen into windows in which multiple applications programs can be displayed and run at the same time. It also allows you to operate the computer using pull-down menus and standardized commands to load programs; call up help; cancel commands; format disks; copy, rename, and erase files; and quit to return to the operating system.

The extended edition contains all the functions of the standard edition as well as a relational database management system. It also improves communications with other computers.

Operating System/2 supports three types of applications programs: DOS programs, family programs, and OS/2 programs. It does this by creating three environments.

- *The DOS environment* of the new system runs applications programs originally designed to run on MS-DOS or PC-DOS.

- *The family environment* takes advantage of some new features of OS/2, but programs developed for this environment can still be run under previous versions of MS-DOS and PC-DOS.

- *The OS/2 environment* runs programs that take full advantage of the new system's features and therefore cannot be run with earlier versions of DOS. In this environment, you can run more than one applications program at the same time.

OPERATING SYSTEM VERSIONS

As computers have evolved, so have operating systems. When major changes are made in the operating system, it is released as a new version. For example, PC-DOS was initially released as version 1.0, and over the years, versions 2.0 and 3.0 have been released. Minor changes also are introduced periodically. These are usually identified with numbers following the decimal point. For example, PC-DOS is available in versions 3.0, 3.1, 3.2, and 3.3. Normally, programs that run on an early version will also run on a later version.

SINGLE-TASKING AND MULTITASKING OPERATING SYSTEMS

Operating systems can be classified as single tasking or multitasking. **Single-tasking operating systems**, the type most commonly used, allow you to run one program at a time. If you want to run another program, you first remove the current program from the computer's memory, and then load the other program. Typical single-tasking operating systems include MS-DOS, PC-DOS, and CP/M.

    Multitasking operating systems, the type most users will soon be using, allow you to run several programs simultaneously. To use more than one program, you load them, one after another, into the computer's memory. You then use the operating system's commands to move between the programs. The program you are currently working on is in the **foreground**. The other programs, which you are not currently working on, are in the **background**. Multitasking operating systems include OS/2.

OPERATING SYSTEM ENVIRONMENTS

Operating system environments like IBM's TopView and Presentation Manager, Digital Research's GEM (Graphics Environment Manager), Quarterdeck's DESQview, and Microsoft's Windows (Figure 2-1) make using the computer easier and more efficient.

    They feature menus you can choose commands from to copy, rename, or delete files; prepare disks for use; and perform many other standard operating system tasks. Using MS-DOS, PC-DOS, or OS/2 without the aid of an operating system environment, you perform these tasks by typing cryptic commands that you must either memorize or look up each time you want to use them.

    Operating system environments also let you split the screen into **windows**, portions of the screen surrounded by a frame. You can run your favorite spreadsheet in one window and your favorite word processor in another.

    With these operating environments, you can copy and move data back and forth between programs. For example, with Microsoft's Windows, you first select the part of the text that you want to copy or move. You then select the operating environment's Cut or Copy command to move or copy the selected text to the clipboard. You then switch to the other program, and use the Paste command to move the text from the clipboard to this program.

FIGURE 2-1
Operating
system
environments

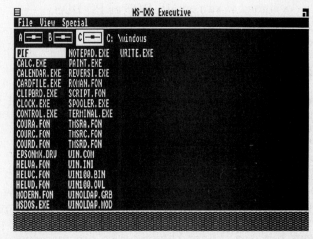

Three levels of compatibility determine how successfully programs will run with an operating environment like Windows.

DOS programs like WordPerfect, Lotus 1-2-3, dBase III Plus, and others have their own unique ways of communicating with the keyboard and display monitor. For these programs to run under an operating enviromnent, the publishers must provide utilities that allow them to do so. Even then, it is unlikely they will take advantage of all the operating environment's capabilities. For example, when these programs are run under an operating environment, they often take over the screen looking just as they do when they run independently. Thus pull-down menus, windows, and other features of the operating environment cannot be used. When moved to the background, DOS programs often do not continue to function, so a database management program cannot be sorting a file in the background while you are working on a memo in the foreground.

Operating-environment-aware programs use the same standard DOS commands as the operating environment to communicate with the monitor and keyboard. These programs will run successfully in the operating environment without modification and can take advantage of its many features like pull-down menus and windows.

Operating-environment-specific programs cannot run without the integrating environment program, which becomes the operating system for these programs. These programs take full advantage of all features offered by the operating environment.

DOS UTILITIES

Normally, the operating system handles its functions without your direct involvement. But all operating systems include several built-in commands and separate utility programs that you must understand to manage your files. You use these commands and utility programs to prepare disks for use on the computer and to copy, rename, erase, and otherwise manage files you have saved on your disks. The several utilities available on MS-DOS and PC-DOS fall into two classes: internal commands and external commands. Table 2-1 lists many commonly used MS-DOS and PC-DOS commands. Here is how to read this table.

To perform this task lists many tasks that you might want to perform.

At this prompt indicates the system prompt that should be on the screen when you perform the task. There are also ways to perform the same tasks with other prompts on the screen, as you will see in the topics in this part.

Insert this disk into drive A specifies the disk that should be in drive A when you first execute the command. Sometimes it specifies N/A, the DOS disk, a source disk, or a target disk. N/A means it does not matter what disk is in drive A.

When it specifies the DOS disk, it means the command is a separate utility program (an external command) and not a utility program that is loaded with the rest of the operating system (an internal command).

- **Internal commands** are built in to the operating system, so they are available whenever the operating system A>, B>, or C> prompt is on the screen. Internal commands are automatically loaded into the computer's memory whenever you load DOS.

- **External commands** are stored in separate program files on the operating system disk until you need them. These commands are used less often than internal commands, so not loading them into memory until they are needed leaves room for other programs and data. To use an external command, you must insert a disk with the necessary file on it into one of the disk drives. You then type the utility program's name and press **Return**.

TABLE 2-1
Summary of MS-DOS and PC-DOS Commands

To perform this task	At this prompt	Insert this disk into drive A	Insert this is disk into drive B	Type this Command and press Return	Topic
Display version of DOS in memory	A>, B>, or C>	N/A	N/A	VER	2
Display of change system date	A>, B>, or C>	N/A	N/A	DATE	2
Display of change system time	A>, B>, or C>	N/A	N/A	TIME	2
To change the default drive to A>	B> or C>	Any disk	N/A	A:	3
To change the default drive to B	A> or C>	N/A	Any disk	B:	3
To change the default drive to C	A> or B>	N/A	N/A	C:	3
List files on disk in drive A	A>	Target disk	N/A	DIR, DIR/P or DIR/W	4
	B>	Target disk	N/A	DIR A:, DIR A:/P or DIR A:/W	4
List files on disk in drive B	A>	N/A	Target disk	DIR B:, DIR B:/P, or DIR B:/W	4
	B>	N/A	Target disk	DIR, DIR/P, or DIR/W	4
Clear the screen display	A>, B>, or C>	N/A	N/A	CLS	4
Send list of files on drive A to printer connected to LPT1	A>	Target disk	N/A	DIR A:>LPT1	4
Format a data disk in drive B	A>	DOS	Blank disk	FORMAT B:	6
Format a system disk in drive B	A>	DOS	Blank disk	FORMAT B:/S	7
Copy a single file from A to B	A>	Source disk	Target disk	COPY FILENAME.EXT B:	8
	B>	Source disk	Target disk	COPY A:FILENAME.EXT	8
Copy all files from A to B	A>	Source disk	Target disk	COPY *.*: B:	8
	B>	Source disk	Target disk	COPY A:*.*	8
Duplicate a disk in A to B	A>	DOS (then source)	Target	DISKCOPY A: B:	9
Compare the disks in A and B	A>	DOS (then source)	Target disk	DISKCOMP A: B:	10
Rename a file on a disk in drive A	A>	Target disk	N/A	RENAME OLDNAME.EXT NEWNAME.EXT	11
	B>	Target disk	N/A	RENAME A:OLDNAME.EXT A:NEWNAME.EXT	11
Erase a single file on disk in drive A	A>	Target disk	N/A	ERASE FILENAME.EXT	12
	B>	Target disk	N/A	ERASE A:FILENAME.EXT	12
Erase all file on disk in drive A	A>	Target disk	N/A	ERASE *.*	12
	B>	Target disk	N/A	ERASE A:*.*	12
Check the files on disk in drive B	A>	DOS	Target disk	CHKDSK B:	13
Make a new directory	B> or C>	N/A	Target disk	MD\DIRECTORY	14
Change to a new directory	B> or C>	N/A	Target disk	CD\DIRECTORY	14
Return to root directory	B> or C>	N/A	Target disk	CD\	14
Move up one level in directories	B> or C>	N/A	Target disk	CD ..	14
Display directories on disk	B> or C>	N/A	Target disk	TREE	14
Display directories and files on disk	B> or >C	N/A	Target disk	TREE/F	14
Create a batch file on disk in drive A	A>	Target disk	N/A	COPY CON FILENAME.BAT	15
Send list of files on drive A to file on disk in drive B	A>	Source disk	Target disk	DIR A:>B:FILENAME.EXT	16
Display an ASCII text file on drive A	A>	Target disk	N/A	TYPE FILENAME.EXT	16
Display an ASCII text file on drive B	A>	N/A	Target disk	TYPE B:FILENAME.EXT	16
Print an ASCII text file on drive B	A>	DOS	Target	PRINT B:FILENAME.EXT	16

If you enter an external DOS command and its program is not on the disk in the drive, the computer tells you it cannot find the command. When this occurs, check to see what commands are on the disk and if you specified the correct command. If you use an external command frequently, copy the appropriate program file from the DOS disk onto an applications program disk so that you do not have to swap disks when you need it.

The source and target disks are the disks you want the task performed on. For example, when you want a listing of the files on a disk, that disk is the target disk. When you copy files from one disk to another, the disk you copy from is the source disk, and the disk you copy to is the target disk.

Insert this disk into drive B specifies the disk that should be in drive B when you first execute the command.

Type this command specifies the command that you type to perform the function. After typing the command, you press **Return** to execute it.

Topic lists the topic in Part 2 where the command is discussed in detail.

QUESTIONS

1. Why does a computer need an operating system?
2. What are the two main functions of an operating system?
3. What is the basic difference between an internal and external DOS command?
4. Using Table 2-1 as a guide, match the following DOS commands with the function they perform:

____ FORMAT	A.	Displays an ASCII text file on the screen
____ COPY	B.	Displays a list of files on the disk
____ DISKCOPY	C.	Compares two disks
____ DISKCOMP	D.	Copies one or more files
____ TYPE	E.	Prints an ASCII text file
____ PRINT	F.	Makes an exact duplicate copy of a disk
____ CHKDSK	G.	Tells you if there are any noncontiguous sectors on a disk
____ DIR	H.	Changes the name of a file
____ RENAME	I.	Prepares a disk so that you can store data on it
____ FORMAT /S	J.	Prepares a self-booting system disk

5. What is the difference between a single-tasking and a multitasking operating system?
6. What are versions of operating systems?

TOPIC 2-1
Getting Ready

In this part, you prepare two data disks, one for a working copy of the files you create and one for backup copies. You also prepare disks to make backup working copies of your original program disks so that you can put the original copies in a safe place. This way, if you inadvertently damage the working copies, you still have the originals to make other working copies from.

After preparing, or formatting, these disks, you copy files to them and explore many DOS commands. After completing all the exercises in this part, you will have two blank data disks ready to store files on in later exercises. You will also have self-booting working copies of each of your program disks so that you can load the programs without first loading DOS from another disk.

Note. If you have to quit before completing all the topics in this part, try to complete the exercise you are working on. Then, just remove your disks, and turn off the computer. When you resume, load DOS as described in Topic 2-2, and then resume where you left off.

To complete the exercises in Part 2, you need the disks, labels, and tape described in the checklist in the Introduction. Before proceeding, be sure you have the necessary number of blank disks, labels, and pieces of write-protect tape.

Note. If you are using full-featured versions of the programs covered in this text instead of the special educational versions provided by the publisher, your checklist will vary slightly.

LABELING YOUR DISKS

An unwritten rule among computer users is that an unlabeled disk contains no valuable files. People often do not take the time to check an unlabeled disk to see what files, if any, it contains. Thus the first step is always to label your disks. Using Figure 2-2 as a guide, write the disk title, WORKING COPY, ORIGINAL WORKING COPY or BACKUP WORKING COPY, your name, the date, and the DOS version you are using on the labels you need for the exercises in this text. The number of labels you need and the labels you prepare depend on the number and type of program disks you are using.

When preparing labels, fill them out before you put them on the disks. If you write on a label that is already on a disk, you can damage the disk if you apply too much pressure. If you must write on a label that is already on a disk, use a felt-tip pen, and write very gently. Do not apply pressure.

Note. Some program disks you cannot back up because they are copy protected. The Lotus 1-2-3 program disks are such disks. If you are using this program, you must use the original disks, so do not prepare labels for backup working copies.

WRITE-PROTECT YOUR PROGRAM DISKS

Most floppy disks have a small square notch on the side of the disk. This is the write-protect notch, and it is very important. If the notch is uncovered, you can save files onto the disk, format the disk, or erase files from it. Any of these actions can damage files if you make a mistake. If the notch is covered by a piece of tape (or if there is no notch on the disk), you can read files on the disk, but you cannot save files on it, format it, or erase files from it. Some disks, like original copies of the DOS disk, have no write-protect notch since they are permanently write-protected.

FIGURE 2-2
Disk labels

```
You must have the following disks

[X]    DOS Disk
       WORKING COPY
       Your Name The Date
       Version Number

[X]    DATA DISK
       ORIGINAL DATA FILES
       Your Name The Date
       Formatted with DOS Version ___

[X]    DATA DISK
       BACKUP DATA FILES
       Your Name The Date
       Formatted with DOS Version ___

You must have one or more of the following disks

[ ]    WORDPERFECT PROGRAM DISK
       WORKING COPY
       Your Name The Date
       Formatted with DOS Version ___

[ ]    THE TWIN PROGRAM DISK
       WORKING COPY
       Your Name The Date
       Formatted with DOS Version ___

[ ]    DBASE III PLUS SYSTEM DISK #1
       WORKING COPY
       Your Name The Date
       Formatted with DOS Version ___

[ ]    DBASE III PLUS SYSTEM DISK #2
       WORKING COPY
       Your Name The Date
       Formatted with DOS Version ___
```

When you have an important disk that you want to protect the files on, cover the write-protect notch with a piece of special write-protect tape. (Not all tape will work because some drives determine if the notch is covered or not with a photoelectric device that sees though some tape.)

Before beginning the remaining topics in Part 2, cover the write-protect notch on each of your original program disks with write-protect tape so that you cannot inadvertently erase files from these disks.

QUESTIONS

1. What would you do if you found an unlabeled disk in the computer lab? Would you use it for your own files, or try to find out whose it is?

2. What is the purpose of the write-protect notch on a floppy disk? What can you do when it is covered with tape, and what can you not do? What can you do when it is not covered?

3. Why would you not use a piece of clear tape to cover the write-protect notch?

4. Why should you write out a label before you stick it onto a disk?

TOPIC 2-2
Loading DOS

In this topic, we introduce you to the following commands:

Command	Description	Type
Ctrl-Alt-Del	Warm-boots the system	System command
VER	Displays DOS version number	Internal
DATE	Displays system date	Internal
TIME	Displays system time	Internal
PROMPT	Changes the system prompt	Internal

BACKGROUND

Before you can use DOS or any applications program, you must first load the operating system (called **booting** the system). When you load DOS, the A> prompt, or system prompt, appears on the screen. You encounter prompts often when working with computers. They are simply requests, displayed on the screen, to supply the computer with information it needs. Some prompts, like the system prompt, are cryptic. Others are more helpful, for example, a prompt that asks *Do you want to save this file? (Y/N)*.

When the A> prompt is displayed, you can either load your applications program or use DOS utility programs to manage your files. There are two ways to boot a computer system, depending on whether the computer is off or on.

- A **cold boot** means the computer is off. You cold-boot the system by inserting a disk with the necessary operating system files into drive A, closing the drive's door, and then turning the computer on.

- A **warm boot** means the computer is on. You warm-boot the system by inserting a disk with the necessary operating system files into drive A, closing the drive's door, and then pressing the keys specified by the computer's manufacturer. For example, on an IBM PC, you hold down the **Ctrl** and **Alt** keys while pressing the **Del** key. This command clears all data from the computer's memory. Since it has almost the same effect as turning the computer off and then back on again, use it with caution.

If you are already running an applications program, you do not have to boot the system to return to DOS since it is already in memory. You just use the applications program's Quit command, and that returns you to the operating system prompt.

EXERCISE 1
Getting Acquainted with DOS

In this exercise, you load DOS and experiment with some basic commands.

Step 1. Insert the Original DOS Disk. DOS comes on its own floppy disk, which you should insert into drive A as follows (Figure 2-3):

■ Hold the DOS disk with the label facing up. (If the disk is in your right hand and your thumb is on the label, you are holding it correctly.)

■ Open the door to disk drive A. (It is usually the one on the left if the drives are side by side or the one on top if one is above the other.)

■ Hold the disk so that the oblong read/write slot is pointing toward the slot in the drive. Insert the disk gently into the drive. Never push hard because the disk will buckle if it gets caught on an obstruction. Carefully jiggle the disk to make sure it is inserted all the way into the disk drive.

■ Gently close the disk drive door. If it will not close all the way, open the door, jiggle the disk, and then close the door again.

Step 2. Load the Operating System. If the computer is off, turn it on to cold-boot it. If the computer is on, warm-boot it using the keys described in the Background section. (Be sure the previous user did not just go to get a cup of coffee, or you may lose a friend when he or she returns to find you have erased an important file.)

Step 3. Enter the Date and Time. If you have just turned on the computer, and it does not have a clock that is set automatically, in a moment, you are asked to enter the date and time.

To enter the date

Prompt reads *Enter new date:*.
    Enter the date as month-day-year (for example, 01-30-89 for January 30, 1989) or as month/day/year (for example, 1/30/89), and then press **Return**.

To enter the time

Prompt reads *Enter new time:*.
    Enter the time as hour:minute (for example, 1:30), and then press **Return**. (You can enter times in twelve-hour or twenty-four-hour formats; for example, you can enter 3 p.m. as 3:00 or as 15:00.)

Result. The operating system A> prompt appears on the screen. You enter all DOS commands from this prompt.

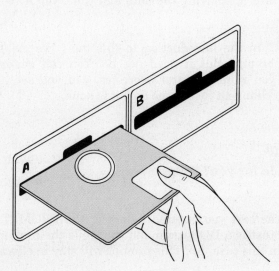

FIGURE 2-3
Inserting disk into
drive A

Step 4. Check the Version Number. After loading DOS 2.0 or later, you can check the version number whenever the system prompt is displayed. This is useful when you have more than one version of DOS and cannot remember which one you loaded into memory. Since you should use the external commands from the same version of DOS as the one in memory, you would not want to load DOS 2.1 into memory and then insert a DOS 3.0 disk to load the program for an external command when you want to format a disk. You can first use this command to find out which version is in memory, and then insert the correct disk when using external commands.

Note. In all the instructions in this text, the characters you type are shown in uppercase letters, but whether you use uppercase or lowercase letters usually does not matter. For example, in the following command, you can type VER, ver, Ver, vEr, or veR, and the computer accepts them all. In this text, when case is important, as when searching and replacing words, we point out the importance at that time. Otherwise, assume you can enter the command in any case.

To check the version number

Type   **VER**, and then press **Return**.

Result. The screen displays the version number of the DOS in memory.

Step 5. Check the Date and Time. If you did not enter the date and time when you first booted the system, or you want to know what the current date and time is, you can use the DATE and TIME commands. These commands display the current date and time and then prompt you to enter a new date and time. You can do so, or you can press **Return** to leave them unchanged. Here, display the date and time, but do not change them.

To display the system date

Type   **DATE**, and then press **Return**.
Press   **Return** to return to the system prompt.

To display the system time

Type   **TIME**, and then press **Return**.
Press   **Return** to return to the system prompt.

Result. When you press **Return** after displaying the date and time, you leave them unchanged.

Step 6. Change the System Prompt. In the introduction to this topic, we mentioned that the DOS system prompt is cryptic. But it need not be. You can change the prompt to read almost anything you want. In later exercises, you will see how to make useful changes, but here you change it just to see how it is done.

To change the system prompt

Type   **PROMPT What can I do for you? pg**.
Press   **Return**.

Result. The prompt changes to the text you entered following the PROMPT command. The pg at the end of the text is a DOS command that tells the computer to display the current default drive, in this case, A>. This prompt will stay in effect until you turn off the computer. If you want to change it back to the way it was, just type **PROMPT**, and then press **Return**.

Step 7. Continue or Quit. You have now completed this exercise. You can either continue to the next exercise or quit for the day. If you want to quit, remove the DOS disk from the drive, put it in its envelope, and then turn off the computer.

QUESTIONS

1. What does booting a computer mean?
2. What is the difference between a warm and a cold boot? How do you do each?
3. Why would you want to use the VER command to find out which version of DOS is in your computer's memory?
4. When typing DOS commands, do you have to be careful with the case of the letters you type?
5. What command do you use to change the system's date?
6. What command do you use to change the system's time?
7. What command do you use to change the system prompt?

TOPIC 2-3
Changing Default Drives

In this topic, we introduce you to the following commands:

Command	Description	Type
A:	Makes drive A the default drive	Internal
B:	Makes drive B the default drive	Internal
Backspace	Deletes typos when entering commands	Internal

BACKGROUND

Since most computers have two or more disk drives, the computer must be told which drive to use, or **address**, when it is running a program or copying, saving, or retrieving a file. When addressing the drive, the operating system spins the disk in the drive so that it can read information from, or write information to, the disk.

When you first turn on your computer and load the operating system, drive A spins. If a disk is in that drive and it contains the necessary operating system files, the operating system is loaded. Drive A operates because the computer's designers have placed a program in the computer's ROM telling it that it should address this drive when first turned on. Since it addresses drive A automatically, drive A is the **default drive**. The DOS prompt indicating that drive A is the default drive is A>.

When you load an applications program, you almost always leave the program disk in drive A because the program's designers have told the program to look for the files it needs on the disk in that drive. Again, they have specified that drive A is the default drive.

When you save files to, or retrieve files from, the data disk, most applications programs will automatically address drive B. This is because the program's designers have specified that drive B is the default drive.

Although you cannot change the default drive that the computer addresses when you first turn it on, and you usually do not want to change the drive the computer looks to for program files, you can, and often do, copy, rename, delete, and save files from a drive other than the default drive. There are two ways to do this.

Changing the Default Drive

When working in DOS, you can quickly change the default drive by typing, at the DOS system prompt, the letter of the drive and a colon and then pressing **Return**. Later, when you run applications programs, you will find that they usually come from the publisher with the default drive for data files set to drive B. But all programs allow you to change the default drive so that when you use a Save or Retrieve command, the computer automatically addresses the drive you specify as the default drive.

Specifying the Other Drive

To copy or save a file to, or copy or retrieve a file from, a drive other than the default drive, you must specify the drive (and, possibly, the directory) in the Copy, Save, or Retrieve command. For example, if the default drive is set to A, and you want to copy a file named LETTER on drive A to drive B, you would type either **COPY A:LETTER B:** or **COPY LETTER B:**. In the first command, you specified both drives, so the command reads "copy the letter in drive A to drive B." In the second command, you did not specify drive A. You do not have to because drive A is the default drive, and you never need to specify the default drive except as a precaution. This command reads "copy the file named LETTER in the default drive to drive B."

Later, when running an applications program, you will use the same procedures. You might begin by issuing the program's Save command. When a prompt appears that reads something like *Name of file to save:*, you type **B:LETTERS**, and then press **Return**. The file is then saved to the disk in drive B. If you just type **LETTERS** and then press **Return**, the file is saved to the default drive.

EXERCISE 2

Specifying Drives

You will be specifying drives in all the exercises that follow, but this exercise briefly introduces you to changing the default drive.

Note. This exercise assumes DOS is loaded and the operating
system A> or B> prompt is on the screen. If this is not so, load DOS as described in Topic 2-2.

Step 1. Getting Ready. Before proceeding with this exercise, insert the DOS disk into drive A and one of the original program disks into drive B. Then close both drive doors.

Step 2. Change the Default Drive. In DOS, specifying default drives is quite simple. You just type the letter of the drive, a colon, and then press **Return**. You can also enter an optional backslash (\) after the colon. (Do not use the slash (/) by mistake. If you do, no harm is done, but it will not work in later exercises.) The backslash separates the drive designation from other information that you use to change a default directory, as you will see in Topic 2-14. As you enter each of the following commands, watch how the system prompt changes from A> to B> and back again. The letter always indicates the default drive.

To change the prompt

Type   **PROMPT**, and then press **Return**.

To change the default drive

Type   **B:**, and then press **Return**.
Type   **A:**, and then press **Return**.
Type   **B:**, and then press **Return**.
Type   **A:**, and then press **Return**.

Result. Each time you type one of these commands, the system prompt changes from A> to B> and back again. When the A> prompt is displayed, drive A is the default drive. When the B> prompt is displayed, drive B is the default drive.

Step 3. Change the Prompt and Then Change the Default Drive. Change the system prompt so that it is more descriptive, and then repeat the same commands you just used to change the default drive. (Remember, you can type commands like PROMPT in all uppercase letters, all lowercase letters, or in a combination of both.) If you make a typo when entering this, or any command, press **Backspace** to delete the incorrect characters, and then type them in correctly before pressing **Return**.

To change the system prompt

Type   **PROMPT The default drive is now pg**.
Press   **Return**.

To change the default drive

Type   **B:**, and then press **Return**.
Type   **A:**, and then press **Return**.
Type   **B:**, and then press **Return**.
Type   **A:**, and then press **Return**.

Result. Each time you type one of these commands, the system prompt changes from *The default drive is now A:\\>* to *The default drive is now B:\\>* and back again. To return your prompt to the way it was, type **PROMPT**, and then press **Return**.

Step 4. Continue or Quit. You have now completed this exercise. You can either continue to the next exercise or quit for the day. If you want to quit, remove your disks from the drives, put them in their envelopes, and then turn off the computer.

QUESTIONS

1. What is the default drive?
2. Using MS-DOS or PC-DOS, how do you change the default drive?
3. What does the A> prompt mean? The B> prompt?

TOPIC 2-4
Listing Files on Disks

In this topic, we introduce you to the following commands:

Command	Description	Type
DIR	Lists files	Internal
DIR/W	Lists files horizontally	Internal
DIR/P	Lists files a page at a time	Internal
Ctrl-PrtSc	Turns screen print on and off	Internal
Shift-PrtSc	Prints the current screen display	Internal
CLS	Clears the screen	Internal
LPT1	Directs output to the printer	Internal

BACKGROUND

Since a disk can hold many files, it is often necessary to find out what files are on a particular disk. The names of the files on a disk are held in a directory, and the DIR command displays the contents of that directory. Besides listing the filenames, the DIR command also displays

- The size of each file in bytes
- The date and time the file was last saved (useful only if you set the date and time each time you turn on the computer)
- The number of files on the disk
- How much free space is left on the disk

In its simplest form, this command lists the directory of the disk in the default drive. For example, with the operating system A> prompt on the screen

- To list the files on the disk in drive A, type **DIR** or **DIR A:**, and then press **Return**.
- To list the files on the disk in drive B, type **DIR B:**, and then press **Return**.

If a list of files is too long to be displayed on the screen, some of the filenames will quickly scroll up and off the screen. Two commands prevent this: DIR/W and DIR/P. The /W and /P following the command are called *switches* and modify the basic command.

- The /W switch tells the DIR command to display the files horizontally instead of vertically. DIR/W drops the file size, date, and time information to make room for a horizontal listing of filenames. Because only the filenames are displayed and they are arranged horizontally on the screen, a good many filenames can be displayed on the screen at one time.
- The /P switch tells the DIR command to display files until the screen is full. To display additional files, simply press any key. Since most screens can display only twenty-three filenames, DIR/P is useful when more than twenty-three files are on a disk. If you use the regular DIR command, the topmost filenames scroll off the screen too quickly to read them.

Listing Files

Since you are going to be working with the files on the original program disks, you begin by finding out what files are on them. To do so, use the DIR command (an internal command).

Note. This exercise assumes DOS is loaded and the operating system A> or B> prompt is on the screen. If this is not so, load DOS as described in Topic 2-2.

Step 1. Getting Ready. Insert the DOS disk into drive A. Although the DIR command is an internal command, and the DOS disk does not have to be in one of the drives, you want to list the files on the disk. Insert one of your original program disks into drive B. Then close both drive doors.

Step 2. Display Filenames on the DOS Disk. Now, display the files on the DOS disk in drive A. Before doing so, change the default drive if the A> prompt is not displayed on the screen.

To change the default drive

Type **A:**, and then press **Return**.

To display a list of all files on drive A

Type **DIR**, and then press **Return**.

Result. All the files on the disk in drive A are listed, and the A prompt reappears. If your disk has all the original DOS files, the list is too long to be displayed on the screen at one time, so the topmost files scroll off the screen to make room for the last files on the disk. Look closely at the information displayed on the screen and see the description in the Background section of this topic.

Step 3. Display Filenames on the Program Disk. In Step 2, you typed **DIR** to display the files on the disk in drive A. You did not have to specify a drive because drive A was the default drive. Here, you want to display the files on the disk in drive B. To do so, first specify the drive in the DIR command; then change the default drive, and use the DIR command again without specifying the drive.

To display a list of all files on drive B

Type **DIR B:**, and then press **Return**.

To change the default drive

Type **B:**, and then press **Return**.

To display a list of all files on drive B

Type **DIR**, and then press **Return**.

Result. The same filenames are listed for both commands. In the first command, you specified drive B because it was not the default drive. In the second command, you did not specify drive B because it was the default drive.

Step 4. Display Files Horizontally. Sometimes disks have so many files that they cannot all be displayed on the screen at the same time. When this happens, you can use the /W switch with the DIR command to display them horizontally. Since the DOS disk has more files than the program disk, let's display the files on that disk. Do not change the default drive back to A; instead, specify it in the command.

To display files horizontally

Type   **DIR A:/W**, and then press **Return**.

Result. The filenames are displayed horizontally across the screen. To make room for them, information about file sizes, dates, and times is not displayed.

Step 5. Display Files a Page at a Time. When there are so many files that they cannot all be displayed on the screen at the same time, you can also use the /P switch with the DIR command to display a page of filenames at a time.

To display files a page at a time

Type   **DIR A:/P**, and then press **Return**.

Result. The first twenty-three files are listed, and if there are more than 23 files, the prompt reads *Strike a key when ready*. Press any key to display the rest of the files.

Step 6. Send a List of DOS Filenames to the Printer. Usually, displaying files on the screen is helpful when performing specific tasks, but a printout of the files on a disk is a more permanent record. Before beginning, turn the printer on; be sure it has paper and the paper is aligned. Then change the default drive back to A> so that you do not have to specify it in the command.

To change the default drive

Type   **A:**, and then press **Return**.

To toggle the printer on

Press   **Ctrl-PrtSc**.

To print a list of filenames

Type   **DIR**, and then press **Return**.

Result. A list of filenames begins printing out on your printer. When the list is finished, press the printer's On Line switch to take the printer off line, and then press the Form Feed switch (sometimes labeled FF) to either advance the paper to the top of the next page or eject the printed page from the printer. When you are finished, press the On Line switch again to put the printer back on line.

Your printed list should look similar to the one in Figure 2-4. There may be slight variations between the two if you are using a different version of DOS.

Step 7. Turn Off the Print Screen Command. The Ctrl-PrtSc command remains in effect until you turn it off. When it is on, everything displayed on the screen is also printed on the printer. To turn it off, you use the same command you used to turn it on.

To toggle the printer off

Press   **Ctrl-PrtSc**.

Result. The screen print function should be turned off. To see that it is, press **Return**. If the system prompt appears on the screen but is not printed, you have correctly turned it off.

Step 8. Send a List of Program Filenames to the Printer. Here, use the DOS command that directs output to the printer connected to LPT1 to print out a list of the files on the program disk in drive B.

To print a list of filenames

Type   **DIR B:>LPT1**, and then press **Return**.

Result. A list of filenames begins printing out on your printer. When the list is finished, press the printer's On Line switch to take the printer off line, and then press the Form Feed switch (sometimes labeled FF) to either advance the paper to the top of the next page or eject the printed page from the printer. When you are finished, press the On Line switch again to put the printer back on line.

Depending on the program disk you inserted into drive B, your printed list will look similar to one of those in Figure 2-4. There may be slight variations because your program files may have been updated by the publisher since the printouts shown in

FIGURE 2-4 a
PC-DOS Version 3.0
directory

```
(a)  PC-DOS Version 3.0 Directory

A:\>DIR A:

 Volume in drive A has no label
 Directory of  A:\

COMMAND  COM    22042   8-14-84   8:00a
ANSI     SYS     1641   8-14-84   8:00a
SORT     EXE     1632   8-14-84   8:00a
SHARE    EXE     8544   8-14-84   8:00a
FIND     EXE     6363   8-14-84   8:00a
ATTRIB   EXE    15123   8-14-84   8:00a
MORE     COM      320   8-14-84   8:00a
ASSIGN   COM      988   8-14-84   8:00a
PRINT    COM     7811   8-14-84   8:00a
SYS      COM     3629   8-14-84   8:00a
CHKDSK   COM     9275   8-14-84   8:00a
FORMAT   COM     9015   8-14-84   8:00a
VDISK    SYS     3080   8-14-84   8:00a
BASIC    COM    17024   8-14-84   8:00a
BASICA   COM    26880   8-14-84   8:00a
FDISK    COM     8076   8-14-84   8:00a
COMP     COM     3471   8-14-84   8:00a
TREE     COM     2473   8-14-84   8:00a
BACKUP   COM     5440   8-14-84   8:00a
RESTORE  COM     5413   8-14-84   8:00a
LABEL    COM     1260   8-14-84   8:00a
DISKCOPY COM     4165   8-14-84   8:00a
DISKCOMP COM     3752   8-14-84   8:00a
KEYBSP   COM     2073   8-14-84   8:00a
KEYBIT   COM     1854   8-14-84   8:00a
KEYBGR   COM     2111   8-14-84   8:00a
KEYBUK   COM     1760   8-14-84   8:00a
KEYBFR   COM     2235   8-14-84   8:00a
MODE     COM     5194   8-14-84   8:00a
SELECT   COM     2079   8-14-84   8:00a
GRAPHICS COM     3111   8-14-84   8:00a
RECOVER  COM     4066   8-14-84   8:00a
EDLIN    COM     7183   8-14-84   8:00a
GRAFTABL COM     1169   8-14-84   8:00a
        34 File(s)     103424 bytes free
```

FIGURE 2-4 b
WordPerfect
educational version
program disk directory

```
        (b) WordPerfect Educational Version Program Disk Directory

       A:\>DIR A:

        Volume in drive A has no label
        Directory of  A:\

       WP        EXE    265286    5-01-87   10:38a
       WPHELP    FIL      1508    5-01-87   10:38a
       LEX       WP       7369    5-01-87   10:38a
       TH        WP       2051    5-01-87   10:38a
       README    WP       1325    5-01-87   10:38a
               5 File(s)         80896 bytes free
```

the figure were made. Save your list because you will be using it to select files to copy, rename, and delete in the following exercises.

Step 9. Print the Current Screen Display. In the previous steps, you experimented with the command that prints anything on the screen until you turn it off. Another command prints only the current screen display.

To print the current screen display

Press   **Shift-PrtSc**.

Result. The current screen display is sent to the printer. Advance the paper or eject it from the printer. When you are finished, press the On Line switch again to put the printer back on line. To clear the current screen display, type **CLS**, and then press **Return**. Only the system prompt remains displayed on the screen.

Step 10. Continue or Quit. You have now completed this exercise. You can either continue to the next exercise or quit for the day. If you want to quit, remove your disks from the drives, put them in their envelopes, and then turn off the computer.

EXERCISE 4
Printing File Directories of Other Program Disks

Make a printout of the directory of each of your remaining original program disks. Remember these steps.

1. Insert each disk in turn into drive A.
2. Type **A:**, and then press **Return** if the system prompt is not A>.

FIGURE 2-4 c
The TWIN introductory
version program disk
directory

```
        (c) The TWIN Introductory Version Program Disk Directory

       A>DIR A:

        Volume in drive A has no label
        Directory of  A:\

       MFONT1    FNT      3712    2-16-87    4:11p
       MFONT3    FNT      6023    2-16-87    4:11p
       MFONT2    FNT      9216    2-16-87    4:11p
       TWIN      EXE    179840    2-16-87    4:11p
       TWIN      OVL    132528    2-16-87    4:11p
       CGA       DRV      5568    2-16-87    4:11p
       SETFULL   COM       264    2-16-87    4:11p
       TWNLOGOM  SCR      4104    2-16-87    4:11p
       TWNLOGOG  SCR      4104    2-16-87    4:11p
       HARDCOPY  COM      2724    2-16-87    4:11p
       PRINTER   DEF       640    2-16-87    4:11p
       TWNHARDW  CFG       259    2-18-87    9:55p
       TWNCOLOR  CFG        28    2-18-87   10:02p
       TWINH     BAT        59    2-16-87    4:11p
       HERC      DRV      3008    2-16-87    4:11p
              15 File(s)         2048 bytes free
```

```
(d) dBASE III Plus System Disk #1 Directory


A>DIR A:

 Volume in drive A is 10605210789
 Directory of  A:\

DBASEINL OVL    27648    3-20-86    4:51p
DBASE    EXE   132608    3-20-86    4:51p
CONFIG   DB        44    3-20-86    4:51p
DBASE    MSG    12276    3-20-86    4:51p
CONFIG   SYS       22    3-20-86    4:51p
CONFI256 SYS       25    3-20-86    4:51p
CONFI256 DB       110    3-20-86    4:51p
INSTALL  BAT     2688    8-22-86    1:52p
ERRSET   COM       71    3-20-86    4:51p
UNINSTAL BAT     2560    3-20-86    4:51p
        10 File(s)     178176 bytes free
```

FIGURE 2-4 d
dBASE III Plus system
disk #1 directory

```
(e) dBASE III Plus System Disk #2 Directory

A>DIR A:

 Volume in drive A is 10605310789
 Directory of  A:\

DBASE    OVL   264704    3-20-86    4:51p
HELP     DBS    66560    3-20-86    4:51p
ASSIST   HLP    17648    3-20-86    4:51p
INSTALL  BAT     2688    8-22-86    1:52p
         4 File(s)      9216 bytes free
```

FIGURE 2-4 e
dBASE III Plus system
disk #2 directory.

```
(f) dBASE III Plus System Disk #1 Directory


A>DIR A:

 Volume in drive A is 10605210789
 Directory of  A:\

DBASEINL OVL    27648    3-20-86    4:51p
DBASE    EXE   132608    3-20-86    4:51p
CONFIG   DB        44    3-20-86    4:51p
DBASE    MSG    12276    3-20-86    4:51p
CONFIG   SYS       22    3-20-86    4:51p
CONFI256 SYS       25    3-20-86    4:51p
CONFI256 DB       110    3-20-86    4:51p
INSTALL  BAT     2688    8-22-86    1:52p
ERRSET   COM       71    3-20-86    4:51p
UNINSTAL BAT     2560    3-20-86    4:51p
        10 File(s)     178176 bytes free
```

FIGURE 2-4 f
dBASE III Plus system
disk #1 directory

```
(g) dBASE III Plus System Disk #2 Directory

A>DIR A:

 Volume in drive A is 10605310789
 Directory of  A:\

DBASE    OVL   264704    3-20-86    4:51p
HELP     DBS    66560    3-20-86    4:51p
ASSIST   HLP    17648    3-20-86    4:51p
INSTALL  BAT     2688    8-22-86    1:52p
         4 File(s)      9216 bytes free
```

Figure 2-4 g
dBASE III Plus system
disk #2 directory

3. Press **Ctrl-PrtSc** to send screen text to the printer.
4. Type **DIR**, and then press **Return**.
5. Press the printer's On Line switch to take it off line.
6. Press the printer's Form Feed switch to advance or eject the page.
7. Press the printer's On Line switch to put it back on line.
8. Insert another disk and repeat steps 4 through 7 until all directories have been printed.
9. Press **Ctrl-PrtSc** to stop sending screen text to the printer.

QUESTIONS

1. What information does the DIR command give you in addition to a list of filenames?
2. What is a switch?
3. What switch do you use to display filenames horizontally across the screen?
4. What switch do you use to display filenames a page at a time?
5. If drive A is the default drive, what command do you use to display a list of files on the disk in that drive? In drive B?
6. If drive B is the default drive, what command do you use to display a list of files on the disk in that drive? In drive A?
7. Is the DIR command an internal or external command?
8. What command do you use to clear the screen?
9. What switch do you use on the printer to take it off line and then put it back on line?
10. What switch on the printer do you press to advance the paper to the top of the next sheet?

TOPIC 2-5
Using Wildcards

In this topic, we introduce you to the following commands:

Command	Description	Type
?	Wildcard for a single character	Internal
*	Wildcard for a group of characters	Internal
F3	Displays the previous DOS command	Internal

BACKGROUND

In many DOS commands, you specify the name of a file. Frequently, however, you want to work with groups of files. For example, when making a backup disk, you might want to copy all the files from one disk to another. Instead of copying one file at a time, you can copy several files at once using wildcards. A **wildcard** is simply a character that stands for one or more other characters, much like a wildcard in a card game. MS-DOS and PC-DOS wildcards are the question mark (?) and the asterisk (*).

The question mark can be used to substitute for any single character.

- BOO?.EXE will stand for any four-character filename that begins with BOO, followed by a single character and the extension .EXE. For example, BOOT.EXE or BOOK.EXE.

- BO??.EXE will stand for any filename with four characters or less that begins with BO, followed by any two characters and the extension .EXE. For example, BOOT.EXE, BOOK.EXE, or BORE.EXE.

- B??.??? will stand for any filename with three characters or less that begins with a B, followed by any three-character or less extension. For example, BIG.33, BA.LST, BOO.BOO, BUG.DOC, or BAD.PRT.

- ????.??? will stand for any filename with four characters or less, followed by any extension of three characters or less (including no extension). For example, LOV.EX, TEXT, TEXT.1, EYE.DOC, WORD.CH6, NAME.LST, or READ.ME.

The asterisk is more powerful; it represents any character in a given position and all following characters.

- *.* will stand for any filename with any extension.

- B*.* will stand for any filename that begins with B, followed by any extension. For example, BOOT.SYS, BOOK.EXE, BORE.SYS, BLOT.TXT, BATTLE.DOC, or BOTTLE.SYS.

- B*.EXE will stand for any filename that begins with B, followed by the extension .EXE. For example, BRAIN.EXE, BOOK.EXE, B.EXE, or BYLAWS.EXE.

- *.EXE will stand for any filename with the extension .EXE. For example, GRAPHICS.EXE or INCOME.EXE.

Using Wildcards

In this exercise, you use wildcards with the DIR command to list specific files on your disks.

Note. This exercise assumes DOS is loaded and the operating system A> or B> prompt is on the screen. If this is not so, load DOS as described in Topic 2-2.

Step 1. Getting Ready. Insert the DOS disk into drive A and one of the original program disks into drive B. Then close both drive doors.

Step 2. Using the * Wildcard. In this step, you display all files that begin with the same letter and then all files that end with the same extension. First follow the instructions to list the files on the DOS disk in drive A. Then, display the files on the program disk you inserted into drive B. The commands you type to display files on the program disk depend on which disk you inserted into drive B. Find your program below, and then type only those commands. Before beginning, change the default drive to A if the A> prompt is not displayed.

To change the default drive

Type   **A:**, and then press **Return**.

To list files on the DOS disk

Type   **DIR**, and then press **Return** to list all files.
Type   **DIR *.***, and then press **Return** to list all files.
Type   **DIR A*.***, and then press **Return** to list all files that begin with the letter A.
Type   **DIR B*.***, and then press **Return** to list all files if any that begin with the letter B.
Type   **DIR *.COM**, and then press **Return** to list all files with the extension .COM.
Type   **DIR *.SYS**, and then press **Return** to list all files with the extension .SYS.
Type   **DIR *.EXE**, and then press **Return** to list all files with the extension .EXE.

To list files on the WordPerfect program disk

Type   **DIR B:**, and then press **Return** to list all files.
Type   **DIR B:*.***, and then press **Return** to list all files.
Type   **DIR B:W*.***, and then press **Return** to list all files that begin with the letter W.
Type   **DIR B:*.WP**, and then press **Return** to list all files with the extension .WP.
Type   **DIR B:*.EXE**, and then press **Return** to list the one file with the extension .EXE.

To list files on The TWIN Educational Version System Disk 1

Type   **DIR B:**, and then press **Return** to list all files.
Type   **DIR B:*.***, and then press **Return** to list all files.
Type   **DIR B:H*.***, and then press **Return** to list all files that begin with the letter H.
Type   **DIR B:M*.***, and then press **Return** to list all files that begin with the letter M.

Type	**DIR B:*.SCR**, and then press **Return** to list all files with the extension .SCR.
Type	**DIR B:*.COM**, and then press **Return** to list all files with the extension .COM.
Type	**DIR B:*.BAT**, and then press **Return** to list all files with the extension .BAT.

To list files on the dBASE III Plus system disk #1

Type	**DIR B:**, and then press **Return** to list all files.
Type	**DIR B:*.***, and then press **Return** to list all files.
Type	**DIR B:C*.***, and then press **Return** to list all files that begin with the letter C.
Type	**DIR B:D*.***, and then press **Return** to list all files that begin with the letter D.
Type	**DIR B:*.BAT**, and then press **Return** to list all files with the extension .BAT.
Type	**DIR B:*.SYS**, and then press **Return** to list all files with the extension .SYS.
Type	**DIR B:*.DB**, and then press **Return** to list all files with the extension .DB.

Result. The wildcards affect the files displayed.

Step 3. Using the ? Wildcard. In this step, you use the ? wildcard to display filenames that vary by a specific number of characters in specific positions in the filenames. You also repeat commands by pressing the **F3** function key. Pressing this key displays the previous DOS command so that you can execute it again by just pressing **Return**.

First follow the instructions to list the files on the DOS disk in drive A. Then, display the files on the program disk you inserted into drive B. The commands you type to display files on the program disk depend on which disk you inserted into drive B. Find your program listed below, and then type only those commands.

To list files on the DOS disk

Type	**DIR**, and then press **Return** to list all files.
Type	**DIR DISKCO??*.COM**, and then press **Return** to list the files DISKCOPY.COM and DISKCOMP.COM.
Type	**DIR MO?E.COM**, and then press **Return** to list the files MODE.COM and MORE.COM (if both are on the disk).
Type	**DIR *.???**, and then press **Return** to list all filenames with any extension of three characters or less.
Type	**DIR ????.***, and then press **Return** to list all filenames with four characters or less and any extension.
Press	**F3**, and then press **Return** to repeat the previous command.

To list files on the WordPerfect program disk

Type	**DIR B:**, and then press **Return** to list all files.
Type	**DIR B:??.***, and then press **Return** to list all filenames with two characters or less and any extension.
Type	**DIR B:??????.***, and then press **Return** to list all filenames with six characters or less and any extension.
Type	**DIR B:W?.***, and then press **Return** to list all filenames with two characters or less that begin with the letter W and have any extension.
Type	**DIR B:*.W?**, and then press **Return** to list any filenames with a extension of two characters or less that begins with the letter W.
Press	**F3**, and then press **Return** to repeat the previous command.

To list files on The TWIN Educational Version System Disk 1

Type	**DIR B:**, and then press **Return** to list all files.
Type	**DIR B:TWNLOGO?.SCR**, and then press **Return** to list all files that begin with TWNLOGO, followed by any other character and the extension .SCR.

Type   **DIR B:TWN?????.***, and then press **Return** to list all filenames with eight characters or less, begin with TWN, and have any extension.
Type   **DIR B:TWIN?.***, and then press **Return** to list all filenames with five characters or less, begin with TWIN, and have any extension.

Press   **F3**, and then press **Return** to repeat the previous command.

To list files on the dBASE III Plus system disk #1

Type   **DIR B:**, and then press **Return** to list all files.
Type   **DIR B:*.??**, and then press **Return** to list all files with an extension of two characters or less.
Type   **DIR B:*.???**, and then press **Return** to list all files with an extension of three characters or less.
Press   **F3**, and then press **Return** to repeat the previous command.

Result. The wildcards affect the files displayed.

Step 4. Repeat the Commands with a Different Disk. For more practice, remove the program disk from drive B, and insert another original program disk. Then repeat Steps 2 and 3 to display the files on those disks.

Step 5. Continue or Quit. You have now completed this exercise. You can either continue to the next exercise or quit for the day. If you want to quit, remove your disks from the drives, put them in their envelopes, and then turn off the computer.

EXERCISE 6

Using Wildcards to Display Additional Filenames

Display additional filenames on your DOS or original program disks. Remember these steps.

1. Change the default drive to the drive that contains the disk you want to list files on.
2. Type **DIR**, followed by a filename containing the ? wildcard to stand for a specific character or the * wildcard to stand for any group of characters.
3. Press **Return**.

DOS disk
- List filenames that begin with the letters S and R (DIR S*.* and DIR R*.*).
- List filenames that begin with the letter S and end with the extension .EXE (DIR S*.EXE).

WordPerfect program disk
- List filenames that begin with the letter W and end with any extension (DIR W*.*).

The TWIN Educational Version System Disk 1
- List filenames with as many as four characters and any extension (DIR ????.*).

dBASE III Plus system disk #1
- List filenames with as many as six characters and any extension (DIR ??????.*).

QUESTIONS

1. What are wildcards used for?

2. What two wildcards are used with MS-DOS and PC-DOS? Describe what each does.

3. What are the advantages of using wildcards? What are the potential disadvantages?

4. Using the programs listed in the table below, display all files beginning with the letters shown. Then, display all files ending with the extensions shown.

Filenames with duplicate first letters

DOS 3.0	A, B, C, D, E, G, K, M, R, S
WordPerfect	W
The TWIN Educational Version System Disk 1	A, H, P, R, T
dBASE III Plus system disk #1	C, D
dBASE III Plus system disk #2	None

Filenames with duplicate extensions

DOS 3.0	COM, EXE, SYS
WordPerfect	WP
The TWIN Educational Version System Disk 1	COM, SCR, BAT, DEF, TXT
dBASE III Plus system disk #1	BAT, DB, SYS
dBASE III Plus system disk #2	None

TOPIC 2-6
Formatting Data Disks

In this topic, we introduce you to the following commands:

Command	Description	Type
FORMAT	Formats a data disk	External
Ctrl-C	Cancels a command in progress	Internal

BACKGROUND

Newly bought floppy disks usually will not run on your computer until you format the disks. Formatting does the following:

■ It checks the disk surface for unusable spots.

■ It divides the disk into tracks and sectors, an invisible magnetic pattern that looks something like a dartboard.

Tracks run in circles around the disk. The number of tracks per inch determines the density of the disk and the amount of data that can be stored on it. A high-density disk has more tracks per inch than a low-density disk and can therefore store more data.

Since tracks can store a great deal of data, the computer divides them into sectors, which makes it easier to find a location on the disk. These sectors are like pie-shaped wedges that radiate out from the center of the disk. Each track is divided into the same number of sectors.

■ It creates a directory that the operating system uses to keep track of files on the disk.

The FORMAT command completely erases any data on a disk. You therefore must be careful with this command. You should never format a previously used disk unless you are sure you will not need any of the files on it. You also should never format a hard disk drive unless you are willing to lose every file on the disk.

EXERCISE 7

Formatting a Data Disk

In this exercise, you format two data disks.

Note. This exercise assumes DOS is loaded and the operating system A> prompt is on the screen. If this is not so, load DOS as described in Topic 2-2, and then change the default drive as described in Topic 2-3.

Step 1. Getting Ready. Insert the DOS disk into drive A because the FORMAT command is an external command. The DOS disk must be in the drive when you first execute this command. Insert the disk labeled DATA DISK -- ORIGINAL DATA FILES into drive B, and then close the door.

Step 2. Load the External Format Program. To format a data disk, you use the FORMAT command. When entering this command (and all others), you may use either upper-case or lowercase letters, but you must strictly observe spaces.

To format a data disk

Type   **FORMAT B:**, and then press **Return**.

Result. In a moment, a prompt asks you to insert the disk to be formatted into drive B and specifies the key you should press to continue.

Step 3. Cancel the Command. When you begin to execute a command and then change your mind, you can cancel it by pressing **Ctrl-C**. Here you cancel the command and then enter it again.

To cancel the command

Press   **Ctrl-C** to return to the system prompt.

To format a data disk

Type   **FORMAT B:**, and then press **Return**.

Result. Pressing **Ctrl-C** cancels the command and returns you to the system prompt. Reentering the command returns you to where you were at the end of the previous step.

Step 4. Format the Original Data Disk. Since you have already put the disk to be formatted into drive B, press the key that the instructions on the screen tell you to press. (Some versions of DOS tell you to press any key, other tell you to press ENTER, which we call **Return**.) Drive B spins as it formats the disk, and the message *Formatting* is displayed on the screen. In a minute or so, the drive stops, and a message tells you how many bytes of total disk space there are and how many are available. (Usually the two numbers are the same; if they are different, DOS may have found bad sectors on the disk. If so, it marked them so no data is store on them.) A prompt asks if you want to format another disk.

Step 5. Format the Backup Data Disk. Remove the disk labeled DATA DISK— ORIGINAL DATA FILES from drive B, and then insert the disk you labeled DATA DISK—BACKUP DATA FILES. A prompt on the screen asks you if you want to format another disk. To format the disk you just inserted, press the letter **Y**, and then press **Return**. The prompt asks you to press a key to continue. Press the requested key. In a minute or so, the same message appears as described in Step 4. Press **N** this time, and then press **Return** since you do not want to format any more disks. The A> prompt reappears.

Step 6. Continue or Quit. You have now completed this exercise. You can either continue to the next exercise or quit for the day. If you want to quit, remove your disks from the drives, put them in their envelopes, and then turn off the computer.

EXERCISE 8
Formatting Additional Data Disks

If you want to format some more data disks, do so. Some of the programs you might be using have two disk so the second disk can be formatted as data disks since you boot the program from the first disk (which you format as a system disk in Topic 2-7). If you are using dBase III Plus or the Educational Version of The Twin, format the following disks as data disks

[ ] dBASE III Plus System Disk #2
[ ] The TWIN Educational Version System Disk 2

Remember these steps.
1. Insert the DOS disk into drive A.
2. Type **A:**, and then press **Return** if necessary to make drive A the default drive.
3. Type **FORMAT B:**, and then press **Return**.
4. Insert the disk to be formatted into drive B, and then press the designated key to continue.
5. Either press **N**, and then press **Return** to quit formatting.

   Or   insert a new disk into drive B, press **Y**, and then press **Return** to display the prompt asking you to insert a new disk. Press the designated key to continue.

QUESTIONS

1. Why do you format a disk?
2. When you format a disk, what three things does DOS do to the disk?
3. Why must you be careful when using the FORMAT command?

TOPIC 2-7
Formatting System Disks

In this topic, we introduce you to the following command:

Command	Description	Type
FORMAT/S	Formats a system disk	External

BACKGROUND

When you want to load a program without first having to load DOS from another disk, you format the program disk as a system disk. This command does the same thing as the regular FORMAT command, but it also copies the necessary operating system files onto the disk. This lets you load DOS directly from the new disk and use all the internal DOS commands. Although the two FORMAT commands are both external commands, they are slightly different. For example, with the DOS disk in drive A, a new disk in drive B, and the A> prompt on the screen

- To format the disk in drive B as a data disk, type **FORMAT B:**, and then press **Return**.
- To format the disk in drive B as a system disk, type **FORMAT B:/S**, and then press **Return**.

The /S switch following the FORMAT command tells DOS to copy the system files to the disk in drive B.

EXERCISE 9
Formatting a System Disk

Now that you have formatted data disks that you can save your files on, you format self-booting disks that you will later copy your program files on to.

Note. This exercise assumes DOS is loaded and the operating system A> prompt is on the screen. If this is not so, load DOS as described in Topic 2-2, and then change the default drive as described in Topic 2-3.

Step 1. Getting Ready. Before proceeding, insert the original DOS disk into drive A. The FORMAT command is an external command, so the DOS disk must be in the drive when you execute this command. Insert the disk labelled DOS Disk — WORKING COPY into drive B, and then close that drive's door.

Step 2. Load the External Format Program. To format a system disk, you first load the FORMAT command from the DOS disk.

To load the DOS FORMAT program

Type   **FORMAT B:/S**, and then press **Return**.

Result. In a moment, a prompt asks you to insert the disk to be formatted into drive B and specifies the key you should press to continue.

Step 3. Format the Working Copy of the DOS Disk. Since the disk is already in the drive, press the designated key to continue.

Result. Drive B spins as it formats the disk. In a minute or so, the drive stops, and a prompt asks you if you want to format another disk. To stop, press **N**, and then press **Return** to return to the A> prompt. The message on the screen tells you how many total bytes are on the disk, how many are used by the system files that are copied to a system disk, and how many remain available for other files.

Step 4. Continue or Quit. You have now completed this exercise. You can either continue to the next exercise or quit for the day. If you want to quit, remove your disks from the drives, put them in their envelopes, and then turn off the computer.

EXERCISE 10

Formatting Additional System Disks

Format any additional system disks you need. You need one for each of the following program disks if you are using them:

[ ] WordPerfect program disk — Working Copy
[ ] dBASE III Plus System Disk #1 — Working Copy
[ ] The TWIN Educational Version System Disk 1 — Working Copy (The TWIN Introductory Version program disk has files so large that there is not room for the DOS system files. You will use the DISKCOPY command to format this disk in Exercise 14 in Topic 2-9.)

Remember these steps.

1 Insert the DOS disk into drive A.
2 Type **A:**, and then press **Return** if necessary to make drive A the default drive.
3 Type **FORMAT B:/S**, and then press **Return**.
4 Insert the disk to be formatted into drive B, and then press the designated key to continue.
5 Either press **N**, and then press **Return** to quit formatting and return to the system prompt.

    Or   insert a new disk into drive B, press **Y**, and then press **Return** to display the prompt asking you to insert a new disk. Press the designated key to continue.

Questions

1. What is the difference between a system disk and a data disk?
2. Why would you want to copy the operating system files to an applications disk?
3. Why is DOS not already on a program disk when you buy it?
4. What files are copied to a system disk?

TOPIC 2-8
Copying Files

In this topic, we introduce you to the following command:

Command	Description	Type
COPY	Copies individual files	Internal

BACKGROUND

When you want a duplicate copy of one or more files, you use the COPY command. This command copies one or more specified files from a disk in one drive or directory to a disk in another drive or directory. The COPY command is often used to make backup copies of important files. It also is used with wildcards to copy more than one file. For example, with the operating system A> prompt on the screen, the disk that files are being copied from in drive A, and the disk that files are being copied to in drive B

■ To copy a file named FILENAME.EXT, type **COPY A:FILENAME.EXT B:**, and then press **Return**.

■ To copy all files, type **COPY A:*.* B:**, and then press **Return**.

■ To copy all files named with the extension .EXT, type **COPY A:*.EXT B:**, and then press **Return**.

EXERCISE 11

Copying Files

In this exercise, you copy the files from your original DOS disk to the DOS Disk—WORKING COPY that you formatted in Topic 2-7. There is a command to copy all files from one disk to another, but you first experiment with copying individual files and then use wildcards to copy groups of files.

Note. This exercise assumes DOS is loaded and the operating system A> prompt is on the screen. If this is not so, load DOS as described in Topic 2-2, and then change the default drive as described in Topic 2-3.

Step 1. Getting Ready. Before proceeding, insert the original DOS disk into drive A and the disk you labeled DOS—WORKING COPY into drive B. Then close both drive doors.

Step 2. Copy a Single File. When you want to copy a single file from one disk to another, you specify its name and the drive you want to copy it from and to. Before beginning, change the default drive to A.

To change the default drive

Type　　**A:**, and then press **Return**.

To copy a single DOS file

Type　　**COPY COMMAND.COM B:**, and then press **Return**.
Type　　**DIR B:**, and then press **Return** to see the filename.

Result. The file you specified has been copied from the disk in drive A to the disk in drive B.

Step 3. Copy All Files Beginning with the Same Letter. In this step, you copy all files that begin with the same letter. The commands you type depend on which disk you inserted into drive A.

To copy a group of files on the DOS disk

Type   **COPY D*.* B:**, and then press **Return** to copy all files that begin with the letter D.
Type   **DIR B:**, and then press **Return** to see the filenames.

Type   **COPY C*.* B:**, and then press **Return** to copy all files that begin with the letter C.
Type   **DIR B:**, and then press **Return** to see the filenames.

Result. The wildcards affect the files copied.

Step 4. Copy All Files with the Same Extension. In this step, you copy all files that end with the same extension.

To copy files on the DOS disk

Type   **COPY *.COM B:**, and then press **Return** to copy all files with the extension .COM.
Type   **DIR B:**, and then press **Return** to see the filenames.
Type   **COPY *.SYS B:**, and then press **Return** to copy all files with the extension .SYS.
Type   **DIR B:**, and then press **Return** to see the filenames.
Type   **COPY *.EXE B:**, and then press **Return** to copy all files with the extension .EXE.
Type   **DIR B:**, and then press **Return** to see the filenames.

Result. The wildcards affect the files copied.

Step 5. Copy Files Using the ? Wildcard. In this step, you use the ? wildcard to copy files that vary by a specific number of characters in specific positions in the filename.

To copy files on the DOS disk

Type   **COPY DISKCO??.* B:**, and then press **Return** to copy the files DISKCOPY. and DISKCOMP.
Type   **DIR B:**, and then press **Return** to see the filenames.

Type   **COPY MO?E.* B:**, and then press **Return** to copy the files MODE. and MORE. (if both are on the disk).
Type   **DIR B:**, and then press **Return** to see the filenames.
Type   **COPY CO??????.* B:**, and then press **Return** to copy all eight-character filenames that begin with CO and have any extension.
Type   **DIR B:**, and then press **Return** to see the filenames.

Result. The wildcards affect the files copied.

Step 6. Copy All Files. Now that you have practiced copying single files and groups of files, copy all files from the original DOS disk to the working copy. Up to now, the default drive has been A, so you have not had to specify it in the command. Let's change the default drive to B, so you now have to specify drive A but no longer have to specify drive B.

To change the default drive

Type   **B:**, and then press **Return**.

To copy all files

Type   **COPY A:*.***, and then press **Return**.
Type   **DIR**, and then press **Return** to see the filenames.

Result. All files are now copied from the disk in drive A to the disk in drive B and have a duplicate copy of the DOS disk.

Step 7. Continue or Quit. You have now completed this exercise. You can either continue to the next exercise or quit for the day. If you want to quit, remove your disks from the drives, put them in their envelopes, and then turn off the computer.

EXERCISE 12

Copying Other Program Disk Files

Make copies of each of the program disks that you formatted data disks for in Topic 2-6 or formatted system disks for in Topic 2-7. You need copies of the following disks in addition to the DOS WORKING COPY you made in Exercise 11 (you will copy The TWIN Introductory Version program disk in Topic 2-9):

[ ] WordPerfect program disk — Working Copy

[ ] dBASE III Plus System Disks #1 and #2 Working Copies

Remember these steps.

1. Insert the source disk (the original disk you are copying from) into drive A.
2. Insert the target disk (the working copy that you are copying to) into drive B.
3. Change the default drive to drive A.
4. Type **COPY *.* B:**, and then press **Return** to copy all files from the disk in drive A to the disk in drive B.
5. Repeat steps 1 through 4 for each disk that you want to copy. (Remember, you can press **F3** to repeat the COPY command.)

QUESTIONS

1. When the default drive is set to A, and you want to copy a file named FILENAME.EXT from drive A to drive B, what command do you enter?

2. When the default drive is set to A, and you want to copy a file named FILENAME.EXT from drive B to drive A, what command do you enter?

TOPIC 2-9
Duplicating Disks

In this topic, we introduce you to the following command:

Command	Description	Type
DISKCOPY	Duplicates a disk	External

BACKGROUND

As you have seen, you can use the COPY command with wildcards to copy all the files from one disk to another to make a backup copy. The DISKCOPY command also lets you make a backup copy of a disk. So why are there two commands to do the same thing?

- The DISKCOPY command does not require you to format the disk you are copying the files to. The DISKCOPY command automatically formats the disk before it begins to copy the files. This means you cannot use this command to copy files to a disk that already contains files unless you want to erase the existing files.

- The COPY command does not make an exact duplicate copy of a disk. It copies the files but not their exact location on the disk. When you want to make an exact duplicate of a disk, use the DISKCOPY command.

If a disk is full and files are stored in noncontiguous sectors (see Topic 2-10), it takes the drive longer to save and retrieve them. The COPY *.* command will copy them so that they are all on contiguous sectors, but the DISKCOPY command will not. If you are making backup copies, it is better to use the COPY *.* command.

EXERCISE 13
Duplicating Disks

In this exercise, you make a duplicate copy of one of your original program disks. (Do not use the DOS disk because it is a system disk, and duplicating it onto a data disk will make the data disk a system disk.) Instead of duplicating one of your program disks onto one of the self-booting disks you made in Topic 2-7, you duplicate it onto one of your data disks that you formatted in Topic 2-6. You do this for two reasons.

- If you duplicated a program disk onto a self-booting disk, the disk would no longer be self-booting because the original program disk is not self-booting.

- After duplicating the program disk onto a data disk, you can erase the files in a later exercise without damaging one of your self-booting program disks.

Note. This exercise assumes DOS is loaded and the operating system A> prompt is on the screen. If this is not so, load DOS as described in Topic 2-2, and then change the default drive as described in Topic 2-3.

Step 1. Getting Ready. Before proceeding, insert the DOS disk into drive A. DISKCOPY is an external command, so the DOS disk must be in the drive when you first execute this command.

Step 2. Execute the DISKCOPY Command. Now, enter the command used to make the backup disk in drive B an exact duplicate of the disk in drive A.

To duplicate the disk in drive A onto drive B

Type   **DISKCOPY A: B:**, and then press **Return**.

Result. In a few moments, a message on the screen tells you to insert the source disk into drive A and the target disk into drive B. The source disk is the disk you are copying from, and the target disk is the disk you are copying to.

Step 3. Insert Disks. Remove the DOS disk from drive A, and then insert one of the original program disks into drive A. Insert the disk labeled DATA DISK— ORIGINAL DATA FILES into drive B. Then close both drive doors.

  Note. It is a good idea to be sure the write-protect notch of the original program disk is covered before using the DISKCOPY command. It will protect you from inadvertently copying in the wrong direction and thereby destroying the very thing you were trying to protect.

Step 4. Begin Duplicating. Now that the disks are in the drives, press any key to continue. Both disk drives operate while the disk in drive B is formatted, and all files on the disk in drive A are copied to the disk in drive B. When copying is complete, the drives stop, and a prompt asks if you want to duplicate another disk. Press the letter **N**, and the A> prompt reappears.

Step 5. Continue or Quit   You have now completed this exercise. You can either continue to the next exercise or quit for the day. If you want to quit, remove your disks from the drives, put them in their envelopes, and then turn off the computer.

EXERCISE 14

Duplicating The TWIN Introductory Version Disk

Now that you have learned how to duplicate a disk, duplicate The TWIN Introductory Version program disk if you will be using it in Part 4 of this text. Remember these steps.

1. Insert the DOS disk into drive A.
2. Type **DISKCOPY A: B:**, and then press **Return**.
3. Insert The TWIN's original program disk into drive A.
4. Insert The TWIN's working copy disk into drive B.
5. Press any key to continue.
6. Either insert the new disk, press **Y**, and then press the suggested key to duplicate additional disks.

    Or   press **N** to stop and return to the system prompt.

Questions

1. When would you not want to use the DISKCOPY command?
2. What are the differences between the commands COPY *.* and DISKCOPY?
3. Why is it preferable to use the COPY command when making a backup copy of files?

TOPIC 2-10
Comparing Disks

In this topic, we introduce you to the following command:

Command	Description	Type
DISKCOMP	Compares duplicated disks	External

BACKGROUND

After you duplicate a disk with the DISKCOPY command, you can use a command to check that the disks are identical. This command does not compare disks copied with the COPY command.

EXERCISE 15
Comparing Disks

In this exercise, you compare the original and working copy disk that you made in Exercise 13. To check that the disk was copied correctly, you use the DISKCOMP command to compare the two disks.

Note. This exercise assumes DOS is loaded and the operating system A> prompt is on the screen. If this is not so, load DOS as described in Topic 2-2, and then change the default drive as described in Topic 2-3.

Step 1. Getting Ready. Before proceeding, insert the DOS disk into drive A. DISKCOMP is an external command, so the DOS disk must be in the drive when you first execute this command.

Step 2. Load the DISKCOMP Program. When you use the DISKCOPY command, you make an exact duplicate of the source disk.

To compare the two disks

Type   **DISKCOMP A: B:**, and then press **Return**.

Result. You are prompted to insert the first disk into drive A and the second disk into drive B.

Step 3. Insert the Original and Working Copy Disks. Remove the DOS disk from drive A, and then insert the original program disk that you duplicated onto the disk labeled DATA DISK—ORIGINAL DATA FILES in Topic 2-9. Insert the disk labeled DATA DISK—ORIGINAL DATA FILES into drive B.

Step 4. Compare the Disks. Press the specified key when ready. The drives spin, and in a few moments, the message reads *Diskettes compare ok* or *Compare OK*. The prompt reads *Compare more diskettes (Y/N)?* or *Compare another diskette (Y/N)*. Press **N** to display the system A> prompt. (If the computer finds tracks that do not match, it beeps and displays the message *Compare error(s)* and indicates the tracks and sides on this disk where the error(s) were found. If this happens, first check that you inserted the correct disks in Step 3 or use DISKCOPY to make another copy.)

Step 5. Continue or Quit. You have now completed this exercise. You can either continue to the next exercise or quit for the day. If you want to quit, remove your disks from the drives, put them in their envelopes, and then turn off the computer.

EXERCISE 16

Comparing The TWIN Introductory Version Original and Working Copy Disks

If you are using The TWIN introductory version and made a duplicate working copy in Exercise 14, compare the working copy with the original program disk. Remember these steps.

1. Insert the DOS disk into drive A.
2. Type **DISKCOMP A: B:**, and then press **Return**.
3. Insert The TWIN's original program disk into drive A.
4. Insert The TWIN's working copy disk into drive B.
5. Press any key to continue.
6. Either insert two new disks, press **Y**, and then press the specified key to compare additional disks.

   Or   press **N** to stop and return to the system prompt.

QUESTIONS

1. Can you use the DISKCOMP command to compare disks you copied with the COPY command?

2. What should you do if the DISKCOMP command finds that your disks do not exactly match each other?

TOPIC 2-11
Renaming Files

In this topic, we introduce you to the following commands:

Command	Description	Type
RENAME	Renames files	Internal
REN	Renames files	Internal

BACKGROUND

There are times when you want to change the name of a file after it has been saved. To do this, you use the RENAME command. For example, when the A> prompt is on the screen and a disk in drive B has a file named OLDNAME.EXT that you want to change to NEWNAME.EXT, you type **RENAME   B:OLDNAME.EXT NEWNAME.EXT**, and then press **Return**.

You can also change the name of a file while copying it. For example, when the A> prompt is on the screen and a disk in drive A has a file named OLDNAME.EXT that you want to change to NEWNAME.EXT and copy to drive B, you type **COPY A:OLDNAME.EXT B:NEWNAME.EXT,** and then press **Return**.

EXERCISE 17

Renaming Files

In this exercise, you rename some of the files you copied to the disk labeled DATA DISK — ORIGINAL DATA FILES with the DISKCOPY command in Topic 2-9. Since the RENAME command is an internal command, it is always available when the system prompt A>, B>, or C> is displayed.

Note. This exercise assumes DOS is loaded and the operating system A> prompt is on the screen. If this is not so, load DOS as described in Topic 2-2, and then change the default drive as described in Topic 2-3.

Step 1. Getting Ready. Before proceeding, insert the disk labeled DATA DISK— ORIGINAL DATA FILES into drive A, and then close the drive's door.

Step 2. Change the Default Directory. Since you will be working on the files on the disk in drive A, make drive A the default drive if it is not already.

To change the default drive

Type   **A:**, and then press **Return**.

Result. The system prompt reads A>.

Step 3. Select the File to Be Renamed. The first step in renaming a file is to select the file and confirm the exact spelling of its filename.

To display filenames

Type   **DIR**, and then press **Return**.

Result. A list of the files on the disk is displayed. Select the file you want to rename. Although you can select any of the filenames, pick one of the smaller ones so that you can copy it later without running out of room on the disk. The size of each file is listed in the column next to the filename's extension.

Step 4. Rename the File. Now change the filename from its original name to NEWNAME.EXT. In the instructions below, enter the name of the file you selected in place of OLDNAME.EXT.

To rename a file

Type   **RENAME OLDNAME.EXT NEWNAME.EXT**, and then press **Return**.

Result. The drive spins, and the file is renamed. Type **DIR**, and then press **Return** to display a list of the files on the disk in drive A. The file no longer is listed under its original name but now is listed as NEWNAME.EXT.

Step 5. Rename Another File. Select another file to be renamed, and use a shorthand version of the RENAME command to change its name to NEWNAME2.EXT. In the instructions below, enter the name of the file you selected in place of OLDNAME.EXT.

To rename a file

Type   **REN OLDNAME.EXT NEWNAME2.EXT**, and then press **Return**.

Result. The drive spins, and the file is renamed. Type **DIR**, and then press **Return** to display a list of the files on the disk in drive A. The file no longer is listed under its original name but now is listed as NEWNAME2.EXT.

Step 6. Copy a File and Change Its Name. There are times when you want to make a copy of a file on the same disk. Since two files on the same disk cannot have the same name, you must specify a new name for the copy. Here, let us copy NEWNAME.EXT and change its name to NEWCOPY.EXT.

To copy a file and change its name

Type   **COPY NEWNAME.EXT NEWCOPY.EXT**, and then press **Return**.

Result. The drive spins, and in a moment, the message *1 File(s) copied* is displayed, and the A> prompt reappears. To see the results, type **DIR**, and then press **Return**. The file NEWCOPY.EXT is now listed in the directory. It is a copy of the file NEWNAME.EXT, which is still on the disk.

Step 7. Continue or Quit. You have now completed this exercise. You can either continue to the next exercise or quit for the day. If you want to quit, remove your disks from the drives, put them in their envelopes, and then turn off the computer.

EXERCISE 18
Review of Renaming Files

Select any of the other files on the disk, and change their names. Remember these steps.

1. Select the name of the file you want to rename.
2. Type **RENAME**, followed by a space, the original name of the file, a space, and then the new name of the file.
3. Press **Return**.

QUESTIONS

1. What commands do you use to rename files on a disk?
2. If you want to make a copy of a file on the same disk as the original file, can you use the same name for both files?

TOPIC 2-12
Erasing Files

In this topic, we introduce you to the following commands:

Command	Description	Type
ERASE	Deletes files from disk	Internal
DEL	Deletes files from disk	Internal

BACKGROUND

Monitoring the amount of free space on a disk is important because many applications programs misbehave when you ask them to save files on a full disk, or they may create temporary files that take up a lot of space. Most people tend to keep files around long after they are useful. It is good practice to occasionally use the DIR command to list the files on a disk and then the ERASE command to delete any files no longer needed. For example, with the A> prompt on the screen and a disk in drive B that you want to erase a file named FILENAME.EXT from, you type **ERASE B:FILENAME.EXT**, and then press **Return**.

You can use wildcards with the ERASE command, but it is dangerous to do so. Miscalculating even slightly the effects that wildcards have can cause the wrong files to be deleted. One way to use them safely is to preview what files will be affected by specifying the planned wildcards with the DIR command (see Topic 2-5). If only the files you want to delete are listed, the same wildcards will be safe to use with the ERASE command.

The ERASE command does not actually erase a file from the disk. It merely removes its name from the directory and no longer reserves the space on the disk. But if you save another file on this disk, it might be saved on top of, and thus erase, the file you "erased" with the ERASE command. If you ever erase a file by mistake, do not save any files on the disk because utility programs are available that you can use to put its name back in the directory so that you can retrieve it from the disk.

EXERCISE 19
Erasing Files

In this exercise, you erase all the DOS files from the disk labeled DATA DISK— ORIGINAL DATA FILES. When you want to erase unwanted files, use the ERASE command. At the end of the exercise, the disk will be blank.

Note. This exercise assumes DOS is loaded and the operating system A> prompt is on the screen. If this is not so, load DOS as described in Topic 2-2, and then change the default drive as described in Topic 2-3.

Step 1. Getting Ready. Before proceeding, insert the disk labeled DATA DISK— ORIGINAL DATA FILES into drive A, and then close the drive's door.

Step 2. Select the Files to Be Erased. Type **DIR**, and then press **Return** to display a directory of the files on the disk. You need to select files to be deleted, and then enter them in the spaces below. Select any files; you will erase them all at the end of this topic, so none are important.

Select one file, and then write its name and extension.

_____.___

Select at least two files, if possible, that have the same extension, and then write the extension.

XXXXXXXX.___

Select at least two files, if possible, with the same extension, but different from the preceding one, and then write the extension.

XXXXXXXX.___

Step 3. Erase a Single File. Begin by erasing the single file you selected above. Although you need not specify the drive in the command, since drive A is now the default drive, do so as an extra precaution. The ERASE command deletes files from the disk, so it is a fairly serious procedure. If you are not careful, you can inadvertently erase a file from the wrong disk. In the instructions below, enter the name of the file you selected in place of FILENAME.EXT.

To erase a single file

Type   **ERASE A:FILENAME.EXT**, and then press **Return**.

Result. The disk in drive A spins momentarily as it erases the file. When it stops and the A> prompt reappears, type **DIR/W**, and then press **Return**. The file is no longer listed in the directory.

Step 4. Erase All Files with the Same Extension. Now, use a wildcard to erase all files with one of the extensions you selected above. To preview the results, type **DIR A:*.EXT** (substitute the extension you selected above in place of EXT), and then press **Return**. The files ending with that extension are listed. Now enter the same command, but this time use **ERASE** instead of **DIR** in the command.

To erase all files with the same extension

Type   **ERASE A:*.EXT**, and then press **Return**.

Result. The disk in drive A spins momentarily. When it stops and the A> prompt reappears, type **DIR**, and then press **Return**. The files are no longer listed in the directory.

Step 5. Erase Files Using DEL Command   Besides the ERASE command, DOS has a DEL command that works the same way. Use it to erase all files with the other extension you selected in Step 2. To preview the results, type **DIR A:*.EXT** (substitute the extension you selected above in place of EXT), and then press **Return**. The files ending with that extension are listed. Enter the same command below, but this time use **DEL** instead of **DIR** in the command.

To erase all files with the same extension

Type   **DEL A:*.EXT**, and then press **Return**.

Result. The disk in drive A spins momentarily. When it stops and the A> prompt reappears, type **DIR**, and then press **Return**. The files are no longer listed in the directory.

Step 6. Erase All Files. You can use wildcards to erase all files from a disk. Be careful when using this command. You can lose a valuable file while erasing everything on the disk.

To erase all files

Type   **ERASE A:*.*,** and then press **Return.**

Result. To make certain you really want to erase everything, the prompt reads *Are you sure (Y/N)?* Press **Y,** and then press **Return** to continue. (If you press **N,** and then press **Return,** you cancel the command.) The drive spins, and all files are erased from the original data disk in drive A. The data disk is now a blank formatted disk. To see this, type **DIR,** and then press **Return.** The prompt reads *File not found.*

Step 7. Continue or Quit. You have now completed this exercise. You can either continue to the next exercise or quit for the day. If you want to quit, remove your disks from the drives, put them in their envelopes, and then turn off the computer.

EXERCISE 20

Review of Erasing Files

Select any unneeded files on any disk, and then erase them. Remember these steps.

1. Select the name of the file you want to erase.
2. Preview the results of the ERASE command by typing **DIR,** followed by a filename. (Use the ? wildcard to stand for a specific character or the * wildcard to stand for any group of characters.) Then specify the drive you want to copy files to.
3. Press **Return** to display the files.
4. Type **ERASE,** followed by the name of the file to be deleted. (If using wildcards, use the ones you entered to preview the results.)
5. Press **Return** to erase the files.

QUESTIONS

1. Why must you be careful when using wildcards to erase files?

2. When using wildcards to erase groups of files, how can you preview the names of the files to be deleted?

3. Can you retrieve a file that you inadvertently erase? What should you do to salvage it?

TOPIC 2-13
Checking Disks

In this topic, we introduce you to the following command:

Command	Description	Type
CHKDSK	Looks for noncontiguous blocks Indicates status of memory Indicates disk space	External
CHKDSK/V	Displays each filename as it is checked	External
CHKDSK/F	Displays a prompt that asks you if you want to correct errors	External

BACKGROUND

When you save a file on a new disk, it is stored neatly on adjacent sectors around adjacent tracks on the disk. But after the disk begins to fill up, the disk drive has to work harder to store a file. It tends to store different parts of the file wherever it can find free sectors. After a while, a file may end up scattered all over the disk. Files stored this way take longer to save and retrieve because the drive's read/write head must keep moving over the disk's surface to reach parts of the file. These files can also become lost if the drive cannot find all the sections.

You can check your disks with the CHKDSK command to see if any files are scattered. The CHKDSK command is an external command, so insert the DOS disk into drive A. To check the status of memory, type **CHKDSK**, and then press **Return**. The screen indicates the following information about the disk:

- The total disk space on the disk
- The number of bytes in your files and the number of files
- The space that remains available on the disk for additional files
- The total amount of memory your computer has
- The amount of memory that is free, that is, not currently used by the programs you have loaded into memory

Then, to check the status of files on a disk in drive B, you type **CHKDSK B:*.***, and then press **Return**. In a moment or so, the screen will tell you if all files are contiguous or show you the files that are noncontiguous, or scattered. Contiguous means the files are stored in adjacent sectors, as they should be. To save the files so that they are contiguous, copy all the files to a new formatted disk with the COPY *.* command. The DISKCOPY command will copy the noncontiguous files exactly as they are, so nothing is gained.

If sectors of a file become scattered, the operating system may not be able to find sections called **clusters**. The CHKDSK command occasionally displays a message telling you the disk has lost clusters and asks if you want them fixed. To do so, you should be familiar with two other variations of the CHKDSK command.

- To have a series of messages displayed as the disk is checked, type **CHKDSK B:/V** (or **CHKDSK B:*.*/V**), and then press **Return**.
- To correct any errors discovered by the CHKDSK command, type **CHKDSK B:/F** (or **CHKDSK B:*.*/F**), and then press **Return**.

The CHKDSK command also tells you how much space remains on your disk and in the computer's memory.

The CHKDSK command also tells you how much space remains on your disk and in the computer's memory.

EXERCISE 21

Checking Disks

In this exercise, you check the program disks you copied the program files to in Topic 2-8.

Note. This exercise assumes DOS is loaded and the operating system A> prompt is on the screen. If this is not so, load DOS as described in Topic 2-2, and then change the default drive as described in Topic 2-3.

Step 1. Getting Ready. Before proceeding, insert the DOS disk into drive A and one of the working copies of your program disks into drive B. Then close both drive doors.

Step 2. Check the Disk in Drive B. You can check the files on the working copy in drive B.

To check the disk in drive B

Type **CHKDSK B:**, and then press **Return**.

Result. The status of the files on the disk in drive B is displayed.

Step 3. Try Other Variations. Other variations of the CHKDSK command look at individual files.

To check individual files

Type **CHKDSK B:*.***, and then press **Return**.
Type **CHKDSK B:/V**, and then press **Return**.

Result. The first command displays a prompt telling you if the files on the disk are all contiguous or not. If all files on the disk are contiguous, a prompt reads *All specified file(s) are contiguous.* If all files on the disk are not contiguous, a prompt reads *xx non-contiguous blocks,* and you could have problems when you try to retrieve files. Normally, files are stored in adjacent sectors on the disk, but when the disk begins to get full, parts of a file may be stored in widely separated, or noncontiguous, sectors. Two problems may result.

- The drive's read/write head will have to move back and forth more frequently, slowing down the save and retrieve operations.
- Some blocks may get lost and not be retrievable. To correct the disk, copy all files onto another disk using the COPY *.* command. Do not use the DISKCOPY command since it will not correct the problem.

The second command lists each file as it is checked. You can also use the two commands together. To do so, you type **CHKDSK B:*.*/V**.

Step 4. Continue or Quit. You have now completed this exercise. You can either continue to the next exercise or quit for the day. If you want to quit, remove your disks from the drives, put them in their envelopes, and then turn off the computer.

Review of Checking Disks

Remember these steps.

☐1 Insert the DOS disk into drive A.

☐2 Insert the disk you want to check into drive B.

☐3 Type **CHKDSK B:**, **CHKDSK B*.***, **CHKDSK B:/S**, or **CHKDSK B:*.*/V**, and then press **Return**.

QUESTIONS

1. What happens to files, when the disk begins to get full, that makes the drive work harder and take longer to retrieve and save the files?

2. If you get a message telling you your files have noncontiguous sectors, what does it mean?

3. If a disk has noncontiguous sectors, how can you fix the files so that they are all in adjacent sectors on the disk?

4. What is the difference between the **CHKDSK** and **CHKDSK *.*** commands.

TOPIC 2-14
Using Directories

In this topic, we introduce you to the following commands:

Command	Description	Type
MD	Creates a new directory	Internal
CD	Changes the default directory	Internal
RD	Removes a directory	Internal
CD\	Returns to the root directory	Internal
CD ..	Returns to one level up	Internal
TREE	Displays a list of directories	External
TREE/F	Displays a list of directories and files	External

BACKGROUND

Most operating systems, including MS-DOS and PC-DOS, are able to divide a hard disk into directories, which help you organize files on these disks. Imagine if you used a file drawer to store all of your memos, letters, and reports. Before long, the drawer would become so crowded that you could not find anything. But with a little organization and planning, the documents could be organized into folders, making it easier to locate the needed document (Figure 2-5).

A hard disk is like an empty drawer in a new filing cabinet: It provides a lot of storage space but no organization (Figure 2-6). To make it easier to find items in the drawer, you can divide it into categories with hanging folders (Figure 2-7). You can file documents directly into the hanging folders, or you can divide them into finer

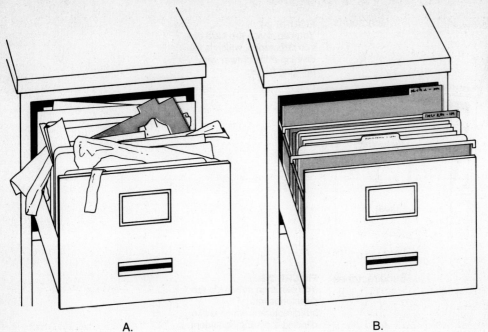

FIGURE 2-5
(a) Unorganized file drawers make it difficult to find files when you need them.
(b) Organized file drawers make it easy to find the file you want.

A.   B.

categories with manila folders (Figure 2-8). A **directory** is like a hanging folder, and a **subdirectory** is like a manila folder within a hanging folder. A file is a letter, report, or other document within either a directory or a subdirectory (Figure 2-9).

Paths

If you are using a computer with a hard disk drive, you not only must specify a defalut drive, you must also specify a default directory. This is essential because most hard disk drives are divided into directories to make them more manageable.

A hard disk drive, usually drive C, may be divided into two subdirectories, named, for example, MEMOS and LETTERS (Figure 2-10). The entire drive, except the subdirectories, is the **root directory**. If the default drive is C, and you do not specify a directory in the save command, the file will be saved to this directory. To save the file to another directory, you have two choices: Make the desired directory the default, or specify a path.

To change default directories, you use the CD (change directory) command. For example, to make MEMOS the default directory, you type **CD C:\MEMOS**, and then press **Return**, or you can use your applications program's command to do the same thing.

To specify a **path** — the location of a file on a hard disk — you must indicate the

Empty File Drawer

FIGURE 2-6
A new hard disk is like an empty file drawer. It has lots of room for files but no organization.

Hard
Disk

Directories

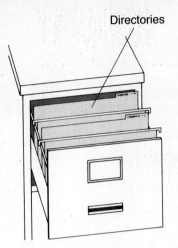

FIGURE 2-7
You can divide the hard disk into directories, which is like dividing a file drawer with hanging folders.

Subdirectories

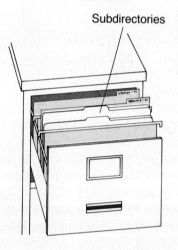

FIGURE 2-8
You can then subdivide the directories into subdirectories, which is like dividing the hanging folders with manila folders.

drive, then the name of the subdirectory, and then the filename. All three must be separated from one another by backslashes (\). For example, to save a memo named JOHN.DOC in the MEMO subdirectory, you might begin by issuing the Save command. When a prompt appears that reads something like *Name of file to save:*, you specify a path in front of the file's name; that is, you type **C:\MEMO\JOHN.DOC**. To save the same file in the LETTER subdirectory, you type **C:\LET-TER\JOHN.DOC**. If you type only **JOHN.DOC**, and then press **Return**, the file is saved to the default directory.

Files

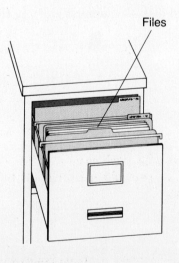

FIGURE 2-9
You can then file documents in any of these subdirectories the same way you would file documents in one of the manila folders.

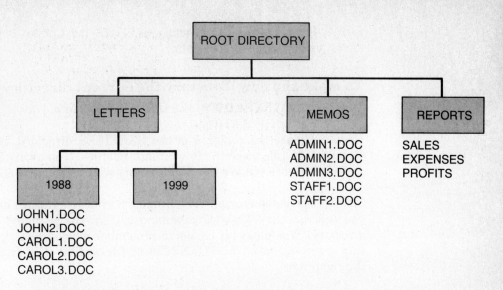

FIGURE 2-10
Paths are instructions to the program that tell it what subdirectory a file should be saved to or retrieved from. It is like telling someone that the last letter to ACME Hardware is in the manila folder labeled ACME in the hanging folder labeled Hardware. These precise instructions make it easy to find the file.

The path to the file CAROL1.DOC is C: \ LETTERS \ 1988 \ CAROL1.DOC
The path to STAFF 1. DOC is C: \ MEMOS \ STAFF1.DOC
The path to SALES is C: \ REPORTS \ SALES

EXERCISE 23

Using Directories

In this exercise, you create subdirectories on the original copy of your data disk and then copy DOS files into them. You then move between directories, erase files, and finally remove directories.

Note. This exercise assumes DOS is loaded and the operating system A> prompt is on the screen. If this is not so, load DOS as described in Topic 2-2, and then change the default drive as described in Topic 2-3.

Step 1. Getting Ready. Before proceeding, insert the DOS disk into drive A and the disk labeled DATA DISK — ORIGINAL DATA FILES into drive B. Then close both drive doors.

Step 2. Create Subdirectories. You create subdirectories with the MD (make directory) command. Here you create three subdirectories, one each for the DOS files that end with the extensions .EXE, .SYS, and .COM.

To change the directory

Type   **B:**, and then press **Return**.

To create subdirectories

Type   **MD\EXEFILES**, and then press **Return**.
Type   **MD\SYSFILES**, and then press **Return**.
Type   **MD\COMFILES**, and then press **Return**.

Result. The disk spins, and then the A> prompt appears after each command. To see the new directories, type **DIR**, and then press **Return**. The new directories are listed and can be identified by the <DIR> following their name.

Step 3. Make the New Subdirectory EXEFILES the Current Directory. To change directories, you use the CD command.

To make the new directory the current directory

Type   **CD\EXEFILES**, and then press **Return**.

Result. To see the contents of the EXEFILES directory, type **DIR**, and then press **Return**. At the moment, it contains no files. The two <DIR>s listed next to the periods indicate you are in a subdirectory with a directory above it.

Step 4. Change the Prompt. The prompt normally indicates only the current drive, but you can use the PROMPT command so that the prompt also indicates the current directory. This makes it easier to remember what directory you are in. You can put this command in an AUTOEXEC.BAT file so that it is executed whenever you boot the computer.

To change the prompt

Type   **PROMPT PG**, and then press **Return**.

Result. The prompt now reads *B:\EXEFILES>*.

Step 5. Move Back to the Root Directory. To move back to the root directory, you type **CD**, and then press **Return** without specifying the name of a directory.

To return to the root directory

Type   **CD**, and then press **Return**.

Result. The prompt now reads *B:\>* to indicate you are in the root directory.

Step 6. To Specify a Path. Let us copy the files from your DOS disk with the extension .EXE to the EXEFILES directory, files with the extension .SYS to the SYSFILES directory, and files with the extension .COM to the COMFILES directory. To begin, insert the DOS disk into drive A, and then close the drive's door.

To copy files into the subdirectory

Type   **COPY A:*.EXE B:\EXEFILES**, and then press **Return**.
Type   **COPY A:*.SYS B:\SYSFILES**, and then press **Return**.
Type   **COPY A:*.COM B:\COMFILES**, and then press **Return**.

Result. The files are copied into the subdirectories. To list the files in the EXEFILES subdirectory, type **DIR B:\EXEFILES**, and then press **Return**. To list the files in the SYSFILES subdirectory, type **DIR B:\SYSFILES**, and then press **Return**. To list the files in the COMFILES subdirectory, type **DIR B:\COMFILES**, and then press **Return**.

Step 7. Display a List of Directories and Files. You can use the TREE command whenever you want to display a list of the directories or both the directories and the files on a disk.

To display a list of directories on the disk

Type   **A:TREE B:**, and then press **Return**.

To display a list of directories and files on the disk

Type   **A:TREE B:/F**, and then press **Return**.

Result. The first command displays only the directories on the disk. The second displays both the directories and files on the disk. To print a list of all directories and files, type **A:TREE B:/F>LPT1**, and then press **Return**.

Step 8. Erase Files in Directories. Now erase the files in the directories. The ERASE command erases only the files in the current default directory (unless you specify another), so first change directories, and then erase the files in them.

To erase files in the EXEFILES directory

Type   **CD\EXEFILES**, and then press **Return**.
Type   **ERASE *.***, and then press **Return**. In a few moments, the prompt reads *Are you sure (Y/N)?*
Press   **Y**, and then press **Return**.

To erase files in the SYSFILES directory

Type   **CD\SYSFILES**, and then press **Return**.
Type   **ERASE *.***, and then press **Return**. In a few moments, the prompt reads *Are you sure (Y/N)?*
Press   **Y**, and then press **Return**.

To erase files in the COMFILES directory

Type   **CD\COMFILES**, and then press **Return**.
Type   **ERASE *.***, and then press **Return**. In a few moments, the prompt reads *Are you sure (Y/N)?*
Press   **Y**, and then press **Return**.

Result. All the directories are now empty.

Step 9. Remove Directories. When you no longer need a directory, you can remove it from the disk. But before you can remove it, you must erase all the files it contains. You have already done that, so here you remove the subdirectories. Since you cannot remove the current default directory, return to the root directory. Here you use the CD .. command, which moves you up one level in directories.

To remove directories

Type   **CD ..**, and then press **Return** to return to the root directory.
Type   **RD\EXEFILES**, and then press **Return**.
Type   **RD\SYSFILES**, and then press **Return**.
Type   **RD\COMFILES**, and then press **Return**.

Result. The directories are now removed. To see the results, type **DIR**, and then press **Return**. Since no files or directories are now on the disk, the message reads *File not found.*

Step 10. Continue or Quit. You have now completed this exercise. You can either continue to the next exercise or quit for the day. If you want to quit, remove your disks from the drives, put them in their envelopes, and then turn off the computer.

Review of Using Directories

Create some new directories on the disk, and then move between them. Remember these commands.

- To create a directory, type **MD**, the name of the directory, and then press **Return**.
- To change the default directory, type **CD**, the name of the directory, and then press **Return**.
- To return to the root directory, type **CD**, and then press **Return**.
- To move up one level, type **CD ..**, and then press **Return**.
- To remove an empty directory, type **RD**, the name of the directory, and then press **Return**.
- To display a list of directories, type **TREE**, and then press **Return**.
- To display a list of directories and the files they contain, type **TREE/F**, and then press **Return**.

QUESTIONS

1. If you want to save a file in a specific directory on a hard disk, what two approaches could you use?

2. In the following examples, you are given the name of a file and the drive and directory it is stored on. Write out the path you would specify to save or retrieve the file.

Filename	Drive	Directory	Path
LETTER1.DOC	C	LETTERS	_____
LETTER2.DOC	D	1987	_____
LETTER3.DOC	C	Root Directory	_____

3. What must you do before you can remove a directory from a hard disk?

TOPIC 2-15
Creating Batch Files

In this topic, we introduce you to the following command:

Command	Description	Type
COPY CON	Copies from console to disk file	External

BACKGROUND

Suppose you have a disk with a word processing program and the operating system files on it. Each time you use this disk to start the system, the computer asks you to enter the date and time. When the A> prompt appears, you must type the name of the program to load it. To speed things up, you can set up the program disk so that the program loads automatically. With batch files, you can tell the computer to do a series of tasks by entering a single command or by just turning on the computer with the disk containing the batch file in drive A.

For example, let us assume you have a program called Clock that automatically answers the computer's prompts for the date and time when you turn it on. You also have two programs on the same disk that you want to load into the computer's memory. One of the programs, Desktop, is a memory-resident program with a built-in phone dialer and appointment calendar. The second program, GOODWORD, is the word processing program that you use. To manually answer the date and time prompts and then load both programs from the keyboard, you would type the following each time you turned on the computer:

Type   **11/10/88**, and then press **Return**.
Type   **11:20**, and then press **Return**.
Type   **DESKTOP**, and then press **Return**.
Type   **GOODWORD**, and then press **Return**.

You can replace these thirty-two keystrokes with a single batch file (AUTOEXEC.BAT) that automatically executes these commands when you turn on the computer.

To see the contents of an AUTOEXEC.BAT file, or any other batch file, use the TYPE command. For example, insert the disk with the batch file into drive B, type **TYPE B:AUTOEXEC.BAT**, and then press **Return**.

EXERCISE 25
Creating Batch Files

In this exercise, you add an AUTOEXEC.BAT file to the working copy of one of your program disks. This batch file will automatically load the program when you turn on the computer with the disk in drive A and enter the date and time.

Note. This exercise assumes DOS is loaded and the operating system A> prompt is on the screen. If this is not so, load DOS as described in Topic 2-2, and then change the default drive as described in Topic 2-3.

Step 1. Getting Ready. Insert one of the following disks into drive A, and then close the drive's door. (You cannot make The TWIN introductory version program disk self-booting because there is not room on the disk for the necessary system files.)

[ ] WordPerfect program disk — Working Copy
[ ] The TWIN Educational Version System Disk 1
[ ] dBASE III Plus system disk #1 — Working Copy

Step 2. Create a Batch File for the WordPerfect Disk. Let's create a batch file that automatically prompts you to enter the date and time and then automatically loads the program.

To create an AUTOEXEC.BAT file for the WordPerfect disk

Type   **COPY CON A:AUTOEXEC.BAT**, and then press **Return**.
Type   **DATE**, and then press **Return**.
Type   **TIME**, and then press **Return**.
Type   **PROMPT PG**, and then press **Return**.
Type   **WP**, and then press **F6** to end the batch file. A ^Z then appears on the screen.
Press   **Return** to save the file.

Result. The drive spins as the file is saved onto the disk, and then the A> prompt reappears.

Step 3. Load the Copy. To see how the AUTOEXEC.BAT file works, you can type **AUTOEXEC**, and then press **Return**, or reboot your computer. Here, execute the batch file by typing its name.

To load WordPerfect

Type   **AUTOEXEC**, and then press **Return**.
Type   the date, and then press **Return**.
Type   the time, and then press **Return** to display a description of the Educational version or the document screen on the full featured version. If the description of the educational version appears, press any key to display the document screen.

To quit WordPerfect

Press   **F7** to exit, and the prompt reads *Save document? (Y/N)*.
Press   **N**, and the prompt reads *Exit WP? (Y/N)*.
Press   **Y** to return to the system prompt.

Result. The commands you entered in the AUTOEXEC.BAT file prompt you for the date and time. When you enter the time and then press **Return**, the program loads automatically. Its name is in the batch file, so you need not type it. When you return to the DOS prompt, it is displayed as A:\> instead of A> because of the prompt command in the batch file.

Step 4. Create a Batch File for The TWIN. Insert The TWIN Educational Version System Disk 1 into drive A. Let's create a batch file that automatically prompts you to enter the date and time and then automatically loads The TWIN program.

To create an AUTOEXEC.BAT file for The TWIN disk

Type   **COPY CON A:AUTOEXEC.BAT**, and then press **Return**.
Type   **DATE**, and then press **Return**.
Type   **TIME**, and then press **Return**.
Type   **PROMPT PG**, and then press **Return**.

Type   **TWIN**, and then press **F6** to end the batch file. A ^Z then appears on the screen.
Press   **Return** to save the file.

Result. The drive spins as the file is saved onto the disk, and then the A> prompt reappears.

Step 5. Load The TWIN Copy. To see how the AUTOEXEC.BAT file works, you can type **AUTOEXEC**, and then press Return, or reboot your computer. Here, execute the batch file by typing its name. Before proceeding, insert the disk labeled DATA DISK—ORIGINAL DATA FILES into drive B and close the drive's door. When you load The TWIN it looks for files on this drive and if a disk is not in the drive, it takes a few minutes to display an error message.

To load The TWIN Educational Version

Type   **AUTOEXEC**, and then press **Return**.
Type   the date, and the press **Return**.
Type   the time, and then press **Return**. In a moment, the copyright screen appears.
            Insert The TWIN System Disk 2 and press **Return** to display the spreadsheet.

To quit The TWIN

Press   **/** (the slash) to display the menu.
Press   **Q** for **Quit** and the prompt reads **No Yes**.
Press   **Y** to return to the system prompt.

Result. The commands you entered in the AUTOEXEC.BAT file prompt you for the date and time. When you enter the time and then press **Return**, the program loads automatically. Its name is in the batch file. so you need not type it. When you use the Quit command, the prompt tells you to insert a disk with the COMMAND.COM file on it. Insert The TWIN system disk 1, and press any key to return to the DOS prompt. It is displayed as A:\> instead of A> because of the prompt command in the batch file.

Step 6. Create AUTOEXEC.BAT Files for the dBASE III System Disk #1. Insert the dBase III System Disk #1 into drive A. Let's create a batch file that automatically prompts you to enter the date and time and then automatically loads the program.

To create an AUTOEXEC.BAT file for the dBASE III Plus System Disk #1

Type   **COPY CON A:AUTOEXEC.BAT**, and then press **Return**.
Type   **DATE**, and then press **Return**.
Type   **TIME**, and then press **Return**.
Type   **PROMPT PG**, and then press **Return**.
Type   **DBASE**, and then press **F6** to end the batch file. A ^Z then appears on the
            screen.
Press   **Return** to save the file.

Result. The drive spins as the file is saved onto the disk, and then the A> prompt reappears.

Step 7. Load the dBASE III Plus Copy. Now, type **AUTOEXEC**, and then press **Return**. Enter the date and time. If you are using the Educational version, in a moment the prompt reads *Press ↵ to assent to the license agreement and begin dBase III*

Plus. Press **Return** or wait a few moments and the prompt reads *Insert Sampler Disk 2 in drive A and a Data Disk in drive B, and press ENTER or press Ctrl-C to abort.* Insert System Disk #2 in drive A, and then press **Return** to continue. In a moment the dBase screen appears with a menu bar across the top and the Set Up menu is pulled down (see Figure 5-1 in Part 5).

To quit the dBASE III Plus program

Press   ↓ to highlight **Quit dBASE III Plus**, and then press **Return**.

Result. If you quit the program, the operating system prompt reappears. Remove your disks and turn off the computer.

Step 8. Continue or Quit. You have now completed this exercise. You can either continue to the next exercise or quit for the day. If you want to quit, remove your disks from the drives, put them in their envelopes, and then turn off the computer.

EXERCISE 26

Creating AUTOEXEC.BAT Files for Other Program Disks

Create autoexec.bat files on other program disks that you might have. Remember these steps.

1. Load the operating system so that the A> prompt is displayed on the screen.
2. Insert the program disk you want to create a batch file on in drive A.
3. Type **COPY CON A:AUTOEXEC.BAT**, and then press **Return**. The COPY CON command tells the computer to copy anything you type on the keyboard to the specified file. The filename specification, A:AUTOEXEC.BAT, indicates the drive the commands you type are copied on to and the name of the file they are to be copied in to. You use the name AUTOEXEC.BAT because this is the file the computer looks for automatically whenever you turn it on.
4. Now you type in the commands you want executed, just as you would normally enter them from the keyboard.

Type   **CLOCK**, and then press **Return**.
Type   **DESKTOP**, and then press **Return**.
Type   **GOODWORD**, (but do not press **Return**).

5. To tell the computer you are finished entering commands, hold down **Ctrl** while you press the letter **Z**. On an IBM PC, you can just press the **F6** function key.
6. To save the commands in the AUTOEXEC.BAT file, press **Return**. The drive spins, and in a moment, the A> prompt reappears. You can now execute the batch file by typing its name AUTOEXEC and then pressing **Return** or by turning on the computer with the disk in which it is stored in drive A. On the IBM PC and compatible computers, you can also hold down **Alt** and **Ctrl** while you press **Del**, which is similar to turning off the computer.

QUESTIONS

1. What are batch files, and what are they used for?
2. What does an AUTOEXEC.BAT file do?

TOPIC 2-16
Displaying and Printing ASCII Text Files

In this topic, we introduce you to the following commands:

Command	Description	Type
TYPE	Displays ASCII text file on screen	Internal
PRINT	Prints ASCII text file	External
FILENAME.EXT	Sends directory to a disk file	Internal
Ctrl-Num Lock	Freezes scrolling screen display	Internal

BACKGROUND

When you save files, you can save them in two, and sometimes three, formats: binary, ASCII, and print file, as you saw in Topic 1-7. Those saved in an ASCII format or printed to the disk can be displayed on the screen printed from DOS using the TYPE and PRINT commands.

When you use the PRINT command, a prompt asks you for the name of the print device and suggests LPT1 (the normal printer port). If your printer is attached to that port, you just press **Return** to print the file. If your printer is attached to a different port, for example, LPT2, COM1, or COM2, you type the name of the port, and then press **Return**.

EXERCISE 27
Displaying and Printing ASCII Text Files

In this exercise, you display and print the batch file you created in Topic 2-15.

Note. This exercise assumes DOS is loaded and the operating system A> prompt is on the screen. If this is not so, load DOS as described in Topic 2-2, and then change the default drive as described in Topic 2-3.

Step 1. Getting Ready. Before proceeding, insert the DOS disk into drive A and one of the program disks you created an AUTOEXEC.BAT file on in Topic 2-15 into drive B. Then close both drive doors.

Step 2. Display a Batch File. The batch files you created in Topic 2-15 are ASCII text files, so you can display them with the TYPE command.

To display the batch file

Type   **TYPE B:AUTOEXEC.BAT**, and then press **Return**.

Result. The batch file appears on the screen just as you entered it.

Step 3. Print a Text File. To print a file from DOS, it must either be in ASCII format or have been printed to the disk from another program.

To print a text file

Type **PRINT B:AUTOEXEC.BAT**, and then press **Return**. The prompt reads *Name of list device [PRN]:*.

Press **Return** to answer the prompt for the name of the list device.

Result. The message then reads *Resident part of PRINT installed, B:AUTOEXEC.BAT is currently being printed.* In a moment, the batch file is printed on your printer, and then the A> prompt reappears.

Step 4. Direct a Listing of Files to a Disk File and Then Print It. You can send a directory to a disk file where it is saved as an ASCII text file. You can then retrieve it with an applications program, display it with the TYPE command, or print it with the PRINT command. To begin, leave the DOS working copy disk in drive A and insert the disk labeled DATA DISK — ORIGINAL DATA FILES into drive B. Be sure the default drive is drive A.

To send a directory to a disk file

Type **DIR>B:FILELIST.TXT**, and then press **Return**.

To display the list of filenames

Type **TYPE B:FILELIST.TXT**, and then press **Return**.

To print the list of filenames

Type **PRINT B:FILELIST.TXT**, and then press **Return**.

Result. When displaying the list of filenames on the screen, if the list of filenames is too long to fit on the screen at one time, you can freeze it by pressing **Ctrl-Num Lock** and then unfreeze it by pressing **Spacebar**. To try this, type **TYPE B:FILELIST.TXT**, and then press **Return**. Then quickly press **Ctrl-Num Lock** to freeze it, and then press **Spacebar** to unfreeze it. If you do not succeed at first, you can press **F3** and then **Return** to repeat the command until you are successful.

Step 5. Continue or Quit. You have now completed this exercise. You can either continue to the next exercise or quit for the day. If you want to quit, remove your disks from the drives, put them in their envelopes, and then turn off the computer.

QUESTIONS

1. What command do you use to display ASCII files?
2. Name one of the two requirements for printing a file from DOS.

WORD PROCESSING APPLICATIONS

PART

THREE

Topic 3-1   Loading the Program

Topic 3-2   Entering, Saving, and Printing Documents

Topic 3-3   Retrieving and Editing Documents

Topic 3-4   Working with Blocks of Text

Topic 3-5   Searching and Replacing

Topic 3-6   Using the Spell Checker and Thesaurus

Topic 3-7   Aligning and Hyphenating Text

Topic 3-8   Emphasizing Text

Topic 3-9   Changing Page Layout

Topic 3-10   Tab Stops and Indents

Topic 3-11   Page Breaks, Page Numbers, and Headers and Footers

Topic 3-12   Merge Printing Form Letters

Topic 3-13   Merge Printing Labels and Envelopes

Topic 3-14   Drawing Lines

Topic 3-15   Entering Special Characters

Topic 3-16   Creating Newspaper-Style Columns

Topic 3-17   Creating Parallel-Style Columns

Topic 3-18   Creating and Using Macros

Topic 3-19   Using Math Functions

Topic 3-20   Creating Automatically Generated Lists

Topic 3-21   Entering Footnotes

Topic 3-22   Sorting Data

Topic 3-23   Creating an Outline

Topic 3-24   Using Superscripts and Subscripts

Topic 3-25   Changing Default Settings

Many word processing programs are on the market. All of them allow you to accomplish basic word processing functions like entering, editing, formatting, and printing text. They differ from one another in two major respects: the features they offer and the procedures you follow to obtain specific results.

The number of features offered by word processing programs increases almost daily. A few years ago, a program that allowed you to enter, edit, format, and print a document was considered sufficient. These functions alone were such an improvement to the typewriter that many people switched to microcomputer-based word processing systems. But newer programs have added built-in spelling checkers and thesauruses and the ability to draw lines, make calculations, print in multiple columns, and so on. These features, once considered exotic, have gradually become standard, and improvements continue.

Keeping abreast of this rapidly developing technology is an adventure. But you cannot keep up unless you have a solid understanding of the many features now offered. In Part 3, we help you gain this understanding. We introduce you to the features now available on all programs and to some features not yet widely available.

To introduce you to word processing procedures, we have organized Part 3 into twenty-five topics. These topics are familiar because they are not limited to microcomputer-based word processing. They discuss the same results you might want to obtain on a typewriter. For example, topics include entering and editing text, entering headers and footers, emphasizing characters, aligning text with margins, and using tab stops and indents. Organizing Part 3 around these familiar topics makes it easier for you to learn the program that you are using.

Each topic explains the principles behind the procedures you follow to obtain the desired result. Understanding these principles prepares you to use any word processing program.

Each topic in this part has at least one and sometimes two or three exercises based on the educational and full-featured versions of WordPerfect 4.2. The first exercise shows you step by step how to use the procedures discussed in the topic. The second and third exercises discuss related procedures and summarize the steps you follow to use them. These exercises assume you know how to enter text, save files, and print documents that you create for the exercise.

Most topics are treated as independent units so that you can refer to them in any order. The first exercises in Topics 3-1, 3-2, and 3-3 (Exercises 28, 31, and 34) are exceptions; these you should complete in sequence before attempting any other exercises so you become familiar with WordPerfect's basic features. Other exceptions are indicated on the Roadmap in the Introduction to this text.

WHAT YOU NEED

The exercises in this part assume your program disk(s) are already installed. To complete all the exercises in this part, you need the following disks:

- A copy of MS-DOS or PC-DOS, version 2.0 or later
- A copy of the educational version of the WordPerfect program disk or the following disks for the full-featured version:
  - ❑ WordPerfect program disk
  - ❑ Learning disk
  - ❑ Speller disk
  - ❑ Thesaurus disk

WORD PROCESSING PROCEDURES —AN OVERVIEW

When you use a word processing program, you follow only a few basic steps. Let's look briefly at how you use a word processing program to create a memo, from loading the program to clearing the screen or quitting. Later in the topics in this part, we explain these procedures in detail.

Step 1. Load the Program

The first step in word processing is loading the program. To do so, you first load the computer's operating system and then the word processing program into the computer's memory from the disks they are stored on. If you are using a computer with floppy disk drives, you also insert a formatted data disk into drive B so that you can save your work (see Topic 3-1).

Step 2. Create a New Document

When you load the program, it usually displays a copyright notice, and then it displays either the document screen (as does WordPerfect) or a Main menu. If a Main menu appears, it lists choices you select, usually by typing the number that precedes your desired choice. When you select the choice for creating a new document, the document screen appears, and you are then ready to enter text (see Topic 3-2).

Step 3. Enter the Document

The document screen always displays a cursor, a one-character wide underline or box. The cursor indicates where the next character you type will appear. When you type a character, it appears on the screen, and the cursor moves one space to the right. The text you enter is not only displayed on the screen, it is also stored in the computer's memory.

Entering text on a word processor is similar to entering it on a typewriter. The main difference is that you do not have to press **Return** at the end of lines; the program automatically does that for you. You have to press **Return** only at the ends of paragraphs and when you want a line to end before the right margin is reached (see Topic 3-2).

Step 4. Edit and Revise the Document

After you enter the text of your document, you proofread it and correct any mistakes. Generally, proofreading a printout of the document is easier than proofreading the document on the screen.

To edit a document on the screen after you have proofread it, you use the cursor movement keys to move the cursor through the text of the document. You can then delete or insert characters, words, or phrases, or you can select blocks—large sections of text—to copy, move, or delete in one step (see Topics 3-3 and 3-4). You can also use advanced editing features like search and replace (see Topic 3-5) and spell checking (see Topic 3-6) to speed up the editing.

Step 5. Format the Document

You format a document to control its appearance (see Topics 3-7 through 3-11). You can format the document before you enter it, while you enter it, or after you enter it. You can change margins or line spacing, emphasize key words by boldfacing them, or indent paragraphs. You need not know much about formatting when you begin word processing since almost every program, including WordPerfect, is already set to print a document single spaced on an 8 1/2-by-11-inch sheet of paper. These default settings anticipate the most frequent applications of these programs—the preparation of memos and letters.

Step 6. Save the Document

When you have completed the document, you save it before printing it. To save the document, you use the program's save command. The document on the screen and in memory is copied to a file on the disk. If the document is long, you would save it several times while entering it so that you would not lose it if the power failed or something else went wrong (see Topic 3-2).

Step 7. Print the Document

You make a printout using the program's print command. This command sends the document to the printer. It is then printed in the format you specified (see Topic 3-2).

Step 8. Continue or Quit

When you finish a document, you have three choices: open a new document, retrieve an existing document, or quit the program (see Topic 3-1).

TOPIC 3-1
Loading the Program

In this topic, we introduce you to the following procedures:

- Loading the program
- Understanding the screen display
- Executing commands
- Quitting the program
- Displaying the tab ruler
- Using windows

BACKGROUND

Before you can use a word processing program, you must turn on the computer and load the operating system (called **booting** the system); you then load the word processing program and use the document screen as a guide when entering text and executing commands.

LOADING THE PROGRAM

The way you load a word processing program like WordPerfect depends on whether you are loading it from a system with floppy disk drives or from a system where the program files have been copied to a hard disk drive.

Loading the Program from a Floppy Disk Drive System

The way you load an applications program on a computer system with two floppy disk drives depends on how your program disk has been set up. There are three basic variations of a program disk.

■ **If your program disk does not contain the operating system files needed to load it**, you must first load the operating system from the operating system disk by booting the system. On the IBM PC, you insert the disk labeled MS-DOS or PC-DOS, and then turn on the computer. You then enter the date and time, and the system prompt, A>, appears. You remove the operating system disk, insert the applications program disk, and type the name you use to load the program. For example, to load WordPerfect, you insert the program disk into drive A (the one on the left if your drives are side by side or the one on top if one drive is above the other), and then close the drive's door. You load the program by typing **WP** and then pressing **Return**.

■ **If the needed operating system files have already been copied to your word processing program disk**, the disk is self-booting. When you format a blank disk as a system disk and then copy the word processing program's files to it, as you did in Part 2, you create a self-booting program disk. You load the program from this disk the same way you do from a non-self-booting disk, but you do not have to insert the DOS disk first and then replace it with the program disk when the A> prompt appears on the screen. You load both the operating system and the applications program from the same disk.

■ **If your disk is self-booting and contains an AUTOEXEC.BAT file** (see Part 2), the operating system and the program are automatically loaded when you boot the program. If your computer does not have a built-in clock, you have to enter only the date and time.

Loading the Program from a Hard Disk Drive System

To load an applications program from a hard disk drive, you first turn on the computer, and then, if necessary, enter the date and time. You then change the default drive and directory to the one containing the program's files if there is not a batch file to load the program in the root directory. For example, if the applications program's files are in a directory named WORDPERF, you type **CD\WORDPERF**, and then press **Return**. If they are in a directory named WP, you type **CD\WP**, and then press **Return**. (To see the name of the current default directory, change the prompt by typing **PROMPT PG**, and then press **Return**.) You then load the program by typing its abbreviated name; for example, to load WordPerfect, you type **WP**, and then press **Return**.

UNDERSTANDING THE DOCUMENT SCREEN

The document screen on some programs, like WordPerfect, appears automatically when you load the program. Except for the bottom line, which displays the current status of the program, the WordPerfect document screen (Figure 3-1) is devoted entirely to the document you create.

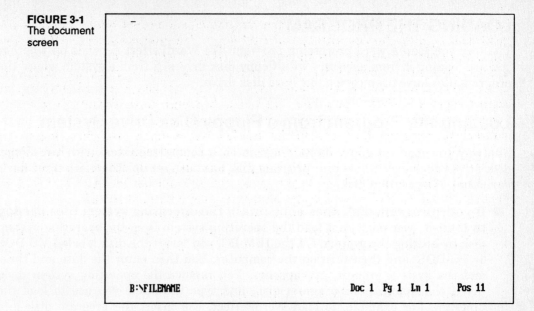

FIGURE 3-1
The document screen

B:\FILENAME   Doc 1 Pg 1 Ln 1   Pos 11

■ The text area is normally set so that you can see twenty- four lines of text eighty characters wide. The left margin is initially set in column 10, and the right margin in column 74, so there is room for sixty-five characters on a line. The cursor indicates where the next character you type will appear.

■ The status line is at the bottom of the screen. The left end of the status line shows the name of the file on the screen, if any. The right end of the status line shows the cursor's position by document (*Doc*), page (*Pg*), line (*Ln*), and column (*Pos*). Prompts and messages also appear on this line when you operate the program.

■ Menus are displayed when you press function keys. Some menus are full screen, and others are displayed only on the status line.

■ Prompts appear at various places on the screen when you execute commands. Frequently, they appear on the status line, but they also appear in various positions on fullscreen menus.

■ Key lock indicators on the status line indicate when **Caps Lock** or **Num Lock** keys are engaged.

Key	When Engaged	When Not Engaged
Caps Lock	*Pos* in uppercase	*Pos* in lowercase
Num Lock	*Pos* flashes	*Pos* does not flash

EXECUTING COMMANDS

To execute most WordPerfect commands, you press function keys to display menus or prompts. Extensive on-line help is available to guide you when using these keys to operate the program. Additional aids include the keyboard template and *Quick Reference* card.

Using Function Keys and Menus

You begin most WordPerfect commands by pressing one of the ten function keys **F1** through **F10** on the keyboard (some newer computers have twelve or more function keys). Since WordPerfect has more than ten commands, these keys are often used in combination with the **Alt**, **Shift**, and **Ctrl** keys. You hold down one of these keys while you press the appropriate function key. When you do this, do not hold down the function key; simply press it firmly and quickly just as if you were typing a character. Since there are so many commands and so many function key combinations, you should have a keyboard template and *Quick Reference* card. These aids are color coded (see Table 3-1). If you do not have a keyboard template, press **F3** once on the educational version and twice on the full-featured version to display one on the screen. On many computers you can print a copy of this template while it is displayed on the screen. To do so, first be sure there is paper in your printer and the printer is on. Then hold down **Shift** while you press the key labeled **PrtSc**. When you are finished, press **Spacebar** or **Return** to return to the document screen.

Note. If you load the full-featured version of WordPerfect from a floppy disk, when you press **F3** for help, a prompt reads *Insert Learning Diskette and press drive letter:*. Insert the Learning disk into drive A or B, and then type the letter of the drive.

When you press one of the function keys alone, or in combination with **Alt**, **Shift**, or **Ctrl**, any one of several things might happen.

- An action is immediately performed; for example, a line is centered.
- An action is begun and then must be stopped; for example, you boldface some text and then change back to regular text.
- A menu is displayed. Some of these menus are displayed on the status line at the bottom of the screen; others are displayed on the full screen. Each choice on the menu is preceded by a number or letter. To make a selection from the menu, press the number or letter that precedes your choice. If you press a number, use the number keys at the top of the keyboard, not the numeric keypad at the right of the keyboard. When you type the response, the cursor often automatically moves to the next prompt. When you finish, the menu may either disappear or remain on the screen in anticipation of your making another choice. To remove the menu and return to the document screen, press **0**, **F1**, or **F7**.
- A prompt is displayed; for example, when saving a file, a prompt asks you to enter or confirm a filename.

Responding to Prompts

When you press a function key or make a choice from a menu, a prompt may appear. Prompts are questions that the program wants you to answer.

- Some prompts you type an answer to. For example, to set the pitch to ten characters per inch, you would type **10**. To save a file named LETTER, you

---

TABLE 3-1
Color Codes on Keyboard Template and Quick Reference

Color	Meaning
Black	Press the indicated function key by itself. If more than one key is listed in black (as they are on the *Quick Reference* card), press the keys in sequence.
Blue	Hold down **Alt** while you press the indicated function key.
Green	Hold down **Shift** while you press the indicated function key.
Red	Hold down **Ctrl** while you press the indicated function key.

would type **LETTER**, **letter**, or **Letter**. (You can use any case.) If you make any typos while typing an answer, press **Backspace** to delete them, and then type the answer correctly. When the response is complete and correct, press **Return** to enter it.

■ Some prompts, when displayed the second and subsequent times in a session, display your previous response. You can press **Return** to accept the suggested response. You can also type a new response or press the arrow keys and **Del** to edit the existing response, and then press **Return**. When editing a response, you can press **Ins** to switch between insert and typeover modes (see Topic 3-3), and you can press **Ctrl-End** to delete all characters from the cursor to the end of the response.

■ Some prompts have a suggested answer, for example, *Delete [Bold]? (Y/N) N.* The N (or Y) following (Y/N) is the suggested response. To accept the suggested response, in this example, No, press **N**, or just press **Return**. To reject the suggested response, press **Y** or any other key on the keyboard.

Canceling a Command in Progress

You can cancel and back out of many commands when a prompt or menu is displayed on the screen by pressing **F1** or **Esc**. You may have to press either key more than once to back entirely out of the command. If a prompt or menu is not displayed, pressing **F1** displays the Undelete menu. If this happens to you by mistake, press **F1** again to remove the Undelete menu and the highlighted text in your document.

CONTINUING OR QUITTING

When you finish a document, you have three choices: open a new document, retrieve an existing document, or quit the program.

■ If you want to open a new document, you first clear the existing document from the screen and the computer's memory. You then open a new document.

■ If you want to retrieve an existing document, you use the retrieve command (see Topic 3-3).

■ If you want to quit the program, you use the exit command. This command removes the program and any document you are working on from the screen and the computer's memory, so you must save it before quitting, or it is lost. Some programs (but not WordPerfect) check documents on the screen to see if any changes have been made that you have not yet saved. If documents like this are found, the program asks if you want to save them before quitting. In a moment, the operating system prompt (usually A>, B>, or C>) reappears.

It is always advisable to quit a program using the commands or menu choices designed for this purpose. Although you can quit a program by simply turning off the computer, this is a bad habit to get into because

■ Some day you will do it without thinking and may lose files as a result.

■ Many programs, including WordPerfect, create temporary files on the disk while you are working. When you quit the program, these files are automatically deleted. If you do not correctly quit the program, for example, if you simply turn off the computer, the document on the disk may not be the same as the one that was on your screen.

If you are quitting for the day (or for any period longer than about an hour), you should do four things.

- Make a backup copy of any files you created so that you have at least the original and one copy.

- Turn off the computer, or if you leave it on, use the display monitor's controls to dim the screen so that an image will not be "burned" into its phosphor surface.

- Open the floppy disk drive doors to lift the disk drives' read/write heads off the disks. This prevents the read/write heads from indenting the disks' surfaces.

- Remove your disks from the disk drives. This prevents their loss, increases security, and ensures that no one mistakenly erases them.

EXERCISE 28

Getting Acquainted with WordPerfect

In this exercise, you load and then quit the WordPerfect program. While the program is loaded, you explore its on-line help. To begin this exercise, the computer must be off.

Step 1. Load WordPerfect. Before you can use the WordPerfect program, you must load it into your computer's memory. These instructions describe how to load the program from a floppy disk.

To load the program from a floppy disk

1 Insert a self-booting system disk into drive A.

- If your WordPerfect program disk *is* self-booting, insert it into drive A.

- If your WordPerfect program disk *is not* self-booting, insert the DOS disk into drive A.

2 Turn the computer on. If your computer does not have a built-in clock that automatically sets the date and time, you are asked to enter it. Enter the date in the format month/day/year (for example, 1/1/88), and then press **Return**. Enter the time in the format hour:minute (for example, 10:15), and then press **Return**. In a moment, the A> prompt is displayed. If you inserted the DOS disk in step 1, remove it from drive A, and then insert the WordPerfect Program disk in that drive.

3 Type **WP** (you can type this and other commands in either uppercase or lowercase letters), and then press **Return**.

4 Insert a formatted disk to save your work on into drive B.

Result. If you are using the educational version, a notice appears on the screen describing how it differs from the full-featured version. Read the notice, and then press any key to display the document screen. If you are using the full-featured version, the document screen appears unless you have not yet installed a printer, in which case the welcome screen appears. If the welcome screen appears, press any key to display the document screen.

Step 2. Explore Help. WordPerfect has an extensive on-line help system that you can display at any time. Take a few minutes to experiment with the help commands. You will find this on-line help very useful. On the educational version, the only help available is an illustration of the keyboard template.

Note. When you execute the help command on the full-featured version on a floppy disk system, the prompt reads *Insert Learning Diskette and press drive letter:*. When this prompt appears, remove the data disk from drive B, insert the Learning disk, and then press **B**.

To display help on the educational version

Press   **F3** to display an illustration of the keyboard template.
Press   **Spacebar** or **Return** to return to the document screen.

To display help on the full-featured version

Press   **F3** to display a screen that introduces you to help.
Press   **F3** again to display an illustration of the keyboard template.
Press   each of the other function keys (labeled **F1** through **F10**) to display a brief description of their function.
Hold down **Alt, Shift,** or **Ctrl** when you press each function key to display help on the commands these key combinations execute.
Press   alphabetical keys (**A** through **Z**) to see an alphabetized list of features. Each key displays a list of topics that begins with the letter you press. To get help on a topic of interest, press the appropriate key. For example, for help on deleting text, press **D**; for help on the go to command, press **G**.
Press   **Spacebar** to return to the document screen.

Result. The document screen reappears. (If you swapped disks, remove the Learning disk from drive B, insert the data disk, and then close the drive's door.)

Step 3. Continue or Quit. You have now completed this exercise. You may either continue on your own document or another exercise or quit and return to the operating system. If you want to work on your own document, feel free to do so. You can return to this step later to see how you quit the program.

To continue or quit

Press   F7, and the prompt reads *Save Document? (Y/N) Y.*
Press   N, and the prompt reads *Exit WP? (Y/N) N.*
Press   Y to quit the program, or press **N** to clear the screen and work on your own document.

Result. If you did not quit the program, the document screen is now blank so that you can enter your own document. If you quit the program, the operating system B> prompt is displayed on the screen. Remove your program and data disks, and then turn off the computer or load another program.

EXERCISE 29
Displaying the Tab Ruler

The tab ruler shows margins and tab stops. Although it is not normally displayed by WordPerfect on the document screen, you can display this information. The tab ruler changes as you move through the document if you have changed tab stops or margins at various places. On the tab ruler, triangles (▲) indicate tab stops, brackets ([and]) indicate the left and right margins, and braces ({ and }) indicate a left or right margin and tab stop in the same position.

To display or remove the tab ruler

1. Press **Ctrl-F3** to display the Screen menu.
2. Press 1 for **Window**.
3. Either press ↑ to display the tab ruler at the bottom of the screen, and the prompt reads # *Lines in this Window: 23.*
   Or   press ↓ to remove a tab ruler you have previously displayed, and the prompt reads # *Lines in this Window: 24.*

4 Press **Return** to return to the document screen.

EXERCISE 30

Using Windows

WordPerfect has two document screens you can switch between or display on the screen at the same time. WordPerfect's windows command allows you to display two different document files if your computer has at least 256KB of memory. The two windows can be displayed above each other or "back to back" so that you can toggle between them.

When you split the screen, it is split with a tab ruler. When the cursor is in the upper window, the triangles indicating tab stop positions point up; when the cursor is in the lower window, the triangles point down.

To display two documents on the same screen

1 Press **Ctrl-F3** to display the Screen menu.

2 Press 1 for **Window**, and the prompt reads # *Lines in this Window: 24.*

3 Either type the number of lines (24 returns you to full- screen display), and then press **Return**.

Or press ↑ or ↓ to move the tab ruler to the desired position, and then press **Return**.

4 Press **Shift-F3** to move the cursor between the windows.

TIPS

■ **If you did not correctly quit the program** the last time you used it, you see the prompt *Are other copies of WordPerfect currently running? (Y/N).* Press **N** to continue. (You press **Y** if you are using the timed backup feature to redirect temporary files into another directory so that you do not overwrite the recoverable temporary files that might contain lost work. For instructions on retrieving the temporary files, see the *WordPerfect Manual.*)

QUESTIONS

1. How do you load a program that does not have the operating system files on it?
2. What is the difference between a warm boot and a cold boot?
3. List the three steps you would follow to load a program from a floppy disk drive.
4. List the three steps you would follow to load a program from a hard disk drive.
5. What is the *Quick Reference* card used for?
6. What is the keyboard template used for?
7. What are help screens?
8. Figure 3-1 shows the WordPerfect document screen. Label each part with the following labels:

Text area
Status line
Cursor
Key lock indicators

TOPIC 3-2
Entering, Saving, and Printing Documents

In this topic, we introduce you to the following procedures:

- Entering text
- Correcting typos
- Specifying drives
- Saving a document
- Printing documents
- Using type-thru mode

BACKGROUND

The basic skills you must know to create documents are those you use to enter text and then to save and print the document.

ENTERING TEXT

Word processing document screens always display a cursor, a one- character wide underline or box. The cursor indicates where the next character you type will appear. When you type a character, it appears on the screen, and the cursor moves one space to the right. The text you enter is not only displayed on the screen, it is also stored in the computer's memory.

Entering Letters and Symbols

To enter uppercase letters, either hold down **Shift** while typing a letter or press **Caps Lock**. Usually, an indicator on the screen shows you if **Caps Lock** is engaged or not. **Caps Lock** is like a toggle switch: If it is not engaged when you press it, it becomes engaged; if it is engaged when you press it, it becomes disengaged.

Entering Numbers

To enter numbers, either use the number keys at the top of the keyboard or, if your computer has one, use the numeric keypad at the right of the keyboard. If some of the keys on the numeric keypad also move the cursor, you must press **Num Lock** to switch back and forth between entering numbers and moving the cursor. Usually, an indicator on the screen shows you if **Num Lock** is engaged or not.

If you are an experienced typist and are used to typing a lowercase L for 1, or an uppercase O for 0 (zero), do not do this on your computer. The computer treats numbers and letters differently, and although you usually will not have problems, you could run into difficulties by disregarding this distinction.

Entering Spaces

To enter spaces, you press **Spacebar**. Some programs (but not WordPerfect) automatically add a second space after a period if you do not enter two yourself.

Correcting Typos

If you make any mistakes—and notice them immediately—press **Backspace** to move the cursor to the left and delete the incorrectly typed characters. You can then correctly type the characters.

Word Wrap

When you are typing paragraphs, you do not have to press **Return** at the end of each line. The program automatically does this for you. Unlike a typewriter, when the end of a line is reached, the word processing program calculates whether the word being entered will fit on the line. If it will not fit, the program automatically begins a new line of text by moving the entire word to the next line. Called **word wrap**, this function is common to all word processing programs.

Carriage Returns

All word processing programs automatically enter soft carriage returns at the end of a line when you type a word that extends past the right margin and wraps to the next line. To enter hard carriage returns, you simply press **Return**. Normally, you do this when you want to

- End lines of text that do not reach the right margin
- End paragraphs
- Insert blank lines
- Return the cursor to the left margin

Soft carriage returns automatically adjust their position when you insert or delete enough text to change the length of lines. Hard carriage returns do not.

Most programs, including WordPerfect, use hard carriage returns to define paragraphs. These programs define a paragraph as any text from the top of the document to the next hard carriage return or any text between two hard carriage returns. Knowing how your program defines paragraphs is important because some of the commands you will learn about involve selecting, copying, moving, or formatting paragraphs.

Scrolling

As you enter text, the screen gradually fills up. When the last line on the screen is filled, the text begins to **scroll**, or move, up a line at a time so that you always see the line you are currently entering. To make room for the new text, text at the top of the document scrolls off the top of the screen. But it is not gone for good; you can scroll back to it whenever you want. You can vertically and horizontally scroll the screen.

- You use **vertical scrolling** when the document is longer than the screen. The effects of vertical scrolling depend on whether the program is document oriented or page oriented; each reacts differently to vertical scrolling.
- You use **horizontal scrolling** when the document is wider than the screen.

Document-Oriented Programs

WordPerfect is a document-oriented program that displays pages as continuous text; that is, as you type, you can see the bottom of one page and the top of the next at the same time. A line of dashes indicates **page breaks**, where one page will end and the next will begin when you print the document.

Page-Oriented Programs

Other programs are page oriented. These programs treat each page like individual sheets of paper. You cannot see the bottom of one page and the top of the next on the screen at the same time. To display another page, you must execute a next page or previous page command. Some of these page-oriented programs hold only the current page in memory. They store all other pages on the disk. When you move from one page to another, the program saves the current page on the disk and retrieves the page you want from the disk into the computer's memory. This slows down the program so that you notice delays when scrolling through a document.

SPECIFYING DRIVES

WordPerfect's default drive is set to drive A, so any files you save are automatically saved to that drive. If you want to save files to or retrieve files from a disk in another drive or directory, you can specify the path to the drive and directory in the save and retrieve command, or you can change the default drive and directory (see Topic 25).

SAVING A DOCUMENT

To save a document, you use the program's save command, and the document on the screen and in memory is copied to a file on the disk. You should frequently save the file you are working on. If you turn off the computer, experience a power failure, encounter hardware problems, or make a mistake, you may lose files that are in the computer's memory. Your files are not safe from these disasters until you save them onto a disk—a more permanent form of storage. When preparing a document, you should always save your file

- Before experimenting with unfamiliar commands
- Before making major revisions
- Before printing (in case something goes wrong during the process)
- Before quitting the program

Most programs, including WordPerfect, provide two commands to save a file.

- One command saves the file but also leaves it in memory and on the screen so that you can continue working on it.
- The other command saves the document in a file on the disk, removes it from memory, and either clears the screen or returns you to the Main menu so that you can then create a new document, select another function, or quit the program.

When you save a file the first time, you must assign it a filename. WordPerfect's filenames follow DOS conventions; that is, they can contain as many as eight characters and be followed by an optional period and extension of as many as three characters. WordPerfect, unlike some other programs, does not automatically add extensions to files.

- The following charachters are INVALID in filenames . " \ / [ ] : | < > + = ; ,
- The following charachters are VALID in filenames A–Z 0–9 $ # & @ ! % ( ) - _ { } ' ' ~ ^

If you are saving the file on the default drive and directory, you have to specify only the filename. But if you are saving the file on a drive or in a directory other than the default drive and directory, you must specify both a path and a filename. For example, to save the file MEMO.WP on the default drive, you just type **MEMO.WP**. To save it on drive B when that is not the default drive, type **B:\MEMO.WP**. To save it in the directory 1986 on drive C when they are not the default drive and directory, type **C:\1986\MEMO.WP**.

When you save a file the second and subsequent times, the program anticipates that you want to save it again under the same name on the same drive and directory and displays that suggestion. You can press **Return** to accept the suggestion, or you can redirect the document into a new drive or directory, save it under a new filename, or both. To do so, enter a new path and filename, or edit the one displayed following the prompt.

- To enter a new path and filename, type them in. The first character you type deletes the entire suggested path and filename.
- To edit the suggested path, press → to enter edit mode, and then insert or delete characters (see Topic 3-3).

When you have finished entering or editing the path and filename, press **Return**.

PRINTING DOCUMENTS

You make a printout using the program's print command. This command sends the document to the printer, where it is printed using the formats you specified.

With WordPerfect, you can print a file displayed on the screen or any file stored on the disk. In both cases, you can print the entire document, and all print jobs are first printed to the disk so that you can return to editing while they are being printed. There are differences between printing files on the screen and printing files on the disk.

- When you print a document on the screen, you can print a specific page or a selected block.
- When you print a file on the disk, you can specify that one or more selected pages be printed. If you print a file on the disk that is also on the screen, be sure they are the same. To be sure, save the file before printing it.

TYPE-THRU MODE

Normally, you enter text, save it to a file on a disk, and print it from that file. But some programs, including WordPerfect, have a **type-thru mode** that you can use when writing brief memos, addressing envelopes, or filling out preprinted forms.

EXERCISE 31
Entering Text

In this exercise, you enter and edit text. To begin this exercise, you must load the program or clear the screen of any document (see Topic 3-1).

Note. If you stop work and turn off the computer after you load the program, any data you have entered is erased from the computer's memory. Your work is then lost unless you have saved the data onto a disk as described in Step 3.

Step 1. Enter the Document. Type in the text for the document shown in Figure 3-2, including the deliberate spelling mistakes in the highlighted words. (Do not try to highlight the words on your own screen.) If you make additional mistakes, do not worry about them; you can fix them later. As you enter the document

FIGURE 3-2
Entering document

Word **processing** is probably the most common application of
microcomputers. The ease with which you can draft and revise
memos, **letters**, **resorts**, and numerous other documents, with a word
processing program increases both the speed and quality of your
writing. You can enter, edit, change, reorganize, format, and
print text without having to retype all of it each time you make
a change. This ease of use encourages you to revise and
reorganize your material more frequently so you can express your
ideas more clearly.

There are many word processing programs on the market. They
differ from one another in the ease with which you can edit text,
and how much more you can do with the program, especially when
formatting documents for printing.

B:\ENTER.WP   Doc 1 Pg 1 Ln 15

- Notice how the cursor moves as you type. It indicates where the next character you type will appear.

- If you make any typos (except the deliberate ones), press **Backspace** to back up the cursor to erase them, and then reenter the correct letter(s).

- Do not press **Return** at the end of lines. WordPerfect's word-wrap feature automatically does that for you. Press **Return** only at the end of each paragraph to end the paragraph and move the cursor to the beginning of the next line. Press it one more time between the first and second paragraphs to insert a blank line between them.

Step 2. Change the Default Drive. WordPerfect's default drive is initially set to drive A. Change the default drive to drive B, the one you want to save the document in. Although your current default drive may be correct because a previous user changed the default setting, complete this step anyway to see how it is done. If you are using a system with a hard disk drive, substitute the complete path for **B:**. For example, to change the default path to the directory LETTERS on drive C, type **C:\LETTERS** instead of **B:**.

Before proceeding, *be sure a formatted disk is in drive B.*

To set the default drive

Press   **F5**, and the status line reads *Dir* followed by the current default drive and directory and the prompt *(Type = to change default Dir)*.

Press   **=**, and the status line reads *New Directory* = followed by the current default drive and directory.

Type   **B:** (or another drive and directory), and then press **Return**. The prompt reads *Dir B:*.*.*

Press   **Return** to display the files, if any, in the default drive and directory.

Press   F1 to return to the document screen.

Result. The document screen is again displayed, but the default drive is now set to drive B.

Step 3. Save the Document. Here, use WordPerfect's command to save the document, but leave the document on the screen and in the computer's memory so that you can continue working on it. Use this save command often—it takes only a few seconds, and you save a great deal of time in the long run.

To save the document in a disk file

Press   F10, and the status line reads *Document to be Saved:.*
Type   ENTER.WP, and then press **Return**.

Result. The disk drive spins as the document is saved onto the disk in drive B. When the drive stops and its red light goes out, you can continue to work on the document.

Step 4. Enter Your Name. Now, enter your name at the bottom of the document.

To enter your name

Press   Home, Home, ↓ to move the cursor to the end of the document.
Press   Return twice to insert a blank line.
Type   your name, and then press **Return**.

Step 5. Save the Document. Now that you have finished editing the document, save the latest version. When you execute the save command this time, the program remembers the name you assigned to the document the last time you saved it (the path in front of the filename may be different if you did not specify drive B in Step 3). You can press **Return** to accept that name, or you can type in a new name, and then press **Return** to save the document under the new name. Here you want to save it under the same name.

To save the document

Press   F10, and the status line reads *Document to be Saved: B:\ENTER.WP.*
Press   Return to accept the default filename, and the status line reads *Replace B:\ENTER.WP? (Y/N) N.*
Press   Y.

Result. The drive spins as the document is saved onto the disk. When the drive stops, you can resume working.

Step 6. Print the Document. Now that you have entered the document, make a printout to see how it looks. Be sure that the printer is on and has paper in it and that the paper is aligned.

To print the document

Press   Shift-F7 to display the Print menu.
Press   1 for **Full Text**.

Result. The printer immediately begins printing. Notice the following about the printout:

- The left edge of the printed document starts ten characters in from the left edge of the paper and six lines down from the top edge of the paper.
- The right margin is justified, that is, neatly aligned.

■ If you are using the educational version, the characters *WPC are printed periodically throughout the document.

These are WordPerfect's default settings. You will see how to change these in later topics.

Step 7. Continue or Quit. You have now completed this exercise. You may either continue on your own document or another exercise or quit and return to the operating system. If you want to work on your own document to practice what you have learned, feel free to do so. You can return to this step later to see how you quit the program.

To continue or quit

Press   **F7**, and the status line reads *Save Document? (Y/N) Y.*
Press   **N**, and the status line reads *Exit WP? (Y/N) N.*
Press   **Y** to quit the program, or press **N** to clear the screen and work on your own document.

Result. If you did not quit the program, the document screen is now blank so that you can enter your own document. If you did quit the program, the operating system B> prompt is displayed on the screen. Remove your program and data disks, and then turn off the computer or load another program.

EXERCISE 32
Printing Files on the Disk

You can also print a file on the disk by pointing to its name on the list files screen (Figure 3-3). Use the following instructions to print the file you saved onto the disk in Exercise 31.

FIGURE 3-3
List of files

```
02/28/87  08:24              Directory C:\WP\*.*
Document Size:        0                          Free Disk Space:     237568

. <CURRENT>    <DIR>                    .. <PARENT>    <DIR>
CONVERT .EXE    36800  12/23/85 11:30   CURSOR  .BAT        9  01/27/87 23:35
CURSOR  .COM     1451  10/28/86 14:47   LEX     .WP    290309  10/20/86 15:51
LINES   .WP      3465  02/18/87 14:56   SPELL   .EXE    52592  10/20/86 15:50
TEST1   .WP      2048  12/10/86 11:48   TEST2   .WP      6144  12/10/86 11:39
TH      .WP    362303  10/20/86 15:58   WP      .EXE   266913  01/27/87 07:24
WPFEED  .FIL     2304  04/08/86 10:10   WPFONT  .FIL     8192  01/08/87 11:59
WPHELP  .FIL    63802  12/23/85 11:30   WPRINTER.FIL     2560  01/08/87 11:59
WPSET   .PIX      780  12/01/86 10:37   WPSUFN  .PIX      910  12/01/86 10:39
{WP}    .BU1        0  02/28/87 08:23   {WP}    .CHK        0  02/28/87 08:23
{WP}    .SPC     4096  02/28/87 08:23   {WP}    .TV1        0  02/28/87 08:23
{WP}LEX .SUP     1264  02/27/87 10:34   {WP}SYS .FIL      419  02/17/87 04:58




1 Retrieve; 2 Delete; 3 Rename; 4 Print; 5 Text In;
6 Look; 7 Change Directory; 8 Copy; 9 Word Search; 0 Exit: 6
```

To print a document on the disk by pointing to it

1. Press **F5**, and then press **Return** to display a list of files in the default directory or to change directories.
2. Move the highlight over the name of the file you want to print.
3. Press **4** for **Print**, and then press **0** for **Exit** to return to the document screen.

EXERCISE 33

Using Type-Thru Mode

WordPerfect lets you switch to type-thru mode so that you can send text to the printer either line by line or character by character as you type. When using this feature, all margin settings are ignored. To begin, align the paper in the printer with the print head over the spot where you want the first character to be printed. You can type lines as long as 250 characters before text will wrap at the end of the line. Always press **Return** to end a line before it reaches the right margin on the paper. If the line is too long to fit on the screen, the screen scrolls as you type. Table 3-2 describes the keys you can use in type-thru mode.

Type-thru mode depends to a certain extent on the kind of printer you have. For example, a laser printer cannot print a character, line, or paragraph at a time; it can print only complete pages. If you want to print out less than a page, you must press the On-Line switch to take the printer off line, and then press the Form-Feed switch to advance the page out of the printer.

To use type-thru mode

1. Align the paper in the printer, and then turn the printer on.
2. Press **Shift-F7** to display the Print menu.
3. Press **5** for **Type-thru**, and the status line reads *Type-thru printing: 1 by line; 2 by character:*.
4. Either press **1** for **by line** to send text to the printer only when you press **Return** at the end of each line.

   Or press **2** for **by character** to send each character to the printer as you type it.
5. Type the text to be sent to the printer using the keys described in Table 3-2, and then press **Return**.
6. Press **F7** or **F1** to exit and return to the document screen.

TABLE 3-2
Keys That Work in Type-Thru Mode

Command	Press
Up	↑
Down	↓
Left one character[a]	↓
Right one character[a]	→ or **Spacebar**
To end line	**Return**
To return previous line to screen for editing	**Ctrl-F4**
To return to document screen	**F7**

[a]On some printers, when using line type-thru, these commands move the print head as well as the cursor.

■ **WordPerfect, like most other word processing programs, allows you to enter soft and hard spaces and soft and hard hyphens.** When you press **Spacebar** or **Hyphen** in a document, it enters a soft space or soft hyphen. If the word following the space or hyphen does not fit on the line, it wraps following the space or hyphen to the next line. Certain phrases, for example, a title like Henry VIII, a time like 8 p.m., an address like 32 Elm Street, or a description like son-in-law, though they contain spaces or hyphens, should not be on different lines. To keep the phrase together, you enter hard spaces or hard hyphens. This way, if the phrase does not fit on one line, it all wraps to the next line. If you are using justified text, hard spaces and hyphens (for minus signs) also prevent the program from inserting unwanted soft spaces in formulas and computer commands. To enter a hard space, press **Home, Spacebar**. To enter a hard hyphen, press **Home, Hyphen**.

■ **The error message** *Disk full - Strike any key to continue* appears when you try to save a file and there is no room for it on the disk. If this happens, either delete some files from the disk and try again, or put a new disk into the drive and save the file; if working from a hard disk, insert a disk into drive A, and then save the file on that drive.

■ **If you want to print, copy, or delete several files that are displayed when you press F5, Return**, you can mark them. Move the highlight over the desired file, hold down **Shift**, and then press the asterisk (*) key. Do the same to remove the mark if you want to unmark a file. You can also press **Alt-F5** to mark all files, and then unmark selected ones using **Shift-***. To unmark all files, press **Alt-F5** a second time.

QUESTIONS

1. What is the difference between hard and soft carriage returns?
2. What is the difference between hard and soft spaces?
3. What is the difference between hard and soft hyphens?
4. You are working on a document named MEMO.DOC and want to save it on a disk or in a directory other than the default. For each of the following, specify the path and filename you would specify:

To save the file on   **I would specify this path**

Drive	Directory	
B:	None	_____
A:	None	_____
C:	Root	_____
C:	LETTERS	_____
C:	LETTERS\1987	_____

5. List three stages at which it is prudent to save your files.
6. Why would you want to abandon a file instead of saving it?

TOPIC 3-3
Retrieving and Editing Documents

In this topic, we introduce you to the following procedures:

- Retrieving a file
- Moving the cursor and scrolling the screen
- Inserting and typing over text
- Displaying hidden characters and codes
- Deleting text and joining lines
- Entering dates and times
- Changing the case of text

BACKGROUND

After you enter the document, you proofread it and correct any mistakes. Generally, proofreading a printout of a document is easier than proofreading the document on the screen. If you saved the document after entering it, and then cleared the screen or quit the program, you first retrieve it from the disk you saved it on.

RETRIEVING FILES

After you have created and saved a file on a disk, you can retrieve it later for further editing. To retrieve the file, you must

- Insert the disk it was saved on into the disk drive if you are working on a floppy disk system.
- Specify the drive and directory it is stored in if it is not stored in the default drive and directory.

When you execute the program's retrieve command, WordPerfect displays a list of the filenames on the disk to guide you (Figure 3-3). You retrieve a file in one of two ways.

- By entering the filename and then pressing **Return** when prompted for the filename
- By pointing to the filename on the List Files screen with a highlight and then pressing **Return** to preview the file or pressing **1** for **Retrieve** from the menu

When the file is retrieved, the disk drive spins, and the computer copies the file from the disk into the computer's memory and displays it on the screen. The copy of the file on the disk remains unchanged until you change the document in memory and then save it back onto the disk, at which time it overwrites the old file.

EDITING DOCUMENTS

To edit a document on the screen after you have proofread it, you use the cursor movement keys to move the cursor through the text of the document. You can then delete or insert characters, words, or phrases, or you can select blocks—large sections of text—to copy, move, or delete in one step (see Topic 3-4). To speed up your editing, you can also use advanced editing features like search and replace (see Topic 3-5) and spell checking (see Topic 3-6).

MOVING THE CURSOR AND SCROLLING THE SCREEN

You can move the cursor a character or line at a time with the directional arrow keys. When you do so, you will notice

- When you move the cursor along a line of text, it moves through the text and does not affect it.
- When you move the cursor past the rightmost character on a line, it usually jumps down to the beginning of the next line.
- When you move the cursor past the leftmost character on a line, it usually jumps up to the rightmost end of the line above.
- If the document is longer than the number of lines displayed on the screen, it can be scrolled into view by moving the cursor to the top or bottom line of the screen and pressing the up or down arrow keys. Instead of moving off the screen, the cursor stays on the top or bottom line, and the text scrolls into view.
- You cannot move the cursor off the screen, and you usually cannot move it past the last line of text, or hard carriage return, in the document.

WordPerfect, like all other word processing programs, also has commands that move the cursor more than a character or line at a time. Table 3-3 describes these cursor movement keys. Since you can move the cursor only though text, some of these keys work only when your document is longer than a single page.

- Many of the commands require that you press arrow keys. On some computers, these keys are on the numeric keypad, which is also used to enter numbers. When pressing these keys to move the cursor, be sure the *Pos* indicator on the

---

TABLE 3-3
Cursor Movement Keys

To Move Cursor	Press
Horizontally	
One character left or right	← or →
One word left or right	**Ctrl–← or Ctrl–→**
To left or right edge of text on screen[a]	**Home,** ← or **Home,** →
To left edge of document when wider than screen	**Home** (two times), ←
To right edge of document when wider than screen	**Home** (two times), →
To beginning of line before codes	**Home** (three times), ←
To end of line	**End**
Vertically	
One line up or down	ì or ↓
To top or bottom line on screen	**Home,** ↑ or **Home,** ↓
To top line of document	**Home** (two times), ↑
To top of document before all codes	**Home (three times), ↑**
To end of document's last line	**Home** (two times), ↓
To end of document after all codes	**Home** (three times), ↓
To bottom line and then to next screen	**Gray+**[a]
To top line and then to previous screen	**Gray-**[a]
To top of next page	**PgDn**
To top of previous page	**PgUp**

[a] The **Gray+** and **Gray-** keys are on the far right of the keyboard.

---

status line is not flashing. If it is, pressing the arrow keys enters numbers. To turn off the flashing indicator, press **NumLock**.

- Pressing the arrow keys moves the cursor a character or line at a time. When you press **Home** and then press an arrow key, or when you hold down **Ctrl** while you press an arrow key, the cursor moves in larger jumps. These keys are like magnifiers. For example, pressing **Home** once and then pressing an arrow key moves the cursor to the top, bottom, left, or right of the screen. Pressing **Home** twice and then pressing the arrow keys moves the cursor to the edges of the document even if it is wider or longer than the screen.

- When you move the cursor through formatted text, pressing the arrow keys sometimes does not move the cursor. This is because the text contains codes that you entered when you formatted it. Normally, these codes are hidden on the screen, but the cursor treats each of them as characters. Although the cursor does not appear to be moving on the screen, it is moving through codes.

INSERTING OR TYPING OVER TEXT

To edit text, you move the cursor through the document and then delete and insert characters as needed. Most word processing programs, including WordPerfect, allow you to **toggle**, or switch, between inserting characters and typing over and replacing characters already there. A command that toggles is like a light switch—it has only two states, on and off. This command changes the program's mode between insert and typeover.

WordPerfect's default setting is the insert mode. To toggle back and forth between insert mode and typeover mode, press **Ins**. The status line reads *Typeover* when you are in typeover mode.

When you set the command to insert mode, the existing text moves over and down to make room for the new text. When you set the command to typeover mode, the new text types over and erases the existing text while text to the right, and below, does not move. This is useful when entering or editing tables or other lists arranged in columns. In typeover mode, you can enter new text without causing characters in columns to the right to shift out of alignment. If you press **Spacebar** in typeover mode, you erase the character highlighted by the cursor.

DISPLAYING HIDDEN CHARACTERS AND CODES

As you create a document, usually just the letters and numbers you type are displayed on the screen. However, on many programs, including WordPerfect, printer control codes are entered whenever you press **Return**, **Tab**, or **Spacebar** or when you use formatting commands, for example, to center, indent, or underline text. These printer control codes usually do not appear on the screen and never in the printout. They control how your text is displayed on the screen and printed on a page.

WordPerfect, like many other programs, allows you to display these codes (Figure 3-4), which makes editing much easier. By displaying the codes, you can see where carriage returns and other formatting codes are located, so it is simple to delete or change them. Hard hyphens and soft hyphens are also displayed differently so that you can tell them apart. The codes displayed vary from program to program, but Table 3-4 lists many of WordPerfect's.

Figure 3-4
The reveal codes
screen display

```
┌──────────────────────────────────────────────────────────────────────┐
│ This is an example of what hidden characters look like when you        │
│ use the reveal codes command. [SRt] is a soft carriage return and      │
│ [HRt] is a hard carriage return. The codes around these words are      │
│ for boldfacing, underlining, and a font change.                        │
│                                                                        │
│      Tab codes are like the one at the beginning of this line.         │
│      Indent codes are like the one at the beginning of this line.      │
│                                         Doc 1  Pg 1  Ln 4      Pos 57   │
│████▲▲▲▲▲▲▲▲▲▲▲▲▲▲▲▲▲]▲▲████████│
│ This is an example of what hidden characters look like when you[SRt]    │
│ use the reveal codes command. [SRt] is a soft carriage return and[SRt] │
│ [HRt] is a hard carriage return. The codes around these words are[SRt] │
│ for [B]boldfacing[b], [U]underlining[u], and a [Font Change:10,4]font change[Fon│
│ t Change:10,1].-[HRt]                                                   │
│ [HRt]                                                                   │
│ [TAB]Tab codes are like the one at the beginning of this line.[HRt]     │
│ [->Indent]Indent codes are like the one at the beginning of this line.  │
│                                                                        │
└──────────────────────────────────────────────────────────────────────┘
```

TABLE 3-4
WordPerfect Codes

Code	Description
_ (blinking)	Current position of cursor
]	Hard space
[-]	Hyphen
-	Soft hyphen
/	Hyphenation canceled
[A] [a]	Tab align or flush right begins/ends
[Adv ▲]	Printer advances up one-half line
[Adv ▼]	Printer advances down one-half line
[Align Char:]	Alignment character
[B][b]	Bold begins/ends
[Block]	Block begins
[BlockPro:On][BlockPro:Off]	Block protection begins/ends
[C][c]	Centering begins/ends
[CenterPg]	Text centered vertically on page
[CndlEOP:n]	Conditional end of page
[Col Def:]	Column definition
[Col On:] [Col Off:]	Text columns begin/end
[Date:n]	Date/time function
[DefMark:Index,n]	Index definition
[DefMark:List,n]	List definition
[DefMark:ToC,n]	Table of contents definition
[Elnd]	End of indent
[EndDef]	End of index, list, or table of contents
[EndMark:List,n]	End of text marked for list
[EndMark:ToC,n]	End of text marked for table of contents
[Font Change:n,n]	New font; n=pitch, font number
[FtnOpt]	Footnote or endnote options
[Hdr/Ft:n,n;text]	Header or footer definition
[HPg]	Hard page break
[Hrt]	Hard carriage return
[Hyph on] [Hyph off]	Hyphenation begins/ends
[Hzone Set:n,n]	Change in hyphenation zone
[—>Indent]	Indent begins

[—>Indent<—]	Left/right indent begins
[Index:heading;subheading]	Index mark
[LnNum:On], [LnNum:Off]	Line numbering begins/ends
[LPI:n]	Lines per inch
[<—Mar Rel:n]	Left margin release; n=columns
[Margin Set:n,n]	Left and right margin settings
[Mark:List,n]	Beginning of text marked for list
[Mark:ToC,n]	Beginning of text marked for table of contents
[Math Def]	Math columns definition
[Math On] [Math Off]	Math columns begin/end
!	Formula calculation
t	Subtotal entry
+	Do subtotal
T	Total entry
=	Do total
*	Do grand total
[Note:End,n;[note#]text]	Endnote; n=number
[Note:Foot,n;[note#]text]	Footnote; n=number
[Ovrstk]	Following character will be typed over preceding character
[Par#:Auto]	Automatic paragraph or outline number
[Par#:n]	Fixed paragraph number; n=level
[Par#Def]	Paragraph numbering definition
[Pg#:n]	New page numbers begin
[Pg#Col:n,n,n]	Page number column positions; n=left, center, right
[Pg Lnth:n,n]	Page length; n=form lines, text lines
[Pos Pg#:n]	Page number position
[RedLn][r]	Redlining begins/ends
[Rt Just On] [Rt Just Off]	Right justification turned on/off
[Set Ftn#:n]	New footnote number
[Smry/Cmnt:]	Document summary or comments code
[Spacing Set:n]	Change in line spacing
[SPg]	Soft page break
[Srt]	Soft carriage return
[StrkOut][s]	Text strikeout begins/ends
[SubScrpt]	Next character is subscripted
[SuprScrpt]	Next character is superscripted
[Suppress:n]	Page formats suppressed
[TAB]	Tab
[Tab Set:]	Tabs reset
[Top Mar:n]	Top margin; n=number of half lines
[U][u]	Underlining begins/ends
[Undrl Style:n]	Underline style change
[W/O On] [W/O Off]	Widow/orphan protection begins/ends

DELETING TEXT

As you have seen, you can delete words a character at a time with **Backspace** or **Del**. On most programs, pressing **Backspace** deletes the character to the left of the cursor, whereas pressing **Del** erases the character highlighted by the cursor. If you hold down either key, the computer's **autorepeat feature** causes it to delete one character after another until you release the key. That is, holding down **Backspace** deletes one character after another to the left of the cursor, and holding down **Del** deletes one character after another to the right of the cursor. You can also use special commands to delete text by word, line, or paragraph (see Topic 3-4). When text is deleted, all text to its right and below moves over and up to fill the space vacated.

Table 3-5 lists the keys you can delete text with. When deleting text, codes you entered to format text are not normally displayed on the screen. If you try to delete

TABLE 3-5
Keys Used to Delete Text

To Delete	Press
Character to left of cursor	**Backspace**
Character above cursor	**Del**
Word containing cursor	**Ctrl-Backspace**
From cursor to beginning of word	**Home, Backspace**
From cursor to end of word	**Home, Del**
From cursor to end of line	**Ctrl-End**
From cursor to end of page	**Ctrl-PgDn**

some of these codes with **Backspace** or **Del**, the status line reads, for example, **Delete [Bold]? (Y/N) N**. Press **Y** if you want to delete the code, or press **N** if you do not. These prompts do not appear if you select and then delete a block that includes codes (see Topic 3-4); instead, the codes are deleted along with the selected text. When editing text containing these codes, it is easier if you display them on the screen with the reveal codes command (**Alt-F3**). When displayed this way, you can delete the codes without first being prompted. If you delete any text by mistake, you can undo the deletion with the undelete command (see Topic 3-4).

JOINING LINES OF TEXT SEPARATED BY CARRIAGE RETURNS

When editing, you often want to delete blank lines, join two lines, or join paragraphs separated by hard carriage returns. Although not necessarily displayed on the screen, hard carriage returns are much like other characters you enter in a document; therefore, you delete them the same way you delete other characters. To reveal the hard carriage returns in a WordPerfect document, press **Alt-F3** to display the reveal codes screen. When you are finished, press any key other than a cursor movement or delete key to return to the document screen.

To join two lines or two paragraphs, move the cursor one space to the right of the punctuation mark at the end of the first line or paragraph. Press **Del** to delete carriage returns until the line or paragraph below jumps up to join the line above. If necessary, you then use **Spacebar** to insert spaces between the last word of the first paragraph and the first word of the second paragraph.

CHANGING CASE

WordPerfect has a command that changes text from uppercase to lowercase and vice versa. To change the case of one or more characters, you first must select the characters (see Topic 3-4). To lowercase all but the first character, for example, when you change the case of a sentence from lowercase to uppercase, include the punctuation mark from the preceding sentence in the selected block. This way, the first letter in the sentence remains uppercased. When you change lowercase text to uppercase, single-letter words like *I* or contractions like *I'm* remain uppercased.

EXERCISE 34
Retrieving and Editing Text

In this exercise, you edit the document you entered in Exercise 31. To begin this exercise, you must load the program or clear the screen of any document (see Topic 3-1).

Step 1. Retrieve the File. After you have created and saved a file on the disk, you can retrieve it later for editing.

WordPerfect has a command that lets you preview the contents of a file before you retrieve it. This command displays the file, but you cannot edit it until you retrieve it. You see how this command works in this step.

To preview and then retrieve a file

Press	**F5**, and the status line reads *Dir* followed by the current default drive and directory and the prompt *(Type = to change default Dir)*.
Press	**=**, and the status line reads *New Directory =* followed by the current default drive and directory.
Type	**B:**, and press **Return** to change the default, and then press **Return** again to display the names of the files in that directory.
Press	the arrow keys to move the highlight over the desired file, in this case, **ENTER.WP**.
Press	**Return** to display the contents of the file, and a message reads *NOTE: This text is not displayed in WordPerfect format.*
Press	any key to continue, and then press **1** for **Retrieve** to retrieve the same file so you can edit it.

Step 2. Move the Cursor. Now that you have edited the document, you can move the cursor through it. Practice moving the cursor with the commands described in Table 3-3, and notice how the cursor moves through the text. Remember that keys connected with hyphens, for example, **Ctrl-←**, are pressed simultaneously, whereas those separated by commas, for example, **Home**, ↑, are pressed sequentially. Hold down some of the keys to see how they repeat until you release them.

Step 3. Correct Mistakes. Now that you know how to move the cursor, let's correct some mistakes. First correct the intentional errors in the document. Figure 3-5 shows the document after editing.

To delete characters

Move	the cursor to under either *c* in *proccessing* on the first line.
Press	**Del** to delete the extra letter *c*.

To insert characters

Move	the cursor to under the *t* in *leters* on the third line.
Type	**t** to insert the missing letter *t*.

To type over characters

Move	the cursor to under the first *s* in *resorts* on the third line.
Press	**Ins** to turn on typeover mode, and the status line reads *Typeover*.
Type	**p** over the letter *s*.
Press	**Ins** to return to insert mode, and *Typeover* disappears from the status line.

To delete a word

Move	the cursor to the beginning of *numerous* on the third line.
Press	**Ctrl-Backspace**.

To break a paragraph into two paragraphs

Move   the cursor to under the *Y* in *You can enter* at the beginning of the third sentence.

Press   **Return** twice to insert a blank line between the two paragraphs.

To join lines separated by carriage returns

Move   the cursor to the right of the period at end of the first paragraph.

Press   **Del** until the two paragraphs are joined.

Press   **Spacebar** if necessary to insert a space between the joined sentences.

Result. Now, using what you have learned, correct any additional mistakes. The editing commands you have just learned, and others, are summarized in Table 3-5. When you have finished, your document should look like Figure 3-5.

Step 4. Change the Case of Characters. Now, use WordPerfect's command that changes the case of characters you have already entered.

To change the case of characters

Move   the cursor under the *W* in *Word processing* at the beginning of the document.

Press   **Alt-F4** to turn on block, and the status line flashes *Block on*.

Press   Ctrl-→ twice to expand the highlight over the entire phrase *Word processing*.

Press   **Shift-F3** to display the Move menu, and the status line reads *Block: 1 Uppercase; 2 Lowercase:*.

Press   1 for **Uppercase** to change the highlighted phrase to all uppercase letters.

Press   **Alt-F4** to turn off block, and the status line no longer flashes *Block on*.

FIGURE 3-5
Edited document

```
WORD PROCESSING is probably the most common application of
microcomputers. The ease with which you can draft and revise
memos, letters, reports, and other documents with a word
processing program increases both the speed and quality of your
writing.  You can enter, edit, change, reorganize, format, and
print text without having to retype all of it each time you make
a change.  This ease of use encourages you to revise and
reorganize your material more frequently so you can express your
ideas more clearly.

There are many word processing programs on the market. They
differ from one another in the ease with which you can edit text,
and how much more you can do with the program, especially when
formatting documents for printing.




B:\ENTER.WP                              Doc 1  Pg 1  Ln 14      Pos 44
```

Result. The two words change from lowercase to uppercase letters.

Step 5. Enter the Date and Time. You can enter the date and time either as text or with functions (special commands that read the date and time from your computer's clock). If you enter the date and time as text, they do not change. They are just like those you type character by character. If you enter the date and time with functions, they change to reflect the current date and time whenever you retrieve or print the document. Here you enter both the date and time using functions.

To enter the date as a function

Press   **Home, Home,** ↑ to move the cursor to the beginning of the document.
Press   **Return** to insert a blank line.
Press   ↑ to move the cursor to the blank line.
Press   **Shift-F5** to display the Date menu.
Press   **3** for **Insert Function**.
Press   **Return** to insert another blank line.

To enter the time as a function

Press   **Shift-F5** to display the Date menu.
Press   **2** for **Format** to display the Date Format menu, and the prompt reads *Date Format:*.
Type   **8:90** to change the format to Hour:Minute followed by am or pm.
Press   **Return** to return to the Date menu.
Press   **3** for **Insert Function**.
Press   **Return** to insert a blank line.

Result. The current date and time are displayed if you entered them correctly when you first turned on the computer. If you did not enter them correctly, you can do so the next time you turn on the computer. The document will then show the current date and time if you retrieve or print it.

Step 6. Save the Document. Now that you have finished editing the document, save the latest version.

To save the document

Press   **F10**, and the status line reads *Document to be Saved: B:\ENTER.WP*.
Press   **Return** to accept the suggested filename, and the status line reads *Replace B:\ENTER.WP? (Y/N) N*.
Press   **Y**.

Result. The drive spins as the document is saved onto the disk. When the drive stops, you can resume working.

Step 7. Print the Document. Now that you have edited the document, make a printout to see how it looks. Be sure that the printer is on and has paper in it and that the paper is aligned.

To print the document

Press   **Shift-F7** to display the Print menu.
Press   **1** for **Full Text**.

Result. The printer immediately begins printing. The time on the printout differs from the time displayed on the screen because the date and time are updated when you retrieve or print the document. The time on the screen remains fixed at the time at which you entered or retrieved the document.

Step 8. Continue or Quit. You have now completed this exercise. You may either continue on your own document or another exercise or quit and return to the operating system. If you want to work on your own document to practice what you have learned, feel free to do so. You can return to this step later to see how you quit the program.

To continue or quit

Press   **F7**, and the status line reads *Save Document? (Y/N) Y*.
Press   **N**, and the status line reads *Exit WP? (Y/N) N*.
Press   **Y** to quit the program, or press **N** to clear the screen and work on your own document.

Result. If you did not quit the program, the document screen is blank. If you did quit the program, the operating system A> or B> prompt is displayed on the screen. Remove your program and data disks, and then turn off the computer or load another program.

EXERCISE 35

Using the Go To Command

WordPerfect has a command that moves the cursor directly to a specific place in a document without your having to scroll to it. To go to a specific place, press **Ctrl-Home**, and the status line reads *Go to*. Then press any of the keys described in Table 3-6. To return to your original position, press **Ctrl-Home** twice. To practice these commands, retrieve the file named ENTER.WP that you created in Exercise 31 and edited in Exercise 34.

TABLE 3-6
Go To Commands

To Move Cursor to	Press
Next occurrence of specific character	The character
Next hard carriage return	**Return**
Specific page	Page number, **Return**
Top of current page	↑
Bottom of current page	↓

EXERCISE 36

Using the List Files Menu

When a list of files is displayed on the screen (Figure 3-3), the screen also displays the names of the files, their size (in bytes), and the date and time they were last saved. A header indicates the current date and time and the name of the directory. The List Files menu at the bottom of the screen lists choices used in file management (see Table 3-7).

    Feel free to experiment with these commands, but be sure you do not delete an important file like ENTER.WP.

TABLE 3-7
List Files Menu

1 Retrieve retrieves the highlighted file onto the screen.

2 Delete deletes the highlighted file.

3 Rename changes the name of the highlighted file.

4 Print prints the highlighted file.

5 Text In retrieves ASCII files.

6 Look displays the contents of the highlighted file or directory. The top of the screen tells you the file's name and size in bytes. If the file is longer than the screen, press ↓, **PgDn**, or **Gray+** to scroll down through it. (You can also move the highlight over a drive and directory, and then press **Return** to look at their contents.) When you are finished looking at the contents of the file or directory, press any other key to return to the list files screen.

7 Change Directory changes the default directory.

8 Copy copies the highlighted file.

9 Word Search helps you locate files by searching for key words in the document. Press **9** for **Word Search**, and the status line reads *Word Pattern:*. Enter, in uppercase or lowercase letters, a word or phrase that you think is in the file you are looking for. Enclose phrases that contain spaces in double quotation marks, for example, "the word". Then press **Return**. The drives spin, and in a moment, only those files containing the specified word or phrase are displayed on the list files screen.

When specifying words to be searched for, you can use the wildcards * and ? and the logical operators semicolon (;), space, and comma (,).

- If you separate two or more words by semicolons or spaces, the program displays the files that contain all the words you specified. For example, entering **John;Dennis** tells word search to look for John *and* Dennis. If they are both in the same file, the file is displayed.

- If you separate two or more words with commas, the program displays the files that contain either or any of the words you specified. For example, entering **John,Dennis** tells word search to look for John *or* Dennis. If either name is in a file, the file is displayed.

- If you want to search for a selected group of files, you can mark them. Move the highlight over each file, hold down **Shift**, and then press the asterisk key (*). Do the same to remove the mark if you want to unmark a file. You can also press **Alt-F5** to mark all files, and then unmark selected ones using **Shift-***. To remove marks from all files, press **Alt-F5** a second time.

0 Exit removes the menu and then returns you to the document screen.

TIPS

- **Backspace acts differently depending on the mode you are in**. In insert mode, **Backspace** deletes the character to the cursor's left and closes up the text. In typeover mode, it erases the character to the left and inserts a space.

- **When you press Spacebar in existing text**, how it behaves depends on whether the program is in insert or typeover mode. In insert mode, it inserts a space, and text to the right of the cursor moves over to make room for it. In typeover mode, it deletes the character, and the cursor moves to the right; text to the right of the cursor does not move over.

- **When you press F5 to list files in a directory**, the status line reads *Dir PATH*.*.* To display only selected files, use wildcards. For example, type **B:*.WP** to list all the files on drive B that end with the extension .WP.

- **You can print a list of the filenames** displayed on the list files screen by pressing **Shift-F7**.

- **When you press F5 and then Return, the list files screen is displayed, and any subdirectory is listed followed by <DIR>.** To move quickly through directories, highlight the directory (including *<CURRENT>* *<DIR>* and *<PARENT>* *<DIR>*, and then press **Return** twice to display the files it contains. When you locate the directory containing the file you want, highlight the file's name, and then press **1** for **Retrieve**. You can also press **7** for **Change Directory**, and then press **Return** twice to make the highlighted directory the current directory.

QUESTIONS

1. If you press **Spacebar** to move the cursor, what happens if the program is in insert mode? In typeover mode?
2. What is the basic difference between insert mode and typeover mode?
3. What are hidden characters? Why would you want to display them?
4. What commands move the cursor to the top of the document? To the bottom?
5. What does the go to command do?
6. List three options offered on the List Files menu.

TOPIC 3-4
Working with Blocks of Text

In this topic, we introduce you to the following procedures:

- Selecting blocks
- Copying, moving, and deleting blocks
- Undoing deletions
- Copying a block to its own file
- Printing a block
- Working with columns

BACKGROUND

If you are revising typewritten copy, at some point, you will likely take a pair of scissors and some glue and reorganize your work by cutting and pasting. But with a word processing program, you do this electronically. Blocks of text are the sections you cut from one place and then move or copy to another.

SELECTING BLOCKS

A **block** of text can be a character, word, phrase, sentence, paragraph, group of paragraphs, or an entire document. Depending on your program, you use one of two approaches to work with a block of text: Either you first select the block, and then indicate the operation you want to perform on it, as in WordPerfect, or you first indicate the operation, and then select the block.

To select a block of text, you indicate the beginning and end of the block. You do this in one of three ways, depending on the program that you are using.

- You highlight the block, as in WordPerfect. To do so, you move the cursor to the beginning or end of the block, and then press a function key (in WordPerfect, you press **Alt-F4**) to enter block mode. You then use the arrow keys or other cursor movement commands to expand the highlight over the text you want included in the block.

- You enter codes at the beginning and end of the block. These codes do not print out; they are used only to mark the block.

- You select a specific type of block by pressing a key that tells the program you want to select the word, sentence, or paragraph the cursor is positioned in. You then press a designated key to copy, move, delete, or format the selected section.

A selected block usually appears highlighted so that it stands out from the text you have not selected. It may be in a different color, dimmer or brighter than the rest of the document, or in reverse video (dark characters against a bright background).

With WordPerfect, and many other programs, you can select three kinds of blocks: lines, columns, and rectangles.

Line Blocks

When working with blocks of text, you usually copy, move, or delete lines of text. A line block begins any place on a line and ends any place on the same line or any other.

Column Blocks

Many word processors, including WordPerfect, allow you to work with columns of text. Called **column mode**, this feature is useful when revising or formatting tables or other text aligned in columns. For example, what if you want to reorganize a table by copying, moving, or deleting one of the columns? If the program works only with lines, you must painstakingly copy, move, or delete the entries in the selected column one line at a time. But with column mode, you can select a column and copy, move, or delete it all at once.

In WordPerfect, a column block is defined as one or more columns separated from adjoining columns by tab stops, tab aligns, indents, or hard carriage returns. You cannot copy, move, or delete columns that were created by entering spaces; to do that, you must copy or move a rectangular block.

Rectangular Blocks

Rectangular blocks are like column blocks, but they have no conditions; that is, you specify them by indicating an upper left-hand and lower right-hand corner. Usually, rectangular blocks are parts of line drawings. When you delete or move a rectangular block, the existing lines do not reform with the margins; rather, each line closes up individually like column blocks. Thus deleting a rectangular block from a paragraph turns it into nonsense. Each line reads correctly up to where the block was deleted and then continues with the text that was on the same line on the other side of the deleted block. It is much like tearing a lengthwise strip out of the middle of a page and pasting the two remaining halves together.

PERFORMING OPERATIONS ON BLOCKS

After selecting a block of text, you can copy, move, or delete it.

- The copy command leaves the existing block intact and copies it into a buffer, or temporary file.
- The move, or cut, command copies the selected block into the buffer and then deletes the block from the document.

After you have moved or copied a block into the buffer, you move the cursor to the new location, and then retrieve the block from the buffer back into the text at the cursor's position. If you copy or move it into existing text, all text moves to the right and down to make room for the retrieved text. If you copy or move a column into existing columns, any columns to the right of the inserted column move over to make room for it.

- The delete command moves the block into a separate buffer from the one used to store copied or moved blocks. This allows you to undo the deletion because the delete command does not replace text in the copy or move buffer. For example, you can move a block into the buffer, delete a block in its buffer, and then still retrieve the first block from the first buffer to insert it where you want it. If you had moved rather than deleted the second block, it would have replaced the first block in the buffer.

UNDOING MISTAKES

Deleting text removes it from the screen and the computer's memory. With many programs, this means you lose the text unless you save it before and not after you delete it. WordPerfect, like many other programs, has an undelete command that stores deletions in a buffer—a small portion of the computer's memory allocated to saving material you delete. You can recover a deletion if you notice the mistake soon enough.

Buffers store only the most recent deletions (and sometimes other commands). They also do not store material permanently; they store it only until you issue another command that uses it again. For example, WordPerfect saves the previous three deletions in a buffer so that you can recover them if necessary. Thus you must undelete mistakes immediately or at least before you make additional deletions that replace the text in the buffer. Depending on the amount of material you have deleted and the size of the undelete buffer, you may be able to recover only part of the deleted material.

EXERCISE 37

Working with Blocks

In this exercise, you copy, move, and delete columns and lines of text. The principles you learn in this exercise can be applied to copying, moving, or deleting rectangles. To begin this exercise, you must load the program or clear the screen of any document (see Topic 3-1).

Step 1. Enter Columns. Before copying, moving, or deleting columns, you first must enter them.

To enter columns

Move	the cursor to the top of the screen.
Type	**Item 1**, and then press **Tab** to move to the next tab stop.
Type	**100**, and then press **Tab** to move to the next tab stop.

Type	200, and then press **Tab** to move to the next tab stop.
Type	300, and then press **Return** to move to the next line.

Type	**Item 2**, and then press **Tab** to move to the next tab stop.
Type	400, and then press **Tab** to move to the next tab stop.
Type	500, and then press **Tab** to move to the next tab stop.
Type	600, and then press **Return** to move to the next line.

Type	**Item 3**, and then press **Tab** to move to the next tab stop.
Type	700, and then press **Tab** to move to the next tab stop.
Type	800, and then press **Tab** to move to the next tab stop.
Type	900, and then press **Return** to move to the next line.

Results. Your screen should look like the one in Figure 3-6.

Step 2. Move Column Blocks. When you want to copy, move, or delete a column, you first select it, and then cut or copy it to a buffer. If you cut the block, it is deleted from the document. You then copy the cut block from the buffer back into the document.

To cut a column

Move	the cursor to under any character in the number 100 in the first row.
Press	**Alt-F4** to turn on block, and the status line flashes *Block on*.
Press	↓ to move the cursor to under any character in the number 700 in the last row.
Press	**Ctrl-F4** to display the Block Move menu.
Press	4 for **Cut/Copy Column**, and the status line reads *1 Cut; 2 Copy; 3 Delete:*.
Press	1 for **Cut** to cut the column into the buffer.

```
Item 1    100  200  300
Item 2    400  500  600
Item 3    700  800  900
```

FIGURE 3-6
Blocks

```
B:\BLOCKS.WP                          Doc 1  Pg 1  Ln 4      Pos 10
```

To move the column

Move	the cursor to the right of the number 300 in the first row.
Press	**Ctrl-F4** to display the Move menu.
Press	**4** for **Column** to copy the column from the buffer.

Result. When you cut the column into the buffer, the column is deleted, and all other columns move over to fill the space. When you then copy it back in from the buffer, it appears as the rightmost column in the table.

Step 3. Copy a Column. When you copy or move columns, you should also include the tab code that you originally inserted to align the columns. To see these, press **Alt-F3** to reveal codes. The screen divides into two parts: The top half shows the actual text, and the bottom half shows both the text and the codes. In this step, you select the column of numbers 200, 500, and 800 and the tab codes to their left. To return to the normal screen display, press **Spacebar**.

To copy a column into the buffer

Move	the cursor to under any character in the number 200 in the first row.
Press	**Alt-F4** to turn on block, and the status line flashes *Block on*.
Press	↓ to move the cursor to under any character in the number 800 in the last row.
Press	**Ctrl-F4** to display the Block Move menu.
Press	**4** for **Cut/Copy Column**, and the status line reads *1 Cut; 2 Copy; 3 Delete:*.
Press	**2** for **Copy** to copy the column into the buffer.

To copy the column from the buffer

Move	the cursor to the right of the number 200 in the first row.
Press	**Ctrl-F4** to display the Move menu.
Press	**4** for **Column**.

Result. The first column is now copied so that there are two identical columns side by side. The other columns moved to the right to make room for the copied column.

Step 4. Copy a Line. You can also copy lines, just as you copy columns of text.

To copy a line into the buffer

Move	the cursor to the Item 1 line.
Press	**Home**, ← to move the cursor to the beginning of the line.
Press	**Alt-F4** to turn on block, and the status line flashes *Block on*.
Press	**End** to highlight the entire line.
Press	**Ctrl-F4** to display the Block Move menu.
Press	**2** for **Copy Block**.

To copy the line from the buffer

Press	**Home, Home,** ↓ to move the cursor to the end of the document.
Press	**Home,** ← to move the cursor to the beginning of the line. (The status line should read *Ln 4 Pos 10*.)
Press	**Ctrl-F4** to display the Move menu.
Press	**5** for **Text**.

Result. The first line is now copied so that there are two identical lines, one at the top of the document and one at the bottom.

Step 5. Delete a Block and Then Undo the Deletion. Now, delete two of the lines in the document, and then undo both deletions.

To delete the first block

Move   the cursor to the Item 1 line.
Press   **Home, ←** to move the cursor to the beginning of the line.
Press   **Alt-F4** to turn on block, and the status line flashes *Block on*.
Press   **End** to highlight the entire line.
Press   **Del**, and the status line reads *Delete Block? (Y/N) N*.
Press   **Y** to delete the block.

To delete the second block

Move   the cursor to the Item 2 line.
Press   **Home, ←** to move the cursor to the beginning of the line.
Press   **Alt-F4** to turn on block, and the status line flashes *Block on*.
Press   **End** to highlight the entire line.
Press   **Del**, and the status line reads *Delete Block? (Y/N) N*.
Press   **Y** to delete the block.

To undo the last deletion

Move   the cursor to the beginning of the second blank row. (Text is restored at the cursor position.)
Press   **F1** to display the Undelete menu and show the most recent deletion in reverse video.
Press   **1** for **Restore**.

To undo the first deletion

Press   **Home, Home, ↑** to move the cursor to the top of the document.
Press   **F1** to display the Undelete menu and show the most recent deletion in reverse video.
Press   **2** for **Show Previous Deletion** repeatedly to cycle through up to three previous deletions.
Press   **1** for **Restore** to restore the desired deletion.

Result. Both deleted blocks are restored, and the document is now as it had been originally.

Step 6. Save the Document. You should now save your document. Here, and in all subsequent exercises, we specify the drive (B:) in front of the filename when giving instructions on saving files. This will save the file on the disk in drive B. If you would rather change the default drive so that you need not specify the drive in the path when saving, feel free to do so. Before proceeding, *be sure a formatted disk is in drive B*.

To save the document

Press   **F10**, and the status line reads *Document to be Saved:*.
Type   **B:\BLOCKS.WP**, and then press **Return**.

Result. The disk drive spins as the document is saved onto the disk in drive B. When the drive stops and its red light goes out, you can continue to work on the document.

Step 7. Print the Document. Now that you have completed the document, make a printout to see how it looks. Be sure that the printer is on and has paper in it and that the paper is aligned.

To print the document

Press   **Shift-F7** to display the Print menu.
Press   **1** for **Full Text**.

Result. The printer immediately begins printing.

Step 8. Continue or Quit. You have now completed this exercise. You may either continue on your own work or quit and return to the operating system.

To continue or quit

Press   **F7**, and the status line reads *Save Document? (Y/N) Y*.
Press   **N**, and the status line reads *Exit WP? (Y/N) N*.
Press   **Y** to quit the program, or press **N** to clear the screen and work on your own document.

Result. If you did not quit the program, the screen is blank. If you did quit the program, the operating system B prompt is displayed on the screen. Remove your program and data disks and then turn off the computer or load another program.

EXERCISE 38

Working with Predefined Blocks

WordPerfect has a shorthand approach to copying or moving sentences, paragraphs, and pages—the most frequent line blocks. A sentence ends with a period (.), question mark (?), or exclamation point (!); a paragraph ends with a hard carriage return; and a page ends with a hard or soft carriage return. Enter some text on your own, or use the text you entered in Exercise 31 to experiment with these commands but don't save the file when you are finished.

To cut, copy, or delete a sentence, paragraph, or page

1. Move the cursor to anywhere in the sentence, paragraph, or page to be copied or moved.
2. Press **Ctrl-F4** to display the Move menu.
3. Either press **1** for **Sentence**.
   - Or   press **2** for **Paragraph**.
   - Or   press **3** for **Page**.
4. Either press **1** for **Cut**.
   - Or   press **2** for **Copy**.
   - Or   press **3** for **Delete**.

To retrieve a cut or copied sentence, paragraph, or page

1. Move the cursor to where you want to insert the text.
2. Press **Ctrl-F4** to display the Move menu.
3. Press **5** for **Text** to copy or move the text.

EXERCISE 39

Copying or Moving Blocks to Their Own Files

Besides copying and moving blocks within a document, you can copy and move them to their own files or append them to the end of already existing files.

- If you copy the block to its own file, it remains unchanged on the screen.
- If you move the block to its own file, it is deleted from the document on the screen.

In either case, a new file with the name you specify is created on the disk, or the block is appended to the end of the file you specified. You can retrieve the new file and edit it just like any other document file. It can also be copied into another position in the document you copied it from or into any other document.

Moving blocks is often used to break large documents into smaller, more manageable files. Working on smaller documents has several advantages.

- You can get around them more easily.
- You can save and retrieve them faster.
- You are less likely to run out of memory.
- You are less likely to lose your entire document if you make a catastrophic mistake.

To practice these commands, enter some paragraphs and then follow the instructions below.

To copy a block to a new file on the disk
1. Press **Alt-F4** to turn on block, and then select the block.
2. Press **F10** to save the block, and the status line reads *Block Name:*.
3. Type the name of the file you want to save the block in, and then press **Return**.
4. Press **Alt-F4** to turn off block.

With WordPerfect, you can print a block of text from the document on the screen.

To print a block from the text on the screen
1. Press **Alt-F4** to turn on block, and then select the block.
2. Press **Shift-F7**, and the status line reads *Print Block? (Y/N) N*.
3. Press **Y**.

TIPS

- **To unselect a block if you change your mind**, either press **Alt-F4** or **F1** to turn off block, or press **Ctrl-Home** twice to return the cursor to the beginning of the block.
- **There are times when you want to perform two or more operations to the same block**, for example, to write it to its own file and then delete it from the document. To select the same block again, press **Alt-F4**, and then press **Ctrl-Home** twice.
- **You can return the cursor to the beginning of a block** after completing a block operation by pressing **Ctrl-Home** and then pressing **Alt-F4**. For example, use this command after moving a block to return the cursor to where you moved the block from.
- **If you undo a deletion of a column or rectangle**, you cannot reinsert it where you deleted it from. To undo a deletion like this, move the cursor to a blank area of the document and undo the deletion. Cut the column or rectangle as described, and then move it to where you cut it from.

QUESTIONS

1. What is the undelete command? Describe how it works.
2. What is a block of text? What kinds of blocks can you work with? What can you do with blocks of text?
3. What is the purpose of column mode?
4. What steps would you take to copy a block to its own file and then copy it into another document?

TOPIC 3-5
Searching and Replacing

In this topic, we introduce you to the following procedures:
- Searching for strings
- Searching and replacing strings
- Using wildcards
- Searching and replacing format codes

BACKGROUND

The ability to search and replace text is a powerful editing tool. With it, you can find and, if you wish, replace text or formatting codes in the document. When you want to find text in a document, you **search** for it. If you want to replace it with new text, you **search and replace** it. You can search for or search and replace any string of characters. Letters, numbers, symbols, codes, words, and sentences that appear in sequence are **strings**. Table 3-8 lists some examples of strings.

SEARCH

When you use the search command, you are prompted to enter the string you want to find. If the specified string is found, the cursor moves to the beginning or end of the string or highlights it in some other way. The program may then display a prompt asking if you want to quit the operation or find the next occurrence. Alternatively, the search operation might end automatically, and you then use another command to continue it. You might search for strings for several reasons.

TABLE 3-8
Examples of Strings

Character	Example
Letters	a
Words	president
Numbers	$100.00
Symbols	¶
Numbers and letters	100 Elm Street
Sentences	Thank you for your consideration.
Codes	[HRt]

- You might want to find a section of a document. In this case, you just enter a key word that appears in the section's title or contents, and the search command finds it.

- You might want to check words that you frequently misspell, especially those you misspell in more than one way. For example, using wildcards (see Exercise 41), you can find all occurrences of the word *similar* even if they have been misspelled *simalar*, *simelar*, and *similer*.

When searching for strings, you can enter the string in several ways to determine which occurrences are found.

- To find whole words only, for example, *the* but not *there*, enter spaces before and after the word when you enter it. This will not find the string if it ends with a period or other punctuation mark. The same procedure can be used with search and replace. For example, searching and replacing *row* with *column* converts *arrow* into *arcolumn* and *rowboat* into *columnboat*. But searching for (space)*row*(space) finds only whole words spelled *row* with a space in front of them and a space behind them. This approach will not find words followed by a punctuation mark. To do so, you must repeat the procedure, this time specifying (space)*row*.

- To find all occurrences, regardless of case, enter the search string in lowercase letters.

- To limit the strings found, enter the appropriate characters in uppercase when specifying the string to be searched for; for example, *The* finds *The* and *THE* but not *the*, whereas *THE* finds only *THE*.

SEARCH AND REPLACE

When you use the search and replace command (sometimes just called replace), you specify the string you want to find and the string you want to replace it with. If the string is found, the program highlights it and usually displays a prompt or menu offering you options; for example, you can

- Replace it
- Leave it unchanged
- Find the next occurrence
- Quit the search and replace operation

Normally, you use search and replace to replace misspelled words with their correct spelling. But it also has other useful applications, including saving typing time. If a word or phrase appears repeatedly in a document, you can substitute it with an unusual character (or characters) that are unlikely to appear elsewhere in the document. Later, you can search and replace these substitute characters with the actual word or phrase. For example, if you often refer to a book title in a long report, you can enter an abbreviation wherever the title is to appear. Then you can search and replace the abbreviation with the actual title.

EXERCISE 40

Searching and Replacing

In this exercise, you enter a document and then use the search and replace command to find and replace strings. To begin this exercise, you must load the program or clear the screen of any other document.

Step 1. Enter the Document. Enter the document shown in Figure 3-7. The first column lists words with all uppercase letters, the second column with only initial uppercase letters, and the third column with all lowercase letters.

To enter the list of words

Type	**THERE**, and then press **Tab**.
Type	**There**, and then press **Tab**.
Type	**there**, and then press **Return**.
Type	**THEIR**, and then press **Tab**.
Type	**Their**, and then press **Tab**.
Type	**their**, and then press **Return**.
Type	**THEM**, and then press **Tab** twice.
Type	**Them**, and then press **Tab** twice.
Type	**them**, and then press **Return**.
Type	**THE**, and then press **Tab** twice.
Type	**The**, and then press **Tab** twice.
Type	**the**, and then press **Return**.
Type	******, and then press **Return**.
Type	******, and then press **Return**.

Result. Your finished list should look like the one in Figure 3-7.

Step 2. Use Case to Specify the Strings. Here, make three passes through the document to see the effects of searching for *THE*, *The*, and *the*. When doing so, notice what words are found for each string.

FIGURE 3-7
Search and replace document

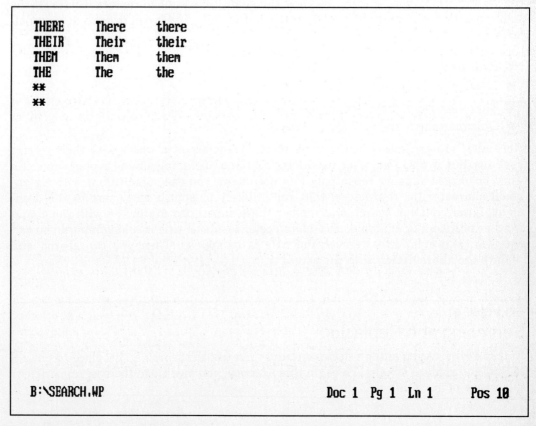

To search for strings

Press	**Home, Home,** ↑ to move the cursor to the beginning of the document.
Press	**F2** to search toward the end of the document, and the status line reads *—> Srch:*.
Type	**THE**.
Press	**F2** to begin the search and move the cursor to the first occurrence of the specified string.

Result. The first word containing a *THE* is highlighted. Press **F2** twice to repeat the command. Continue until no occurrence is found and the status line reads * *Not Found* *. Notice how the program only finds words that contain uppercase *THE*s in the first column. Move the cursor back to top of the document and repeat the commands, first specifying *The* and then *the* instead of *THE*. When you specify *The*, the program finds words that are all uppercase or begin with an uppercase letter. When you specify *the*, the program finds all words.

Step 3. Search for Strings in Both Directions. You can search from the cursor toward the top or bottom of the document. Here, search for the word *THEM* from the top and then the bottom of the document.

To search for strings toward the end of the document

Press	**Home, Home,** ↑ to move the cursor to the beginning of the document.
Press	**F2** to search toward the end of the document, and the status line reads *—> Srch: the*.
Type	**THEM**, and then press **F2**.

To search for strings toward the beginning of the document

Press	**Home, Home,** ↓ to move the cursor to the end of the document.
Press	**Shift-F2** to search toward the beginning of the document, and the status line reads *<— Srch: THEM*.
Press	**F2** to begin the search using the suggested string.

Result. Both commands highlight the same word but find it searching from opposite ends of the document.

Step 4. Search and Replace All Strings. When you want to replace all occurrences of a string, you tell the program to replace all occurrences without asking you to confirm each replacement.

To search and replace strings

Press	**Home, Home,** ↑ to move the cursor to the beginning of the document.
Press	**Alt-F2**, and the status line reads *w/Confirm? (Y/N) N*.
Press	**N** to automatically replace the string throughout the document, and the status line reads *—> Srch: THEM*.
Type	**the**, and then press **F2**. The status line reads *Replace with:*.
Type	**she**, and then press **F2** to begin the search and replace operation.

Result. Since you specified the search string in lowercase and answered no to *w/Confirm?*, all strings are replaced automatically. Obviously, you can create havoc with this combination of commands. Press **Home, Home,** ↑ to move the cursor to the beginning of the document and repeat the command, but specify *she* as the string to search for and *The* as the string to replace with. This partially restores the file, but the second and third characters in each word in the first column are no longer uppercased.

Step 5. Search and Replace Strings One at a Time. You can confirm replacements so that you do not make serious mistakes like those demonstrated here. Now, selectively replace *The* with *THE* to restore the words in the first column to all uppercase.

To search and replace strings

Press	**Home, Home,** ↑ to move the cursor to the beginning of the document.
Press	**Alt-F2**, and the status line reads *w/Confirm? (Y/N) N.*
Press	**Y** to confirm each replacement, and the status line reads —> *Srch: the.*
Type	**The**, and then press **F2**. The status line reads *Replace with:.*
Type	**THE**, and then press **F2** to begin the search and replace operation.

Result. Since you answered yes to *w/Confirm?*, when the first occurrence of the string is found, the cursor flashes under the string, and the status line reads *Confirm? (Y/N) N.* To replace the string, press **Y**; to leave it unchanged, press **N**. The cursor then immediately jumps to the next occurrence. Replace only the strings in the first column. After all occurrences of the string have been found, the prompt no longer appears. When you are finished, your document should look as it did originally (Figure 3-7).

Step 6. Search and Replace for Strings in a Selected Block. When you do not want to search and replace throughout the entire document, you can select just the part of the text you want to search and replace. Here you replace the pairs of asterisks with a book title.

To search and replace strings in a block

Press	**Home, Home,** ↑ to move the cursor to the beginning of the document.
Press	**F2** to search toward the end of the document, and the status line reads —> *Srch: The.*
Type	****, and then press **F2** to move the cursor to the right of the first pair of asterisks.
Press	← twice to move the cursor to under the first asterisk.
Press	**Alt-F4** to turn on block.
Press	**Return** twice to highlight the last two lines of the list.
Press	**Alt-F2**, and the status line reads *w/Confirm? (Y/N) N.*
Press	**N** to automatically replace throughout the document, and the status line reads —> *Srch: **.*
Press	**F2** to confirm the suggested search string, and the status line reads *Replace with:.*
Type	**WordPerfect Users Manual**, and then press **F2**.

Result. Both pairs of asterisks are immediately replaced with the title.

Step 7. Delete Strings. To delete strings, enter the string to be deleted when prompted for the string to search for, but leave the replacement prompt blank. Here, delete all occurrences of the string *their* regardless of case.

To delete strings

Press	**Home, Home,** ↑ to move the cursor to the beginning of the document.
Press	**Alt-F2**, and the status line reads *w/Confirm? (Y/N) N.*
Press	**N** to automatically replace throughout the document, and the status line reads —> *Srch: **.*
Type	**their**, and then press **F2**. The status line reads *Replace with:.*

Press   **F2** to begin the search and replace operation without specifying a replacement string.

Result. Since you specified the search string in lowercase, did not enter a replacement string, and answered no to *w/Confirm?,* all strings on the second line are deleted automatically.

Step 8. Save the Document. You should now save your document. Before proceeding, *be sure a formatted disk is in drive B.*

To save the document

Press   **F10**, and the status line reads *Document to be Saved:*.
Type   **B:\SEARCH.WP**, and then press **Return**.

Result. The disk drive spins as the document is saved onto the disk in drive B. When the drive stops and its red light goes out, you can continue to work on the document.

Step 9. Print the Document. Now that you have completed the document, make a printout to see how it looks. Be sure that the printer is on and has paper in it and that the paper is aligned.

To print the document

Press   **Shift-F7** to display the Print menu.
Press   1 for **Full Text**.

Result. The printer immediately begins printing.

Step 10. Continue or Quit. You have now completed this exercise. You may either continue on your own work or quit and return to the operating system.

To continue or quit

Press   **F7**, and the status line reads *Save Document? (Y/N) Y.*
Press   **N**, and the status line reads *Exit WP? (Y/N) N.*
Press   **Y** to quit the program, or press **N** to clear the screen and work on your own document.

Result. If you did not quit the program, the screen is blank. If you did quit the program, the operating system B> prompt is displayed on the screen. Remove your program and data disks and then turn off the computer or load another program.

EXERCISE 41
Using Wildcards

When searching for strings or searching and replacing them, you can use wildcards. To match any character, press **Ctrl-V**, and then press **Ctrl-X** at the appropriate spot in the search string, and the ^X wildcard is displayed on the screen. Do not use this wildcard as the first character or when searching for format codes.

To experiment with this command, enter the following strings, and then search for them using the specified strings that include one or more wildcards.

List 1
Enter: tee toe the tie
Search for: t^Xe

List 2
Enter: hat hut hit hot
Search for: h^Xt

List 3
Enter: take tape time tree tune tale tide true type
Search for: t^X^Xe

EXERCISE 42

Searching for Formatting Codes

When editing a document, you frequently want to find formatting codes so that you can delete or change them. With WordPerfect, you can specify the codes listed in Table 3-9 in the search and replace strings.

To experiment with this command, enter the following document, and then search and replace the suggested codes. (Press **Return** or **Spacebar** where indicated when the prompt reads *Srch* and *Replace with*.) When you are finished, the returns are replaced with spaces.

Enter: List-1 **Return** List-2 **Return** List-3 **Return**
Srch: press **Return**
Replace with: press **Spacebar**
Now, search and replace the spaces with carriage returns to return the list to its original form.

Srch: press **Spacebar**
Replace with: press **Return**

TIPS

■ **When you want to search for text entered in headers, footers, footnotes, or endnotes,** press **Home, F2** (to search forward); **Home, Shift-F2** (to search backward); or **Home, Alt-F2** (to replace). These extended search commands display these entries on the screen if the string being searched for is found in them. If this happens when searching, repeat the extended search command to continue, or press **F7** to exit and return to the document screen.

TABLE 3-9
Codes You Can Specify in the Search and Replace String

Code	Press
Advance up and advance down	**Shift-F1**
Math operators	***, -, +, /**
Center page	**Shift-F6**
Merge codes	**Alt-F9**
Merge ^E	**Shift-F9**
Columns on/off	**Alt-F7**
Overstrike	**Shift-F1**
Hyphenation cancel	**Shift-F8**
Hard space	**Home-Spacebar**
Hyphen	**Home-Hyphen**
Soft hyphen	**Ctrl-Hyphen**
Justification on/off	**Ctrl-F8**
Subscript/superscript	**Shift-F1**
Math on/off	**Alt-F7**
Widow/orphan	**Alt-F8**

- **You can search for soft and hard carriage returns and soft and hard page breaks.** When the status line reads —> *Srch:*, press **Ctrl-V** to make the character visible, and then press **Ctrl-M** to find a soft carriage return, **Ctrl-J** to find a hard carriage return, **Ctrl-K** to find a soft page break, or **Ctrl-L** to find a hard page break.

- **To search or replace format codes that come in pairs**, when prompted to enter the string to be searched for or replaced, press the format key, type the string, and then press the format key again. For example, to replace a boldfaced **the** with an underlined <u>the</u>, when prompted to enter the search string, press **F6**, type **the**, and then press **F6** again. When prompted to enter the replace string, press **F8**, type **the**, and then press **F8** again.

QUESTIONS

1. What is the difference between the search command and the search and replace command?
2. List and describe three options available when you want to search or search and replace?
3. How are wildcards helpful when using search or search and replace?
4. What is a string?
5. If you entered *The* as a string to be searched for, would the program find *THE*? Would it find *the*?

TOPIC 3-6
Using the Spell Checker and Thesaurus

In this topic, we introduce you to the following procedures:

- Checking spelling
- Adding words to a dictionary
- Looking up synonyms in a thesaurus
- Counting words

BACKGROUND

Spelling checkers and thesauruses are invaluable aids when you are editing important documents.

SPELLING CHECKERS

Spelling checkers check all words in a file against a main dictionary and any supplemental dictionaries that you specify. For example, WordPerfect's spelling checker compares words in your document to a list of words stored in the file LEX.WP. This file contains two lists, a main word list and a common word list. When you run a spelling check, the program looks in the common word list first. If it cannot find the word there, it looks in the main word list. This quickens the spell checking of words.

Any words not found in the dictionaries are either flagged with special characters or highlighted. You can then decide whether to change them, leave them as is, or in some cases, add them to the dictionary. Good spelling checkers do not simply flag questionable words; they also list spelling suggestions that you can accept or reject.

When Misspelled Words Are Found

Misspellings are generally found either when you type them or when you run the spelling checker program.

A spelling checker that finds misspellings as you type monitors each word and immediately flags any word it does not find in its dictionary.

Most spelling checkers, like WordPerfect's, find misspellings only when you load the spelling checker program and execute a command. Some of these programs stop at each word they do not find in their dictionaries and offer you options.

How Misspelled Words Are Found

Spelling checkers compare your text to either a root word dictionary or a literal dictionary.

- A **root word dictionary** contains only word roots; it does not include prefixes and suffixes.
- A **literal dictionary** contains exact spellings of complete words. They are much longer than root word dictionaries because they contain a variety of entries for each root word.

How would these two types of dictionaries deal with the word *preplan*? If you spelled it incorrectly as *preplane*, the root word dictionary would assume it was spelled correctly because the word's root, *plane*, is spelled correctly. But the literal dictionary would flag it because the word *preplane* would not be found in the dictionary.

What Misspelled Words Are Not Found

Spelling checkers are nice, but you cannot rely on them entirely. They check only spelling, not usage. For example, spelling checkers would find no problems in the sentence *Eye wood like two except you invitation, butt can not. Unfortunately, their are another things i half too due.*

It may be an exceptionally fine example of bad grammar, but each word is spelled correctly. Because of this limitation, you must carefully proofread your documents for content and context. This cannot be stressed enough.

Spell Checking Options

When a word is flagged because the spelling checker program cannot find it in its dictionary, the program offers you options. Table 3-10 describes the options offered by WordPerfect.

TABLE 3-10
Check Menu Choices

1 Skip Once skips the word, and spell checking continues. If the same word is found again, it is highlighted.

2 Skip skips the word, and spell checking continues. If the same word is found again, it is not highlighted.

3 Add Word saves the word in the supplemental dictionary {WP}LEX.SUP.

3 Delete 2nd appears when the same word is repeated in sequence, for example, *the the*.

3 Ignore words containing numbers appears when any word contains a number, for example, *F3* or *3D*. If you choose this option, all subsequent words containing numbers are ignored.

4 Change Dictionary is used to specify a different main or supplemental dictionary. The prompt reads *Enter new main dictionary name: LEX.WP*. Type a new dictionary (the default is LEX.WP), or press **Return** to accept the default. The prompt reads *Enter new supplementary dictionary name: {WP}LEX.SUP*. Type a new supplemental dictionary (the default is {WP}LEX.SUP), or press **Return** to accept the default and return to the Check menu.

4 Edit moves the cursor to the word so that you can correct it. When you are finished, press **Return**. If your correction does not match a word in the dictionary, the word remains highlighted.

5 Look Up displays the prompt *Word Pattern:*. Type the word you want to confirm the spelling of. You can use wildcards to display a list of words that match a specified pattern. The question mark (?) substitutes for a single letter, and the asterisk (*) substitutes for zero or more characters in sequence. For example, if you want to find how to spell *category,* you can enter **cat*** to display all words beginning with those three letters or **cat?gory** if you are unsure of only a single character.

5 Disable double word checking appears on the menu when the same word is repeated in sequence.

6 Phonetic displays a list of words that sound like the highlighted word.

THESAURUS

When using a thesaurus, you can highlight a word and request a list of synonyms. For example, when the word *wicked* is highlighted, the thesaurus may display such synonyms as *sinful, malevolent, nefarious, wayward, dissolute, vile,* and *vicious.* You can then select one of the suggested words to replace the highlighted word, look up another word, or quit the thesaurus and return to the document screen.

The WordPerfect thesaurus contains 10,000 headwords (words that can be looked up) and many references (a word or phrase found under a headword, including synonyms and antonyms). To use the thesaurus, your computer must have at least 256KB of memory.

When you position the cursor in a word and execute the thesaurus command, the thesaurus screen and menu are displayed if the word you highlight is in the thesaurus. The word you looked up (the headword) is displayed on the screen border. Often, nouns (n), verbs (v), adjectives (a), and antonyms (ant) are listed under separate categories. The words displayed for each form of the headword are called references and are preceded by letters. Those references preceded by bullets are also headwords, so you can press the letter in front of them to look up additional words. References with the same connotation are grouped together into numbered sub-groups.

You use the menu to operate the thesaurus. Table 3-11 describes the Thesaurus menu choices. You can also use the cursor movement keys described in Table 3-12 to move the numbers and lists displayed on the thesaurus screen.

TABLE 3-11
Thesaurus Menu Choices

1 Replace Word replaces the word in the document with one of the words displayed on the list.
   1. Press → or ← to move the menu selection letters (*A, B, C* and so on) to the column containing your choice if necessary. (Table 3-12 describes other keys you can use to move the cursor through a long list.)
   2. Press **1**, and the status line reads *Press letter for word*.
   3. Type the letter of the replacement, and the document screen reappears.

2 View Doc returns the cursor to the document so that you can scroll through the document to see the word in context before choosing a replacement. Press **F7** to return to the thesaurus.

3 Look Up Word displays the prompt *Word:* so that you can enter a word to be looked up.

4 Clear Column clears subgroups from the thesaurus screen. (You can also press **Backspace** or **Del** to do the same.)

TABLE 3-12
Thesaurus Screen Cursor Movement Keys

Code	Press
Move menu selection letters between columns	→ or ←
View subgroups too long to fit on screen	↑ or ↓
Move column up or down	**PgUp** or **PgDn**
	Gray+ or **Gray-**
Move to first subgroup	**Home**, Home, ↑
Move to last subgroup	**Home, Home,** ↓
Move to specific subgroup	**Ctrl-Home**

EXERCISE 43

Checking Spelling

In this exercise, you use WordPerfect's spell checker. To begin this exercise, you must load the program or clear the screen of any other document.
Note. The full-featured version of WordPerfect has the spelling checker (and thesaurus) on separate disks. They are not loaded along with the program. When you execute the commands for either, the program is loaded into the computer's memory. If you are working on a floppy disk system, you should do two things before using these commands.

   1. Remove the data disk from drive B, and then insert the Speller or Thesaurus disk.

   2. Change the default drive to B. To do so, press **F5**, press the equal sign (**=**), type **B:**, and then press **Return**. Press **F7** to return to the document screen.

After completing the procedure, remove the Speller or Thesaurus disk from drive B, and reinsert your data disk.

Step 1. Enter a Document. Enter the document shown in Figure 3-8. Be sure to misspell the words that are highlighted. (Do not highlight them in your own document.)

FIGURE 3-8
Spell check document

We hold theese truths to be self-evedent, that all men are are
created equal, they are endoud by their Creator with certain
unalienable Rights, that among these are Life, Liberty, and the
prusuit of Happiness. That to secure these rights, Goverments are
instituted among Men, deriving their just powers from the consent
of the governed.

B:\SPELL.WP   Doc 1 Pg 1 Ln 1   Pos 10

Step 2. Spell Check the Document. Now, spell check the words in the document.

To spell check a document

Press   **Home, Home,** and ↑ to move the cursor to the beginning of the
             document.
Press   **Ctrl-F2** to display the Check menu.
Press   **3** for **Document.**

Result. The status line reads * *Please Wait* * while the spelling checker program is
loaded into memory. If a word on the screen, like *theese,* is not found in the program's
dictionary, the prompt reads *Not Found!,* the word is displayed in reverse video, and
a menu of choices and a list of words appears (Figure 3-9).

To replace the word in the document with one of the words in the displayed list,
type the letter that precedes the replacement. After you correct a word, the next
misspelled word is displayed. When two identical words appear next to each other,
such as *then then,* press **3** for **Delete 2nd.** Correct each word until the status line
reads *Word Count: 56 Press any key to continue.* Press any key to return to editing
the document. Notice that the case of a corrected word remains unchanged. If it
began with an uppercase letter, it is replaced with an uppercase letter.

Step 3. Print the Document. Be sure that the printer is on and has paper in it and that
the paper is aligned.

Note. If you are using the full-featured version on a floppy disk drive system,
remove the Speller disk from drive B, insert the data disk, and then close the drive's
door.

To print the document

Press   **Shift-F7** to display the Print menu.
Press   **1** for **Full Text.**

FIGURE 3-9
Spell check screen

```
We hold theese truths to be self-evedent, that all men are are
created equal, they are endoud by their Creator with certain
unalienable Rights, that among these are Life, Liberty, and the
prusuit of Happiness. That to secure these rights, Governents are
instituted among Men, deriving their just powers from the consent
of the governed.


============================================================================

A. these




Not Found!  Select Word or Menu Option (0=Continue): 0
1 Skip Once; 2 Skip; 3 Add Word; 4 Edit; 5 Look Up; 6 Phonetic
```

Result. The printer immediately begins printing the corrected document.

Step 4. Save and Continue or Quit. You have now completed this exercise. Save the document and clear the screen so that you can continue working, or quit WordPerfect and return to the operating system.

To save the document and clear the screen or quit

Press	**F7**, and the status line reads *Save Document? (Y/N) Y*.
Press	**Y**, and the status line reads *Document to be Saved:*.
Type	**B:\SPELL.WP**, and then press **Return**. The status line reads *Exit WP? (Y/N) N*.
Press	**N** to clear the screen or **Y** to quit the program.

Result. If you cleared the screen, it is blank just as it was when you began this exercise. If you quit the program, the operating system B prompt is displayed on the screen. Remove your program and data disks, and then turn off the computer or load another program.

EXERCISE 44

Looking Up Synonyms

WordPerfect also has a thesaurus program that you can use to look up synonyms and antonyms. Enter the sentence *Fools rush in where angels fear to tread*, and then, using the thesaurus program, look up each of the words.

    Note. If you are using the full-featured version of WordPerfect, before you execute the thesaurus command on a floppy disk system, insert the Thesaurus disk into drive B, and then close the drive's door. Drive B should also be the default drive.

To look up words in the thesaurus

1. Move the cursor to any position in the word to be looked up.
2. Press **Alt-F1** to display the Thesaurus menu and a list of words (Figure 3-10).
3. Press the letters in front of the headwords (the words preceded by bullets) to display additional synonyms or antonyms. (Press **4** for **Clear Column** twice to remove the additional columns.)

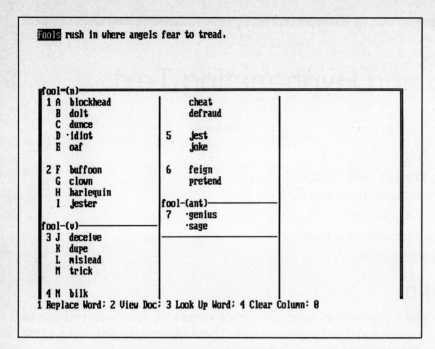

FIGURE 3-10
Thesaurus screen

```
Fools rush in where angels fear to tread.

fool-(n)
 1 A  blockhead          cheat
   B  dolt               defraud
   C  dunce
   D ·idiot         5    jest
   E  oaf                joke

 2 F  buffoon       6    feign
   G  clown              pretend
   H  harlequin
   I  jester       fool-(ant)
                    7    ·genius
fool-(v)                 ·sage
 3 J  deceive
   K  dupe
   L  mislead
   M  trick

 4 N  bilk
1 Replace Word; 2 View Doc; 3 Look Up Word; 4 Clear Column: 0
```

4. Press 1 for **Replace Word,** and the status line reads *Press letter for word.*
5. Press the letter preceding a word to replace the word in the document.

EXERCISE 45

Counting Words

When you spell check a document, WordPerfect displays the number of words in the document. There is also a separate command that does the same thing; it counts the words in a document or in a selected block of text. This command is useful when preparing documents with strict length limitations. Typical applications are when typing assigned reports and other school-related projects or when processing articles for magazines and newspapers.

To count words

1. Press **Ctrl-F2** to display the Check menu.
2. Press **6** for **Count** to count all the words in the document.
3. Press **any key**, then press **F7** to return to editing.

QUESTIONS

1. What is the purpose of a spelling checker?
2. What is a thesaurus used for?
3. If you use words that are not found in the program's dictionary, which Check menu choice do you use to add them to the dictionary so that they are not highlighted in subsequent spelling checks?
4. If the spelling checker program flags a misspelled word, how do you correct it?
5. What is a headword? A reference word?
6. What kinds of words will a spell checker not catch? Give two examples.

TOPIC 3-7
Aligning and Hyphenating Text

In this topic, we introduce you to the following procedures:

- Justifying and unjustifying text
- Aligning text with the right margin
- Centering text between the margins
- Centering text on a column
- Centering text vertically on a page
- Hyphenating a document

BACKGROUND

Among the most useful features of word processing programs are those you use to align text with the margins and to hyphenate text. These commands give you a great deal of control over the way your printed document looks.

ALIGNING TEXT

Unlike a typewriter, a word processing program allows you to experiment with alignments. If you do not like the result you get with one alignment, you can change it without having to reenter the text. How you align text varies from program to program.

- On some programs, you select the text to be aligned, and then execute an alignment command.
- On other programs, you enter codes or format lines wherever you want to change the alignment.

WordPerfect uses both approaches. WordPerfect's default alignment is for justified text, but you can turn this off and on anywhere in the document, align text with the right margin, or center text.

- **Justified text** is aligned flush with both the left and right margins. To justify text so that it aligns with both margins, the program inserts spaces of varying width between words to expand the lines. The result is that, in some situations, large white spaces are occasionally inserted between words to justify lines.

  A few programs can insert spaces as small as 1/120 of an inch between words and letters to expand the line. This is called **microjustification**, and when supported by the program and printer, gives a finished appearance to printed text. If your program and printer do not support microjustification, you may decide, after comparing printouts of justified text with unjustified text, that unjustified text looks better and is easier to read.

- When you turn justification off, the text is automatically left-aligned with a ragged-right margin.

- You can align lines or paragraphs flush with the right margin, as when entering dates or addresses. If you right-align a paragraph longer than a single line, it will have a ragged-left margin.

- You can center text between the margins or on a column. Centering text on a specific column is useful when preparing tabular material.

■ You can also center text vertically on the page between the top and bottom margins, for example, to center the text on a title page. The effects of vertical alignment are usually seen only when you print the document.

After you change the alignment of text, you may change your mind. You can easily return the text to its original default alignment. To do this, you delete the codes you entered when you changed the alignment.

HYPHENATION

Hyphenation can improve the appearance of justified text. If when you enter text, a word does not fit on a line, the entire word wraps to the next line. If your text is justified, you may have large gaps between words. If your text is unjustified, you may have a very ragged-right margin. For a neater appearance, hyphenate the document just before you print it out. Hyphenation inserts soft hyphens that disappear and do not print out if you revise the text, and they no longer fall at the end of lines.

When a program hyphenates a document, it uses a **hyphenation zone**, a setting that determines the length of words that are candidates for hyphenation. Some programs, including WordPerfect, let you revise the default hyphenation zone, an area on either side of the right margin. The finer the setting, the shorter the words that are hyphenated and the greater the number of words that are hyphenated. A finer setting reduces the spaces between words when justification is on and the raggedness of the right margin when it is off (WordPerfect's default setting is seven characters on the left side of the right margin and zero on the right side.) When setting the hyphenation zone, keep the following points in mind:

■ Words that are candidates for hyphenation begin before or at the left edge of the hyphenation zone and extend past the right edge of the zone.

■ Words that begin after the left edge of the zone and extend past the right margin are automatically wrapped to the next line.

■ Some lines may print past the right margin if the right hyphenation-zone setting is greater than zero.

EXERCISE 46

Aligning Text with Margins

In this exercise, you align text with the left and right margin and center it between the margins. To begin this exercise, you must load the program or clear the screen of any other document.

Step 1. Enter the Document. Enter the document shown in Figure 3-11. Remember to press **Return** once at the end of lines that do not reach the right margin (like the headings) and twice at the end of paragraphs to insert a blank line. The line of equal signs (=) across the screen indicates a hard page break. Type the text above the hard page break, press **Ctrl-Return** to enter the hard page break, and then type the four lines of text below it.

Step 2. Turn Justification Off. Since the default setting is for justified text, you need not turn on justification for the first paragraph, but you must turn off justification for the second paragraph.

To turn justification off

Move	the cursor to under the *U* in the heading *Unjustified Text*.
Press	**Ctrl-F8** to display the Print Format menu.
Press	**3** for **Turn off** to turn off justification.

FIGURE 3-11
Aligning document

```
Justified Text (the default)
Justified text is aligned flush with both the left and right
margins of the printed page. To justify text so it is even with
both margins, the program inserts spaces between the words.
Justified text does not appear justified on the screen, only on
the printout.

Unjustified Text
Unjustified text is flush with the left margin but has a ragged-
right margin. For example, text that you enter on a typewriter is
unjustified.

Centered Text
Centered text is centered between the margins.

Right-aligned Text
Right-aligned text is flush with the right margin.

==============================================================================
Vertically Centered Text
is
centered between the
top and bottom margins.

B:\ALIGN.WP                                 Doc 1  Pg 2  Ln 5     Pos 10
```

Press   **0** to return to the document screen.

Result. No change is obvious on the screen because justified text is not shown as such on the screen.

Step 3. Center Text Horizontally. Now, center a line of text between the margins.

To center new text between the margins

Move   the cursor to under the *C* in *Centered* in the sentence below the heading *Centered Text.*
Press   ***Shift-F6*** to center the text.
Press   ↓ to align the line.

Result. The line is now centered between the margins.

Step 4. Right Align Text. Now, align a line of text with the right margin.

To right-align single lines of text

Move   the cursor to under the *R* in *Right* in the sentence below the heading *Right-aligned Text.*
Press   ***Alt-F6*** to right-align the text.
Press   ↓ to align the line.

Result. The line aligns with the right margin.

Step 5. Center a Block of Text Vertically. Now center text between the top and bottom margins. Since the block is simulating a title page, you also center it horizontally by selecting the entire block before executing the center command.

To center text vertically on the page

Press   **Ctrl-Home**, and the prompt reads *Go To*.

Type   **2**, and then press **Return** to move the cursor to the top of the second page.

Press   **Alt-F8** to display the Page Format menu.

Press   **3** for **Center Page Top to Bottom** to vertically center the text.

Press   **0** to return to the document screen.

To center a block of existing text

Move   the cursor to under the *V* in *Vertically*.

Press   **Alt-F4** to turn on block, and the status line flashes *Block on*.

Press   **Return** four times to highlight the entire block.

Press   **Shift-F6**, and the status line reads *[Center]? (Y/N) N*.

Press   **Y** for **Yes**.

Result. The block is centered horizontally and vertically, but vertical centering will be seen only when you print the document.

Step 6. Save the Document. You should now save your document. Before proceeding, *be sure a formatted disk is in drive B*.

To save the document in a disk file

Press   **F10**, and the status line reads *Document to be Saved:*.

Type   **B:\ALIGN.WP**, and then press **Return**.

Result. The disk drive spins as the document is saved onto the disk in drive B. When the drive stops and its red light goes out, you can continue to work on the document.

Step 7. Print the Document. Now that you have completed the document, make a printout to see how it looks. Be sure that the printer is on and has paper in it and that the paper is aligned.

To print the document

Press   **Shift-F7** to display the Print menu.

Press   **1** for **Full Text**.

Result. The printer immediately begins printing. The first paragraph is justified. The second paragraph has a ragged-right margin. The third is centered, and the forth is aligned with the right margin. On the second page, the text is centered both vertically and horizontally.

Step 8. Continue or Quit. You have now completed this exercise. Either continue on your own work, or quit and return to the operating system.

To continue or quit

Press   **F7**, and the status line reads *Save Document? (Y/N) Y*.

Press   **N**, and the status line reads *Exit WP? (Y/N) N*.

Press   **Y** to quit the program, or press **N** to clear the screen and work on your own document.

Result. If you did not quit the program, the screen is blank. If you did quit the program, the operating system B> prompt is displayed on the screen. Remove your program and data disks, and then turn off the computer or load another program.

Hyphenating Text

You can turn hyphenation on and off at any point in the document if you want some text hyphenated and some not. You can select aided or auto hyphenation.

- Aided hyphenation displays each candidate for hyphenation so that you can accept the suggested hyphen location, move it, or choose not to hyphenate the word.

- Auto hyphenation automatically hyphenates all words according to rules built into the program. It displays only those words that do not fit its rules.

Enter a few new paragraphs of text, or use the text you entered in Exercise 46, and then use WordPerfect's hyphenation commands to hyphenate it.

To turn hyphenation on and hyphenate the document

1. Move the cursor to the top of the document or the beginning of the text to be hyphenated.

2. Press **Shift-F8** to display the Line Format menu.

3. Press **5** for **Hyphenation**.

4. Press **3** for **Set H-Zone**, and the prompt reads *to Left =*.

5. Type **3**, and then press **Return**, and the prompt reads *Right =*.

6. Type **0**, and then press **Return**.

7. Either press **4** for **Aided** to confirm hyphenation choices.

    Or   press **5** for **Auto** to automatically hyphenate the document.

8. Press **1** for **On** to turn on hyphenation.

9. Press **0** to return to the document screen.

10. Press the cursor movement keys to scroll down through the document. If you specified aided hyphenation and the program finds a word that might be hyphenated (or if you selected auto hyphenation and the program cannot find a word in the hyphenation dictionary), the status line reads *Position hyphen press Esc* followed by the word. A flashing cursor indicates the suggested hyphen position. Either press **Esc** to hyphenate where suggested; press ← or → to reposition the hyphen, and then press **Esc**; or press **F1** to wrap the entire word to the next line.

Centering Text in Columns and Aligning Blocks of Existing Text

You can center text on columns instead of between the margins. You can also select blocks of text and right-align them. When centering text on columns, move the cursor in several columns from the left margin, and keep the text short; otherwise, it might disappear off the left edge of the screen.

To center new text on tab stop

1. Move the cursor to the column you want the text centered on.

2. Press **Shift-F6**.

3. Type the text, and then press **Return** to end underlining and return the cursor to the left margin.

To right-align a block of existing text

1. Select a block of text that ends with a hard carriage return.
2. Press **Alt-F6**, and the status line reads *[Aln/FlshR]? (Y/N) N*.
3. Press **Y** to align the block of text flush right.

TIP

- Text is justified only if the line or paragraph ends with a hard carriage return. Therefore, always press **Return** after entering the last line or paragraph in a document, or it will not be justified.

QUESTIONS

1. What is the major characteristic of hyphenated text?
2. What kinds of hyphens are inserted when you hyphenate a document? What happens to them when they fall at the end of a line? When they do not?
3. What is a hyphenation zone?
4. What are the four main types of alignment?
5. What is the difference between aided hyphenation and auto hyphenation?

TOPIC 3-8
Emphasizing Text

In this topic, we introduce you to the following procedures:

- Boldfacing text
- Underlining text
- Editing and deleting format codes
- Striking out text

BACKGROUND

Word processing programs offer several ways of emphasizing text. For example, you can boldface or underline headings, key words, disclaimers, and book titles. You can emphasize individual characters, words, lines, paragraphs, or entire documents. You can also combine formats; for example, you can both boldface and underline a heading.

How you assign these formats varies. On some programs, you select the text and then choose the format from a menu. On others, like WordPerfect, you enter codes at the beginning and end of the text to be boldfaced or underlined. If you are using the latest dot-matrix printers (including laser printers), you achieve the same result by changing fonts.

BOLDFACE

Boldfaced text is darker than regular text. Impact printers produce boldfaced characters by striking the character two or three times. Laser printers must have access to a separate boldfaced font since they cannot strike the same characters to create a darker image.

UNDERLINE

There are a two basic underline styles, continuous and noncontinuous, and some programs offer you a choice. Continuous style underlines words and the spaces between the words. To obtain continuous underlining in WordPerfect, you must enter hard spaces between the words (see Topic 3-2). Noncontinuous style underlines words but not the spaces between the words.

Some programs, including WordPerfect, also offer both single and double underline options. These are useful when you are creating financial statements and other documents with subtotals and totals. Although some programs offer these options, they also must be supported by the printer type element or font.

STRIKEOUT

Strikeout can indicate where deletions have been made when one person edits the text and another reviews the changes. Most programs use the hyphen (-) or slash (/) to strike out text, but WordPerfect and some others let you choose the character. On some programs, including WordPerfect, struckout text can be automatically deleted after review.

COMBINATIONS

You can use boldfacing and underlining in combination. For example, to both boldface and underline a phrase, you individually enter the command for each format.

EXERCISE 49

Using Boldfacing and Underlining

In this exercise, you boldface and underline text. To begin this exercise, you must load the program or clear the screen of any other document.

Step 1. Enter the Document. Enter the sentence in the instruction below.

To enter the document

Type	**You can boldface and underline text as you enter it or after you enter it.**
Press	**Return.**

Step 2. Boldface Text. First, boldface text that has already been entered, and then boldface text as you enter it.

To boldface existing text

Move	the cursor to under the *b* in *boldface*.
Press	**Alt-F4** to turn on block, and the status line flashes *Block on*.
Press	**Spacebar** to highlight the word.
Press	**F6** to boldface the word.

To boldface new text

Press	**Home, Home,** ↓ to move the cursor to the end of the document.
Press	**Return** to insert a blank line.
Type	**This word was,** and then press **Spacebar.**
Press	**F6** to begin boldfacing.
Type	**boldfaced.**
Press	**F6** to end boldfacing.
Press	**Spacebar.**
Type	**as it was being entered.** Then press **Return.**

Result. The word you boldfaced in the existing sentence and the word you boldfaced in the new sentence should both stand out from the rest of the text and be similarly highlighted. If they do not stand out, adjust your screen's brightness and contrast. If they are not similarly highlighted, press **Alt-F3** to see the codes on either side of the words. Press any key to return to the document screen.

Step 3. Underline Text. Now, underline text that has already been entered, and then underline text as you enter it.

To underline existing text

Move	the cursor to under the *u* in *underline.*
Press	**Alt-F4** to turn on block, and the status line flashes *Block on.*
Press	**Spacebar** to highlight the word.
Press	← to position the cursor under the letter e.
Press	**F8** to underline the word.

To underline new text

Press	**Home, Home,** ↓ to move the cursor to the end of the document.
Press	**Return** to insert a blank line.
Type	**This word was,** and then press **Spacebar.**
Press	**F8** to begin underlining.
Type	**underlined.**
Press	**F8** to end underlining.
Press	**Spacebar.**
Type	**as it was being entered.** Then press **Return.**

Result. The word you underlined in the existing sentence and the word you underlined in the new sentence should both stand out from the rest of the text and be similarly highlighted. If they do not stand out, adjust your screen's brightness and contrast. If they are not similarly highlighted, press **Alt-F3** to see the codes on either side of the words. Press any key to return to the document screen.

Step 4. Boldface and Underline Text. Here, both boldface and underline text that has already been entered, and then both boldface and underline text as you enter it.

To boldface and underline existing text

Move	the cursor to under the *t* in *text.*
Press	**Alt-F4** to turn on block.
Press	t four times to highlight the words up to the *t* in the first *it.*
Press	**F6** to boldface the text.
Press	**Alt-F4** to turn on block.
Press	**Ctrl-Home** twice to highlight the same block again.
Press	**F8** to underline the text.

To boldface and underline new text

Press	**Home, Home,** ↓ to move the cursor to the end of the document.
Press	**Return** to insert a blank line.
Type	**These words were,** and then press **Spacebar.**
Press	**F6** to begin boldfacing.
Press	**F8** to begin underlining.
Type	**boldfaced and underlined.**
Press	**F6** to end boldfacing.
Press	**F8** to end underlining.
Press	**Spacebar.**
Type	**as they were being entered.** Then press **Return.**

Result. The words you boldfaced and underlined in the existing sentence and the words you boldfaced and underlined in the new sentence should stand out from the rest of the text and be similarly highlighted. If they do not stand out, adjust your screen's brightness and contrast. If they are not similarly highlighted, press **Alt-F3** to see the codes on either side of the words. Press any key to return to the document screen.

Step 5. Change the Type of Underlining. You can select from several underlining styles. The default is noncontinuous single, which means the spaces between words are not underlined. Change the type of underlining above the last sentence so that it is printed with continuous single underlining.

To change the kind of underline

Move	the cursor to the blank line above the last sentence.
Press	**Ctrl-F8** to display the Print Format menu.
Press	**7** for **Continuous Single.**
Press	**0** to return to the document screen.

Result. No change is obvious on the screen, but you will see it when you print the document. (The educational version may not support this option on your printer.)

Step 6. Save the Document. You should now save your document. Before proceeding, *be sure a formatted disk is in drive B.*

To save the document in a disk file

Press	**F10,** and the status line reads *Document to be Saved:.*
Type	**B:\EMPHASIS.WP,** and then press **Return.**

Result. The disk drive spins as the document is saved onto the disk in drive B. When the drive stops and its red light goes out, you can continue to work on the document.

Step 7. Print the Document. Now that you have completed the document, make a printout to see how it looks. Be sure that the printer is on and has paper in it and that the paper is aligned.

To print the document

Press	**Shift-F7** to display the Print menu.
Press	**1** for **Full Text.**

Result. The printer immediately begins printing. The words you boldfaced should be darker than the rest of the text, and the words you underlined should have a line under them. The last sentence may or may not be continuously underlined depending on whether your printer supports this option.

Step 8. Continue or Quit. You have now completed this exercise. Either continue on your own work, or quit and return to the operating system.

To continue or quit

Press   **F7**, and the status line reads *Save Document? (Y/N) Y.*
Press   **N**, and the status line reads *Exit WP? (Y/N) N.*
Press   **Y** to quit the program, or press **N** to clear the screen and work on your own document.

Result. If you did not quit the program, the screen is blank. If you did quit the program, the operating system B> prompt is displayed on the screen. Remove your program and data disks, and then turn off the computer or load another program.

EXERCISE 50

Editing and Deleting Formatting Codes

To change formats you entered with codes, you delete the codes. This returns the text to the default format. For example, if you have indented, boldfaced, superscripted, or centered text, or if you have changed margins, tab stops, or page numbers, you can restore them to their default settings by deleting the codes you entered. If you delete codes inserted in pairs, you usually have to delete only one of the codes, and the other is automatically deleted. The easiest way to delete codes is to use the reveal codes command (**Alt-F3**) so that you can see them on the screen.

- If you try to delete a code on the normal screen with **Backspace** or **Del**, the status line reads, for example, *Delete [Bold]? (Y/N) N?*. If you press **N**, continue to press **Backspace** or **Del**, or press any key other than Y, the code is not deleted.
- If you select a block of text that contains codes and then delete the block, the codes within the block are also deleted (see Topic 3-4).
- If you have to find or delete several codes, you can use the search and replace commands (see Topic 3-5). Table 3-4 lists and describes all codes.

Using the document you created in Exercise 49, delete the codes you entered to boldface and underline words.

To delete format codes

1. Press **Alt-F3** to display the reveal codes screen. The lower half of the screen shows the text with codes, whereas the upper half shows the same text without codes.
2. Move the cursor with the cursor movement keys to the left or right of the code.
3. Either press **Del** to delete the code to the right of the cursor.
   Or   press **Backspace** to delete the code to the left of the cursor.
4. Press any other key to return to the document screen.

EXERCISE 51

Using Redlining and Strikeout

Redlining and strikeout are related features. If you want to highlight a section of a document to draw another person's attention to it, you can use WordPerfect's redline command. This inserts a vertical line (|) in the left margin of the redlined section. You see the redlining only when you print your document. But when you are editing and the cursor is under a redlined character, a plus sign (+) appears at the far right of the status line.

You can also strike out existing text. Again, you do not see the results until you make a printout, but when the cursor is under a character you are striking out, a hyphen (-) appears at the far right of the status line. After editing, you can use a command that automatically removes all redlining and deletes any text that has been struckout.

Step 1. Enter the Document. Enter the following two sentences:
This sentence is redlined.
This sentence has been struck out.

Step 2. Redline Text. Now, select the first sentence and redline it.

To redline text

Press   **Alt-F4** to turn on block, and then select the first sentence.
Press   **Alt-F5** to display the Mark Text menu.
Press   **3** for **Redline** to redline the selected block.

Result. When you move the cursor under any character in the first sentence a plus (+) sign is displayed following the *Pos* indicator column number.

Step 3. Strikeout Text. Now, strikeout the second sentence.

To strike out text

Press   **Alt-F4** to turn on block, and then select the second sentence.
Press   **Alt-F5** to display the Mark Text menu.
Press   **4** for **Strikeout** to strike out the selected block.

Result. When you move the cursor under any character in the second sentence a minus (-) sign is displayed following the *Pos* indicator column number.

Step 4. Print the Document. Print the document to see how your printer indicates redlined and struckout text.

To print the document

Press   **Shift-F7**.
Press   **1** for **Full Text**.

Result. The first sentence should be printed with a line in the left margin to indicate it has been redlined. The second sentence should have slashes printed through each word.

Step 5. Remove Redlining and Delete Struckout Text. This command is used after you have confirmed that redlined text should be retained and struckout text deleted from the final copy.

To remove all redlining and delete text that has been struckout

Press   **Alt-F5** to display the Mark Text menu.
Press   **6** for **Other Options**.
Press   **6** for **Remove all Redline Markings and all Strikeout text from document**, and the status line reads *Delete Redline markings and Strikeout text? (Y/N) N*.
Press   **Y** to remove redline markings and delete strikeout text.

Step 8. Continue or Quit. You have now completed this exercise. Either continue on your own work, or quit and return to the operating system.

To continue or quit

Press   **F7**, and the status line reads *Save Document? (Y/N) Y.*
Press   **N**, and the status line reads *Exit WP? (Y/N) N.*
Press   **Y** to quit the program, or press **N** to clear the screen and work on your own document.

Result. If you did not quit the program, the screen is blank. If you did quit the program, the operating system B> prompt is displayed on the screen. Remove your program and data disks, and then turn off the computer or load another program.

TIPS

■ **To see what format has been assigned**, move the cursor under any character. The number following the *Pos* indicator on the status line indicates the text's character attributes. The number is displayed the same way the text is. For example, if underlined text appears underlined in the document, the number appears underlined, and if underlined text in the document appears dim, the number appears dim. This is especially useful when you want to determine if your cursor is inside or outside a pair of codes.

QUESTIONS

1. How does boldfaced text differ from regular text?
2. What two kinds of underlining styles are offered by programs like WordPerfect?
3. If you boldface or underline text and then change your mind, how do you remove the boldfacing or underlining?
4. Why would you want to strike out text?
5. Why would you want to redline text?

TOPIC 3-9
Changing Page Layout

In this topic, we introduce you to the following procedures:

- Changing left and right margins
- Changing page offset and binding width
- Calculating horizontal layout
- Changing lines per inch
- Changing lines per page
- Changing page length
- Changing line spacing
- Calculating vertical layout
- Changing pitch

BACKGROUND

Most programs, including WordPerfect, are set to print on 8 1/2- by 11-inch pages with 1-inch margins on both sides and at the top and bottom. You can change these margins for the entire document or change the left and right margins for sections of the document. You can also change other settings that affect the lines per page or per inch.

HORIZONTAL PAGE LAYOUT

Margin settings and page offset commands determine where the first and last characters on a line are printed.

Left and Right Margins

The left and right margin settings determine the length of lines printed. The left margin determines how far in from the left edge of the page the text is printed. The right margin determines how far in from the right edge of the page the text stops printing. The line length is the total page width minus the left and right margins.

Binding Width and Margins

Some word processing programs, like WordPerfect, can treat margins on the screen and margins on the printout separately. On these programs, text aligned with column 1, the far left margin on the screen, is printed in column 1, the left edge of the paper, unless you specify how many columns it should be offset. On WordPerfect, the binding width command is used when you want to reproduce bound copies of a document that is printed or copied on both sides of the pages and then bound, for example in a three-ring binder. This command shifts the text to the right on pages with odd numbers and to the left on pages with even numbers to increase the width of the margin by a specified amount on the side of the pages to be bound or three-hole punched. For example, if the left margin setting is 1 inch, and you set the binding width to $^1/_2$ inch, the margin is 1 1/2 inches on alternate pages. The binding width command is a printer command and affects the entire document.

Calculating Horizontal Layout

On many programs, you specify margin settings in characters, for example, you set the left margin in column 10 and the right margin in column 75. To calculate the number of characters to specify for a given setting, you can use a regular ruler.

For example, here is how you would calculate a left margin setting.

1. Measure the distance from the left edge of the paper to where you want the first character of text to print. Let's say it is 1 1/2 inches.

2. Determine the pitch, that is, how many characters per inch you will be printing. This can be controlled from your program or printer, but it is usually set to 10 or 12 unless you specify otherwise.

3. Multiply the desired margin spacing in inches by the pitch. For example,
   1.5 inches x 10 characters per inch = 15 characters
   or
   1.5 inches x 12 characters per inch = 18 characters

4. Set the left margin to the calculated number of characters. When you print the document, the first character in each line will now print in column 15 or 18 on the paper.

VERTICAL PAGE LAYOUT

Top and bottom margins determine the number of lines left blank at the top and bottom of a page and the line that the first line of text prints on. These margins, the page length setting, and the lines printed per inch all affect the number of text lines printed on the page.

Lines Per Inch

A printer normally prints six lines per inch. You can change this setting for individual paragraphs or for an entire document.

Lines Per Page

The total number of lines per page is calculated by multiplying the length of the page in inches by the number of lines printed per inch. For example, if the page is 11 inches long and the printer prints six lines per inch, the total number of printable lines per page is sixty-six. If the printer prints eight lines per inch, the total number of printable lines per page is eighty-eight. Three variables determine the number of text lines actually printed on a page.

- The length of the paper
- How many lines the printer prints per inch
- How many lines are reserved for the top and bottom margins

If you print six lines per inch on an 11-inch long page, you can print a maximum of sixty-six lines. If you reserve six lines for the top margin and six lines for the bottom margin, you print only fifty-four lines on the page. If you use only three lines for both the top and bottom margins, you can print sixty lines per page.

Page Length

The page length setting determines where the printer stops printing and advances to the top of the next form. When using continuous form paper, envelopes, or labels, you measure the page length from the top of one sheet to the top of the next. If this measurement is 11 inches, you set the page length to 11 inches or the equivalent number of lines, and then the top, bottom, and number of lines per page settings are adjusted for the new page length.

Line Spacing

You can change line spacing for an entire document or for individual paragraphs. Some programs display the specified line spacing on the screen; other programs always display single spacing on the screen to make it faster to scroll through the document. When you print the document, the line spacing is whatever you have specified.

Calculating Vertical Layout

Settings that control vertical layout on the page are usually given in lines, but you generally measure in inches. To calculate vertical spacing settings, you can use a regular ruler and simple arithmetic to convert inches to lines. If, for example, you want the first line of a letter to print below a letterhead, here is how you do it. (Although you are calculating the top margin setting, the same method is used to set the bottom margin or page length.)

1. Measure the vertical distance from the top of the paper to where you want the top of the first line of text to print. Let's say the distance is 1 1/2 inches.
2. Find out how many lines per inch your program and printer prints. Unless you have specified otherwise, this is usually set to 6 lines per inch.
3. Multiply the vertical distance by the number of lines per inch. For example,
    1.5 inches x 6 lines per inch = 9 lines
    or
    1.5 inches x 8 lines per inch = 12 lines
4. Set the top margin settings to the calculated number of lines (9 or 12 lines in this example). If the program asks you to specify the first line that text is printed on, add 1 to either setting; for example, enter line 10 or line 13. When the page is printed, the printer advances that number of lines before printing the first line of text.

In WordPerfect, you set the top margin in half lines. To calculate the number of lines, multiply the distance in inches times 6 to find the number of lines per inch. Then, divide that answer by 2 to calculate the setting in half lines. You calculate the top margin setting at six lines per inch even if you change the lines per inch to eight.

EXERCISE 52

Changing Page Layout

In this exercise, you change margins. To begin this exercise, you must load the program or clear the screen of any other document.

Step 1. Enter a Document. Enter the document shown in Figure 3-12. Remember to press **Return** twice at the end of paragraphs to insert a blank line. The line of equal signs (=) across the screen indicates a hard page break. Type the text above the hard page break, press **Return** a few times, press **Ctrl-Return** to enter the hard page break, and then type the text below it.

Step 2. Change the Left and Right Margins. You can change margins for the entire document or for just sections of it. Here, change the margins at the beginning of the second paragraph, and then restore them to their original settings at the end of the paragraph.

FIGURE 3-12
Page layout
document

```
This exercise introduces you to page layout. It includes changing
the left and right margins, lines per inch, line spacing, and the
top margins.

Left and right margins can be changed for the entire document or
for selected sections. This paragraph has had its margins
changed.

Lines per inch can also be changed for the entire document or
just sections. You can choose between six (the default) and eight
lines per inch. This paragraph is printed at eight lines per
inch.

Line spacing, like the other settings in this exercise, can be
changed for the entire document or for just sections. This
paragraph is printed double spaced.
===============================================================================
The top margin can be changed for the entire document or just for
selected pages. The top margin on this page is changed from 1
inch (the default) to 3 inches.



B:\LAYOUT.WP                              Doc 1  Pg 2  Ln 3      Pos 41
```

To change the left and right margins

Move   the cursor to under the *L* in *Left* at the beginning of the second paragraph.
Press   **Shift-F8** to display the Line Format menu.
Press   **3** for **Margins**, and the status line reads *[Margin Set] 10 74 to Left =*.
Type   **20**, and then press **Return**. The status line reads *[Margin Set] 10 74 to Left = 20 Right =*.
Type   **64**, and then press **Return**.

To restore the left and right margins

Move   the cursor to the blank line between the second and third paragraphs.
Press   **Shift-F8** to display the Line Format menu.
Press   **3** for **Margins**, and the status line reads *[Margin Set] 20 64 to Left =*.
Type   **10**, and then press **Return**. The status line reads *[Margin Set] 10 64 to Left = 10 Right =*.
Type   **74**, and then press **Return**.

Result. The second paragraph is indented 10 spaces from both the left and right margins.

Step 3. Change the Lines Printed per Inch. Now, change the lines per inch to 8 for the third paragraph. Then, reset them to their original 6 lines per inch setting at the end of the paragraph.

To change the lines printed per inch

Move   the cursor to under the *L* in *Lines per inch* at the beginning of the third paragraph.
Press   **Ctrl-F8** to display the Print Format menu.
Press   **2** for **Lines per Inch**, and the cursor moves to the lines-per-inch setting.

Press	**8,** and then press **Return.**
Press	**0** to return to the document screen.

To restore the lines printed per inch

Move	the cursor to the blank line between the third and fourth paragraphs.
Press	**Ctrl-F8** to display the Print Format menu.
Press	**2** for **Lines per Inch,** and the cursor moves to the lines-per-inch setting.
Press	**6,** and then press **Return.**
Press	**0** to return to the document screen.

Result. No change is seen on the screen, but the results will be seen in your printout if your printer and version of the program supports this feature.

Step 4. Change the Line Spacing. Now, change line spacing for the fourth paragraph from single spacing to double spacing.

To change line spacing

Move	the cursor to under the *L* in *Line spacing* at the beginning of the fourth paragraph.
Press	**Shift-F8** to display the Line Format menu.
Press	**4** for **Spacing,** and the status line reads *[Spacing Set]* followed by the current line spacing.
Type	**2,** and then press **Return.**

To restore the line spacing

Move	the cursor to the space following the period at the end of the fourth paragraph.
Press	**Shift-F8** to display the Line Format menu.
Press	**4** for **Spacing,** and the status line reads *[Spacing Set] 2.*
Type	**1,** and then press **Return.**

Result. All text in the fourth paragraph is double spaced.

Step 5. Change the Top Margin. Finally, change the top margin on the second page to 2 inches. Since the setting is calculated at 6 lines per inch, you need 12 lines to make a 2-inch margin. Because you enter the line needed in half lines, enter 24 for the top margin.

To change the top margin

Move	the cursor to under the *t* in *top margin* at the top of the second page.
Press	**Alt-F8** to display the Page Format menu.
Press	**5** for **Top Margin,** and the status line reads *Set half-lines (12/inch) from 12 to.*
Type	**24,** and then press **Return.**
Press	**0** to return to the document screen.

Result. No change is seen on the screen, but the new top margin will appear on the printout.

Step 6. Save the Document. You should now save your document. Before proceeding, *be sure a formatted disk is in drive B.*

To save the document

Press   **F10**, and the status line reads *Document to be Saved:*.
Type   **B:\LAYOUT.WP**, and then press **Return**.

Result. The disk drive spins as the document is saved onto the disk in drive B. When the drive stops and its red light goes out, you can continue to work on the document.

Step 7. Print the Document and Change Binding Width. Now that you have completed the document, make a printout to see how it looks. You also change the binding width so that alternate pages are offset from the left margin by an additional 3/10 inch. Be sure that the printer is on and has paper in it and that the paper is aligned.

To change binding width

Press   **Shift-F7** to display the Print menu.
Press   **3** for **Options**.
Press   **3** for **Binding Width (1/10 in.)**.
Type   **3** (for 3/10 inch), and then press **Return**.
Press   **0** to return to the Print menu.
Press   **1** for **Full Text**.

Result. The second paragraph is indented from both margins, the third paragraph is printed 8 lines per inch (if supported by your program and printer), and the forth paragraph is printed double spaced. The top margin on the second page is 2 inches instead of 1 inch. Now tear the two sheets apart, and hold them up back to back (as they would appear if copied or printed on both sides of a page) to see how the binding width increased the margins on the side that you would bind or three-hole punch.

Step 8. Continue or Quit. You have now completed this exercise. Either continue on your own work, or quit and return to the operating system.

To continue or quit

Press   **F7**, and the status line reads *Save Document? (Y/N) Y*.
Press   **N**, and the status line reads *Exit WP? (Y/N) N*.
Press   **Y** to quit the program, or press **N** to clear the screen and work on your own document.

Result. If you did not quit the program, the screen is blank. If you did quit the program, the operating system B> prompt is displayed on the screen. Remove your program and data disks, and then turn off the computer or load another program.

EXERCISE 53

Changing Pitch

You can change pitch (the default is 10) and font (the default is 1). You can also specify fixed pitch or proportional spacing. Your printer must support the fonts and pitch you select, and your program must be installed for your printer to print the correct results.

When you change pitch, you should also change the left and right margins. For example, in 10 pitch, margins set in columns 10 and 74 give you even 1-inch margins. In 12 pitch, margins should be set in columns 12 and 89 to retain the same 1-inch margins.

To experiment with pitch, type the following three lines, and then change the pitch for the second and third lines. Print the document to see if your version of the program and your printer support these changes.

This line is printed using 10 pitch.
This line is printed using 12 pitch.
This line is printed using 15 pitch.

To change pitch or fonts

1. Move the cursor to where you want to change pitch or fonts.
2. Press **Ctrl-F8** to display the Print Format menu, and the prompt reads *Selection:*.
3. Press 1 for **Pitch/Font**, and the cursor jumps to the pitch setting.
4. Either type the number of characters per inch you want (type * following the number for proportional spacing), and then press **Return** to move the cursor to the font setting.

   Or   press **Return** to leave the pitch unchanged and move the cursor to the font setting.
5. Type the number of the font you want to use, and then press **Return** twice to return to the document screen.

EXERCISE 54

Entering Text to the Left of the Left Margin

When you set the left margin setting in any column other than the first, the cursor does not automatically move to columns to the left of the margin. When words wrap or when you press **Return**, the cursor always returns to the left margin setting. To enter text to the left of the left margin, you use the margin release command. This command moves the cursor left, from tab stop to tab stop. To control the distance it moves to the left of the tab stop, you must change the tab stop settings (see Topic 3-10).

To enter text to the left of the left margin

1. Move the cursor to the left margin on the line you want entered or moved to the left of the left margin.
2. Press **Shift-Tab** to move the cursor to the next tab stop to its left. (Each time you press this command, the cursor, as well as the line, moves one more tab stop to the left.)
3. Type in any new text, and then press **Return** at the end of the line or paragraph.

TIPS

- **If you specify your own page length or the number of text lines per page, or if you change the number of lines printed per inch,** you must calculate the necessary settings for the top margin and number of text lines. To do so, begin by measuring the length of the page you will print on, the top margin, and the bottom margin. Then, decide on the number of lines (six or eight) you want to print per inch. With these four variables, you can calculate the settings you need to make for the top margin, page length, and number of text lines. Table 3-13 shows the formulas and some examples for making these calculations.

TABLE 3-13
Vertical Spacing Calculations

Measurements		*Examples*				
		A	B	C	D	E
PL Page length in inches		11	11	14	14	3
TM Top margin in inches		1	1	1	1	0.5
BM Bottom margin in inches		1	1	1	1	0.5
LPI Lines to be printed per inch		6	8	6	8	6

Calculations	*Formulas*					
Text length in inches (TL)	PL - (TM + BM)	9	9	12	12	2
Page length in single-spaced lines [a]	PL x 6	66	66	84	84	18
Total actual lines per page	PL x LPI	66	88	84	112	18
Number of half lines for top margin [a]	(TM x 6) / 2	12	12	12	12	6
Number of text lines printed	LPI x TL[b]	54	72	72	96	12
Lines left for bottom margin	BM x LPI	6	8	6	8	3

Explanation of Examples
A This is the default setting.
B The lines per inch is changed from 6 to 8.
C The paper length is changed from 11 to 14 inches.
D Both the paper length and lines per inch are changed.
E The paper length and the top and bottom margins are changed (much as they would be to print mailing labels).

[a] Always calculated at 6 lines per inch
[b] Text length in inches

QUESTIONS

1. What is a binding width margin?
2. What is pitch?
3. How do you calculate the number of lines on a page?
4. If you want to print on a sheet of letterhead, how many lines should the top margin be if you want it to be 2 inches and your printer prints 6 lines per inch?
5. If you want to print a memo on a 6-by-9-inch sheet of paper so that a 1-inch margin is on all four sides, what would your left, right, and top margin settings be, and what page length would you specify if your printer prints 6 lines per inch and you use 10 pitch?

TOPIC 3-10
Tab Stops and Indents

In this topic, we introduce you to the following procedures:

- Aligning text with tab stops
- Setting tab stops
- Indenting paragraphs

BACKGROUND

When you want to align text in columns, for example, to create tables or indent paragraphs, you use tab stops.

TAB STOPS

Tab stops on a word processor are much like those on a typewriter. You can position them at intervals across the width of the screen and beyond. When you press **Tab** in insert mode, the cursor jumps to the next tab stop. When you press **Backtab,** the cursor jumps to the previous tab stop.
WordPerfect's tab stops are originally set to every five columns, and text tabbed to these tab stops is left-aligned.

- You can change these tab stop settings anywhere in the document and specify if the text aligned with the tab stops is left-aligned, right-aligned, or centered.

- The tab stops you enter affect all alignments until the end of the document or until you enter another tab setting code below them.

On most programs, including WordPerfect, you can set both text tabs and decimal tabs. You can then use these tab settings to align columns, including numbers with decimal points, or indent paragraphs.

Text Tabs

You use text tabs to indent paragraphs or lists or to create tables with aligned columns. You can align text with tab stops as you enter the text or after you enter it.

- To align text as you are entering it, press **Tab** until the cursor is in the desired tab column, and then type the text. If you type enough text to reach past the right margin, the second and subsequent lines wrap back to and align with the left margin, not with the tab stop.

- To align text that has already been entered, position the cursor under the first character in the text to be aligned. When you then press **Tab** or **Ins** and then **Tab**, the cursor and all text to its right moves to the next tab stop. On many programs, you must be in insert mode to do this. If you are in typeover mode, pressing **Tab** may just move the cursor through the text.

Decimal Tabs

Columns of numbers, including those containing decimal points, can be aligned with programs, like WordPerfect, that include a decimal tab feature. All programs allow you to align decimal points, but WordPerfect, as well as some others, allows you to change the alignment character. Although the program's default setting is to align decimal points (periods), you can change the alignment character to, for example, commas (,), pound signs (#), dollar signs ($), or any other character. This is useful when you want to align dollar signs ($) or when you are writing to a foreign country that uses commas where we use decimal points and decimal points where we use commas (for example, where we write $1,000.50, in some countries, they write $1.000,50). To align numbers with decimal tabs

1. Position decimal tab stops in the desired columns. With WordPerfect, you can also align the decimals with ordinary text tab stops.
2. Press **Tab**, or another designated key, to move the cursor to the decimal tab position. On many programs, an indicator on the screen shows when the cursor is in a decimal tab column.
3. Enter the part of the number preceding the decimal point. As you do so, the numbers you enter move to the left while the cursor remains in the decimal tab column.
4. Enter a decimal point (using the period key or other alignment character you have specified).
5. Type the numbers that follow the decimal point. As you do so, the decimal remains fixed in place, and all numbers are entered to the right of it.

Setting Tab Stops

Most word processing programs have default tab stops set every five columns. You can change these settings by adding or deleting tab stops. There are two ways to do this.

- You can change the tab stops for part or all of an individual document.
- You can change the system defaults so that new default tab settings appear when you open a new document.

To change tab stops, you usually display a ruler or format line, move the cursor to it, and use the appropriate commands to revise the current tab settings. Most programs have several tab stop settings that you can enter. Table 3-15 describes WordPerfect's options.

When you have changed the position of tab stops, you may want to return them to their original default settings. How you do this varies from program to program.

- Some programs have a command that does this automatically.
- Other programs require that you move, delete, or insert tabs individually.

Most programs allow you to change tab settings throughout a document by entering a new format line where you want the settings to change. The tab stops on this format line affect all text that follows until either the end of the document or the next format line. Tables 3-14 and 3-15 summarize WordPerfect's commands to enter tab stops.

TABLE 3-14
Tab Stop Editing Commands

To Display a Ruler Line	Press Shift-F8, 1
To Move the Cursor on the Tab Ruler Line to	
Column 0 on tab line	Press **Home, Home,** ←
Left edge of screen	Press **Home,** ←
Right edge of screen	Press **Home,** →
Column 250	Press **End**
To Enter Tab Stops	
At cursor position	Type code listed in Table 3-15.
At specified column	Type column number, and then press **Return**.
At regular intervals	Type beginning column number, comma, and interval in columns, and then press **Return**. For example, type **0,10**, and then press **Return** to set tab stops every ten columns beginning at column 0.
	The type of tab stops set with this command depends on the type of tab stop set in the beginning column. If no tab is set there, this command enters left-aligned tabs (L). To set another type, enter that type in the starting column before using this command. Forn example, type **D** in column 0; then type **0,10**, and then press **Return** to set decimal tab stops every ten columns.
To Delete Tab Stops	
At cursor position	Press **Del**
From cursor to end of line	Press **Ctrl-End**
All tab stops	Press **Home,** Home, ←, and then **Ctrl-End**

TABLE 3-15
Tab Stop Codes

Alignment	Code
Text left-aligns	L
Text right-aligns	R
Text aligns with decimal (or other specified align character)	D
Text left-aligns (with dot leader)	L then . (period)
Text right-aligns (with dot leader)	R then . (period)
Text aligns with decimal (with dot leader or other specified align character)	D then . (period)

INDENTS

As Figure 3-13 shows, you can indent paragraphs in many ways. The number of characters you indent is a matter of personal choice, but five characters is the standard text indent. Normally, when you enter text, you execute the indent command, and it stays in effect until you press **Return**. At that point, text aligns with the original margins. The way you indent text that is already entered varies. On some programs, you select blocks of text, and use an indent command. On others, you change margin settings, or insert a format line.

FIGURE 3-13
Indents

Indents can take a number of forms. You can indent the first line of a paragraph (a) or the entire paragraph (b) from the left margin. You can indent the paragraph from both margins (c) or create a hanging indent so the first line is flush with the left margin and the rest of the paragraph is indented (d).

A.

Indents can take a number of forms. You can indent the first line of a paragraph (a) or the entire paragraph (b) from the left margin. You can indent the paragraph from both margins (c) or create a hanging indent so the first line is flush with the left margin and the rest of the paragraph is indented (d).

B.

Indents can take a number of forms. You can indent the first line of a paragraph (a) or the entire paragraph (b) from the left margin. You can indent the paragraph from both margins (c) or create a hanging indent so the first line is flush with the left margin and the rest of the paragraph is indented (d).

C.

Indents can take a number of forms.

(a) You can indent the first line of a paragraph a specified number of characters from the left margin.
(b) You can indent the entire paragraph a specified number of characters from the left margin.
(c) You can indent the paragraph a specfied number of characters from both margins.
(d) You can create a hanging indent so the first line is flush with the left margin and the rest of the paragraph is indented.

D.

On most programs, including WordPerfect, indents are made to tab stops. To change indents, you may have to change tab stops. On other programs, the indents are specified independently of the tab stop settings.

EXERCISE 55
Using Tab Stops

In this exercise, you change tab stops and align text and decimals. To begin this exercise, you must load the program or clear the screen of any other document.

Step 1. Display the Tab Ruler. Begin by displaying the tab ruler so that you can get a better idea of what happens when you work with tab stops.

To display the tab ruler

Press   **Ctrl-F3** to display the Screen menu.
Press   **1** for **Window**, and the status line reads # *Lines in this Window: 24.*
Press   ↑ to display the tab ruler at the bottom of the screen.
Press   **Return** to return to the document.

Result. The tab ruler is displayed at the bottom of the screen. (For a complete description of this tab ruler, see Exercise 29.)

Step 2. Enter New Tab Stops. When entering columnar material, you can align the columns with tab stops. The default tab stops are set every five columns, as the tab ruler shows. In this step, you change these tab stops.

To enter new tab stops

Press   **Home, Home,** ↑ to move to the beginning of the document.
Press   **Shift-F8** to display the Line Format menu.

Press	**1** for **Tabs** to display the tab settings screen (Figure 3-14).
Press	**Home** twice, and then press ← to move the cursor to the beginning of the line.
Press	**Ctrl-End** to delete all tab stops.
Press	→ to move the cursor to column 20.
Press	**L** to enter a left-aligned tab stop.
Press	→ to move the cursor to column 40.
Press	**D** to enter a decimal tab stop.
Press	→ to move the cursor to column 60.
Press	**R** to enter a right-aligned tab stop.
Press	**F7** to return to the document.

Result. The new tab stops appear on the tab ruler at the bottom of the screen. Press **Alt-F3** to display the code that has changed the tab settings. Press ← to move the cursor to the left of the code, and watch the tab ruler in the middle of the screen. The tabs to the left of (or above) the code are the original default tab stops. Press → to move the cursor to the right of the code, and watch the tab ruler. The tabs to the right of (or below) the code are the revised tab stops. Press **Spacebar** to return to the normal screen. Watch the tab ruler at the bottom of the screen while you press **Home three times, and then press** ↑ to move the cursor to the beginning of the document in front of all codes. The tab ruler shows tab stops every five columns. Now press → or ↓ to move the cursor to the right of (or below) the code. The tab ruler now displays the new tab stops. When you enter the table, be sure your cursor is to the right of (or below) the tab code so that the new tab settings are in affect on the tab ruler.

Step 3. Enter Table. Now that you have set tab stops, you can enter a table to see the way they work.

To enter the table

Type	**U.S. Prices**, and then press **Return**.
Press	**Tab** to move the cursor to the first tab stop.
Type	**Computer**, and then press **Tab**. The status line reads *Align Char =* to indicate that the cursor is in a decimal tab column.
Type	**$2,000.50**, and then press **Tab** to move the cursor to the next tab stop.
Type	**5000 in stock**, and then press **Return** to end the line.

Figure 3-14
TAB SETTINGS SCREEN

```
L....L....L....L....L....L....L....L....L....L....L....L....L....L....L....L....
01234567890123456789012345678901234567890123456789012345678901234567890123456789012345678
        20        30        40        50        60        70        80
Delete EOL (clear tabs); Enter number (set tab); Del (clear tab);
Left; Center; Right; Decimal; .= Dot leader; Press EXIT when done.
```

Press	**Tab** to move the cursor to the first tab stop.
Type	**Printer**, and then press **Tab**. The status line reads *Align Char =* .
Type	**600.25**, and then press **Tab** to move the cursor to the next tab stop.
Type	**100 in stock**, and then press **Return** to end the line.

Press	**Tab** to move the cursor to the first tab stop.
Type	**Modem**, and then press **Tab**. The status line reads *Align Char =* .
Type	**275.76**, and then press **Tab** to move the cursor to the next tab stop.
Type	**24 in stock**, and then press **Return** to end the line.

Result. Your table should look like the one in Figure 3-15. The product names are left-aligned with the first tab stop, the prices are aligned on their decimal points in the decimal tab column, and the numbers in stock are right-aligned with the last tab stop.

Step 4. Change Alignment Character and Enter Another Table. Now let's change the alignment character to a comma and enter the same table, this time specifying prices in French francs.

To change the alignment character

Press	**Return** a few times to insert blank lines below the first table.
Press	**Shift-F8** to display the Line Format menu.
Press	**6** for **Align Char**, and the status line reads *Align Char =*.
Press	**,** (the comma).

To enter another table

Type	**French Prices**, and then press **Return**.

Press	**Tab** to move the cursor to the first tab stop.

FIGURE 3-15
Table 1

```
U.S. Prices
      Computer    $2,000.50    5000 in stock
      Printer        600.25     100 in stock
      Modem          275.76      24 in stock
```

```
B:\TABS.WP                           Doc 1  Pg 1  Ln 5      Pos 10
[      ▲                ▲                ▲            ]
```

Tab Stops and Indents

207

Type	**Computer**, and then press **Tab**. The status line reads *Align Char =*.
Type	**8.000,50**, and then press **Tab** to move the cursor to the next tab stop.
Type	**5000 in stock**, and then press **Return** to end the line.

Press	**Tab** to move the cursor to the first tab stop.
Type	**Printer**, and then press **Tab**. The status line reads *Align Char = .*
Type	**2.400,25**, and then press **Tab** to move the cursor to the next tab stop.
Type	**100 in stock**, and then press **Return** to end the line.

Press	**Tab** to move the cursor to the first tab stop.
Type	**Modem**, and then press **Tab**. The status line reads *Align Char = .*
Type	**1.000,76**, and then press **Tab** to move the cursor to the next tab stop.
Type	**24 in stock**, and then press **Return** to end the line.

Result. Your table should look like the one in Figure 3-16. It is identical to the previous table, but now the numbers are aligned with the commas in the decimal tab columns.

Step 5. Save and Print. Now that you have completed the exercise, save your revised document. You can then make a printout of your result by pointing to the filename on the list of files. Be sure that the printer is on and has paper in it and that the paper is aligned.

To save the document

| Press | **F10**, and the status line reads *Document to be Saved:*. |
| Type | **B:\TABS.WP**, and then press **Return**. |

To print the document

| Press | **F5**, and then press **Return** to display a list of files. |

FIGURE 3-16
Table 2

```
U.S. Prices
        Computer      $2,000.50      5000 in stock
        Printer          600.25       100 in stock
        Modem            275.76        24 in stock


French Prices
        Computer      f8,000,50      5000 in stock
        Printer        2,400,25       100 in stock
        Modem          1,000,76        24 in stock













B:\TABS.WP                                      Doc 1  Pg 1  Ln 11      Pos 10
[          ▲                  ▲                  ▲                  ]
```

Move	the highlight over *TABS.WP*.
Press	**4** for **Print**.
Press	**F7** to return to the document screen.

Result. The tables printout on the printer. To remove the tab ruler from
of the screen, press **Ctrl-F3** to display the Screen menu, and then pres
dow. The status line reads # *Lines in this Window: 23*. Press ↓, an
Return.

Step 6. Continue or Quit. You have now completed this exercise. Either continue on
your own work, or quit and return to the operating system.

To continue or quit

Press	**F7**, and the status line reads *Save Document? (Y/N) Y*.
Press	**N**, and the status line reads *Exit WP? (Y/N) N*.
Press	**Y** to quit the program or **N** to clear the screen.

Result. The operating system A> or B> prompt is displayed on the screen. Remove
your program and data disks, and then turn off the computer or load another
program.

Indenting Paragraphs

Experiment with WordPerfect's indent commands. You can either enter the
paragraphs and then indent them or indent the paragraphs as you enter them.

- Indent commands (other than **Tab**) affect the text you are entering until you
  press **Return**. This automatically ends the indent and returns the cursor to the
  left margin.
- When indenting existing text, the indent affects all text up to the next hard
  carriage return.

To indent the first line of a paragraph

1. Move the cursor to the beginning of the new or existing text you want to indent.
   (Press **Ins** if the status line reads *Typeover* to change to insert mode.)
2. Press **Tab** to move the cursor to the desired tab stop.
3. Either type the new text.
   Or   press ↓ to reform the existing text.

To indent an entire paragraph

1. Move the cursor to the beginning of the new or existing text you want to indent.
2. Press **F4** to move the cursor to the desired tab stop.
3. Either type the new text, and then press **Return** to return the cursor to the left
   margin.
   Or   press ↓ to reform the existing text.

To double indent a paragraph

1. Move the cursor to the beginning of the new or existing text you want to indent.
2. Press **Shift-F4** to move the cursor to the desired tab stop.
3. Either type the new text, and then press **Return** to return the cursor to the left
   margin.
   Or   press ↓ to reform the existing text.

To enter a hanging indent in new text

1. Press **F4** to move the cursor to the desired tab stop.
2. Press **Shift-Tab** to move the cursor back to the left margin.
3. Type the new text.
4. Press **Return** to return the cursor to the left margin.

To enter a hanging indent in existing text

1. Move the cursor to the beginning of the second line of the paragraph you want to indent.
2. Press **F4**.
3. Press ↓ to reform the rest of the paragraph.

TIPS

- Tab acts differently depending on the mode you are in. In insert mode, **Tab** inserts a tab code and pushes text ahead of it to the next tab stop. In typeover mode, **Tab** moves the cursor through the text to the next tab stop without entering tab codes.

QUESTIONS

1. When would you use text tabs?
2. When would you use decimal tabs?
3. What is the difference between a text tab and a decimal tab?
4. What does left-aligned mean? Right-aligned?
5. What is an alignment character? Give three examples of alignment characters.
6. What is a double indent?
7. Describe a hanging indent. When are they useful?
8. How does **Tab** work in insert mode? In typeover mode?

TOPIC 3-11
Page Breaks, Page Numbers, and Headers and Footers

In this topic, we introduce you to the following procedures:

- Controlling page breaks
- Adding page numbers
- Entering and editing headers and footers
- Previewing documents before printing

BACKGROUND

When working on long documents, like reports and term papers, you can control where page breaks fall, add page numbers, and enter headers and footers to identify pages and sections.

PAGE BREAKS

Soft page breaks, indicated on the screen with single-dashed lines (-----), are automatically entered as you type enough lines of text to fill a page. They also automatically adjust their position if you insert or delete enough text to change the number of lines in the document. If soft page breaks do not fall where you want them to, you have three ways to control them.

- You can enter a hard page break, indicated on the screen with double-dashed lines (=====), to force a page break anywhere in the document.
- You can protect a block of text with a conditional page break. WordPerfect offers two ways to enter a conditional page break: You can select the block and then protect it, or you can specify the number of lines to be protected.
- When printing documents longer than a single page, you can turn on widow and orphan protection so that at least two lines at the beginning or end of paragraphs are kept together at the bottom and top of each page.

PAGE NUMBERS

The default setting for WordPerfect is for page numbers not to be printed. But you can turn page numbers on and then back off anyplace in a document. When you do so, you can also specify where on the page they are to be printed. Page numbers are not displayed on the screen but are added as the document is being printing.

- If you turn on page numbers, you can then suppress them on selected pages, for example, where you want to insert an illustration. Page numbers then resume printing on the following pages. For example, if your document has five pages and you suppress the page number on page 3, pages 1, 2, 4, and 5 are still numbered.
- You can start a new page number sequence anywhere in your document. You can also choose whether numbers are printed as Arabic numerals (1, 2, 3) or lowercase Roman numerals (i, ii, iii). You can use Roman numerals, for example, to number a table of contents and then start the body of the document with an Arabic 1.
- You can change the column that page numbers print in. The default settings are left = 10, center = 42, and right = 74. If you do change the columns, you can return them to their original positions elsewhere in the document.

HEADERS AND FOOTERS

You can add headers and footers to your document. **Headers** are text printed at the top of the page in the space reserved for the top margin, or with WordPerfect, where the first line of text normally prints. **Footers** are text printed at the bottom of the page in the space reserved for the bottom margin, or with WordPerfect, where the last line of text normally prints. The advantage of using the header and footer command is that you enter the text only once, and it is then printed on any pages you specify. Headers and footers can be printed on a single page or on every page of a document. When printed on more than one page of the document, they are called **running heads** and **running feet**.

When you enter headers and footers, the program normally aligns them flush left on a specific line of the page. You can change this alignment or use other variations. For example, with WordPerfect, you can define two headers and two footers (Figure 3-17) anywhere in a document (see Table 3-16). To change them, enter new headers and footers where you want them to change. If you do enter headers or footers, you can suppress them on selected pages.

Many programs can automatically number, date, and time-stamp pages of a document as it is printed. These features are special forms of headers or footers. Unlike headers and footers that simply repeat text, these features are calculated by the program. You enter special codes into headers or footers, and these codes calculate and print the current page number or read the current date and time from the computer's clock. The advantage of using the clock is that the dates and times change automatically each time the document is printed so that it is easier to keep track of different versions of the same document.

EXERCISE 57

Entering and Editing Headers and Footers

In this exercise, you enter headers and footers. To begin this exercise, you must load the program or clear the screen of any other document.

Step 1. Enter a Document. Enter the document shown in Figure 3-18. Remember to press **Return** twice at the end of paragraphs to insert a blank line. The line of equal signs (=) across the screen indicates a hard page break. Type the text above the hard page break, press **Ctrl-Return** to enter the hard page break, and then type the text below it.

Step 2. Turn Page Numbers On. You can turn page numbers on anywhere in your document. Here, you enter the page code at the top of the first page so that all pages are numbered in the upper right-hand corner.

To turn page numbers on

Press   **Ctrl-Home**, and then press ↑ to move the cursor to the beginning of the page where page numbers are to be turned on or off.

FIGURE 3-17
Headers and footers
screen

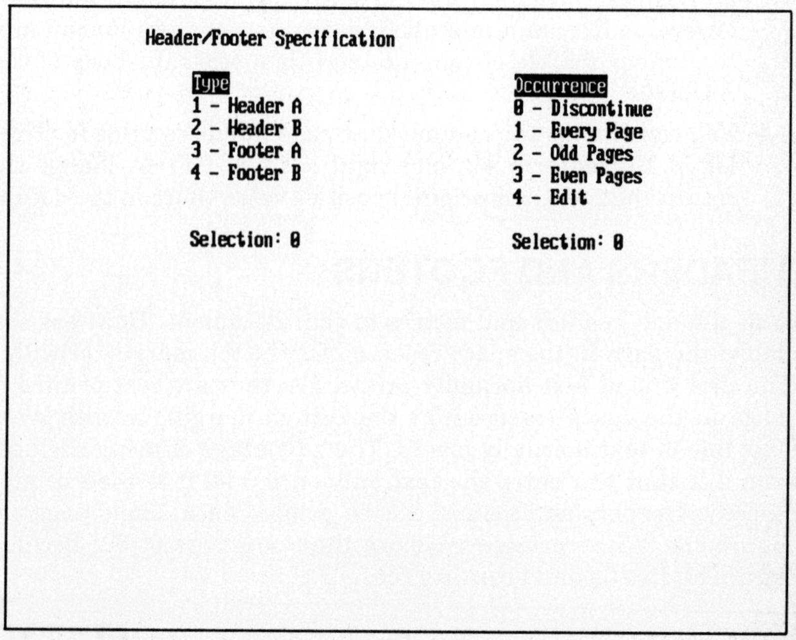

```
                    Header/Footer Specification

                    Type                          Occurrence
                    1 - Header A                  0 - Discontinue
                    2 - Header B                  1 - Every Page
                    3 - Footer A                  2 - Odd Pages
                    4 - Footer B                  3 - Even Pages
                                                  4 - Edit

                    Selection: 0                  Selection: 0
```

TABLE 3-16
Header and Footer Specifications

Type	Description
1 - Header A	Prints header at top of page where first line of text normally prints
2 - Header B	Prints second header at top of page where first line of text normally prints
3 - Footer A	Prints footer at bottom of page where last line of text normally prints
4 - Footer B	Prints second footer at bottom of page where last line of text normally prints

Occurrence	Description
0 - Discontinue	Discontinues headers or footers for rest of document
1 - Every Page	Prints headers or footers on every page
2 - Odd Pages	Prints headers or footers only on odd pages
3 - Even Pages	Prints headers or footers only on even pages
4 - Edit	Displays header or footer for editing

Press **Alt-F8** to display the Page Format menu.
Press **1** for **Page Number Position**.
Press **3** for **Top right of every page**.
Press **0** to return to the document screen.

Result. No change is seen on the screen, but page numbers will print in the upper right-hand corner when you print the document.

Step 3. Enter a Header. When entering headers, the code must be at the top of the page it is to begin on. If it is not at the top of the page, it will not print until the next page, if there is a next page. To be sure the code stays at the top of the page, enter a hard page break before it.

FIGURE 3-18
Headers and footers document

```
You can enter and then change headers and footers anywhere in
your document. Headers print at the top of the page, and footers
print at the bottom. If you want, you can also enter page numbers
and dates into either headers or footers.


================================================================================
When you enter headers and footers, they begin printing on the
page on which you enter them and on all following pages.
```

```
B:\HEADERS.WP                          Doc 1  Pg 2  Ln 3      Pos 10
```

To enter a header

Press   **Home, Home,** ↑ to move the cursor to the top of the first page.
Press   **Alt-F8** to display the Page Format menu.
Press   **6** for **Headers or Footers** to display the Header/Footer Specification menu, and the prompt reads *Selection:*.
Press   **1** for **Header A**, and the prompt reads *Selection:*.
Press   **1** for **Every Page**, and the header/footer screen appears.
Type   **This is a header.**
Press   **F7** to save the header text and return to the Page Format menu.
Press   **0** to return to the document screen.

Result. No change is seen on the screen.

Step 4. Enter a Footer. Here you enter a footer that prints both the date and the page number at the bottom of every page.

To enter a footer

Press   **Home, Home,** ↑ to move the cursor to the top of the first page.
Press   **Alt-F8** to display the Page Format menu.
Press   **6** for **Headers or Footers** to display the Header/Footer Specification menu, and the prompt reads *Selection:*.
Press   **3** for **Footer A**, and the prompt reads *Selection:*.
Press   **1** for **Every Page**, and the header/footer screen appears.
Type   **Date:**, press **Spacebar**, and then press **Shift-F5** to display the Date menu.
Press   **3** for **Insert Function**.
Press   **Alt-F6** to align the cursor with the right margin.
Type   **Page:**, press **Spacebar**, and then press **Ctrl-B** to enter a code to number pages.
Press   **F7** to save the footer text and return to the Page Format menu.
Press   **0** to return to the document screen.

Result. No change is seen on the screen.

Step 5. Edit the Header. Most format commands work in headers and footers just as they do in normal text. You can boldface or underline text, center it or align it with the right margin, and so on. Here you just edit the text, but if you want to boldface or underline words in the header, feel free to do so.

To edit a header or footer

Move   the cursor down a few lines in the document. (The program searches from the cursor toward the top of the document for the next header or footer code, and that is the header or footer displayed.)
Press   **Alt-F8** to display the Page Format menu.
Press   **6** for **Headers or Footers** to display the Header/Footer Specification menu, and the prompt reads *Selection:*.
Press   **1** for **Header A**, and the prompt reads *Selection:*.
Press   **4** for **Edit** to display the text for the next header above the cursor.
Edit   the header text so that it reads **This is an edited header**.
Press   **F7** to save the header text and return to the Page Format menu.
Press   **0** to return to the document screen.

Result. The revised header is saved, and no change is seen on the screen.

Step 6. Save the Document. You should now save your document. Before proceeding, *be sure a formatted disk is in drive B*.

To save the document

Press	**F10**, and the status line reads *Document to be Saved:*.
Type	**B:\HEADERS.WP**, and then press **Return**.

Result. The disk drive spins as the document is saved onto the disk in drive B. When the drive stops and its red light goes out, you can continue to work on the document.

Step 7. Print the Document. Now that you have completed the document, make a printout to see how it looks. Be sure that the printer is on and has paper in it and that the paper is aligned.

To print the document

Press	**Shift-F7** to display the Print menu.
Press	1 for **Full Text**.

Result. The header prints at the top of the page and is aligned with the left margin. The page numbers print in the upper right- hand corner of the document. The footer prints both the date and page number using the codes you entered.

Step 8. Continue or Quit. You have now completed this exercise. Either continue on your own work, or quit and return to the operating system.

To continue or quit

Press	**F7**, and the status line reads *Save Document? (Y/N) Y*.
Press	**N**, and the status line reads *Exit WP? (Y/N) N*.
Press	**Y** to quit the program, or press **N** to clear the screen and work on your own document.

Result. If you did not quit the program, the screen is blank. If you did quit the program, the operating system B> prompt is displayed on the screen. Remove your program and data disks, and then turn off the computer or load another program.

EXERCISE 58

Previewing a Document

You can preview your document on the screen before you print it. The preview command shows headers, footers, footnotes, endnotes, margins, page numbers, and right justification (if justified text is not also set for proportional spacing). Neither font styles nor pitch is displayed with the preview command, which creates only a temporary document (Doc. 3). Although you cannot edit this file, you can scroll through it and switch back and forth to check its layout before you print it. Follow the commands below to preview the documents you created in Exercises 46 (ALIGN.WP) or 52 (LAYOUT.WP).

To preview a document

1. Retrieve the document that you want to preview.
2. Press **Shift-F7** to display the Print menu.
3. Press **6** for **Preview**, and the status line reads *Preview: 1 Document; 2 Page*.

4. Either press **1** for **Document**, and the status line reads *PREVIEW*.
  Or   press **2** for **Page**, and the status line reads *PREVIEW*.
5. Scroll through the document or page.
6. Press **F7** to return to the original document.

EXERCISE 59

Printing Headers or Footers on Bound Documents

To print headers or footers on a document to be printed or copied on both sides of the paper, align them so that they are on the outside corners. To do so, enter an A header or footer, align it flush left, and then specify odd pages. Then, enter a B header or footer, align it flush right (**Alt-F6**), and then specify even pages. Keep the header and footer short so that they do not overlap.

TIPS

- To change the line a header or footer prints on, press **Return** when the header or footer is displayed on the screen to insert blank lines above or below it.

- Since headers and footers print where the first and last lines of text normally print, you can change their position by changing the top margin and number of text lines (see Topic 3-9). For example, you normally have six lines for the top and bottom margins and fifty-four lines of text. If you print a header, it prints on line 7, and a blank line prints below it, leaving fifty-two text lines. If you change the top margin to four lines (six half lines) and specify fifty-six lines of text, the header prints on line 5, and there are still fifty-four lines of text.

- **If you change the margins of your document after entering a header or footer that is longer than the new margins**, you must display it as if you were editing it, but just press **F7** to exit and return to the document. This wraps the header or footer to the new margins.

- **To search or replace text in headers and footers**, use the extended search command by pressing **Home** before the search or replace command (see Topic 3-5).

QUESTIONS

1. What is a soft page break?
2. What is a conditional page break?
3. What is a widow? An orphan?
4. What is a header? Why would you use one?
5. What is a footer? Why would you use one?
6. On what line does WordPerfect normally print a header? A footer?
7. What does the preview command show?

TOPIC 3-12
Merge Printing Form Letters

In this topic, we introduce you to the following procedures:

- Coding a primary document
- Creating a secondary file
- Merge printing
- Assembling documents on screen

BACKGROUND

Instead of individually entering and editing tens, hundreds, or thousands of letters or other documents, **merge printing** lets you enter one document and then enter personalized data into each copy as it is being printed. This can greatly increase your speed in preparing repetitive documents like form letters for billing or scheduling appointments that are essentially the same except for minor changes from copy to copy. For example, you can maintain a mailing list of existing or prospective customers and regularly send them personalized letters using merge printing.

The first step in merge printing form letters is to create the needed files. You enter the information to be printed in every document in the **primary document**. Data to be inserted into this primary document to personalize each copy when it is printed are called **variables**. You can enter these variables directly from the keyboard or store them in a second file, a **secondary file**. When you then merge print the primary document, it is printed over and over again with the variables specific to each copy entered manually from the keyboard or inserted automatically from the secondary file.

THE PRIMARY DOCUMENT

The primary document contains the unchanging parts, sometimes called boilerplate, of the document. You also enter codes into this document to indicate where the variables are to be inserted during printing.

If data is being inserted from a secondary file, these codes refer to fields in that file. For example, one code might indicate that the person's name is to be inserted from the secondary file, and another code might indicate that the person's street address is to be inserted. The codes are entered in the primary document where this data is to be inserted. When you merge print the documents, data from the fields in each record in the secondary file are inserted into each copy in place of the codes that refer to them.

You may refer to all the fields in the secondary file or just to some of them. For example, a primary document used to print letters might refer to a field in which you have stored salutations for each person, but a primary document used to print envelopes from the same secondary file would not refer to the salutation field because salutations are not used on envelopes.

Table 3-17 describes typical WordPerfect codes you can insert. You can type codes directly into the document without selecting them from the Merge Codes menu (Figure 3-19). To do so, hold down **Ctrl**, and then press the appropriate code; for example, press **Ctrl-T** to merge a field from a secondary file, and **Ctrl-D** to enter a code for the date. When specifying a field, press **Shift-^** (caret) to enter the closing caret after entering the field number.

TABLE 3-17
Merge Codes

Code	Description
^C	Stops the printer so that you can type in information from the keyboard. When you encounter this code during merge printing, the printer stops until you press **F9** to continue. Press **C**, and the code ^C appears on the screen.
^D	Reads the system's clock, and inserts the current date into each document. Press **D**, and the code ^D appears on the screen.
^F	Specifies what data is to be inserted from the secondary file. Press **F**, and the prompt reads *Field Number?* Type the number of the field number to be merged at this position from the secondary file, and then press **Return**. Fields in secondary files are entered on lines. For example, you enter the name on the first line of each record, the company on the second, the street on the third, the city on the fourth and so on. To insert names from the secondary file, type **1**; to insert companies, type **2**; to insert streets, type **3**; to insert cities, type **4**. The code ^F#^ appears on the screen where the number of the field you specified appears in place of the #. You can enter a question mark (?) following the field number to close up the line if that field happens to be empty in any record. The code ^F#?^ appears on the screen.
^G	Starts a macro at the end of the merge. For example ^GMERGE^G would start the macro named MERGE.
^N	Directs the merge to the next record. When you encounter this code during the merge, the program goes to the next record in the secondary file. If no such record exists, the merge ends. Press **N**, and the code ^N appears on the screen.
^O	Displays a prompt on the screen during the merge. You can use prompts along with the stop codes to remind yourself or another operator what information to enter. These prompts appear only on the screen; they do not print out. Press **O**, and the code ^O appears on the screen. Type a message to appear on the screen. Press **Alt-F9** to display the Merge Codes menu, and then press **O** again to end the message.
^P	Instructs the program to start over using another primary file or to resume the merge using the same primary file. Press **P**, and the code ^P appears on the screen. Type the name of the primary file to be used when merge printing is done again, press **Alt-F9**, and then press **P** again to end the filename. You can also press **Alt-F9** and then press **P** again without entering a filename to continue with the same primary file. For example, if you are coding a primary document named PRIMARY1, the code ^PPRIMARY2^P starts the merge over using the primary document PRIMARY2. Using the code without specifying a filename, for example, ^P^P, starts the merge over using the primary document PRIMARY1.
^Q	Ends the merge. You can enter this code in either the primary or secondary file. Press **Q**, and the code ^Q appears on the screen.
^S	Like ^P, but starts the merge over using a new secondary file.
^T	Sends merged text to the printer. If you do not insert this code at the end of the primary document, the copies appear on the screen when you merge print the document. You can then edit or format the copies for printing. If you do insert this code, each copy is sent to the printer. Press **T**, and the code ^T appears on the screen.
^U	Clears the screen. Press **U**, and the code ^U appears on the screen.

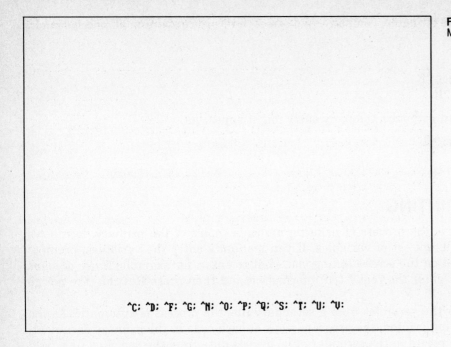

FIGURE 3-19
Merge codes menu

^C; ^D; ^F; ^G; ^N; ^O; ^P; ^Q; ^S; ^T; ^U; ^V;

THE SECONDARY FILE

The secondary file stores the variables that you want inserted into each copy of the primary document when you merge print it. The variables you enter in a secondary file must be organized so that the program can easily find it when you merge print. To understand how a program finds the needed information to insert into the copies, you must first understand how data is stored in fields and records in a secondary file.

Fields

A **field** is a specific piece of information, for example, a person's name. Other fields can be names (Smith), numbers (100.10), names and numbers (100 Main Street), or formulas (100*3). When you first create a record file, you should plan ahead so that the data is effectively organized.

- If you want to be able to sort a mailing list by ZIP codes, they must be entered in a separate field.
- If you want to use the last name in the salutation, it must be in a separate field. If you have only one field for the entire name, your letter might read "Dear Mr. John Smith" instead of "Dear Mr. Smith."
- The number of lines used in addresses varies. One address might require only three lines, and another might require five. Set up your fields for the maximum number of lines. If a particular address is shorter than others, you can leave those fields blank.

Records

A **record** is several related fields, for example, a person's name, address, and phone number. Each record must have the same fields, and data must be entered in the same order in each record. The fields in each record are separated from each other by a **delimiter**, usually a comma, colon, or special character. WordPerfect uses the special character ^R. If a field is to be left empty in a record, the delimiter still must be entered so that the program knows the field exists but is empty. For example, if you have three fields for name, company, and street, a record containing all entries might be

John Smith^R
Word Corporation^R
100 Elm Street^R

whereas a record without a company entry might appear as

Mary Hernandez^R
^R
200 Main Street^R

MERGE PRINTING

Merge printing is the process of printing multiple copies of the primary document, each with a different set of variables. If you manually enter the variables, prompts can be displayed on the screen telling you what to enter, for example, *Enter amount due:*. When you enter the requested information and then press **Return**, the merge continues.

If you enter the variables from a secondary file, the process is automatic. As the first letter is being printed, the program stops at each code in the primary document, goes to the first record in the secondary file, inserts data from the specified field, and then continues printing. After all the requested fields from the first record have been inserted, the first copy advances from the printer, and the second copy is printed. But this time the program inserts data from the second record in the secondary file. This process continues until all records in the secondary file have been used.

EXERCISE 60
Merge Printing a Form Letter

In this exercise, you merge print form letters. To begin this exercise, you must load the program or clear the screen of any other document.

Step 1. Create the Secondary File. The secondary file contains three records, each of which has five fields. The fields have to be the same in each record. You use the following fields:

Field 1	Name
Field 2	Company Name
Field 3	Street Address
Field 4	City, State, and ZIP Code
Field 5	Salutation

If one field in a record is empty (for example, the person does not have a company affiliation), that field is left blank. Enter the three records shown in Figure 3-20.

To enter the first record

Type	**Mr. Robert Smith**, and then press **F9** to enter a ^R code.
Type	**Alf Industries**, and then press **F9** to enter a ^R code.
Type	**100 Elm Street**, and then press **F9** to enter a ^R code.
Type	**Boston, MA 00120**, and then press **F9** to enter a ^R code.
Type	**Mr. Smith**, and then press **F9** to enter a ^R code.
Press	**Shift-F9** to enter a ^E code and end the first record.

To enter the second record

Type	**Ms. Wendy Lewis**, and then press **F9** to enter a ^R code.
Press	**F9** to enter a ^R code for an empty field.

FIGURE 3-20
Secondary
document

```
Mr. Robert Smith^R
Alf Industries^R
100 Elm Street^R
Boston, MA 00120^R
Mr. Smith^R
^E
Ms. Wendy Lewis^R
^R
400 Main Street^R
Los Angeles, CA 90020^R
Wendy^R
^E
Mrs. Mary Lockhart^R
Curtis & Mathers^R
1000 Oak Road^R
Chicago, IL 30010^R
Mrs. Lockhart^R
^E




B:\SECOND.WP                    Doc 1  Pg 1  Ln 1      Pos 10
```

Type	400 Main Street, and then press F9 to enter a ^R code.
Type	Los Angeles, CA 90020, and then press F9 to enter a ^R code.
Type	Wendy, and then press F9 to enter a ^R code.
Press	Shift-F9 to enter a ^E code and end the second record.

To enter the third record

Type	Mrs. Mary Lockhart, and then press F9 to enter a ^R code.
Type	Curtis & Mathers, and then press F9 to enter a ^R code.
Type	1000 Oak Road, and then press F9 to enter a ^R code.
Type	Chicago, IL 30010, and then press F9 to enter a ^R code.
Type	Mrs. Lockhart, and then press F9 to enter a ^R code.
Press	Shift-F9 to enter a ^E code and end the third record.

To print the secondary file

Press	Shift-F7 to display the Print menu.
Press	1 for Full text.

Result. The printer immediately begins printing the secondary file. Carefully compare the printout against Figure 3-20.

To save the secondary file and clear the screen

Press	F7, and the status line reads *Save Document? (Y/N) Y.*
Press	Y, and the status line reads *Document to be Saved:.*
Type	B:\SECOND.WP, and then press Return. The status line reads *Exit WP? (Y/N) N.*
Press	N.

Result. The secondary file is saved on the disk, and the screen is now blank so that you can create the primary document.

Step 2. Create and Code the Primary Document. Now, create and code the primary document shown in Figure 3-21. Since the second field in the second record is blank, enter the question mark code following the field number so that a blank line is not printed where the blank field occurs.

To code the primary document

Press	**Alt-F9** to display the Merge Codes menu.
Press	**D** for **^D**, and then press **Return** twice.
Press	**Alt-F9** to display the Merge Codes menu.
Press	**F** for **^F**, type **1**, and then press **Return** twice.
Press	**Alt-F9** to display the Merge Codes menu.
Press	**F** for **^F**, type **2?**, and then press **Return** twice.
Press	**Alt-F9** to display the Merge Codes menu.
Press	**F** for **^F**, type **3**, and then press **Return** twice.
Press	**Alt-F9** to display the Merge Codes menu.
Press	**F** for **^F**, type **4**, and then press **Return** three times.
Type	**Dear**, and then press **Spacebar**.
Press	**Alt-F9** to display the Merge Codes menu.
Press	**F** for **^F**, type **5**, and then press **Return**.
Type	**,** (a comma), and then press **Return** twice.
Type	**I am pleased to confirm your appointment.** Then press **Return** twice.
Type	**Sincerely yours**, and then press **Return** four times.
Type	**Ms. Melba Stuart**, and then press **Return**.

FIGURE 3-21
Primary document

```
^D

^F1^
^F2?^
^F3^
^F4^

Dear ^F5^,

I am pleased to confirm your appointment.

Sincerely yours,



Ms. Melba Stuart
```

```
B:\PRIMARY.WP                          Doc 1  Pg 1  Ln 18      Pos 18
```

To print the primary document

Press   **Shift-F7** to display the Print menu.
Press   **1** for **Full text**.

Result. The printer immediately begins printing. Carefully compare the printout against Figure 3-21.

To save the primary document and clear the screen

Press   **F7**, and the status line reads *Save Document? (Y/N) Y*.
Press   **Y**, and the status line reads *Document to be Saved:*.
Type   **B:\PRIMARY.WP**, and then press **Return**. The status line reads *Exit WP? (Y/N) N*.
Press   **N**.

Result. The primary document is saved on the disk, and the screen is now blank.

Step 3. Merge the Files on the Screen. Now that you have created a primary and secondary file, you can merge the two files.

To merge print the primary and secondary files

Press   **Ctrl-F9** to display the Merge/Sort menu.
Press   **1** for **Merge**, and the status line reads *Primary file:*.
Type   **B:\PRIMARY.WP**, and then press **Return**. The status line reads *Secondary file:*.
Type   **B:\SECOND.WP**, and then press **Return**.

Result. The status line reads ** Merging **, and in a moment, the three personalized letters appear on the screen although you cannot see them all at the same time. Press **PgUp** and **PgDn** to scroll through the three letters you merged, and notice the following:

- The date was automatically entered when you placed the ^D code. (If the time is entered instead of the date, it is because you changed the date format in a previous exercise. If this has happened, press **Shift-F5** to display the Date menu, then press **2** for **Format**, and the prompt reads *Date Format:*. Type **3 1, 4**, and then press **Return** to change the format. Then press **0** to return to the document screen. Clear the screen, and then repeat Step 3 to merge print the files again.)

- The fields were automatically filled from the secondary file. In the one record without a company name, that field has been left blank and the line closed up because you entered a question mark code following the field name in the primary document.

Step 4. Print the Files. You can print the files on the screen just like any other document.

To print the merged files

Press   **Shift-F7** to display the Print menu.
Press   **1** for **Full text**.

Result. The documents print out on the printer.

Step 5. Add Operator Input. You can pause the merge function at selected points to enter information from the keyboard. When you do this, you can also display prompts on the status line to remind you what information to enter. Let's revise the primary document to see how this works. You also add a code at the end of the document that sends each letter to the printer as you complete it.

To clear the screen

Press	**F7**, and the status line reads *Save Document? (Y/N)*.
Press	**N**, and the status line reads *Exit WP? (Y/N)*.
Press	**N** to clear the screen.

To retrieve the primary document

Press	**Shift-F10**, and the status line reads *Document to be Retrieved:*.
Type	**B:\PRIMARY.WP**, and then press **Return**.

To add operator input

Move	the cursor to under the period following *appointment*.
Press	**Spacebar.**
Type	**at my office at**, and then press **Spacebar**.
Press	**Alt-F9** to display the Merge Codes menu.
Press	**O** for **^O** to begin a prompt.
Type	**Enter time:**, and then press **Spacebar**.
Press	**Alt-F9** to display the Merge Codes menu.
Press	**O** for **^O** to end a prompt.
Press	**Alt-F9** to display the Merge Codes menu.
Press	**C** for **^C** to enter a stop code.
Press	**Spacebar**, type **on**, and then press **Spacebar** again.
Press	**Alt-F9** to display the Merge Codes menu.
Press	**O** for **^O** to begin a prompt.
Type	**Enter date:**, and then press **Spacebar**.
Press	**Alt-F9** to display the Merge Codes menu.
Press	**O** for **^O** to end a prompt.
Press	**Alt-F9** to display the Merge Codes menu.
Press	**C** for **^C** to enter a stop code.

To code the primary document so copies print as they are merged

Press	**Home, Home**, ↓ to move the cursor to the end of the document.
Press	**Alt-F9** to display the Merge Codes menu.
Press	**T** for **^T** to send merged text to the printer.
Press	**Alt-F9** to display the Merge Codes menu.
Press	**N** for **^N** to tell the program to go to the next record in the secondary file.
Press	**Ctrl-P** twice to enter a *^P^P* code that tells the program to use the same primary document.

Result. Your documents should now look like the one shown in Figure 3-22. To save the revised document, press **F7**, **Y**, and then **Return**. To replace the existing file, press **Y**. To clear the screen, press **N**.

Step 6. Merge the Files to the Printer. Unlike the last time you printed the files, this time you send them to the printer one at a time, as you enter information.

FIGURE 3-22
Primary document
with operator input

```
^D

^F1^
^F2?^
^F3^
^F4^

Dear ^F5^,

I am pleased to confirm your appointment at my office at ^OEnter
time: ^O^C on ^OEnter date: ^O^C.

Sincerely yours,




Ms. Melba Stuart
^T^N^P^P
```

To print the merged files

Press	**Ctrl-F9** to display the Merge/Sort menu.
Press	1 for **Merge**, and the prompt reads *Primary file:*.
Type	**B:\PRIMARY.WP**, and then press **Return**. The prompt reads *Secondary file:*.
Type	**B:\SECOND.WP**, and then press **Return**.

Result. The first letter immediately appears on the screen. The date has been entered automatically. The record is for Robert Smith from Alf Industries. The cursor pauses at the first ^C code, and the status line reads *Enter time:*.

To fill out the first form letter

Type	**10:00 a.m.**, and then press **F9** to continue.
Type	**June 10**, and then press **F9** to continue. (The first letter begins printing, and the cycle starts over with the second letter).

To fill out the second form letter

Type	**11:00 a.m.**, and then press **F9** to continue.
Type	**June 10**, and then press **F9** to continue. (The second letter begins printing, and the cycle starts over with the third letter.)

To fill out the third form letter

Type	**12:00 noon**, and then press **F9** to continue.
Type	**June 10**, and then press **F9** to continue.

Result. The third letter begins printing, and then the screen clears. Check your three letters to see if the correct information was entered into each.

Step 7. Continue or Quit. You have now completed this exercise. Either clear the screen and continue to work, or quit and return to the operating system. You do not have to save any documents because they were saved in previous steps.

To clear the screen or quit without saving the file

Press   **F7**, and the status line reads *Save Document? (Y/N) Y.*
Press   **N**, and the status line reads *Exit WP? (Y/N) N.*
Press   **N** to clear the screen, or press **Y** to quit.

Result. If you cleared the screen, it is blank just as it was when you began this exercise. If you quit the program, the operating system A> or B> prompt is displayed on the screen. Remove your program and data disks, and then turn off the computer or load another program.

EXERCISE 61

Assembling Documents on the Screen

You can assemble a document on the screen from two or more files on the disk. This is especially useful when you prepare a report, term paper, or book in sections, parts, or chapters that are stored in their own files. You can assemble them on the screen and print them from there. When you do so, all pages are numbered consecutively.

To retrieve a file into the document on the screen

1. Move the cursor to where you want the first file to appear. (Text below the cursor will move down to make room for the file you retrieve.)
2. Retrieve the file using any of the retrieve commands (see Topic 3-3).
3. Move the cursor to the end of the file on the screen, and retrieve another file. Repeat this step until all files are displayed on the screen.

TIPS

- **Sorting records to be printed.** You can sort secondary merge files into ascending or descending order (see Topic 3-22).

- **To stop a merge in progress,** press **Shift-F9**.

- **If you want to merge print only part of a secondary file,** for example, names from A–N, you can enter a ^Q code at the point in the secondary document where you want the merge to end. Just press **Alt-F9**, and then press **N** for **^N**.

QUESTIONS

1. What is merge printing?
2. Name three practical uses for merge printing.
3. What information does the primary document hold?
4. What information is stored in the secondary document?
5. What is a merge code? Which document do you insert merge codes into?
6. What is the difference between a field and a record? What is each used for?
7. What steps do you take for assembling two or more files before printing them as one document?

TOPIC 3-13
Merge Printing Labels and Envelopes

In this topic, we introduce you to the following procedures:

- Merge printing 1-up labels
- Merge printing 3-up labels
- Merge printing envelopes

BACKGROUND

If you maintain a list of names and addresses, you can use it not only to address letters but also to print envelopes and mailing labels. Envelopes can be fed to the printer from a bin or by using continuous form envelopes. Mailing labels normally come in several kinds of forms, called 1-up, 2-up, 3-up, and so on, depending on how many labels are across the sheet. If you print on 1-up labels, you simply code the primary document as you did the form letter. You then specify a new page length and the top and bottom margin settings, and then you begin printing.

If you print on 2-up or 3-up labels, the program must print labels side by side. To do so, the program must be able to work with the record file so that it can print a line of just names and then a line of just addresses. Instead of proceeding through each field in a record, as it would with a letter, it must access the same field in several records before it moves down to the next line. Some programs like Word Perfect are capable of doing this, but many are not.

With WordPerfect, you format the primary file or merge the files to the screen and format that file before printing. If you merge to a printer, you must use continuous form envelopes. If you merge to the screen and then print from there, you can use either continuous form or individual envelopes. If you use individual envelopes, you must define the printer as hand fed.

To format a primary document to print 1-up or 3-up labels, you follow these steps.

To format a file to print 1-up labels

1. Measure the labels from the top of one label to the top of another. Multiply times 6 to calculate the number of lines in the form length.
2. Determine the number of lines you want to print on each label. Subtract this from the form length to calculate the number of lines available for the top margin.
3. Enter a code at the top of the document to set the top margin and form length (see Topic 3-12).
4. Measure the distance from the left edge of the labels to where you want the first character on each line to print. Multiply this times the pitch to calculate the left margin in columns.
5. Measure the distance from the left edge of the labels to where you want the last character on each line to print. Multiply this times the pitch to calculate the left margin in columns.
6. Enter a code at the top of the document to set the left and right margins (see Topic 3-12).

To format a file to print 3-up labels

☐1 Format the margins as described in the instructions above for 1-up labels.

☐2 Define the columns as newspaper style, and then turn the columns on (see Topic 3-16). For example, specify three evenly spaced columns, with three spaces between the columns.

EXERCISE 62

Merge Printing Labels

In this exercise, you create a primary document to merge names from the SECOND.WP file you created in Exercise 60. You then format the merged names and addresses to print 1-up and 3-up mailing labels. You print the labels on normal paper, but the effect is the same as if you were printing on continuous form paper. To begin this exercise, you must first complete Exercise 60 (Topic 3-12); then load the program or clear the screen of any other document.

Step 1. Code and Save the Primary Document. Begin by coding the primary document so that only fields 1 through 4 are merged from the secondary file.

To code the primary document

Press	**Alt-F9** to display the Merge Codes menu.
Press	**F** for **^F**, type **1**, and then press **Return** twice.
Press	**Alt-F9** to display the Merge Codes menu.
Press	**F** for **^F**, type **2?**, and then press **Return** twice.
Press	**Alt-F9** to display the Merge Codes menu.
Press	**F** for **^F**, type **3**, and then press **Return** twice.
Press	**Alt-F9** to display the Merge Codes menu.
Press	**F** for **^F**, type **4**, and then press **Return**.

To save the primary document and clear the screen

Press	**F7**, and the status line reads *Save Document? (Y/N) Y*.
Press	**Y**, and the status line reads *Document to be Saved:*.
Type	**B:\LABELS.WP**, and then press **Return**. The status line reads *Exit WP? (Y/N) N*.
Press	**N**.

Result. The primary document is saved on the disk, and the screen is now blank.

Step 2. Merge the Files on the Screen. Now that you have created a primary and secondary file, you can merge the two files.

To merge print the primary and secondary files

Press	**Ctrl-F9** to display the Merge/Sort menu.
Press	**1** for **Merge**, and the prompt reads *Primary file:*.
Type	**B:\LABELS.WP**, and then press **Return**. The prompt reads *Secondary file:*.
Type	**B:\SECOND.WP**, and then press **Return**.

Result. The status line reads ** Merging **, and in a moment, the three names and address appear on the screen.

Step 3. Format for 1-Up Labels. Let's assume you are printing on labels 2 inches deep and 4 inches across.

To format the margins

Press	**Home, Home,** ↑ to move the cursor to the beginning of the document.
Press	**Shift-F8** to display the Line Format menu.
Press	**3** for **Margins**, and the status line reads *[Margin Set] 10 74 to Left =*.
Press	**5**, and then press **Return**. The status line reads *[Margin Set] 10 74 to Left = 5 Right =*.
Press	**35**, and then press **Return**.

To format the page length and top margin

Press	**Alt-F8** to display the Page Format menu.
Press	**4** for **Page Length**.
Press	**3** for **Other**, and the prompt reads *Form Length in Lines (6 per inch):*.
Type	**12**, and then press **Return**. The prompt reads *Number of Single Spaced Text Lines:*.
Type	**9**, and then press **Return** to return to the Page Format menu.
Press	**5** for **Top Margin**, and the status line reads *Set half- lines (12/inch) from 12 to*.
Type	**0**, and then press **Return**.
Press	**F7** to return to the document screen.

Step 4. Print the Labels. You print the labels just as you do any other document. Be sure that the printer is on and has paper in it. Align the paper so that the print head is on the same line as the first line of text to be printed.

To print the merged files

Press	**Shift-F7** to display the Print menu.
Press	**1** for **Full text**.

Result. The labels are printed. If you measure the labels vertically, you find the first lines of each address are 2 inches apart.

To save the file and clear the screen

Press	**F7**, and the status line reads *Save Document? (Y/N) Y*.
Press	**Y**, and the status line reads *Document to be Saved:*.
Type	**B:\1-UP.WP**, and then press **Return**. The status line reads *Exit WP? (Y/N) N*.
Press	**N.**

Result. The names and addresses formatted for printing 1-up labels are saved on the disk, and the screen is now blank.

Step 5. Merge the Files on the Screen. Now let's merge print the two files again so that you can format the merged file for printing 3-up labels.

To merge print the primary and secondary files

Press	**Ctrl-F9** to display the Merge/Sort menu.
Press	**1** for **Merge**, and the prompt reads *Primary file:*.
Type	**B:\LABELS.WP**, and then press **Return**. The prompt reads *Secondary file:*.
Type	**B:\SECOND.WP**, and then press **Return**.

Result. The status line reads * *Merging* *, and in a moment, the three names and address appear on the screen.

Step 6. Format for 3-Up Labels. Let's assume you are printing on labels 1 inch deep and 2 1/2 inches across on a sheet 8 1/2 inches wide.

To format the margins

Press	**Home, Home,** ↑ to move the cursor to the beginning of the document.
Press	**Shift-F8** to display the Line Format menu.
Press	**3** for **Margins**, and the status line reads *[Margin Set] 10 74 to Left =.*
Press	**3**, and then press **Return**. The status line reads *[Margin Set] 10 74 to Left = 3 Right =.*
Press	**85**, and then press **Return**.

To format the page length and top margin

Press	**Alt-F8** to display the Page Format menu.
Press	**4** for **Page Length**.
Press	**3** for **Other**, and the prompt reads *Form Length in Lines (6 per inch):.*
Type	**6**, and then press **Return**. The prompt reads *Number of Single Spaced Text Lines:.*
Type	**6**, and then press **Return** to return to the Page Format menu.
Press	**5** for **Top Margin**, and the status line reads *Set half- lines (12/inch) from 12 to.*
Type	**0**, and then press **Return**.
Press	**F7** to return to the document screen.

To format the labels in columns

Press	**Alt-F7** to display the Math/Columns menu.
Press	**4** for **Column Def**, and the prompt reads *Do you wish to have evenly spaced columns? (Y/N) N.*
Press	**Y**, and the prompt reads *If yes, number of spaces between columns:.*
Press	**3**, and then press **Return**. The prompt reads *Type of columns:.*
Press	**1** for **Newspaper**, and the prompt reads *Number of text columns (2-24):.*
Press	**3**, and then press **Return**.
Press	**F7** to return to the Math/Columns menu.
Press	**3** for **Column On/Off**.
Press	**PgDn** to reform the labels.

Result. The labels are now displayed on the screen in three columns.

Step 7. Print the Labels. You print the labels just as you do any other document. Be sure that the printer is on and has paper in it. Align the paper so that the print head is on the same line as the first line of text to be printed.

To print the merged files

Press	**Shift-F7** to display the Print menu.
Press	**1** for **Full text**.

Result. The labels are printed three across, just as they would be if you were printing on labels.

To save the file and clear the screen

Press	**F7**, and the status line reads *Save Document? (Y/N) Y.*
Press	**Y**, and the status line reads *Document to be Saved:.*
Type	**B:\3-UP.WP**, and then press **Return**. The status line reads *Exit WP? (Y/N) N.*
Press	**N**.

Result. The names and addresses formatted for printing 3-up labels are saved on the disk, and the screen is now blank.

Step 8. Continue or Quit. You have now completed this exercise. Either continue on your work, or quit and return to the operating system. You do not have to save any documents because they were saved in previous steps.

To quit without saving document

Press   **F7**, and the status line reads *Save Document? (Y/N) Y.*
Press   **N**, and the status line reads *Exit WP? (Y/N) N.*
Press   **N** to clear the screen, or press **Y** to quit.

Result. If you quit the program, the operating system A> or B> prompt is displayed on the screen. Remove your program and data disks, and then turn off the computer or load another program.

EXERCISE 63

Merge Printing Envelopes

To print envelopes from a secondary file, you must create a primary file that indicates the fields to be merged. Create a primary file to print envelopes using the same secondary file you created in Exercise 60 (Topic 3-12).

To format a file to print envelopes

1. Press **Ctrl-F9** to merge print the envelope primary file and the name and address secondary file onto the screen.
2. Set the top margin to zero.
3. Calculate and then set the left and right margins.
4. Enter the merge codes, and then save the file.
5. Adjust the continuous form envelopes so that the print head is over the line where printing is to begin. If hand feeding envelopes, roll the first envelope into the printer to the same point.

QUESTIONS

1. What do 1-up, 2-up, and 3-up refer to when talking about labels?
2. Why is printing 2-up and 3-up labels more complicated than printing 1-up labels?
3. How would you format the margins for 1-up labels that measure 3 by 5 inches?
4. If you want to merge print envelopes, what information goes in the primary file? What goes in the secondary file?

TOPIC 3-14
Drawing Lines

In this topic, we introduce you to the following procedures:

■ Drawing lines
■ Repeating commands

BACKGROUND

Many word processing programs, including WordPerfect, have line drawing capability. The IBM PC character set has several graphics characters that you can use to create lines and boxes. This line drawing can highlight headings, create organization charts, and make attractive tables.

To create lines or boxes, you first select the character you want to work with. You then use the directional arrow keys to move the cursor around the screen. As you move the cursor, you paint a line with the selected character. Other commands let you erase any lines you have mistakenly entered. Table 3-18 describes the Word-Perfect line draw menu commands.

To print line drawings, you must have the IBM extended character set in the font you are using. On some printer fonts, these characters have been replaced with italic typefaces or foreign characters. If your line drawings do not print, try changing fonts.

EXERCISE 64

Drawing Lines

In this exercise, you practice WordPerfect's line drawing features. To begin this exercise, you must load the program or clear the screen of any other document.

Note. To print the results of this exercise, your printer must support the IBM extended character set. If you are unsuccessful when printing, ask your instructor if changing fonts will help. If so, ask for instructions on how to change them.

TABLE 3-18
Line Draw Menu Commands

Command	Description
1 ¦	Selects the character that draws single lines.
2 ‖	Selects the character that draws double lines.
3 *	Selects the character that draws lines with asterisks or any other character specified with the change command.
4 Change	Displays a list of additional characters you can draw with. When you select a character, it replaces the asterisk on the Line Draw menu. Type the number of your choice, and you return to the Line Draw menu. If you press **9** for **Other**, the status line reads **Solid Character:**. Hold down **Alt**, and then, using the numeric keypad, type any character's ASCII code. Figure 1-15 shows the ASCII codes for the IBM character set.
5 Erase	Erases lines when the cursor is moved through them.
6 Move	Allows you to move the cursor around the screen without drawing or erasing lines.

Step 1. Draw Lines. You can draw straight lines or closed boxes with line draw characters. When you draw a box and turn a corner, the corner is automatically added. Here you see how to draw boxes and how to use **Esc** to repeat line draw commands.

To draw a box with a single line

Press	**Ctrl-F3** to display the Screen menu.
Press	**2** for **Line Draw** to display the Line Draw menu.
Press	**1** for I.
Press	→ twenty times until the status line reads *Pos 30*.
Press	**Esc**, and the status line reads *n = 8*.
Press	↓ to draw a line down eight lines.
Press	**Esc**, and the status line reads *n = 8*.
Type	**20**, and then press ←.
Press	**Esc**, and the status line reads *n = 8*.
Press	↑ to close the box.
Press	**F7** to remove the Line Draw menu.

To draw a box with a double line

Press	**Home, Home,** ↓ to move the cursor to the end of the document.
Press	**Return** twice to enter blank lines.
Press	**Ctrl-F3** to display the Screen menu.
Press	**2** for **Line Draw** to display the Line Draw menu.
Press	**2** for II.
Press	**Esc**, and the status line reads *n = 8*.
Type	**20**, and then press →. (The status line reads *Pos 30*.)
Press	**Esc**, and the status line reads *n = 8*.
Press	↓ to draw a line down eight lines.
Press	**Esc**, and the status line reads *n = 8*.
Type	**20**, and then press ←.
Press	**Esc**, and the status line reads *n = 8*.
Press	↑ to close the box.
Press	**F7** to remove the Line Draw menu.

Result. Your line drawings should look like those in Figure 3-23.

Step 2. Edit Line Draw Characters. You can erase characters or move the cursor without affecting a line drawing.

To edit a line

Move	the cursor onto any line on either box.
Press	**Ctrl-F3** to display the Screen menu.
Press	**2** for **Line Draw** to display the Line Draw menu.
Press	**5** for **Erase**.
Press	→, ↑, ←, or ↓ to erase the characters.
Press	**6** for **Move**.
Press	→, ↑, ←, or ↓ to move the cursor through the characters without erasing them. When finished, return the cursor to where the first character was erased.
Press	**1** for I or **2** for II, and then press the arrow keys to restore the erased characters.
Press	**F7** to remove the Line Draw menu.

FIGURE 3-23
line draw boxes

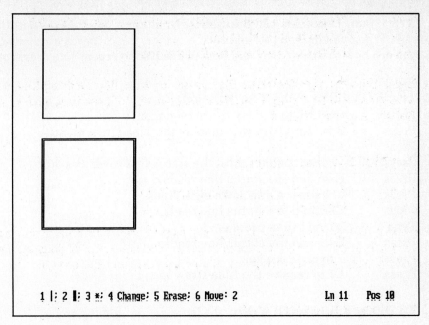

Step 3. Change the Line Draw Character. The menu normally displays three characters you can use to draw lines. The third character can be changed to a different character.

To change the line draw character

Press	**Home, Home,** ↓ to move the cursor to the end of the document.
Press	**Return** twice to enter blank lines.
Press	**Ctrl-F3** to display the Screen menu.
Press	**2** for **Line Draw** to display the Line Draw menu.
Press	**4** for **Change** to display a list of characters that can replace *, the default character.
Press	**1** for , and you return to the Line Draw menu.
Press	**3** for .
Press	→, ↑, ←, or ↓ to move the cursor and draw with the new character.
Press	**F7** to remove the Line Draw menu.

Step 4. Draw Boxes around Text. You can draw boxes around text, for example, to ornament cover pages and chapter headings.

To enter text

Press	**Home, Home,** ↓ to move the cursor to the end of the document.
Press	**Return** four times to enter blank lines.
Press	**Spacebar** three times, and then type **WORD PROCESSING**.

To draw a box around the text

Press	Home, ← to move the cursor to the beginning of the line.
Press	**Ctrl-F3** to display the Screen menu.
Press	**2** for **Line Draw** to display the Line Draw menu.
Press	**1** for │.
Press	↑ twice.
Press	**Esc,** and status line reads $n = 8$.
Type	**20,** and then press →. (The status line reads *Pos 30.*)
Press	↓ four times.
Press	**Esc,** and the status line reads $n = 8$.

Type	**20**, and then press ←. (The status line reads *Pos 10.*)
Press	↑ once to close the box.
Press	**F7** to remove the Line Draw menu.

Step 5. Print the Line Drawings. Now that you have finished the line drawings, make a printout to see how they look. Be sure that the printer is on and has paper in it and that the paper is aligned.

To print the line drawing

Press	**Shift-F7** to display the Print menu.
Press	**1** for **Full text**.

Result. The printer immediately begins printing. The results depend on whether or not your printer supports the line draw characters. If it does and your boxes have dashed vertical lines, change lines per inch to 8 to close them up.

To change lines per inch

Press	**Home, Home,** ↑ to move the cursor to the beginning of the document.
Press	**Ctrl-F8** to display the Print Format menu.
Press	**2** for **Lines per Inch**.
Type	**8**, and then press **Return**.
Press	**F7** to return to the document screen.

To print the line drawing

Press	**Shift-F7** to display the Print menu.
Press	**1** for **Full text**.

Result. The line drawings should now print with solid vertical lines. When you do this with your own work, remember the reduced line spacing causes single-spaced text to overlap and boxes to be shorter. To compensate for this, you must double space text, with hard carriage returns at the end of each line, and draw boxes with exaggerated height on the screen.

Step 6. Continue or Quit. You have now completed this exercise. Either clear the screen and continue to work, or quit and return to the operating system. In either case, you should first save the document.

To save the document and clear the screen or quit

Press	**F7**, and the status line reads *Save Document? (Y/N) Y.*
Press	**Y**, and the status line reads *Document to be Saved:.*
Type	**B:\DRAW.WP**, and then press **Return**. The status line reads *Exit WP? (Y/N) N.*
Press	**N** to clear the screen, or press **Y** to quit.

Result. If you cleared the screen, it is blank, just as it was when you began this exercise. If you quit the program, the operating system A> or B> prompt is displayed on the screen. Remove your program and data disks, and then turn off the computer or load another program.

EXERCISE 65

Using the Repeat Command

WordPerfect has a repeat command you use to repeat a character or command a specified number of times. For example, you can use it to repeat the hyphen (-) or equal sign (=) characters to enter a dashed line across the screen. You can also repeat commands like **Ctrl-Backspace** to delete several words. Table 3-19 describes the commands you can repeat with this command.

The default setting for the number of times a character or command repeats is eight. You can change the default setting for a single command or for the entire session to any number you wish. If you change it for the session, the change lasts until you change it again or until you quit and then reload the program.

To repeat characters or commands

1. Press **Esc** to turn on repeat mode, and the status line reads *n = 8.*
2. Either press the key or command you want repeated.

   Or   type the number of times you want it to repeat (the default is 8), and then press the key or command you want repeated.

To change the default repeat setting

1. Press **Esc** to turn on repeat mode, and the status line reads *n = 8.*
2. Type the number of times you want it to repeat (the default is 8), and then press **Return.**

TIPS

■ **You can copy or move sections of line drawings** with the rectangular block commands.

■ **You can search for or search and replace graphics characters.** When the status line reads —> *Srch:,* hold down **Alt,** and then type the decimal equivalent of the graphic character. Figure 1-15 lists the equivalent decimal character.

TABLE 3-19
Commands You Can Repeat

Command	Press
Move cursor by characters or lines	→, ←, ↑, ↓
Move cursor word to left	**Ctrl-←**
Move cursor word to right	**Ctrl-→**
Move up document by pages	**PgUp**
Move down document by pages	**PgDn**
Move up document by screens	**Gray-**
Move down document by screens	**Gray+**
Delete words	**Ctrl-Backspace**
Execute macro	**Alt-F10**

QUESTIONS

1. What would you use line drawings for?

2. What feature must your printer have to support line drawings?

3. If your printer prints vertical lines as dashes rather than solid lines, what might be causing this, and how would you remedy it?

4. What is a repeat command? Give three examples of repeat commands, and explain their effects on a document.

TOPIC 3-15
Entering Special Characters

In this topic, we introduce you to the following procedures:

- Creating special characters by backspacing the printer
- Entering special characters with the numeric keypad
- Assigning special characters to **Alt** and **Ctrl**

BACKGROUND

Special characters are any characters not on the computer keyboard. These include graphic symbols, Greek letters, foreign currency symbols, and foreign language accents. To print these special characters, you must be able to display them on the screen, and they must be supported by your printer. Special characters can be created by backspacing one character over another with the printer, entered using their ASCII three-digit code, or selected from a menu and assigned to specified key combinations. WordPerfect allows you to create special characters in all three ways.

BACKSPACING THE PRINTER TO PRINT SPECIAL CHARACTERS

What if you are preparing a report on international sales and have to express some amounts in pounds sterling? The symbol for this is the pound symbol (£), a character not found on many keyboards or supported by many printers. To simulate the character, you can print an uppercase L with a superimposed hyphen. The end result, £, is achieved by printing the two characters one over the other. Called **overstriking**, this technique is accomplished by telling the printer to back up one space after it prints the first character so that it can print the second character in the same position.

TYPING ASCII CODES

The IBM PC has 254 characters in its character set, and each of these characters is assigned a three-digit ASCII code. To enter a special character, you hold down **Alt** while you, using the numeric keypad, type its three-digit code.

ASSIGNING SPECIAL CHARACTERS TO OTHER KEYS

On some programs, including WordPerfect, you can display a menu of the special characters available in the computer's character set. (The IBM character set includes many characters not found on the keyboard.) From this menu, you can select the special characters you want to use. You then assign the desired characters to a combination of keys. For example, you might assign a right arrow symbol (→) to the keys Alt-R. Whenever you hold down **Alt** and press the letter **R**, the right arrow symbol is entered into the document at the cursor position.

EXERCISE 66

Entering Special Characters

In this exercise, you practice creating special characters. To begin this exercise, you must load the program or clear the screen of any other document.

Note. To print the results of this exercise, your printer must support the IBM extended character set. If you are unsuccessful when printing, ask your instructor if changing fonts will help. If so, ask for instructions on how to change them.

Step 1. Enter Special Characters. If you regularly use special characters, you can assign them to **Alt** or **Ctrl** key combinations. For example, you can assign the four arrow symbols in the IBM character set to **Ctrl** key combinations. You can assign them so that you can enter them into a document by pressing **Alt-U** (for ↑), **Alt-D** (for ↓), **Alt-R** (for →), and **Alt-L** (for ←).

To display the character menu

Press **Ctrl-F3** to display the Screen menu.
Press **3** for **Ctrl/Alt keys** to display the Ctrl/Alt Keys menu.

Result. A menu of characters appears on the screen (Figure 3-24). At the top is a list of possible **Alt** and **Ctrl** key combinations you can assign special characters to. At the bottom is a table of the special characters. To read the table, first you read the numbers on the left side and then the numbers across the top. For example, the happy face symbols on the first line are numbers 01 and 02. The up arrow is 024, and the down arrow is 025.

To create special characters

Press **Alt-U** to specify the keys the character is assigned to.
Type **024**, and then press **Return** to assign an up arrow.

FIGURE 3-24
The Ctrl/Alt key screen

Key	Value	Key	Value	Key	Value	Key	Value
Alt-A	196 –	Alt-N	0	Ctrl-A	0	Ctrl-N	0
Alt-B	232 ⌠	Alt-O	0	Ctrl-B	0	Ctrl-O	0
Alt-C	0	Alt-P	0	Ctrl-C	0	Ctrl-P	0
Alt-D	25 ↓	Alt-Q	0	Ctrl-D	0	Ctrl-Q	0
Alt-E	0	Alt-R	26 →	Ctrl-E	0	Ctrl-R	0
Alt-F	0	Alt-S	0	Ctrl-F	0	Ctrl-S	0
Alt-G	0	Alt-T	0	Ctrl-G	0	Ctrl-T	0
Alt-H	0	Alt-U	24 ↑	Ctrl-H	0	Ctrl-U	0
Alt-I	0	Alt-V	0	Ctrl-I	0	Ctrl-V	0
Alt-J	0	Alt-W	0	Ctrl-J	0	Ctrl-W	0
Alt-K	0	Alt-X	0	Ctrl-K	0	Ctrl-X	0
Alt-L	27 ←	Alt-Y	0	Ctrl-L	0	Ctrl-Y	0
Alt-M	0	Alt-Z	0	Ctrl-M	0	Ctrl-Z	0

```
           0123456789112345678921234567893123456789412345678 9
  0 -  ☺☻♥♦♣♠•◘○◙♂♀♪♫☼►◄↕‼¶§▬↨↑↓→←∟↔▲▼
100 -                                 ⌐ÇüéâäàåçêëèïîìÄÅÉæÆôöò
150 - ûùÿÖÜ¢£¥₧ƒáíóúñÑªº¿⌐¬½¼¡«»░▒▓│┤╡╢╖╕╣║╗╝╜╛┐└┴┬├─┼╞╟╚╔╩╦╠═╬╧
200 - ╨╤╥╙╘╒╓╫╪┘┌█▄▌▐▀αßΓπΣσµτΦΘΩδ∞φε∩≡±≥≤⌠⌡÷≈°∙
250 - √ⁿ²■
```

Press key to be defined (Press Exit to return):

WORD PROCESSING APPLICATIONS

Press	**Alt-D** to specify the keys the character is assigned to.
Type	**025**, and then press **Return** to assign a down arrow.
Press	**Alt-R** to specify the keys the character is assigned to.
Type	**026**, and then press **Return** to assign a right arrow.
Press	**Alt-L** to specify the keys the character is assigned to.
Type	**027**, and then press **Return** to assign a left arrow.
Press	**F7** to return to the document screen.

To enter the new characters

Press	**Alt-U** to enter ↑.
Press	**Alt-D** to enter ↓.
Press	**Alt-R** to enter →.
Press	**Alt-L** to enter ←.
Press	**Return** to insert a blank line.

Result. The arrows appear on your screen.

Step 2. Create Character by Backspacing Printer. You can create characters while printing by backing the printer up to strike one character over another. Here you see how to create the character ñ using the letter n and the tilde (~).

To backspace the printer

Type	**n.**
Press	**Shift-F1** to display the Super/Subscript menu.
Press	**3** for **Overstrike.**
Press	**Shift-~** (the tilde) and then press **Return.**

Result. Only the last character is displayed on the screen. Press **Alt-F3** to reveal codes, and you can see both characters separated by the code. Press any key to continue. You will see the final results when you print the document.

Step 3. Print the Special Characters. Be sure that the printer is on and has paper in it and that the paper is aligned.

To print the special characters

Press	**Shift-F7** to display the Print menu.
Press	**1** for **Full text.**

Result. The printer immediately begins printing. Check the results to see which, if any, of the special characters are supported by your printer. Many printers substitute another character or print nothing at all.

Step 4. Continue or Quit. You have now completed this exercise. Either clear the screen and continue to work, or quit and return to the operating system. In either case, you should first save the document.

To save the document and clear the screen or quit

Press	**F7**, and the status line reads *Save Document? (Y / N) Y.*
Press	**Y**, and the status line reads *Document to be Saved:.*
Type	**B:\SPECIAL.WP**, and then press **Return**. The status line reads *Exit WP? (Y / N) N.*
Press	**N** to clear the screen, or press **Y** to quit.

Result. If you cleared the screen, it is blank, just as it was when you began this exercise. If you quit the program, the operating system A> or B> prompt is displayed on the screen. Remove your program and data disks, and then turn off the computer or load another program.

EXERCISE 67

Using ASCII Codes to Enter Special Characters

Using the ASCII codes shown in Figure 1-15, enter any special character shown by holding down **Alt** while you, using the numeric keypad, type its three-digit code. When you release **Alt**, the character appears on the screen.

TIPS

■ **You can search for or search and replace special characters**. When the prompt reads —> *Srch:*, hold down **Alt**, and then press the numbers on the numeric keypad that you used to enter the special character. If the character does not appear, press **Ctrl-V** to make the characters visible, and then try again.

QUESTIONS

1. What are special characters?
2. What is overstriking, and how is it done?
3. Why would you want to assign special characters to key combinations?
4. What feature must your printer have in order to print the special characters that you can display on the screen?

TOPIC 3-16
Creating Newspaper-Style Columns

In this topic, we introduce you to the following procedures:

■ Creating newspaper-style columns
■ Entering text in newspaper-style columns
■ Editing text in newspaper-style columns

BACKGROUND

Newspaper-style columns are like those you see in newspapers, newsletters, and books. Text flows from column to column. As you enter text, it gradually fills the first column. When that column is full, text flows into the next column. When the last column on the page is full, text starts to fill the first column on the next page. If you add text to or delete text from any of the columns, the remaining text adjusts to keep the columns full.

There are three basic steps to creating newspaper-style columns with Word-Perfect.

1. Define the columns, and then turn them on.
2. Enter or retrieve text if it has not already been entered.
3. Turn off columns if you want to enter single-column text below them. When you turn them off, you can turn them back on again further down in the document. When you turn them back on, you do not have to define them again unless you want to change the column layout.

After entering text in columns, you can use the commands described in Table 3-20 to move between and around the columns.

EXERCISE 68

Creating Newspaper-Style Columns

In this exercise, you create and edit newspaper-style columns. To begin this exercise, you must load the program or clear the screen of any other documents.

Step 1. Enter Heading. To begin, turn justification off, set a tab stop to indent an enumerated list, enter a centered heading, and double space the text to be entered.

To turn justification off

Press	**Ctrl-F8** to display the Print Format menu.
Press	**3** for **Turn off**.
Press	**F7** to return to the document screen.

To set a tab stop

Press	**Shift-F8** to display the Line Format menu.
Press	**1** for **Tabs**.
Type	**13,** and then press **Return** to set a tab stop in column 13.
Press	**F7** to return to the document screen.

To enter a centered heading

Press	**Shift-F6** to begin centering.
Press	**F8** to begin underlining.
Type	**NEWSPAPER-STYLE COLUMNS.**
Press	**F8** to end underlining.
Press	**Return** twice to enter blank lines.

TABLE 3-20
Column Editing Commands

To	Press
Start new column[a]	**Ctrl-Return**
Move cursor to previous column	**Ctrl-Home, ←**
Move cursor to next column	**Ctrl-Home, →**
Move cursor to first column	**Ctrl-Home, Home-←**
Move cursor to last column	**Ctrl-Home, Home-→**

[a]You need to start new columns only when entering text in parallel-style columns, but you can also use this command to force text to start in the next column when using newspaper-style columns.

To double space text

Press   **Shift-F8** to display the Line Format menu.
Press   **4** for **Spacing**, and the status line reads *[Spacing Set] 1*.
Press   **2** for double spacing, and then press **Return**.

Step 2. Define Newspaper-Style Columns. Here you define the layout of the columns.

To define newspaper-style columns

Press   **Alt-F7** to display the Math/Columns menu (Figure 3-25).
Press   **4** for **Column Def**, and the prompt reads *Do you wish to have evenly spaced columns? (Y/N) N*.
Press   **Y** to have columns evenly spaced, and the prompt reads *If yes, number of spaces between columns:*.
Type   **3**, and then press **Return**. The prompt reads *Type of columns:*.
Press   **1** for **Newspaper**, and the prompt reads *Number of text columns (2-24):*.
Type   **2**, and then press **Return**. The cursor jumps to the column margins list.
Press   **F7** to accept the suggested column margin settings and return to Math/Column menu.
Press   **3** for **Column On/Off** and to remove the Math/Columns menu.

Result. The columns are now defined.

Step 3. Enter Text. Type in the text shown in Figure 3-26. As you do so, notice the following:

- To indent the first two paragraphs beginning with letters, you type **A.** (or **B.**), press **F4** to insert an indent code, and then type the paragraph.

- When you reach the bottom of the first column, the cursor automatically jumps to the top of the next column.

- When you finish, you press **Alt-F7** to display the Math/Columns menu, and then press **3** for **Column On/Off**. This enters a soft page break at the end of the columns.

FIGURE 3-25
Column definition
screen

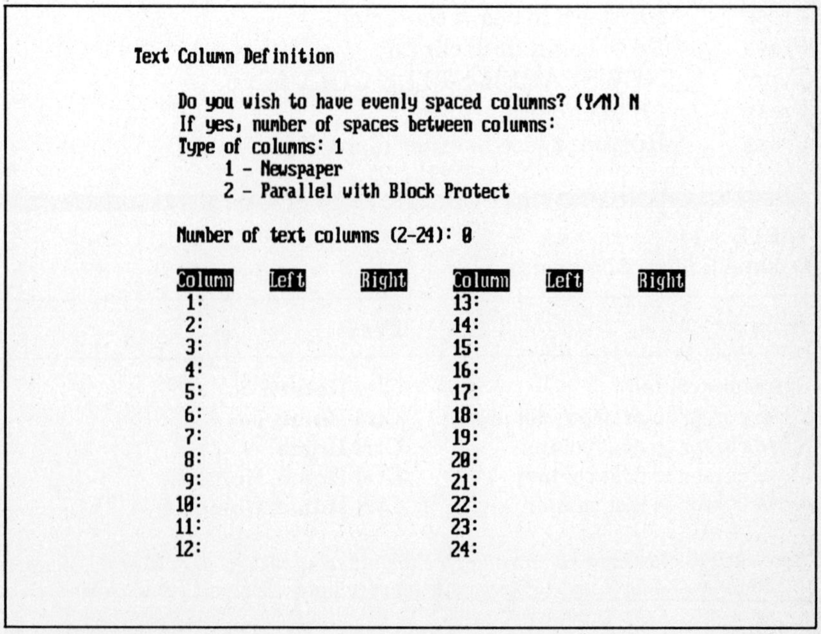

```
Text Column Definition

    Do you wish to have evenly spaced columns? (Y/N) N
    If yes, number of spaces between columns:
    Type of columns: 1
        1 - Newspaper
        2 - Parallel with Block Protect

    Number of text columns (2-24): 0

    Column   Left    Right    Column   Left    Right
      1:                       13:
      2:                       14:
      3:                       15:
      4:                       16:
      5:                       17:
      6:                       18:
      7:                       19:
      8:                       20:
      9:                       21:
     10:                       22:
     11:                       23:
     12:                       24:
```

FIGURE 3-26
Newspaper-style
columns

```
                    NEWSPAPER-STYLE COLUMNS

WordPerfect offers two kinds of      it has not already been
columns, parallel style and          entered.
newspaper style.                     3.    Turn columns off.


A.   Newspaper-style columns are     After entering text in columns,
     used for text like              you can use the keys described
     newsletters and reports.        in Table 3-20 to move between
B.   Parallel-style columns are      and around the columns.
     useful for lists arranged
     in columns, like name and       To edit text arranged in more
     address files. They are         than one column, you use the
     also useful for text that       same commands you use when text
     must appear side by side,       is arranged in a single column.
     as when showing direct          The only differences are the
     translations or annotating      commands you use to move the
     a script with notes.            cursor around and between the
                                     columns of text.
There are three basic steps to
creating columns.                    Practice using the editing
                                     commands described in Table 3-
1.   Define the columns and turn     20 and those you have learned
     them on.                        in previous exercises. Feel
2.   Enter or retrieve text if       free to experiment.
```

Step 4. Save the Document. In a few steps, you will edit the document. But before doing so, you should save the document in case you make a mistake.

To save the document

Press   **F10**, and the status line reads *Document to be Saved:*.
Type   **B:\NEWSCOLS.WP**, and then press **Return**.

Result. The document is saved onto the disk.

Step 5. Print the Document. Be sure that the printer is on and has paper in it and that the paper is aligned.

To print the document

Press   **Shift-F7** to display the Print menu.
Press   **1** for **Full text.**

Result. The printer immediately begins printing.

Step 6. Edit Columns of Text. To edit text arranged in more than one column, you use the same commands you use when text is arranged in a single column. The only differences are the commands you use to move the cursor around and between the columns of text. Practice using the editing commands described in Table 3-20 and those you learned in previous exercises. Feel free to experiment. Do not worry about the changes you make because you will not be saving the document at the end of the exercise.

Step 7. Continue or Quit. You have now completed this exercise. Either clear the screen and continue to work, or quit and return to the operating system.

To clear the screen or quit

Press   **F7**, and the status line reads *Save Document? (Y/N) Y.*
Press   **N**, and the status line reads *Exit WP? (Y/N) N.*
Press   **N** to clear the screen, or press **Y** to quit.

Result. If you cleared the screen, it is blank, just as it was when you began this exercise. If you quit the program, the operating system A> or B> prompt is displayed on the screen. Remove your program and data disks, and then turn off the computer or load another program.

QUESTIONS

1. When might you want to produce text in newspaper-style columns?
2. What are the three basic steps to creating newspaper-style columns?
3. If you deleted a paragraph of text from a newspaper-style column, how would the surrounding text behave?
4. What commands do you use to edit text in newspaper-style columns?

TOPIC 3-17
Creating Parallel-Style Columns

In this topic, we introduce you to the following procedures:

- Creating parallel-style columns
- Entering text in parallel-style columns
- Editing text in parallel-style columns

BACKGROUND

Parallel-style columns align text side by side. This style is used when showing the same text in two languages; annotating a script with marginal notes; creating lists of names and address; or creating tables of text for schedules, product descriptions, and the like. Text does not flow from one column to another, as in newspaper-style columns. You enter and edit text in each column independently.

There are three basic steps to creating parallel-style columns with WordPerfect just as their are with newspaper-style columns.

1. Define the columns, and then turn them on.
2. Enter or retrieve text if it has not already been entered.
3. Turn off columns if you want to enter single column text below them. When you turn them off, you can turn them back on again further down in the document. When you turn them back on, you do not have to define them again unless you want to change the column layout.

After entering text in columns, you can use the commands described in Table 3-20 to move between and around the columns.

EXERCISE 69
Creating Parallel-Style Columns

This exercise describes creating and editing parallel-style columns. To complete this exercise you must load the program and clear the screen or other documents.

Step 1. Define and Start Parallel-Style Columns. To begin, define the columns as parallel columns, and then turn them on.

To enter a heading

Press	**Shift-F6** to begin centering.
Press	**F6** to begin boldfacing.
Press	**F8** to begin underlining.
Type	**NAMES AND ADDRESSES.**
Press	**F6** to end boldfacing.
Press	**F8** to end underlining.
Press	**Return** twice to enter blank lines.

To define parallel-style columns

Press	**Alt-F7** to display the Math/Columns menu.

Press	**4** for **Column Def**, and the prompt reads *Do you wish to have evenly spaced columns? (Y/N) N.*
Press	**N** to define your own columns, and the prompt reads *Type of columns:.*
Press	**2** for **Parallel with Block Protect**, and the prompt reads *Number of text columns (2-24):.*
Type	**3**, and then press **Return**. The cursor jumps to the column margins list.
Type	**10** for **Left**, and then press **Return**.
Type	**32** for **Right**, and then press **Return**.
Type	**35** for **Left**, and then press **Return**.
Type	**57** for **Right**, and then press **Return**.
Type	**60** for **Left**, and then press **Return**.
Type	**82** for **Right**, and then press **Return** to return to the Math/Columns menu.
Press	**3** for **Column On/Off** and to remove the Math/Columns menu.

Step 2. Enter Names and Addresses. Now that you have defined the columns, you enter three names and addresses. After completing the entry in a column, press **Ctrl-Return** to move the cursor to the next column. This command does not enter a hard page break when working with multiple columns.

To enter first name

Type	**Dennis Hogan**, and then press **Ctrl-Return** to move the cursor to the next column.
Type	**Lakeside Industries**, and then press **Return**.
Type	**100 Elm Street**, and then press **Return**.
Type	**Westfield, NY 10010**, and then press **Ctrl-Return** to move the cursor to the next column.
Type	**716-555-1212**, and then press **Ctrl-Return** to move the cursor down and back to the first column.

To enter second name

Type	**Nancy Benjamin**, and then press **Ctrl-Return** to move the cursor to the next column.
Type	**Wordcraft, Inc.**, and then press **Return**.
Type	**52 Seneca Road**, and then press **Return**.
Type	**Oakland, CA 90020**, and then press **Ctrl-Return** to move the cursor to the next column.
Type	**403-555-1212**, and then press **Ctrl-Return** to move the cursor down and back to the first column.

To enter third name

Type	**Catherine Rossbach**, and then press **Ctrl-Return** to move the cursor to the next column.
Type	**Real Estate Inc.**, and then press **Return**.
Type	**1500 Main Street**, and then press **Return**.
Type	**Muncie, IN 47305**, and then press **Ctrl-Return** to move the cursor to the next column.
Type	**313-555-1212**, and then press **Ctrl-Return** to move the cursor down and back to the first column.

Result. Your results should match those shown in Figure 3-27.

```
┌────────────────────────────────────────────────────────────────┐
│                    ▓NAMES AND ADDRESSES▓                         │
│                                                                  │
│   Dennis Hogan          Lakeside Industries    716-555-1212      │
│                         100 Elm Street                           │
│                         Westfield, NY  10010                     │
│                                                                  │
│   Nancy Benjamin        Wordcraft, Inc.        403-555-1212      │
│                         52 Seneca Road                           │
│                         Oakland, CA  90020                       │
│                                                                  │
│   Catherine Rossbach    Real Estate Inc.       313-555-1212      │
│                         1500 Main Street                         │
│                         Muncie, IN  47305                        │
│                                                                  │
│                                                                  │
│   NOTE: This list of names and addresses is current as of January│
│   1, 1988. Any changes can be found by calling Dennis Hogan.     │
│                                                                  │
│                                                                  │
│                                                                  │
│                                                                  │
│                                                                  │
│   B:\PARCOLS.WP                       Doc 2  Pg 1  Ln 1    Pos 10 │
└────────────────────────────────────────────────────────────────┘
```

FIGURE 3-27
Parallel-style columns

Step 3. Turn Columns Off and Enter Single-Column Text. Once you have defined columns, you can turn them on and off at any point below the definition code.

To turn columns off

Press	**Alt-F7** to display the Math/Columns menu.
Press	**3** for **Column On/Off** and to remove the Math/Columns menu.
Type	**NOTE: This list of names and addresses is current as of January 1, 1988. To learn of any changes, call Dennis Hogan.**
Press	**Return.**

Result. The new sentence wraps at the original right margin and not at the column margins.

Step 4. Save the Document. In a few steps, you will edit the document. But before doing so, you should save the document in case you make a mistake.

To save the document

Press	**F10**, and the status line reads *Document to be Saved:*.
Type	**B:\PARCOLS.WP**, and then press **Return**.

Result. The document is saved onto the disk.

Step 5. Print the Document. Be sure that the printer is on and has paper in it and that the paper is aligned.

To print the document

Press	**Shift-F7** to display the Print menu.
Press	**1** for **Full text**.

Result. The printer immediately begins printing.

Step 6. Edit the Columns. To edit text arranged in more than one column, you use the same commands you use when text is arranged in a single column. The only differences are the commands you use to move the cursor around and between the columns of text. Practice using the editing commands described in Table 3-20 and those you learned in previous exercises. Feel free to experiment. Do not worry about the changes you make because you will not be saving the document at the end of the exercise.

Step 7. Continue or Quit. You have now completed this exercise. Either clear the screen and continue to work, or quit and return to the operating system.

To clear the screen or quit

Press   **F7**, and the status line reads *Save Document? (Y/N) Y.*
Press   **N**, and the status line reads *Exit WP? (Y/N) N.*
Press   **N** to clear the screen, or press **Y** to quit.

Result. If you cleared the screen, it is blank just as it was when you began this exercise. If you quit the program, the operating system A> or B> prompt is displayed on the screen. Remove your program and data disks, and then turn off the computer or load another program.

QUESTIONS

1. When might you want to produce text in parallel-style columns?
2. What are the three basic steps to creating parallel-style columns?
3. What commands do you use to edit text in parallel-style columns?

TOPIC 3-18
Creating and Using Macros

In this topic, we introduce you to the following procedures:

- Recording keystrokes
- Playing back recorded keystrokes

BACKGROUND

Since many of the tasks you perform while word processing are repetitive, you often find yourself pressing the same sequence of keys to save, retrieve, or print files; indent paragraphs; boldface words; and so on. Some programs, including WordPerfect, allow you to use **macros** to automate these repetitive tasks. Macros record a series of keystrokes so that you can then play them back with just a few keystrokes. Recording and playing back keystrokes is easy and can save you a lot of time if you use the same series of keystrokes over and over again. With keystrokes, you can

- Record sections of text.
- Record and then execute a series of commands. If you must press five or six keys to execute a command, you can store those keystrokes in a macro and execute it by pressing as few as two keys.
- Enter a pause in a macro when you record it. When you play back the macro, it executes all keystrokes up to the pause and then waits for you to enter text or other keystrokes from the keyboard. When you do so and then press **Return**, the macro continues. This is useful when all but a few of the keystrokes are the same. For example, you can record all the keystrokes needed to retrieve a file from the disk but enter a pause so that you can type in the desired file's name.

There are usually four steps to recording keystrokes.

1. You issue a command to begin recording keystrokes.
2. You assign keystrokes a name or to an **Alt**-letter key combination.
3. You type the keys you want to record.
4. You issue a command to terminate recording keystrokes.

When you want to play back the keystrokes (execute the macro), if you assigned them a name, press **Alt-F10**, and then enter the name. If you assigned them to an **Alt**-letter key combination, hold down **Alt**, and then press the letter (A-Z) you assigned them to.

EXERCISE 70

Creating and Using Macros

In this exercise, you use WordPerfect's macro features. To begin this exercise, you must load the program or clear the screen of any other document.

Step 1. Record Keystrokes. Let's record the keystrokes you would use to close a typical business letter.

To record keystrokes

Press   **Ctrl-F10** to turn on record mode, and the status line reads *Define Macro:*.

Type   **CLOSE**, and then press **Return**. The status line flashes *Macro Def*.

Type   **Sincerely yours**, and then press **Return** four times.

Type   **your name**, and then press **Return**.

Press   **Ctrl-F10** to turn off record mode, and the status line no longer flashes *Define Macro:*.

Result. When you record a macro, it is stored in a file on the current default drive (unless you specify another path when naming it). To see the filename you recorded the macro in, press **F5**, and then press **Return**. The macro is stored under CLOSE.MAC, the name you assigned to it. (The program automatically adds the extension .MAC.) Press **F7** to return to the document screen.

Step 2. Play Back Keystrokes. Once you have recorded keystrokes, you can play them back at any time.

To play back the recorded keystrokes

Press   **Home, Home,** ↓ to move the cursor to the end of the document.

Press   **Return** twice to enter blank lines.

Press   **Alt-F10**, and the status line reads *Macro:*.

Type   **CLOSE**, and then press **Return**.

Result. The macro is played back, and the close is entered at the cursor position. You can insert this information anywhere in your document by moving the cursor to the desired spot and playing back the recorded keystrokes.

Step 3. Record Keystrokes with a Pause. Macros are usually executed so fast that you cannot see them happen; you just see the final results. But WordPerfect has a pause command that lets you specify a delay between keystrokes. You can do this at any time after you enter the macro's name by pressing **Ctrl-PgUp**, entering a delay value when the computer beeps, and then pressing **Return**. The delay value can be any number from 0 to 254 in increments of one tenth of a second. For example, if you enter 10, there is a 1-second pause between keystrokes; if you enter 254, there is a 25.4-second pause between keystrokes. To return a macro to full speed after entering a delay value, press **Ctrl- PgUp**, and then type 255. The macro resumes running at full speed without prompts and messages being displayed. If you enter 0, the macro runs at full speed, but prompts and messages are displayed.

     Now record the same keystrokes as in Step 1, but this time add a pause.

To record keystrokes with a pause

Press   **Ctrl-F10** to turn on record mode, and the status line reads *Define Macro:*.

Type   **SLOW**, and then press **Return**. The status line flashes *Macro Def*.

Press   **Ctrl-PgUp** to enter a pause, and the computer beeps.

Type   **3**, and then press **Return**.

Type   **Sincerely yours**, and then press **Return** four times.

Type   **your name**, and then press **Return**.

Press   **Ctrl-F10** to turn off record mode, and the status line no longer flashes *Define Macro:*.

Result. The macro is stored under the name SLOW.MAC.

Step 4. Play Back Slow Keystrokes. You play back the keystrokes the same way you did the original series.

To play back the recorded keystrokes

Press	**Alt-F10** to display the prompt *Macro:*.
Type	**SLOW**, and then press **Return**

Result. The macro is played back a character at a time. Use **Alt-F10** to play back the macro CLOSE again, and watch the difference in speed. As we said, 10 equals a second, so the 3 you entered specifies that three characters be played back a second. If you entered 10, the pause between each character would be one second; if you entered 100, the pause between each character would be ten seconds.

Step 5. Link Macros. You can link macros to one another so that when one is finished, another plays back. Lets create a new macro that moves the cursor to the end of the document, enters two blank lines, and then executes the SLOW macro. This time, instead of assigning it a name, you assign it to the **Alt-C** combination so that you can execute it by just pressing **Alt-C**.

To record keystrokes

Press	**Ctrl-F10** to turn on record mode, and the status line reads *Define Macro:*.
Press	**Alt-C**, and the status line flashes *Macro Def*.
Press	**Home, Home,** ↓ to move the cursor to the end of the document.
Press	**Return** twice.
Press	**Alt-F10**, and the status line reads *Macro:*.
Type	**SLOW**, and then press **Return** to execute that macro from within the new one.
Press	**Ctrl-F10** to turn off record mode, and the status line no longer flashes *Define Macro:*.

To play back the recorded keystrokes

Press	**Home, Home,** ↑ to move the cursor to the beginning of the document.
Press	**Alt-C** to execute the macro.

Result. The cursor moves to the end of the document, and then the SLOW macro is automatically executed.

Step 6. Repeat Macros. You can use the repeat command to repeat a macro a specified number of times. Let's try it, using it to enter your name.

To record keystrokes

Press	**Home, Home,** ↓ to move the cursor to the end of the document.
Press	**Return** twice.
Press	**Ctrl-F10** to turn on record mode, and the status line reads *Define Macro:*.
Type	**NAME**, and then press **Return**. The status line flashes *Macro Def*.
Type	**your name**, and then press **Return**.
Press	**Ctrl-F10** to turn off record mode, and the status line no longer flashes *Define Macro:*.

To play back the recorded keystrokes

Press	**Esc**, and the status line reads *n = 8*.
Type	**10**.
Press	**Alt-F10**, and the status line reads *Macro:*.
Type	**NAME**, and then press **Return**.

Result. The macro repeats twenty times.

Step 7. Print the Document. Be sure that the printer is on and has paper in it and that the paper is aligned.

To print the document

Press   **Shift-F7** to display the Print menu.
Press   1 for **Full text**.

Result. The printer immediately begins printing.

Step 8. Continue or Quit. You have now completed this exercise. Either clear the screen and continue to work or quit and return to the operating system. There is no need to save this document since the macros are already saved on the disk and can be used with any document you create.

To clear the screen or quit without saving the document

Press   **F7**, and the status line reads *Save Document? (Y/N) Y*.
Press   **N**, and the status line reads *Exit WP? (Y/N) N*.
Press   **N** to clear the screen, or press **Y** to quit.

Result. If you cleared the screen, it is blank, just as it was when you began this exercise. If you quit the program, the operating system A> or B> prompt is displayed on the screen. Remove your program and data disks, and then turn off the computer or load another program.

EXERCISE 71

Pausing a Macro for Keyboard Input

To have a macro pause for keyboard input, for example, to enter a person's name in a salutation, or a filename in a save or retrieve macro, press **Ctrl-PgUp** while recording the macro. When the beep sounds, press **Return** twice. When you run the macro, it pauses at the point where you pressed **Return** twice. When you then enter text and press **Return**, the macro resumes. Try to use this command to retrieve a file (using **Shift-F10**) from the disk. Have it pause at the point where you enter the file's name.

TIPS

- **Macros are normally stored in the default drive and directory when they are recorded.** When recording one, you can specify a path in front of the macro's name to store the macro in another drive and directory. When playing one back, either make the drive and directory it is stored in the default, or specify a path when prompted to enter the macro's name.

- **You can use the repeat command** to repeat a macro a specified number of times (see Topic 3-14).

- **To stop a macro in progress**, press **F1**.

■ **If you press an Alt-letter key combination** when the status line reads *Define Macro:* and have assigned a special character to the same key combination (see Topic 3-15), the special character appears following the prompt. Press **Backspace** to delete the special character and enter a new combination. If this does not work, press **F1** to cancel the command and then try it again, this time entering a new combination of keys.

QUESTIONS

1. What is a macro? What is the advantage of using macros?
2. What are the four basic steps to creating a macro?
3. Why might you want to add a pause to a macro you are recording?
4. How do you slow down playing back a macro?

TOPIC 3-19
Using Math Functions

In this topic, we introduce you to the following procedures:

- Calculating numbers in rows and columns
- Calculating formulas

BACKGROUND

When using a word processing program, you often have columns or tables of numbers that require totals and subtotals. At other times, you have two or more numbers that you want to add, subtract, multiply, or divide. WordPerfect and other programs with built-in math functions let you make these calculations on the screen without a separate calculator. Some programs also have advanced math functions that calculate averages or percentages.

CALCULATING NUMBERS IN ROWS AND COLUMNS

One math feature automatically totals rows and columns of numbers. You enter these numbers in a document, and then tell the program what rows or columns to total and where to place the answer.

WordPerfect's math feature allows you to make calculations based on numbers you enter into columns of your document. You can enter numbers as described in Table 3-21 and then calculate subtotals, totals, and grand totals for the numbers. To make calculations, you enter codes that tell the program what to add and where to place the result. You then use the calculate command to determine the answers. If you change any of the numbers, all you do is recalculate, and the program displays the new answers.

TABLE 3-21
Entering Numbers in Numeric Columns

Positive and Negative Numbers
You can enter positive or negative numbers. Positive numbers do not require a sign, but negative numbers do. You can enter negative numbers with a minus sign, for example, -100, or in parentheses, for example, (100). You can enter numbers with or without commas separating thousands and with or without dollar signs.

Percentages
You can enter numbers as decimal points or follow them by percent signs. For example, to enter 10 percent, type **.1** or **10%**; to enter 20 percent, type **.2** or **20%**; and to enter 1 1/2 percent, type **.015** or **1.5%**.

Subtotals and Totals
You can enter subtotals and totals directly so that they are included in calculations by totals and grand totals. To do so, you type a lowercase *t* to indicate a subtotal, and an uppercase *T* to indicate a total, followed by the number. For example, to enter a subtotal for $1,000, type **t$1,000 or t1000**; to enter a total of $3,000, type **T$3,000 or T3000**.

CALCULATING FORMULAS

You can also define as many as four columns as calculation columns and use math operators to build formulas that add, subtract, multiply, divide, and average numbers entered in other columns. The formulas can refer to numbers entered or calculated in other columns. For example, you could enter sales in column A and then enter a formula A*.10 in column B to calculate a 10 percent commission on sales entered in column A.

All columns are initially defined as numeric columns, and you need not redefine them unless you want to define calculation columns or the way numbers are displayed.

Without changing column definitions, you can add numbers and calculate subtotals, totals, and grand totals.

Calculated numbers are displayed with two numbers to the right of the decimal point (for example, 200.00), and negative numbers are enclosed in parentheses (for example, (200). You can change the number of decimal places from zero to four and display negative numbers preceded by a minus sign.

When entering numbers or defining math columns, you can use or define twenty-four columns, A through X. Column A is the first tab stop in the document that falls to the right of the left margin setting. Columns to the left of the left margin, or between the left margin and the first tab stop, are not math columns; they can be used for labels only.

To calculate formulas, you should understand two basic principles: operators and the order of operations.

Operators

To calculate formulas with some programs, you enter **operators**, symbols that tell the program what calculations to perform. Along with numbers, operators are used to create formulas. Table 3-22 describes WordPerfect's math operators. You should be familiar with operators from arithmetic. A typical arithmetic problem might be written as 2+2. The plus sign is the operator, and it tells you the numbers should be added. You use the same operators with WordPerfect, but the symbols are a little different. For example, the division operator is a slash (/), and the multiplication operator is an asterisk (*).

TABLE 3-22
WordPerfect's Math Operators

Operation	Operator	Example	Answer
Addition	+ or nothing	100+100 or 100 100	200
Subtraction	- or ( )	200-100 or 200 (100)	100
Multiplication	*	2*2	4
Division	/	4/2	2
Percentage	. or %	.28*100 or 28%*100	28

Order of Operations

When constructing formulas that contain more than one operator, another concept, **the order of operations**, becomes important. Every program has a specific order in which operators are calculated.

- Some programs like WordPerfect automatically calculate operations from left to right in the order they appear in the formula, unless you use parentheses, in which case the numbers in parentheses are calculated first.

- Other programs follow algebra's rules of precedence; that is, those operators with a higher level of precedence are performed before those with a lower level. For example, multiplication and division have equal precedence but a higher precedence than addition and subtraction, which also have equal precedence. Operators with the same level of precedence are calculated from left to right.

Let us see how the order of operations works in practice. Assume you want to add the numbers 1 and 1/2. To do this, you enter them as 1+1/2. This formula contains two operators: one to add (+) and one to divide (/).

- If calculations are performed from left to right, the answer is 1. First addition is performed, so 1+1 = 2, then division is performed, so 2/2 = 1.

- If algebra's rules of precedence are followed, the answer is 1.5. First division is performed, so 1/2 = 0.5, then addition, which has a lower precedence, is performed, so 1+0.5 = 1.5.

ENTERING CALCULATION CODES

To make calculations with WordPerfect, you enter codes that define columns and codes that tell the program what to calculate. Initially, the first column is defined as a label column, and all other columns are defined as numeric columns. But you can change the definition of any of these columns (except the first) to calculation, label, or total columns. Table 3-23 describes the types of columns you can assign.

After defining columns, you enter codes in the columns that define what calculations are to be made. Table 3-24 describes the available codes and the calculations they perform.

EXERCISE 72

Using Math Functions

In this exercise, you use WordPerfect's math features. To begin this exercise, you must load the program or clear the screen of any other document.

Step 1. Set Tabs. Here, you create a table showing the sales and returns for two items. Before creating the table, change the tab stops so that there are three columns, one for labels, one for numbers, and one for calculations. The leftmost column is never considered a numeric column; you always use it only for labels.

To display the tab ruler

Press	**Ctrl-F3** to display the Screen menu.
Press	**1** for **Window**, and the status line reads # *Lines in this Window: 24.*
Press	↑ to display the tab ruler at the bottom of the screen.
Press	**Return** to return to the document.

To change tab stops

Press	**Home, Home,** ↑ to move the cursor to the beginning of the document.
Press	**Shift-F8** to display the Line Format menu.
Press	**1** for **Tabs** to display the tab ruler.
Press	**Ctrl-End** to delete all tab stops.
Type	**10,30** and then press **Return** to set tab stops every thirty columns beginning in column 10.
Press	**F7** to return to the document.

Result. The tab ruler shows the new tab stop settings in columns 40 and 70.

Step 2. Enter Table Headings. Enter the table headings shown in Figure 3-28. Press **Spacebar** once to indent the Item and Total labels.

TABLE 3-23
Math Definition Menu Choices

---

0 = Calculation
Calculation columns are for entering formulas in. These formulas can refer to numbers entered or calculated in other columns. You create formulas with operators that tell the program you want to add, subtract, multiply, or divide. These operators can be used in combinations or by themselves. There are also special operators that calculate averages and the like that must be used alone; you cannot combine them with other operators or values. After entering a formula, press **Return**.

Operators That Can Be Used in Combinations
+	Adds, for example, 100+200 or A+B (to add numbers in column A and numbers in column B)
-	Subtracts, for example, 200-100 or B-A (to subtract numbers in column A from numbers in column B)
*	Multiplies, for example, .1*100 or .1*A (to multiply 10% by the numbers in column A)
/	Divides, for example, 200/100 or B/A (to divide the numbers in column A into the numbers in column B)

Operators That Must Be Used by Themselves
+	Adds numbers in the numeric columns on the same row as the operator
+/	Averages numbers in the numeric columns on the same row as the operator
=	Adds numbers in the total columns on the same row as the operator
=/	Averages numbers in the total columns on the same row as the operator

1 = Text
Text columns are for descriptive labels. Numbers in these columns are not calculated.

2 = Numeric
Numeric columns are for calculating subtotals, totals, and grand totals.

3 = Total
Total columns are for calculating and displaying totals of the numbers in the columns to their immediate left.

TABLE 3-24
Entering Calculation Codes in Numeric Columns

Code	Description
+	To calculate a subtotal, enter a plus sign (+) in the column and on the line immediately below the numbers to be added.
=	To calculate a total, enter an equal sign (=) in the column and on the line immediately below the numbers to be added. To calculate a total, you must first enter codes to calculate one or more subtotals.
*	To add one or more totals (a grand total), enter an asterisk (*) in the column and on the line immediately below the numbers to be added. To calculate a grand total, you must first enter codes to calculate one or more totals.
N	To force any calculation to be displayed and treated as a negative number, type an uppercase *N* in front of any subtotal, total, or grand total code; for example, type **N+**, **N=**, or **N***. This is useful on certain types of financial statements where columns of added numbers, although positive, should be treated as negative in subsequent calculations.

FIGURE 3-28
Math document table
headings

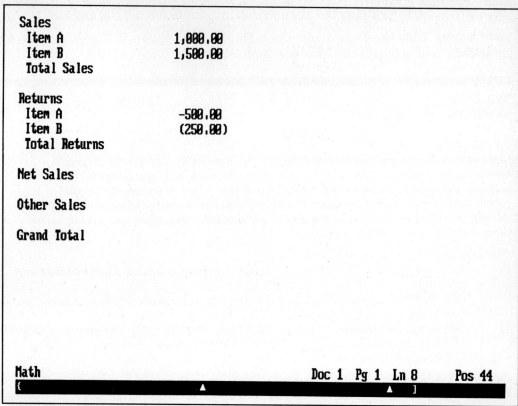

```
Sales
  Item A              1,000.00
  Item B              1,500.00
  Total Sales

Returns
  Item A              -500.00
  Item B              (250.00)
  Total Returns

Net Sales

Other Sales

Grand Total




Math                        Doc 1  Pg 1  Ln 8      Pos 44
```

Step 3. Turn Math On and Off. Enter codes at the top and bottom of the table to turn math mode on and off.

To turn on math mode

Press   Home, Home, ↑ to move the cursor to the beginning of the document.

Press   **Alt-F7** to display the Math/Columns menu.

Press   **1** for **Math On**, and the status line reads *Math*.

To turn off math mode

Press   **Home, Home,** ↓ to move the cursor to the end of the document.

Press   **Return** if necessary to move the cursor to the line below the Grand Total line.

Press   **Alt-F7** to display the Math/Columns menu.

Press   **1** for **Math Off**, and the status line no longer reads *Math*.

Result. Math mode is on within the lines covered by the table. Move the cursor to the last blank line, and the indicator *Math* on the status line disappears. Move it back to the Grand Total line, and it reappears.

Step 4. Enter Numbers. The first column is always defined as a text column. To do calculations, you must enter numbers in a numeric column (Figure 3-29). The default setting is for all columns except the first to be numeric.

To enter numbers

Move   the cursor to the Item A line under the Sales heading.

Press   **End** to move the cursor to the right end of the line.

Press   **Tab** to move the cursor to the tab stop. (The status line reads *Align Char =.* when the cursor is in the correct column.)

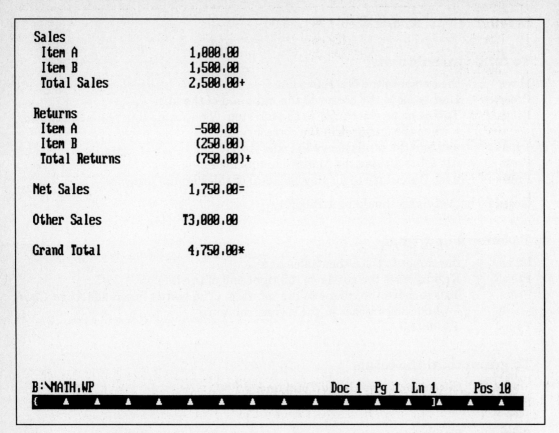

```
Sales
  Item A               1,000.00
  Item B               1,500.00
  Total Sales          2,500.00+

Returns
  Item A                -500.00
  Item B                (250.00)
  Total Returns         (750.00)+

Net Sales              1,750.00=

Other Sales           T3,000.00

Grand Total            4,750.00*




B:\MATH.WP                          Doc 1  Pg 1  Ln 1        Pos 10
{     ▲     ▲     ▲     ▲     ▲     ▲     ▲     ▲     ▲     ▲     ▲   ]▲    ▲     ▲
```

FIGURE 3-29
Math document
numbers

Type   **1,000.00.**

Result. The number aligns in the decimal tab column. Use the same steps to enter the rest of the sales and returns numbers, including the commas and decimal points, shown in Figure 3-29. Notice that you can enter negative numbers preceded by a minus sign or enclosed in parentheses.

Step 5. Enter Operators and Calculate. Now enter operators that specify the calculations to be performed.

To subtotal two numbers

Move   the cursor to the Total Sales on the fourth line.
Press   **End** to move the cursor to the right end of the line.
Press   **Tab** to move the cursor to the tab stop. (The status line reads *Align Char* = when the cursor is in the correct column.)
Type   **+** to add the numbers above the operator.
Press   **Alt-F7** to display the Math/Columns menu.
Press   **2** for **Calculate** to display the total sales of items A and B.

Result. The Total Sales should be 2,500.00+.

To subtotal two negative numbers

Move   the cursor to the Total Returns line.
Press   **End** to move the cursor to the right end of the line.
Press   **Tab** to move the cursor to the tab stop. (The status line reads *Align Char* = when the cursor is in the correct column.)
Type   **+** to add the numbers above the operator.
Press   **Alt-F7** to display the Math/Columns menu.
Press   **2** for **Calculate** to display the total returns of items A and B.

Result. The Total Returns should be (750.00)+.

To total two subtotals

Move	the cursor to the Net Sales line.
Press	**End** to move the cursor to the right end of the line.
Press	**Tab** to move the cursor to the tab stop. (The status line reads *Align Char* = when the cursor is in the correct column.)
Type	= to add the totals above the operator.
Press	**Alt-F7** to display the Math/Columns menu.
Press	**2** for **Calculate** to display the total of sales minus returns.

Result. The Net Sales should be 1,750.00=.

To enter a new total

Move	the cursor to the Other Sales line.
Press	**End** to move the cursor to the right end of the line.
Press	**Tab** to move the cursor to the tab stop. (The status line reads *Align Char* = when the cursor is in the correct column.)
Type	**T3,000.00.**

To grand total the totals

Move	the cursor to the Grand Total line.
Press	**End** to move the cursor to the right end of the line.
Press	**Tab** to move the cursor to the tab stop. (The status line reads *Align Char* = when the cursor is in the correct column.)
Type	* (that is, press **Shift-***) to add the totals above the operator.
Press	**Alt-F7** to display the Math/Columns menu.
Press	**2** for **Calculate** to display the grand total of the subtotals and the other sales.

Result. The Grand Total should be 4,750.00*. All your results should match those shown in Figure 3-30.

FIGURE 3-30
Math document final results

```
Sales
   Item A              1,000.00                    0.21!
   Item B              1,500.00                    0.32!
   Total Sales         2,500.00+                   0.53!

Returns
   Item A               -500.00                   (0.11)!
   Item B               (250.00)                  (0.05)!
   Total Returns        (750.00)+                 (0.16)!

Net Sales             1,750.00=                    0.37!

Other Sales           T3,000.00                    0.63!

Grand Total           4,750.00*                    1.00!




Math                                  Doc 1  Pg 1  Ln 1      Pos 10
```

Step 6. Define a Calculation Column. You can define as many as four columns to perform additional calculations. To do so, display and modify the settings on the math definition screen. Let's define the second numeric column, the one to the right of the current numbers, as a calculation column. You then enter a formula that divides each of the numbers by $4,750, the grand total.

To display the math definitions screen

Press   **Home, Home, Home,** ↑ to move the cursor to the beginning of the document above any codes. (The status line should not read *Math*.)

Press   **Alt-F7** to display the Math/Columns menu.

Press   **2** for **Math Def.**

Result. The math definitions screen appears (Figure 3-31). The second line lists columns A through X. The third line shows the current type of each column. They are all defined as 2, that is, numeric columns.

To define a calculation column

Press   → to move the cursor to under the 2 in column B.

Type   **0** for **Calculation,** and the cursor jumps to the line that reads *Calculation 1*.

Type   **A/4750,** and then press **Return.**

Press   **F7** to return to the Math/Columns menu.

Press   **0** to remove the Math/Columns menu and return to the document.

Result. No result is immediately obvious on the screen, but you have defined the last column beginning in column 70 as a calculation column. The formula you specified for this column will divide the number in column A, the first numeric column (remember the first column is not considered a math column), by 4750, the grand total.

Step 7. Calculate the Results. To calculate the results, begin by moving the cursor to the right of each number, and then press **Tab** to move the cursor to the next tab stop. The status line reads *Pos 70,* and an exclamation mark (!) appears to indicate a number will be calculated in that position.

FIGURE 3-31
Math definition screen

```
Math Definition          Use arrow keys to position cursor

Columns                  A B C D E F G H I J K L M N O P Q R S T U V W X

Type                     2 2 2 2 2 2 2 2 2 2 2 2 2 2 2 2 2 2 2 2 2 2 2 2

Negative Numbers         ( ( ( ( ( ( ( ( ( ( ( ( ( ( ( ( ( ( ( ( ( ( ( (

# of digits to           2 2 2 2 2 2 2 2 2 2 2 2 2 2 2 2 2 2 2 2 2 2 2 2
the right (8-4)

Calculation    1
Formulas       2
               3
               4

Type of Column:
      0 = Calculation    1 = Text     2 = Numeric    3 = Total

Negative Numbers
      ( = Parenthesis (50.00)       - = Minus Sign  -50.00

Press EXIT when done
```

To calculate the formulas in column B

Move	the cursor to the Item A line.
Press	**End** to move the cursor to the right end of the line.
Press	**Tab** to move the cursor to the tab stop. (An exclamation point appears in front of the cursor when it is in the correct column.)
Press	**Alt-F7** to display the Math/Columns menu.
Press	**2** for **Calculate**.

Result. The status line reads * *Please Wait* *, and in a moment, the calculated results are displayed followed by exclamation points. Use the same steps to calculate the rest of the percentages shown in Figure 3-32.

To remove the tab ruler from the bottom of the screen, press **Ctrl-F3** to display the Screen menu. Press **1** for **Window**, and the status line reads # *Lines in this Window: 23*. Press ↓, and then press **Return**.

Step 8. Print the Results. Be sure that the printer is on and has paper in it and that the paper is aligned.

To print the table

Press	**Shift-F7** to display the Print menu.
Press	**1** for **Full text**.

Result. The printer immediately begins printing. Operators displayed on the screen are not printed.

Step 9. Continue or Quit. You have now completed this exercise. Either clear the screen and continue to work, or quit and return to the operating system. In either case, you should first save the document.

To save the document and clear the screen or quit

Press	**F7**, and the status line reads *Save Document? (Y/N) Y*.
Press	**Y**, and the status line reads *Document to be Saved:*.
Type	**B:\MATH.WP**, and then press **Return**. The status line reads *Exit WP? (Y/N) N*.
Press	**N** to clear the screen, or press **Y** to quit.

FIGURE 3-32
Calculation column
results

```
Total Sales         2,500.00+              0.53!

Returns
Item A               -500.00              (0.11)!
Items B              (250.00)             (0.05)!
Total Returns        (750.00)+            (0.16)!

Net Sales           1,750.00=              0.37!

Other Sales         T3,000.00             0.63!

Grand Total         4,750.00*             1.00!




Math                               Doc 1  Pg 1  Ln 15      Pos 69
[                        ▲                      ▲  ]
```

Result. If you cleared the screen, it is blank, so you can continue with your own work. If you quit the program, the operating system A> or B> prompt is displayed on the screen. Remove your program and data disks, and then turn off the computer or load another program.

TIPS

■ **If columns are so narrow that numbers overlap,** your calculations will be incorrect. Reset the tab stops to allow more room.

QUESTIONS

1. What are math functions used for?
2. What math functions can word processing programs generally perform? What additional functions can they perform if they have advanced features?
3. What is an operator?
4. Why is the order of operations important?
5. Which operators can be used in combinations? Which must be used by themselves?
6. What is the difference between a numeric column and a text column?
7. How can you enter negative numbers?

TOPIC 3-20
Creating Automatically Generated Lists

In this topic, we introduce you to the following procedures:

■ Creating a table of contents
■ Creating an index
■ Creating lists

BACKGROUND

When working on a long document with many sections, you often need to prepare a table of contents or an index to help readers find the information they need. Both of these lists refer to subjects in the document and provide page numbers for them. Manually preparing these references takes a great deal of time, and if any revisions are made to the document, all page number references might have to be changed. Many word processing programs now allow you to automatically prepare these lists.

In a program that allows you to automatically create indexes and tables of contents, you first enter codes to indicate which items in the text are to be listed. You then generate and print a table of contents, an index, or another kind of list, for example, a list of all illustrations or tables in the document. With WordPerfect, you can automatically generate a table of contents, an index, and as many as six lists.

- Tables of contents can have as many as five levels. Each level is indented one tab stop from the previous level.
- Indexes can list words or phrases appearing in your document.
- As many as six lists can catalog various items in a document. When you generate the lists, entries are listed in the order they appear in.

To create automatically generated lists, you normally follow three steps: coding, definition, and generation.

CODING

To specify the entries to appear in the automatically generated list, you must code the appropriate sections in the document. You can specify the level of the heading so that subtopics are listed and indented under topics assigned a higher level; for example, your document may have parts, and each part may have sections. You would specify that the part headings are a level 1 entry, and the section headings are a level 2 entry. When you generate the table of contents or index, the level 2 entries are indented under the level 1 entries.

DEFINITION

To define the automatically generated list, you move the cursor to where in the document you want it to appear. You then specify the type of list it is, for example, a table of contents, an index, or a list. You can also specify how many levels to include and whether to indicate page numbers. Some programs automatically generate the index, table of contents, or other list at the end of the document or even store it in another file.

GENERATION

Once you have defined the automatically generated list and coded the entries, you execute the command that generates the list. The program then searches through the document for the coded entries, calculates their level and page numbers, and displays the list where you entered the definition code or at the end of the document. If you make changes to the document, you must generate the lists again to update them.

EXERCISE 73

Creating a Table of Contents

In this exercise, you code, define, and generate a table of contents. To begin this exercise, you must load the program or clear the screen of any other document.

Step 1. Enter Document. Enter the document shown in Figure 3-33. You can center the heading by pressing **Shift-F6** before typing it.

Step 2. Code Entries for Table of Contents. Now that you have entered headings for the document you can code them.

To code level 1 entries for the table of contents

Move	the cursor to the first *T* in *TABLE OF CONTENTS*.
Press	**Alt-F4**, and the status line flashes *Block on:*.
Press	**End** to highlight the line.

```
                    DOCUMENT

TABLE OF CONTENTS
Coding Headings for the Table of Contents
Defining the Table of Contents
Generating the Table of Contents
INDEXES
Coding Entries for the Index
Defining the Index
Generating the Index










B:\TOC.WP                        Doc 1  Pg 1  Ln 11      Pos 10
```

FIGURE 3-33
Document for table
of contents

Press   **Alt-F5** to display the Mark Text menu.
Press   **1** for **ToC**, and the status line reads *ToC Level:*.
Press   **1.**
Move   the cursor to the *I* in *INDEXES*.
Press   **Alt-F4**, and the status line flashes *Block on:*.
Press   **End** to highlight the line.
Press   **Alt-F5** to display the Mark Text menu.
Press   **1** for **ToC**, and the status line reads *ToC Level:*.
Press   **1.**

To code level 2 entries for the table of contents

Move   the cursor to the first *C* in *Coding Headings for the Table of Contents*.
Press   **Alt-F4**, and the status line flashes *Block on:*.
Press   **End** to highlight the line.
Press   **Alt-F5** to display the Mark Text menu.
Press   **1** for **ToC**, and the status line reads *ToC Level:*.
Press   **2.**

Result. You have coded only one level 2 heading. Repeat these same steps to code each of the other level 2 headings (those not entirely in uppercase). Nothing is obvious on the screen, but if you press **Alt-F3** to reveal codes, you see the table of contents codes. The code *[Mark:ToC,1]* begins each level 1 entry, and *[EndMark:ToC,1]* ends each. The code *[Mark:ToC,2]* begins each level 2 entry, and *[EndMark:ToC,2]* ends each. Press any key to return to the document.

Step 3. Define the Table of Contents. Now you define the table of contents. You enter the definition code where you want the table of contents to appear.

To define the table of contents

Press	**Home, Home,** ↑ to move the cursor to the beginning of the document.
Press	**Ctrl-Return** to enter a hard page break.
Press	↑ to move the cursor to the new first page.
Press	**Shift-F6** to center the cursor, and then type **TABLE OF CONTENTS**.
Press	**Return** twice.
Press	**Alt-F5** to display the Mark Text menu.
Press	**6** for **Other Options** to display the Other Mark Text Options menu.
Press	**2** for **Define Table of Contents**, and the prompt reads *Number of levels in table of contents (1-5):*.
Press	**2**, and the prompt reads *Display last level in wrapped format? (Y/N) N.*
Press	**N**, and the cursor jumps to the **Page Number Position** column.
Press	**Return** twice to accept the suggested settings and return to the document screen.

Step 4. Generate Table of Contents. Now that the entries have been coded and the table of contents defined, you can generate a table of contents.

To generate the table of contents

Press	**Alt-F5** to display the Mark Text menu.
Press	**6** for **Other Options** to display the Other Mark Text Options menu.
Press	**8** for **Generate Tables and Index**, and the status line reads *Existing tables, lists, and indexes will be replaced. Continue? (Y/N): Y.*
Press	**Y** since you have not yet created them.

Result. The status line reads *Generation in progress* and displays a counter to keep you informed that progress is being made. In a moment, the table of contents appears below the heading on the first page (Figure 3-34). If you were working on a long document, and made revisions that affected its length, you would use this command to generate a new, up-to-date, table of contents. You would delete the existing table of contents first, or type **N** when the prompt reads *Have you deleted your old Table of Contents, Lists and Index? (Y/N) N*. The current table of contents would then be highlighted, and a prompt would ask if you wanted to delete it.

FIGURE 3-34
Generated table of contents

```
                          TABLE OF CONTENTS


TABLE OF CONTENTS . . . . . . . . . . . . . . . . . . . . . .   2
      Coding Headings for the Table of Contents . . . . . . .   2
      Defining the Table of Contents . . . . . . . . . . . .    2
      Generating the Table of Contents . . . . . . . . . . .    2


INDEXES . . . . . . . . . . . . . . . . . . . . . . . . . . .   2
      Coding Entries for the Index . . . . . . . . . . . . .    2
      Defining the Index . . . . . . . . . . . . . . . . . .    2
      Generating the Index . . . . . . . . . . . . . . . . .    2


===============================================================
                          DOCUMENT

TABLE OF CONTENTS
Coding Headings for the Table of Contents
Defining the Table of Contents
Generating the Table of Contents
INDEXES
Coding Entries for the Index
Defining the Index
Generating the Index
B:\TOC.WP                            Doc 1  Pg 1  Ln 1      Pos 18
```

Step 5. Print the Results. Be sure that the printer is on and has paper in it and that the paper is aligned.

To print the table

Press   Shift-F7 to display the Print menu.

Press   **1** for **Full text**.

Result. The printer immediately begins printing.

Step 6. Continue or Quit. You have now completed this exercise. Either clear the screen and continue to work, or quit and return to the operating system. In either case, you should first save the document.

To save the document and clear the screen or quit

Press   **F7**, and the status line reads *Save Document? (Y/N) Y*.

Press   **Y**, and the status line reads *Document to be Saved:*.

Type   **B:\TOC.WP**, and then press **Return**. The status line reads *Exit WP? (Y/N) N*.

Press   **N** to clear the screen, or press **Y** to quit.

Result. If you cleared the screen, it is blank, so you can continue with your own work. If you quit the program, the operating system A> or B> prompt is displayed on the screen. Remove your program and data disks, and then turn off the computer or load another program.

EXERCISE 74

Creating an Index

You can code the entries in a document so that they are listed in the index as headings or subheadings. For example, if your index consists of a straight listing of entries, code each as a heading, and do not specify a subheading. If you want to group selected entries under a broader heading, specify a heading, and then code the entry as a subheading. When you generate the index, all subheadings appear under the heading you specified. Try entering a paragraph and indexing key terms in it using the following instructions:

To code entries for an index

1. Either move the cursor to under any character in the word to be included in the index.

    Or   select more than one adjacent word (including any format codes to be included).

2. Press **Alt-F5** to display the Mark Text menu.

3. Press **5** for **Index**, and the status line reads *Index Heading:* followed by the selected text.

4. Either press **Return** if the entry is not to appear under a heading.

    Or   type the name of the heading the entry is to be listed under in the index, and then press **Return**.

    The status line reads *Subheading:*.

5. Either press **Return** if the entry is not to appear under a heading or if it is to appear under a heading as is.

    Or   press **Return** to specify another subheading, and then press **Return** to return to the document screen.

6. Repeat steps 1 through 5 for each entry.

To define an index

1. Move the cursor to where the beginning of the index is to appear.
2. Press **Alt-F5** to display the Mark Text menu.
3. Press **6** for **Other Options** to display the Other Mark Text Options menu.
4. Press **5** for **Define Index**, and the status line reads *Concordance Filename (Enter=none):*.
5. Either press **Return** to continue without a concordance file.

   Or   type the name of the concordance file, and then press **Return**.

   The Index Definition menu appears.
6. Press **1** through **5** to select the kind of numbering you want to use, and you then return to the document screen.

To generate an index

1. Press **Alt-F5** to display the Mark Text menu.
2. Press **6** for **Other Options** to display the Other Mark Text Options menu.
3. Press **8** for **Generate Tables and Index**, and the status line reads *Existing tables, lists, and indexes will be replaced. Continue? (Y/N): Y.*
4. Press **Y** to continue.

EXERCISE 75

Creating a List

Frequently, reports, term papers, and other manuscripts have figure titles, table titles, or other repetitive elements that you might want to list separately, perhaps in a list following the table of contents or the end of the document. With WordPerfect, you can create as many as six lists much as you create a table of contents. Create a document and try listing its elements using the following instructions:

To code entries for a list

1. Select the block, including any format codes to be included.
2. Press **Alt-F5** to display the Mark Text menu.
3. Press **2** for **List**, and the status line reads *List #:*.
4. Type the number of the list (you can define as many as five), and you then return to the document screen.
5. Repeat steps 1 through 4 for each entry.

To define a list

1. Move the cursor to where the beginning of the list is to appear.
2. Press **Alt-F5** to display the Mark Text menu.
3. Press **6** for **Other Options** to display the Other Mark Text Options menu.
4. Press **3** for **Define List**, and the status line reads *Enter List Number (1-5):*.
5. Press **1** through **5** to define any one of five lists and display the List Definition menu for that list.
6. Press **1** through **5** to select the kind of numbering you want to use, and you then return to the document screen.

To generate a list

1. Press **Alt-F5** to display the Mark Text menu.
2. Press **6** for **Other Options** to display the Other Mark Text Options menu.
3. Press **8** for **Generate Tables and Index**, and the status line reads *Existing tables, lists, and indexes will be replaced. Continue? (Y/N): Y.*
4. Press **Y** to continue.

- **If you boldface or underline entries to be included in a table of contents, index, or list**, the placement of the codes is important. If the boldface and underline codes are inside the codes that mark the entries, the entries will be boldfaced or underlined when you generate the lists. If they are outside the codes, the entries will not be affected by them.

- **Tables of contents with more than one level automatically indent to tab stops**. If you want to change the indent, revise the tab stops above the table of contents definition code.

- **You can generate tables of contents at different levels**. For example, you can code entries as many as five levels deep but define the table of contents so that it generates only the first level of entries. You can then delete the definition code and redefine it for any other number of levels. This is helpful when working on long projects where you want to address organization at several levels.

- **When creating an index, you can code each entry in the text or create a concordance**. A concordance is a master list of words that you want listed in the index. You create this list and save it just like a normal document. When you generate the index, you can specify the name of this file, and the program searches the current document for the words listed in the concordance and adds them to the index. When creating the concordance file, keep the following rules in mind:

  - Each word or phrase must end with a hard carriage return.

  - You can add index marks to any entry. They should follow the word or phrase but precede the hard carriage return. If you do not enter any index marks, the phrase appears in the index as a major heading. If you do enter index marks, the word or phrase itself is not listed, but the page number the word or phrase appears on is listed under the heading or subheading you enter in the index marks.

  - A word or phrase may be as long as needed.

  - The number of entries in the file is limited by your computer's memory. If you have too many entries, an error message reads *Not enough memory to use entire concordance file. Continue? (Y/N)*. Press **Y** to use the part of the concordance file that does fit into memory, or press **N** to exit from index generation.

  - **Always save your file before using the command that generates tables, indexes and lists**. If you have incorrectly placed codes, you can loose your entire file.

QUESTIONS

1. What three kinds of automatically generated lists can you generate in a long document?
2. What are the three basic steps to creating automatically generated lists?
3. What is the difference between a level 1 heading and a level 2 heading?
4. What is a concordance?
5. Why is it important to save your work before using the command that generates tables, indexes, and lists?

TOPIC 3-21
Entering Footnotes

In this topic, we introduce you to the following procedures:

- Entering footnotes
- Editing footnotes
- Changing footnote options

BACKGROUND

Footnotes are numbered references printed at the bottom of the page. The numbers in the footnotes match the numbers in the text that refer to the footnotes. For example, when typing a term paper your document may cite an author. Immediately following the author's name, you can enter a footnote reference number. At the bottom of the same page, you then enter the same number followed by the title of the book, publisher, publication date, and page number cited. Endnotes are just like footnotes, but instead of being entered at the bottom of the same page as the reference number, they are entered at the end of a section or chapter.

Many programs, including WordPerfect, allow you to enter footnotes and endnotes any place in the document. The program then automatically numbers the footnote references in the document and either prints footnotes on the same page as the references to them or prints endnotes at the end of the document.

The procedures for entering footnotes vary. On some programs, you enter the footnote on a specific footnote page and then enter a code in the document where you want its reference number to appear. On other programs, you position the cursor where you want the footnote reference number to be printed and execute the footnote command. A special footnote screen appears on which you type, edit, and format your footnote. When you are finished, you quit the footnote procedure, and the document screen reappears.

When you print the document, the codes entered in the document are converted into a series of sequential numbers, and the footnotes they refer to are printed on the bottom of the same page. To do this, the program first has to calculate the length of the footnote, in lines, and then stop printing the text so that enough lines are available to print the footnote.

When you insert new footnotes or delete old ones, all footnote references in the document are automatically renumbered.

When you use WordPerfect's command to edit a footnote or an endnote, the program searches for the next note following the cursor and asks if you want to edit that note. You can either accept it or enter a new number.

EXERCISE 76

Entering Footnotes

In this exercise, you enter footnotes. To begin this exercise, you must load the program or clear the screen of any other document.

Step 1. Create Document. Begin by entering the paragraph shown in Figure 3-35.

Step 2. Enter a Footnote. You can enter footnotes anywhere in the document. Here you enter a footnote that follows the MLA guidelines. Underline the title in the footnote by pressing **F8** to begin underlining and then again to end it.

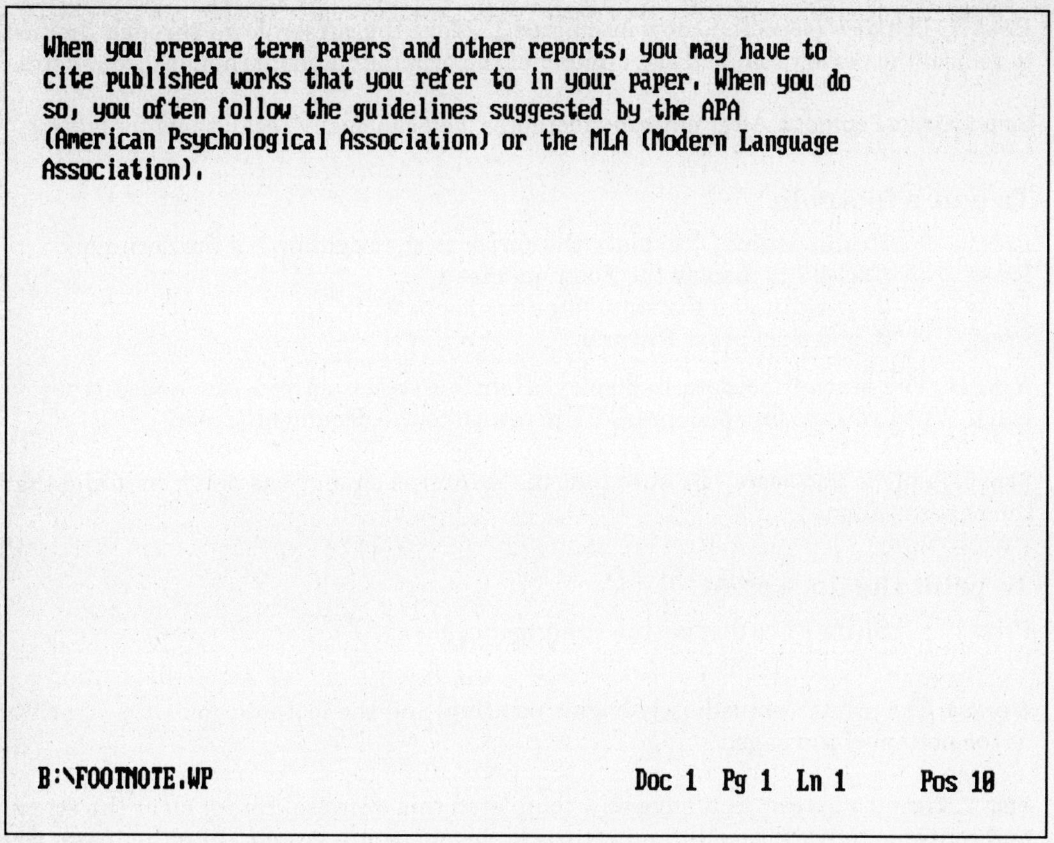

FIGURE 3-35
Document for
footnotes

```
When you prepare term papers and other reports, you may have to
cite published works that you refer to in your paper. When you do
so, you often follow the guidelines suggested by the APA
(American Psychological Association) or the MLA (Modern Language
Association).




















B:\FOOTNOTE.WP                        Doc 1  Pg 1  Ln 1      Pos 10
```

To enter a footnote

Move	the cursor to the space following the abbreviation MLA.
Press	**Ctrl-F7** to display the Footnote menu.
Press	**1** for **Create**, and the screen goes blank except for the number 1.
Type	**Troyka, Lynn Quitman. <u>Simon & Schuster Handbook for Writers</u>. Englewood Cliffs: Prentice Hall, 1987.**
Press	**F7** to return to the document screen.

Result. The number 1 at the cursor position is the footnote number.

Step 3. Reveal Codes. To see the footnote code, press **Alt-F3**. The code begins with *[Note:Foot,1;[Note#1,* followed by the first fifty characters of the footnote. It ends with *...],* indicating there is more to the footnote that is not displayed. Press **Spacebar** to return to the document screen.

Step 4. Enter Another Footnote. Enter another footnote above the first one to see how the program automatically numbers them. Here you enter the same footnote you entered in Step 2, but this time you use the APA guidelines.

To enter a footnote

Move	the cursor to the space following the closing parenthesis after (American Psychological Association).
Press	**Spacebar**, and then type **(Troyka, 1987)**.
Press	**Ctrl-F7** to display the Footnote menu.
Press	**1** for **Create**, and the screen goes blank except for the number 1.
Type	**Troyka, L (1987). <u>Simon & Schuster Handbook for Writers.</u> Englewood Cliffs: Prentice Hall.**
Press	**F7** to return to the document screen.

Result. The new footnote is now numbered 1. Move the cursor down through the text to reform the paragraph, and the number of the original footnote changes from 1 to 2.

Step 5. Edit a Footnote. After entering footnotes, you can easily recall them for editing.

To edit a footnote

Press	**Home, Home,** ↑ to move the cursor to the beginning of the document.
Press	**Ctrl-F7** to display the Footnote menu.
Press	**2** for **Edit**, and the status line reads *Ftn #? 1.*
Press	**2**, and then press **Return**.

Result. The second footnote is displayed on the screen so you can revise it if you want. When you are finished, press **F7** to return to the document screen.

Step 6. Print the Document. Be sure that the printer is on and has paper in it and that the paper is aligned.

To print the document

| Press | **Shift-F7** to display the Print menu. |
| Press | **1** for **Full text**. |

Result. The printer immediately begins printing, and the footnote you entered prints at the bottom of the page.

Step 7. Clear the Screen. You have now completed this exercise. Either clear the screen and continue to work, or quit and return to the operating system. In either case, you should first save the document.

To save the document and clear the screen or quit

Press	**F7**, and the status line reads *Save Document? (Y/N) Y.*
Press	**Y**, and the status line reads *Document to be Saved:.*
Type	**B:\FOOTNOTE.WP**, and then press **Return**. The status line reads *Exit WP? (Y/N) N.*
Press	**N** to clear the screen, or press **Y** to quit.

Result. If you cleared the screen, it is blank, just as it was when you began this exercise. If you quit the program, the operating system A> or B> prompt is displayed on the screen. Remove your program and data disks, and then turn off the computer or load another program.

EXERCISE 77

Changing Footnote Options

When you enter footnotes, they are printed using the program's default settings. But you can change these default settings using the options provided. Using the document you created in Exercise 76, change some of the options, and then print the document so that you can see the results.

To change footnote and endnote options

1. Press **Ctrl-F7** to display the Footnote menu.
2. Press **4** for **Options** to display the Footnote Options menu (Figure 3-36).
3. Make any of the changes described in Table 3-25.
4. Press **0** to return to the document screen.

FIGURE 3-36
Footnote options
screen

```
Footnote Options

        1 - Spacing within notes           1
        2 - Spacing between notes          1
        3 - Lines to keep together         3
        4 - Start footnote numbers each page   N
        5 - Footnote numbering mode        0
        6 - Endnote numbering mode         0
        7 - Line separating text and footnotes  1
        8 - Footnotes at bottom of page    Y
        9 - Characters for notes           *
        A - String for footnotes in text      [SuprScrpt][Note]
        B - String for endnotes in text       [SuprScrpt][Note]
        C - String for footnotes in note           [SuprScrpt][Note]
        D - String for endnotes in note       [Note],

    For options 5 & 6:          For option 7:
        0 - Numbers                 0 - No line
        1 - Characters              1 - 2 inch line
        2 - Letters                 2 - Line across entire page
                                    3 - 2 in, line w/continued strings


    Selection: 0
```

TIPS

- **To delete an endnote or a footnote,** delete the code you entered to create it. Table 3-4 lists footnote and endnote codes.

- **If you change the margins in your document** after entering footnotes and endnotes, you must reset their margins. You can automatically do this by spell checking the document (see Topic 3-6), counting the words in the document (see Topic 3-6), or editing each note so that it appears on the screen and then exiting.

- **Endnotes print below the last hard carriage return on the last page of the document.** To print endnotes on a separate page, put a hard page break (**Ctrl-Return**) after the last line of text in the document. To add a heading, type it on the last page, and then press **Return** two or three times so that the first endnote prints that number of lines below the heading.

- **To override automatic numbering and change a footnote or endnote reference number,** move the cursor under the reference number in the document, and then press **Ctrl-F7**. Press **3** for **New #,** and the status line reads *Note #?* Type the new number, and then press **Return**. All the following numbers change to reflect the change in the renumbered reference.

- **To search or search and replace in footnotes and endnotes,** press **Home, F2** to use the extended search command (see Topic 3-5).

QUESTIONS

1. How does a footnote differ from an endnote?
2. When you reveal codes, you may see a footnote code that ends with ...*].* What does this indicate?
3. When you execute the command to edit a footnote, in which direction from the cursor does the program look for a footnote code.
4. List and describe four things you can change with footnote options.

TABLE 3-25
Footnote and Endnote Options

1 - *Spacing within notes* controls the line spacing within the note.

2 - *Spacing between notes* controls the line spacing between notes when more than one appears on the same page.

3 - *Lines to keep together* controls the number of lines kept together on the same page when the footnote spills onto another page. (The default is 3.) It also controls the number of lines kept together when an endnote spills onto another page.

4 - *Start footnote numbers each page* controls whether footnote numbers run consecutively throughout the document or start over on each page of the document. (The default is N for consecutive numbering.)

5 - *Footnote numbering mode* controls the way footnotes are numbered. 0 is for numbers, 1 is for characters, and 2 is for letters. (The default is 0 for numbers.)

6 - *Endnote numbering mode* controls the way endnotes are numbered. 0 is for numbers, 1 is for characters, and 2 is for letters. (The default is 0 for numbers.)

7 - *Line separating text and footnotes* controls whether a line separates footnotes from the last line of the document. 0 is for no line, 1 is for a 2-inch line, 2 is for a line across the entire page, and 3 is for a 2-inch line, and if the footnote continues to the next page, it prints "Continued..." on the last line of the first page and "...Continued" on the first footnote line of the following page above where the footnote continues. (The default is 1 for a 2-inch line.)

8 - *Footnotes at bottom of page* controls where footnotes print when the page is not full. (The default is for them to print immediately after the last line of text, not at the bottom of the page.)

9 - *Characters for notes* controls the characters used as references when you select character mode for footnotes or endnotes. You can specify as many as five characters. (The default is a single asterisk.) If you specify a single character, like the asterisk, the number of characters indicates the sequence. For example, * indicates the first reference, ** the second, *** the third, and so on. If you specify more than one character, they cycle to indicate the sequence. For example, if you specify * and #, the first reference is *, the second #, the third **, the fourth ##, and so on.

A - *String for footnotes in text* controls the style of your notes. For example, you can change character attributes (boldface, underline, and the like), superscript and subscript, or enter spaces to indent them from the left margin.

B - *String for endnotes in text* is the same as *A - String for footnotes in text*. (The default is for superscripted numbers.)

C - *String for footnotes in note* is the same as *A - String for footnotes in text*. (The default is for superscripted numbers and a five-space indent from the left margin.)

D - *String for endnotes in note* is the same as *A - String for footnotes in text*. (The default is for numbers followed by periods.)

TOPIC 3-22
Sorting Data

In this topic, we introduce you to the following procedures:

- Sorting lines and paragraphs
- Sorting secondary files
- Selecting specific records

BACKGROUND

Many programs, like WordPerfect, allow you to **sort**, or arrange, tables, lists, paragraphs, or record files in a desired order. To sort a file, you first determine what information to arrange in order. On most programs, you can sort either the entire document or just a specific section.

After deciding what to sort, you must specify the sort keys and the order of the sort.

SORT KEYS

When you sort a document, you must specify what the program is to use as the basis of the sort. For example, if you want to sort a table that has three columns--name, department, and extension-- you can sort it by any column. Perhaps you want the names in alphabetic order to use as a phone directory or the extensions in numeric order for the maintenance department. When you sort, you must tell the program which column you want to sort by. The column you specify is called a **key**. When you select a key and sort the document, it is sorted based on the key, and all lines, paragraphs, or records are rearranged, not just the column that contains the keys. When you sort using a single key, it is the primary key. You can often also specify a secondary key.

The **primary key** is the field the document is first sorted by. Ideally, a primary key contains unique information, for example, a drivers license number, an employee number, or a social security number. But sometimes a unique field does not exist or serve your purpose, for example, when you sort a file by names. In these cases, a perfect sort is not achieved using only a primary key.

A **secondary key** is specified to break ties after the data has been sorted by the primary key. For example, if you are sorting a file that contains names, you may have more than one Smith or Jones in the file. If you enter their first and last names in separate fields, you can use the secondary key to arrange all the Smiths or Jones into ascending order using their last names as the primary key and their first names as the secondary key.

Some programs provide for more than one secondary key; if any ties occur in the first two sorts, they can be broken by using a third key.

SORT ORDER

The way data is sorted depends on how the program is set up, but usually you must specify either an ascending order or a descending order (see Table 3-26). For example, if you specify an ascending sort, the file is arranged so that any special characters are at the top of the document, followed by numbers arranged from 0 to the highest number, followed by words beginning with uppercase letters from *A* to *Z*, followed by words beginning with lowercase letters from *a* to *z*. If you specify a descending sort, the order of the file is reversed.

TABLE 3-26
Ascending and Descending Sorts

Characters	Ascending	Descending
Special characters	1 (first)	4 (last)
Numbers	2	3
Uppercase letters	3	2
Lowercase letters	4 (last)	1 (first)

SORTING WITH WORDPERFECT

With WordPerfect, you can sort lines, paragraphs, or secondary merge files. To sort only selected sections in a document or secondary merge file, you can select the block to be sorted. When you sort, you are sorting records. The definition of a record depends on whether you are sorting lines, paragraphs, or secondary merge files. Typical records are

- Lines ending in hard or soft carriage returns
- Paragraphs ending with two or more hard carriage returns.
- Secondary merge files separated by ^E (see Topic 3-12).

When you sort, the program displays the Sort by Line menu (Figure 3-37), which lists the options described in Table 3-27. Always save your document before sorting in case something goes wrong. This allows you to exit from the document and retrieve the original file from the disk.

EXERCISE 78

Sorting Data

In this exercise, you use WordPerfect's sorting features. To begin this exercise, you must load the program or clear the screen of any other document.

FIGURE 3-27
Sort by line menu

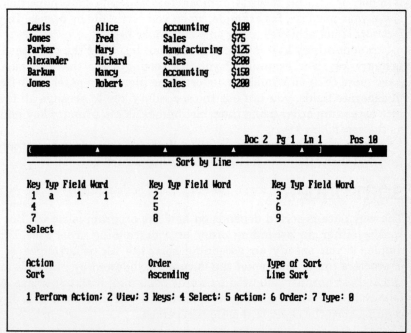

TABLE 3-27
Sort by Line Menu Options

1 Perform Action begins the sort.

2 View lets you scroll through the document.

3 Keys defines the keys' type (alphanumeric or numeric) and indicates their location by field, line, and word. You can enter as many as nine keys. The document is sorted by the first key; if there are any ties, they are broken by the second key and so on through the nine keys. To enter keys, use the left and right arrow keys to move the cursor through the keys. Press **Del** to delete all keys from the cursor to the end of the key listings (expect the first key, where pressing **Del** returns it to the default settings). When specifying keys, you must specify the following:

Type is either alphanumeric or numeric. Alphanumeric types are words made up of numbers and letters of the same length, like phone or social security numbers. Numeric types are numbers of any length that contain only numerals, commas, dollar signs, or periods.

Fields are lines in secondary merge files that end with ^R or text separated by tabs or indents in lines and paragraphs. You count them from top to bottom in secondary merge files, or from left to right in lines and paragraphs.

Lines end in hard or soft carriage returns. To specify lines, you count them from top to bottom, and then enter the line number; or you count them from bottom to top, and then enter a negative line number.

Words are separated by spaces. To specify words, you count them from right to left, and then enter the position of the word on the line or paragraph; or you count them from right to left, and then enter a negative number.

4 Select moves the cursor to *Select* so that you can enter a select statement with logical operators (see Table 3-28). You use this command to select records from a file. For example, you can select only those records that have amounts due of more than $1,000 or that are in the 01945 ZIP code area. The selected records match the criteria you specify. When you enter the select statement, you must enter spaces between keys but not between words and symbols.

To select all records in a file where the ZIP code in field 2 is 01945, enter the select statement **KEY2=01945.**

To select all records where the ZIP code in field 2 is either 01945 or 01946, enter **KEY2=01945 +KEY2=01946.**

To select all records where the ZIP code in field 2 is 01945 and the amount in field 3 is equal to or greater than $100, enter **KEY2=01945 * KEY3>=100.**

To select all records that contain a key word, specify the letter *g* after a key, for example, enter **KEYg=SMITH.**

5 Action chooses between *Select and sort* and *Select only*. Selection occurs only if you have created a select statement.

6 Order specifies ascending or descending sort.

7 Type specifies if sort is a line, paragraph, or merge sort.

TABLE 3-28
Sort Criteria Operators

Operator	Description
+ (OR)	Selects records that match either criteria
* (AND)	Selects records that match both criteria
=	Equal to
<>	Not equal to
	Greater than
<	Less than
=	Greater than or equal to
<=	Less than or equal to

Step 1. Set Tabs. Before creating a table, change the tab stops so that they are every fifteen columns beginning in column 10.

To display the tab ruler

Press	**Ctrl-F3** to display the Screen menu.
Press	**1** for **Window**, and the status line reads *# Lines in this Window: 24.*
Press	↑ to display the tab ruler at the bottom of the screen.
Press	**Return** to return to the document.

To change tab stops

Press	**Home, Home,** ↑ to move the cursor to the beginning of the document.
Press	**Shift-F8** to display the Line Format menu.
Press	**1** for **Tabs** to display the tab ruler.
Press	**Ctrl-End** to delete all tab stops.
Type	**10,15,** and then press **Return** to set tab stops beginning in column 10 every 15 columns.
Press	**F7** to return to the document.

Result. The tab ruler shows the new tab stop settings.

Step 2. Enter List. Using **Tab** to move between the new tab stops, enter the list shown in Figure 3-38.

Step 3. Save the List. When sorting documents, you can easily get unexpected results. Some of these results are difficult or impossible to recover from. Always save a document before you sort it so that you can retrieve the unsorted document if something goes wrong.

To save the list

Press	**F10** to display the prompt *Document to be Saved:.*
Type	**B:\SORT.WP,** and then press **Return**.

Step 4. A Simple Sort by Lines. Here you first select the block you want to sort; in this case, the lines containing the names, departments, and amounts (not the column headings). If you do not select a block, the entire document is sorted.

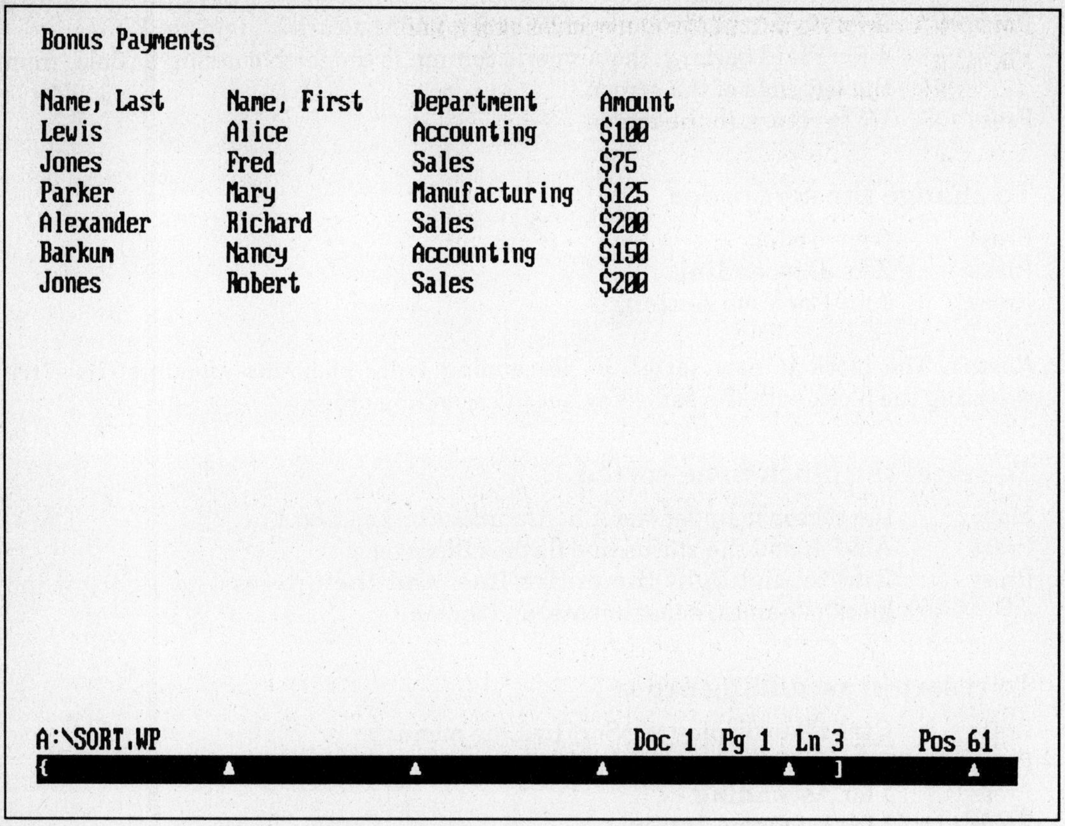

```
Bonus Payments

Name, Last      Name, First     Department       Amount
Lewis           Alice           Accounting       $100
Jones           Fred            Sales            $75
Parker          Mary            Manufacturing    $125
Alexander       Richard         Sales            $200
Barkum          Nancy           Accounting       $150
Jones           Robert          Sales            $200




A:\SORT.WP                              Doc 1  Pg 1  Ln 3        Pos 61
```

FIGURE 3-38
Sort document

To select the block to be sorted

Move   the cursor to under the *L* in *Lewis* on the first line.
Press   **Alt-F4**, and the status line flashes *Block on*.
Press   **End to highlight the entire line, and then press** ↓ to highlight the block of names, departments, and amounts.

To sort the block

Press   **Ctrl-F9** to display the Sort by Line menu.
Press   1 for **Perform Action**.

Result. The sort arranges the rows so that the names in the leftmost column are in alphabetical order because these are the default settings.

Step 5. Change the Sort Key and Order of the Sort. Now change the sort key and order so that the block is sorted by amount in descending order. When specifying keys, the fields are columns separated by tabs and they are counted from left to right.

To select the block to be sorted

Move   the cursor to under the *A* in *Alexander* on the first line.
Press   **Alt-F4**, and the status line flashes *Block on*.
Press   **End to highlight the entire line, and then press** ↓ to highlight the block of names, departments, and amounts.

To change the sort key

Press   **Ctrl-F9** to display the Sort by Line menu.
Press   3 for **Keys**, and the cursor jumps to the definition of key number 1 so that you can describe the type of sort.

Press	**n** for **Typ** to perform a numeric sort, and the cursor jumps to *Field*.
Press	**4** for **Field** because the numeric column is the forth column, or field, from the left edge of the screen.
Press	**F7** to return to the menu.

To change the sort order

Press	**6** for **Order**.
Press	**2** for **Descending**.
Press	**1** for **Perform Action**.

Result. The block is now sorted in descending order of bonus amounts. Now try resorting the block with the same key but in ascending order.

To select the block to be sorted

Move	the cursor to under the *A* in *Alexander* on the first line.
Press	**Alt-F4**, and the status line flashes *Block on*.
Press	**End to highlight the entire line, and then press** ↓ to highlight the block of names, departments, and amounts.

To resort in ascending order

Press	**Ctrl-F9** to display the Sort by Line menu.
Press	**6** for **Order**.
Press	**1** for **Ascending**.
Press	**1** for **Perform Action**.

Result. The block is now sorted in ascending order of bonus amounts.

Step 6. Print the Document. Be sure that the printer is on and has paper in it and that the paper is aligned.

To print the document

Press	**Shift-F7** to display the Print menu.
Press	**1** for **Full text**.

Result. The printer immediately begins printing.

Step 7. Select Records. Frequently, you maintain a master document, from which you select records based on criteria. For example, what if you wanted to send a letter to those people who earned a bonus of $200 or more. To do so, you can select records that meet this criteria from the master list.

To select the block to be sorted

Move	the cursor to under the *J* in *Jones* on the first line.
Press	**Alt-F4**, and the status line flashes *Block on*.
Press	**End to highlight the entire line, and then press** ↓ to highlight the block of names, departments, and amounts. (You may have to press → to highlight the last digit in the amount on the last line.)

To select records

Press	**Ctrl-F9** to display the Sort by Line menu.
Press	**4** for **Select**, and the cursor jumps to *Select*.

Type	key1>=200.
Press	**F7** to return to the menu.
Press	**1** for **Perform Action**.

Result. Only two records remain, both of which have bonuses of $200 or more. The other records are lost. (That is why you saved the document before you began to experiment.) Print the document on the screen.

Step 8. Continue or Quit. You have now completed this exercise. Either clear the screen and continue to work, or quit and return to the operating system.

To clear the screen or quit without saving the document

Press	**F7**, and the status line reads *Save Document? (Y/N) Y*.
Press	**N**, and the status line reads *Exit WP? (Y/N) N*.
Press	**N** to clear the screen, or press **Y** to quit the program.

Result. If you cleared the screen, it is blank, just as it was when you began this exercise. If you quit the program, the operating system A> or B> prompt is displayed on the screen. Remove your program and data disks, and then turn off the computer or load another program.

EXERCISE 79

Sorting a Secondary File

If you completed Exercise 60 (Topic 3-12), you can retrieve the file SECOND.WP to see how you can sort a secondary file. Begin by inserting the disk on which you saved the file SECOND.WP into drive B.

To retrieve the secondary file

Press	**F5**, and the status line reads *Dir B:*.*. (If it does not, press =, type **B:**, and then press **Return** to change the directory.)
Press	**Return**.

Result. A list of files appears on the screen. Highlight SECOND.WP, and then press **1** for **Retrieve**.

To sort the secondary file

Press	**Ctrl-F9** to display the Merge/Sort menu.
Press	**2** for **Sort**, and the status line reads *Input file to sort: (Screen)*.
Press	**Return** to sort the file on the screen, and the status line reads *Output file for sort: (Screen)*.
Press	**Return** to sort to the screen and display the Sort by Line menu.

To delete the select criteria you entered previously

Press	**4** for **Select**, and the cursor jumps to *Select*.
Press	**Del** repeatedly to delete Key1>=200 if it is in the *Select* field.
Press	**F7** to return to the menu.

To change the sort key

Press	**3** for **Keys**, and the cursor jumps to the definition of key number 1 so that you can describe the type of sort.
Press	**a** for **Typ** to perform an alphabetic sort, and the cursor jumps to *Field*.

Press	1 for **Field** because the names are in the first field in each record.
Press	**F7** to return to the menu.

To sort the file

Press	7 for **Type**.
Press	1 for **Merge**.
Press	1 for **Perform Action**.

Result. The file is sorted so that all the records are arranged in descending order by name. Since the name is preceded by a courtesy title, they are arranged in the order or Mr., Mrs., and Ms. Let's sort them again by company.

To sort the secondary file

Press	**Ctrl-F9** to display the Merge/Sort menu.
Press	2 for **Sort**, and the status line reads *Input file to sort: (Screen)*.
Press	**Return** to sort the file on the screen, and the status line reads *Output file for sort: (Screen)*.
Press	**Return** to sort to the screen and display the Sort by Line menu.

To change the sort key

Press	3 for **Keys**, and the cursor jumps to the definition of key number 1 so that you can describe the type of sort.
Press	a for **Typ** to perform a numeric sort, and the cursor jumps to *Field*.
Press	2 for **Field** because the company is listed in the second field in each record.
Press	**F7** to return to the menu.

To sort the file

Press	7 for **Type**.
Press	1 for **Merge**.
Press	1 for **Perform Action**.

Result. The records are now sorted by company. The record with no company listed is at the top of the file, followed by Alf Industries, and then Curtis & Mathers.

QUESTIONS

1. What three steps allow you to set up a sort?
2. What is a sort key?
3. What is the difference between a primary key and a secondary key?
4. Why should you try to enter unique information in the primary field?
5. What are the two orders you can specify for a sort? How does each work?
6. Why should you always save the file before sorting?

TOPIC 3-23
Creating an Outline

In this topic, we introduce you to the following procedures:

- Creating an outline
- Numbering paragraphs

BACKGROUND

Word processing programs have two kinds of outlining functions. You use an **outline** to create numbered and indented outlines. An **outliner** is more powerful, you can use it to organize the actual text in the document because the headings in the outline and the body text are linked.

OUTLINES

When you want to create an outline, you use numbers and indents to identify the levels in the outline. The numbering style can take any one of several forms. Indenting is used to reinforce the numbering system—the lower the level of the outline entry, the more the indent.

WordPerfect's outline feature lets you create enumerated paragraphs or outlines as many as seven levels deep. If you add or delete entries, all the following numbers are automatically updated.

If you specify more than one level for your outline, each level is indented from the previous one. To change the amount each level is indented, change the tab stops (see Topic 3-10).

OUTLINERS

Outliners (not available on Word Perfect) allow you to organize your ideas and text before and during writing. Outlines created with an outliner have levels that are automatically numbered and linked to text in the document. The hallmark of an outliner is its ability to display your entire text, **document view**, or just the headings, **outline view**. The ability to switch between a view of the headings, which is just like an outline, and the entire document is a powerful feature when you work on long, complicated reports.

- When the document is displayed in outline view, you can highlight one or more adjacent headings and move, copy, or delete them. When you do this, you also move, copy, or delete the text you have entered under those headings.

- You can analyze on two levels, by content and by organization. When the document is displayed in document view, the text can be entered and edited just like a normal document. When it is displayed in outline view, the headings can be moved up or down levels or elsewhere in the outline at the same level. Text can then be entered using the outline as a guide.

- As you get ideas, you can enter them under existing headings, or you can add new headings.

- You can move around a long document quickly because moving through the outline is faster than moving through the text. You display the document in outline view, move the cursor to the heading of the section you want, and then display the document in document view.

NUMBERING PARAGRAPHS

You can number paragraphs with automatic or fixed numbers. In both cases, if you insert or delete a paragraph number, the numbers automatically change to reflect the new sequence.

- An automatic number changes levels when you insert a tab in front of it.
- A fixed number does not change when you insert or delete tabs in front of it. This is ideal when you want to keep all paragraph numbers aligned with the left margin.
- You can also change the numbering style of the outline.

EXERCISE 80

Creating an Outline

In this exercise, you make and edit outlines. To begin this exercise, you must load the program or clear the screen of any other document.

Step 1. Turn Outline Mode On. The first step in creating an outline is to move the cursor to where the outline is to begin and turn outline mode on.

To turn outline mode on

Press   **Alt-F5** to display the Mark Text menu.
Press   **1** for **Outline**, and the status line reads *Outline*.

Result. The message *Outline* indicates outline mode is on.

Step 2. Enter the Outline. With outline mode on follow the instructions below and enter the outline shown in Figure 3-39.

FIGURE 3-39
Outline document

```
1. THIS IS A LEVEL 1 HEADING
     1.1. This Is a Level 2 Heading
     1.2. This Is Another Level 2 Heading
          1.2.1. This is a level 3 heading
     1.3. This Is Another Level 2 Heading
2. THIS IS ANOTHER LEVEL 1 HEADING




B:\OUTLINE.WP                    Doc 1  Pg 1  Ln 7      Pos 44
```

To enter the outline

Press	**Return** to display the first outline number.
Press	**Spacebar** to insert a space.
Type	**THIS IS A LEVEL 1 HEADING**, and then press **Return**.

Press	← to move the cursor to the left of number II.
Press	**F4** to indent to the next tab stop.
Press	→, and then press **Spacebar**.
Type	**This Is a Level 2 Heading**, and then press **Return**.

Press	← to move the cursor to the left of number II.
Press	**F4** to indent to the next tab stop.
Press	→, and then press **Spacebar**.
Type	**This Is Another Level 2 Heading**, and then press **Return**.

Press	← to move the cursor to the left of number II.
Press	**F4** twice to indent to the second tab stop.
Press	→, and then press **Spacebar**.
Type	**This is a level 3 heading**, and then press **Return**.

Press	← to move the cursor to the left of number II.
Press	**F4** to indent to the next tab stop.
Press	→, and then press **Spacebar**.
Type	**This Is Another Level 2 Heading**, and then press **Return**.

Press	**Spacebar**.
Type	**THIS IS ANOTHER LEVEL 1 HEADING.**

Result. Your finished outline should look like Figure 3-39. Continue experimenting with this feature since it is very useful. When you are finished, turn outline mode off. To do so, press **Alt-F5** to display the Mark Text menu, and then press **1** for **Outline**. The status line no longer reads *Outline*.

Step 3. Change the Numbering. You can choose from a variety of outline numbering systems. Let's change the way the outline is numbered to legal style.

To change outline numbering

Press	**Home, Home, Home,** ↑ to move the cursor to the beginning of the document above the Outline On code.
Press	**Alt-F5** to display the Mark Text menu.
Press	**6** for **Other Options** to display the Other Mark Text Options menu.
Press	**1** for **Define Paragraph/Outline Numbering** to display the paragraph numbering definition screen (Figure 3-40).
Press	**3** for **Legal Numbering**, and the prompt reads *Starting Paragraph Number (in Legal Style):*.
Press	**1**, and then press **Return** to start numbering at 1 and return to the document screen.
Press	↓ to move the cursor down through the outline to renumber each entry.

Result. The outline is automatically renumbered in a legal style.

Step 4. Save the Outline. In the next step, you edit the outline, so save it now in case anything goes wrong.

FIGURE 3-40
Paragraph numbering
definition screen

```
Paragraph Numbering Definition

      1 - Paragraph Numbering, e.g. 1. a. i. (1) (a) (i) 1)
      2 - Outline Numbering, e.g. I. A. 1. a. (1) (a) i)
      3 - Legal Numbering, e.g. 1. 1.1. 2.2.1 etc.
      4 - Other

   Selection: 0

   Levels:            1   2   3   4   5   6   7
     Number Style:    0   2   4   3   4   3   1
     Punctuation:     1   1   1   1   3   3   2

   Number Style                              Punctuation
   0 - Upper Case Roman                      0 - 1
   1 - Lower Case Roman                      1 - 1.
   2 - Upper Case Letters                    2 - 1)
   3 - Lower Case Letters                    3 - (1)
   4 - Numbers
   5 - Numbers with previous levels separated by a period

   Starting Paragraph Number (in Legal Style): 1
```

To save the outline

Press   **F10**, and the status line reads *Document to be Saved:*.

Type   **B:\OUTLINE.WP**, and then press **Return**.

Result. The outline is saved onto the disk. You can retrieve it if anything goes wrong with the outline on the screen.

Step 5. Edit the Outline. One of the reasons to use outline mode when creating numbered outlines is that the numbers are automatic. If you add or delete entries, the numbers automatically adjust to reflect the new sequence.

To delete an entry

Move   the cursor to the line numbered 1.1.

Press   **Home, Home, Home,** ← to move the cursor to the beginning of the line.

Press   **Ctrl-End** to delete the line.

Press   **Del** to delete the blank line.

Result. The items below the deleted number are automatically renumbered. Sometimes when you delete entries, those below change levels. To correct this, you may have to press **Del** an extra time to restore them to their proper levels. Continue deleting, and try adding new entries, and watch the numbers adjust.

Step 6. Continue or Quit. You have now completed this exercise. Either clear the screen and continue to work, or quit and return to the operating system. In either case, you should save the document under a new name since it is now different from the one you saved in Step 6.

To save the document and clear the screen or quit

Press   **F7**, and the status line reads *Save Document? (Y / N) Y*.

Press   **Y**, and the status line reads *Document to be Saved: B:\OUTLINE.WP*.

Press   → to move the cursor to under the period separating the filename and its extension.

Type   **2** (to change the name to OUTLINE2.WP), and then press **Return**. The status line reads *Exit WP? (Y / N) N*.

Press   **N** to clear the screen, or press **Y** to quit.

Result. If you cleared the screen, it is blank, just as it was when you began this exercise. If you quit the program, the operating system A> or B> prompt is displayed on the screen. Remove your program and data disks, and then turn off the computer or load another program.

EXERCISE 81

Numbering Paragraphs

If you have paragraphs in a document that you want to number, you can easily do so. Enter several paragraphs, and then use the instructions below to number them.

To number paragraphs

1. Move the cursor to the left of the paragraph to be numbered (on the first line).
2. Press **Alt-F5** to display the Mark Text menu.
3. Press **2** for **Para #**, and the status line reads *Paragraph Level (ENTER for automatic):.*
4. Either press **Return** to enter an automatic number and then press **Spacebar**.

   Or type the level of the number (1-7), and then press **Return** to enter a fixed number, and then press **Spacebar**.

TIPS

■ **When you define paragraph or outline numbering, you can specify a starting number.** This is useful if you are entering two or more numbered sections in the same document or carrying a numbered section across two or more files.

■ When you number indented paragraphs, the numbering automatically calculates the indent as a level, and reflects this in the numbering.

QUESTIONS

1. What is the difference between an outline and an outliner?
2. What happens when you delete a numbered outline entry?
3. How are outline levels indicated?
4. What is one advantage of displaying a long document in outline view before displaying it in document view?
5. How are automatic numbers different from fixed numbers when numbering paragraphs?

TOPIC 3-24
Using Superscripts and Subscripts

In this topic, we introduce you to the following procedures:

- Entering superscripts
- Entering subscripts

BACKGROUND

Most word processors, especially those used by technical, scientific, and engineering writers and typists, allow you to enter superscripts above and subscripts below the normal line of text. Superscripts and subscripts can be used to print fractions, formulas, trademark symbols, copyright symbols, registration marks, temperature degrees, and footnote symbols.

- Some programs do not allow you to control the distance above and below lines that superscripts and subscripts print, so you may have to double space the text to provide enough room for them. To use superscripts and subscripts with these programs, your printer must also be capable of printing them in the desired position. That is, it must be able to advance the paper forward and backward to print characters above and below the line it is currently printing.

- Other programs print the superscripts and subscripts on the same line as the text but in smaller type. The superscript on these programs is printed in small type above the center of the line, and the subscript is printed in small type below the center of the line.

You can format characters so they are superscripted or subscripted as you type text, or later. When you format superscripts or subscripts as you type text, the command affects only the next character you type. When you format existing text, the entire selected block is superscripted or subscripted.

EXERCISE 82

Entering Superscripts and Subscripts

In this exercise, you use WordPerfect's superscripting and subscripting commands. To begin this exercise, you must load the program or clear the screen of any other document. Superscripts and subscripts may not be supported by your version of WordPerfect or your printer.

Step 1. Enter a Document. Enter the document in Figure 3-41.
Press **Return** at the end of each line.

Step 2. Superscript Characters. Now, select and superscript all characters that are to print above the line.

To superscript existing text

Move	the cursor to under the 1 in 1/2 on line 1.
Press	**Alt-F4**, and the status line flashes *Block on*.
Press	→ to highlight just the number 1.
Press	**Shift-F1** to display the Super/Subscript menu.
Press	1 for **Superscript**.

```
1. 1/2
2. Trademarktm
3. RegistrationR
4. 30oF
5. H2O
6. 1-3/4=1/4




D:\SATEXT\DISK\SCRIPT.WP                  Doc 2  Pg 1  Ln 1        Pos 10
```

FIGURE 3-41
Superscript and
subscript document

Result. No change is seen on the screen, but as you move the cursor to the left, back under the 1, an *S* appears at the far left of the status line to indicate the character has been superscripted. Now, select each of the other characters to be superscripted, and use the same command to superscript them. They include the tm at the end of line 2, the R at the end of line 3, the o following the 30 on line 4, and the 3 in 3/4 and the 1 in 1/4 on line 6.

Step 3. Subscript Characters. Now, subscript all characters that are to print below the line.

To subscript existing text

Move	the cursor to under the 2 in 1/2 on line 1.
Press	**Alt-F4**, and the status line flashes *Block on.*
Press	→ to highlight just the number 2.
Press	**Shift-F1** to display the Super/Subscript menu.
Press	**2** for **Subscript**.

Result. No change is seen on the screen, but as you move the cursor to the left, back under the 2, an *s* appears at the far left of the status line to indicate the character has been subscripted. Now, select each of the other characters to be subscripted, and use the same command to subscript them. They include the 2 in H_2O on line 5 and the two 4s on line 6.

Step 4. Save the Document. You should now save your document. Before proceeding, *be sure a formatted disk is in drive B.*

To save the document

Press	**F10**, and the status line reads *Document to be Saved:.*
Type	**B:\SCRIPTS.WP**, and then press **Return**.

Using Superscripts and Subscripts   289

Result. The disk drive spins as the document is saved onto the disk in drive B. When the drive stops and its red light goes out, you can continue to work on the document.

Step 5. Print the Document. Now that you have completed the document, make a printout to see how it looks. Be sure that the printer is on and has paper in it and that the paper is aligned.

To print the document

Press   **Shift-F7** to display the Print menu.
Press   1 for **Full Text**.

Result. The printer immediately begins printing. Your document should look like Figure 3-42.

Step 6. Continue or Quit. You have now completed this exercise. Either continue on your own work, or quit and return to the operating system.

To continue or quit

Press   **F7**, and the status line reads *Save Document? (Y/N) Y.*
Press   **N**, and the status line reads *Exit WP? (Y/N) N.*
Press   **N** to clear the screen, or press **Y** to quit.

Result. If you did not quit the program, the screen is blank. If you did quit the program, the operating system B> prompt is displayed on the screen. Remove your program and data disks, and then turn off the computer or load another program.

QUESTIONS

1. Give three examples of superscripts. Of subscripts.
2. When you enter a superscript or subscript command as you type text, how many characters are affected by the command?

FIGURE 3-42
Superscript and subscript printed results

1. $^1/_2$
2. Trademark^{tm}
3. Registration^R
4. 30^oF
5. H_2O
6. $1{-}^3/_4 = ^1/_4$

TOPIC 3-25
Changing Default Settings

In this topic, we introduce you to the following procedures:

- Customizing your color or graphics screen display
- Changing default settings for your program

BACKGROUND

Using WordPerfect's Set-up menu, you can change many of the default format settings like tab stops and margins, have back copies automatically created when you save a file or have them periodically saved, and use menu commands to customize your display.

CUSTOMIZING YOUR DISPLAY MONITOR

You can customize your display monitor by changing its colors if you are using a color monitor or by changing the way it displays boldfaced or underlined text if you are using a black and white monitor.

- On a color monitor, you can change the colors for background, normal text, underlined text, boldfaced text, and boldfaced and underlined text.
- On a black and white graphics monitor, you can change the way boldfaced text and underlined text are displayed.

CHANGING SYSTEM DEFAULTS

Many of the formatting commands you use override the default settings entered by the publisher of the program. If you find you are frequently changing these settings to meet your own needs, you can permanently change them using the Set-up menu. The settings you enter as the defaults should be those you use most often. The settings you can change are

- The drive or directory the dictionary and thesaurus files are stored in.
- The default settings for many features. For example, you can change tab stops, margins, line spacing, align character, page number position, date formats, and insert or typeover mode.
- Screen options, including the number of rows or columns displayed, the character displayed when you press **Return**, and the filename displayed on the status line. You can also turn the beeper on or off when the * *Not Found* * message appears during search and replace operations, when you commit an error, or when hyphenating a document.
- You can set WordPerfect so that it saves the file you are working on at timed intervals. You also can turn the feature that saves a back copy on or off. When you use the timed backup and original backup commands, you protect your work from loss due to power failures. Both of these commands save versions of the file on the disk that you can retrieve in case something goes wrong. The timed backup feature saves your work in temporary files, either {WP}BACK.1 (for document 1) or {WP}BACK.2 (for document 2). Normally, these files are deleted when you correctly exit from the program, but they remain on the disk if there is a power failure. To retrieve them to get access to your lost text, rename them,

and then use the retrieve command. The original backup feature renames the previous version of your file with the extension .BK! whenever you save your work. If you make a serious mistake, you can rename the file so that it does not have the .BK! extension and then retrieve it with the retrieve command.

EXERCISE 83

Changing Your Display

In this exercise, you change the colors on your screen if you are using a color monitor or the way underlined and boldfaced text is displayed if you are using a monochrome graphics monitor. If you are using a character display, like IBM's, you cannot use this procedure. To begin this exercise, you must load the program.

To change your color monitor

1. Press **Shift-F3** to display the screen you want to change.
2. Press **Ctrl-F3** to display the Screen menu.
3. Press **4** for **Colors**. (The status line reads *Not a Color Monitor* if you are not using a color monitor.)
4. Press **1** for **Color Monitor**, and the prompt reads *Fast text display? (may cause snow) N.*
5. Press **N** or **Y** to display the Color Selection screen (Figure 3-43).
6. Enter the letter for the desired background, foreground, underline, underlined background, bold, and bold and underline colors while observing the effect of your choices on the sample text to the right of the menu choices.
7. Press **F7** to save your changes and return to the document screen.

To change your black and white graphics monitor

1. Press **Ctrl-F3** to display the Screen menu.
2. Press **4** for **Colors**. (The status line reads *Not a Color Monitor* if you are not using a graphics monitor.)
3. Press **2** for **Single Color Monitor (eg. Black & White or Compaq)**, and the prompt reads *Fast text display? (may cause snow) N.*

FIGURE 3-43
Color selection screen

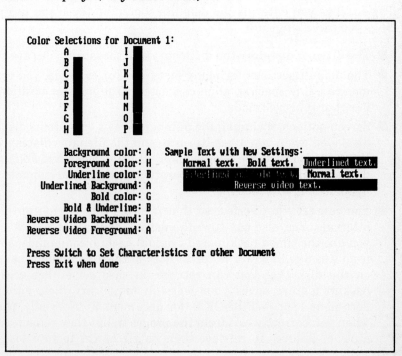

WORD PROCESSING APPLICATIONS

4 Press **N** or **Y**.

5 Press **1** for **Underline Displayed as Reverse Video,** or press **2** for **Underline Displayed as Underline**. (On some monitors, text may appear dimmer instead of underlined.)

6 Press **F7** to save your changes and return to the document screen.

EXERCISE 84

Changing Default Settings

Many of the default format settings can be changed on the full- featured version of WordPerfect.

To display the set-up menu

1 Load DOS so that the A> prompt is displayed.

2 Load WordPerfect with the WP/S command to display the Set-up menu (Figure 3-44).

The Set-up menu lists five choices (0-4). You can exit from the menu at any time by pressing **F1**.

To specify drives and directories

1 Press **1** for **Set Directories or Drives for Dictionary and Thesaurus Files,** and the prompt reads *Where do you plan to keep the dictionary (LEX.WP)?*

2 Type the path (including the name of the dictionary, LEX.WP), and then press **Return**. The prompt reads *Where do you plan to keep the supplementary dictionary file?*

3 Type the path (including the name of the supplementary dictionary, {WP}LEX.SUP), and then press **Return**. The prompt reads *Where do you plan to keep the thesaurus (TH.WP)?*

4 Type the path (including the name of the thesaurus, TH.WP), and then press **Return** to return to the Set-up menu.

5 Either make another selection from the Set-up menu.

   Or   press **0** to display the document screen.

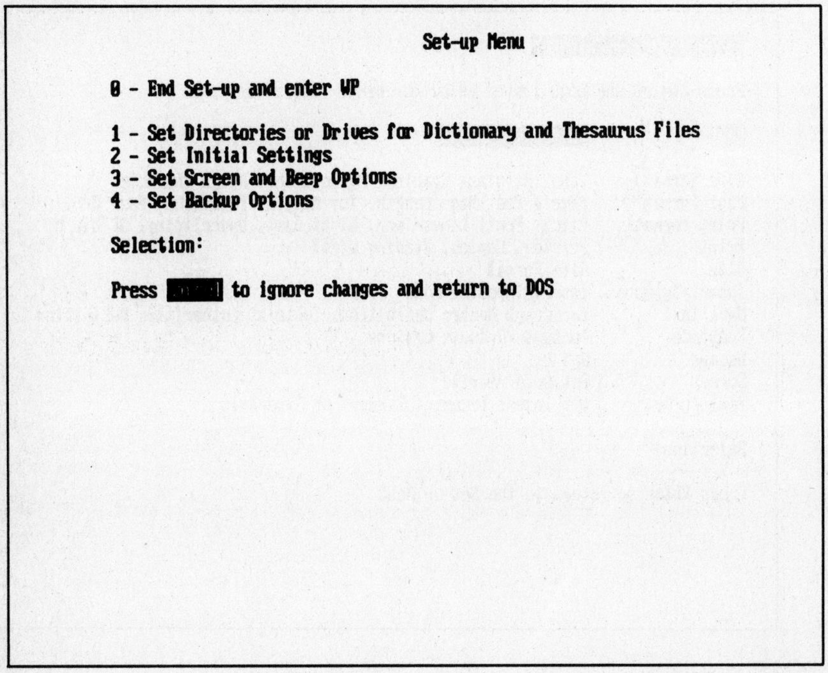

FIGURE 3-44
The set-up menu

```
                          Set-up Menu

      0 - End Set-up and enter WP

      1 - Set Directories or Drives for Dictionary and Thesaurus Files
      2 - Set Initial Settings
      3 - Set Screen and Beep Options
      4 - Set Backup Options

      Selection:

      Press ▮▮▮▮ to ignore changes and return to DOS
```

To set initial settings

- **1** Press **2** for **Set Initial Settings** to display the initial settings screen (Figure 3-45).
- **2** Press the desired function key(s), and then enter new settings.
- **3** Press **Return** to return to the Set-up menu.
- **4** Either make another selection from the Set-up menu.

    Or   press **0** to display the document screen.

To set screen and beep options

- **1** Press **3** for **Set Screen and Beep Options**, and the prompt reads *Number of rows: 25.*
- **2** Type the number of rows on your display monitor, and then press **Return**. The prompt reads *Number of columns: 80.*
- **3** Type the number of columns, and then press **Return**. The prompt reads *Hard return displayed as ascii value: 32.*
- **4** Type the ASCII value of the character you want to appear on the screen when you press **Return**, and then press **Return**. The prompt reads *Display filename on status line? (Y/N) Y.*
- **5** Press **Y** or **N**, and the prompt reads *Beep when search fails? (Y/N) Y.*
- **6** Press **Y** or **N**, and the prompt reads *Beep on error? (Y/N) Y.*
- **7** Press **Y** or **N**, and the prompt reads *Beep on hyphenation? (Y/N) Y.*
- **8** Press **Y** or **N**, and you return to the Set-up menu.
- **9** Either make another selection from the Set-up menu.

    Or   press **0** to display the document screen.

To save files automatically and save back copies

- **1** Press **4** for **Set Backup Options**, and the prompt reads *Number of minutes between each backup: 0.*
- **2** Either type the number of minutes between file saves, and then press **Return**.

    Or   press **Return**, and the prompt reads *Backup the original document? (Y/N) N.*

FIGURE 3-45
Initial settings screen

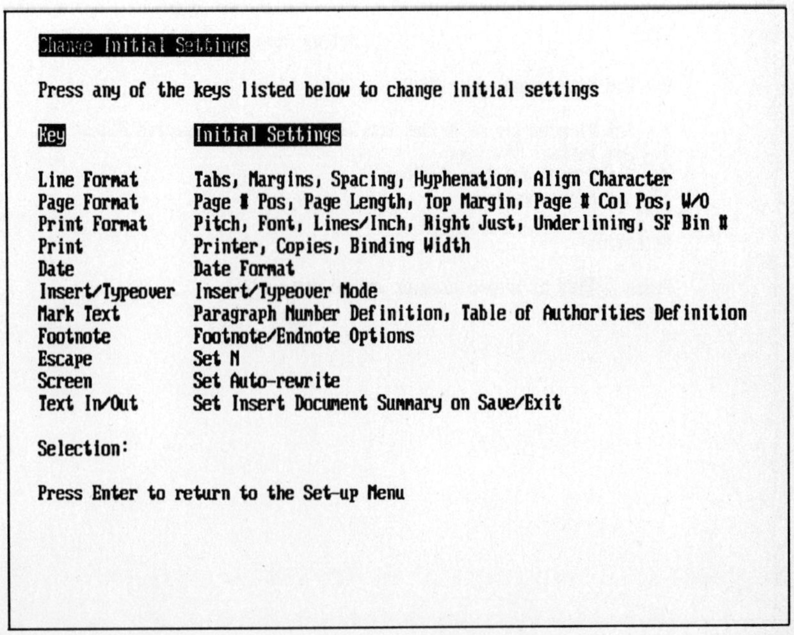

```
Change Initial Settings

Press any of the keys listed below to change initial settings

Key                  Initial Settings

Line Format          Tabs, Margins, Spacing, Hyphenation, Align Character
Page Format          Page # Pos, Page Length, Top Margin, Page # Col Pos, W/O
Print Format         Pitch, Font, Lines/Inch, Right Just, Underlining, SF Bin #
Print                Printer, Copies, Binding Width
Date                 Date Format
Insert/Typeover      Insert/Typeover Mode
Mark Text            Paragraph Number Definition, Table of Authorities Definition
Footnote             Footnote/Endnote Options
Escape               Set N
Screen               Set Auto-rewrite
Text In/Out          Set Insert Document Summary on Save/Exit

Selection:

Press Enter to return to the Set-up Menu
```

3 Either press **Y** if you want previously saved versions saved as backup copies.

Or press **N** if you do not want back copies saved.

4 Press **0** to save changes and display the document screen.

TIPS

- **You can also set the backup time** when you load the program. To load the program, type **WP/B#**. (# is the number of minutes between automatic backups.)

- **When back copies are saved**, the extension is ignored. If you have two files, one named REPORT.WP and one named REPORT, and you save both, only the most recently saved is in the file named REPORT.BK!.

QUESTIONS

1. What are some of the default settings you can change using WordPerfect's Set-up menu?

2. In what ways can you customize a color monitor?

3. In what way can you customize a black and white graphics monitor?

4. How do you display the Set-up menu?

SPREADSHEET APPLICATIONS

PART

FOUR

Topic 4-1   Getting Acquainted with Your Program

Topic 4-2   Entering Labels and Numbers and Saving Files

Topic 4-3   Entering Formulas and Functions

Topic 4-4   Retrieving and Editing Models

Topic 4-5   Printing Models

Topic 4-6   Changing a Model's Appearance

Topic 4-7   Copying and Moving Data

Topic 4-8   Using Relative and Absolute Cell References

Topic 4-9   Using Windows and Fixed Titles

Topic 4-10   Using Recalculation Methods

Topic 4-11   Using Lookup Tables

Topic 4-12   Using Data Tables

Topic 4-13   Using Date and Time Functions

Topic 4-14   Using Protection and Security

Topic 4-15   Combining and Extracting Files

Topic 4-16   Creating and Printing Graphs

Topic 4-17   Creating and Using Macros

Topic 4-18   Creating Menus

Topic 4-19   Using Data Management

Until recently, accounting, financial analysis, and other mathematical calculations were done by entering numbers on pages of an accountant's ruled ledger pad, or spreadsheet. These spreadsheets have ruled lines across and down the page that labels and numbers are written into to keep financial records or do financial analysis. Calculating subtotals, totals, and other formulas all had to be done manually, so spreadsheets took time to prepare. If any changes were then made in the data, the calculations all had to be redone.

But the development of the microcomputer and spreadsheet applications programs has taken much of the drudgery out of analysis. It may still take as much time to gather the data needed to analyze a situation or solve a problem, but that is where the similarity between the old and new ways ends. You can quickly create a model of the financial situation on a spreadsheet program by entering labels, numbers, and formulas. You can also use the program's built-in functions to perform complicated operations like calculating interest earned and monthly payments on a loan. The completed model can then be used to explore **what-if analyses**, any changes in any variables, such as in price, discount, or sales patterns. What-if analyses cause your model to automatically recalculate the figures and display the new result.

You can save a spreadsheet model and use it again whenever you or others need it. Never again will you forget how a specific analysis was done and have to reconstruct it from scratch the next time you need to use it. Often, when you work with an existing model, you will find ways to make it better and more efficient. Your models will grow in power and simplicity. You can save each revision to provide the base for the next step forward in your understanding and analysis.

There are hundreds of spreadsheet applications programs to choose from, and more are sure to come. Although each of these spreadsheets is slightly different from all of the others, several features are common to most of them.

ONE POINT BEFORE WE BEGIN

You may think spreadsheets require a strong background in mathematics; after all, they are primarily used to manipulate numbers. Relax—you could not be further from the truth. Spreadsheets use math, but they do the laborious calculations, not you. Many spreadsheets also contain functions that simplify complex calculations. Spreadsheets allow you to approach problems logically because they make it possible to focus on the problem, not the calculations. You will begin to see numbers in a new light, as tools to be used, not theories and calculations to be avoided. Spreadsheets put tools for analysis and problem solving, once useful only to professionals, within the reach of any interested user.

SPREADSHEET APPLICATIONS

Spreadsheet applications are limited by only two things: your understanding of the problem being analyzed and your knowledge of the spreadsheet techniques you need to use to create the necessary model. Let's take a look at some typical spreadsheet applications.

- *Financial analysis.* Any problems that can be quantified can be solved or analyzed with a spreadsheet. In business, spreadsheets analyze the performance of products, sales people, or dealers. They compare costs, prices, and gross margins on individual products in a product line. They also calculate prices, forecast and make budgets for sales, predict expenses and profits, and make cash flow projections.

- *Downloading from mainframe or on-line computers.* In many corporations, large databases of valuable information are stored on mainframe computers. The cost of designing programs that can uniquely analyze this data for departments or individuals usually outweighs the benefits, at least as viewed by top management. But with the right computer system, users can gain access to this information and copy it from the mainframe to their own computers (called downloading), where it can then be analyzed using a spreadsheet. When downloaded, the numbers do not have to be manually entered into the spreadsheet. This saves time and eliminates the possibility of introducing errors.

Outside databases holding vast amounts of information are also available to companies and individuals. All you need to obtain information for analysis is a modem, a communications program, and the willingness to pay the service's usage fees. These services include such well-known ones as Dow Jones News/Retrieval Service and The Source.

- *Development of data for graphs and charts.* Graphs are powerful analytical tools. They can show trends and relationships between series of numbers that would otherwise be missed. For example, a spreadsheet may show sales and costs are both rising. But the relative rates of change are much more obvious on a graph. If sales are rising faster than expenses, profits will increase; if they are rising more slowly, profits will fall. Spreadsheets are an ideal tool to develop the numbers that are then graphed. The spreadsheet-graphics combination is so useful that many spreadsheet programs now come with an integrated graphics capability. This feature makes it so easy to create graphs that they become a valuable tool for exploring what-if analyses, not just for presenting the finished results to others.

- *Data management models for listing, sorting, and extracting any information* that *can be organized by rows and columns.* Mailing lists, inventory items, and employee payroll records can be stored in spreadsheet files. Once entered, you can instantly sort data into ascending or descending order. On some programs, you can also extract data that matches a specific criteria. For example, you can list the names and phone extensions of all employees in the marketing department or list all customers in the state of Ohio.

UNDERSTANDING MODELS

One of the primary uses of spreadsheets is to build models. You use models to simulate real-world situations. Just as a plastic model of an airplane represents, or simulates, a real plane, a spreadsheet model simulates financial or other situations. When using a spreadsheet, you should understand three basic terms: *spreadsheet, model,* and *template.*

- A **spreadsheet**, sometimes called a worksheet, is the arrangement of horizontal rows and vertical columns that appears on the screen when you first load the program.

- A **model** is the data you enter into the spreadsheet to solve a problem or perform an analysis. To create a model, you use two basic types of entries: labels and values. **Labels** describe or identify parts of the model. **Values** are numbers to be analyzed and formulas and built-in functions that perform analysis.

- A **template** is a model from which all the numbers have been removed. Since it still retains all the labels, formulas, and functions, you can enter new numbers and calculate an answer. Mastering a spreadsheet and the business principles needed to analyze a problem takes time. In many firms, people who understand the principles behind an application often collaborate with those who understand a spreadsheet to develop templates of great value to others in the firm. These templates are designed to be used over and over again by anyone who knows how to move the cursor and enter the numbers to be analyzed.

SPREADSHEET PROCEDURES—AN OVERVIEW

Let's look at a typical model, one that you might use to help you plan the purchase of a new car. What if you want to buy a new car and you have between $2,000 and $2,500 for a down payment and feel you can afford a monthly payment of about $170? How much could you spend on a car, and what combination of interest rates and loan periods would achieve that monthly payment? This is a typical problem that you can quickly solve on a spreadsheet. But first you must be sure you understand the problem so that you can create an accurate model. Remember, you cannot use a computer to solve a problem you do not understand. In this case, you know you have between $2,000 and $2,500 for the down payment. You also know you want to explore how the cost of the car, down payment, interest rate, and period of the loan affect the monthly payment. The model you need to create then, must have places where you can enter these four variables, cost, down payment, interest rate, and loan term. You also need a formula that calculates the monthly payment based on these four variables.

Step 1. Load the Program

The first step in creating a model is to load the program so that the spreadsheet is displayed on the screen (Figure 4-1). If you are planning to save your work, you also insert a formatted data disk into drive B, and then close that drive's door. The spreadsheet on the screen is divided into rows and columns much like a ledger pad (see Topic 4-1). Each of the rectangles where rows and columns intersect is a **cell**. It is into these cells that you enter labels, numbers, formulas, and functions.

Step 2. Enter Labels

You enter labels to identify the contents of rows and columns so that you, and others, can understand the model (Figure 4-2). Labels are nothing more than text characters, much like those you would enter on a word processing program. On rows 3, 5, and 8, ruled lines have been entered into cells to separate different parts of the model.

FIGURE 4-1
The spreadsheet screen display

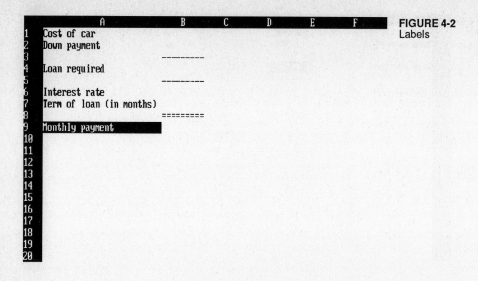

FIGURE 4-2
Labels

	A	B	C	D	E	F
1	Cost of car					
2	Down payment					
3		————				
4	Loan required					
5		————				
6	Interest rate					
7	Term of loan (in months)					
8		========				
9	Monthly payment					

Step 3. Enter Numbers

You enter numbers to be used in calculations (Figure 4-3). Numbers can be added, subtracted, multiplied, and divided. The numbers entered in the model include the cost of the car ($10,000), the down payment ($2,000), the interest rate (13%), and the term of the loan (36 months).

Step 4. Enter Formulas

You enter a formula to calculate the amount of the loan required (Figure 4-4). Since you know the cost of the car is $10,000 and your down payment is $2,000, you could subtract the two numbers and enter the result. But if you did this, the number would not change if you changed either the cost of the car or the down payment. If you enter a formula that refers to the two cells those numbers are entered in, the loan you re-

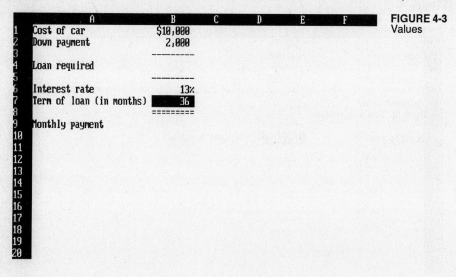

FIGURE 4-3
Values

	A	B	C	D	E	F
1	Cost of car	$10,000				
2	Down payment	2,000				
3		————				
4	Loan required					
5		————				
6	Interest rate	13%				
7	Term of loan (in months)	36				
8		========				
9	Monthly payment					

FIGURE 4-4
Formulas

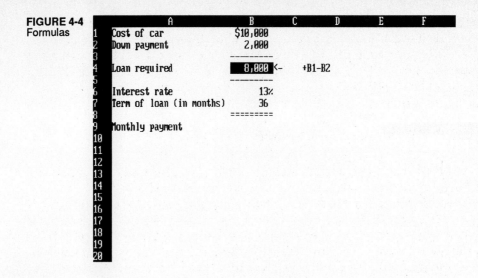

	A	B	C	D	E	F
1	Cost of car	$10,000				
2	Down payment	2,000				
3		-------				
4	Loan required	8,000	<-	+B1-B2		
5		-------				
6	Interest rate	13%				
7	Term of loan (in months)	36				
8		=========				
9	Monthly payment					

quire does change if you change the cost of the car or the down payment.

Here, the formula +B1-B2 in cell B4 tells the spreadsheet program to subtract the value in cell B2 from the value in cell B1. The result calculated by the formula is 8,000 (10,000 cost − 2,000 down payment). As you can see, the spreadsheet displays the calculated result, not the formula entered into the cell to calculate it. Moreover, the computer remembers the cells you want subtracted, not their values. This way, if you change the values in either cell, the program automatically calculates a new answer.

Step 5. Enter a Function

Formulas, like the one that calculates the amount of the loan required, are powerful, but spreadsheets have a special type of formula called a **function** that is even more so. Functions are built into the program and are designed to replace very complicated formulas. In this step, you enter a function that calculates the monthly payment on the loan (Figure 4-5).

FIGURE 4-5
Functions

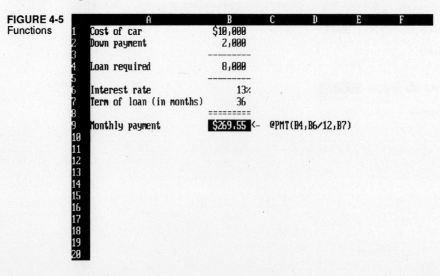

	A	B	C	D	E	F
1	Cost of car	$10,000				
2	Down payment	2,000				
3		-------				
4	Loan required	8,000				
5		-------				
6	Interest rate	13%				
7	Term of loan (in months)	36				
8		=========				
9	Monthly payment	$269.55	<-	@PMT(B4,B6/12,B7)		

The function in cell B9 is @PMT(B4,B6/12,B7). In English, this function reads "calculate and display the monthly payment based on the amount of the loan in cell B4, the annual interest rate in cell B6 (divided by 12 to convert the annual rate into a monthly rate), and the term of the loan in cell B7." The calculated answer is $269.55, way above your goal of $170 a month.

Step 6. Explore What-If Analyses

So far, the only exciting things you have seen are when you entered a formula and a function that performed calculations. Not much to write home about. But now we explore the real power of a spreadsheet; its ability to instantly reflect the changes made in variables—called sensitivity, or what-if, analysis. Since the monthly payment is more than what you want to pay, let's see if we can achieve your goal of $170 a month. As Figure 4-6 shows, you can change the terms of the loan or the price of the car until you find monthly payments that are within a few dollars of your goal. You can easily explore more what-ifs to either find even lower monthly payments or to compare two or more different deals.

- What if you increase the term of the loan from 36 to 48 months (Figure 4-6a)? To change the term of the loan, you move the cursor to cell B7, type **48** over the current 36 months, and then press **Return**. The function in cell B9 calculates and displays the new monthly payment of $214.62.

- What if you increase the down payment from $2,000 to $2,500 (Figure 4-6b)? If you increase the down payment by $500, the loan required falls from $8,000 to $7,500, and the monthly payment decreases to $201.21.

- What if you reduce the cost of the car from $10,000 to $9,000 (Figure 4-6c)? If you change the cost of the car, the loan required falls from $7,500 to $6,500, and the monthly payment falls to $174.38.

- What if you go to a bank that offers a lower interest rate (Figure 4-6d)? If you lower the interest rate by 1%, the monthly payment drops to $171.17.

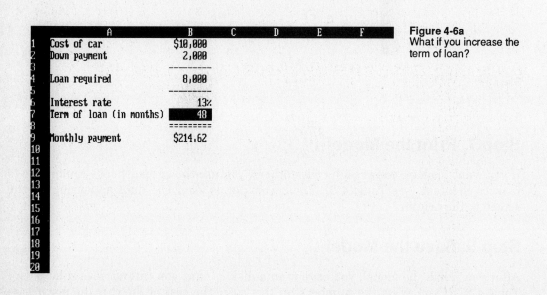

Figure 4-6a
What if you increase the term of loan?

FIGURE 4-6b
What if you increas the down payment?

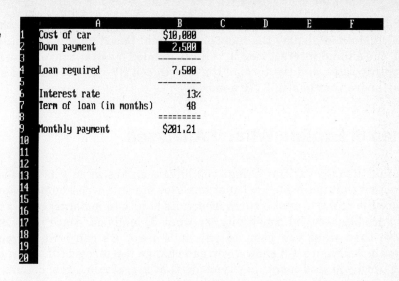

	A	B	C	D	E	F
1	Cost of car	$10,000				
2	Down payment	2,500				
3		---------				
4	Loan required	7,500				
5		---------				
6	Interest rate	13%				
7	Term of loan (in months)	48				
8		=========				
9	Monthly payment	$201.21				
10						

FIGURE 4-6c
What if you buy a less expensive car?

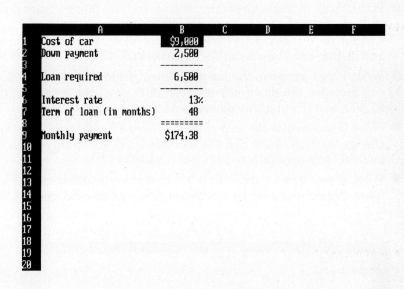

	A	B	C	D	E	F
1	Cost of car	$9,000				
2	Down payment	2,500				
3		---------				
4	Loan required	6,500				
5		---------				
6	Interest rate	13%				
7	Term of loan (in months)	48				
8		=========				
9	Monthly payment	$174.38				

Step 7. Print the Model

If you want to share your results with others, you use the spreadsheet's commands to make a printout (see Topic 4-5). These commands send the data appearing on the screen to the printer.

Step 8. Save the Model

After you finish the model, you save it on a disk so that you can retrieve it later (see Topic 4-2). If you erase the numbers (in this case, the cost of the car, the down payment, the interest rate, and the term of the loan) and then save it, you convert the model into a template. Anyone can then retrieve the blank template, enter their own data, and analyze their own car purchase plans.

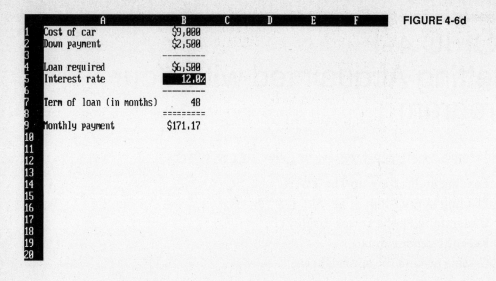

FIGURE 4-6d

	A	B	C	D	E	F
1	Cost of car	$9,000				
2	Down payment	$2,500				
3						
4	Loan required	$6,500				
5	Interest rate	12.0%				
6						
7	Term of loan (in months)	48				
8						
9	Monthly payment	$171.17				

Step 9. Quit or Clear the Screen

You quit a program when you want to return to the operating system or use another program (see Topic 4-1). If you want to stay in the program and begin working on a new model, you just clear the old model off the spreadsheet using the program's clear or erase commands (see Topic 4-1). If the new model you want to work on has already been created and saved on a disk, you can retrieve it from the disk (see Topic 4-4).

QUESTIONS

1. What are some of the most common spreadsheet applications?
2. What is the difference between a spreadsheet and a model?
3. What is what-if analysis? Give an example.
4. What similarities are there between an accountant's ledger pad and a spreadsheet program?
5. If you want to use a model developed on one spreadsheet program on another, what must usually be done first?
6. What is a template, and how does it differ from a model?
7. List the three types of data included under the term *value*.
8. What is a cell, and what is it used for?
9. What is the difference between a label and a value?

TOPIC 4-1
Getting Acquainted with Your Program

In this topic, we introduce you to the following procedures:

- Loading and setting up The TWIN
- Loading Lotus 1-2-3
- Understanding the screen display
- Executing commands
- Getting around the spreadsheet

BACKGROUND

When you load a spreadsheet program, the spreadsheet is immediately displayed on the screen. One exception is the Lotus 1-2-3 program, which lets you first load the Lotus Access System. This is simply a menu from which you can load the spreadsheet or load the program that prints graphs, converts files, or performs other tasks.

THE SPREADSHEET SCREEN DISPLAY

Spreadsheet screen displays have two major areas: the working area where you enter labels, values, formulas, and functions to create models, and the control panel where menus, prompts, and messages are displayed. Figure 4-7(a) shows The TWIN's screen display, and Figure 4-7(b) shows Lotus 1-2-3's screen display.

The Working Area

The working area, also called a worksheet, is a window on the underlying spreadsheet (Figure 4-8) where you create your models. It contains the following elements:

FIGURE 4-7a
The TWIN screen display

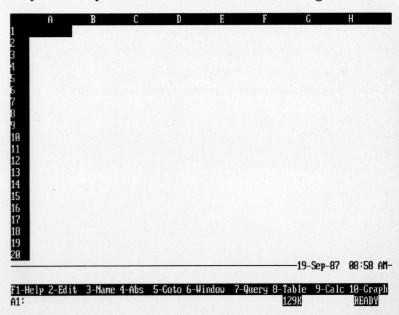

SPREADSHEET APPLICATIONS

09-Nov-87 10:50 AM

- A border with column letters across the top of the spreadsheet and row numbers down the left side.

- Columns run vertically down a spreadsheet and are labeled consecutively with letters. The first 26 columns are labeled A to Z, the next 26 are labeled AA to AZ, the next 26 are labeled BA to BZ, and so on.

- Rows run horizontally across a spreadsheet and are labeled consecutively with numbers, starting with row 1 at the top of the spreadsheet.

- Cells, the basic working units on a spreadsheet, fall at the intersection of each column and row. They are initially empty when the program is loaded and are referred to by their coordinates, or

ce

ll

add

ress. Cell addresses are indicated by specifying the column letter(s) followed by the row number.

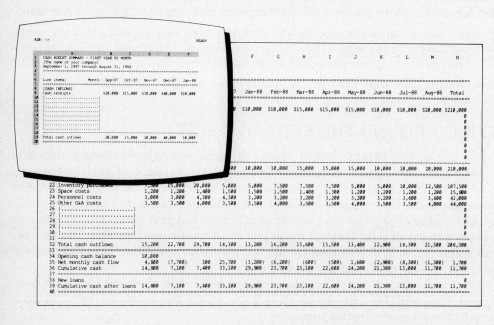

Figure 4-8
The screen is a
window on the
spreadsheet

TABLE 4-1
Cell Entries

Entry	Description
Labels	Identify models or individual rows and columns of data
Numbers	Can be used in calculations when referred to by formulas
Formulas	Can calculate numbers entered in the formula itself, or entered into other cells to which the formula refers
Formats	Control the way numbers are displayed on the screen and the way labels are aligned in their cells

■ The working area contains a bright reverse video highlight, called the cursor, cell pointer, or cell marker. You move this cursor by pressing the cursor movement keys to point to cells when you want to enter, delete, copy, move, or print data. The cell the cursor is positioned in is the active or current cell. Table 4-1 briefly describes some of the things you can enter into a spreadsheet's cells.

The Control Panel

The control panel, also called the status area, is at the bottom of The TWIN screen and the top of the Lotus 1-2-3 screen. It displays the following information:

■ *The status line* provides information about the cell the cursor is positioned in. For example, it indicates the cell's address, contents, and format. If the cell contains a formula, the formula, not the calculated result, is displayed.

The TWIN, but not Lotus 1-2-3, also displays an indicator that tells you how much memory is left for your model. As you enter data into the spreadsheet, the amount of available memory decreases. When no memory is left, you cannot expand your model any further.

■ *The prompt line* displays prompts or messages when the program wants you to provide information, for example, the cell coordinates you want to print, the name of the file you want to save or retrieve, or the width you want to set a column to. The TWIN, but not Lotus 1-2-3, also displays a brief description of the ten function keys on this line when prompts or messages are not being displayed.

■ *The edit line* displays the characters that you type as you enter them or when you use the edit command. When you press **Return**, the characters displayed on this line are entered into the cell that contains the cursor.

■ *The current date and time* are also displayed on The TWIN and Lotus 1-2-3 Release 2.

GETTING AROUND THE SPREADSHEET

If you ever use an accountant's ledger pad for financial analysis, you soon realize that even those with only 20 or so columns are unwieldy because of their large size. Spreadsheet programs come in a variety of sizes, all of them much larger than the largest ledger pads. The number of cells on a spreadsheet can be calculated by multiplying the number of rows by the number of columns. But just because a spreadsheet has a given number of cells does not mean you can actually use them all. The number you can actually use is determined by the memory your computer has, the shape of the spreadsheet you build, and the data you enter.

What if some typical spreadsheets were printed out in their entirety with each cell 1 inch wide and 1/4 inch deep? How large would the printouts be? The sizes shown in Table 4-2 may surprise you.

TABLE 4-2
Spreadsheet Sizes

Programs	Columns	Rows	Cells	Size If Printed Width (in feet)	Height (in feet)
SuperCalc 3	63	254	16,002	5	5
MultiPlan	63	254	16,065	5	5
The TWIN	256	2,048	524,288	21	43
1-2-3					
Release 1A	256	2,048	524,288	21	43
Release 2	256	8,192	2,097,152	21	171
Excel	256	16,384	4,194,304	21	341

Moving the Cursor

When you want to enter data into cells or execute other commands, you point to cells. The four directional arrow keys move the cursor a cell at a time and repeat if you hold them down. Other keys, or combinations of keys, move the cursor in larger jumps. The larger your models are, the more important these keys and commands become.

For example, the **Goto** key moves the cursor quickly to a specific cell. On both The TWIN and Lotus 1-2-3, pressing **Goto (F5)** displays a prompt that asks you what cell you want to go to. You just type in the cell coordinates, press **Return**, and the cursor immediately jumps to the specified cell. On many computers, pressing **PgUp** and **PgDn** scrolls you through the spreadsheet a screen page at a time, and pressing **Home** moves the cursor to cell A1 at the upper left-hand corner of the spreadsheet.

Most other commands involve a combination of keys. For example, when using The TWIN or Lotus 1-2-3 on an IBM PC, pressing **Home** moves the cursor to cell A1. But pressing **End** and then **Home** moves the cursor to the lower right-hand corner of the working area of the model. The keys used to make these larger moves depend on both the program and computer you are using. Table 4-3 lists the cursor movement keys for The TWIN and Lotus 1-2-3.

TABLE 4-3
Cursor Movement Keys

To Move Cursor	Press
Right or left one column	→ **or** ←
Up or down one row	↑ or ↓
Right one full screen	**Tab** or **Ctrl-→**
Left one full screen	**Shift-Tab** or Ctrl-←
Up or down one full screen	**PgUp** or **PgDn**
To upper left-hand corner (cell A1)	**Home**
To next nonblank cell in row or column followed or preceded by blank cell	**End, Arrow**
To lower right-hand corner of working area	**End, Home**
To specified cell	**Goto (F5)**, cell coordinates, **Return**
To named range (see Topic 4-6)	**Goto (F5)**, range name, **Return**
To other window (see Topic 4-9)	**Window (F6)**
To freeze cursor and scroll spreadsheet	**Scroll Lock**

Scrolling the Screen

The display screen is just a small window on a large spreadsheet, but you can scroll it around the underlying spreadsheet with the cursor movement keys. As you move the cursor down a column or along a row, it eventually runs into one of the boundaries of the screen display. The next time you press the same key, the cursor stays against the edge of the screen (it cannot be moved off the screen), but the screen display scrolls to reveal the next row or column of the spreadsheet. As it does so, the leftmost column or topmost row scrolls off the other side of the screen. You can see this happen if you watch the row and column labels change as you scroll the screen. If the cursor runs into one of the boundaries of the spreadsheet, the computer beeps the next time you press the arrow key that points toward the boundary.

On some programs, you can engage **Scroll Lock** to keep the cursor in the same cell. When you then press the arrow keys, the screen scrolls. When the cursor reaches the edge of the screen, it stays there, and the spreadsheet scrolls under it.

EXECUTING COMMANDS

To execute commands, you use the spreadsheet's menus (Table 4-4). For example, when using The TWIN or Lotus 1-2-3, you press the slash key (/) to display the Main menu at the top or bottom of the screen. One choice in the menu is always highlighted, and a brief description of the highlighted choice is displayed on the line below the menu. You can make choices from the menu in one of two ways.

- You can type the first letter in the menu choice's name.

- You can press → or ← to move the highlight, sometimes called a menu pointer, over your choice, and then press **Return**. If you position the highlight over the first or last choice on the menu and then press the arrow key one more time, the highlight wraps around to the other end of the menu. You can quickly move to the first or last menu choice by pressing **Home** or **End**.

There is occasionally a slight variation in the commands listed on The TWIN and different versions of Lotus. For example, when using Lotus 1-2-3 Release 1A, you press **/WCS** (for Worksheet, Column-Width, Set). The same command on Release 2 selects the commands Worksheet, Column, Set-Width. There is also a difference in the command that aligns labels. The TWIN and Lotus 1-2-3 Release 1A refer to it as the Label-Prefix command whereas Lotus 1-2-3 Release 2 refers to it as the Label command. When these differences do occur, this text uses just the first part of the menu command, for example, Column, Set or Label when it describes the command.

TABLE 4-4
Keys Used with Menu Commands

Key	Function
/	Displays Main menu
Arrow keys	Moves highlight along menu
Home	Moves highlight to first selection on menu
End	Moves highlight to last selection on menu
Esc	Cancels menu selection by backing you out of menu one step at a time
Ctrl-Break	Cancels command
Return	Selects highlighted menu choice

TABLE 4-5
Function Key Commands

Key	Function
Help (F1)	Displays help screens *(not available on the introductory version of The TWIN)*
Edit (F2)	Displays the contents of the cell containing the cursor for editing (see Topic 4-4)
Name (F3)	Lists all range names assigned to cells in the spreadsheet (works in point mode only) (see Topic 4-6)
Abs (F4)	Specifies if cell references in formulas are relative, absolute, or mixed (see Topic 4-8)
Goto (F5)	Moves the cursor to a specific location
Window (F6)	Moves the cursor between windows when the screen is divided with the Worksheet Window command (see Topic 4-9)
Query (F7)	Repeats the most recent Data Query command (see Topic 4-19)
Table (F8)	Repeats the most recent Data Table command (see Topic 4-12)
Calc (F9)	Recalculates all formulas in the model (see Topic 4-10); if the program is in value or edit mode, converts formulas into their calculated values
Graph (F10)	Displays the most recently displayed or created graph on the screen (see Topic 4-16)

Answering Prompts

When the program wants you to supply information, it displays a prompt on the prompt line. You can answer prompts by typing your response with uppercase or lowercase letters. If you make a mistake while typing your response, press **Backspace** to delete the mistake, or press **Esc** to clear the current entry and retype a new one.

Canceling Commands

In many cases, selecting an option from the Main menu displays another menu or a prompt. If you decide you want to cancel the command at some point during these steps, you can either press **Esc** to back up through the sequence of commands you entered, or you can press **Ctrl-Break** to cancel the command.

The Function Keys

The TWIN and Lotus 1-2-3 use the function keys to perform ten frequently used commands (see Table 4-5). The actual keys assigned to these commands vary depending on the computer you are using. Table 4-5, and all references to the function keys in this text, show the keys used by the IBM PC (and compatible computers) in parentheses following the name of the key. If you are using a different type of computer, refer to the manual or plastic template included with the computer for the key assignments.

Special Keys

Besides the function keys, several other keys on the keyboard perform specific tasks. Table 4-6 describes these keys.

TABLE 4-6
Special Key Functions

Key	Function
Alt	When pressed together with a letter, executes the macro assigned to that letter
Esc	When editing, deletes everything from the edit line; when using a menu, backs up to the last command entered
Backspace	When entering or editing data, erases the character to the left of the cursor; when pointing to a range, returns the cursor to the cell where the pointing was started
Del	When editing, erases the character at the cursor

Mode Indicators

A spreadsheet program can perform only one task at a time. It can be accepting a new label you are typing, but it cannot also be recalculating, printing, or saving a file. For this reason, the current mode is displayed so that you know what the program is doing or what information it is ready to accept. You do not have to select modes; that is done automatically based on the steps you are performing at the moment.

The mode indicator displays *READY* when you first load the program and then changes as you perform various tasks. For instance, when you press the slash key (/) to display the Main menu on The TWIN or Lotus 1-2-3, the mode indicator reads *MENU*. Table 4-7 lists the most common mode indicators on The TWIN and Lotus 1-2-3.

Error Messages

If The TWIN or Lotus 1-2-3 encounters any errors, the computer beeps and displays an error message. You must then press **Esc** or **Return** before you can enter any further commands or data.

TABLE 4-7
Mode Indicators

Indicator	Meaning
READY	Displayed when no commands are in progress.
VALUE	Displayed when entering a number, formula, or function. For example, it is displayed when the first character that you type is a number or one of the symbols +, @, −, #, ., $, or ((see Topic 4-3).
LABEL	Displayed when entering a label, for example, when the first character you type is a letter or any symbol not included in the value symbol list (see Topic 4-2).
EDIT	Displayed when you press **Edit** (**F2**) to return the data in a cell to the edit line for editing. When this indicator is displayed, you can move the edit cursor through the data to insert or delete characters as needed (see Topic 4-4).
POINT	Displayed when moving the cursor during a command to point to a range and when you press the **Goto** (**F5**) key (see Topic 4-3).
MENU	Displayed when you press the slash key (/) to display the Main menu and remains displayed until you complete or cancel the command.
FIND	Displayed when you use the Data Query Find command (see Topic 4-19).
HELP	Displayed when you press the **Help** (**F1**) key.
ERROR	Displayed when the program detects an error. To remove the indicator and continue, press **Esc** or **Return**.
WAIT	Displayed when the program is calculating, printing, or otherwise engaged internally. Wait for the *READY* indicator before typing.

HELP WHENEVER YOU NEED IT

The TWIN (full-featured version only) and Lotus 1-2-3 contain extensive built-in help facilities that you can display at any time by pressing the **Help (F1)** key. When pressed in the middle of a command, the program tries to anticipate the information you need and respond with the appropriate help screen. Each help screen lists additional help topics. You can select a topic by highlighting it and then pressing **Return** or by using any of the keys described on the screen.

CLEARING THE SCREEN

You need not turn off the computer to erase a spreadsheet. You use the Worksheet Erase command to erase all data on the spreadsheet from the screen and the computer's memory. Before you use this command, be sure you have saved the file with the File Save command (see Topic 4-2). If you erase data from the spreadsheet without first saving it, the data is lost.

QUITTING THE PROGRAM

When you are finished with a TWIN or Lotus 1-2-3 session, you quit the program with the Quit command. You should always use the program's Quit command rather then just turn off the computer for the following reasons:

■ Selecting the Quit command returns you to the system A> prompt. If you turn off the computer, you must reboot it before running another program.

■ If you just open the drive doors and turn off the computer, it is slightly faster than quitting, but someday you will do it by reflex and lose unsaved file into.

EXERCISE 85

Loading and Setting Up The TWIN

In this exercise, you load and set up The TWIN to run on your computer system. To begin this exercise, your computer must be turned off.

Step 1. Load the Operating System. Since the introductory version of The TWIN cannot be made self-booting, you must first load the operating system from the DOS disk.

To load the operating system

Insert   the DOS disk into drive A, and then turn on the computer. If your computer does not have a built-in clock, you are asked to enter the date.

Type   the date in the format month/day/year (for example, 1/1/86), and then press **Return**. A prompt asks you to enter the time.

Type   the time in the format hour:minute (for example, 14:40), and then press **Return**.

Result. In a moment, the A> prompt is displayed.

Step 2. Load The TWIN. With the operating system prompt on the screen, you can load The TWIN. Remove the DOS disk, and then insert The TWIN Program disk into drive A. Insert a formatted disk into drive B. If you load The TWIN without a data disk in drive B, the drive spins for a long time before the spreadsheet appears.

FIGURE 4-9a
The TWIN setup screen 1

```
                              HARDWARE CONFIGURATION              (Page 1 of 2)

Default Data Pathname B:\

System Drive Letter A  (currently ignored)

Display Boards in Computer 3     1 = Color/Graphics Board
                                 2 = IBM Monochrome Board
   (The program automatically    3 = BOTH Mono and Color Boards (IBM PC only)
    determines this setting.)     4 = Hercules or Monochrome Graphics
   If you have an Epson Equity or Leading Edge Model D, please read ADDENDUM.TXT

Video Monitor #1 2               1 = -NONE-
                                 2 = IBM Monochrome Monitor
Video Monitor #2 3               3 = High Resolution Graphics (B&W)
                                 4 = Medium Resolution Graphics (Color)

                                 1 = -NONE-          6 = HP LaserJet
Printer Attached 2               2 = Epson MX/FX/RX   7 = IBM Color
                                 3 = IBM Graphics (B&W) 8 = No Graphics
Only IBM and Epson supported     4 = Okidata 92       9 = IBM ProPrinter
for Hercules - use HARCOPY.COM   5 = Dataproducts 8050/8070 (IDS Prism)

PgDn for next page, <CTRL> ENTER to save, <ESC> to cancel,
                                                                  FORMS
```

To load The TWIN

Type   **TWIN**, and then press **Return**.

Result. The drive spins as the program is loaded and in a few moments, the copyright screen appears.

- If you are loading the introductory version, a prompt asks you to *Press any key to continue.* Press any key.

- If you are loading the educational or full-featured versions, the prompt reads *Place System 2 disk in A: drive, press Enter, or Esc to quit.* Remove System Disk 1 from drive A, insert System Disk 2, and then press **Return**.

In a few moments, The TWIN's spreadsheet (Figure 4-7a) appears on the screen.

Step 3. Set Up The TWIN. Before you can print out models and graphs, you must set up The TWIN for your hardware. You specify the default drive the files are saved on, the drive the program disk is in, the graphics board in your computer, and the printer you are using.

To set up The TWIN

Press   **/WGH** (for Worksheet, Global, Hardware) to display the first setup screen.

Result. The first setup screen appears (Figure 4-9a). Type in your selections. Press **Tab, Shift-Tab,** and the arrow keys to move the cursor from one field to another.

- *Default Data Pathname* specifies the drive where you want to store data files. It should be set to B:\ if you are using a system with two floppy disk drives.
- *System Drive Letter* specifies the drive that contains the program disk and should be set to A.
- *Display boards in computer* specifies the type of display you are using.
- *Video Monitor #1* specifies the monitor on which you display the spreadsheet. *Video Monitor #2* specifies a second monitor connected to your computer, if any.
- *Printer attached* specifies the printer on which you want to print your models.

When you are finished with the first screen, press **PgDn** (if necessary) to display the next setup screen (Figure 4-9b).

FIGURE 4-9b
The TWIN setup screen 2

```
                HARDWARE CONFIGURATION              (Page 2 of 2)

                              1 = -NONE-          4 = Strobe 260
        Plotter Attached ▮    2 = HP7470 2-pen    5 = EMUPLOT printer
        (Serial port only, non-network)  3 = HP7475 6-pen    6 = HI DMP-29/DMPL

        Device                I/O Port
         Printer ▮            1 = -NONE-
         Plotter ▮            2 = Parallel Port #1 (LPT1:)
         (reserved) ▮         3 = Parallel Port #2 (LPT2:)
                              4 = Serial Port #1   (COM1:)
         (Indicate which port each  5 = Serial Port #2   (COM2:)
          device is attached to.)

        Default Printer Settings     Serial Port Baud Rate    Baud Rate Choices:
        Page Length (20-100) ▮6
        Left Margin  (0-240) ▮       Serial Port #1 ▮       1 = 110   5 = 1200
        Right Margin (0-240) ▮6      Serial Port #2 ▮       2 = 150   6 = 2400
        Top Margin    (0-10) 2                             3 = 300   7 = 4800
        Bottom Margin (0-10) 2                             4 = 600   8 = 9600
        Wait Between Printing Pages (Y/N) ▮
        Printer Setup String ████████████████████████████

        PgUp for the previous page. <CTRL> ENTER to save. <ESC> to cancel.
                                                          [FORMS]
```

■ *Plotter attached* specifies a plotter attached, if any.

■ *Device* specifies the ports to which the printer and plotter are attached.

■ *Printer settings* specifies default printer settings for page length and margins.

When you have entered all settings, hold down **Ctrl**, and then press **Return** to save them. If you have not made any changes, press **Esc** to cancel the command and return to the spreadsheet.

Step 4. Continue or Quit. You have now completed this exercise. Either continue to the next exercise, or quit the program.

To quit the program

Press   /**Q** (for Quit), and the prompt reads *No Yes*.

Press   **Y** (for Yes).

Result. If you quit the program, the operating system prompt reappears.

Note. If you are using The TWIN introductory version, there is no room on the disk for the COMMAND.COM file, so a prompt reads *Insert COMMAND.COM disk in drive A and strike any key when ready*. In this, and all subsequent exercises, if you are quitting for the day, remove your disks, and then turn off the computer. If you want to work on another program, insert any disk with the COMMAND.COM file on it, and then press any key to return to the system prompt.

EXERCISE 86

Loading and Setting Up Lotus 1-2-3

In this exercise, you load Lotus 1-2-3. To display or print graphs your Lotus 1-2-3 program must be installed to work with the equipment in your system. This text assumes that your program has been installed. If your program has not been installed, see the manual that accompanies the program for instructions on how to install it. To begin this exercise, your computer must be turned off.

Step 1. Load the Operating System. This step describes how to load Lotus 1-2-3 from a disk that is not self-booting. If your disk is self-booting, insert it instead of the DOS disk in the instructions below, type **123**, and then press **Return**. Then, follow the instructions on entering the date and time.

To load the operating system

Insert   the DOS disk into drive A, and then turn on the computer. If your computer does not have a built-in clock, you are asked to enter the date.

Type   the date in the format month/day/year (for example, 1/1/86), and then press **Return**. A prompt asks you to enter the time.

Type   the time in the format hour:minute (for example, 10:15), and then press **Return**.

Result. In a moment, the A> prompt is displayed.

Step 2. Load Lotus 1-2-3. With the operating system prompt on the screen, you can load Lotus 1-2-3. Remove the DOS disk, and then insert the Lotus 1-2-3 System disk into drive A. Insert a formatted disk into drive B.

To load Lotus 1-2-3

Type   **123**, and then press **Return**.

Result. The drive spins as the program is loaded. In a few moments, the copyright screen appears. If you are using Release 2, the spreadsheet then appears. If you are using Release 1A, a prompt asks you to *Press Any Key to Continue.* Press any key, and in a few moments, the Lotus 1-2-3 spreadsheet (Figure 4-7b) appears on the screen.

Step 3. Specify the Default Drive. Before saving models, you should be sure your default drive is set to the drive into which you insert the data disk. If you are using a system with two floppy disk drives, the default drive should be set to B:\. You can make this change and save it so you don't have to change it each time you load the program.

To set the default drive

Press   **/WGDD** (for Worksheet, Global, Default, Directory) and the drive indicated following the prompt indicates the current default drive.

Press   **Esc** to delete the current entry.

Type   **B:**, and then press **Return**.

To save the setting

Press   **U** (for Update) to save the setting.

Press   **Q** (for Quit) to return to the spreadsheet.

Result. The new default drive is now saved in a configuration file so the default drive will be B whenever you load the program.

Step 4. Continue or Quit. You have now completed this exercise. Either continue to the next exercise, or quit the program.

To quit the program

Press   **/Q** (for Quit), and the prompt reads *No Yes.*

Press   **Y** (for Yes).

Result. If you quit the program, the operating system prompt reappears. Remove your disks, and then turn off the computer.

Getting to Know Your Program

In this exercise, you get to know your program's screen display, menus, key indicators, spreadsheet, and commands. To begin this exercise, the program must be loaded, and the spreadsheet must be displayed on the screen.

Step 1. Explore the Program's Screen Display. The screen display has two major areas: the worksheet and the control panel or status area. Find each area on the screen.

Step 2. Explore the Menus. To see the menus, press the slash key (/). The menu appears, and the mode indicator at the right end of the status line reads *MENU* to indicate you are in the program's command menus. Menu choices appear in the control panel. Press → to move the menu highlight along the list of choices. As you do so, the line below the menu displays detailed descriptions about each menu choice. If you press **Return**, the highlighted choice is executed. To see this, highlight Worksheet, and then press **Return**. A new menu, called a submenu, appears. Press **Esc** twice to remove the menus from the screen so that the mode indicator reads *READY*. You can always press **Esc** to back out of menus if you change you mind.

Step 3. Explore the Key Indicators. Indicators are displayed if you press **Num Lock**, **Scroll Lock**, or **Caps Lock**. To see them, press each of these keys once to turn on their indicators. The indicators for each key appear on the bottom line of the screen display. Before continuing, press each of the keys again to turn them off. The indicators no longer appear on the screen display.

Step 4. Explore Getting around the Spreadsheet. Let's explore the keys used to move the cursor around the spreadsheet.
1. Press → once. The cursor moves one cell to the right. The cell address indicator on the status line now reads *B1:*, indicating the coordinates of the cell the cursor is positioned in.
2. Press ↓ three times. The cursor moves down one cell at a time. The cell address indicator now reads *B4:*.
3. Hold down →. It automatically repeats. When you press → with the cursor against the right edge of the screen, the screen begins to scroll. The column letters in the border area change when you scroll past the right edge of the screen.
4. Press **Home**. The cursor immediately returns to cell A1, the upper left-hand corner of the spreadsheet.
5. Hold down ←. Beep, beep, beep!!! You cannot move the cursor off the spreadsheet.
6. Hold down ↓. See what it does.
7. Lost? Just press **Home**. It always takes you back to cell A1.
8. Want to see how big the spreadsheet is? Press **End**. The program displays the *END* indicator (*E* in the TWIN) in the lower right-hand corner of the screen. Now press →. You jump instantly to the last column on your spreadsheet. (The column varies depending on the program and version you are using.) Now press **End** again, and then press ↓. The cursor moves to the last row in the last column, the lower right-hand corner of the spreadsheet. Pressing **End** tells the program to move the cursor in the direction of the next key you press until it runs into a boundary. The boundary can be the edge of the spreadsheet or the boundary between a blank cell and a cell with data. You will find these key combinations a great help when you navigate large models because they can quickly move you to the end of a row or column of numbers.

9. Press **Home** to return to cell A1. Then press **PgDn**. It moves you a screen, or twenty rows, at a time. You can page quickly through a model this way to examine or create it. Now press **PgUp**. It does the same thing but in the opposite direction.

10. Press **Goto (F5)**, and a prompt asks you to enter the cell address you want to go to. Type **M30**, and then press **Return**. The cursor immediately jumps to cell M30.

11. Now experiment with some of the other cursor movement keys (see Table 4-3).

12. When you have finished experimenting, press **Home**, and the cursor returns to cell A1.

Step 5. Explore the Commands. With the cursor in cell A1 (press **Home** if it is not), type **Entry**. The characters you type appear on the edit line. Now, press **Return** to enter the characters into the cell. The status line now reads *A1: 'Entry,* indicating that the cursor is positioned in column A on row 1 and that the cell contains the indicated label. The apostrophe preceding the label is a label alignment character (see Topic 4-2).

Now, use the program's command that erases cell entries. Press the slash key (/) to display the menu. Press **R** (for Range) to display the Range submenu. Press → to move the highlight over the Erase choice, and then press **Return** to display a prompt that asks you what range to erase. Press **Return** to erase the suggested range—the cell that contains the cursor.

Step 6. Continue or Quit. You have now completed this exercise. Either clear the screen, continue to the next exercise, or quit the program.

To clear the screen

Press   **/WE** (for Worksheet, Erase), and the prompt reads *No Yes.*

Press   **Y** (for Yes) to clear the screen.

To quit the program

Press   **/Q** (for Quit), and the prompt reads *No Yes.*

Press   **Y** (for Yes).

Result. If you quit the program, the operating system prompt reappears. Remove your disks, and then turn off the computer.

QUESTIONS

1. What is a cell, and how are cell addresses given? What is the address of the cell in column 8 and row 30?

2. What are the two areas of the spreadsheet? Give two names for each area.

3. Where does the **Home** key move the cursor on many spreadsheet programs?

4. The typical spreadsheet program has three lines on the control panel: the status line, the prompt line, and the edit line. What is each line used for?

5. How do you calculate the number of cells in a spreadsheet?

6. What type of information can you enter into spreadsheet cells?

7. What are modes? Name a few common spreadsheet modes.

8. What is the purpose of **F5**, the Goto key?

9. Where does the **End** key move the cursor on many spreadsheet programs?

TOPIC 4-2
Entering Labels and Numbers and Saving Files

In this topic, we introduce you to the following procedures:

- Entering labels
- Entering numbers
- Saving files

BACKGROUND

You enter data into a spreadsheet by moving the cursor to the cell and then typing in the data. Entries are displayed on the edit line as you type them. You complete the entry by pressing **Return**, which moves the entry from the edit line to the cell the cursor is positioned in. If the cell already contains an entry, you can replace it by typing a new entry over it and then pressing **Return**.

You can use any of the cursor movement keys to complete an entry instead of pressing **Return**. For instance, to enter a number into a cell and automatically move down one row, press ↓ instead of **Return** after typing the number. When making several entries along a row or down a column, it is faster to enter data using one of the arrow keys because they enter the data and automatically move the cursor one cell in the direction of the arrow saving you a keystroke each time.

When you enter data, spreadsheet programs make a distinction between labels and values (numbers, formulas, and functions) since they can use values but not labels in calculations. When you type the first character, the program makes an assumption about which you are entering. For example, both The TWIN and Lotus 1-2-3 assume you are entering a value if you type any of the characters in Table 4-8. If you type any other character, the programs assume you are entering a label.

ENTERING LABELS

To enter a label, you move the cursor to the cell you want to enter it in, type the label, and then press **Return**. This is a straightforward procedure with one exception, labels that begin with numbers or certain other characters used in formulas and functions. If the first character you type is one of those listed in Table 4-8, the program assumes you are entering a value. Although this assumption on the part of the program usually saves you time, you sometimes have to override it.

TABLE 4-8
Characters That Spreadsheets Assume Are Values

0–9	(numbers)
+	(addition)
–	(subtraction)
*	(multiplication)
@	
(	
$	
#	

TABLE 4-9
Label Prefix Characters

Character	Effect on Label
"	Right-aligns label
^	Centers label
'	Left-aligns label (the default)

You can override the program's assumptions by typing a designated key or symbol before you type the entry's first character. If you want to enter a label that begins with a number, for example, 100 Elm Street, you first type a **label prefix** such as an apostrophe ('). This puts the program into *LABEL* mode. You then enter the label by typing it and pressing **Return**. The TWIN and Lotus 1-2-3 have three label prefix characters that you can use to enter labels beginning with numbers. You can also use these label prefixes with labels that begin with letters because they also control the alignment of the label in the cell. Table 4-9 describes the three label prefix characters.

When you are entering a label, check the mode indicator after typing the first character; the *READY* indicator should change to *LABEL*. If the mode indicator shows *VALUE,* the character you entered is one used to begin a number.

When entering labels, keep the following points in mind:

- Labels can be as long as 240 characters.

- Unless you enter a label prefix, the label is aligned with the default global setting (see Topic 4-6).

- If a label is longer than its cell is wide, it overflows into the next cell if that cell is empty. If the cell next to it is not empty, the label appears truncated; only the display is truncated, not the actual entry. To display the entire label, you can widen the column (see Topic 4-6).

Spreadsheet programs have a command that lets you repeat a specified character so that it fills the entire width of a cell or row. These commands are ideal for entering ruled lines to separate parts of a model. On The TWIN and Lotus 1-2-3, you press the backslash key (\) to repeat the next character you type until the cell is full. For example, pressing \ and then – **fills a cell with a single-ruled line. Pressing \ and** then = fills a cell with a double-ruled line. You can then copy the ruled line to other cells on the row to underline more than one column (see Topic 4-7). The nice thing about repeated labels is that if you change column widths, the labels automatically adjust so that they are always as wide as the columns, no wider or narrower.

ENTERING NUMBERS

To enter numbers, you move the cursor to the desired cell, type the number, and then press **Return**. If the first character you type is one of those listed in Table 4-8, entering numbers is automatic because the program recognizes them as values, and the mode indicator changes from *READY* to *VALUE*.

When entering numbers, keep the following points in mind:

- If you enter a number that is too long for the cell, it is displayed as a row of asterisks or other symbols. To display the entire number, you must widen the column or change the number's format (see Topic 4-6).

- Numbers are always right-aligned. You can change the alignment on a number by entering it as a label, but you cannot then use that number in calculations.

- Regardless of how they are displayed, numbers are always stored in memory with fifteen-digit precision. For example, you can format the number 1000.1425 so that it is displayed as $1,000, $1,000.14, 1000.142, and so on, but it is always calculated by any formulas that refer to it as 1000.1425 (see Topic 4-6). This is done so that calculations can be as exact as possible. If you want to change the precision of calculation, use the @RND function (see Topic 4-3).

- Numbers cannot be entered with spaces, commas, or dollar signs. For example, enter one thousand dollars as 1000, not $1,000.00. If you want to format the number, for example, to display dollar signs or commas, use the Range Format and Global Format commands (see Topic 4-6). The format commands can display the number as 1,000, $1,000, or $1,000.00.

- Long numbers can be entered in scientific notation to save space and avoid typing errors. For example, to enter the number 1,000,000, type **1e6**. If the column is wide enough, the full number is displayed.

- To enter a percentage, type the number followed by a percent sign, or type in its decimal equivalent. Either way, you must format the cell as a percentage if you want it displayed with the percent sign (see Topic 4-6). When you enter a percentage as a whole number followed by a percent sign, the program automatically converts it into a decimal by dividing the number by 100. For example, entering a percentage as 10% is the same as entering it as 0.1 or as 10/100.

USING DATA FILL

The Data Fill command *(not available on the introductory version of The TWIN)* enters an equally incremented series of numbers in a row, column, or block of cells. You decide what number to start with, what increment to increase or decrease that number by, and what number to stop at.

- When the Data Fill command is used a second time, the program remembers the previous settings, including the range. You can change a setting by reentering it or keep the setting by pressing **Return**.

- The start, step (increment), and stop numbers can be positive or negative numbers or formulas.

- Both the fill range and the stop number you enter determine the results. The Data Fill command continues to enter numbers until it reaches the end of the range or the stop number, whichever comes first.

SAVING FILES

When creating models, save them often, not just when you finish them. Turning off the computer, power failures, hardware problems, or making mistakes can cause you to lose files that are in the computer's memory. Files are not safe from these kinds of disasters until you have saved them on a disk, a more permanent form of storage.

To save a model, you first assign it a filename acceptable to your computer's operating system and then execute the program's save command. If the file has been saved before, you have a choice to make. You can save it under the same filename, in which case it overwrites and erases the previous version. Or you can save it under a different filename, in which case a series of versions are saved, enabling you to recall any earlier version.

EXERCISE 88
Entering a College Budget

In this exercise, you enter labels and numbers. To begin this exercise, you must load the program or clear the screen of any other model.

FIGURE 4-10
The BUDGET model

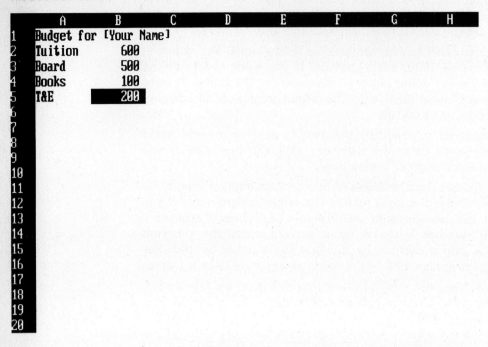

Your finished model should look like Figure 4-10. Refer to this figure to check your results as you complete the steps in this exercise.

Note. You may not be able to complete this exercise in one lab period. If you stop work and turn off the computer, any data you have entered is erased from the computer's memory. Your work is then lost unless you have saved the data on a disk. Step 5 describes saving your work. If you must quit, refer to that step. When you are ready to resume work, load the program (see Topic 4-1); then retrieve the unfinished model (see Topic 4-4).

Step 1. Enter Labels. Let's enter a one-year college budget using some made up numbers. In this step, enter each label by pressing **Return**, and then press ↓ to move the cursor to the next cell.

To enter labels

Press	**Home** to move the cursor to cell A1.
Type	**Budget for,** press **Spacebar**, type **your name**, and then press **Return**.
Press	↓ to move the cursor to cell A2.
Type	**Tuition,** and then press **Return**.
Press	↓ to move the cursor to cell A3.
Type	**Board,** and then press **Return**.
Press	↓ to move the cursor to cell A4.
Type	**Books,** and then press **Return**.
Press	↓ to move the cursor to cell A5.
Type	**T&E,** and then press **Return**.

Results. Your labels should match the labels shown in Figure 4-10.

322   SPREADSHEET APPLICATIONS

Step 2. Enter Numbers. Now enter the numbers. In the instructions that follow, Goto tells you to move the cursor to the indicated cell by pressing the appropriate arrow keys. Up until now, you have typed data, pressed **Return** to enter it, and then pressed the arrow keys to move to the next cell. Here, try another technique. Use the arrow keys to both *enter* the data and *move* the cursor. When practicing this technique, watch the status line to be sure you are in the correct cells before entering the numbers.

To enter numbers

Goto   B2, type **600**, and then press ↓ to move the cursor to cell B3.

Type   **500**, and then press ↓ to move the cursor to cell B4.

Type   **100**, and then press ↓ to move the cursor to cell B5.

Type   **200**, and then press **Return**.

Results. Your numbers should match the numbers shown in Figure 4-10.

Step 3. Change the Numbers. The numbers you entered in the previous step were made up. Here, move the cursor to each number, and type in numbers that more accurately reflect your own situation. As you type new numbers into cells that already contain numbers, the new ones replace the old when you press **Return**.

Step 4. Print the Model. Now make a printout of the model. Turn on the printer, and be sure it has paper in it. If for any reason you want to stop the printer while it is printing, press **Ctrl-Break**.

Note. If you are using The TWIN (in this and all subsequent exercises), you need not specify a range if you want to print the entire model. The program automatically prints the entire model when you press **/PPG** (for Print, Printer, Go) from the Print menu.

To print the model

Press   **/PPR** (for Print, Printer, Range), and the prompt asks you to enter the range you want to print.

Type   **A1.B5**, and then press **Return**.

Press   **AG** (for Align, Go).

Result. The printer begins printing out the model. When the printer stops, press **P** (for Page) to advance the paper out of the printer. When the menu reappears, press **Q** (for Quit) to leave the Print menu.

Step 5. Save the Model. Now that you have finished the model, save it into a file on the disk so that you can retrieve it later. Before proceeding, *be sure a formatted disk is in drive B and the drive's door is closed.*

To save the model

Press   **/FS** (for File, Save), and the prompt asks you for the name to save the file under.

Type   **BUDGET**, and then press **Return**.

Result. The disk drive spins, and the model is saved on the disk in drive B.

Step 6. Continue or Quit. You have now completed this exercise. Either clear the screen and continue to the next exercise, or quit the program if you have finished.

To clear the screen

Press   **/WE** (for Worksheet, Erase), and the prompt reads *No Yes*.

Press   **Y** (for Yes) to clear the screen.

To quit the program

Press   **/Q** (for Quit), and the prompt reads *No Yes*.

Press   **Y** (for Yes).

Result. If you quit the program, the operating system prompt reappears. Remove your disks, and then turn off the computer.

EXERCISE 89

Entering a Series of Numbers

In this exercise, you use the Data Fill command *(not available on the introductory version of The TWIN)*. To begin this exercise, you must load the program or clear the screen of any other model.

In this exercise, you are asked by the program to specify a range. Ranges are discussed in detail in Topic 4-6. They are simply a group of adjacent cells. To indicate what cells are included in the group, you type the cell address of the cell in the upper left-hand corner of the range, type a period (the program displays two on the screen), and then type the address of the cell in the lower right-hand corner.

Step 1. Fill a Column. Begin by using the Data Fill command to fill a column with numbers. When you specify the range here, the cells that define the range are the topmost and bottommost cells in the column.

To fill a column with the data fill command

Press   **Home** to move the cursor to cell A1.

Press   **/DF** (for Data, Fill), and the prompt asks you to enter the range to be filled.

Type   **A1.A20**, and then press **Return**. The prompt asks you to enter the number to start with and suggests the number 0.

Press   **Return** to accept the suggested start value, and the prompt asks you to enter the step, or increment value, and suggests the number 1.

Press   **Return** to accept the suggested step value, and the prompt asks you to enter the number to stop at.

Press   **Return** to accept the suggested stop value.

Result. The column fills with a series of numbers starting at 0, increasing by 1 in each cell, and stopping in the last cell you specified as the range. To see this, press **End**, and then press ↓ to move the cursor to the last number in the column. Press ↓ to scroll the screen up to see that the numbers do not continue past row 20.

Step 2. Fill a Row. Now, fill a row with numbers. When you specify the range here, the cells that define the range are the leftmost and rightmost cells in the row.

To fill a row with the data fill command

Press   **Home** to move the cursor to cell A1.

Press   **/DF** (for Data, Fill), and the prompt asks you to enter the range to be filled and highlights the previous range.

Type	**A1.H1**, and then press **Return**. The prompt asks you to enter the number to start with and suggests the number 0.
Press	**Return** to accept the suggested start value, and the prompt asks you to enter the step, or increment value, and suggests the number 1.
Press	**Return** to accept the suggested step value, and the prompt asks you to enter the number to stop at.
Press	**Return** to accept the suggested stop value.

Result. The row fills with a series of numbers starting at 0, increasing by 1 in each cell, and stopping in the last cell you specified as the range. To see this, press **End**, and then press → to move the cursor to the last number on the row. Press → to scroll the screen to the left to see that the numbers do not continue past column H.

Step 3. Fill a Range. Finally, fill a range of cells with numbers. When you specify the range here, the cells that define the range are the upper left-hand and lower right-hand cells in the block.

To fill a range with the data fill command

Press	**Home** to move the cursor to cell A1.
Press	**/DF** (for Data, Fill), and the prompt asks you to enter the range to be filled and highlights the previous range.
Type	**A1.H20**, and then press **Return**. The prompt asks you to enter the number to start with and suggests the number 0.
Type	**1**, and then press **Return** to begin the sequence with the number 1. The prompt asks you to enter the step, or increment value, and suggests the number 1.
Type	**10**, and then press **Return** to change the step to 10. The prompt asks you to enter the number to stop at.
Type	**1500**, and then press **Return** to end the sequence with the number 1500.

Result. The block fills with a series of numbers starting at 1, increasing by 10 in each cell, and stopping at the number 1491 because the stop value was reached before the end of the range was. The number is 1491 and not 1501 because the later value is greater than the stop value that you specified. To move the cursor to the lower-right corner of the active area of the spreadsheet, press **End**, and then press **Home** to move the cursor to cell H20, the cell where the last row and column containing data intersect.

Step 4. Continue or Quit. You have now completed this exercise. There is no need to save or print the model. Either clear the screen and continue to the next exercise, or quit the program if you have finished.

To clear the screen

Press	**/WE** (for Worksheet, Erase), and the prompt reads *No Yes*.
Press	**Y** (for Yes) to clear the screen.

To quit the program

Press	**/Q** (for Quit), and the prompt reads *No Yes*.
Press	**Y** (for Yes).

Result. If you quit the program, the operating system prompt reappears. Remove your disks, and then turn off the computer.

TABLE 4-10
Typical Line Patterns

To Enter	Press
_____	\-
=============	\=
***************	*
....	\.
_____	_

EXERCISE 90

Using Ruled Lines and Borders

Ruled lines are most commonly used to separate sections of a model. The best way to enter horizontal ruled lines is with the repeat command (the backslash, followed by the character you want to repeat). If you change the column width, the character repeats to fill the new width. Try entering the ruled lines shown in Table 4-10 using the commands described in that table. To do so, just move the cursor to an empty cell, press the backslash key, the indicated character, and then press **Return**. In later topics, you see how to copy ruled lines like these to other cells. When finished, refer to Step 4 in Exercise 89 for instructions on clearing the screen or quitting.

TIPS

- **If you enter a label that does not conform to the program's rules**, the computer beeps, and you are automatically placed in edit mode (see Topic 4-4). For example, if you type the label **123 Main St.** without a label prefix, when you press **Return**, the computer beeps and the program changes to edit mode. To enter a label prefix, press **Home**, type ', and then press **Return**.

- **Cells containing labels have a numeric value of 0 when referred to by a formula** on The TWIN and Lotus 1-2-3 Release 1A. On Release 2, Lotus introduced the ability to manipulate strings (see Topic 4-3). Since labels can be manipulated on this program, you cannot refer to them in some types of formulas or functions or you will get an error message.

- **To change the alignment on a range of labels**, use the Range Label-Prefix command (see Topic 4-6).

QUESTIONS

1. What is the difference between a label and a value?
2. What is a label prefix, and why would you need to use it?
3. What is a repeating label? What can they be used for?
4. How would you enter the number $6,580.00?
5. How do you enter a label that begins with a number?
6. What happens when you enter a number followed by a percent sign?
7. What does the Data Fill command do?
8. What is a range?
9. How would you enter a label so it is aligned with the left edge of the cell? So it aligns with the right edge? So it is centered?

TOPIC 4-3
Entering Formulas and Functions

In this topic, we introduce you to the following procedures:

- Entering formulas
- Using built-in functions
- Using strings

BACKGROUND

You can enter formulas and functions in spreadsheet cells that either calculate numbers directly or refer to cells elsewhere on the spreadsheet into which you enter numbers or other formulas and functions.

FORMULAS

When entering formulas, you must understand a few principles, namely, how operators and the order of operations work and the difference between constants and variables. Once you understand these principles, you can enter formulas (and functions) by typing them in or by pointing.

Operators

When building formulas, certain keys (and the symbols they generate on the screen) tell the program what calculations to perform. These symbols, or **operators**, are used along with numbers or cell references to create formulas. Table 4-11 lists the typical spreadsheet operators, and Table 4-12 shows how you can use these operators to create formulas.

The Order of Operations

When entering formulas that contain more than one operator, another concept, **the order of operations**, becomes important. Every program has a specific order that operators are calculated in. Table 4-13 shows the order of operations followed by The TWIN and Lotus 1-2-3.

- Some programs automatically calculate operations from left to right in the order they appear in the formula unless you use parentheses, in which case the numbers in parentheses are calculated first.

TABLE 4-11
Spreadsheet Operators

Operator	Use
+	Addition
−	Subtraction
*	Multiplication
/	Division
^	Exponent

TABLE 4-12
Spreadsheet Formulas

Formula	Displayed Result
10+10	20
10*4	40
30–5	25
200/5	40
+A1+A2	The value in cell A1 plus the value in cell A2
+A1*A2	The value in cell A1 times the value in cell A2
+A1–A2	The value in cell A1 minus the value in cell A2
+A1/A2	The value in cell A1 divided by the value in cell A2
10+A1	10 plus the value entered in cell A1
2*A1	2 times the value entered in cell A1
4–A1	4 minus the value entered in cell A1
200/A1	200 divided by the value entered in cell A1
10^2	100 — 10 raised to the second power
10^A1	10 raised to the power entered in cell A1

■ Other programs follow algebra's rules of precedence; that is, those operators with a higher level of precedence are performed before those with a lower level. For example, multiplication and division have equal precedence but a higher precedence than addition and subtraction, which also have equal precedence. Operators with the same level of precedence are calculated from left to right.

Let's see how the order of operations works in practice. Assume you want to add the numbers 1 and 1/2. To do this, you can enter the formula as 1+1/2. The formula contains two operators: one to add (+) and one to divide (/).

■ If calculations are performed from left to right, the answer is 1. First addition is performed, so 1+1 = 2; then division is performed, so 2/2 = 1.

■ If algebra's rules of precedence are followed, the answer is 1.5. First division is performed, so 1/2 = 0.5; then addition, which has a lower precedence, is performed, so 1+0.5 = 1.5.

TABLE 4-13
Order of Operations

Operator	Description	Precedence Level
^	Exponentiation	7
+	Unary plus sign (for example, +A1>A4)	6
–	Negation (for example, -A1>-A4)	6
*	Multiplication	5
/	Division	5
+	Addition	4
–	Subtraction	4
=	Equal to	3
<	Less than	3
	Greater than	3
<=	Less than or equal to	3
=	Greater than or equal to	3
<>	Not equal to	3
#NOT#	Logical NOT	2
#AND#	Logical AND	1
#OR#	Logical OR	1

You can enter formulas so that operations occur in the desired sequence, but it is usually easier to use parentheses to control the order of calculations regardless of the rules followed by the program. For example, entering the formula as 1+(1/2) calculates the correct answer since the operations within the parentheses are always performed first. If parentheses are nested, for example, 1+(1/(1/2)), the operations are performed from the innermost parentheses outward; in this formula, the answer is 3.

Constants and Variables

When you enter formulas, they can contain both constants and variables.

Constants are numbers you do not expect to change. For this reason, you can embed them in formulas. The formula 5*10 contains only numbers; there are no references to other cells. Numbers contained in formulas are called constants because you can change them only with some difficulty, either by reentering or editing the formula, for example, by changing it to 6*10.

Variables are numbers you do expect to change. The formula 6*A1 contains a constant and a cell reference. The number in the cell referred to by the formula can be easily changed. These numbers are called variables because you expect to change them to see what effect different numbers have on the outcome.

When creating a model, you first decide what variables you want to explore, and then structure your models accordingly, using the following combinations of constants and variables:

- Formulas can be all constants (Figure 4-11a). To build formulas, you might type 100*2 in cell A3, and the number 200 is calculated and displayed. But these formulas do not take advantage of a spreadsheet's unique feature to explore what-ifs. To change a formula entered in this way, you must edit or reenter it. You build more powerful models by entering formulas that refer to other cells. This way, you can change the values in the cells the formula refers to, and it calculates them just as if they were part of the formula.

- Formulas can be part constant and part variable (Figure 4-11b). To enter a formula like this into cell A9, you might type 100*A8 and then enter the number 2 into cell A8. Here, too, the number 200 is calculated, and it is displayed in cell A9. The difference is that part of the formula refers to another cell so the number in that cell becomes a variable you can change to explore what-ifs. If you change the number in cell A8, the formula in cell A9 automatically recalculates and displays the new result.

FIGURE 4-11
Formulas with constants and variables

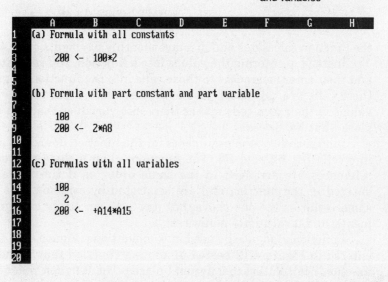

- Formulas can be all variables (Figure 11c). For example, you might break out another variable and enter 100 into cell A14 and 2 into cell A15 and then a formula into cell A16 that reads +A14*A15.

You should consider almost every number a variable for three reasons.

- Embedding a number in a formula is making an assumption either that it should not or cannot be changed or that it is unimportant to the outcome of the analysis. When exploring the model, you may find it is very sensitive to changes in that number—a phenomenon you would never discover if the number were embedded in a formula.

- The next time you use the model, you may forget there is an embedded number and not take it into consideration.

- Printouts of models generally print out only the displayed values, not the formulas behind them. Anyone else trying to follow your analysis might get lost if too many numbers were embedded in formulas rather than displayed on the printout.

BUILT-IN FUNCTIONS

All spreadsheet programs contain built-in functions designed to perform commonly used calculations. Many of the calculations they can perform are quite complicated, so functions simplify model building by simplifying the formula building you must enter.

The Structure of Functions

Functions have a structure, or syntax, that you must follow.

- A prefix must begin every function. Frequently, the prefix is an @ sign followed by a contraction of the function, for example, @SUM (sum), @AVG (average), and @PMT (payment).

- Arguments must follow the prefix and be enclosed in parentheses. Arguments can be numbers, cell references, ranges, formulas, or other functions. If the function contains more than one argument, each part is separated from the other by commas.

For example, to calculate monthly payments on a loan, the function syntax is @PMT(Principle, Interest, Period). The prefix is @PMT (for PayMenT). The arguments are Principle, Interest, and Period and are separated by commas and enclosed in parentheses. If you substitute numbers in the function, for example

@PMT(10000,.14,48)

the function calculates and displays monthly payments of $1,402.60.

Instead of entering the values into a function, you can enter them into other cells, and then enter references to those cells into the function (Figure 4-12). The values in these cells are calculated just as if they were a part of the function. Entering the values in their own cells makes them into variables that you can easily change to explore what-ifs.

In Figure 4-12, the arguments for the function described above have been entered into cells B1, B2, and B3. The functions then include references to those cells. The references are arranged in the same order as if the values themselves had been entered in the function and are separated by commas. The function calculates the same result as the one above, but now you can easily change any of the three arguments, and it calculates a new result.

Functions can also be used in combinations. Figure 4-13 shows the same function entered in Figure 4-12 nested in another function that rounds the result of the first function's calculation to 0 decimal places. The function reads "Round the value of the

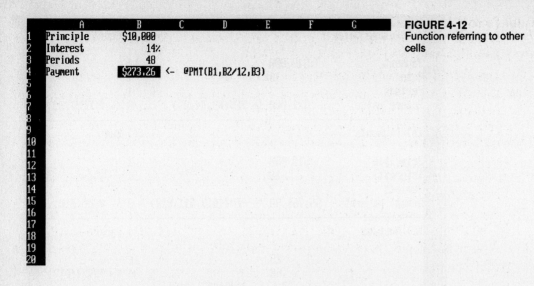

FIGURE 4-12
Function referring to other cells

	A	B	C	D	E	F	G
1	Principle	$10,000					
2	Interest	14%					
3	Periods	48					
4	Payment	$273.26	<- @PMT(B1,B2/12,B3)				

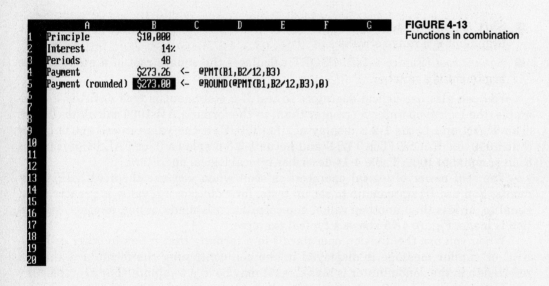

FIGURE 4-13
Functions in combination

	A	B	C	D	E	F	G
1	Principle	$10,000					
2	Interest	14%					
3	Periods	48					
4	Payment	$273.26	<- @PMT(B1,B2/12,B3)				
5	Payment (rounded)	$273.00	<- @ROUND(@PMT(B1,B2/12,B3),0)				

function @PMT(B1,B2/12,B3) to 0 decimal places". The original function calculates the value $273.26, but the new one rounds it to $273.00.

The number and types of functions vary from program to program, as does the exact name of the function and the way its arguments are structured. Figure 4-14 illustrates some of the functions available on most programs. (The introductory version of The TWIN has only the @PMT function.)

■ *Future value* (Figure 4-14a). @FV calculates the future value of an annuity. The arguments are the regular payment, interest rate, and period.

■ *Mortgage payments* (Figure 4-14b). @PMT calculates the monthly payments needed to amortize a loan. The arguments are the principle, interest rate, and period.

■ *Average* (Figure 4-14c). @AVG calculates the average value of a range of values. The argument is a range of values.

■ *Count* (Figure 4-14d). @COUNT calculates the number of nonblank cells in a range. The argument is a range of values.

Entering Formulas and Functions

331

FIGURE 4-14
Typical functions

```
       A              B              C            D       E         F
1  (a) Future Value                          (d) Count
2
3  Payment        $10,000                     1
4  Rate              10%                      1
5  Periods            2                       1
6  Future value   $21,000 <- @FV(B3,B4,B5)    3 <- @COUNT(D3..D5)
7  -----------------------------------------------------------------
8  (b) Payments                              (e) Sum
9
10 Principle      $10,000                     1
11 Interest          10%                      1
12 Periods            2                       1
13 Annual payments $5,761.90 <- @PMT(B10,B11,B12) 3 <- @SUM(D10..D12)
14 -----------------------------------------------------------------
15 (c) Average                               (f) Square Root
16
17                  25                       16
18                  50                        4 <- @SQRT(D17)
19                37.5 <- @AVG(B17..B18)
20
```

- *Sum* (Figure 4-14e). @SUM calculates the total sum of a range of values. The argument is a range of values.

- *Square root* (Figure 4-14f). @SQRT calculates the square root of a number. The argument is a number.

You can also use logical operators to test if a statement is true or false. For example, the logical operator > (greater than) in the formula A1>1000 calculates TRUE (The TWIN and Lotus 1-2-3 display a 1 for TRUE) if the value in cell A1 is larger than 1000 and FALSE (The TWIN and Lotus 1-2-3 display a 0 for FALSE) if it is less than or equal to 1000. Table 4-14 describes typical logical operators.

The real power of logical operators is seen when you use them with IF statements. You use IF statements to set up tests; for example, if a value is greater than, equal to, or less than another value, one calculation is made; if not, another calculation is made. Figure 4-15 shows a typical example.

When you use the division operator (/) in a formula that refers to other cells, an ERR or similar message is displayed in the cell containing the formula if the cell referred to in the denominator is blank, as it may be in a template. For example, if

FIGURE 4-15
Logical operators

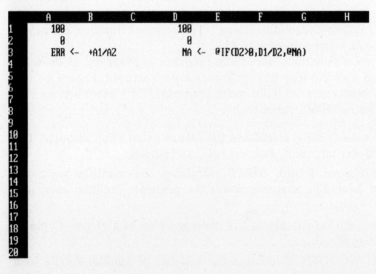

```
      A      B      C      D      E      F      G      H
1    100                  100
2     0                    0
3   ERR <-  +A1/A2        NA <-  @IF(D2>0,D1/D2,@NA)
4
5
6
7
8
9
10
11
12
13
14
15
16
17
18
19
20
```

TABLE 4-14
Typical Logical Operators

Operator	Description
=	Tests if values are equal. For example, @IF(A1=1,1,0) displays a 1 if the value in cell A1 is equal to 1, and a 0 if it is not.
<>	Tests if values are not equal. For example, @IF(A1<>1,1,0) displays a 0 if the value in cell A1 is equal to 1, and a 1 if it is not.
<	Tests if one value is less than another. For example, @IF(A1<1,1,0) displays a 1 if the value in cell A1 is less than 1, and a 0 if it is 1 or larger.
>	Tests if one value is greater than another. For example, @IF(A1>1,1,0) displays a 1 if the value in cell A1 is greater than 1, and a 0 if it is 1 or smaller.
<=	Tests if one value is less than or equal to another. For example, @IF(A1<=1,1,0) displays a 1 if the value in cell A1 is less than or equal to 1, and a 0 if it is larger than 1.
>=	Tests if one value is greater than or equal to another. For example, @IF(A1>=1,1,0) displays a 1 if the value in cell A1 is greater than or equal to 1, and a 0 if it is less than 1.
AND	Sets up tests where two or more conditions must be satisfied before a calculation is made. For example, @IF(A1<1#AND#A2>2,1,0) displays a 1 if the value in cell A1 is less than 1 *and* the value in cell A2 greater than 2. It displays a 0 if the value is between 1 and 2.
OR	Sets up tests where one of two or more conditions must be satisfied before a calculation is made. For example, @IF(A1=1#OR#A1=2,1,0) displays a 1 if the value in cell A1 is equal to 1 *or* 2. It displays a 0 if the value is anything else.

you enter the formula A1/A2 into a cell, it displays an error message if cell A2 is blank. To prevent error messages, you can embed the formula in an IF statement. For example, in cell D3 the formula is @IF(D2>0,D1/D2,@NA). This formula now reads "If the value in cell D2 is greater than 0, then divide the value in cell D1 by the value in cell D2, otherwise display an @NA."

ENTERING FORMULAS AND FUNCTIONS

There are two ways to enter formulas and functions: by typing them in and, if they refer to other cells, by pointing to the cells with the cursor.

■ You can type in a formula that refers to another cell, for example, A1*A2. But this formula begins with a letter, so if you type that letter first, the program assumes a label is being entered. To enter formulas like this that begin with letters, you must first type the plus sign (+) to enter the formula as +A1*A2. You can also begin formulas with any of the value characters listed in Table 4-8.

■ You can use cursor pointing to point to cells referred to in the formula. Pointing is especially useful when working on larger spreadsheets where the cells you want to refer to are not displayed on the screen. Experienced users almost always build formulas by pointing because it is faster, more accurate, and easier than typing. Figure 4-16 shows how cursor pointing is used with The TWIN and Lotus 1-2-3 to enter a formula.

In Figure 4-16, the numbers 3 and 4 have been entered into cells A1 and A2. Let's say you want to use cursor pointing to enter a formula into cell A3 that adds the value in cell A2 to the value in cell A1.

FIGURE 4-16
Entering formula

1. Move the cursor to cell A3, and then press the plus sign (+) to begin the formula. The edit line reads +, and the mode indicator reads *VALUE* (Figure 4-16a).

2. Press ↑ twice to move the cursor to cell A1. The formula displayed on the edit line now reads *+A1*, and the mode indicator reads *POINT* (Figure 4-16b).

3. Press the plus sign (+). The formula displayed on the edit line now reads *+A1+*, and the cursor returns to cell A3 (Figure 4-16c).

☐4 Press ↑ to point to cell A2, the cell you want to add to A1. The formula displayed on the edit line now reads *+A1+A2* (Figure 4-16d).

☐5 Press **Return** to complete the entry, and the formula leaves the edit line and is entered into cell A3. It calculates and displays the result 7 (Figure 4-16e).

When entering formulas, keep the following points in mind:

■ Formulas can be as long as 240 characters.

■ To display a formula on the edit line, move the cursor to the cell that contains the formula. If the formula is too long to be fully displayed, press **Edit** (**F2**), and then use → and ← to move along the line. When you are finished, press **Esc** to return to the spreadsheet and leave the formula unchanged.

■ When entering formulas that begin with a letter (formulas that refer to other cells, for instance), you must begin the formula with one of the value characters (**+ − * @ # $ (.**). Otherwise, the formula is treated as a label.

EXERCISE 91

Adding Formulas and Functions to the Budget Model

In this exercise, you enter formulas and functions. To begin this exercise, you must load the program or clear the screen of any other model. This exercise uses the BUDGET model you created in Exercise 88. You must complete that exercise before you can begin this one.

Your finished model should look like Figure 4-17. Refer to this figure to check your results as you complete the steps in this exercise.

Step 1. Retrieve the Model. When you use the File Retrieve command, any work on the screen is erased. Be sure to save your work before retrieving a new file. Before retrieving the BUDGET file, insert the disk you saved it on into drive B, and then close the drive's door.

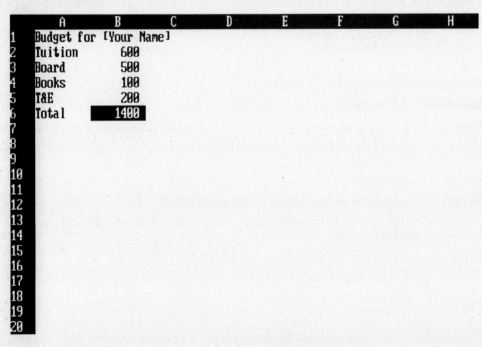

FIGURE 4-17
The revised BUDGET model

To retrieve a file

Press   **/FR** (for File, Retrieve), and the prompt asks you for the name of the file you want to retrieve. A list of files on the disk is displayed.

Press   → if necessary to move the highlight over BUDGET (it may be followed by an extension that the program automatically adds to its files), and then press **Return**.

Result. The BUDGET model appears on the screen.

Step 2. Type a Formula to Add the Numbers. Let's type in a formula that adds the numbers in each of the cells in column B. Before doing so, however, restore the original numbers if you changed them so your results match ours.

To restore the original numbers

Goto   B2, type **600**, and then press ↓ to move the cursor to cell B3.

Type   **500**, and then press ↓ to move the cursor to cell B4.

Type   **100** , and then press ↓ to move the cursor to cell B5.

Type   **200**, and then press **Return**.

To add a label

Goto   A6, type **Total**, and then press **Return**.

To type in a formula

Goto   B6, type **+B2+B3+B4+B5**, and then press **Return**.

Result. The total of the numbers in the four cells appears in cell B6.

Step 3. Use Cursor Pointing to Enter a Formula. Now, enter the same formula by pointing to the cells to be added.

To enter a formula by pointing

Goto   B6, and press **+**. (The edit line displays +.)

Press   ↑ four times to move the cursor to cell B2. (The edit line displays *+B2*.)

Press   +, and the cursor jumps back to cell B6.

Press   ↑ three times to move the cursor to cell B3. (The edit line displays *+B2+B3*.)

Press   +, and the cursor jumps back to cell B6.

Press   ↑ two times to move the cursor to cell B4. (The edit line displays *+B2+B3+B4*.)

Press   +, and the cursor jumps back to cell B6.

Press   ↑ to move the cursor to cell B5. (The edit line displays *+B2+B3+B4+B5*.)

Press   **Return** to enter the formula.

Result. The same formula and the same result is entered into cell B6.

Step 4. Enter a Function. As you have seen, entering formulas that refer to each cell can take a lot of time. It is faster to use a function to add a column of numbers.

To enter a function by pointing

Goto   B6, and type **@SUM(**.

Press   ↑ four times to move the cursor to cell B2 and the edit line displays *@SUM(B2*.

Press   . (the period) to anchor the range and the edit line displays *@SUM(B2..B2*.

Press   ↓ three times to move the cursor to cell B5 and the edit line displays *@SUM(B2..B5*.

Press   ) to complete the function, and then press **Return** to enter the function.

Result. The same result is calculated, but this time by a function, not a formula.

Step 5. Print the Model. Now make a printout of the model. Turn on the printer, and be sure it has paper in it.

To print the model

Press   **/PPR** (for Print, Printer, Range), and the prompt asks you to enter the range you want to print.

Type   **A1.B6**, and then press **Return**.

Press   **AG** (for Align, Go).

Result. The printer begins printing out the model. When the printer stops, press **PQ** (for Page, Quit) to advance the paper out of the printer and leave the Print menu.

Step 6. Save the Model. Now that you have finished the model, save it in a file on the disk so that you can retrieve it later. Before proceeding, *be sure a formatted disk is in drive B and the drive's door is closed.*

To save the model

Press   **/FS** (for File, Save), and the prompt asks you for the name to save the file under and suggests the name BUDGET.

Press   **Return** to accept the suggested name, and the prompt reads *Cancel Replace*.

Press   **R** (for Replace).

Result. The drive spins, and the revised model is saved on the disk.

Step 7. Continue or Quit. You have now completed this exercise. Either clear the screen and continue to the next exercise or quit the program if you have finished.

To clear the screen

Press   **/WE** (for Worksheet, Erase), and the prompt reads *No Yes*.

Press   **Y** (for Yes) to clear the screen.

To quit the program

Press   **/Q** (for Quit), and the prompt reads *No Yes*.

Press   **Y** (for Yes).

Result. If you quit the program, the operating system prompt reappears. Remove your disks, and then turn off the computer.

Figure 4-18
The AUTOLOAN Model

```
            A                B        C       D       E       F
1    AUTOLOAN model
2    Cost             10000
3    Down              2000
4    Loan              8000
5    Interest          0.12
6    Term                48
7    Monthly payment 210.6706
8    Total payments  10112.19
9
10
11
12
13
14
15
16
17
18
19
20
```

EXERCISE 92

Creating an Auto Loan Model

In this exercise, you enter formulas and functions. To begin this exercise, you must load the program or clear the screen of any other model.

Over the past few years, car dealers have used special financing terms to attract buyers to their showrooms. Advertisements proclaim "Low Interest," "Low Monthly Payment," "Cash Rebates," "Discounts," and other enticements. Here, you create a model to evaluate these offers. The model calculates the monthly and total payments due on a loan based on the principle, interest, and term of the loan.

Your finished model should look like Figure 4-18. Refer to this figure to check your results as you complete the steps in this exercise.

Step 1. Enter Labels. Let's begin the auto loan model by entering labels to identify rows.

To enter labels

Goto   A1 (press **Home**), type **AUTOLOAN model**, and then press ↓ to move the cursor to cell A2.

Type   **Cost**, and then press ↓ to move the cursor to cell A3.

Type   **Down**, and then press ↓ to move the cursor to cell A4.

Type   **Loan**, and then press ↓ to move the cursor to cell A5.

Type   **Interest**, and then press ↓ to move the cursor to cell A6.

Type   **Term**, and then press ↓ to move the cursor to cell A7.

Type   **Monthly payment**, and then press ↓ to move the cursor to cell A8.

Type   **Total payments**, and then press **Return**.

Result. Your labels should look like those in Figure 4-18.

Step 2. Change Column Widths. If you look closely at the labels you entered in column A, you notice many of them are wider than the column. Initially, column widths are always set to 9 characters but you can easily widen them so that the labels are not hidden when you enter data in the next column.

To widen column A

Press   **Home** to move the cursor to column A.

Press   **/WCS** (for Worksheet, Column, Set), and the prompt asks you to enter the column width.

Press   → to scroll the column wider, or press ← to scroll it narrower.

Result. As you press → or ←, the number following the prompt indicates the current column width. Practice scrolling it in both directions. When you are finished experimenting, scroll the column so that the prompt indicates it is twenty-five characters wide, and then press **Return**.

Step 3. Enter Numbers. Now enter numbers for a new car purchase. Let's assume you are thinking of buying a $10,000 car and have $2,000 to put down.

To enter numbers

Goto   B2, type **10000** , and then press ↓ to move the cursor to cell B3.

Type   **2000** , and then press ↓ twice to move the cursor to cell B5.

Type   **.12**, and then press ↓ to move the cursor to cell B6.

Type   **48**, and then press **Return**.

Result. Your numbers should look like those in Figure 4-18.

Step 4. Enter a Formula. Now enter a formula that calculates the loan required by subtracting the down payment in cell B3 from the cost of the car in cell B2.

To enter a formula

Goto   B4, type **+B2–B3**, and then press **Return**.

Result. The formula calculates and displays 8000.

Step 5. Enter a Function. Now enter a function to calculate the monthly payment. A function is a small program within a program that performs complicated calculations. The function you enter here calculates the monthly payment based on three variables, the amount of the loan, the interest rate (divided by 12 to convert it from an annual into a monthly rate), and the term of the loan.

To enter a function

Goto   B7, type **@PMT(B4,B5/12,B6)**, and then press **Return**.

Result. The formula calculates and displays 210.6706.

Step 6. Enter a Formula by Pointing. Now enter a formula that calculates the total payments by multiplying the period of the loan by the monthly payment. Instead of typing in the formula as you did the last time, you use cursor pointing to create the formula.

To enter a formula by pointing

Goto   B8, and then type **+**. (The edit line displays +.)

Press   ↑ to point to cell B7. (The edit line displays +*B7*.)

Type	*. (The edit line displays +B7*.)
Press	↑ two times to point to cell B6. (The edit line displays +B7*B6.)
Press	**Return**.

Result. The formula calculates and displays 10112.19. The model now shows you pay more than $10,000 to pay back an $8,000 loan given the interest rate and term you entered.

Step 7. Save Your Work. Now save your work. Before proceeding, *be sure a formatted disk is in drive B and the drive's door is closed.*

To save the model

Press	**/FS** (for File, Save), and the prompt asks you for the name to save the file under.
Type	**AUTOLOAN**, and then press **Return**.

Result. The disk drive spins, and the model is saved onto the disk in drive B.

Step 8. Print the Model. Turn on the printer, and be sure it has paper in it.

To print the model

Press	**/PPR** (for Print, Printer, Range), and the prompt asks you to enter the range you want to print.
Type	**A1. B8** , and then press **Return**.
Press	**AG** (for Align, Go).

Result. The printer begins printing out the model. When the printer stops, press **PQ** (for Page, Quit) to advance the paper out of the printer and leave the Print menu.

Step 9. Explore What-Ifs. You built this model to explore the financing terms that car dealers are offering. Let's explore some what-ifs to see just how favorable those car loan terms really are. The ads are stressing 2.4 percent interest. But the dealer may not be as willing to negotiate on price. You might also find the monthly payments are high because the term of the loan is so short. The dealer may switch you to a longer period to lower the monthly payments, but then the interest rate is higher. Enter the following interest rates and loan periods into your model, a pair at a time, and then record the monthly and total payments.

To enter the numbers, move the cursor to the appropriate cell, type in the number, and then press **Return**. The new number overwrites and erases any number currently in the cell. Do not forget to enter percentages as decimals, for example, 2.4% as .024, 9.4% as .094, and so on.

INTEREST RATE	TERM	MONTHLY PAYMENT	TOTAL PAYMENTS
2.4%	24		
9.4%	36		
10.5%	48		
13%	60		

What terms do you think you would want? What if a bank was willing to loan you what you needed at 12 percent for 48 months? What price would you try to negotiate to make the monthly payment and total payments better than the terms you were willing to accept from the dealer?

Step 10. Continue or Quit. You have now completed this exercise. Either clear the screen and continue to the next exercise or quit the program if you have finished. There is no need to save the file since you saved it in Step 7. If you do save it, you will save the changes you entered while exploring what-ifs and your results may not match ours in later exercises.

To clear the screen

Press   **/WEY** (for Worksheet, Erase, Yes).

To quit the program

Press   **/QY** (for Quit, Yes).

Result. If you cleared the screen, it looks just as it did when you first loaded the program. If you quit the program, the system A> prompt appears on the screen. Remove your disks, and then turn off the computer.

EXERCISE 93

Using Strings

Some programs, like Lotus 1-2-3 Release 2, have the ability to handle **strings**, any series of characters used as labels. For example, 100, 100 Elm Street, and John Lewis are all strings. If you are using a program that can manipulate strings (The TWIN and Lotus 1-2-3 Release 1A do not have this ability), try entering the strings shown

	A	B	C	D	E
1		First	Second	Result	Formula in
2		string	string		column D
3					
4					
5	(a)	String 1		String 1	+B5
6					
7	(b)	String 1	String 2	String 1String 2	+B7&C7
8					
9	(c)	String 1	String 2	String 1 String 2	+B9&" "&C9
10					
11	(d)	String 1	String 2	String 1 – String 2	+B9&" – "&C9
12					
13					
14					
15	(e)	Sales	$10,000		
16		Action	Promote	<- @IF(C15<10000,"Fire","Promote")	
17					
18					
19					
20					

FIGURE 4-19
Strings

in Figure 4-19. To do so, enter the labels shown in columns B and C, and then enter the indicated formula in column D.

The ability to manipulate strings has several applications. You can use strings to copy labels or combine labels. You can also use them in formulas, for example, to display messages in cells when designated conditions are met.

- If you use the same labels over and over again on a model, you can save time by entering the labels once and then entering references to those cells wherever you want the label to be repeated. In Figure 4-19(a), a string is entered into cell B5 and a reference to that cell is entered into cell D5. The cell reference carries the string to the cell it is entered into just as it would carry a value. The advantage of using this approach is not limited to saving time. If the string is changed, all cells referring to it will automatically change, making revision easier and faster.

- Strings can be added together into longer strings by **concatenation** (often informally called gluing). To glue strings in this way, the cell references are combined with an ampersand (&), or **text operator**. In Figure 4-19(b), strings have been entered into cells B7 and C7. The formula +B7&C7 is then entered into cell D7. The two strings are displayed joined as *String 1String 2* in this cell. To add a space between the strings, you can include the space in the string formula. As shown in Figure 4-19(c), the formula +B9&" "&C9, with the space enclosed in double quotes, results in the string *String 1 String 2* being displayed. If you include a minus sign (–) inside the double quotes so that the formula read +B9&" – "&C9 (Figure 4-19c), the displayed string is *String 1 – String 2*.

- You can include strings in formulas by enclosing them in double quotes (Figure 4-19e). For example, you could create an @IF function using strings as follows:

@IF(C15<10000,"Fire","Promote")

This formula reads "If sales in cell C15 are less than $10,000, then display the string Fire, if not display the string Promote." Change the number in cell C15 to 9000, and the displayed string reads Fire. When the number is 10000 or higher, it displays Promote.

TIPS

- On The TWIN and Lotus 1-2-3, you can convert formulas into their calculated values so that they do not change during subsequent recalculations if the cells they refer to are changed. To do this, move the cursor to the cell containing the formula, press the **Edit** (**F2**) key to move the formula to the edit line, and then press the **Calc** (**F9**) key. To enter the calculated value into the cell, press **Return**. To cancel the command and leave the formula unchanged, press **Esc**.

- **If a formula or function is entered that does not conform to the program's rules, you are automatically placed in edit mode** (see Topic 4-4). When this happens, the program moves the cursor to where in the line it thinks the error is. For example, if you try to enter the formula **+A1+A** and press **Return**, the computer beeps, the cursor goes to the second A, and you are placed in edit mode. To edit the formula, press → to move the cursor to the right of the A, type **2**, and then press **Return**.

QUESTIONS

1. How do you enter a formula that multiplies the values in cells A1 and C3 in a spreadsheet?

2. What will the function SUM(B4..B6) do? What is the reference B4..B6 called?

3. Why do some programs require you to type a plus sign before entering the first character in a formula, for example, +B2–B3?

4. What are operators? List and describe the functions of four of them.

5. What is the order of operations?

6. What is the difference between a constant and a variable?

7. What is a function in a spreadsheet program? What is it used for?

8. How would you enter a function to round the value 1.11234? To round the value in cell B4? To round the sum of the values in the range A1..A3?

9. How would the formula @IF(A27>0,A1/A2,0) read if you translated it into normal English?

10. Identify the notation used for five logical operators, and describe how they are used.

11. What is a string? What does it mean to concatenate a string?

TOPIC 4-4
Retrieving and Editing Models

In this topic, we introduce you to the following procedures:

■ Retrieving files
■ Editing cell contents
■ Erasing cell contents
■ Inserting and deleting rows

BACKGROUND

If you want to improve or expand a model, you can retrieve it from the disk it is stored on. You can then insert or delete rows and columns or edit the contents of cells.

RETRIEVING FILES

After you have saved a model into a file on the disk, you can retrieve it later with the File Retrieve command. Retrieving a file from the disk automatically erases any file already on the screen.

EDITING CELL CONTENTS

The procedure you use to edit the contents of a cell depends on whether you notice the mistake while entering it or after having entered it.

Editing Data That Is Being Entered

If you notice a mistake while entering data, you generally have four choices.

■ Press **Backspace** to delete one or more characters to the left of the cursor. The key repeats if you hold it down so that you can delete characters one after another.

TABLE 4-15
Keys That Move the Edit Cursor and Delete Characters

To Move the Edit Cursor	Press
One character to left or right	← or →
To beginning of line	**Home**
To end of line	**End**
Five spaces to right	**Tab** or **Ctrl-→**
Five spaces to left	**Shift-Tab** or **Ctrl-←**

To Delete	Press
Character to left of cursor	**Backspace**
Character directly over cursor	**Del**
All characters on edit line	**Esc**

- Press **Esc** to abandon the entry and start again.
- Press **Edit (F2)** to enter edit mode.
- Press **Return** to complete the entry, and then reenter it correctly.

Editing Data That Has Already Been Entered

If you notice a mistake after having entered data, that is, after having pressed **Return** to enter data into a cell, you can return the data to the edit line for editing. To do this, you move the cursor to the cell you want to edit, and then press **Edit (F2)**. This puts the program into edit mode (the mode indicator reads *EDIT*), and displays the cell's contents on the edit line along with a cursor, called the edit cursor. In edit mode, you can move the edit cursor freely through the data and insert or delete characters as needed. Table 4-15 describes the keys you can use to move the cursor and delete characters.

ERASING CELL CONTENTS

You can erase the contents of one or more cells. For example, on The TWIN and Lotus 1-2-3, you press **/RE** (for Range, Erase), and a prompt asks you to specify the range to be erased. When you do so and then press **Return**, the contents of the cells in the range are erased. This command erases only the labels, numbers, or formulas, not the formats assigned to the cells (see Topic 4-6).

INSERTING AND DELETING ROWS AND COLUMNS

One of the advantages of working with spreadsheet models is being able to revise and improve them as you gain more experience with the program and more understanding of an analysis.

Inserting Rows and Columns

Often, you may find it necessary to insert rows or columns into the middle of an existing model. You can do this easily, and all formulas below the inserted rows, or to the right of the inserted columns, automatically adjust so that they continue to refer to the correct cells.

When inserting rows and columns, keep the following points in mind:

- Rows are inserted above the cursor.
- Columns are inserted to the left of the cursor.

- The cursor can be in any cell in the row or column you want to insert.

- If there is data in the last row or column, and you enter a row or column, a message appears telling you the spreadsheet is full.

- You can press **Esc** to abandon the entry and start again.

- You can type in a range of rows or columns or point to them when prompted to enter the range to be inserted.

- If rows or columns are inserted within a print range or a range referred to by a formula, the range expands to include the new rows or columns. If rows or columns are inserted on the edge of the range, they are not included.

Deleting Rows and Columns

Deleting one or more rows and columns has almost the same effect as inserting them. The spreadsheet closes up, and all formulas automatically adjust to refer to the correct cells.

There is one exception to the way formulas automatically adjust. If you delete any cells that formulas that are not deleted refer to, those formulas display error messages to tell you the cells they refer to have been deleted. For this reason, it is wise to save a model before making deletions. After making deletions, be sure to recalculate the spreadsheet to see if any error messages appear in the cells. If you have any doubts, save the model under a new filename so that you do not store it on top of and erase the original. You may also want to convert formulas that refer to parts of the model to be deleted into their currently displayed values before deleting the cells they refer to.

When deleting rows and columns, keep the following points in mind:

- You can type in a range of rows or columns to delete or point to them when prompted to enter the range to be deleted.

- If you do not delete the upper left-hand or lower right-hand corner of a range, the range contracts or expands to accommodate the change. If these corners are deleted, the range name is erased, and formulas referring to it display the ERR message.

- To keep from deleting cells included in formulas elsewhere on the spreadsheet, enter ruled lines to separate those ranges. This way you can delete rows between the ruled lines without affecting the formulas (see Topic 4-2).

EXERCISE 94

Retrieving and Editing the AUTO LOAN Model

In this exercise, you edit the contents of cells and insert rows and columns. To begin this exercise, you must load the program or clear the screen of any other model. This exercise uses the AUTOLOAN model you created in Exercise 92. You must complete that exercise before you can begin this one.

Your finished model should look like Figure 4-20. Refer to this figure to check your results as you complete the steps in this exercise.

Step 1. Retrieve the Model. When you use the File Retrieve command, any work on the screen is erased. Be sure to save your work before retrieving a new file. Before retrieving the AUTOLOAN file, insert the disk you saved it on into drive B, and then close the drive's door.

To retrieve a file

Press   **/FR** (for File, Retrieve), and the prompt asks you for the name of the file you want to retrieve. A list of files on the disk is displayed.

FIGURE 4-20
Edited AUTOLOAN model

```
                A               B       C       D       E       F
1   AUTOLOAN model
2   Cost of car                10000
3   Down payment                2000
4                          ----------
5   Loan required               8000
6   Interest rate               0.12
7                          ----------
8   Term of loan (in months)      48
9                          ==========
10  Monthly payment         210.6706
11  Total payments          10112.19
12
13
14
15
16
17
18
19
20
```

Press   → if necessary to move the highlight over AUTOLOAN, and then press **Return**.

Result. The AUTOLOAN model appears on the screen.

Step 2. Edit an Entry While Entering It. When you want to enter new data into a cell that already contains data, you just type it in and then press **Return**. Here, enter a new label into cell B2, and then deliberately make a mistake so that you can correct it before you press **Return**.

To correct a mistake while entering

Goto   A2, and then type **Cost for**.

Press   **Backspace** three times to delete *for*.

Type   **of car**, and then press **Return**.

Result. The new label is inserted into cell B2.

Step 3. Edit Entries After They Have Been Entered. After you press **Return** to complete an entry, you must return it to the edit line before you can revise it.

To correct mistakes after entering

Goto   A3, and then press **F2** to move the contents of the cell to the edit line.

Press   **Spacebar**, type **payment**, and then press **Return**.

Goto   A4, and then press **F2** to move the contents of the cell to the edit line.

Press   **Spacebar**, type **required**, and then press **Return**.

Goto   A5, and then press **F2** to move the contents of the cell to the edit line.

Press   **Spacebar**, type **rate**, and then press **Return**.

Goto   A6, and then press **F2** to move the contents of the cell to the edit line.

Press	**Spacebar**, type **of loan (in months)**, and then press **Return**.

Result. The new labels should match those in Figure 4-20 though the cell addresses do not match because rows are inserted in the next step.

Step 4. Insert Rows and Add Ruled Lines. Ruled lines are useful to separate sections of a model to make it easier to read. To enter ruled lines, you use the repeat command. Any character you type after pressing the backslash key (\) is repeated across the width of a column. Here, you insert rows and use the minus sign (-) to enter single-ruled lines and the equal sign (=) to enter a double-ruled line.

To insert rows and enter ruled lines

Goto	B4, type **/WIR** (for Worksheet, Insert, Row), and the prompt asks you to enter the range of rows to insert.
Press	**Return** to insert a row above the cursor.
Type	**\-**, and then press **Return** to enter a single-ruled line.
Goto	B7, type **/WIR** (for Worksheet, Insert, Row), and the prompt asks you to enter the range of rows to insert.
Press	**Return** to insert a row above the cursor.
Type	**\-**, and then press **Return** to enter a single-ruled line.
Goto	B9, type **/WIR** (for Worksheet, Insert, Row), and the prompt asks you to enter the range of rows to insert.
Press	**Return** to insert a row above the cursor.
Type	**\=**, and then press **Return** to enter a double-ruled line.

Result. Your ruled lines should look like those in Figure 4-20.

Step 5. Print the Model. Now make a printout of the model. Turn on the printer, and be sure it has paper in it.

To print the model

Press	**/PPR** (for Print, Printer, Range), and the prompt asks you to enter the range you want to print and highlights the previous range you specified.
Press	**Return** to accept the suggested range.
Press	**AG** (for Align, Go).

Result. The printer begins printing out the model. When the printer stops, press **PQ** (for Page, Quit) to advance the paper out of the printer and leave the Print menu.

Step 6. Save the Model. Now that you have finished the model, save it in a file on the disk so that you can retrieve it later. Before proceeding, *be sure a formatted disk is in drive B and the drive's door is closed.*

To save the model

Press	**/FS** (for File, Save), and the prompt asks you for the name to save the file under and suggests the name AUTOLOAN.
Press	**Return** to accept the suggested name, and the prompt reads *Cancel Replace.*
Press	**R** (for Replace).

Result. The disk drive spins, and the model is saved on the disk in drive B.

Step 7. Continue or Quit. You have now completed this exercise. Either clear the screen and continue to the next exercise, or quit the program if you have finished.

To clear the screen

Press   /**WEY** (for Worksheet, Erase, Yes).

To quit the program

Press   /**QY** (for Quit, Yes).

Result. If you quit the program, the operating system prompt reappears. Remove your disks, and then turn off the computer.

EXERCISE 95

Safely Inserting and Deleting Columns And Rows

When a function like @SUM totals a range of cells, you can generally delete rows or columns within the range, and the function adjusts automatically. But if you delete the upper left-hand or lower right-hand corner of the range, the cell displays an error message and must be reentered. In these cases, if you move the cursor to the cell containing the error message and look at the formula, it reads something like @SUM(B3..ERROR), indicating which cell in the formula has been deleted.

If you add ruled lines to separate ranges on your models, functions like @SUM that refer to ranges can refer to the lines, instead of to the top and bottom rows of numbers in the range. This helps guide you; you can safely insert or delete rows anywhere between the ruled lines without affecting any of the functions.

To see how this works, clear the screen, and then enter a ruled line into cell A1. (Press \–, and then press **Return**.) Enter the number 100 into cell A2 and the same number into cell A3. Into cell A4, enter another ruled line. Into cell A5, enter the function @**SUM(A1.A4)**, and then press **Return**. Now insert rows anywhere within the ruled lines, and then move the cursor to the cell that contains the function so that it is displayed on the status line. The cells it refers to have changed. Enter new numbers on any of the new rows in column A, and the function automatically totals them.

TIPS

- Rows and columns cannot be deleted when cell protection is enabled (see Topic 4-14).

- On some programs, rows and columns can be deleted to free up memory for new data on a model. After deleting, save the file. When the saved file is retrieved, the available memory increases.

QUESTIONS

1. What sequence of commands is necessary to retrieve a model?
2. When you retrieve a file, what happens to the currently displayed file?
3. How do you change data in a cell?
4. Explain the two ways of editing the contents of a cell.
5. How do you insert blank rows in a spreadsheet model?
6. What happens when you delete cells that existing formulas refer to?

TOPIC 4-5
Printing Models

In this topic, we introduce you to the following procedure:

■ Printing models

BACKGROUND

When you want to print a model, you can print the entire model or only a selected range to a printer or to an ASCII text file. You print to a file when you want to retrieve the file into a word processing document or print it from DOS. The only difference between the two commands is that you must specify a name for the file when you print to the disk. In either case, you initiate the print command by pressing /P (for Print). You then

1. Specify if the model is to be printed to the disk or to the printer. To print the model to the printer, you press **P** (for Printer). To print the model to a file, you press **F** (for File). This displays the Print menu (after you specify a filename if printing to the disk).

2. Select the Range command to type in the coordinates of, or use the cursor to point to, the upper left-hand and lower right-hand cells in the range. On The TWIN, you need not specify a range if you are printing the entire model; on Lotus 1-2-3, you must specify the range.

3. Select the Options command to control the layout and appearance. Both The TWIN and Lotus 1-2-3 automatically print on 8 1/2-by-11-inch continuous form paper using the settings described in Table 4-16.

4. Select the Align command to align the paper in the printer, and then select the Go command to begin printing. When you are finished printing, select the Page command to advance the paper out of the printer. Table 4-17 describes the choices on the Print menu.

TABLE 4-16
Default Printer Settings

Setting	Default
Top margin	Lines 1–2
Header	Line 3
Header margin	Lines 4–5
Lines for model to print on	Lines 6–61
Footer margin	Lines 62–63
Footer	Line 64
Bottom margin	Lines 65–66
Paper length	Sixty-six lines
Right margin	Column 4
Left margin	Column 76

TABLE 4-17
Printer Commands

Menu Choice	Description
Range	Specifies the part of the model to be printed.
Line	Advances the paper in the printer one line each time it is selected. If selecting the Line command causes the paper to reach the bottom of a page, the paper advances to the top of a new page.
Page	Advances paper in the printer one full page each time it is selected. This command advances the paper out of the printer and prints a footer on the bottom of the page if you specified one.
Options	Changes the page margins, page length, print font, and several other formats.
Clear	Clears some or all print settings previously specified.
Align	Tells the program you have adjusted the paper in the printer, and it is now at the top of the page. When you first load the program, the Align command is executed automatically. If you adjust the paper in the printer after beginning a session, be sure to use the Align command to reset the top of the page.
Go	Starts printing. On Lotus 1-2-3 this command works only if you have specified a range. On The TWIN, this command prints the entire model unless you specified a different range.
Quit	Leaves the Print menu and returns to *READY* mode.

OPTIONS

Both The TWIN and Lotus 1-2-3 give you a great deal of control over the layout of your printouts. Getting a printout just right can sometimes require some experimenting to get the best results. After getting the results you want, you should save the model because most programs save the print settings along with the file. The next time you use the model, you do not have to reenter the print settings.

Headers and Footers

Headers and footers as long as 240 characters can be added to the model to identify it. These may also include page numbers, dates, and times, as Table 4-18 describes. (A footer is not printed on the last page until you select the Page command from the Print menu.)

Margins

Left, right, top, and bottom margins can be changed. These settings are useful when switching between 8 1/2-by-11-inch and 11-by-14-inch paper. You can tell the program you have changed the paper size or you want to change the layout of a print range by changing the margin settings described in Table 4-19.

Borders

Borders are used when a model is too wide to print on a single sheet of paper. For example, if you use column 1 for labels and print a wide model, column 1 appears only on the first page of the printout. This makes it hard to identify the contents of the rows on the second and subsequent pages. The same is true if you use row 1 for labels

Table 4-18
Possible Header and Footer Contents

Entry	Description
Text	Prints as text.
@	Prints current date in the DD-MMM-YY format. Can be combined with text, for example, Date: @.
#	Prints a page number. Can be combined with text, for example, Page: #.
I	Aligns contents within header or footer. Can be used in combination with text or the date and page number symbols to achieve different effects. For example, **Date: @|text|Page: #** left-aligns the date, centers the text, and right-aligns the page number. If used individually in front of an entry, a single I centers the following text, and I I right-aligns it.

and print a long model. The labels appear only at the top of the first page. In either case, if you specify that these columns or rows be treated as borders, they are printed on each page of the printout. When you set borders, be sure they do not overlap the print range, or duplicate rows and columns will be printed.

Setup

You can send printer setup codes to the printer to change the type size if you are using a dot matrix printer. Using compressed type allows you to print 132 characters on an 8 1/2-by-11-inch sheet of paper instead of the normal 85 characters, so you can squeeze a lot more data onto the sheet of paper.

Unfortunately, different printers use different setup codes. You need to refer to your printer's manual to find the codes used to control printing. You enter setup strings as three-digit decimal ASCII numbers preceded by a backslash (\). For example, on an Epson printer (Table 4-20), the code for compressed print is 015. To use

TABLE 4-19
Margin Settings

Margin	Default Setting	Possible Range
Left	Column 4	0–240
Right	Column 76	0–240
Top	Two lines	0–10
Bottom	Two lines	0–10

TABLE 4-20
Typical Epson Setup Strings

Print Control	Setup String
Compressed print on	\015
Compressed print off	\018
Double strike on	\027\071
Double strike off	\027\072
Set line spacing to 8 lpi	\0270
Set line spacing to 6 lpi	\0272

TABLE 4-21
Other Printing Formats

Menu Option	Description
As-Displayed	Prints exactly what is displayed in the print range. This is the default appearance of a printout.
Cell-Formulas	Prints cell entries as a list showing the cell coordinates, the format and protection status, and the cell contents. If cells contain formulas, the formulas are printed instead of the calculated results.
Formatted	Uses all printing specifications selected from the Print menu, including headers, footers, and borders. This is the default printing format.
Unformatted	Suppresses margins, headers, and footers and prints the range in one continuous strip with no page breaks. Use this command to print a text file on the disk that can be read by other programs.

this as a setup string, you would enter **\015**. If you are entering more than one setup code, enter them one after another. For example, on an Epson printer, the setup string \027\071 turns on double-strike printing.

Once a setup string is sent to the printer, the printer remains in that mode. To cancel the setup string, turn the printer off and then back on again. On Lotus 1-2-3 Release 2, you can use a pair of split vertical bars (| |) to enter setup strings in cells in the worksheet. This allows you to print different sections of the document using different typestyles. For example, on an Epson printer you can enter | | \015 in a cell to print the first part of a model in compressed type and | | \018 in another cell to print the remainder in normal type.

Page Length

The page length can be set to print between twenty and one hundred lines per page. The default length is sixty-six lines on 11-inch paper (six lines per inch). The number of lines from the print range actually printed depends on the top and bottom margins you have set and the space reserved for the headers and footers.

Other

Normally when you make a printout, it looks the same way it does when displayed on the screen. But you can choose any of the printing formats described in Table 4-21.

PRINTING MULTIPAGE MODELS

Some models are simply too large to be printed on a single page. But if your document is too wide or long, you may be able to print it out on a single page, or reduce the total number of pages required, by altering the print options.

■ If the document is too wide to print on a single page, try making some columns narrower so that more columns fit on the screen and on a printed page. You can also reduce the left margin, increase the right margin, print the model in compressed type, or print the document by specifying several individual ranges that do fit on the page.

■ If the material is too long to print on a single page, you can reduce the top and bottom margins, use a setup string to print the document eight lines per inch, or print the document by specifying several individual ranges that do fit on the page.

STOPPING THE PRINTER

To stop the printer while it is printing, hold down **Ctrl** while you press **Break**. This stops any further text from being sent to the printer.

- The printer may not stop immediately when you press **Ctrl-Break** because some printers have buffers that store sections of the text before they are printed. When you press **Ctrl-Break**, the text stored in the printer's buffer prints, and then the printer stops.

- If you turn off the printer after pressing **Ctrl-Break**, the printer's buffer is cleared. After you realign the paper, turn the printer back on, and then use the Align command on the Print menu to tell the program you have reset the top of the page.

EXERCISE 96

Printing a Model

In this exercise, you use print options when printing a model. To begin this exercise, you must load the program or clear the screen of any other model. This exercise uses the AUTOLOAN model you created in Exercise 92. You must complete that exercise before you can begin this one.

Note. This exercise has you enter a setup string that prints your model in compressed type. Before beginning, ask your instructor or lab assistant what the setup string for compressed type is for your printer.

Step 1. Retrieve the Model. When you use the File Retrieve command, any work on the screen is erased. Be sure to save your work before retrieving a new file. Before retrieving the AUTOLOAN file, insert the disk you saved it on into drive B, and then close the drive's door.

To retrieve a file

Press   **/FR** (for File, Retrieve), and the prompt asks you for the name of the file you want to retrieve. A list of files on the disk is displayed.

Press   → if necessary to move the highlight over AUTOLOAN, and then press **Return**.

Result. The AUTOLOAN model appears on the screen.

Step 2. Enter Print Options. Headers print at the top of the page. Here, enter a header that prints the date left-aligned, some centered text, and the page number right-aligned. Enter the string that will compress print on your printer. If you do not know what this string is, enter **\015** to see if it works.

To enter a header

Press   **/PPOH** (for Print, Printer, Options, Header), and prompt asks you to enter the header.

Type   **Date: @ | Your Name | Page: #**, and then press **Return** to return to the Print Options menu.

To enter a setup string

Press   **S** (for Setup), and the prompt asks you to enter the setup string.

Type   **\015**, and then press **Return** to return to the Print Options menu.

Press   **Q** (for Quit) to return to the Print menu.

To print the model

Press   **AG** (for Align, Go) to print the model.

Result. The printer begins printing out the model. When the printer stops, press **PQ** (for Page, Quit) to advance the paper out of the printer and leave the Print menu.

Step 3. Print the Model's Formulas. Up until now you have printed model's just as they are displayed on the screen. But when you are troubleshooting models or want a record of the formulas they contain, you might want to print out a list of the model's formulas.

To print the model's formulas

Press   **/PPOOC** (for Print, Printer, Options, Other, Cell-Formulas).

Press   **Q** (for Quit) to return to the Main Print menu.

Press   **G** (for Go) to print the model.

Result. The model's cell contents print out. When the printer stops, press **PQ** (for Page, Quit) to advance the paper out of the printer and leave the Print menu. To cancel compressed print, turn off the printer, and then turn it back on. Be sure to use the Align command before you print again.

Step 4. Continue or Quit. You have now completed this exercise. There is no need to save the model. (If you do, you will save the print options you have entered, and that might cause problems in later exercises.) Either clear the screen and continue to the next exercise, or quit the program if you have finished.

To clear the screen

Press   **/WEY** (for Worksheet, Erase, Yes).

To quit the program

Press   **/QY** (for Quit, Yes).

Result. If you quit the program, the operating system prompt reappears. Remove your disks, and then turn off the computer.

TIPS

- On some programs, you can set a column width to 0 so that its contents do not appear in the printout. On other programs, you can achieve the same effect by hiding the contents of cells. For example, on Lotus 1-2-3 Release 2, you type **/RFH** (for Range, Format, Hidden), specify the range to be hidden, and then press **Return**.

- When printing to a text file, you can print several different ranges in the same model by specifying a new range after each Go command. The ranges are printed to the same text file, one after the other. You can continue adding ranges to the text file until you press the Print menu's Quit command. Once you quit the print session, the text file is closed.

QUESTIONS

1. When making a printout, must you print the entire model?
2. Why might you want to print your model to a file on the disk?

3. What are the advantages of including headers and footers in a printout of a model?

4. What are borders used for?

5. What is a setup string?

6. How do you stop the printer while it is printing? What is a print buffer?

TOPIC 4-6
Changing a Model's Appearance

In this topic, we introduce you to the following procedures:

- Understanding ranges
- Changing column widths
- Formatting labels
- Formatting values

BACKGROUND

When you want your models, whether on the screen or in printouts, to be attractive and easy to read, you use formats to align labels and format numbers. When you do this, you can use the Global Format or Range Format commands.

- A global format affects all cells on the spreadsheet. Generally, you select a global format based on the format that will be used most frequently in a model and then override it in selected cells to display them as desired.

- To override the global format in selected cells, you use range formats.

Range formats have priority over global formats. For example, if you use a Range command to format a group of cells and then change the global format, the format of the cells you formatted with the Range command does not change. To make the cells in the range respond to Global commands again, you must first reset them to the global format using a command designed for this purpose.

UNDERSTANDING RANGES

When you use Range Format commands, you specify rectangular ranges of cells. Understanding ranges is important because you also use ranges in formulas and when copying, moving, printing, or erasing groups of cells.

A **range** is a group of adjacent cells. Ranges can be as small as a single cell or as large as the entire spreadsheet. The only rule is that the range must be rectangular. There are essentially four rectangular shapes of ranges (Figure 4-21).

- Individual cells
- Rows or parts of rows
- Columns or parts of columns
- Blocks of cells

FIGURE 4-21
Types of ranges

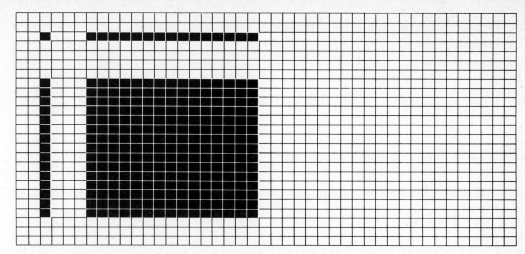

When you use Range commands, you must specify the range of cells to be affected by the command. Usually, the sequence you follow is

1. Initiate the command
2. Specify the range
3. Complete the command

You specify a range in one of two ways: by typing in the coordinates of, or by using the cursor to point to, the cells indicating the range. Figure 4-21 highlights the cells you specify for each type of range.

■ To select a range by typing, you type two cell address that define the range, the upper left-hand and lower right-hand cells in the range (see Figure 4-21). When more than one cell is in the range, you type two cell addresses separated by a delimiter, usually a period. For example, on The TWIN and Lotus 1-2-3 you type **A1.C3** to indicate the cells falling in the columns between A and C and the rows 1 and 3.

■ To select a range by pointing, you move the cursor to one of the corners of the range, and then press the period (.) to anchor that corner of the range. You then use the cursor movement keys to highlight the desired range.

Both The TWIN and Lotus 1-2-3 let you assign names to ranges. This way you can refer to the name, rather than specify cell addresses, when formatting, printing, copying, or moving the range. To assign a name, you press **/RNC** (for Range, Name, Create), specify the range name, and then indicate the range the name is applied to. Table 4-22 describes the commands on the Range Name menu.

TABLE 4-22
Range Name Menu

Command	Description
Create	Assigns names to ranges.
Delete	Deletes names assigned to ranges.
Labels	Assigns labels entered into columns or rows to the cells to their right or left, or above or below.
Reset	Removes all names assigned to ranges.
Table	Creates table of range names that gives both the name of the range and the cell address or addresses to which they have been assigned. You have to specify a range for the table in a blank area of the spreadsheet.

COLUMN WIDTHS

The width of a column, as measured in characters, determines how many characters can be displayed in cells falling in the column. When you first load a spreadsheet, all columns are nine characters wide. You can change the width of any or all columns to between one and the maximum width specified by your program. For example, with The TWIN and Lotus 1-2-3 Release 1A, you can set columns up to 72 characters wide. On Lotus 1-2-3 Release 2, you can set them up to 240 characters wide.

You can change the width of individual columns or of all columns on the spreadsheet, and you can change them before or after you enter data in them. If you use a Global command, it changes the width of all columns except those previously changed with a Range command.

Narrow columns let you see more on the screen and squeeze more into a printout, so columns should be as narrow as possible. Since column width is always set for an entire column—it cannot be wider or narrower at the top than at the bottom—a column must be set to the width required by the longest entry in the column.

Once you change the width of an individual column, it no longer responds to the Global command to change column widths unless you first execute the command that resets it to the global setting.

Column Widths and Labels

If you enter a label that is longer than the column is wide, the entire label is displayed only if the adjoining cell is empty. If the adjoining cell contains data, the label is truncated—that is, only the part that fits in the cell is displayed. The entry appears on the status line in its entirety if you position the cursor in the cell. If a label is too long, you can widen the column, justify the label, or if the adjoining cell is blank, leave the label as is.

Column Widths and Values

The width of columns also affects whether numbers, entered directly or calculated by formulas, are displayed correctly. If a number is too large to be displayed in a cell, the program might do one of the following:

- Display it in scientific notation, for example, display 100,000 as 1.00E+5
- Fill the cell with symbols, for example ******, >>>>>>, ######, !!!!!!

This does not affect the value of the number, only its display. To properly display the number, change the column width of the cell, or change the format of the number. The column width required to correctly display numbers depends on

- The size of the number. Programs usually require columns to be at least one character wider than the largest value so that there is room to display a negative sign if needed.
- The format used. Formats that display commas or add dollar signs or percent signs require additional room for these characters.
- The number of decimal places specified when formatting.

For example, the number 12000 needs a column six characters wide, but if formatted as currency to two decimal places $12,000.00, the same number needs eleven characters. If the number might be displayed as a negative value, the columns widths should each be one-character wider, for example –12000 requires seven characters, and ($12,000.00) requires twelve characters.

Changing Column Widths

To change the width of all columns on The TWIN or Lotus 1-2-3, you press **/WGC** (for Worksheet, Global, Column). When changing the width of all columns, the position of the cursor is not important. To change the width of a single column, position the cursor anywhere in the column and press **/WCS** (for Worksheet, Column, Set). When you execute the global or individual column width command, a prompt asks you to enter the new column width. You can either type it in or press → or ← to scroll it wider or narrower. Scrolling is especially useful when making final adjustments to column widths after labels and data have been entered since it lets you see what happens as the width is changed.

Resetting Column Widths

If individual column widths have been changed, they do not respond when the Worksheet Global Column command is used unless they are reset with the Worksheet Column Reset command. Resetting sets the column to the current global width.

FORMATTING LABELS

You can align labels (and on some programs, numbers) in cells. They can be aligned with the right edge of the cell, the left edge of the cell, or centered in the cell. On The TWIN and Lotus 1-2-3, you can also justify labels.

If you enter a label without a label-prefix character, The TWIN and Lotus 1-2-3 aligns it based on the global setting (the default setting is left-aligned) and adds the global label-prefix character. If you want to change the alignment of labels, you can do so as you enter them, or you can use the range and global alignment commands after entering them.

Aligning Labels During Entry

You can align individual labels as you enter them by typing one of the label-prefix characters described in Table 4-23 before typing the first character in the label.

Aligning All Labels to Be Entered

You can change the alignment of all labels to be entered on the spreadsheet by pressing **/WGL** (for Worksheet, Global, Label) and then specifying a new default alignment from the menu choices described in Table 4-24. The new alignment affects all labels entered after the change is made unless a different label prefix is entered with the label, or it is realigned with a Range Format command.

TABLE 4-23
Label Prefixes

To Align a Label	Type
With left edge of cell (default)	' (apostrophe)
With right edge of cell (with one-space margin)	" (double quote)
Centered in cell	^ (caret)

TABLE 4-24
Label-Prefix Menu Choices

To Align All Labels	Choose
With left edge of cells	*Left*
With right edge of cells (with one-space margin)	*Right*
Centered in cells	*Center*

Aligning Previously Entered Labels

You can override the global label alignment to realign a label in a cell or range of cells. To align previously entered labels, you press /RL (for Range, Label). Blank cells included in the range are not affected by this command. Future labels entered into the range are aligned according to the global prefix.

Aligning Labels That Begin with a Number

Spreadsheets use the first character you type to anticipate the kind of information you are entering. If you type a number first, spreadsheet programs assume the cell is to contain a value. If you type a label that begins with a number, one of the label prefixes must be used. If you begin a label with a number or any of the other characters listed in Table 4-8 without first entering a label prefix, the computer beeps, and the program switches to edit mode. The entry is not allowed until you begin it with a label prefix.

Once a number is entered with a label prefix, it cannot be used in mathematical operations. Be careful when entering labels that could also be values. Telephone numbers and ZIP codes, in particular, could cause confusion if entered without a label prefix. For example, if you enter the phone number 555-1212, the last digits of the number are subtracted from the first digits, and the result, −657, is displayed. No error message results because the program assumes you are entering a formula.

Justifying Long Labels

Labels can be entered and then justified. Unlike word processing where justifying refers to both margins being even, on spreadsheet programs, it refers to a command that wraps a long label so that it fits within a specified range of cells.

- If you indicate a range that is only one row deep, The TWIN and Lotus 1-2-3 extends the row range to the first cell that is blank or contains a number or formula.

- If you indicate a range that is not large enough to include the justified entry, a message appears telling you the range is full. Press **Esc**, and then specify a larger range.

- Do not use the Range Justify command when cell protection is enabled (see Topic 4-14). If protected cells are included in the justify range, a message appears telling you a cell is protected.

FORMATTING VALUES

Spreadsheet programs provide several formats you can use when formatting values on your spreadsheet (Table 4-25). You can also specify the number of decimal places (usually up to fifteen) to be displayed. The names of these formats vary from program to program but generally include those shown in the table. Formatting numbers does not affect the way they are used in formulas. Numbers are always calculated with

TABLE 4-25
Value Formats

Format	Description
Fixed	Displays numbers to a specified number of decimal places.
Scientific	Displays numbers as exponential scientific notation, for example, 1E+01.
Currency	Adds a dollar sign ($) before the number, separates thousands with commas, and displays negative numbers in parentheses, for example, ($1,000). Some programs also allow you to display foreign currency symbols, for example, Deutsche marks, pounds sterling, and yen, but these may not print out if not supported by your printer.
, (comma)	Separates thousands with commas and displays negative numbers in parentheses, for example, (1,000).
General	Displays numbers to the calculated number of decimal places up to the limit imposed by the program. If the column is not wide enough, numbers are displayed in scientific notation or as an overflow value, for example, ******.
+/−	Displays positive numbers as a row of +'s and negative numbers as a row of −'s to create simple bar graphs (see Exercise 102).
Percent	Displays numbers as percentages followed by a percent sign (%) and multiplies the decimal equivalent by 100 to display the number as a whole number. For example, 10% is displayed as 0.1. When formatted, it is displayed as 10% (0.1*100), but it is still used in formulas as 0.1.
Date	There are three date formats (see Topic 4-13).
Text	Formulas are displayed as entered instead of as current value. This is helpful when tracing the relationships among cells.
Hidden	Suppresses cell display (only available on Lotus 1-2-3 Release 2).
Reset	Resets the range to the global format.

accuracy up to fifteen decimal places. For example, as we mentioned earlier, you can format the number 1000.1425 so that it is displayed as $1,000, $1,000.14, 1000.142, and so on, but it is always calculated by any formulas that refer to it as 1000.1425.

Formatting Numbers

When changing the format of all cells, the position of the cursor is not important, but to change the format of a range of cells, you must position the cursor in the upper left-hand corner of the range. When you execute the Global Format or Range Format command, a prompt asks you to specify the range. You can either type it in, or press the cursor movement keys to highlight it. Changing the global column width does not affect columns set with the Worksheet Column Set command unless they are first reset.

EXERCISE 97
Formatting the AUTOLOAN Model

In this exercise, you format cells in a model. To begin this exercise, you must load the program or clear the screen of any other model. This exercise uses the AUTOLOAN model you created in Exercise 92. You must complete that exercise before you can begin this one.

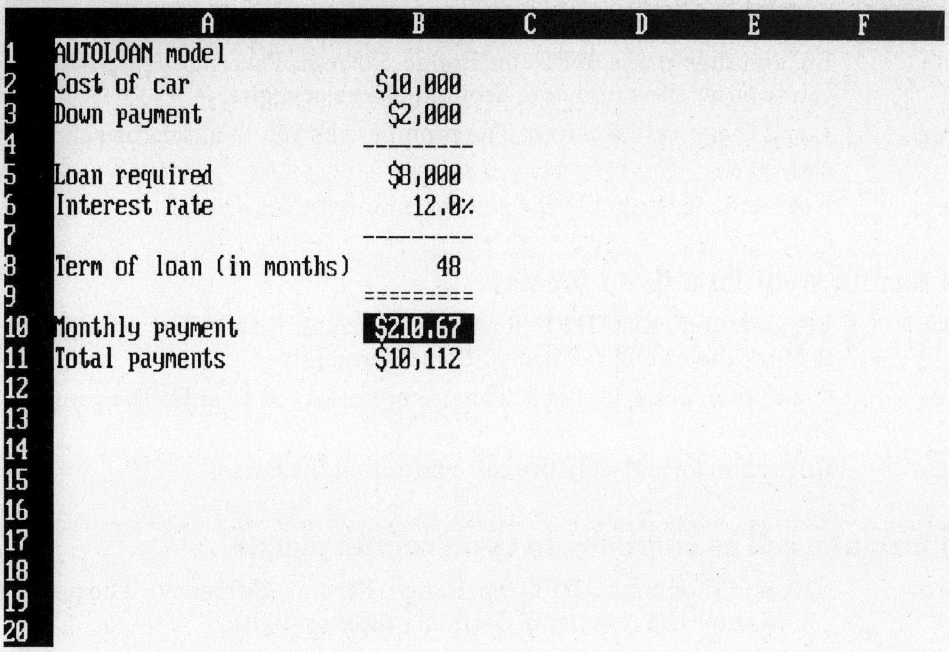

FIGURE 4-22
Formatted AUTOLOAN
model

```
        A           B       C       D       E       F
1  AUTOLOAN model
2  Cost of car        $10,000
3  Down payment        $2,000
4                     ----------
5  Loan required       $8,000
6  Interest rate        12.0%
7                     ----------
8  Term of loan (in months)   48
9                     ==========
10 Monthly payment    $210.67
11 Total payments     $10,112
12
13
14
15
16
17
18
19
20
```

Your finished model should look like Figure 4-22. Refer to this figure to check your results as you complete the steps in this exercise.

Step 1. Retrieve the Model. When you use the File Retrieve command, any work on the screen is erased. Be sure to save your work before retrieving a new file. Before retrieving the AUTOLOAN file, insert the disk you saved it on into drive B, and then close the drive's door.

To retrieve a file

Press   **/FR** (for File, Retrieve), and the prompt asks you for the name of the file you want to retrieve. A list of files on the disk is displayed.

Press   → if necessary to move the highlight over AUTOLOAN, and then press **Return**.

Result. The AUTOLOAN model appears on the screen.

Step 2. Change the Global Format. Begin by changing the format of all numbers (the global format) so that they are displayed with dollar signs, commas separating thousands, and no decimal places.

To change the global format

Press   **/WGFC** (for Worksheet, Global, Format, Currency), and the prompt asks you to enter the number of decimal places or digits.

Type   **0**, and then press **Return**.

Result. All numbers in the model are now displayed with dollar signs and have no decimal places.

Step 3. Format Ranges. Now, format individual numbers so that they are displayed differently from the global format.

To format a cell as a percentage

Goto   B6, and then press **/RFP** (for Range, Format, Percent). The prompt asks you to enter the number of decimal places or digits.

Type   1, and then press **Return**. The prompt asks you to enter the range to format.

Press   **Return** to format only the cell containing the cursor.

To format a cell in a fixed format

Goto   B8, and then press **/RFF** (for Range, Format, Fixed). The prompt asks you to enter the number of decimal places or digits.

Type   0, and then press **Return**. The prompt asks you to enter the range to be formatted.

Press   **Return** to format only the cell containing the cursor.

To format a cell as currency to two decimal places

Goto   B10, and then press **/RFC** (for Range, Format, Currency). The prompt asks you to enter the number of decimal places or digits.

Press   **Return** to accept the suggested setting of two decimal places, and the prompt asks you to enter the range to be formatted.

Press   **Return** to format only the cell containing the cursor.

Result. Your model should look like Figure 4-22.

Step 4. Print the Model. Now make a printout of the model. Turn on the printer, and be sure it has paper in it.

To print the model

Press   **/PPR** (for Print, Printer, Range), and the prompt asks you to enter the range you want to print and highlights the range you specified previously.

Press   **Return** to accept the suggested range.

Press   **AG** (for Align, Go).

Result. The printer begins printing out the model. When the printer stops, press **PQ** (for Page, Quit) to advance the paper out of the printer and leave the Print menu.

Step 5. Save the Model. Now that you have finished the model, save it in a file on the disk so that you can retrieve it later. Before proceeding, *be sure a formatted disk is in drive B and the drive's door is closed.*

To save the model

Press   **/FS** (for File, Save), and the prompt asks you for the name to save the file under and suggests the name AUTOLOAN.

Press   **Return** to accept the suggested name, and the prompt reads *Cancel Replace.*

Press   **R** (for Replace).

Result. The drive spins, and the revised model is saved onto the disk.

Step 6. Continue or Quit. You have now completed this exercise. Either clear the screen and continue to the next exercise, or quit the program if you have finished.

To clear the screen

Press   /WEY (for Worksheet, Erase, Yes).

To quit the program

Press   /QY (for Quit, Yes).

Result. If you quit the program, the operating system prompt reappears. Remove your disks, and then turn off the computer.

EXERCISE 98

Exploring Formats

In this exercise, you use Global Format and Range Format commands. To begin this exercise, you must load the program or clear the screen of any other model.

Your finished model should look like Figure 4-23. Refer to this figure to check your results as you complete the steps in this exercise.

Step 1. Change Column Widths. If you look closely at the labels you entered in column A, you notice that many of them are wider than the column. You can easily widen the column so that the labels are not hidden when you enter data in the next column.

To widen column A

Press   **Home** to move the cursor to column A.

Press   **/WCS** (for Worksheet, Column, Set), and the prompt asks you to enter the column width.

Press   → to scroll the column wider, or press ← to scroll it narrower.

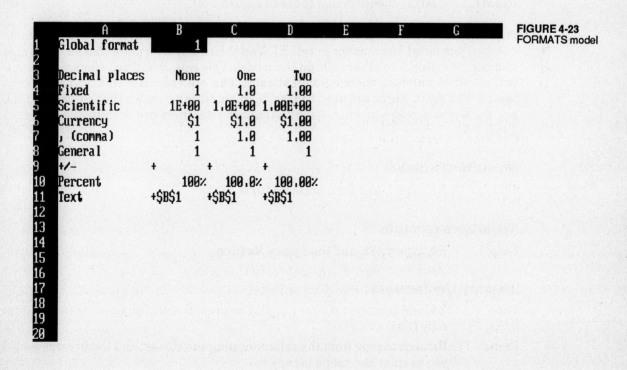

FIGURE 4-23
FORMATS model

	A	B	C	D	E	F	G
1	Global format	1					
2							
3	Decimal places	None	One	Two			
4	Fixed	1	1.0	1.00			
5	Scientific	1E+00	1.0E+00	1.00E+00			
6	Currency	$1	$1.0	$1.00			
7	, (comma)	1	1.0	1.00			
8	General	1	1	1			
9	+/-	+	+	+			
10	Percent	100%	100.0%	100.00%			
11	Text	+$B$1	+$B$1	+$B$1			
12							
13							
14							
15							
16							
17							
18							
19							
20							

Result. As you press → or ←, the number following the prompt indicates the current column width. Scroll the column so that the prompt indicates it is fifteen characters wide, and then press **Return**.

Step 2. Enter Labels. Now, enter the labels for your model.

To enter row labels

Goto	A1, type **Global format**, and then press ↓ twice to move the cursor to cell A3.
Type	**Decimal places**, and then press ↓ to move the cursor to cell A4.
Type	**Fixed**, and then press ↓ to move the cursor to cell A5.
Type	**Scientific**, and then press ↓ to move the cursor to cell A6.
Type	**Currency**, and then press ↓ to move the cursor to cell A7.
Type	**, (comma)**, and then press ↓ to move the cursor to cell A8.
Type	**General**, and then press ↓ to move the cursor to cell A9.
Type	**'+/−** (do not forget the label prefix), and then press ↓ to move the cursor to cell A10.
Type	**Percent**, and then press ↓ to move the cursor to cell A11.
Type	**Text**, and then press **Return**.

To enter column labels

Goto	B3, type **"None**, and then press → to move the cursor to cell C3.
Type	**"One**, and then press → to move the cursor to cell D3.
Type	**"Two**, and then press **Return**.

Result. Your labels should match those in Figure 4-23.

Step 3. Enter a Number and Formulas. To see the effect of different formats on the same number, you enter one number in cell B1. You then enter a formula that refers to this number, and copy it to other cells on the model. This way, when you change the number, all other numbers change automatically. The cell reference that you enter contains dollar signs. These are used to specify an absolute reference that determines the cell the formula refers to when copied. Absolute references are described in detail in Topic 4-8.

To enter a number

Goto	B1, type **1**, and then press **Return**.

To enter a formula

Goto	B4, type **$B$1**, and then press **Return**.

To copy the formula

Goto	B4, and then type **/C** (for Copy). The prompt asks you to enter the range to copy from.
Press	**Return** to copy from the cell containing the cursor, and the prompt asks you to enter the range to copy to.
Type	**B4.D11**, and then press **Return**.

Result. All the cells in the model display the same value.

Step 4. Change the Global Format. Before changing range formats, change the global format a few times to see how it affects all cells. As you make the changes, notice the results each format has.

To change the global format

Press	**/WGFC** (for Worksheet, Global, Format, Currency), and the prompt asks you to enter the number of decimal places or digits.
Press	**Return** to accept the suggested setting.
Press	**/WGFP** (for Worksheet, Global, Format, Percent), and the prompt asks you to enter the number of decimal places or digits.
Type	**0**, and then press **Return**.
Press	**/WGFG** (for Worksheet, Global, Format, General).

Result. Each time you change the global format, all numbers on the model change formats.

Step 5. Format Individual Cells. Now, use a range format to format each number in the model (except the global number in cell B1). We explain only the first format. To do the others, move the cursor to each cell, and use the format specified in column A and the number of decimal places on row 3.

Note. The General, +/–, and Text formats, unlike the others, do not prompt you for the number of decimal places or digits.

To format a cell

Goto	B4, and then press **/RFF** (for Range, Format, Fixed). The prompt asks you to enter the number of decimal places or digits.
Type	**0**, and then press **Return**. The prompt asks you to enter the range to format.
Press	**Return** to format only the cell containing the cursor.

Result. After you have formatted each of the numbers, your model should match the one in Figure 4-23.

Step 6. Change the Number. Now you have a model you can use to experiment with. Enter numbers like, 10, 100, 1000, 10000, and 100000 in cell B1, and see the effects the size of the number has on the numbers displayed on the model. When one or more cells display a row of asterisks, try widening the columns as described in Step 1 or change the global column width by pressing **/WGC** (for Worksheet, Global, Column), press the right and left arrow keys to adjust the column widths, and then press **Return**. Do not bother to widen the columns to remove the asterisks from the +/– row since the number of characters is directly related to the number you enter in cell B1. For example, it you enter the number 100, you have to set the column width to 100 to display the results on this row (a column width that is larger than most programs provide).

Step 7. Change the Global Format. Change the global format a few times. Notice how the cells you formatted with a range format do not respond? Only the number in cell B1, which you did not format with a range format, changes. This is because range formats have precedence over global formats.

Step 8. Print the Model. Now make a printout of the model. Turn on the printer, and be sure it has paper in it.

To print the model

Press   **/PPR** (for Print, Printer, Range), and the prompt asks you to enter the range you want to print.

Type   **A1.D11** and then press **Return**.

Press   **AG** (for Align, Go).

Result. The printer begins printing out the model. When the printer stops, press **PQ** (for Page, Quit) to advance the paper out of the printer and leave the Print menu.

Step 9. Save the Model. Now that you have finished the model, save it into a file on the disk so that you can retrieve it later. Before proceeding, *be sure a formatted disk is in drive B and the drive's door is closed.*

To save the model

Press   **/FS** (for File, Save), and the prompt asks you for the name to save the file under.

Type   **FORMAT**, and then press **Return**.

Result. The drive spins, and the model is saved on the disk.

Step 10. Continue or Quit. You have now completed this exercise. Either clear the screen and continue to the next exercise, or quit the program if you have finished.

To clear the screen

Press   **/WEY** (for Worksheet, Erase, Yes).

To quit the program

Press   **/QY** (for Quit, Yes).

Result. If you quit the program, the operating system prompt reappears. Remove your disks, and then turn off the computer.

EXERCISE 99
Using Data and Label Entry Spaces

When creating models to be used over again (sometimes called templates), it helps to indicate where new labels or data should be entered. Parentheses or square brackets can mark the space, and a dollar, number, or percent symbol can be added to identify the kind of data to be entered.

If you are using The TWIN or Lotus 1-2-3 Release 1A, you can use these characters anywhere on the spreadsheet. But Lotus 1-2-3 Release 2 has a string function, so some formulas and many functions that refer to these labels, display an ERR message.

Experiment with the data and label entry spaces described in Table 4-26. When entering them, keep the following points in mind:

- If you use parentheses in data entry spaces, The TWIN and Lotus 1-2-3 assume you are entering a formula unless you first enter a label-prefix character: ' aligns the data entry space with the left edge of the cell, " aligns it with the right edge, and ^ centers it.

TABLE 4-26
Typical Data Entry and Label Entry Spaces

Numbers	Percentages	Dollars	Labels
(#.....)	(%)	($____)	( )
[#.....]	[%]	[$____]	[ ]
#____	____%	$____	____

■ The square brackets [ ] are treated by The TWIN and Lotus 1-2-3 as labels, so no prefix is required unless you want to specially align the label.

EXERCISE 100

Checking a Spreadsheet's Status

The Worksheet Status command displays the current global settings for recalculation, format, label prefix, column width, and protection. It also displays the current available memory. This command is helpful when working on large models to find out how much memory is available. Press **/WS** to check your program's status, and then press any key to return to the spreadsheet.

TIPS

■ Each of the settings listed by Worksheet Status (except the memory) can be changed with the Worksheet Global commands.

■ Formats entered with the Range Format command are not erased by the Range Erase command. Any new numbers entered into those cells are displayed in the same format.

QUESTIONS

1. What is a range? Describe some typical shapes of ranges.
2. Describe two ways you select ranges. What is a delimiter?
3. If a cell displays a row of symbols, for example, ****** or >>>>>>, what is the cause? How do you correct it?
4. If a cell displays a number in scientific notation, for example, 1.00E+5, what is the cause? How do you correct it?
5. What is the difference between a global format and a range format?
6. If you formatted cells with a Range command and then change the global format, what happens to the cells formatted with the Range command?
7. What is a label prefix, and when do you use it?

TOPIC 4-7
Copying and Moving Data

In this topic, we introduce you to the following procedures:

■ Copying data
■ Moving data

BACKGROUND

You can copy or move the contents of cells to other locations on a spreadsheet. These are two of the most powerful spreadsheet features. Copying allows you to save time by entering a formula once and then copying it as needed. Moving allows you to reorganize models as you create or revise them.

COPYING DATA

When you copy a range of cells, a duplicate set of the range's contents and formats is copied from the original cells, called the **source range**, to a new location called the **target** or **destination range**, and the data in the cells in the source range is left unchanged (Figure 4-24a). If any cells in the target range contain data, it is overwritten by the copied data. Copying allows you to enter formulas once and then copy them where needed, greatly speeding up the process of model building. For example, you can create a monthly budget by entering the necessary formulas in the first monthly column and then copying them to the other monthly columns.

■ When you copy the contents of cells to which formulas in other cells refer, those formulas continue to refer to the original cells, not to the copies.

■ When you copy ranges, you must specify cell addresses that define the source and target ranges (Figure 4-24b). The cells you specify to identify the source and target ranges depend on the shape of the range you are copying. In the figure, the cells you use to specify as the source and target ranges are shaded. Some combinations of source and target ranges are not possible, for example, copying a

FIGURE 4-24a
Copying ranges

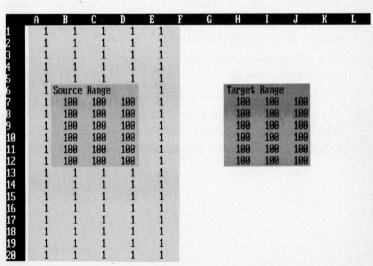

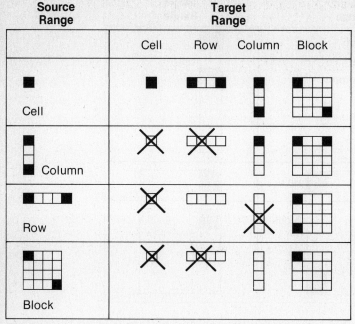

Source Range | **Target Range**

FIGURE 4-24b
Source and target
ranges when copying

column to a cell. These impossible combinations are crossed out on the figure. (Lotus 1-2-3 Release 2 has a Range Transpose command that allows you to copy data from columns to rows and vice versa.)

MOVING DATA

When you move a range of cells, a duplicate of the cell's contents and formats is moved to the target range, and then the contents of the cells in the source range is automatically deleted (Figure 4-25a). If the cells in the target range contain any data, it is overwritten by the data that is moved in. If any formulas refer to cells in the target range, they display error messages. When you move the contents of cells, you must specify cells that define the source and target ranges. The cells you specify vary depending on the shape of the range (Figure 4-25b).

■ If you are moving a single cell, the source range is the address of that cell, and the target range is the address of the cell you move it to.

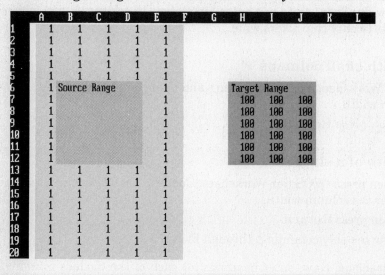

FIGURE 4-25a
Moving ranges

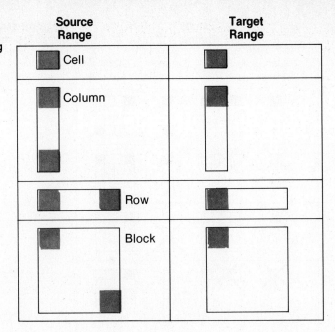

Figure 4-25b
Source and Target
Ranges When Moving

Source Range   **Target Range**

Cell

Column

Row

Block

- If you are moving a column, you specify the top and bottom cells in the source range and only the top cell in the source range.

- If you are moving a row, you specify the first and last cells in the source range and only the first cell in the target range.

- If you are moving a block, you specify the upper left-hand and lower right-hand cells in the source range and only the upper left-hand cell in the target range.

EXERCISE 101

Calculating Grade Point Averages

In this exercise, you copy formulas and other data. To begin this exercise, you must load the program or clear the screen of any other model.

Your finished model should look like Figure 4-26. Refer to this figure to check your results as you complete the steps in this exercise.

Step 1. Change the Column Widths. Here you first widen all the columns so that they are eleven characters wide. Then, since you enter long labels in column A, you widen that column so that it is twenty characters wide.

To change the width of all columns

Press   **/WGC** (for Worksheet, Global, Column), and the prompt asks you to enter the column width.

Type   **11**, and then press **Return**.

To change the width of a single column

Goto   A1, and then press **/WCS** (for Worksheet, Column, Set). The prompt asks you to enter the column width.

Type   **25**, and then press **Return**.

Result. You should now see only columns A through E on the screen.

Step 2. Enter Column Headings. Now, enter headings for each of the model's columns. To enter labels, move the cursor to the indicated cell, type the label shown, press **Return**, and then move to the next cell.

FIGURE 4-26
GPA model

	A	B	C	D	E
1	Courses taken	Credit	Letter	Grade	Total
2		hours	grades	points	GPs
3	===				
4	Biology	4	A	4.00	16.00
5	English lit.	3	A	4.00	12.00
6	Intro. to microcomputers	3	A	4.00	12.00
7	===				
8	Totals	10			40.00
9	===				
10	Grade point average (GPA)	4.00			
11					
12					
13					
14					
15					
16					
17					
18					
19					
20					

To enter column headings

Goto   A1, type **Courses taken**, and then press **Return**.

Goto   B1, type **Credit**, and then press **Return**.

Goto   B2, type **hours**, and then press **Return**.

Goto   C1, type **Letter**, and then press **Return**.

Goto   C2, type **grades**, and then press **Return**.

Goto   D1, type **Grade**, and then press **Return**.

Goto   D2, type **points**, and then press **Return**.

Goto   E1, type **Total**, and then press **Return**.

Goto   E2, type **GPs**, and then press **Return**.

Result. Your column headings should look like those in Figure 4-26 although they may be aligned differently.

Step 3. Enter Ruled Lines. Ruled lines separate key sections of the model so that it is neater and easier to read. Here you enter the first line, and then assign it a name so that you can use the name when copying instead of specifying the cell's coordinates.

To enter a ruled line in a cell

Goto   A3, press **\=**, and then press **Return** to fill the cell.

To copy the ruled line to other columns on the row

Press   /C (for Copy), and the prompt asks you to enter the range to copy from and suggests A3.

Press   **Return** to accept the suggested range, and the prompt asks you to enter the range to copy to.

Type   **B3.E3**, and then press **Return**.

To name the ruled line

Press	**/RNC** (for Range, Name, Create), and the prompt asks you to enter the range name.
Type	**2** (for double-ruled line), and then press **Return**. The prompt asks you to enter the range to be named.
Press	**End**, → to highlight the ruled line, and then press **Return**.

To copy the named ruled line to row 7

Goto	**A7**, and then press **/C** (for Copy). The prompt asks you to enter the range to copy from.
Type	**2**, and then press **Return**. The prompt asks you to enter the range to copy to.
Press	**Return**.

To copy the named ruled line to row 9

Goto	**A9**, and then press **/C** (for Copy). The prompt asks you to enter the range to copy from.
Type	**2**, and then press **Return**. The prompt asks you to enter the range to copy to. Press **Return**.

Result. Your ruled lines should look like those in the Figure 4-26.

Step 4. Enter Row Labels. In this step, you enter labels for rows.

To enter the row labels

Goto	**A4**, type **Biology**, and then press **Return**.
Goto	**A5**, type **English lit.**, and then press **Return**.
Goto	**A6**, type **Intro. to microcomputers**, and then press **Return**.
Goto	**A8**, type **Totals**, and then press **Return**.
Goto	**A10**, type **Grade point average (GPA)**, and then press **Return**.

Result. Your course labels should look like those in the Figure 4-26.

Step 5. Enter the Credit Hours. In this step, you enter credit hours as numbers.

To enter credit hours

Goto	**B4**, type **4**, and then press ↓ to move to cell B5.
Type	**3**, and then press ↓ to move to cell B6.
Type	**3**, and then press **Return**.

Step 6. Enter the Letter Grades. You enter letter grades as labels in column C. In this case, you want the letter grades to be aligned with the right edge of the cell (the default is the left edge), so use the double quote ("). (The single quote (') aligns labels with the left edge, and the caret (^) centers them).

To enter the letter grades

Goto	**C4**, type **"A**, and then press ↓ to move to cell C5.
Type	**"A**, and then press ↓ to move to cell C6.

Type   "**A**, and then press **Return**.

Result. Your letter grades should look like those in Figure 4-26.

Step 7. Enter Grade Points. You enter grade points for each course as numbers in column D.

To enter grade points

Goto   D4, type **4**, and then press ↓ to move to cell D5.

Type   **4**, and then press ↓ to move to cell D6.

Type   **4**, and then press **Return**.

Result. Your results should match those in Figure 4-26 except the numbers are formatted differently.

Step 8. Enter Formulas. You enter formulas to calculate total grade points in column E, totals on row 8, and the grade point average on row 10.

To enter and copy formulas that calculate total GPs

Goto   E4, type **+B4*D4**, and then press **Return**.

To copy the formula to rows 5 and 6 in column E

Goto   E4, and then press **/C** (for Copy). The prompt asks you to enter the range to copy from.

Press   **Return**, and the prompt asks you to enter the range to copy to.

Press   ↓ to move the cursor to E5.

Type   **.** (the period) to anchor the range.

Press   ↓ to move the cursor to E6, and then press **Return**.

To enter a formula that calculates totals on row 8

Goto   B8, type **@SUM(B3.B7)**, and then press **Return**.

To copy the formula to column E

Press   **/C** (for Copy), and the prompt asks you to enter the range to copy from and suggests B8.

Press   **Return** to accept the suggested range, and the prompt asks you to enter the range to copy to.

Type   **E8**, and then press **Return**.

To enter a formula that calculates the GPA

Goto   B10, type **+E8/B8**, and then press **Return**.

Result. Your results should match those in Figure 4-26 except the numbers are formatted differently. Formulas in the Total GPs column multiply credit hours times grade point on each row to calculate total grade points. A formula on the bottom row divides total grade points by total credit hours to calculate the grade point average.

Step 9. Format Numbers. The format for numbers can be changed for the entire spreadsheet or for selected cells.

To change the global format

Press   **/WGFF** (for Worksheet, Global, Format, Fixed), and the prompt asks you to enter the number of decimal places or digits.

Press   **Return** to accept the suggested setting of 2.

To format credit hours in column B

Press   **/RFF** (for Range, Format, Fixed), and the prompt asks you to enter the number of decimal places or digits.

Type   **0**, and then press **Return**. The prompt asks you to enter the range to format.

Type   **B4.B8**, and then press **Return**.

Result. All of your numbers should now look exactly like those in Figure 4-26.

Step 10. Align Labels. Labels can be justified (aligned) so that they are flush with the left or right edges of their cells or
centered in their cells.

To align column heading labels in their cells

Press   **/RLR** (for Range, Label, Right), and the prompt asks you to enter the range of labels to be aligned.

Type   **B1.E2**, and then press **Return**.

Result. All of your column labels should now look exactly like those in Figure 4-26.

Step 11. Print the Model. Now make a printout of the model. Turn on the printer, and be sure it has paper in it.

To print the model

Press   **/PPR** (for Print, Printer, Range), and the prompt asks you to enter the range you want to print.

Type   **A1.E10** and then press **Return**.

Press   **AG** (for Align, Go).

Result. The printer begins printing out the model. When the printer stops, press **PQ** (for Page, Quit) to advance the paper out of the printer and leave the Print menu.

Step 12. Save the Model. Now that you have finished the model, save it in a file on the disk so that you can retrieve it later. Before proceeding, *be sure a formatted disk is in drive B and the drive's door is closed.*

To save the model

Press   **/FS** (for File, Save), and the prompt asks you for the name to save the file under.

Type   **GPA**, and then press **Return**.

Step 13. Explore What-Ifs. Let's explore some what-ifs to see how the GPA changes when some of the variables are changed. To print out your what-ifs, press **/PPG** (for Print, Printer, Go), (You have already specified the range, so you need not specify it again.) When the printer stops, press **PQ** (for Page, Quit) to advance the paper out of the printer and quit the Print menu.

What-If 1. Let's see what happens if you get a B in one of your courses. To make a change of this kind, just move the cursor to the relevant cell, and type in a new label or number. The previous contents of the cell are deleted, so be careful.

To change the grade in English lit.

Goto   C5, type **"B**, and then press → to move to cell D5.

Type   **3**, and then press **Return**.

Result. Total GPs for English lit. in cell F5 drop from 12 to 9. Cell B10 shows a B in English lit. causes a drop in the grade point average from the previous perfect 4.0 to 3.7.

What-If 2. Now let's explore the effect of credit hours and grades on the GPA by changing the grade in Biology, a four credit hour course, to a B. But first restore the letter grade and grade points in English lit. to their original values.

To restore the model

Goto   C5, type **"A**, and then press → to move to D5.

Type   **4**, and then press **Return**.

To change the letter grade and grade points in Biology

Goto   C4, type **"B**, and then press → to move to D4.

Type   **3**, and then press **Return**.

Result. You see immediately that the B causes a drop in the grade point average (cell B10) from the original 4.0 to 3.6. When you compare this to the previous what-if, you find your grade point average is 3.6 as opposed to 3.7. You have discovered the credit hours have an affect on the grade point average.

Step 14. Expand the Model. Now that the model is finished, you can easily expand it to use for your own courses.

To delete the example data

Press   **/RE** (for Range, Erase), and the prompt asks you to enter the range to erase.

Type   **A4.D6**, and then press **Return**.

To insert rows

Press   **/WIR** (for Worksheet, Insert, Row), and the prompt asks you to enter the range to be inserted.

Type   **A7.A16**, and then press **Return**.

To copy the formulas in column E to the new rows

Press   **/C** (for Copy), and the prompt asks you to enter the range to copy from.

Type   **E6**, and then press **Return**. The prompt asks you to enter the range to copy to.

Type   **E7.E16**, and then press **Return**.

Result. The model now fills the screen and has rows to enter as many as thirteen courses. You can insert as many additional rows as you need.

Step 15. Revise the GPA Formula. The GPA formula in cell B20 displays an error message because it divides the Total GPs in cell E18 by the credit hours in cell B18. Whenever B18 is 0, as it is now, the formula displays an error message. To correct this, edit the formula so it is nested in an IF statement.

To edit the formula in cell B20

Goto   B20, and press **Edit (F2)** to display the formula on the edit line.

Press   **Home** to move the edit cursor to the beginning of the formula.

Type   **@IF(B18=0,@NA,** (Be sure to include the comma after @NA).

Press   **End** to move the cursor to the end of the formula.

Type   ), and then press **Return**.

Result. With the cursor in cell B20 the formula displayed on the status line should read @IF(B18=0,@NA,+E18/B18).

Step 16. Save Your Work. As you have seen, the second time you save a model, the program remembers its name and checks the disk for a file with a similar name. If it finds one, it asks you if you want to replace it. You can either replace it, as you have up till now, or change the name so that you save both the original and the current versions on the disk. Before proceeding, *be sure a formatted disk is in drive B and the drive's door is closed.*

To save the model under a new name

Press   **/FS** (for File, Save), and the prompt asks you to enter the name of the file and suggests the name GPA.

Type   **GPAREV**, and then press **Return**.

Result. The disk drive spins, and the model is saved on the disk in drive B. You now have two versions on the disk, the original one and the expanded one to enter your own grades into.

Step 17. Continue or Quit. You have now completed this exercise. Either clear the screen and continue to the next exercise, or quit the program if you have finished. In either case, be sure to save your work if you want to keep it; otherwise, it is lost.

To clear the screen

Press   **/WEY** (for Worksheet, Erase, Yes).

To quit the program

Press   **/QY** (for Quit, Yes).

Result. If you quit the program, the operating system A> prompt appears on the screen. Remove your disks, and then turn off the computer.

EXERCISE 102

Copying Formulas and Creating a Simple Graph

In this exercise, you copy formulas and format a range of numbers to create a simple graph. To begin this exercise, you must load the program or clear the screen of any other model.

Your finished model should look like Figure 4-27. Refer to this figure to check your results as you complete the steps in this exercise.

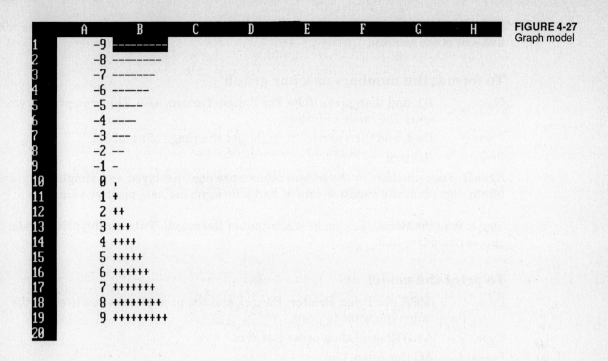

FIGURE 4-27
Graph model

Step 1. Enter a Number and Formulas. Begin by entering a number and then a formula that adds 1 to it. You then copy this formula to other rows in the column.

To enter a number and formula

Goto   A1, type **–9**, and then press **Return**.

Goto   A2, type **1+A1**, and then press **Return**.

To copy the formula

Press   **/C** (for Copy), and the prompt asks you to enter the range to copy from and suggests cell A2.

Press   **Return** to copy from the cell that contains the cursor, and the prompt asks you to enter the range to copy to.

Type   **A3.A19**, and then press **Return**.

To copy the formulas to the next column

Press   **/C** (for Copy), and the prompt asks you to enter the range to copy from.

Type   **A1.A19** and then press **Return**. The prompt asks you to enter the range to copy to.

Type   **B1**, and then press **Return**.

Result. The two columns are filled with numbers from –9 to +9.

Step 2. Format the Numbers as a Graph. The +/– format can be used to create simple bar graphs of numbers on the spreadsheet. The number of + or – signs is determined by the size of the integer in the number. If the integer is zero, a period (.) is displayed.

These signs create crude bar charts since the number of asterisks indicates the relative size of the number.

To format the numbers as a bar graph

Goto   B1, and then press **/RF+** (for Range, Format, +/–). The prompt asks you to enter the range to format.

Press   **End**, and then press ↓ to highlight the range of numbers.

Press   **Return**.

Result. Your numbers in the second column are now displayed as a simple bar graph. Minus signs indicate negative values, and plus signs indicate positive values.

Step 3. Print the Model. Now make a printout of the model. Turn on the printer, and be sure it has paper in it.

To print the model

Press   **/PPR** (for Print, Printer, Range), and the prompt asks you to enter the range you want to print.

Type   **A1.B19** , and then press **Return**.

Press   **AG** (for Align, Go).

Result. The printer begins printing out the model. When the printer stops, press **PQ** (for Page, Quit) to advance the paper out of the printer and leave the Print menu.

Step 4. Save the Model. Now that you have finished the model, save it in a file on the disk so that you can retrieve it later. Before proceeding, *be sure a formatted disk is in drive B and the drive's door is closed*.

To save the model

Press   **/FS** (for File, Save), and the prompt asks you for the name to save the file under.

Type   **GRAPH**, and then press **Return**.

Step 5. Continue or Quit. You have now completed this exercise. Either clear the screen and continue to the next exercise, or quit the program if you have finished.

To clear the screen

Press   **/WEY** (for Worksheet, Erase, Yes).

To quit the program

Press   **/QY** (for Quit, Yes).

Result. If you quit the program, the operating system A> prompt reappears. Remove your disks, and then turn off the computer.

QUESTIONS

1. What is the difference between copying and moving and a range?
2. When copying or moving cells, how to you specify the range to be moved?
3. If you enter the formula +B3 in cell D4 and then copy it to cell G6, what cell will it refer to in its new position?

TOPIC 4-8
Using Relative and Absolute Cell References

In this topic, we introduce you to the following procedures:
- Using relative references
- Using absolute references
- Using mixed references

BACKGROUND

If you typed in every formula you needed, you would not have to be concerned about relative and absolute cell references. But they become very important when you enter a formula in one cell and then copy it to others to save time.

RELATIVE REFERENCES

When you create formulas, they often refer to other cells on the spreadsheet. The program does not "remember" the actual cell coordinates (for example, A1); instead, it remembers the position relative to the cell in which the formula is entered, for example, one column to the left and two rows up. When you copy the formula to another cell, it refers not to the original cell but to whatever cell is one column to the left and two rows up from the cell you copied it to.

For example, in Figure 4-28, when you enter the cell reference +A1 into cell B3, the value contained in cell A1 is carried to cell B3. But when you copy the formula to cell E6, it no longer refers to cell A1 but to cell D4 because the formula refers to the cell one column over and two rows up.

This automatic adjustment occurs because the reference to the cell is relative; that is, the position of the cell referred to is relative to the position of the formula. These relative references are the program's default setting; all formulas you enter have relative references unless you specify otherwise.

ABSOLUTE REFERENCES

You do not always have to keep references to cells relative. You can also make them absolute so that a formula refers to the same cell regardless of where it is copied on the spreadsheet.

FIGURE 4-28
Relative references

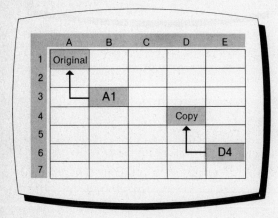

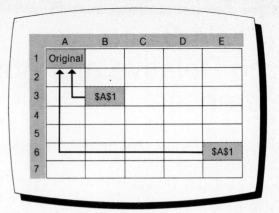

FIGURE 4-29
Absolute references

For example, in Figure 4-29, when you enter the formula +$A$1 into cell B3 (the dollar signs indicate both the row and column references are absolute), it has the same result as entering +A1, but it behaves differently when you copy it. It no longer remembers the cell it refers to relative to its position. It remembers the absolute position, in this case, cell A1. When you copy it to another cell, say, cell E6, it still refers to cell A1.

MIXED REFERENCES

You can also use mixed references that keep the reference to the row or column relative while making the other reference absolute.

For example, in Figure 4-30(a), you enter the formula +$A1 (the column reference is absolute, but the row is relative) into cell B3. When you copy the cell reference to cell E6, part of it changes, and part of it does not.

FIGURE 4-30
Mixed references

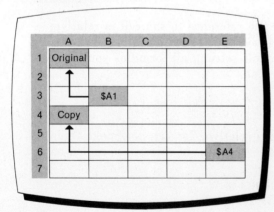
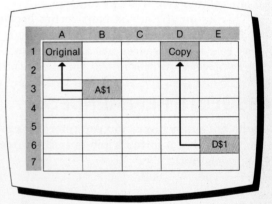

- The column reference, which was made absolute by adding a dollar sign in front of it, does not change when copied. It always refers to column A.
- The row reference, the part of the formula you made relative, does change. It always refers to a cell two rows up, just as it did in the original position.

In Figure 4-30(b), when you enter the formula +A$1 into cell B3 and copy it to another cell, say, cell E6, it always refers to the cell one column to its left (the relative reference) and on the same row as the original position (the absolute reference).

SPECIFYING REFERENCES

The way you specify that a cell reference is absolute varies from program to program. On The TWIN and Lotus 1-2-3, you specify absolute references by adding dollar signs ($) in front of the column or row references.

The TWIN and Lotus 1-2-3 also assign a function key the task of cycling through the four possible combinations so that when you are using cursor pointing to build a formula, you can point to a cell and press the key to select the type of reference you want. When you are pointing to a cell in point mode (the mode indicator reads *POINT*), the cell reference you are pointing to changes its reference each time you press the **Abs** (**F4**) key. Table 4-27 describes the sequence of choices.

TABLE 4-27
Absolute and Relative Cell References

Cell Reference	Column	Row
A1	Relative	Relative
$A1	Absolute	Relative
A$1	Relative	Absolute
$A$1	Absolute	Absolute

EXERCISE 103

Creating a Five-Year Plan

In this exercise, you use relative and absolute references. To begin this exercise, you must load the program or clear the screen of any other model.

Your finished model should look like Figure 4-31. Refer to this figure to check your results as you complete the steps in this exercise.

Step 1. Set the Global Format. Since most of the numbers you enter in the model are dollars, you set the global format so that all numbers are displayed with commas separating thousands and with no decimal places displayed.

To set the global format

Press   /WGF, (for Worksheet, Global, Format, ,), and the prompt asks you to enter the number of decimal places or digits.

Type   0, and then press **Return**.

Result. No results are visible on the screen until you enter a number.

Step 2. Change the Column Widths. Here you first widen all the columns so that they are ten characters wide. Then, since you enter long labels in column A, you widen that column so that it is twenty characters wide.

To change the width of all columns

Press   **/WGC** (for Worksheet, Global, Column), and the prompt asks you to enter the column width.

Type   **10**, and then press **Return**.

To change the width of a single column

Goto   A1, and then press **/WCS** (for Worksheet, Column, Set). The prompt asks you to enter the column width.

Type   **20**, and then press **Return**.

Result. You see only columns A through F on the screen.

Step 3. Enter Labels. Let's enter labels in column A to identify the numbers and formulas you enter in the next steps. (Remember, you can press ↓ instead of **Return** after typing each label.)

To enter labels

Goto   A1, type **Part 1. Variables:**, and then press **Return**.

Goto   A2, type **Initial sales**, and then press **Return**.

Goto   A3, type **Sales growth rate**, and then press **Return**.

Goto   A4, type **Cost of goods sold**, and then press **Return**.

Goto   A6, type **Part 2. Model:**, and then press **Return**.

Goto   A7, type **Year**, and then press **Return**.

Goto   A8, type **Sales**, and then press **Return**.

Goto   A9, type **Cost of goods sold**, and then press **Return**.

Goto   A10, type **Gross margin**, and then press **Return**.

Result. Your results should match those in Figure 4-31.

Step 4. Enter Numbers. Now let's enter some numbers as beginning variables. Two of the numbers are percentages. Although percentages are almost always entered as decimals, you can enter them as whole numbers followed by the percent sign (%). Here we try both ways.

To enter numbers in the variables section

Goto   B2, type **1000**, and then press **Return**.

Goto   B3, type **.10**, and then press **Return**.

Goto   B4, type **56%**, and then press **Return**.

Result. Your results should match those shown in Figure 4-31, except that the percentage figures in cells B3 and B4 are displayed as 0 and 1, respectively, because the global format has been set to display all numbers as whole numbers.

Step 5. Format Numbers. Let's format the percentages so that they are displayed differently from the global format.

To format the cells containing percentages

Goto   B3, and then press **/RFP** (for Range, Format, Percent). The prompt asks you to enter the number of decimal places or digits.

FIGURE 4-31
The 5YRPLAN model.

```
        A              B        C        D        E        F
1   Part 1. Variables:
2   Initial sales       1,000
3   Sales growth rate     10%
4   Cost of goods sold    56%
5
6   Part 2. Model:
7   Year               1988     1989     1990     1991     1992
8   Sales              1,000    1,100    1,210    1,331    1,464
9   Cost of goods sold   560      616      678      745      820
10  Gross margin         440      484      532      586      644
11
12
13
14
15
16
17
18
19
20
```

Type	0, and then press **Return. The prompt asks you to enter the range to format.**
Press	↓ to point to cell B4, and then press **Return**.

Result. Both percentage figures are displayed as percentages as shown in Figure 4-31.

Step 6. Enter the First Year's Formulas. Now that you have entered labels and numbers, you enter data for the first year of the model in Part 2. First, enter the date for the column to identify the period covered, and then enter three formulas, the first by typing it in and the second and third by pointing with the cursor.

To enter a date for the first annual period

Goto	B7, type **1988**, and then press **Return**.

To carry down opening sales from part 1

Goto	B8, type **+B2**, and then press **Return**.

To enter a formula that calculates cost of goods sold

Goto	B9, and then type **+**.
Press	↑ five times to point to cell B4 (Cost of goods sold).
Type	*****.
Press	↑ to point to cell B8 (Sales), and then press **Return**.

To enter a formula that calculates gross margin

Goto	B10, and then type **+**.

Press	↑ two times to point to cell B8 (Sales).
Type	– (the minus sign).
Press	↑ to point to cell B9 (Cost of goods sold), and then press **Return**.

Result. Your results should match those shown in Figure 4-31 with one exception. The year 1988 is displayed as 1,988. Do you know why? Can you change it?

It is displayed as 1,988 because this is the global format. To change it, use a Range Format command. It should be formatted as a fixed number to zero decimal places. Move the cursor to cell B7, press **/RFF** (for Range, Format, Fixed), type **0** (for zero decimal places), and then press **Return** two times.

Step 7. Enter the Second Year's Formulas. The second year's formulas are similar to those you entered in Step 6. But because you copy this column, you specify absolute cell references in some of the formulas. When you enter the formula for sales, enter a dollar sign ($) to specify an absolute reference. When you enter the formula for cost of goods, specify an absolute reference by pressing **F4** to cycle through the four possible options.

To enter a formula that dates the second annual period

| Goto | C7, type **+B7+1**, and then press ↓ Return. |

To enter a formula that calculates sales

| Goto | C8, type **+B8+($B3*B8)**, and then press **Return**. |

To enter a formula that calculates cost of goods sold

Goto	C9, type **+**, and then press the arrow keys to point to cell B4.
Press	**F4** three times to display the formula on edit line as *+$B4*. (If you go past it, just press **F4** a few more times to cycle through to it again.)
Type	*.
Press	↑ to point to cell C8, and then press **Return**.

To copy the formula that calculates gross margin

Goto	B10, and then press **/C** (for Copy). The prompt asks you to enter the range to copy from.
Press	**Return**, and the prompt asks you to enter the range to copy to.
Type	**C10**, and then press **Return**.

Result. Your results should match those in Figure 4-31. Format the year in cell C7 the same way you formatted the one in cell B7.

Step 8. Copy the Second Year's Formulas. Now the hard work is finished and the fun begins. With just a few keystrokes, all the formulas you entered in column C are copied to the next three columns.

To copy the formulas

Goto	C7, and then press **/C** (for Copy). The prompt asks you to enter the range to copy from.
Press	↓ to highlight down to cell C10, and then press **Return**. The prompt asks you to enter the range to copy to.
Press	→ to move the cursor to cell D7, and then press . (the period) to anchor the range.

Press   → two times to move the cursor to column F, and then press **Return**.

Result. If you entered all the formulas and copied them correctly, your results should match those in Figure 4-31. Take a moment to move the cursor to other cells so that their contents are displayed on the status line. This way you can see what happens when formulas with absolute references are copied. All formulas on rows 8 and 9 that refer to cells on rows 2 through 5 should continue to refer to the same cells after being copied because they were absolute references. All references to cells on rows 7 through 10 should refer to the column to their left because they were relative references.

Step 9. Print the Model. Now make a printout of the model. Turn on the printer, and be sure it has paper in it.

To print the model

Press   **/PPR** (for Print, Printer, Range), and the prompt asks you to enter the range you want to print.

Type   **A1.F10**, and then press **Return**.

Press   **AG** (for Align, Go).

Result. The printer begins printing out the model. When the printer stops, press **PQ** (for Page, Quit) to advance the paper out of the printer and leave the Print menu.

Step 10. Save the Model. Now save the model. Before proceeding, *be sure a formatted disk is in drive B and the drive's door is closed*.

To save the finished model

Press   **/FS** (for File, Save), and the prompt asks you to enter the name of the file.

Type   **5YRPLAN**, and then press **Return**.

Result. When the drive stops and the mode indicator changes to *READY*, a copy of the model on the screen has been saved on the disk under the filename 5YRPLAN.

Step 11. Print Out a Section of the Model. You saw in Topic 4-6 that you can print either an entire model or a section of a model. Here you print a section of the 5YRPLAN model.

To print out a selected section of the model

Press   **/PPR** (for Print, Printer, Range), and the prompt asks you to enter the range to print and highlights the range you specified earlier.

Type   **A7.F10**, and then press **Return**.

Type   **G** (for Go).

Result. The printer begins printing out the model. When the printer stops, press **PQ** (for Page, Quit) to advance the paper out of the printer and leave the Print menu. Now that you have specified a range, the next time you print the model, that range is printed.

Step 12. Explore What-Ifs. Now use the finished model to explore some alternative outcomes.

What-If 1. Let's see what happens if the sales growth rate increases from 10 to 15 percent. To make a change of this kind, just move the cursor to the relevant cell, and then type in a new number. The previous contents of the cell are deleted, so be careful where you do this. Remember that percentages are entered as decimals. To enter 10%, you type **.1** or **.10.**

To change the sales growth rate

Goto   B3, type **.15**, and then press **Return.**

Result. Sales increase in all but the first year by 15 percent instead of the original 10 percent. Cost of goods also increases but remains a constant 56 percent of sales. Gross margins increase because sales are increasing faster than cost of goods.

What-If 2. Let's see what happens if the cost of goods increases from 56 to 60 percent.

To change the cost of goods sold

Goto   B4, type **.60**, and then press **Return.**

Result. Sales stay the same as in the previous what-if but are still higher than in the original example in all but the opening year where they remain unchanged. Cost of goods also increases and is higher than the original example because it is now 60 percent of sales instead of 56 percent. Gross margins are lower than in the previous what-if but are higher than in the original example. If your goal was to obtain higher gross margins despite increases in cost of goods (perhaps because of increased prices), you have discovered the way you can achieve this—increase sales sufficiently to achieve the increase in gross margins despite the increased cost of goods.

Step 13. Continue or Quit. You have now completed this exercise. There is no need to save the model. (If you do, you will save your what-if numbers in place of the original numbers, and that might cause problems in later exercises.) Either clear the screen and continue to the next exercise, or quit the program if you have finished.

To clear the screen

Press   **/WEY** (for Worksheet, Erase, Yes).

To quit the program

Press   **/QY** (for Quit, Yes).

Result. If you quit the program, the operating system A> prompt appears on the screen. Remove your disks, and then turn off the computer.

EXERCISE 104

Exploring Absolute and Relative Cell References

In this exercise, you enter and copy the cell references described in Figures 4-28 through 4-30. After copying the formulas, move the cursor to the cells to which you copied them to display the formulas on the status line. Compare your results with the descriptions of these three figures given at the beginning of this topic.

TIPS

- You can move or copy data from one model to another. You first copy or move it to its own file on the disk. You then can use the program's commands to combine it with another spreadsheet on the screen (see Topic 4-15).

QUESTIONS

1. What is the difference between a relative and an absolute cell reference?
2. What are mixed references?
3. How do you specify absolute references on The TWIN and Lotus 1-2-3?
4. What key do you use on these two programs to cycle through the four possible combinations of cell references?
5. If you enter the formula +$B$3 (the $ indicates an absolute reference) in cell D4 and then copy it to cell G6, what cell will it refer to in its new position?
6. If you enter the formula +$B3 (the $ indicates an absolute reference) in cell D4 and then copy it to cell G6, what cell will it refer to in its new position?
7. If you enter the formula +B$3 in cell D4 and then copy it to cell G6, what cell will it refer to in its new position?

TOPIC 4-9
Using Windows and Fixed Titles

In this topic, we introduce you to the following procedures:

- Using windows
- Using fixed titles

BACKGROUND

When you work with models that are too large to be displayed on the screen, you use windows and fixed titles to view parts of the model at the same time.

WINDOWS

Both The TWIN and Lotus 1-2-3 allow you to divide the screen into two horizontal or vertical **windows** so that you can display widely separated sections of the spreadsheet on the screen at the same time (Figure 4-32). When the screen is divided into two windows, you press the Window key (**F6**) to move the cursor back and forth between them.

The two parts of the spreadsheet displayed in the windows can be scrolled together (called synced) or separately (called unsynced) so that you can bring together the sections of the model you want to compare on the screen at the same time. Windows are especially effective if you want to explore what-if situations. For example, to see the effect of changes in sales and expenses on profits, you create a window that displays the cells you want to monitor and another window that displays the cells you want to change.

When using windows, keep the following points in mind:

- Entering data in either window affects the underlying spreadsheet as a whole.
- Titles, column widths, global formats, and label prefixes can be set differently in each window (but not on The TWIN). When the windows are cleared, the format of the upper or left window becomes the format for the entire spreadsheet.

FIGURE 4-32
Windows

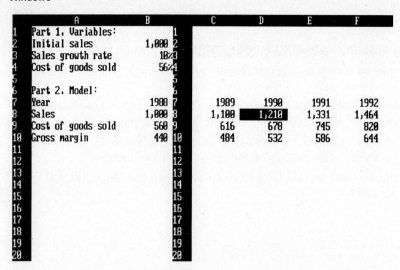

To create windows with The TWIN and Lotus 1-2-3, you press **/WW** (for Worksheet, Window), and then select any of the options described in Table 4-28.

TABLE 4-28
Choices Offered on Windows Menu

Menu Choice	Effect
Horizontal	Splits the screen horizontally so the row containing the cursor becomes the top row in the lower window; cursor moves to upper window
Vertical	Splits the screen vertically so the column containing the cursor becomes the leftmost column in the right window; cursor moves to left window
Sync	Synchronizes scrolling (the default setting) so the two windows scroll together
Unsync	Unsynchronizes scrolling so the two windows scroll independently
Clear	Returns to full screen view and any format changes in the top or left window affect the spreadsheet as a whole

FIXED TITLES

Since the topmost rows and leftmost columns are frequently used for labels identifying the contents of rows and columns, scrolling can make them temporarily disappear from the screen. Many programs allow you to prevent this by **fixing**, or locking, these titles into position so that the rest of the model scrolls under them (Figure 4-33). The TWIN and Lotus 1-2-3 allow you to fix any rows and columns on the screen; others fix only column A and row 1.

For example, you can fix columns A and B as in Figure 4-33(a). When you position the cursor in the rightmost column of the screen, columns A through F are displayed. When, in Figure 4-33(b), you press → a number of times, the spreadsheet scrolls to the left to bring column K into view. Columns A and B have not scrolled off the other side of the screen, but columns C through I have scrolled under the fixed columns and are no longer visible.

If you are using fixed titles, you can use the Goto key (**F5**) to move the cursor into the titles area. This causes a duplicate of the title rows and columns to appear outside the fixed area.

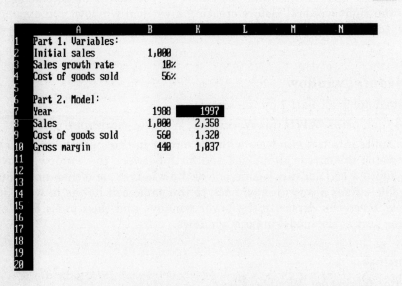

(a)

FIGURE 4-33
Fixed titles

F6:   READY

	A	B	C	D	E	F
1	Part 1. Variables:					
2	Initial sales	1,000				
3	Sales growth rate	10%				
4	Cost of goods sold	56%				
5						
6	Part 2. Model:					
7	Year	1988	1989	1990	1991	1992
8	Sales	1,000	1,100	1,210	1,331	1,464
9	Cost of goods sold	560	616	678	745	820
10	Gross margin	440	484	532	586	644
11						
12						
13						
14						
15						
16						
17						
18						
19						
20						

(b)

K7: (F0) +J7+1   READY

	A	B	K	L	M	N
1	Part 1. Variables:					
2	Initial sales	1,000				
3	Sales growth rate	10%				
4	Cost of goods sold	56%				
5						
6	Part 2. Model:					
7	Year	1988	1997			
8	Sales	1,000	2,358			
9	Cost of goods sold	560	1,320			
10	Gross margin	440	1,037			
11						
12						
13						
14						
15						
16						
17						
18						
19						
20						

To create fixed titles with The TWIN and Lotus 1-2-3, you press /WT (for Worksheet, Titles), and then select any of the options described in Table 4-29.

TABLE 4-29
Choices Offered on the Titles Menu

Menu Choice	Effect
Both	Fixes the columns to the left of and the rows above the cursor
Horizontal	Fixes the rows above the cursor
Vertical	Fixes the columns to the left of the cursor
Clear	Unfixes all titles

Using Windows and Fixed Titles

In this exercise, you use windows and fixed titles. To begin this exercise, you must load the program or clear the screen of any other model. This exercise uses the 5YRPLAN model you created in Exercise 103. You must complete that exercise before you can begin this one.

Step 1. Retrieve the 5YRPLAN. When you use the File Retrieve command, any work on the screen is erased. Be sure to save your work before retrieving a new file.

To retrieve a file

Press   **/FR** (for File, Retrieve), and the prompts asks you to enter the name of the file to be retrieved. A list of files on the disk is displayed.

Press   → if necessary to move the highlight over 5YRPLAN, and then press **Return**.

Result. The 5YRPLAN model appears on the screen.

Step 2. Create Windows. You can divide the screen into horizontal or vertical windows. The Window Horizontal command splits the screen so that the row the cursor is positioned in becomes the topmost row in the lower window. The Window Vertical command splits the screen so that the column the cursor is positioned in becomes the leftmost column in the right window. Before creating a vertical window, you expand the five-year plan into a ten-year plan. You can return the display to a single window at any time.

To create a horizontal window

Press   **Home** to display all Part 1 on the screen.

Goto   A6, and then press **/WWH** (for Worksheet, Window, Horizontal).

Result. The screen splits into two windows with the cursor in the top window. Press **F6** repeatedly and watch the cursor jump back and forth between the windows. Now move the cursor to another cell address within one of the windows, and then press **F6** a few more times. The cursor always jumps back to the same cell it was in when it last left the window. Move the cursor to the lower window, and then press **Home**. You can see the same part of the model in both windows.

To clear the window

Press   **/WWC** (for Worksheet, Window, Clear).

To expand the plan to ten years

Press   **/C** (for Copy), and the prompt asks you to enter the range to copy from.

Type   **F7.F10**, and then press **Return**. The prompt asks you to enter the range to copy to.

Type   **G7.K7**, and then press **Return**.

To create a vertical window

Goto   column C, and then press **/WWV** (for Worksheet, Window, Vertical).

Result. The screen splits vertically. Press **F6** to move the cursor into the right window. Press → to scroll through the last nine years of the plan to compare them to the first year. To clear the windows, press **/WWC** (for Worksheet, Window, Clear).

Step 3. Use Fixed Titles. Fixed titles keep selected rows and columns from scrolling off the screen when you move the cursor around the spreadsheet. The command fixes rows above the cursor and columns to its left.

To fix columns A–B and rows 1-4 on the screen

Press **Home** to move the cursor to cell A1.

Goto C5, and then press **/WTB** (for Worksheet, Titles, Both).

Result. No change is obvious on the screen. Now press → five times. The columns scroll, but columns A and B remain fixed on the screen. Now press **PgDn**. The rows scroll, but rows 1 through 4 remain fixed on the screen. Press ↑ until Part 2 of the model comes back into view. Continue experimenting with the cursor movement keys to see how the fixed titles work.

To clear the fixed titles

Press **/WTC** (for Worksheet, Titles, Clear).

Result. You can now move freely around the model.

Step 4. Continue or Quit. You have now completed this exercise. There is no need to save or print the model. Either clear the screen and continue to the next exercise, or quit the program if you have finished.

To clear the screen

Press **/WEY** (for Worksheet, Erase, Yes).

To quit the program

Press **/QY** (for Quit, Yes).

Result. If you quit the program, the operating system A> prompt reappears. Remove your disks, and then turn off the computer.

EXERCISE 106

Formatting Cells Differently in Each Window

In this exercise, you use different formats in both windows (*not available on The TWIN*). To begin this exercise, you must load the program or clear the screen of any other model.

This exercise uses the 5YRPLAN model you created in Exercise 103. You must complete that exercise before you can begin this one.

Step 1. Retrieve the 5YRPLAN. When you use the File Retrieve command, any work on the screen is erased. Be sure to save your work before retrieving a new file.

To retrieve a file

Press **/FR** (for File, Retrieve), and the prompt asks you to enter the name of the file to be retrieved. A list of files on the disk is displayed.

Press → if necessary to move the highlight over 5YRPLAN, and then press **Return**.

Result. The 5YRPLAN model appears on the screen.

Step 2. Create Windows. Divide the screen into horizontal vertical windows.

To create a horizontal window

Press   **Home** to display all Part 1 on the screen.

Goto   A11, and then press **/WWH** (for Worksheet, Window, Horizontal).

Result. The screen splits into two windows with the cursor in the top window.

Step 3. Format the Lower Window to Display All Formulas as Text. You can format the two windows differently. Here, format the lower window as text so that you can see the formulas instead of the calculated results.

To format the lower window

Press   **F6** to move the cursor to the lower window.

Press   **Home** to display the model in the lower window.

Press   **/WGFT** (for Worksheet, Global, Format, Text).

Result. The formulas in the lower window are now displayed as text. Press **/WGC** (for Worksheet, Global, Column), press → to scroll the columns to fifteen characters wide so that you can see the formulas in their entirety, and then press **Return**. Move the cursor between the windows with **F6**, and then use the cursor movement keys to scroll the windows so that you can compare the formulas in each cell in the lower window with their calculated results in the upper window. When you are finished, press **/WWC** (for Worksheet, Window, Clear) to return the screen to a single window. The formats you entered in the lower window disappear because those in the upper window are the ones that affect the entire spreadsheet.

Step 4. Continue or Quit. You have now completed this exercise. There is no need to save or print the model. Either clear the screen and continue to the next exercise, or quit the program if you have finished.

To clear the screen

Press   **/WEY** (for Worksheet, Erase, Yes).

To quit the program

Press   **/QY** (for Quit, Yes).

Result. If you quit the program, the operating system A> prompt reappears. Remove your disks, and then turn off the computer.

QUESTIONS

1. What are windows? What are they used for?
2. What are fixed titles? What are they used for?
3. What does the Sync command do? The Unsync command?
4. When you format two windows differently and then clear the screen, which window's formatting remains in effect if you had two horizontal windows? If you had two vertical windows?

TOPIC 4-10
Using Recalculation Methods

In this topic, we introduce you to the following procedure:

■ Using recalculation methods

BACKGROUND

Most spreadsheets automatically recalculate all the formulas in your model every time you enter a new formula or value so that any cells referring to a new or changed value display correct results. The larger your model becomes, the longer it takes to recalculate it. The Recalculation command allows you to change the method used to recalculate the model. This is especially important if your model contains forward or circular references.

FORWARD REFERENCES

When a formula refers to a cell in any column to its right or on any row below it, it is a **forward reference**. When a spreadsheet is set to some types of recalculation, a correct answer is not calculated because the formula refers forward to a cell that has not yet been recalculated. To display the correct result, the spreadsheet must be recalculated a second time. To do this on The TWIN and Lotus 1-2-3, you press the Calc key **F9**.

CIRCULAR REFERENCES

Circular references occur when a formula refers either directly or indirectly to itself. Some programs display an indicator if the model contains one or more circular references to warn you they exist. If they do exist, you must recalculate the spreadsheet more than once to get the correct result. Circular references that eventually give a correct result are said to converge. Unfortunately, some circular references diverge; that is, each time the spreadsheet is recalculated, the answer is further from the correct result. Other circular references continue to display new values each time the spreadsheet is recalculated or toggle between two results and never reach a correct one.

CHANGING THE PROGRAM'S RECALCULATION

When you first load your spreadsheet program, the default setting controls the type of recalculation used. On The TWIN and Lotus 1-2-3, the default settings are Natural and Automatic. On these programs, you press **/WGR** (for Worksheet, Global, Recalculation) to change the recalculation order or method. Table 4-30 describes the recalculation options.

EXERCISE 107

Changing Recalculation

In this exercise, you change recalculation. To begin this exercise, you must load the program or clear the screen of any other model. This exercise does not work with The Twin the same way it works with Lotus 1-2-3 because The TWIN does not calculate

TABLE 4-30
Recalculation Menu Options

Menu Choice	Description
Natural	When a formula is recalculated, all other formulas it refers to are recalculated first. Forward references can be used on Lotus 1-2-3 (but not The TWIN) models when the spreadsheets is set to this mode without having to recalculate the spreadsheet more than once to calculate the correct result.
Columnwise	Recalculation begins in cell A1, recalculates column A, then goes to B1, recalculates column B, and so on (Figure 4-34a).
Rowwise	Recalculation begins in cell A1, recalculates row 1, then goes to A2, recalculates row 2, and so on (Figure 4-34b).
Automatic	Recalculates the entire model every time any data is entered in a cell.
Manual	Recalculation occurs only when you press the Calc key (**F9**). When recalculation is set to manual and you enter any data, Lotus 1-2-3 displays a *CALC* indicator, and The TWIN displays a @. This is to remind you to press **F9** for the correct current values in cells containing formulas.
Iteration	When a model has circular references or forward references, the iteration determines the number of times the recalculation cycle is repeated. This setting is ignored if there are no circular references and Natural order is used.

FIGURE 4-34a
Recalculation by rows

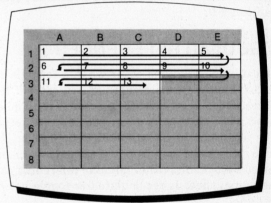

FIGURE 4-34b
Recalculation by columns

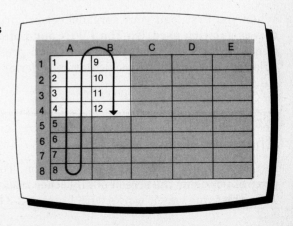

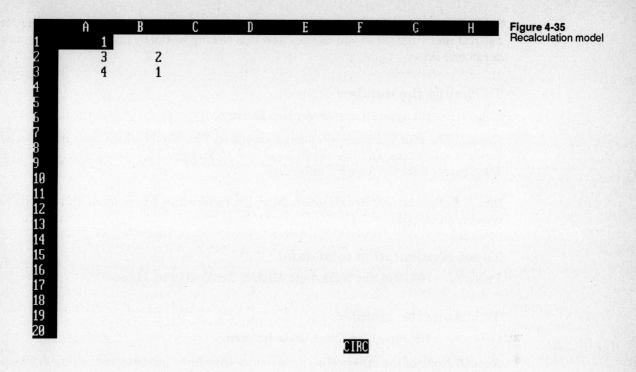

Figure 4-35
Recalculation model

forward references when recalculation is set to Natural. Complete the exercise anyway, ignoring Step 3.

Your finished model should look like Figure 4-35. Refer to this figure to check your results as you complete the steps in this exercise.

Step 1. Enter a Circular Reference. Enter a formula in cell A1 that refers to itself.

To enter a circular reference

Goto   **A1**, type **1+A1**, and then press **Return**.

Result. Since the formulas refers to itself, it is a circular reference. The circular reference indicator is displayed on the bottom of the screen (*CIRC* on Lotus 1-2-3 and @ on The TWIN). Each time you recalculate the spreadsheet, the formula adds 1 to the currently displayed value—essentially acting as a counter displaying the number of times the spreadsheet is recalculated. Press **F9** a few times, and watch the formula calculate. Each time you press **F9**, the number increases by 1.

Step 2. Enter a Series of Numbers. Enter a series of formulas that refer to cells above them and to their right.

To enter a series of numbers

Goto   B3, type **1**, and then press **Return**.
Goto   B2, type **1+B3**, and then press **Return**.
Goto   A2, type **1+B2**, and then press **Return**.
Goto   A3, type **1+A2**, and then press **Return**.

Result. The four numbers 1 through 4 are displayed on the screen in a counter-clockwise order.

Step 3. Explore Natural Recalculation. The program is initially set to automatic and natural recalculation so you can see how this setting works by just changing the number in cell B3.

To change the number

Goto   B3, type **10**, and then press **Return**.

Result. The four numbers all change except on The TWIN which does not calculate forward references, and the sequence is now 10 through 13. If using The TWIN press **F9** to recalculate the forward references.

Step 4. Explore Manual Recalculation. Now, set recalculation to manual and change the number in cell B3.

To set recalculation to manual

Press   **/WGRM** (for Worksheet, Global, Recalculation, Manual).

To change the number

Goto   B3, type **1**, and then press **Return**.

Result. None of the other cells change since they have not been recalculated. The indicator on the bottom line of the screen reads *!* on The TWIN and *CALC* on Lotus 1-2-3 to remind you formulas have not been recalculated. To recalculate them, press **F9** (on The TWIN, press it twice). To return recalculation to automatic, press **/WGRA** (for Worksheet, Global, Recalculation, Automatic).

Step 5. Explore Recalculation by Column. Now, change recalculation from Natural to Columnwise and enter a new number.

To change recalculation to columnwise

Press   **/WGRC** (for Worksheet, Global, Recalculation, Columnwise).

To enter a new number

Goto   B3, type **10**, and then press **Return**.

Result. Only the formula in column B displays the correct result. This is because the two formulas in column A were calculated before column B, so they used the previous value from cell B2. To get the correct result, press **F9** to recalculate the model one more time. (On The TWIN you cannot get the correct result with recalculation set to Columnwise because column A is always recalculated before column B.)

Step 6. Explore Recalculation by Row. Now, change recalculation to Rowwise and enter another number.

To change recalculation to rowwise

Press   **/WGRR** (for Worksheet, Global, Recalculation, Rowwise).

To enter a new number

Goto   cell B3, type **1**, and then press **Return**.

Result. Only the formula in column B displays the correct result. This is because the formula in cell A1 that refers to the formula in cell B2 was calculated first, so it used the previous value from cell B2. To get the correct result, press **F9** to recalculate the model one more time.

Step 7. Explore Iteration. You have seen how you must press the Calc key (**F9**) to recalculate the model to get the correct result when recalculation is set to Columnwise or Rowwise in this model. There is another way to automatically do this by changing the iteration from 1 to 2 so that the spreadsheet recalculates twice each time a number is entered.

To change the number of iterations

Press   /**WGRI** (for Worksheet, Global, Recalculation, Iteration), and a prompt
            asks you to enter the number of iterations.
Type   **2**, and then press **Return**.

To change the number

Goto   B3, type **10**, and then press **Return**.

Result. The correct result is displayed (except on The TWIN) even though recalculation is still by row because the spreadsheet calculated twice when you entered the new number. If you press **F9** while you watch the recalculation counter that you entered into cell A1, you see it increments by two each time.

Step 8. Save the Model. Now that you have finished the model, save it into a file on the disk so that you can retrieve it later. Before proceeding, *be sure a formatted disk is in drive B and the drive's door is closed.*

To save the model

Press   /**FS** (for File, Save), and the prompt asks you for the name to save the file
            under.
Type   **CALC**, and then press **Return**.

Step 9. Continue or Quit. You have now completed this exercise. Either clear the screen and continue to the next exercise, or quit the program if you have finished.

To clear the screen

Press   /**WEY** (for Worksheet, Erase, Yes).

To quit the program

Press   /**QY** (for Quit, Yes).

Result. If you quit the program, the operating system A> prompt reappears. Remove your disks, and then turn off the computer.

TIPS

- You can check the current recalculation method with the Worksheet Status command (see Topic 4-6).
- To recalculate a single formula on a large model with many formulas, set recalculation to manual, move the curson to the cell containing the correct formula, press **F2**, and then press **Return**.

- Use rowwise and columnwise recalculation only when you need to explicitly control the order of recalculation (if there is a circular reference in your model, for example).

QUESTIONS

1. What are forward references? Circular references?
2. What types of recalculation are there?
3. In what order can recalculation be performed?
4. What is natural recalculation?
5. What is the difference between columnwise and rowwise recalculation?
6. How do you change the current recalculation method?

TOPIC 4-11
Using Lookup Tables

In this topic, we introduce you to the following procedures:
- Using vertical lookup tables
- Using horizontal lookup tables

BACKGROUND

What if you are calculating taxes due, and the tax rate varies depending on the net income earned? If your program uses lookup tables, you do not have to manually enter the tax rate after calculating the net income. The TWIN and Lotus 1-2-3 have two kinds of lookup tables: vertical and horizontal. The function of these tables is quite simple: You use them to look up a value on a table. A lookup function

- Looks for a specified value on a row or column of the table
- Selects a corresponding value in an adjoining row or column

Figure 4-36 shows how you would create a vertical lookup table. Horizontal lookup tables work the same way as vertical lookup tables, but the function looks up a value on one row of a table and then selects values in the same column on adjoining rows.

Let's say you have a business that offers different discounts based on the number of items a customer ordered. If a customer orders 1 unit, the discount is 20 percent; if the customer orders 100 or more units, it is 25 percent; and if the customer orders 1,000 or more units, it is 30 percent. You can easily create a model and lookup table to calculate the total price based on the number of units the customer orders.

In Figure 4-36(a), the model is designed so that you enter the quantity and the list price. A lookup function in cell B3 then looks up the quantity entered in cell B1 on the first column of the lookup table (column D) and carries the corresponding discount in the discount column to cell B3. Here the quantity is 1, so the discount is 20%. Let's look at the function entered in cell B3. The actual function is

$$@VLOOKUP (B1, D2.E4, 1)$$

The function may look complicated, but it has only three simple arguments, separated from one another by commas. When the function is calculated, here is what happens.

- B1 is a reference to cell B1, in which you enter the quantity. This is the value the function looks for on the lookup table.

- D2.E4 is the next argument; it tells the function the table is located in the range with D2 as the upper left-hand corner and E4 as the lower right-hand corner. The table is arranged vertically, so it looks in the leftmost column (D) of the table for a value equal to the value in cell B1. All lookup functions assume the search range is in ascending order, so it looks at the values from the top of the range down.

- 1 is the offset. When the function finds the value in the lookup table, in this case, the 1 in cell D2, the offset tells the function to select the corresponding value from the cell one column to the right, here, the 20% in cell E2.

When you change the quantity to 100, the lookup function automatically looks up that quantity on the lookup table and changes the discount to 25% (Figure 4-36b).

When you change the quantity to 1,000, the lookup function automatically looks up that quantity on the lookup table and changes the discount to 30% (Figure 4-36c).

FIGURE 4-36
Lookup tables

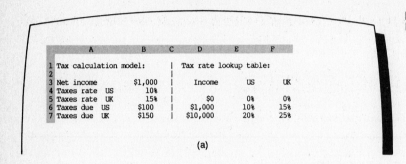

	A	B	C	D	E	F
1	Tax calculation model:			Tax rate lookup table:		
2						
3	Net income	$1,000		Income	US	UK
4	Taxes rate US	10%				
5	Taxes rate UK	15%		$0	0%	0%
6	Taxes due US	$100		$1,000	10%	15%
7	Taxes due UK	$150		$10,000	20%	25%

(a)

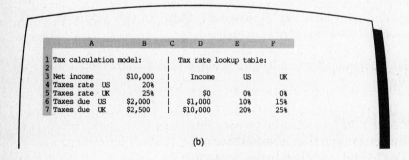

	A	B	C	D	E	F
1	Tax calculation model:			Tax rate lookup table:		
2						
3	Net income	$10,000		Income	US	UK
4	Taxes rate US	20%				
5	Taxes rate UK	25%		$0	0%	0%
6	Taxes due US	$2,000		$1,000	10%	15%
7	Taxes due UK	$2,500		$10,000	20%	25%

(b)

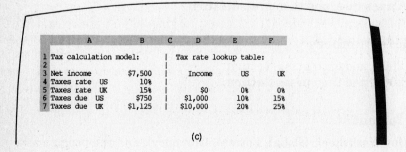

	A	B	C	D	E	F
1	Tax calculation model:			Tax rate lookup table:		
2						
3	Net income	$7,500		Income	US	UK
4	Taxes rate US	10%				
5	Taxes rate UK	15%		$0	0%	0%
6	Taxes due US	$750		$1,000	10%	15%
7	Taxes due UK	$1,125		$10,000	20%	25%

(c)

FIGURE 4-37
Taxes lookup model

	A	B	C	D	E	F	G	H
1	Summer	$2,000			Income	Tax rate	Tax rate	
2	Part-time	$2,000						
3		=========			$1,000	20%	10%	
4	Total	$4,000			$2,000	21%	11%	
5	Tax rate	13%			$3,000	22%	12%	
6	Taxes due	$520			$4,000	23%	13%	
7					$5,000	24%	14%	
8					$6,000	25%	15%	
9	Switch	2			$7,000	26%	16%	
10					$8,000	27%	17%	
11					$9,000	28%	18%	
12					$10,000	29%	19%	
13								
14								
15								
16								
17								
18								
19								
20								

EXERCISE 108

Using a Lookup Table for Taxes

In this exercise, you use a lookup table for taxes *(not available on the introductory version of The TWIN)*. To begin this exercise, you must load the program or clear the screen of any other model.

Your finished model should look like Figure 4-37. Refer to this figure to check your results as you complete the steps in this exercise.

Step 1. Create the Model. To demonstrate a lookup table, create a short model that calculates income taxes due.

To enter the model's labels

Goto	A1, type **Summer**, and then press **Return**.
Goto	A2, type **Part-time**, and then press **Return**.
Goto	B3, type **\=**, and then press **Return**.
Goto	A4, type **Total**, and then press **Return**.
Goto	A5, type **Tax rate**, and then press **Return**.
Goto	A6, type **Taxes due**, and then press **Return**.

To enter the model's numbers

Goto	B1, type **2000**, and then press **Return**.
Goto	B2, type **2000**, and then press **Return**.

To set the global format

Press	**/WGFC** (for Worksheet, Global, Format, Currency), and the prompt asks you to enter the number of decimal places or digits.
Type	**0**, and then press **Return**.

400   SPREADSHEET APPLICATIONS

Step 2. Create the Lookup Table. In this exercise, you use a vertical lookup table. Your model looks up the income you have earned in the first column of the table and selects a tax rate on the same row from the column to the right. In this step, you also name the table so that you can refer to the name, instead of the cell coordinates, when you enter the lookup function.

To enter the lookup table's labels

Goto   E1, type **Income**, and then press **Return**.
Goto   E2, type **\-**, and then press **Return**.
Goto   F1, type **Tax rate**, and then press **Return**.
Goto   F2, type **\-**, and then press **Return**.

To enter the lookup table's numbers

Goto   E3, type **1000**, and then press **Return**.
Goto   E4, type **1000+E3**, and then press **Return**.
Goto   F3, type **.2**, and then press **Return**.
Goto   F4, type **.01+F3**, and then press **Return**.

To copy the formulas

Press   **/C** (for Copy), and the prompt asks you to enter the range to copy from.
Type   **E4.F4**, and then press **Return**. The prompt asks you to enter the range to copy to.
Type   **E5.E12**, and then press **Return**.

To format the lookup tables percentages

Press   **/RFP** (for Range, Format, Percent), and the prompt asks you to enter the number of decimal places or digits.
Type   **0**, and then press **Return**. The prompt asks you to enter the range to format.
Type   **F3.F12**, and then press **Return**.

To name the lookup table

Press   **/RNC** (for Range, Name, Create), and the prompt asks you to enter the range name.
Type   **TABLE**, and then press **Return**. The prompt asks you to enter the range to be named.
Type   **E3.F12**, and then press **Return**.

Step 3. Enter Formulas and a Function. Here you enter a formula that calculates total income. You then enter the lookup function in cell B5 that looks up the total income (cell B4) on the lookup table and carries the appropriate tax rate to cell B5. You then enter a formula that multiples the tax rate by the total income to calculate your taxes due.

To enter a formula that calculates total income

Goto   B4, type **+B1+B2**, and then press **Return**.

To enter the lookup function

Goto   B5, type **@VLOOKUP(B4,TABLE,1)** and then press **Return**.
Press   **/RFP** (for Range, Format, Percent), type **0** (zero), and then press **Return** two times.

To enter a formula that calculates taxes due

Goto   B6, type **+B5*B4**, and then press **Return**.

Result. The lookup function in cell B5 looks up the total income (cell B4) on the leftmost column of the lookup table and carries the percentage on that row one column to the right to cell B5. The formula in cell B6 then multiples this percentage by total income to calculate total taxes due. Change the income on rows 1 and 2, and watch these two cells change.

Step 4. Revise the Lookup Function and Table. Now let's revise the table and lookup function so that you can look up values in more than one column.

To add a "switch"

Goto   A9, type **Switch**, and then press **Return**.
Goto   B9, type **1**, and then press **Return**.
Press   **/RFF** (for Range, Format, Fixed), type **0** (zero), and then press **Return** two times.

To revise the function

Goto   B5, and then press **F2**.
Press   ← two times to move the cursor to under the 1.
Press   **Del** to delete the 1.
Type   **B9**, and then press **Return**.

Result. The function should now read @VLOOKUP(B4,TABLE,B9).

To copy the formulas

Press   **/C** (for Copy), and the prompt asks you to enter the range to copy from.
Type   **F1.F12**, and then press **Return**. The prompt asks you to enter the range to copy to.
Type   **G1**, and then press **Return**.

To change the values in column G

Goto   G3, type **.1**, and then press **Return**.

To revise the name of the table

Press   **/RNC** (for Range, Name, Create), and the prompt asks you to enter the range name.
Press   →, if necessary, to highlight the range name **TABLE**, and then press **Return**. The prompt asks you to enter the range to name.
Press   → to expand the highlight to column G, and then press **Return**.

Result. The table now has two columns, and the switch in cell B9 can be used to select the offset, the column the lookup function selects the value from. Change your income so that the total income is $4,000. When the switch is 1, the tax rate is 23%. Change the switch to 2. The tax rate is now 13% because the lookup function is carrying the value from the second column on the table.

Step 5. Print the Model. Now make a printout of the model. Turn on the printer, and be sure it has paper in it.

To print the model

Press   **/PPR** (for Print, Printer, Range), and the prompt asks you to enter the range you want to print.

Type   **A1.G12**, and then press **Return**.

Press   **AG** (for Align, Go).

Result. The printer begins printing out the model. When the printer stops, press **PQ** (for Page, Quit) to advance the paper out of the printer and leave the Print menu.

Step 6. Save Your Work. Now that the model has been finished, you should save it.

To save the model

Press   **/FS** (for File, Save), and the prompt asks you to enter the name of the file.

Type   **TAXES**, and then press **Return**.

Result. The disk drive spins, and the model is saved onto the disk in drive B.

Step 7. Continue or Quit. You have now completed this exercise. Either clear the screen and continue to the next exercise, or quit the program if you have finished.

To clear the screen

Press   **/WEY** (for Worksheet, Erase, Yes).

Result. The screen clears and looks just as it did when you first loaded the program.

To quit the program

Press   **/QY** (for Quit, Yes).

Result. The operating system A> prompt appears on the screen. Remove your disks, and then turn off the computer.

QUESTIONS

1. What is a lookup table? What does a lookup function do?
2. Describe briefly the difference between horizontal and vertical lookup tables.
3. Give some examples of where lookup tables might be used.
4. What is the function of an offset? A switch?

TOPIC 4-12
Using Data Tables

In this topic, we introduce you to the following procedures:

- Using Data Table 1
- Using Data Table 2

BACKGROUND

Data tables speed up the process of exploring what-ifs. They allow you to run a series of values through a cell in a model and capture the output from one or more other cells. The TWIN and Lotus 1-2-3 have two kinds of data tables, 1 and 2.

- The Data Table 1 command runs a series of values through a single cell on the model and captures the output from as many as eight other cells (Figure 4-38).

- The Data Table 2 command runs two series of numbers through two different cells and captures the output from a single cell (Figure 4-39).

EXERCISE 109

Using Data Table 1

In this exercise, you use the Data Table 1 command *(not available on the introductory version of The TWIN)*. To begin this exercise, you must load the program or clear the screen of any other model.

This exercise uses the AUTOLOAN model you created in Exercise 92 and revised in Exercise 94. You must complete those exercises before you can begin this one.

Your finished model should look like Figure 4-38. Refer to this figure to check your results as you complete the steps in this exercise.

When you run Data Table 1, the series of loan amounts in column D is run through cell B6 one at a time. The program then captures the output of cells B10 and B11 and puts the values on the same row as the input amount that caused them.

FIGURE 4-38
Data table 1 model

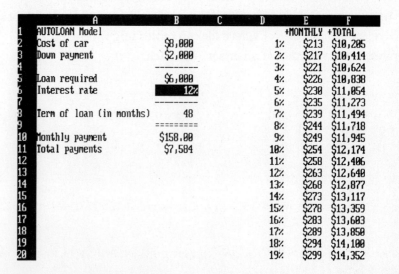

	A	B	C	D	E	F
1	AUTOLOAN Model				+MONTHLY	+TOTAL
2	Cost of car	$8,000		1%	$213	$10,205
3	Down payment	$2,000		2%	$217	$10,414
4		---------		3%	$221	$10,624
5	Loan required	$6,000		4%	$226	$10,838
6	Interest rate	12%		5%	$230	$11,054
7		---------		6%	$235	$11,273
8	Term of loan (in months)	48		7%	$239	$11,494
9		=========		8%	$244	$11,718
10	Monthly payment	$158.00		9%	$249	$11,945
11	Total payments	$7,584		10%	$254	$12,174
12				11%	$258	$12,406
13				12%	$263	$12,640
14				13%	$268	$12,877
15				14%	$273	$13,117
16				15%	$278	$13,359
17				16%	$283	$13,603
18				17%	$289	$13,850
19				18%	$294	$14,100
20				19%	$299	$14,352

	A	B	C	D	E	F
21	+MONTHLY	12	24	36	48	60
22		1%	$670	$337	$226	$170	$137
23		2%	$674	$340	$229	$174	$140
24		3%	$678	$344	$233	$177	$144
25		4%	$681	$347	$236	$181	$147
26		5%	$685	$351	$240	$184	$151
27		6%	$689	$355	$243	$188	$155
28		7%	$692	$358	$247	$192	$158
29		8%	$696	$362	$251	$195	$162
30		9%	$700	$365	$254	$199	$166
31		10%	$703	$369	$258	$203	$170
32		11%	$707	$373	$262	$207	$174
33		12%	$711	$377	$266	$211	$178
34		13%	$715	$380	$270	$215	$182
35		14%	$718	$384	$273	$219	$186
36		15%	$722	$388	$277	$223	$190
37		16%	$726	$392	$281	$227	$195
38		17%	$730	$396	$285	$231	$199
39		18%	$733	$399	$289	$235	$203
40		19%	$737	$403	$293	$239	$208

FIGURE 4-39
Data table 2 model

Step 1. Retrieve the AUTOLOAN Model. When you use the File Retrieve command, any work on the screen is erased. Be sure to save your work before retrieving a new file.

To retrieve a file

Press   /FR (for File, Retrieve), and the prompt asks you to enter the name of the file.

Press   → if necessary to move the highlight over AUTOLOAN, and then press **Return**.

Result. The AUTOLOAN model appears on the screen. To be sure your results match ours, enter a cost of 10000 (cell B2), a down payment of 2000 (B3), an interest rate of 12% (B6), and a term of 48 months (B8).

Step 2. Enter the Series of Interest Rates. You want to run a series of interest rates from 1 to 19 percent through cell B5 to see how your payments are affected by changes in the interest rate.

To enter a series of numbers

Goto   D2, type **.01**, and then press **Return**.

Goto   D3, type **.01+D2**, and then press **Return**.

Press   /C (for Copy), and the prompt asks you to enter the range to copy from and suggests cell D3.

Press   **Return** to accept the suggested range, and the prompt asks you to enter the range to copy to.

Type   **D4.D20**, and then press **Return**.

Result. Column D fills with $0s because the global format is currency to 0 decimal places.

Step 3. Format Values. Let's format the input values so that they are displayed as percentages with no decimal places.

To format a range as percentages

Goto	D2, and then press **/RFP** (for Range, Format, Percent). The prompt asks you to enter the number of decimal places or digits.
Type	**0** (zero), and then press **Return**. The prompt asks you to enter the range to format.
Press	**End**, ↓ to highlight the range of cells, and then press **Return**.

Result. The range of input values is now displayed correctly, ranging from 1% to 19%.

Step 4. Enter the Output Cells. The TWIN and Lotus 1-2-3 allow you to capture the output from as many as eight cells. Here you enter cell references so that you capture the output from monthly payment (cell B10) and total payments (cell B11). You then format the cell references as text, and name the output cells to see the effects these commands have.

To enter the output cells

Goto	E1, type **+B10**, and then press **Return**.
Goto	F1, type **+B11**, and then press **Return**.

Result. The cells references display the current values in the cells they refer to.

To format the output cells as text

Press	**/RFT** (for Range, Format, Text), and the prompt asks you to enter the range to format.
Type	**E1.F1**, and then press **Return**.

Result. The text format displays the cell references as text so that you can see what cells are referred to.

To name the output cells

Goto	B10, and then press **/RNC** (for Range, Name, Create). The prompt asks you to enter the range name.
Type	**MONTHLY**, and then press **Return**. The prompt asks you to enter the range to name.
Press	**Return.**
Goto	B11, press **/RNC** (for Range, Name, Create). The prompt asks you to enter the range name.
Type	**TOTAL**, and then press **Return**. The prompt asks you to enter the range to name.
Press	**Return.**

Result. When you name the cells, the names are displayed in cells E1 and F1 instead of the cell coordinates. If they are not, press **F9**.

Step 5. Run the Data Table. Now let's run the data table to see what happens. When you run it the first time, you must specify the table range and input cell. The table range must include both the column of values and the output cells. To do this, the range starts in the empty cell at the intersection of the column and row containing these items. The input cell is the cell the values are run through, in this case, the interest rate cell (B5).

To run the data table

Press   /DT1 (for Data, Table, 1), and the prompt asks you to enter the table range.

Type   D1.F20, and then press **Return**. The prompt asks you to enter the input cell 1.

Type   B6, and then press **Return**.

Result. The mode indicator reads *WAIT* while the program enters each of the values in column A into cell B6, recalculates the model, and stores the results from the output cells in the data table. In a moment, the calculated results are displayed (Figure 4-38). If you entered .12 (12%) into cell B6, compare the results for 12% on the table, you see the monthly payments and total payments on the data table are the same as in column B. The other rows on the data table show how these outputs are affected by changes in the interest rate.

Step 6. Run the Data Table Again. Once you specify the table range and input cells, you need not do so again (unless you want to change them). You change variables in the model and run the data table again by pressing the Table key (**F8**).

To change a variable

Goto   B2, type **12000**, and then press **Return**.

To run the data table again

Press   **F8** to run the data table.

Result. In a few moments, the table is filled with new values based on the new loan required.

Step 7. Save Your Work Again. Now that the model has been revised, you should save it again.

To save the model

Press   /FS (for File, Save), and the prompt asks you to enter the name of the file and suggests AUTOLOAN.

Press   **Return** to accept the suggested name, and the prompt reads *Cancel Replace*.

Press   **R** (for Replace).

Result. The disk drive spins, and the model is saved onto the disk in drive B. It overwrites and erases the previously saved version.

Step 8. Continue or Quit. You have now completed this exercise. Either clear the screen and continue to the next exercise, or quit the program if you have finished.

To clear the screen

Press   /WEY (for Worksheet, Erase, Yes).

Result. The screen clears and looks just as it did when you first loaded the program.

To quit the program

Press   /QY (for Quit, Yes).

Result. The operating system A> prompt appears on the screen. Remove your disks, and then turn off the computer.

Using Data Table 2

In this exercise, you use the Data Table 2 command *(not available on the introductory version of The TWIN)*. To begin this exercise, you must load the program or clear the screen of any other model.

This exercise uses the AUTOLOAN model you created in Exercise 92 and revised in Exercise 94 and 109. You must complete those exercises before you can begin this one.

Your finished model should look like Figure 4-39. Refer to this figure to check your results as you complete the steps in this exercise.

Step 1. Retrieve the AUTOLOAN Model. When you use the File Retrieve command, any work on the screen is erased. Be sure to save your work before retrieving a new file.

To retrieve a file

Press	**/FR** (for File, Retrieve), and the prompt asks you to enter the name of the file to retrieve.
Press	→ if necessary to move the highlight over AUTOLOAN, and then press **Return**.

Result. The AUTOLOAN model appears on the screen. To be sure your results match ours, enter a cost of 10000 (cell B2), a down payment of 2000 (B3), an interest rate of 12% (B6), and a term of 48 months (B8).

Step 2. Enter the Output Cell. The output cell is the cell from which you want to capture changes in the values in the input cells. It is always entered in the upper left-hand corner of the data table. After entering the cell's coordinates, you format it as text, and then name it to display its name. To move back and forth between the two sections, press **PgDn** and **PgUp**. To keep the screen in alignment, press **Home** before pressing **PgDn** to move to the Data Table 2.

To enter the output cell

Goto	A21, type **+B10**, and then press **Return**.

To format the output cell as text

Press	**/RFT** (for Range, Format, Text), and the prompt asks you to enter the range to format.
Press	**Return** to display the cell's contents as *+MONTHLY* (the name you assigned it in Exercise 109).

Result. The reference in cell A21 is displayed as *+MONTHLY*.

Step 3. Enter the Values to Be Run Through the Two Input Cells. You want to run two series of values through the model. The first series is run through the cell containing the interest rate (B5), and the second is run through the cell containing the period of the loan (B7).

To enter the interest rate to be run through input cell 1

Goto	A22, type **.01**, and then press **Return**.
Goto	A23, type **.01+A22** , and then press **Return**.

To copy the formula

Press	**/C** (for Copy), and the prompt asks you to enter the range to copy from.

| Type | A23, and then press **Return**. The prompt asks you to enter the range to copy to. |
| Type | A24.A40, and then press **Return**. |

To format the values

Press	/RFP (for Range, Format, Percent), and the prompt asks you to enter the number of decimal places or digits.
Type	0 (zero), and then press **Return**. The prompt asks you to enter the range to format.
Type	A22.A40, and then press **Return**.

To enter the loan periods to be run through input cell 2

| Goto | B21, type **12**, and then press **Return**. |
| Goto | C21, type **12+B21**, and then press **Return**. |

To copy the formula

Press	/C (for Copy), and the prompt asks you to enter the range to copy from.
Type	C21, and then press **Return**. The prompt asks you to enter the range to copy to.
Type	D21.F21, and then press **Return**.

To format the values

Press	/RFF (for Range, Format, Fixed), and the prompt asks you to enter the number of digits or decimal places.
Type	0 (zero), and then press **Return**. The prompt asks you to enter the range to format.
Type	B21.F21, and then press **Return**.

Result. The interest rates (column A) to be run through input cell 1 (B6) range from 1% to 19%. The loan periods (row 21) to be run through input cell 2 (B8) range from 12 to 60 in increments of 12 months.

Step 4. Run the Data Table. Now that the table has been constructed, you can run the data table. When doing so for the first time, you specify the table range and the two input cells. The table range has the output cell (B21) as its upper left-hand corner and covers both series of input values. When you run this table, it remembers the table range and input cells you used for Data Table 1. To prevent these from being highlighted, and distracting you, you reset the data table.

To reset the data table

| Press | /DTR (for Data, Table, Reset). |

To run the data table

Press	/DT2 (for Data, Table, 2), and the prompt asks you to enter the table range.
Type	A21.F40, and then press **Return**. The prompt asks you to enter input cell 1.
Type	B6, and then press **Return**. The prompt asks you to enter input cell 2.
Type	B8, and then press **Return**.

Result. The mode indicator reads *WAIT* as the program runs the two series of values through the input cells. In a few moments, the table is filled with values showing how the monthly payments are affected by changes in interest rates and loan periods (Figure 4-39).

Step 5. Run the Data Table Again. Now that the table has been run once, you can change other variables in the model and run it again by pressing **F8**.

To change a variable

Press	**Home** to move the cursor to cell A1.
Goto	B2, type **8000,** and then press **Return**.

To run the data table again

Press	**PgDn** to move to Part 2.
Press	**F8**.

Result. In a few moments, the table is filled with new values based on the new loan required.

Step 6. Print the Model. Now make a printout of the model. Turn on the printer, and be sure it has paper in it.

To print the model

Press	**/PPR** (for Print, Printer, Range), and the prompt asks you to enter the range you want to print.
Type	**A1.F40,** and then press **Return**.
Press	**AG** (for Align, Go).

Result. The printer begins printing out the model. When the printer stops, press **PQ** (for Page, Quit) to advance the paper out of the printer and leave the Print menu.

Step 7. Save Your Work Again. Now that the model has been revised, you should save it again.

To save the model

Press	**Home** to move the cursor to cell A1.
Press	**/FS** (for File, Save), and the prompt asks you to enter the name of the file and suggests AUTOLOAN.
Press	**Return** to accept the suggested name, and the prompt reads *Cancel Replace.*
Press	**R** (for Replace).

Result. The disk drive spins, and the model is saved onto the disk in drive B. It overwrites and erases the previously saved version.

Step 8. Continue or Quit. You have now completed this exercise. Either clear the screen and continue to the next exercise, or quit the program if you have finished.

To clear the screen

Press	**/WEY** (for Worksheet, Erase, Yes).

To quit the program

Press	**/QY** (for Quit, Yes).

Result. If you quit the program, the operating system A> prompt reappears. Remove your disks, and then turn off the computer.

QUESTIONS

1. What is the purpose of data tables?
2. What is the difference between the Data Table 1 command and the Data Table 2 command?
3. When you run a data table for the first time, what information must you specify?
4. What is the table range? The input cell?
5. Name three practical uses for data tables.
6. What key do you press to run a data table the second and subsequent times?

TOPIC 4-13
Using Date and Time Functions

In this topic, we introduce you to the following procedures:

■ Calculating dates and times
■ Using date and time arithmetic

BACKGROUND

Some programs, including The TWIN and Lotus 1-2-3, provide functions to display and calculate dates and times (Table 4-31). These programs assign a numeric value to days and times so that you can add and subtract dates and times, for example, to find the number of days between two dates or the numbers of hours, minutes, and seconds between two times. Days are usually counted from a date at the turn of the century (for example, Lotus 1-2-3 counts from December 31, 1899, and SuperCalc 3 from March 1, 1900). Date and time functions can be formatted to display a serial number or a variety of other formats.

What if you were born on June 3, 1970, and wanted to find out how many days you have lived through October 1, 1989? You would enter these two dates and then subtract the earliest from the latest to calculate the number of days. Figure 4-40 shows a model you can create to do this. It shows the functions and formulas and how the calculated dates appear when unformatted and formatted.

TABLE 4-31
Date and Time Functions

Function	Description
@TODAY	Displays the current date or time if it was entered into the computer system's clock when starting up
@DATE (YEAR,MONTH,DAY)	Enters dates that are actually numbers so that they can be used in calculations; for example, @DATE(86,10,30)-@DATE(85,10,30) is 365 days
@TIME (HOUR,MINUTE,SECOND)	Enters times that are actually numbers so that they can be used in calculations; for example, @TIME(12,0,0)-@TIME(11,0,0) is 1 hour

FIGURE 4-40
Date and time formats

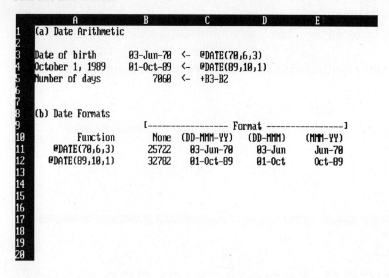

```
        A              B           C          D          E
1  (a) Date Arithmetic
2
3  Date of birth      03-Jun-70  <-  @DATE(70,6,3)
4  October 1, 1989    01-Oct-89  <-  @DATE(89,10,1)
5  Number of days        7060    <-  +B3-B2
6
7
8  (b) Date Formats
9                          [-------------- Format --------------]
10          Function     None (DD-MMM-YY)  (DD-MMM)   (MMM-YY)
11     @DATE(70,6,3)     25722  03-Jun-70   03-Jun     Jun-70
12     @DATE(89,10,1)    32782  01-Oct-89   01-Oct     Oct-89
13
14
15
16
17
18
19
20
```

You enter the function @DATE(70,6,3) in cell B3 and the function @DATE(89,10,1) in cell B4. Their arguments are (Year,Month,Day). You then format the dates so they are displayed in the format DD- MMM-YY. The formula +B4-B3 calculates the number of days between the two dates.

Figure 4-40(b) shows the results of formatting dates that are calculated with date functions. All columns on rows 11 and 12 have the same functions. In column A they are displayed as text. In column B, they are displayed unformatted. The numbers indicate the number of days since the turn of the century. The next three columns show how they are displayed when formatted with one of the programs date formats.

EXERCISE 111

Calculating Dates and Times

In this exercise, you use date and time functions. To begin this exercise, you must load the program or clear the screen of any other model.

Your finished model should look like Figure 4-41. Refer to this figure to check your results as you complete the steps in this exercise.

Step 1. Enter and Format Dates. Your program has several date functions. The interesting thing about these functions is their dates can be added and subtracted.

To enter a date

Goto   A1, type **@DATE(88,1,1)** and then press **Return**.

Result. The number 32143 is displayed in the cell. This is the number of days since December 31, 1899.

To format the date

Goto   A1, and then press **/RFD** (for Range, Format, Date). The prompt asks you to enter the format.

Press   1 (for DD-MMM-YY), and the prompt asks you to enter the range to format.

Press   **Return.**

Result. The cell is filled with asterisks. This indicates the column is not wide enough for the number and format you have entered. To widen the column, press **/WCS** (for

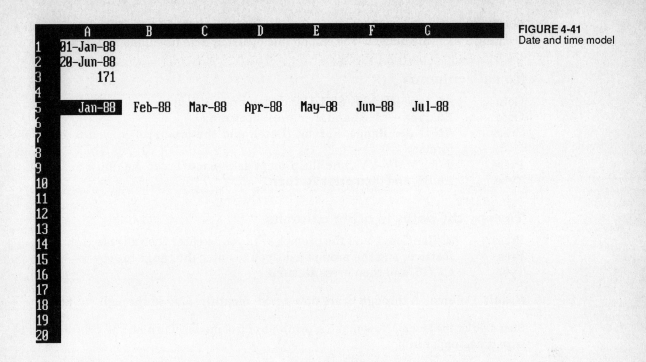

FIGURE 4-41
Date and time model

	A	B	C	D	E	F	G
1	01-Jan-88						
2	20-Jun-88						
3	171						
4							
5	Jan-88	Feb-88	Mar-88	Apr-88	May-88	Jun-88	Jul-88

Worksheet, Column, Set). Press → to widen the column until the date is displayed, and then press **Return**. The date is displayed as 01-Jan-88. Now let's enter a second date in cell A2.

To enter and format a date

Goto   A2, type **@DATE(88,6,20)** and then press **Return**.
Goto   A2, and then press **/RFD** (for Range, Format, Date). The prompt asks you to enter the format.
Press   **1** (for DD-MMM-YY), and the prompt asks you to enter the range to format.
Press   **Return.**

Result. The date 20-Jun-88 is displayed.

Step 2. Manipulate Dates. Dates entered with functions are always values, the number of days since December 31, 1899. Because they are values, you can add and subtract them. Here, enter a formula that calculates the number of days between these two dates.

To enter a formula

Goto   A3, type **+A2-A1**, and then press **Return**.

Result. There are 171 days between the two dates. To find out how many days you have been alive, enter your birth date in cell A1 and today's date in cell A2. The format of the date function is @DATE(year,month,day). You enter the year using only the last two digits. You enter the month as 1 through 12, where January is 1, February is 2, March is 3, and so on. You enter the day as its number. If you were born on April 3, 1963, the function is @DATE(63,4,3). When you are finished, enter formulas that calculate the number of weeks, hours, and minutes you have lived. To calculate weeks, divide the number of days by 7. To calculate hours, multiply the days by 24. To calculate minutes, multiply the hours by 60.

Step 3. Date Columns. Often, you want to date several columns, for example, when creating a monthly budget. You can do this by using date functions and formulas.

To date columns

Goto	A5, type **@DATE(88,1,1)** and then press **Return**.
Goto	B5, type **+A5+31** and then press **Return**.
Press	**/RFD** (for Range, Format, Date), and the prompt asks you to enter the format.
Press	**3** (for MMM-YY), and the prompt asks you to enter the range to format.
Type	**A5.B5**, and then press **Return**.

To copy the dates to other columns

Press	**/C** (for Copy), and the prompt asks you to enter the range to copy from.
Press	**Return**, and the prompt asks you to enter the range to copy to.
Type	**C5.G5**, and then press **Return**.

Result. Columns A through G are now dated, monthly, Jan-88 through Jul-88.

Step 4. Print the Model. Now make a printout of the model. Turn on the printer, and be sure it has paper in it.

To print the model

Press	**/PPR** (for Print, Printer, Range), and the prompt asks you to enter the range you want to print.
Type	**A1.G5**, and then press **Return**.
Press	**AG** (for Align, Go).

Result. The printer begins printing out the model. When the printer stops, press **PQ** (for Page, Quit) to advance the paper out of the printer and leave the Print menu.

Step 5. Save the Model. Now that you have finished the model, save it into a file on the disk so that you can retrieve it later. Before proceeding, *be sure a formatted disk is in drive B and the drive's door is closed.*

To save the model

Press	**/FS** (for File, Save), and the prompt asks you for the name to save the file under.
Type	**DATES**, and then press **Return**.

Result. The model is saved into a file on the disk.

Step 6. Continue or Quit. You have now completed this exercise. Either clear the screen and continue to the next exercise, or quit the program if you have finished.

To clear the screen

Press	**/WEY** (for Worksheet, Erase, Yes).

To quit the program

Press	**/QY** (for Quit, Yes).

Result. If you quit the program, the operating system A> prompt reappears. Remove your disks, and then turn off the computer.

QUESTIONS

1. What is a date function?
2. What is date arithmetic?
3. What are the three date and time functions? When would you use them?
4. If a column fills with asterisks when you enter a date format, what does it indicate? How do you display the date?
5. Describe the model you would build to calculate the number of days you have been at college so far.

TOPIC 4-14
Using Protection and Security

In this topic, we introduce you to the following procedures:
- Protecting global and range data
- Hiding cells and windows
- Assigning passwords

BACKGROUND

Many spreadsheet programs provide several options you can use to ensure the integrity and security of your models.

CELL PROTECTION

When you initially create a model, none of the spreadsheet's cells are protected so that you can enter data into them. As you have seen, entering data into a cell deletes any data that was there. If you enter a number or label into a cell containing a formula, the formula is deleted. This can seriously damage a template.

After you have completed a model, you can protect part or all of it so that you (or another user) cannot inadvertently delete, change, or enter data. You can protect cells so that they cannot be edited, overwritten with new data (by typing, copying, or moving cells into their range), or deleted unless you first remove their protection. If you are planning to use the model as a template, shared by other users, protection is

Unprotected Cells   Protected Cells

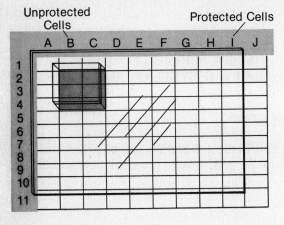

FIGURE 4-42
Cell protection

especially important. Others may be less familiar with the model or unfamiliar with the program, thus increasing the likelihood of mistakes.

Protecting cells is like placing a protective shield over the model (Figure 4-42). Over those cells where you still allow data to be entered or changed, "holes" open up in this shield. Many programs display unprotected cells in a different intensity or color so that you can distinguish them from protected cells. On The TWIN and Lotus 1-2-3 all cells are protected, but only if you turn protection on. You can also selectively unprotect cells. When protection is off, changes can be made anywhere on the spreadsheet. When protection is on, changes cannot be made anywhere, except in those cells you have specifically designated as unprotected.

HIDING CELLS OR WINDOWS

Occasionally, you work at display terminals that people can see as they walk by, or you make printouts that are to be widely circulated, or you share your models with other users. What if there is sensitive data on the model, perhaps a list of salaries? You can hide this data from other users by hiding the cells or windows the data is displayed in. The simplest way of doing this is to set the column width to zero so that the data is not displayed on the screen or in printouts. However, unlike other spreadsheets, neither The Twin nor Lotus 1-2-3 provide this option. Some programs, like 1-2-3 Release 2, allow you to hide ranges of cells. Hidden cells cannot be seen or printed.

PASSWORDS

Protecting and hiding cells does not provide absolute security. Experienced users can often easily disable protection or reveal hidden data. Some programs, but not The TWIN or Lotus 1-2-3, provide a higher level of security by allowing you to assign passwords. Without the password, cell protection cannot be disabled, and hidden cells cannot be unhidden. If you assign a password and then forget it, you cannot see data or remove protection, so use passwords you will remember.

EXERCISE 112
Protecting Your Work

In this exercise, you protect and unprotect cells in your templates. To begin this exercise, you must load the program or clear the screen of any other model.

This exercise uses the 5YRPLAN model you created in Exercise 103. You must complete that exercise before you can begin this one.

Step 1. Retrieve the 5YRPLAN. When you use the File Retrieve command, any work on the screen is erased. Be sure to save your work before retrieving a new file.

To retrieve a file

Press /FR (for File, Retrieve), and the prompt asks you to enter the name of the file to be retrieved. A list of files on the disk is displayed.

Press → if necessary to move the highlight over 5YRPLAN, and then press **Return**.

Result. The 5YRPLAN model appears on the screen.

Step 2. Turn on Global Protection. The TWIN and Lotus 1-2-3 allow you to protect cells so that no data can be entered into them. This is a good way to protect labels and formulas you do not want deleted by mistake.

To turn on protection

Press   /WGPE (for Worksheet, Global, Protection, Enable) to turn on protection.

Result. All cells on the spreadsheet are now protected. Try entering data anywhere. On The TWIN, the computer beeps when you try to type in a number. On Lotus 1-2-3, the computer beeps when you press **Return** to enter a number into a cell, and it displays the error message *Protected cell*. Press **Esc** to clear the message.

Step 3. Unprotect a Range of Cells. When protection is enabled, you can selectively unprotect those cells you want to enter data into. Here, unprotect the data entry cells in Part 1 of the model.

To unprotect a range of cells

Press   /RU (for Range, Unprotect), and the prompt asks you to enter the range to unprotect.

Type   **B2.B4**, and then press **Return**.

Result. The input cells are now unprotected. When you move the cursor to an unprotected cell, *U* (for Unprotected) appears on the status line. You can now enter numbers in cells B2, B3, and B4 but no where else.

Step 4. Turn off Global Protection. If you want to make changes elsewhere on the spreadsheet, you turn off protection.

To turn off protection

Press   /WGPD (for Worksheet, Global, Protection, Disable) to turn off protection.

Step 5. Check the Status of Protection. You can always check your current settings with the Worksheet Status command.

To check your worksheet's status

Press   /WS (for Worksheet, Status) to check your worksheet's status.

Result. A screen appears indicating the current setting for protection and other global commands. Press any key to return to the model.

Step 6. Continue or Quit. You have now completed this exercise. There is no need to save or print the model. Either clear the screen and continue to the next exercise, or quit the program if you have finished.

To clear the screen

Press   /WEY (for Worksheet, Erase, Yes).

To quit the program

Press   /QY (for Quit, Yes).

Result. If you quit the program, the operating system A> prompt reappears. Remove your disks, and then turn off the computer.

TIPS

■ The Range Input command can be used to prevent the cursor from moving to protected cells (see Topic 4-6).

QUESTIONS

1. In what circumstances is cell protection useful?
2. How does cell protection affect your model?
3. Give two ways in which cell protection may work.
4. What is a password used for on some programs?
5. What two ways are there to hide the data in cells?

TOPIC 4-15
Combining and Extracting Files

In this topic, we introduce you to the following procedures:

- Combining models
- Extracting data from files
- Linking models

BACKGROUND

Most spreadsheet programs allow you to combine all or part of another file on the disk with the model you are working on. This is useful when you want to consolidate budgets or speed up model building.

COMBINING FILES

To combine files, you use a command to copy a file, or part of a file, on the disk with a model displayed on the screen. When you do this, for example, to consolidate budgets, the models you want to combine must be designed so that the combined data appears in the right place on the model on the screen. You can do this by creating a template and making copies for others to use. To combine the files

1. Save the file you are working on. This way if anything goes wrong, you can retrieve the model and try again.
2. Move the cursor to the upper left-hand cell where the data is to be combined. The data that is combined overwrites and erases any data in the range of cells it is combined in, so the position of the cursor and the design of the models is important.
3. Execute the File Combine commands (see Table 4-32).
4. Answer any prompts that appear on the screen.

EXTRACTING FILES

The File Xtract command copies a part of a model to its own file on a disk. You can then combine this extracted file with any other model or retrieve it directly. You may be offered the option of extracting the formulas in the range you are extracting or just their calculated values. If you extract any formulas that refer to cells that are not also extracted, these formulas refer to empty cells when the extracted file is retrieved.

TABLE 4-32
Combine Command Menu Choices

Menu Choice	Description
Copy	Copies the contents of the file on the disk to the file on the screen; you may be offered the option to copy the formulas or just their calculated values
Add	Copies only the calculated values from the file on the disk and adds them to the values in the cells they are copied to; normally does not copy labels from the file on the disk, just the values
Subtract	Copies only the calculated values from the file on the disk and subtracts them to the values in the cells they are copied to; normally does not copy labels from the file on the disk, just the values

LINKING MODELS

Some programs, but not The TWIN or Lotus 1-2-3, allow you to design models so that one model (the master, or summary model) summarizes the results of several other models (supplemental, or detailed models). These supplemental models contain detailed breakdowns of the items summarized on the master model.

For example, you might have a series of supplemental models, one for each product category in a store. One might list each brand of skis in inventory, another each brand of tennis rackets. The total from each of these supplemental models is transferred to a master model that has a single line for skis and a single line for rackets.

Although creating models this way keeps models to a manageable size, it also creates problems. A change on any of the supplemental models must be transferred to the master model because each model is in a separate file. A few programs allow you to link models so that this data is transferred automatically. Here is how this works.

1. You enter references in the master model that specify the name of the supplemental model and the cell addresses on that model you want data to be transferred from. You then save the master file.

2. You retrieve the supplemental file and make changes. You then save the revised file.

3. You retrieve the master file. When it is retrieved from the disk, the program checks to see if it contains any references to cells on any other files. If it does, it updates the cells containing those references using the current calculated values in the cells on the model it refers to.

When you link models in this way, the order you update and retrieve them in becomes important. For example, what if you linked three models so that model 1 is linked to model 2, and model 2 is linked to model 3? If you make a change to model 3, save it, and then retrieve model 1, it is not updated. To update it, you must first retrieve model 2 so that it becomes updated. You then save model 2 and retrieve model 1.

EXERCISE 113
Combining and Extracting Files

In this exercise, you combine and extract data. To begin this exercise, you must load the program or clear the screen of any other model.

This exercise uses the 5YRPLAN model you created in Exercise 103. You must complete that exercise before you can begin this one.

Step 1. Retrieve the 5YRPLAN Model. Before retrieving the 5YRPLAN model, insert the disk you saved it on into drive B, and then close the drive's door.

To retrieve a file

Press   **/FR** (for File, Retrieve), and the prompt asks you for the name of the file you want to retrieve. A list of files on the disk is displayed.

Press   → if necessary to move the highlight over 5YRPLAN, and then press **Return**.

Result. The 5YRPLAN model appears on the screen.

Step 2. Extract the Data into its Own Disk File. Let's begin by extracting the data on rows 8 through 10 and then save it in a file on the disk.

To extract a range of numbers

Goto   B8, and then press **/FXV** (for File, Xtract, Values). The prompt asks you to enter the name of the file the extracted data will be saved in.

Type   **EXTRACT**, and then press **Return**. The prompt asks you to enter the range to be extracted.

Type   **B8.F10**, and then press **Return**.

Result. The drive spins as the extracted range is copied to the file named EXTRACT on the disk.

Step 3. Erase Existing Data. Now that the numbers have been extracted, you can erase them from the template.

To erase the existing data

Press   **/RE** (for Range, Erase), and the prompt asks you to enter the range to erase.

Type   **B8.F10**, and then press **Return**.

Result. The range is erased.

Step 4. Copy the File. Now, use the Combine command to copy the numbers back into the template. The cursor's position is important because the file you are combining from the disk will appear with its upper left-hand corner in the cell you position the cursor in.

To combine the files

Goto   B8, and then press **/FCCE** (for File, Combine, Copy, Entire-File). The prompt asks you to enter the name of the file to be combined.

Type   **EXTRACT**, and then press **Return**.

Result. The numbers you extracted reappear in the template. Move the cursor around them and you will see they are now numbers and not formulas. This is because when you extract values, the calculated numbers are extracted, not the formulas in the cells.

Step 5. Add the File. You just used the Combine command that reads in numbers. If other numbers are in the cells they are copied in, they overwrite and erase them. The

Combine command also has a choice that let's you add the numbers that are combined to the numbers already in the cells.

To add numbers

Goto   B8, and then press **/FCAE** (for File, Combine, Add, Entire-File). The prompt asks you to enter the name of the file to be combined.

Type   **EXTRACT**, and then press **Return**.

Result. The original numbers you stored in the EXTRACT file are added to the numbers in the range on the template.

Step 6. Subtract the File. You can also subtract the combined numbers from the numbers already in the range.

To subtract numbers

Goto   B8, and then press **/FCSE** (for File, Combine, Subtract, Entire-File). The prompt asks you to enter the name of the file to be combined.

Type   **EXTRACT**, and then press **Return**.

Result. The original numbers you stored in the EXTRACT file are subtracted from the numbers in the range on the template.

Step 7. Continue or Quit. You have now completed this exercise. You do not want to save the file because when you combined data, you erased the formulas. Either clear the screen and continue to the next exercise, or quit the program if you have finished.

To clear the screen

Press   **/WEY** (for Worksheet, Erase, Yes).

To quit the program

Press   **/QY** (for Quit, Yes).

Result. If you quit the program, the operating system A> prompt reappears. Remove your disks, and then turn off the computer.

QUESTIONS

1. Why might you want to combine files?
2. What are the four basic steps in combining files?
3. What does it mean to link files? If you link models why is the order they are updated and retrieved in so important?
4. What is the disadvantage of using supplemental models?
5. When updating linked models, what order must you follow?
6. If you combined two files and wanted to add the values, how would you do this?

TOPIC 4-16
Creating and Printing Graphs

In this topic, we introduce you to the following procedures:
- Creating and printing graphs with The TWIN
- Creating and printing graphs with Lotus 1-2-3

BACKGROUND

Charts and graphs created on business graphics programs can be used to analyze financial and statistical data. For example, you can use graphs to find trends and relationships between sets of numbers like sales, expenses, and profits over a period. The final results can then be printed out for distribution to others or for inclusion in a report.

Graphics for analysis programs are integrated into spreadsheets like The TWIN and Lotus 1-2-3 so that data generated on the program can be quickly and easily displayed as a graph. This integration increases the speed with which you can generate graphs and allows the graph to be automatically updated when data in the spreadsheet changes. Thus you can use graphs as analytical tools for viewing the results of different scenarios rather than simply presenting final results to others.

CREATING GRAPHS

The power of The TWIN's and Lotus 1-2-3's graphs is that they graph ranges of cells and not just actual values. When any of the values in those cells are changed, the graphs immediately and automatically reflect those changes.

Graphs are easy to create. To create a simple graph, there are only five steps.

1. Press /G (for Graph) to display the Graph menu. Table 4-33 describes the choices on The TWIN's Graph menu, and Table 4-34 describes the choices on Lotus 1-2-3's Graph menu.

TABLE 4-33
The TWIN's Graph Menu Commands

Menu Choice	Description
Type	Selects one of the eight graph types: Line, XY, Horizontal Bar, Vertical Bar, 3D Bar, Pie, #D Pie, and Pie-Bar
X (range)	Sets the X-axis range, the range all other ranges are plotted against
1 - 8	Specifies as many as eight data ranges plotted against the X range
Label	Defines labels, X axis, and bar tops
Options	Specifies various options for enhancing the graph, including titles, sizes, footnotes, labels, and colors
Display	Displays the current graph
Plot	Prints the graph on a pen plotter
GPrint	Prints the current graph or retrieves and saves printer slides
Name	Names a graph so that it can be viewed at a later time
Reset	Cancels all graph settings for the current graph
Slide	Saves the graph as a slide or displays an existing slide
V	Displays the current graph (only available on the introductory and educational versions of The TWIN)
Quit	Exits from the Graph menu and returns to *READY* mode

TABLE 4-34
Lotus 1-2-3's Graph Menu Commands

Menu Choice	Description
Type	Selects one of the five graph types: Line, Bar, XY, Stacked-Bar, and Pie
X (range)	Sets the X-axis range, the range all other ranges are plotted against
A - F	Specifies as many as six data ranges plotted against the X range
Reset	Cancels all graph settings for the current graph
View	Displays the current graph
Save	Saves the current graph in a file (can be printed from the Printgraph program)
Options	Specifies various options for enhancing the graph, including legends, formats, titles, and scaling
Name	Names a graph so that it can be viewed at a later time
Quit	Exits from the Graph menu and returns to *READY* mode

Note. If your computer does not have the hardware necessary to display graphs on the screen, the computer beeps when you select Display (on The TWIN), Display or V (on the introductory and educational versions of The TWIN), or View (on Lotus 1-2-3). The only way you can see graphs without replacing or updating the hardware is to print them.

2. Type in or point to an X-axis range.

3. Type in or point to at least one data range.

4. Select a graph type.

5. Display the graph with the Display or View command from the Graph menu.

EXERCISE 114

Creating and Printing Graphs on The TWIN

In this exercise, you create and print graphs on The TWIN. To begin this exercise, you must load the program or clear the screen of any other model.

This exercise uses the 5YRPLAN model you created in Exercise 103. You must complete that exercise before you can begin this one.

Step 1. Retrieve the 5YRPLAN Model. When you use the File Retrieve command, any work on the screen is erased. Be sure to save your work before retrieving a new file.

To retrieve a file

Press   **/FR** (for File, Retrieve), and the prompt asks you to enter the name of the file. A list of files on the disk is displayed.

Press   → if necessary to move the highlight over 5YRPLAN, and then press **Return.**

Result. The 5YRPLAN model appears on the screen. To be sure your results match ours, enter 1000 as the initial sales (cell B2), 10% as the sales growth rate (B3), and 56% as cost of goods sold (B4).

Step 2. Create a Line Graph. You now create a graph that plots cost of goods sold and gross margins over the five-year period of the plan.

To display the graph menu

Press   **/G** (for Graph).

FIGURE 4-43
The TWIN line graph

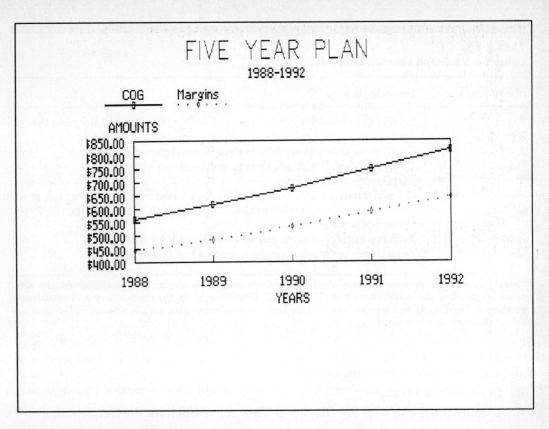

To select the graph type

Press   **TA** (for Type, A Line).

To set the graph's x axis

Press   **X**, and the prompt reads *Data range for X:*.
Type   **B7.F7**, and then press **Return**.

To set the data ranges

Press   **1**, and the prompt reads *Data range for 1:*.
Type   **B9.F9**, and then press **Return**.
Press   **2**, and the prompt reads *Data range for 2:*.
Type   **B10.F10**, and then press **Return**.

To display the graph

Press   **V** (for View—on the full-featured version of The TWIN, press **D** for Display) to display the graph.

Result. The graph appears on your screen (Figure 4-43). There are no labels on the X axis. Press **Spacebar** to clear the graph and return to the Graph menu.

Step 3. Label the X Axis. Let's label the X axis with the years on row 7.

To label the x axis

Press   **LX** (for Label, X), and the prompt reads *Data label range for X:*.
Type   **B7.F7**, and then press **Return** to return to the main Graph menu.
Press   **V** (for View—on the full-featured version of The TWIN, press **D** for Display) to display the revised graph.

Result. The years on row 7 are now displayed as labels on the X axis. Press **Spacebar** to remove the graph and return to the Graph menu.

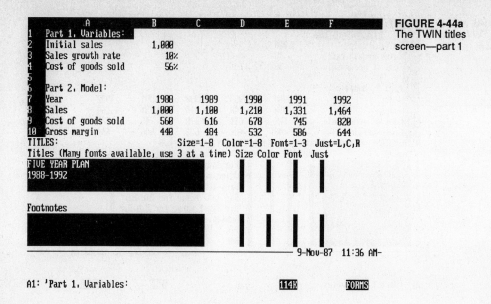

FIGURE 4-44a
The TWIN titles
screen—part 1

Step 4. Add Titles and Legends. The graph contains all the data, but it does not have enough information for anyone but you to understand it. Here you add titles and legends that improve the graph's ability to communicate. You add titles to the top of the graph and to the X axis. You then add legends explaining what each bar represents.

To display the options menu

Press   **O** (for Options) to display the titles screen (Figure 4-44a). The prompt reads *Titles*.

To add titles

Type   **FIVE YEAR PLAN**, and then press **Return**.
Type   **1988-1992**, and then press **PgDn** to move to the next page (Figure 4-44b). The prompt reads *X-Axis Label*.

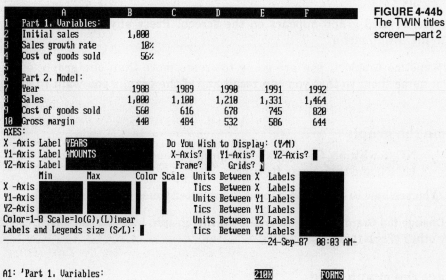

FIGURE 4-44b
The TWIN titles
screen—part 2

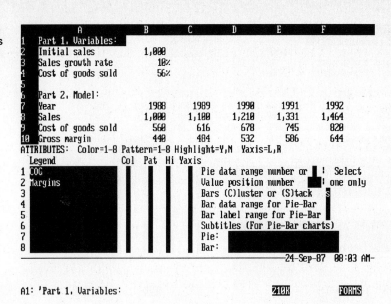

FIGURE 4-44c
The TWIN titles
screen—part 3

	A	B	C	D	E	F
1	Part 1. Variables:					
2	Initial sales	1,000				
3	Sales growth rate	10%				
4	Cost of goods sold	56%				
5						
6	Part 2. Model:					
7	Year	1988	1989	1990	1991	1992
8	Sales	1,000	1,100	1,210	1,331	1,464
9	Cost of goods sold	560	616	678	745	820
10	Gross margin	440	484	532	586	644

ATTRIBUTES: Color=1-8 Pattern=1-8 Highlight=Y,N Yaxis=L,R

	Legend	Col	Pat	Hi	Yaxis	
1	COG					Pie data range number or ▮ ┆ Select
2	Margins					Value position number ▮ ┆ one only
3						Bars (C)luster or (S)tack S
4						Bar data range for Pie-Bar
5						Bar label range for Pie-Bar
6						Subtitles (For Pie-Bar charts)
7						Pie:
8						Bar:

—24-Sep-87 08:03 AM—

A1: 'Part 1. Variables: `210K`   `FORMS`

To add labels

Type   **YEARS,** and then press **Return** to move to the prompt *Y1-axis Label*.

Type   **AMOUNTS,** and then press **PgDn** to move to the next page (Figure 4-44c). The prompt reads *1*.

To add legends

Type   **COG,** and then press **Return**. The prompt reads *2*.

Type   **Margins.**

To save the titles, labels, and legends

Press   **Ctrl-Home** to return to the spreadsheet.

To display the revised graph

Press   **V** (for View—on the full-featured version of The TWIN, press **D** for Display).

Result. The revised graph appears on the screen. Press any key to remove it and return to the Graph menu.

Step 5. Name the Graph. If you are going to create more than one graph, as we are here, you name them so that you can recall any of the graphs you want to display or print.

To name the graph

Press   **NC** (for Name, Create), and the prompt reads *Graph to create:.*

Type   **LINE,** and then press **Return**.

Result. You see how to recall the named graph after you create a new graph.

Step 6. Change the Graph Type. You created a line graph, but you can easily convert it into any other graph type.

To select the graph type

Press   **TD** (for Type, D VBar).

To display the graph

Press   **V** (for View—on the full-featured version of The TWIN, press **D** for Display) to display the graph.

Result. The graph is now displayed as a stacked bar graph (Figure 4-45). Press **Spacebar** to clear the graph and return to the Graph menu.

To name the bar graph

Press   **NC** (for Name, Create), and the prompt reads *Graph to create:*.
Type   **BAR**, and then press **Return**.

Result. You have now created, displayed, and named the stacked bar graph. You can recall it at any time using the Graph Name Use command, as you see in the next step.

Step 7. Print Your Graphs. Lets first recall the line graph and then print out a copy. When that is done, you can print out the bar graph. Before you begin, be sure your printer is on and has paper in it.

To retrieve the line graph

Press   **NU** (for Name, Use), and the prompt reads *Graph to use:*.
Press   → to display the named graphs one at a time until LINE appears.
Press   **Return** to select it.

To print the line graph

Press   **Spacebar** to return to the graph menu.
Press   **GP** (for Gprint, Printer), and the prompt asks if your printer is on line and has paper.
Press   **Y** (for Yes).

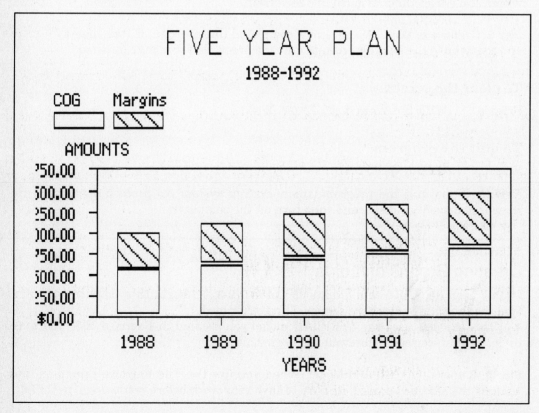

FIGURE 4-45
The TWIN stacked bar graph

Result. The graph begins printing. If it does not, you have not selected a printer. (To do so, see Exercise 85.) When the graph is finished printing, print the bar graph, or press **Q** (for Quit) to leave the Graph menu. To print out the bar graph, you first must make it the current graph. Advance the paper in your printer to the top of a new sheet.

To retrieve the named bar graph

Press   **NU** (for Name, Use), and the prompt reads *Graph to use:*.
Press   → to display the named graphs one at a time until BAR appears.
Press   **Return** to select it.

To print the bar graph

Press   **GP** (for Gprint, Printer), and the prompt asks if your printer is on line and has paper.
Press   **Y** (for Yes).

Result. The graph begins printing. When it is finished, press **Q** (for Quit) to leave the Graph menu.

Step 8. Save Your Work Again. Now that the model has been revised, you should save it again.

To save the model

Press   **/FS** (for File, Save), and the prompt asks you to enter the name of the file and suggests 5YRPLAN.
Press   **Return**, and the prompt reads *Cancel Replace*.
Press   **R** (for Replace).

Result. The disk drive spins, and the model is saved onto the disk in drive B. It over-writes and erases the previously saved version.

Step 9. Continue or Quit. You have now completed this exercise. Either clear the screen and continue to the next exercise, or quit the program if you have finished.

To clear the screen

Press   **/WEY** (for Worksheet, Erase, Yes).

To quit the program

Press   **/QY** (for Quit, Yes).

Result. If you quit the program, the operating system A> prompt appears on the screen. Remove your disks, and then turn off the computer.

EXERCISE 115

Creating Graphs on Lotus 1-2-3

In this exercise, you create graphs on Lotus 1-2-3. To begin this exercise, you must load the program or clear the screen of any other model.

    This exercise uses the 5YRPLAN model you created in Exercise 103. You must complete that exercise before you can begin this one.

Step 1. Retrieve the 5YRPLAN Model. When you use the File Retrieve command, any work on the screen is erased. Be sure to save your work before retrieving a new file.

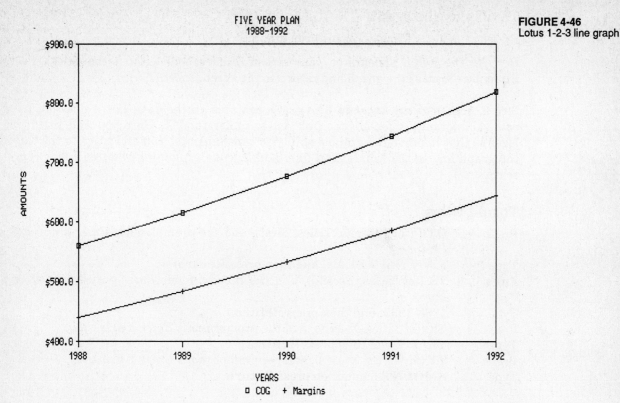

FIGURE 4-46
Lotus 1-2-3 line graph

To retrieve a file

Press   **/FR** (for File, Retrieve), and the prompt asks you to enter the name of the file. A list of files on the disk is displayed.

Press   → if necessary to move the highlight over 5YRPLAN, and then press **Return**.

Result. The 5YRPLAN model appears on the screen. To be sure your results match ours, enter 1000 as the initial sales (cell B2), 10% as the sales growth rate (B3), and 56% as cost of goods sold (B4).

Step 2. Create a Line Graph. You now create a graph that plots cost of goods sold and gross margins over the five-year period of the plan.

To display the graph menu

Press   **/G** (for Graph).

To select the graph type

Press   **TL** (for Type, Line).

To set the graph's x axis

Press   **X**, and the prompt reads *Enter X axis range:*.
Type   **B7.F7**, and then press **Return**.

To set the data ranges

Press   **A**, and the prompt reads *Enter first data range:*.
Type   **B9.F9** , and then press **Return**.
Press   **B**, and the prompt reads *Enter second data range:*.
Type   **B10.F10** and then press **Return**.

To display the graph

Press   **V** (for View) to display the graph.

Result. The graph appears on your screen (Figure 4-46 without the titles). Press **Spacebar** to clear the graph and return to the spreadsheet.

Step 3. Add Titles and Legends. The graph contains all the data, but it does not have enough information for anyone but you to understand it. Here you add titles and legends that improve the graph's ability to communicate. You add titles to the top of the graph and to the X axis. You then add legends explaining what each bar represents.

To add titles

Press   **OTF** (for Options, Titles, First), and the prompt reads *Enter graph title, top line:.*

Type   **FIVE YEAR PLAN**, and then press **Return**.

Press   **TS** (for Titles, Second), and the prompt reads *Enter graph title, second line:.*

Type   **1988-1992**, and then press **Return**.

Press   **TX** (for Titles, X-Axis), and the prompt reads *Enter X axis title:.*

Type   **YEARS**, and then press **Return**.

Press   **TY** (for Titles, Y-Axis), and the prompt reads *Enter Y axis title:.*

Type   **AMOUNTS**, and then press **Return**.

To add legends

Press   **LA** (for Legend, A), and the prompt reads *Enter legend for A range:.*

Type   **COG**, and then press **Return**.

Press   **LB** (for Legend, B), and the prompt reads *Enter legend for B range:.*

Type   **Margins**, and then press **Return**.

To format the y-axis values

Press   **SYFC** (for Scale, Y Scale, Format, Currency), and the prompt reads *Enter number of decimal places (0..15):.*

Type   **1**, and then press **Return**.

Result. To display your titles, press **Q** (for Quit) twice to return to the Graph menu, and then press **V** (for View). The graph now looks exactly like the one in Figure 4-46. Press **Spacebar** to clear the graph and return to the spreadsheet.

Step 4. Name the Graph. If you are going to create more than one graph, as we are here, you name them so that you can recall any of the graphs you want to display or print.

To name the graph

Press   **NC** (for Name, Create), and the prompt reads *Enter graph name:.*

Type   **LINE**, and then press **Return**.

Result. You see how to recall the named graph after you create a new graph.

Step 5. Change the Graph Type. You created a line graph, but you can easily convert it into any other graph type.

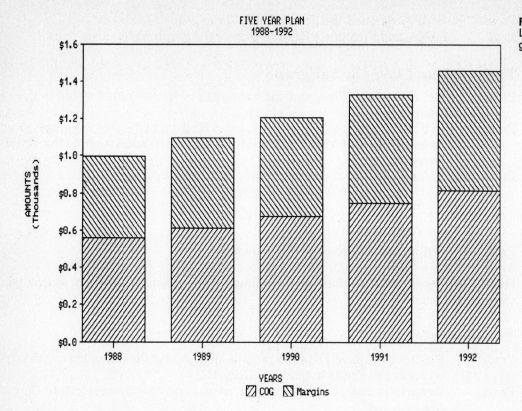

FIGURE 4-47
Lotus 1-2-3 stacked bar
graph

To select the graph type

Press   **TS** (for Type, Stacked-Bar).

To display the graph

Press   **V** (for View) to display the graph.

Result. The graph is now displayed as a stacked bar graph (Figure 4-47). Press **Spacebar** to clear the graph and return to the spreadsheet.

To name the bar graph

Press   **NC** (for Name, Create), and the prompt reads *Enter graph name:*.
Type   **BAR**, and then press **Return**.

Result. You have now created, displayed, and named the stacked bar graph. You can recall it at any time using the Graph Name Use command, as you see in the next step.

Step 6. Save the Graphs. The graph save command saves the current graph, that is, the one you viewed most recently. If your computer is not equipped to display graphs, you do not see the graph, but the command works nonetheless. Before proceeding, *be sure a formatted disk is in drive B and the drive's door is closed.*

To display and save the line graph

Press   **NU** (for Name, Use), and the prompt asks for the name of the graph to make current.
Press   → if necessary to highlight LINE, press **Return** to display the graph, then press **Spacebar** to remove it from the screen and return to the Graph menu.

| Press | S (for Save), and the prompt reads *Enter graph file name:*. |
| Type | **LINE**, and then press **Return** to save the graph on the disk. |

To display and save the bar graph

Press	**NU** (for Name, Use), and the prompt asks for the name of the graph to make current.
Press	→ if necessary to highlight BAR, press **Return** to display the graph, then press the **Spacebar** to remove it from the screen and return to the Graph menu.
Press	S (for Save), and the prompt reads *Enter graph file name:*.
Type	**BAR**, and then press **Return** to save the graph on the disk.

To quit the graph menu

| Press | **Q** (for Quit) to leave the Graph menu. |

Step 7. Save the Model. Now that you have finished the graphs, save them so that you can view them later.

To save the model

Press	**/FS** (for File, Save), and the prompt asks you for the name to save the file under and suggests the name 5YRPLAN.
Press	**Return** to accept the suggested name, and the prompt reads *Cancel Replace*.
Press	**R** (for Replace).

Result. The drive spins, and the revised model is saved onto the disk.

Step 8. Continue or Quit. You have now completed this exercise. Either clear the screen and continue to the next exercise, or quit the program if you have finished.

To clear the screen

| Press | **/WEY** (for Worksheet, Erase, Yes). |

To quit the program

| Press | **/QY** (for Quit, Yes). |

Result. If you quit the program, the operating system A> prompt appears on the screen. Remove your disks, and then turn off the computer.

EXERCISE 116

Printing Graphs on Lotus 1-2-3 Release 1a

In this exercise, you print graphs on Lotus 1-2-3 Release 1A. To begin this exercise, you must display the operating system A> prompt.

This exercise uses the graphs you created and saved in Exercise 115. You must complete that exercise before you can begin this one.

Step 1. Load the Printgraph Program. You print graphs with the Lotus printgraph program. Normally, you can load Lotus 1-2-3 by typing **LOTUS** from the system prompt to load the Lotus Access System (see TIPS below). The Access System menu allows you to move between the 1-2-3 worksheet and the printgraph program.

FIGURE 4-48
Lotus 1-2-3 release 1a
printgraph screen

```
Copyright 1982, 1983 Lotus Development Corp. All Rights Reserved.      MENU
-------------------------------------------------------------------------
Select  Options  Go  Configure  Align  Page  Quit
Select pictures
=========================================================================
SELECTED GRAPHS   COLORS              SIZE   FULL        DIRECTORIES

                  Grid:     Black     Left Margin:   .500   Pictures
                  A Range:  Black     Top Margin:    .250   B:\
                  B Range:  Black     Width:        6.852   Fonts
                  C Range:  Black     Height:       9.445   A:\
                  D Range:  Black     Rotation:    90.000
                  E Range:  Black                           GRAPHICS DEVICE
                  F Range:  Black     MODES
                                                            Epson MX80/2
                  FONTS               Eject: Yes            Parallel
                                      Pause: No
                  1: ROMAN2                                 PAGE SIZE
                  2: BLOCK1
                                                            Length  11.000
                                                            Width    8.000
```

You can also load the printgraph program directly from the operating system prompt as you do here. To begin, insert the Printgraph disk into drive A, type **GRAPH** and then press **Return**. The drive spins, and in a moment, the Printgraph menu appears on the screen (Figure 4-48).

Step 2. Select and Preview the Graph. You select a graph from a list of the graphs on the disk. Press ↓ or ↑ to highlight the desired graph, and then press **Spacebar** to select it. (The same command will "unselect" a previously selected graph.)

To select and preview a graph

Press   **S** (for Select) to display a list of the graphs on the disk in drive B.
Press   ↓ if necessary to highlight LINE, and then press **Spacebar** to select the graph and place a symbol in front of it to indicate it has been selected.
Press   **F10** to preview the graph (if your computer is equipped to display graphics).
Press   **Spacebar** to clear the graph, and then press **Return** to return to the Printgraph menu.

Step 3. Select a Font and Size. You must select a font for the labels before you can print a graph. We also select a small size for the graph so that it prints more quickly.

To select a font

Press   **OF** (for Options, Font), and the prompt reads *1 2*.
Press   1, highlight any font, press **Spacebar** to select it, and then press **Return**.
Press   **F** (for Font), and the prompt reads *1 2*.
Press   2, highlight any font, press **Spacebar** to select it, and then press **Return**.

To specify the size of the graph

Press   **SH** (for Size, Half).
Press   **Q** (for Quit) two times to return to the Graph Options menu.

Step 4. Eject the Page. Specify that the page be ejected from the printer when the graph is finished printing.

To eject the page from the printer

Press   **EYQ** (for Eject, Yes, Quit).

Step 5. Print the Graph. Now that you have selected a graph and specified the fonts and graph's size, you can print it. Be sure your printer is on and has paper in it.

To print the graph

Press   **AG** (for Align, Go).

Result. After a few moments, the graph begins printing. When it is finished printing, press **QY** (for Quit, Yes) to return to the system prompt. You have now completed this exercise. Either reload Lotus 1-2-3, or remove your disks, and then turn off the computer.

EXERCISE 117

Printing Graphs on Lotus 1-2-3 Release 2

In this exercise, you print graphs on Lotus 1-2-3 Release 2. To begin this exercise, you must display the operating system A> prompt.

    This exercise uses the graphs you created and saved in Exercise 115. You must complete that exercise before you can begin this one.

Step 1. Load the Printgraph program. You print graphs with the Lotus printgraph program. Normally, you can load Lotus 1-2-3 by typing **LOTUS** from the system prompt to load the Lotus Access System (see TIPS below). The Access System menu allows you to move between the 1-2-3 worksheet and the printgraph program.

    You can also load the printgraph program directly from the operating system prompt as you do here. To begin, insert the Printgraph disk into drive A and type **PGRAPH** and then press **Return**. The drive spins, and in a moment, the Printgraph menu appears on the screen (Figure 4-49).

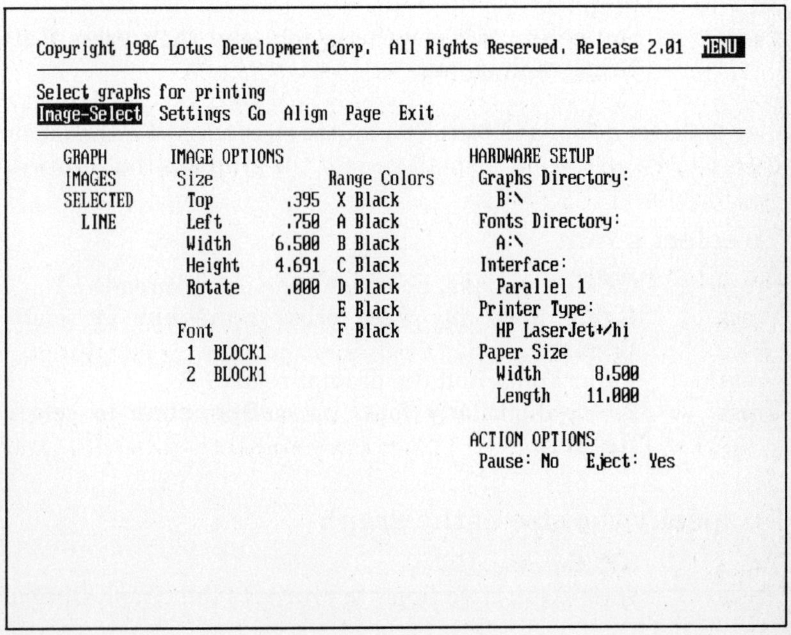

FIGURE 4-49
Lotus 1-2-3 release 2 printgraph screen

```
Copyright 1986 Lotus Development Corp. All Rights Reserved. Release 2.01  MENU

Select graphs for printing
Image-Select  Settings  Go  Align  Page  Exit

   GRAPH      IMAGE OPTIONS                    HARDWARE SETUP
   IMAGES     Size             Range Colors   Graphs Directory:
   SELECTED   Top       .395   X Black           B:\
   LINE       Left      .750   A Black        Fonts Directory:
              Width    6.500   B Black           A:\
              Height   4.691   C Black        Interface:
              Rotate    .000   D Black           Parallel 1
                               E Black        Printer Type:
              Font             F Black           HP LaserJet+/hi
              1  BLOCK1                        Paper Size
              2  BLOCK1                           Width     8.500
                                                 Length   11.000

                                              ACTION OPTIONS
                                              Pause: No   Eject: Yes
```

Step 2. Change Settings. To print graphs you have to specify the drive the graphs are stored on, and the printer you want to print them on. (To select a printer, you must first install the program so that printer drivers are copied to the PrintGraph disk.)

To specify the drive the graphs are stored on

Press **SHG** (for Settings, Hardware, Graphs-Directory).
Type **B:**, and then press **Return**.

To specify a printer

Press **P** (for Printer).
Press ↓ if necessary to highlight the desired printer, press **Spacebar** to select it, and then place a # in front of it.
Press **Return** to return to the Hardware menu.
Press **Q** (for Quit) two times to return to the main Printgraph menu.

Result. The main Printgraph menu reappears.

Step 3. Select and Preview the Graph. You select a graph from a list of the graphs on the disk. Press ↓ or ↑ to highlight the desired graph, and then press **Spacebar** to select it. (The same command will "unselect" a previously selected graph.)

To select and preview a graph

Press **I** (for Image-Select) to display a list of the graphs on the disk in drive B.
Press ↓ if necessary to highlight LINE, and then press **Spacebar** to select the graph and place a # symbol in front of it to indicate it has been selected.
Press **F10** to preview the graph (if your computer is equipped to display graphics).
Press **Spacebar** to clear the graph, and then press **Return** to return to the Printgraph menu.

Step 4. Select Size. Graphs are normally printed full-size, but select a smaller size for the graph so that it prints more quickly.

To change the size of the graph

Press **SISH** (for Settings, Image, Size, Half), and the new size is indicated under the heading *IMAGE OPTIONS*.
Press **Q** (for Quit) three times to return to the main graph menu.

Step 5. Eject the Page. Specify that the page be ejected from the printer when the graph is finished printing.

To eject the page from the printer

Press **SAEY** (for Settings, Actions, Eject, Yes).
Press **Q** (for Quit) twice to return to the main Printgraph menu.

Step 6. Print the Graph. Now that you have selected a graph and specified the fonts and graph's size, you can print it. Be sure your printer is on and has paper in it.

To print the graph

Press **AG** (for Align, Go).

Result. After a few moments, the graph begins printing. When it is finished printing, press **EY** (for Exit, Yes) to return to the system prompt. You have now completed this exercise. Either reload Lotus 1-2-3, or remove your disks, and then turn off the computer.

TIPS

- **On the full-featured Lotus 1-2-3 program, you can load the Lotus Access System** to make it easier to move between the worksheet and printgraph program. To do so, insert the Lotus 1-2-3 System disk into drive A, type **LOTUS** and then press **Return** to display the Lotus Access System. Press **1** (for 1-2-3) to display the spreadsheet or **P** for **PrintGraph** to display the Printgraph menu. When you quit either program, the Access System menu reappears so that you can move to the other program.

QUESTIONS

1. What is the value of graphs when created from spreadsheets?
2. What is the particular power of The TWIN's and Lotus 1-2-3's graphs?
3. What are the five basic steps in creating a graph?
4. What is The TWIN command for displaying the current graph? The Lotus 1-2-3 command?
5. What are The TWIN commands for specifying data ranges? The Lotus 1-2-3 commands?
6. What types of graphs can you create on The TWIN? On Lotus 1- 2-3?
7. What is the difference between titles and legends?
8. Before you can print a Lotus 1-2-3 graph, what must you do?

TOPIC 4-17
Creating and Using Macros

In this topic, we introduce you to the following procedure:

■ Using macros

BACKGROUND

Macros are simply a way to store keystrokes so that they can be played back later. They can save you from having to rekey repetitive data or commands. On the TWIN and Lotus 1-2-3, macros are created using a macro language. The language contains key words (see Table 4-35) that indicate keys on the keyboard. Let's look at an example.

To print a model on The TWIN or Lotus 1-2-3, you must press the slash key (/) and then select Print, Printer, Align, Go, Page, and Quit. You can create a macro so that this same series of commands is executed when you hold down **Alt** and press the letter **P** (or any other key you assign the series of keystrokes to). The macro you would write to do this would be written as

{HOME}/ppagpq

{HOME}, enclosed in braces, tells the program to move the cursor to cell A1. The slash (/) calls up the Main menu, and the sequence of letters (ppagpq) is the same sequence you would type to print the model from the keyboard. After entering the

---

TABLE 4-35
Macro Key Words

Key	Macro Key Word Equivalent
Function Keys	
Edit (F2)	{edit}
Name (F3)	{name}
Abs (F4)	{abs}
Goto (F5)	{goto}
Window (F6)	{window}
Query (F7)	{query}
Table (F8)	{table}
Calc (F9)	{calc}
Graph (F10)	{graph}
Other Keys	
←	{left}
→	{right}
↑	{up}
↓	{down}
Home	{home}
End	{end}
Backspace	{bs}
Del	{del}
Esc	{esc}
Return	~

---

macro, you assign it a name; in this example, you name it so that it is executed when you hold down **Alt** and press the letter **P**. It is like making a piano into a player piano; the only difference is the computer's keys do not move up and down—it is all done electronically.

When entering macros, keep the following points in mind:

■ You must enter macros as labels. Some keys like the slash key (/) must be preceded by a label-prefix character if they are the first character on a line. Lotus 1-2-3 ignores the label-prefix character when it reads the contents of the cell. If you want a label-prefix character to be used at the beginning of a line, you must enter two prefixes; the first converts the second into a label.

■ Until you have all commands memorized, the best way to create a macro is to enter the entire command keystroke by keystroke, recording the keys you press on a sheet of paper. Then enter the keystrokes needed as a label and name the label.

■ Macros are easier to read and understand if you selectively use uppercase and lowercase letters. For example, put all keystrokes in lowercase, and all range names, cell contents, and cell coordinates in uppercase. A macro that prints a range named page1 is easier to read when entered as '/pprPAGE1~agpq than when entered as '/PPRPAGE1~AGPQ.

■ Macros usually should not refer to cell coordinates because inserting or deleting rows and columns can change those coordinates and confuse the macro. Use range names to refer to blocks of cells.

■ To end a macro so that you return to *READY* mode after it has been executed, leave a nonlabel cell at the end (below the last cell containing the macro), or enter a /XQ command in the last macro cell.

■ The first cell in a macro is the only cell that needs to be included in the range name. You can include the rest of the cells, but it is not necessary. The TWIN and Lotus 1-2-3 automatically reads each row until it reaches a nonlabel cell or a cell containing the /XQ command. Macro names consist of the backslash key (\) followed by a letter of the alphabet or the number zero.

■ Macros named \0 (the number zero, not the letter O) are automatically executed when the model is retrieved. A macro with this name cannot be used from the keyboard. To use the macro, assign it a second name (\A through \Z).

■ Macros containing cursor movement key words ({right}, {left}, and so on) may not work the same when **Scroll Lock** is engaged. Always be sure **Scroll Lock** is not engaged before executing a macro containing these commands.

■ Always save a file after creating a macro. If a file is not saved after the macro has been created, the macro is not saved.

■ Always save a file before executing a new macro. That way if anything changes as a result of the macro (intentionally or not), you have a copy of the original file.

■ To stop a macro while it is executing and return to *READY* mode, press **Ctrl-Break**. Macros also stop when a /XQ command or a nonlabel cell is encountered.

■ To work through a macro one step at a time, press the **Step** key. The **Step** key you use to enter and leave step mode depends on the program you are using. For example, on The TWIN and Lotus 1-2-3 Release 1A, you press **Alt-F1**. On Lotus 1-2-3 Release 2, you press **Alt-F2**. When you are in step mode, a *STEP* indicator is displayed on the Lotus 1-2-3 screen and a dollar sign is displayed in front of the *$READY* mode indicator on The TWIN. Then when you invoke a macro, press any key to execute it one keystroke at a time. The *SST* indicator is displayed when a macro is invoked while in step mode. To leave step mode, press **Alt-F1** or **Alt-F2** again. If **Alt-F1** or **Alt-F2** is pressed during the execution of a macro in step mode, pressing any key executes the rest of the macro.

TABLE 4-36
Macro Commands That Pause for Operator Input

Command	Description
{?}	Causes a pause for operator input when encountered anywhere in a macro. The macro continues only after pressing **Return**. The {?} command is followed by a tilde ({?}~) since pressing **Return** once completes the entry but does not resume the macro.
/XL(message)~(location)~	Displays a message of as many as thirty-nine characters on the second line of the control panel and pauses so that you can enter a label. After pressing **Return**, the label typed is entered in the location cell using a left-align prefix character.
/XN(message)~(location)~	Displays a message of as many as thirty-nine characters on the second line of the control panel and pauses so that you can enter a number, formula, range name, or function. After pressing **Return**, the numeric value of the entry is stored at the location.

USING OPERATOR INPUT

Macros can be made to pause during execution and accept operator input with the {?}~ command or with one of the following /X commands. Table 4-36 describes these commands.

BRANCHING MACRO COMMANDS

Macros can be made to continue reading macro keystrokes at other locations on a spreadsheet. This is called branching, and it is useful when using macros to create menus (see Topic 4-18). Table 4-37 describes these branching commands.

EXERCISE 118
Creating A Macro That Enters a Label

In this exercise, you create and execute a macro *(not available on the introductory version of The TWIN)*. To begin this exercise, you must load the program or clear the screen of any other model.

TABLE 4-37
Branching Macro Commands

Command	Description
/XG(location)~	The macro jumps to the specified location and continues reading keystrokes.
/XC(location)~	The macro jumps to the specified location and continues reading keystrokes, remembering where it left off. When a /XR command is encountered, the macro returns to where it left off. The subroutines can be nested as many as sixteen levels deep.
/XR	If a macro branched as a result of a /XC command, it returns to where it left off when /XR is encountered.
/XI(formula)	If the formula is TRUE (not zero), the macro continues reading keystrokes in the same cell; otherwise, it reads the keystrokes in the cell below.
/XM(menu name)~	The macro jumps to the cell containing the menu name and displays the menu on the screen.

Step 1. Enter a Macro. Enter a macro that enters your name.

Remember these points when creating a macro menu.
- Enter the quote mark (') where indicated so that you enter the commands as labels. If you do not do this, you execute the commands.
- Use lowercase letters for commands and uppercase letters for what you would normally type in response to prompts. This makes the macros easier to understand and troubleshoot.
- Enter the tilde (~) wherever indicated. This is the macro command for pressing **Return**.

To enter a macro

Press   **Home** to move the cursor to cell A1.
Type   **{goto}D1~Your Name~**, and then press **Return**.

Step 2. Name the Macro. Use the Range Name command to name the cell. A macro name is always a letter of the alphabet preceded by the backslash key (\), for example, \T or \R.

To name the macro

Goto   A1, and then press **/RNC** (for Range, Name, Create). The prompt asks you to enter the range name.
Type   **\N**, and then press **Return**. The prompt asks you to enter the range.
Press   **Return** to name the cell containing the cursor.

Step 3. Execute the Macro. You execute a macro by holding down **Alt** and pressing the letter used in the macro name.

To execute the name macro

Press   **Alt-N.**

Result. The macro automatically moves to cell D1 and enters your name.

Step 4. Add a Loop to the Macro. Now, add a loop to the macro so that it continues to enter your name again and again until you press **Ctrl-Break** to stop it. A loop is a sequence of commands, the last one of which refers the program back to the first so the commands repeat themselves over and over until stopped.

To enter a loop in the macro

Goto   A2, type **{down}Your Name~**, and then press ↓ to move the cursor to cell A3.
Type   **'/xgA2~**, and then press **Return**.

Step 5. Execute the Macro. Before executing this macro, locate the **Ctrl** and **Break** keys on your keyboard. You must press these keys together to stop the macro.

To execute the name macro

Press   **Alt-N.**

Result. The macro automatically moves to cell D1 and enters your name just as it did the last time. The second line of the macro then moves the cursor down one cell and enters your name again. The third line tells the macro to read the keystrokes in cell A2 again so that it continues to execute the second line, and each time it does, the third line loops it back to the second line and executes those keystrokes again. Press

Ctrl-Break to stop the macro. Then press **Esc** to continue, and press **Home** to return to cell A1.

Step 6. Create a Macro to Erase a Range. Now, add a macro that erases the names (regardless of how many) entered by the **Alt-N** macro.

To enter a macro

Goto   A6, type **{goto}D1~/re**, and then press ↓ to move the cursor to cell A7.

Type   **'.{end}{down}~**, and then press **Return**.

To name the macro

Goto   A6, and then press **/RNC** (for Range, Name, Create). The prompt asks you to enter the range name.

Type   **\E**, and then press **Return**. The prompt asks you to enter the range.

Press   **Return** to name the cell containing the cursor.

To execute the macro

Press   **Alt-E.**

Result. When you execute the macro, it moves the cursor to cell D1 and enters the Range Erase command. It then presses the period to anchor the range, presses **End** and then ↓ to highlight the range, and then presses **Return** to complete the command.

Step 7. Execute the Macros a Step at a Time. When you execute the macro, it happens so fast you cannot really see what happens. But you can use step mode to execute the macro a keystroke at a time. The commands you use to enter and leave step mode depend on the program you are using. For example, on The TWIN and Lotus 1-2-3 Release 1A, you press **Alt-F1**. On Lotus 1-2-3 Release 2, you press **Alt-F2**.

To execute the macro in step mode

Press   **Alt-F1** or **Alt-F2** or to display the step indicator (*$READY* on The TWIN and *STEP* on Lotus 1-2-3).

Press   **Alt-N** to display the *SST* indicator.

Result. Press **Return** repeatedly to enter the macro a keystroke at a time. Each time you press it, another keystroke or key word is executed. After pressing it enough times to enter your name three or four times, press **Ctrl-Break**, and then press **Esc** to cancel the macro. Then, press **Alt-E** to execute the erase macro, and press **Return** to execute it a step at a time. After erasing the range, press **Alt-F1** or **Alt-F2** to return to *READY* mode.

Step 8. Save the Model. Now that you have finished the model, save it into a file on the disk so that you can retrieve it later. Before proceeding, *be sure a formatted disk in drive B and the drive's door is closed.*

To save the model

Press   **/FS** (for File, Save), and the prompt asks you for the name to save the file under.

Type   **MACRO1**, and then press **Return**.

Step 9. Continue or Quit. You have now completed this exercise. Either clear the screen and continue to the next exercise, or quit the program if you have finished.

To clear the screen

Press   /**WEY** (for Worksheet, Erase, Yes).

To quit the program

Press   /**QY** (for Quit, Yes).

Result. If you quit the program, the operating system A> prompt reappears. Remove your disks, and then turn off the computer.

Creating a Macro That Widens Columns

In this exercise, you create a macro that widens columns *(not available on the introductory version of The TWIN)*. To begin this exercise, you must load the program or clear the screen of any other model.

Step 1. Create a Macro That Widens Columns. Enter a macro that automatically widens individual columns.

To enter a macro

Goto   A1, type '/**wcs20~{right}**, and then press **Return**.

To name the macro

Goto   A1, and then press /**RNC** (for Range, Name, Create). The prompt asks you to enter the range name.

Type   **C**, and then press **Return**. The prompt asks you to enter the range.

Press   **Return.**

Result. The macro is now finished. To operate it, hold down **Alt** and press **C**. The column containing the cursor is widened, and the cursor moves one column to the right. Press it again to widen the next column.

Step 2. Save the Model. Now that you have finished the model, save it into a file on the disk so that you can retrieve it later. Before proceeding, *be sure a formatted disk is in drive B and the drive's door is closed.*

To save the model

Press   **Home** to return the cursor to cell A1.

Press   /**FS** (for File, Save), and the prompt asks you for the name to save the file under.

Type   **MACRO2**, and then press **Return**.

Step 3. Continue or Quit. You have now completed this exercise. Either clear the screen and continue to the next exercise, or quit the program if you have finished.

To clear the screen

Press   /**WEY** (for Worksheet, Erase, Yes).

To quit the program

Press   /**QY** (for Quit, Yes).

Result. If you quit the program, the operating system A> prompt appears on the screen. Remove your disks, and then turn off the computer.

EXERCISE 120

Printing a Model with a Macro

In this exercise, you create a macro to print a single-page model *(not available on the introductory version of The TWIN)*. To begin this exercise, you must load the program or clear the screen of any other model.

Step 1. Retrieve a Model. Retrieve any model you have previously created, like the 5YRPLAN model.

Step 2. Create a Macro to Print a Model. Move the cursor to column A on the first blank row below the model, and then move down one more row. Enter this macro.

To enter a macro

Goto   a blank row below the model.

Type   **'/ppr{home}.{end}{home}~agpq,** and then press **Return**.

To name the macro

Goto   the cell you entered the macro in.

Press   **/RNC** (for Range, Name, Create), and the prompt asks you to enter the range name.

Type   **\P**, and then press **Return**. The prompt asks you to enter the range.

Press   **Return.**

Result. The macro is now finished. To operate it, be sure the printer is on and has paper in it. Then, hold down **Alt** and press **P** to print the document and advance the paper out of the printer. It also prints out the macro because it is included in the range. To remove the line, revise the macro so that it reads

'/ppr{home}.{end}{home}{up}~agpq

To see how the macro works, press **Alt-F1** (on The TWIN and Lotus 1-2-3 Release 1A) or press **Alt-F2** (on Lotus 1-2-3 Release 2) to enter step mode. Press **Alt-P** and then press **Return** repeatedly to execute the macro a step at a time. When finished printing the second copy, press **Alt-F1** or **Alt-F2** to turn off step mode.

Step 3. Save the Model. Now that you have finished the model, save it into a file on the disk so that you can retrieve it later. Before proceeding, *be sure a formatted disk is in drive B and the drive's door is closed.*

To save the model

Press   **/FS** (for File, Save), and the prompt asks you for the name to save the file under and suggests the name you originally saved the file under.

Type   **MACRO3**, and then press **Return** to save it under a new name.

Result. The drive spins, and the revised model is saved onto the disk under the new name.

Step 4. Continue or Quit. You have now completed this exercise. Either clear the screen and continue to the next exercise, or quit the program if you have finished.

To clear the screen

Press   **/WEY** (for Worksheet, Erase, Yes).

To quit the program

Press   **/QY** (for Quit, Yes).

Result. If you quit the program, the operating system A> prompt appears on the screen. Remove your disks, and then turn off the computer.

QUESTIONS

1. What is a macro?
2. When might you use macros?
3. What kind of data must macros be entered as?
4. Why should you selectively use uppercase and lowercase letters when entering macros?
5. What is the macro command for pressing **Return**?
6. Describe the macro command {?}.
7. Do macros often refer to cell coordinates? Why or why not?
8. How do you end a macro so that you return to *READY* mode after the macro has been executed? Can you think of two ways to do this?
9. It is important to save a file both after creating a macro and before executing a macro. Why is this?
10. How do you stop a macro while it is executing?
11. How do you work through a macro a step at a time?
12. What are branching macro commands used for?

TOPIC 4-18
Creating Menus

In this topic, we introduce you to the following procedure:

■ Creating menus

BACKGROUND

Programs that provide you with a macro language, like The TWIN and Lotus 1-2-3, also allow you to create your own menus.

These user-defined menus (Figure 4-50) can be displayed and executed just like the menus built into the spreadsheet program. They are useful additions for models used over and over again or by many people. For example, you can create a menu that lists commands to print the model, display graphs, or even display areas of the spreadsheet where you have entered text describing the model.

Menus need at least two names. The cell containing the /XM command must be attached to a keystroke, and the name following the /XM command must be assigned to the first cell in the actual menu.

The basic steps in creating a macro, or user-defined, menu are

1. **Create the macro that calls up the menu.** The /XM(menu name)~ command is used to call up a menu. The cell containing the command is named following the rules for naming a macro—a backslash (\) followed by a letter or a zero. The

```
A1: [W20] 'Part 1. Variables:
Quit-menu Save Print Line Bar
Return to model
          A        B        C        D        E        F
1  Part 1. Variables:
2  Initial sales      1,000
3  Sales growth rate    10%
4  Cost of goods sold   56%
5
6  Part 2. Model:
7  Year               1988     1989     1990     1991     1992
8  Sales              1,000    1,100    1,210    1,331    1,464
9  Cost of goods sold   560      616      678      745      820
10 Gross margin         440      484      532      586      644
11
12
13
14
15
16
17
18
19
20
```

FIGURE 4-50
User-defined menus

first cell in the list of menu selections is named using the same name used in the /XM command. When the macro is executed, the menu is displayed on the second line of the screen.

2. **Enter the menu selections and their descriptions.** The first row of the menu contains the main selections (as many as eight). The second row contains an extended description of each selection.

■ There cannot be blank cells between menu selections.

■ The cell after the last menu selection must be empty. If that cell contains data, an error message is displayed.

■ Begin each menu item with a different letter. Macro menus work the same way The TWIN's and Lotus 1-2-3's built-in menus do. You can select the menu option desired by pointing to it and pressing **Return** or by typing the first letter of the option. If the macro menu has two options beginning with the same letter, typing that letter executes the leftmost entry.

■ Since all menu selections are displayed on the screen at once, the length of the menu selection names is important. If the total length of the combined names does not fit on the control panel, an error message is displayed.

3. **Name the macro that calls up the menu.** You use a backslash and a letter so that you can display the menu by holding down **Alt** while pressing the letter you used to name it.

4. **Name the menu.** The /XM command that displays the menu refers to a menu name. You assign that name to the leftmost entry in the menu.

5. **Create the macros that perform each separate menu selection.** The macros begin on the third row of the menu, immediately under the extended description. To return to the menu after finishing an option, copy the /XM command to the last cell in each menu macro entry.

EXERCISE 121
Create a Menu That Automates the 5YRPLAN Model

In this exercise, you create a menu that saves and prints a model and displays graphs. (*Macros are not available on the introductory version of The TWIN.*) To begin this exercise, you must load the program or clear the screen of any other model.

	O	P	Q	R	S
1	/xmMENU˜	{goto}\M˜			
2					
3					
4					
5	Quit-menu	Save	Print	Line	Bar
6	Return to model	Save file as 5YRPLAN	Print model	Display line graph	Display bar graph
7		/fs5YRPLAN˜r	/pprA1.F10˜agpq	/gnuLINE˜vq	/gnuBAR˜vq
8		/xmMENU˜	/xmMENU˜	/xmMENU˜	/xmMENU˜

FIGURE 4-51
5YRPLAN menu macro

This exercise uses the 5YRPLAN model you created in Exercise 103 and added graphs to in Exercise 114 (The TWIN) or 115 (Lotus 1-2- 3). You must complete those exercises before you can begin this one.

Your finished menu should look like Figure 4-51. Refer to this figure to check your results as you complete the steps in this exercise.

Step 1. Retrieve the 5YRPLAN Model. When you use the File Retrieve command, any work on the screen is erased. Be sure to save your work before retrieving a new file.

To retrieve a file

Press   **/FR** (for File, Retrieve), and the prompt asks you to enter the name of the file. A list of files on the disk is displayed.

Press   → if necessary to move the highlight over 5YRPLAN, and then press **Return**.

Result. The 5YRPLAN model appears on the screen. Since you want to enter data on the spreadsheet, press **/WGPD** (for Worksheet, Global, Protection, Disable) to turn off protection.

Step 2. Create a Menu That Automates the Model. Remember these points when creating a macro menu.

■ Enter the quote mark (') where indicated so that you enter the commands as labels. If you do not do this, you execute the commands.

■ Use lowercase letters for commands and uppercase letters for what you would normally type in response to prompts. This makes the macros easier to understand and troubleshoot.

■ Enter the tilde (~) where indicated. This is the macro command for pressing **Return**.

You may want to widen columns after you enter macros in them so that the entire macro is displayed.

To enter the menu command

Goto   O1, type **'/xmMENU~**, and then press **Return**.

To enter the menu's quit choice

Goto   O5, type **Quit-menu**, and then press **Return**.
Goto   O6, type **Return to model**, and then press **Return**.

To enter the menu's save choice

Goto   P5, type **Save**, and then press **Return**.
Goto   P6, type **Save file as 5YRPLAN**, and then press **Return**.
Goto   P7, type **'/fs5YRPLAN~r** and then press **Return**.
Goto   P8, type **'/xmMENU~** and then press **Return**.

To enter the menu's print choice

Goto   Q5, type **Print**, and then press **Return**.
Goto   Q6, type **Print model**, and then press **Return**.
Goto   Q7, type **'/pprA1.F10~agpq** and then press **Return**.
Goto   Q8, type **'/xmMENU~** and then press **Return**.

To enter the menu's line graph choice

Goto   R5, type **Line**, and then press **Return**.
Goto   R6, type **Display line graph**, and then press **Return**.
Goto   R7, type **'/gnuLINE~vq**, and then press **Return**.
Goto   R8, type **'/xmMENU~** and then press **Return**.

To enter the menu's bar graph choice

Goto   S5, type **Bar**, and then press **Return**.
Goto   S6, type **Display bar graph**, and then press **Return**.
Goto   S7, type **'/gnuBAR~vq** and then press **Return**.
Goto   S8, type **'/xmMENU~** and then press **Return**.

To name the macro

Goto   O1, and then press **/RNC** (for Range, Name, Create). The prompt asks you to enter the range name.
Type   **\M**, and then press **Return**. The prompt asks you to enter the range.
Press   **Return.**

To name the menu

Goto   O5, and then press **/RNC** (for Range, Name, Create). The prompt asks you to enter the range name.
Type   **MENU**, and then press **Return**. The prompt asks you to enter the range.
Press   **Return.**

Result. The menu is now finished.

Step 3. Create a Goto Macro. You can use the **Goto** key (**F5**) to move the cursor to a named range. Here you enter a macro that uses this feature to return you to your menu whenever you want to revise it.

To enter a macro

Goto   P1, type **{goto}\M~**, and then press **Return**.

To name the macro

Goto   P1, and then press **/RNC** (for Range, Name, Create). The prompt asks you to enter the range name.
Type   **\G**, and then press **Return**. The prompt asks you to enter the range.
Press   **Return.**

Result. The macro is now finished.

Step 4. Save Your Work. Now that the model has been revised, you should save it. If something unexpected happens, you can retrieve the model from the disk and try to find the problem.

To save the model

Press /FS (for File, Save), and the prompt asks you to enter the name of the file and suggests 5YRPLAN.

Press **Return** to accept the suggested name, and the prompt reads *Cancel Replace*.

Press **R** (for Replace).

Result. The disk drive spins, and the model is saved onto the disk in drive B. It overwrites and erases the previously saved version.

Step 5. Run the Menu. Press **Home** to return to the model. Hold down **Alt** and press **M** to display the menu on the screen (Figure 4- 50). Press the first letter in any of the choices, or move the highlight over them and press **Return** to execute them. Before using the Print command, be sure your printer is on and has paper in it. When using the Graph commands, press **Spacebar** to return to the menu (you may have to press it twice). Press **Q** (for Quit-menu) when you are done. Then, to see how the goto macro works, hold down **Alt** and press **G**. The cursor jumps to the macros you just created.

Step 6. Continue or Quit. You have now completed this exercise. Either continue to the next exercise, or quit the program if you have finished.

To clear the screen

Press /WEY (for Worksheet, Erase, Yes).

To quit the program

Press /QY (for Quit, Yes).

Result. If you quit the program, the operating system A> prompt appears on the screen. Remove your disks, and then turn off the computer.

QUESTIONS

1. What are the five basic steps in creating a macro menu?
2. Why might you want to create a user-defined menu?
3. Macro menus need at least two names. What are they?
4. Which branching macro command is used to call up a menu?
5. How many main selections can a macro menu accommodate?
6. Why is the length of menu selection names important?

TOPIC 4-19
Using Data Management

In this topic, we introduce you to the following procedures:

- Creating a database
- Sorting a database
- Querying a database
- Finding records in a database
- Extracting records from a database

BACKGROUND

Spreadsheet databases (actually record files) are ideal for organizing and analyzing tables containing sales figures, inventory, mailing or distribution lists, customer accounts, check registers, or any other data that needs to be collected, sorted, and analyzed. Databases are created with most of the same commands used to create a model. In fact, a **database** is just a model organized into fields and records (see Table 4-38); it is a range of cells containing one or more columns and at least two rows.

SORTING A DATABASE

Databases can be quickly sorted into ascending or descending order. You can specify which columns are to be used as the primary and secondary sort keys. The secondary sort key is specified when there is a possibility of duplicate data in the primary sort key. For example, if you were sorting a database by name, you would want to use the Lastname field as the primary sort key and the Firstname field as the secondary sort key. When the data is sorted, any records with the same last name are subsorted by first name.

When you use primary and secondary sort keys, select the keys in descending order of importance. The primary sort key should be the more important field, and the secondary sort key should be the less important field. For example, to sort a database by state and name, specify the state as the primary key if that is the more important field.

TABLE 4-38
Key Parts of a Database

Part	Description
Field names	Field names are placed on the first row and are used to label the columns where data is entered.
Records	Records are entered on the second and subsequent rows. Records are sets of related data, much like Rolodex cards that contain a person's name, address, and phone number.
Fields	Fields are the columns of information that make up a record. A record consists of the information contained within the fields of the database. For example, on a Rolodex card, the fields might be the person's name, street address, city, state, ZIP code, and phone number. A record includes the data for all these fields that pertains to one person.

To sort a database, you need to specify only the range to be sorted. When specifying the range to sort, include only the data records. Do not include field names, or they are sorted along with the data.

QUERYING THE DATABASE

You can use a The TWIN and Lotus 1-2-3 databases as a major record keeping and analysis tool. The Data Query command can be used to

- Find records meeting specified criteria
- Delete records meeting specified criteria
- Delete duplicate records
- Create a new database containing only selected records or fields

To use the Data Query commands, you must first specify an input range, criterion range, and output range.

Creating the Input Range

The input range specifies the range of cells the program looks in during a data query. The input range is either the database itself or some portion of it.

Creating the Criterion Range

The criterion range specifies the range where the query specifications are listed. The criterion range must be at least two rows. The first row contains some or all of the database's field names; the remaining rows are used to enter criteria to be used in the query.

- If you enter more than one criterion on the same row, matches occur only if *all* criteria are met.
- If you enter criteria on adjacent rows, records are found if *any* criterion is met.
- Blank rows in the criterion range cause all records to be found.
- You can use the wildcard symbols to find records containing labels. The asterisk substitutes for any characters from the position of the asterisk to the end of the label. For example, the entry John* in the criterion range would find any records that contained John as the first four letters in the appropriate field, including John, Johnny, and John Jacob. The ? stands for any single character. For example, h?t would find hut, hat, hot, and hit.

Creating the Output Range

The output range specifies where data extracted during a query is stored. An output range is necessary only if you are using the Extract or Unique commands from the Query menu.

Finding Records in a Database

The Query Find command highlights selected records in the input range that meet the requirements specified in the criterion range.

- If more than one record meets the requirements specified in the criterion range, it is highlighted one at a time. Press ↑ and ↓ to move the highlight to subsequent records.
- The **Query** key (**F7**) repeats the most recent Query operation performed. If you want to find several different groups of data, all you need to do is change the criteria and press **F7**.

Extracting Records from a Database

The Query Extract command copies records in the input range that meet selected criteria from the criterion range to the output range. You can use the Extract command to copy selected parts of a database to another range in the spreadsheet. That range can then be printed or saved as a separate model.

Extracting Only Unique Records

The Query Unique command extracts records that meet selected criteria into the output range. If duplicate records exist, only the first one is extracted. You can use the Unique command as a fast way of deleting all duplicate records in a database. Using the Unique command with a blank line in the criterion range copies all nonduplicate records to the output range. You can copy the output range to a new file and use it as the new database.

Deleting Unneeded Records

The Query Delete command deletes records in the input range that meet the requirements specified in the criterion range. Delete "closes up" the database, deleting empty rows. Each time you try a delete, you are given the choice to cancel the command or continue. If you continue, the records are permanently deleted. Before you use the delete option, first extract the records you are considering deleting. This gives you the opportunity of checking the records before erasing them. It also gives you a temporary back-up copy of the records in the output range. The output range can be copied to another file for later reference, or they can be erased.

USING CRITERION FORMULAS IN A DATABASE

When entering criteria in a database, you can enter logical operators to show relationships (Table 4-39). Criterion formulas are recalculated once for each record in the database. If the formula evaluates as true (not equal to zero) for a record, that record is accepted as a match.

TABLE 4-39
Operators Used in a Criterion Formula

Operator	Description	Precedence in Action
<	Less than	3
<=	Less than or equal to	3
	Greater than	3
=	Greater than or equal to	3
=	Equal to	3
<>	Not equal to	3
#AND#	Logical AND	1
#OR#	Logical OR	1
#NOT#	Logical NOT	2

TABLE 4-40
Database Statistical Functions

Function	Description
@DAVG	Averages the values in the selected field that match the specified criteria
@DCOUNT	Counts all nonblank cells of records in the selected field that match the specified criteria
@DMAX	Selects the largest value in the selected field that matches the specified criteria
@DMIN	Selects the smallest value in the selected field that matches the specified criteria
@DSTD	Finds the standard deviation of the selected field that matches the specified criteria
@DSUM	Totals the values in the selected field that match the specified criteria
@DVAR	Find the variance in the selected field that matches the specified criteria

USING DATABASE STATISTICAL FUNCTIONS

The database statistical functions (Table 4-40) are similar to the regular statistical functions except they are used specifically with a database.

Database statistical functions are entered in the form @Function(Input Range, Offset, Criterion Range)

- The input and criterion ranges are the same as those used in the Data Query commands.

- The offset is the number of the field (column) in the database that contains the specified data. To calculate the offset number, start at the leftmost column in the database and count across, beginning with zero. For example, if your three fields in a database were Name, Price, and Sales, the offset number of the first field (Name) would be 0, the next field would be 1, and the last field 2.

Select a cell or cells where you want to store the values generated by the functions. Do not use cells included in a data output range because they would be overwritten by any Extract commands.

EXERCISE 122

Exploring Data Management

In this exercise, you explore data management *(not available on the introductory version of The TWIN)*. To begin this exercise, you must load the program or clear the screen of any other model.

Your finished model should look like Figure 4-52. Refer to this figure to check your results as you complete the steps in this exercise.

Step 1. Enter a Database. Change columns widths, and enter a heading for the database.

To change column widths

Press	**/WGC** (for Worksheet, Global, Column), and the prompt asks you to enter the column width.
Type	**12** and then press **Return**.

To enter a heading for the section

Goto	A1, type **INPUT RANGE:** and then press **Return**.

FIGURE 4-52
Data management model
1

	A	B	C	D	E	F
1	INPUT RANGE:					
2	Dept.	Course	Instructor	Day	Time	Bldg.
3	Math	136	Davis	T,T	9:00	Stoner
4	Math	200	Davis	M,W,F	9:00	Widner
5	English	124	Jones	T,T	12:00	Drew
6	Biology	101	Smith	M,W,F	10:00	Hayes
7						
8	CRITERION RANGE:					
9	Dept.	Course	Instructor	Day	Time	Bldg.
10						
11						
12						
13	OUTPUT RANGE:					
14	Dept.	Course	Instructor	Day	Time	Bldg.
15						
16						
17						
18						
19						
20						

Result. Enter the data shown on rows 1 through 6 in Figure 4-52. When entering the numbers in the course and time columns, enter them as labels by pressing ' (a single quote) before typing the number. When finished, your database looks like rows 1 through 6 in Figure 4-52.

Step 2. Set up the Database to Extract Data. To extract data from a database, you need to add two additional ranges. The criterion range is used to enter the criteria that establish which records are extracted from the database. The output range is the place on the spreadsheet where the records are extracted to. Both ranges use the same labels as the input range.

To enter the criterion range

Goto	A8, type **CRITERION RANGE:**, and then press **Return**.
Press	**/C** (for Copy), and the prompt asks you to enter the range to copy from.
Type	**A2.F2**, and then press **Return**. The prompt asks you to enter the range to copy to.
Type	**A9**, and then press **Return**.

To enter the output range

Goto	A13, type **OUTPUT RANGE:**, and then press **Return**.
Press	**/C** (for Copy), and the prompt asks you to enter the range to copy from.
Type	**A2.F2**, and then press **Return**. The prompt asks you to enter the range to copy to.
Type	**A14**, and then press **Return**.

Result. Your criterion and output ranges should look like those in Figure 4-52.

Step 3. Extract Data from the Database. Once the input, criterion, and output ranges are entered, you tell the program where they are, and then use the criterion range to specify the records to be extracted.

To specify the ranges

Press	**/DQI** (for Data, Query, Input), and the prompt asks you to enter the input range.
Type	**A2.F6**, and then press **Return**.
Press	**C** (for Criterion), and the prompt asks you to enter the criterion range.
Type	**A9.F10**, and then press **Return**.
Press	**O** (for Output), and the prompt asks you to enter the output range.
Type	**A14.F14**, and then press **Return**.
Press	**Q** (for Quit).

To extract the data

Goto	C10, type **Davis**, and then press **Return**.
Press	**/DQE** (for Data, Query, Extract).

Result. The two records with Davis as the instructor are extracted and listed in the output range on rows 15 and 16. Press **Q** (for Quit). To experiment, go to C10, press **/RE** (for Range, Erase), and then press **Return** to delete Davis. Go to any other column on row 10, enter any Dept, Course, Instructor, Day, Time, or Bldg. that appears in the same column in the input range, and then press Query (**F7**). For example, enter T,T in cell D10 and press Query key (**F7**) to display all classes on tuesday and thursday. You see that you can extract any records in this way.

Step 4. Extract Data That Meets More Than One Criteria. You can extract data that meets more than one criteria. To do this, you enter the criteria on the same row of the criterion range. To delete any entries you made in previous steps, press **/RE** (for Range, Erase). When the prompt asks you to enter the range to erase, type **A10.F10**, and then press **Return**. In this step, you run the data extraction again just by pressing **F7**.

To extract the data

Goto	C10, type **Davis**, and then press **Return**.
Goto	F10, type **Stoner**, and then press **Return**.
Press	**F7**.

Result. Only one record is extracted because only one record contains both Davis and Stoner in the appropriate columns. Try other combinations on your own. To do so, erase the entries in the criterion range using the Range Erase command, enter some of your own criteria, and then press **F7**.

Step 5. Extract Data That Meets One Criterion or Another. In the previous step, you extracted data that matched one or more criteria. Here you extract data that matches one criteria or another. To do this, you enter the criteria on different rows below the criterion headings and then change the criterion range to include them. Begin by erasing any criterion you entered in the previous step.

To extract the data

Goto	A11, type **Biology**, and then press **Return**.
Goto	C10, type **Jones**, and then press **Return**.
Press	**/DQC** (for Data Query Criterion), and the prompt asks you to enter the criterion range.
Press	↓ to highlight down to row 11, and then press **Return**.
Press	**Q** (for Quit).
Press	**F7**.

Result. Two records are extracted. One meets the criteria Jones, and the other meets the criteria Biology. Erase the entries in the criterion range using the Range Erase command, and enter some of your own. Just enter criteria on each row, and then press **F7**.

Step 6. Save Your Work. Now that the model has been revised, you should save it.

To save the model

Press   /FS (for File, Save), and the prompt asks you to enter the name of the file.
Type   **DATA1**, and then press **Return**.

Result. The disk drive spins, and the model is saved onto the disk in drive B.

Step 7. Continue or Quit. You have now completed this exercise. Either clear the screen and continue to the next exercise, or quit the program if you have finished.

To clear the screen

Press   /WEY (for Worksheet, Erase, Yes).

To quit the program

Press   /QY (for Quit, Yes).

Result. If you quit the program, the operating system A> prompt appears on the screen. Remove your disks, and then turn off the computer.

EXERCISE 123
Creating a Database

In this exercise, you create and use a database. *(not available on the introductory version of The TWIN).* To begin this exercise, you must load the program or clear the screen of any other model.

Your finished model should look like Figure 4-53. Refer to this figure to check your results as you complete the steps in this exercise.

Step 1. Widen Columns. Change the global column width to twelve characters.

To widen columns

Press   /WGC (for Worksheet, Global, Column), and the prompt asks you to enter the column width.
Type   **12**, and then press **Return**.

Step 2. Enter Field Names. Our database will contain information concerning money due from customers. In this step, you create the field names.

To enter field names

Goto   A1, type **First Name**, and then press → to move the cursor to cell B1.
Type   **Last Name**, and then press → to move the cursor to cell C1.
Type   **Amount**, and then press **Return**.

Step 3. Enter Data. Now we can enter the data into the database. Each row will represent a different record.

FIGURE 4-53
Data management model
2

```
        A           B           C           D           E           F
1   First Name  Last Name   Amount      First Name  Last Name   Amount
2   John        James            $23
3   John        James            $23
4   John        Smith            $35
5   Martha      Smith            $42
6
7
8
9
10  First Name  Last Name   Amount
11
12
13
14
15
16
17
18
19
20
```

To enter the first record

Goto   A2, type **Martha**, and then press → to move the cursor to cell B2.

Type   **Smith**, and then press → to move the cursor to C2.

Type   **42**, and then press **Return**.

To enter the second record

Goto   A3, type **John**, and then press → to move the cursor to cell B3.

Type   **Smith**, and then press → to move the cursor to cell C3.

Type   **35**, and then press **Return**.

To enter the third record

Goto   A4, type **John**, and then press → to move the cursor to cell B4.

Type   **James**, and then press → to move the cursor to cell C4.

Type   **23**, and then press **Return**.

To enter the fourth record

Goto   A5, type **John**, and then press → to move the cursor to cell B5.

Type   **James**, and then press → to move the cursor to cell C5.

Type   **23**, and then press **Return**.

Step 4. Format the Amount Field. You now format the Amount field.

To format the amount field

Press   **/RFC** (for Range, Format, Currency), and the prompt asks you to enter the number of decimal places or digits.

Type   **0**, and then press **Return**. The prompt asks you to enter the range to format.

Type	C2.C5, and then press **Return**.

Result. The entries in your database should look like those Figure 4-53, but it is not yet sorted.

Step 5. Sort the Database. Sort the entire database (excluding the field names) using the Last Name field as the primary sort key.

To sort the database

Goto	A2, and then press **/DSD** (for Data, Sort, Data-Range). The prompt asks you to enter the data range.
Type	**A2.C5**, and then press **Return** to return to the Sort menu.
Press	**P** (for Primary-Key), and the prompt asks you to enter the primary sort key.
Press	[→] to move to cell B2, and then press **Return**. The prompt asks you to enter the sort order.
Press	**A** (for Ascending), and then press **Return**.
Press	**G** (for Go).

Result. The database is sorted in ascending order by last name. Notice, though, that records with the same last names are not in alphabetical order by first name. Martha Smith precedes John Smith (except on The TWIN).

Step 6. Sort Using a Secondary Key. To sort by first name within the last names, we need to select a secondary key.

To sort using a secondary key

Press	**/DSS** (for Data, Sort, Secondary-Key), and the prompt asks you to enter the secondary sort key.
Press	**Return** to make column A the secondary key, and the prompt asks you to enter the sort order.
Press	**A** (for Ascending), and then press **Return**.
Press	**G** (for Go).

Result. The database is sorted by last name, with the same last names now sorted by first name. John Smith now precedes Martha Smith (Figure 4-53).

Step 7. Set Up Criterion and Output Ranges. In the next few steps, you query the database. To do so, you must set up the criterion and output ranges.

To copy field names to the criterion range

Press	**/C** (for Copy), and the prompt asks you to enter the range to copy from.
Type	**A1.C1**, and then press **Return**. The prompt asks you to enter the range to copy to.
Type	**D1**, and then press **Return**.

To copy field names to the output range

Press	**/C** (for Copy) and the prompt asks you to enter the range to copy from.
Type	**D1.F1**, and then press **Return**. The prompt asks you to enter the range to copy to.
Type	**A10**, and then press **Return**.

To specify the input range

Type	**/DQI** (for Data, Query, Input), and the prompt asks you to enter the input range.

| Type | **A1.C5**, and then press **Return** to return to the Query menu. |

To specify the criterion range

| Press | **C** (for Criterion), and the prompt asks you to enter the criterion range. |
| Type | **D1.F2**, and then press **Return** to return to the Query menu. |

To specify the output range

Press	**O** (for Output) and the prompt asks you to enter the output range.
Type	**A10.C10** and then press **Return**.
Press	**Q** (for Quit) to return to the worksheet.

Result. The database is now ready for query commands. It should look like Figure 4-53.

Step 8. Specify the Criterion to Be Found. First, you search for any records that contain the last name Smith.

To specify a criterion

| Goto | E2, type **Smith**, and then press **Return**. |

Result. This enters a criterion into the criterion range. We want any records that contain the last name Smith, so we do not need to specify criteria for the other fields.

Step 9. Use Data Query to Search the Database. Now that you have specified the input, criteria, and output ranges, you can query the database.

To find records that match the criteria

| Press | **/DQF** (for Data, Query, Find). |

Result. The first record in the database that contains the last name Smith is highlighted. To check for other matching records, press ↓. When the computer beeps, you have reached the last matching record. Try using ↑ and ↓ to move around the database. The highlight should remain only on those records that match the specified criteria. Press **Esc** several times to return to *READY* mode.

Step 10. Use an AND Criteria. Change the criteria, and then search the database again. Here, first try entering two criteria on the same row so that the found record must match both.

To change the criteria

| Goto | F2, type **42**, and then press **Return**. |
| Press | F7 to repeat the previous Query command. |

Result. Martha Smith is highlighted because only she meets both criteria. You cannot move the cursor off her name with the arrow keys. Press **Esc** to return to *READY* mode.

Step 11. Use an OR Criteria. Change the criteria, and then search the database again. Here, first try entering two criteria on different rows so that the found record must match either. You also must reset the criterion range to include both rows.

To change the criteria

| Goto | F2, press **/RE** (for Range, Erase), and then press **Return** to erase the existing criteria. |

| Goto | F3, type **42**, and then press **Return**. |

To reset the criterion range

Press	**/DQC** (for Data, Query, Criterion) and the prompt asks you to enter the criterion range and highlights the existing range.
Press	↓ to include row 3, and then press **Return**.
Press	**F** (for Find) to find records that match the criteria.

Result. You can move the cursor between both Smiths because they each match one of the criteria. Press **Esc** several times to return to *READY* mode.

Step 12. Extract Data. Using the same criteria you specified in the preceding step, use the Extract command to copy the matching records from the database into the output range.

To copy matching records into the output range

| Press | **/DQE** (for Data, Query, Extract). |

Result. The matching records are copied into the output range.

Step 13. Change the Criteria. Change the criteria in the criterion range, and then extract the new matching records. Use the last name James as your criterion. Use the Query Unique command to copy the matching records from the database to the output range without copying duplicates.

To erase existing criteria

Press	**Q** (for Quit) to leave the Query menu.
Press	**/RE** (for Range, Erase), and the prompt asks you to enter the range to erase.
Type	**D2.F3**, and then press **Return**.

To enter a new criterion

| Goto | E2, type **James**, and then press **Return**. |

To reset the criterion range

Press	**/DQC** (for Data, Query, Criterion), and the prompt asks you to enter the criterion range and highlights the existing range.
Press	↑ to move the bottom of the range back to row 2, and then press **Return**.
Press	**U** (for Unique) to extract the records that match the criteria.

Result. The matching record is copied to the output range. Only one of the two similar records is copied.

Step 14. Erase the Criteria. Press **Q** (for Quit) to leave the Query menu, and then use the Range Erase command to clear the criteria in the criterion range. (Do not erase the field names.)

To erase existing criteria

| Press | **/RE** (for Range, Erase), and the prompt asks you to enter the range to erase. |
| Type | **D2.F2**, and then press **Return**. |

Result. If you do not enter a criterion and then use the Unique command, all records in the database are copied, except duplicates. Press **F7** to repeat the previous Query command, and you see this happen.

Step 15. Save the File. This is a back-up measure to protect the original file. If you want to keep the file as it looks after you delete records, you can save it again.

To save the file

Press   **/FS** (for File, Save), and the prompt asks you for the name to save the file under.

Type   **DATA2**, and then press **Return**.

Step 16. Specify the Criteria to Delete Records. Use the first name John as your criterion. First, erase the previous criteria. Use the Query Delete command to delete any records that match the criteria. All records with the first name John will be deleted.

To enter a new criterion

Goto   D2, type **John**, and then press **Return**.

To delete records that match the criteria

Press   **/DQD** (for Data, Query, Delete), and the prompt reads *Cancel Delete*.

Press   **D** (for Delete) to erase matching records.

Result. The first three records of the database are deleted, and the fourth record has moved up to fill the vacant space. Press **Q** (for Quit) to leave the Query menu.

Step 17. Retrieve the Original Database. Use the File Retrieve command to retrieve the original DATA2 file you saved before deleting records.

Step 18. Enter a Criterion Formula. What if you want to extract any records with an amount greater than $30? The formula is written as a test of the first record in the database. The cell that contains the first amount field is C2, so that is the cell you refer to in the formula.

To specify a criterion formula

Goto   F2, type **+C2>30**, and then press **Return**.

Result. A 0 (zero) indicating FALSE is displayed in cell F2 if the current value in cell C2 is 30 or less. A 1 indicating TRUE is displayed if the value is larger than 30. You put the formula in cell F2, but it could have been entered in any cell in the criterion range.

Step 19. Extract Matching Records. Use the Query Extract command to select all records matching the formula.

To extract records that match the criteria

Press   **/DQE** (for Data, Query, Extract).

Press   **Q** (for Quit).

Result. The output range contains the two records in your database that include an amount greater than $30.

Step 20. Change the Criteria. Change the criteria to include all records with an amount greater than $30 and the first name Martha.

To change the criteria

Goto   D2, type **Martha**, and then press **Return**.
Press   **F7**.

Result. The extracted data includes only those records that meet both criteria.

Step 21. Use a Database Statistical Function. Enter the criteria to be specified for the functions used. Select all records with the last name Smith as your criteria. First, enter a label for the function, and then enter a database statistical function that sums a field. The first argument to the function is the input range coordinates, the second argument is the offset of the Amount field, and the third argument is the criterion range.

To erase existing criteria

Press   **/RE** (for Range, Erase), and the prompt asks you to enter the range to erase.
Type   **D2.F2**, and then press **Return**.

To enter a new criterion

Goto   E2, type **Smith**, and then press **Return**.

To enter an output range

Goto   D7, type **"Total:**, and then press **Return**.
Goto   D8, and then press **/RFC** (for Range, Format, Currency). The prompt asks you to enter the number of decimal places or digits.
Type   **0** (zero), and then press **Return** two times.
Type   **@DSUM (A1.C5, 2, D1.F2)**, and then press **Return**.

Result. The amount $77 is displayed because that is the sum of the records that match the criterion Smith. Change the criterion to James, and the amount changes to $46.

Step 22. Save the Model. Now that you have finished the model, save it into a file on the disk so that you can retrieve it later. Before proceeding, *be sure a formatted disk is in drive B and the drive's door is closed.*

To save the model

Press   **/FS** (for File, Save), and the prompt asks you for the name to save the file under and suggests the name DATA2.
Press   **Return** to accept the suggested name, and the prompt reads *Cancel Replace.*
Press   **R** (for Replace).

Result. The drive spins, and the revised model is saved onto the disk.

Step 23. Continue or Quit. You have now completed this exercise. Either clear the screen and continue to the next exercise, or quit the program if you have finished.

To clear the screen

Press   **/WEY** (for Worksheet, Erase, Yes).

To quit the program

Press   **/QY** (for Quit, Yes).

Result. If you quit the program, the operating system A> prompt reappears. Remove your disks, and then turn off the computer.

QUESTIONS

1. What are some reasons for organizing data in a spreadsheet database?
2. What are the three key parts of a database?
3. Where are field names entered on a database? Where are records entered?
4. What is a primary sort key? A secondary sort key?
5. What does the Data Query command allow you to do?
6. To use the Data Query command, what must you first specify?
7. What does the input range specify? The criterion range? The output range?
8. When must you use an output range?

DATABASE MANAGEMENT APPLICATIONS

Topic 5-1   Getting to Know Your Program

Topic 5-2   Defining a Database File

Topic 5-3   Entering Records

Topic 5-4   Displaying Records

Topic 5-5   Using Criteria to Display Records

Topic 5-6   Adding, Updating, and Deleting Records

Topic 5-7   Joining Database Files

Topic 5-8   Sorting Records

Topic 5-9   Indexing Records

Topic 5-10 Making Calculations

Topic 5-11 Printing Reports

Topic 5-12 Restructuring the Database

Topic 5-13 Writing Programs

The concept behind database management programs is simple. They allow you to store information in your computer, retrieve it when you need it, and update it when necessary. These programs can do the same things you can do with a set of index cards, but they allow you to do more and to do it faster and more easily. You can store large amounts of information like mailing lists, inventory records, or billing and collection information in files. You can then manipulate the information in these files with the database management program. For example, you can

- Enter information
- Add new information
- Find specific information
- Update information that has changed
- Sort the information into a specified order
- Delete information that is no longer needed
- Print out reports containing all, or some of, the information contained in the file(s)

Because of the power and flexibility of these programs, the applications are almost endless.

- You can maintain mailing lists for sales and marketing purposes. Names and addresses stored using a database management program can be easily kept up to date. The data can also be used to automatically print letters, envelopes, and mailing labels.

- Inventory can be managed by recording inventory moving into and out of a business. The program can give you answers to questions like, "How many widgits are left in inventory?" or "How many were shipped this month?"

- Assets like stock portfolios or collections can be managed so that you always know what you have and what their value is. You can ask the program questions like, "What IBM stocks do I have?" "What stocks have increased in value since I bought them?" or "What stocks have I sold this year?"

- You can maintain a file of frequently used names, addresses, and phone numbers. You can then ask the program questions like, "What phone numbers are listed for SMITH?" or "What phone numbers are listed in area code 617?"

- You can enter a list of your record albums and the songs on each and then use the program to answer questions like, "What album contains the song 'Born in the USA?'" or "What Beatles albums do I have in my collection?"

- Some database management programs allow you to store and retrieve illustrations. These can be either photographs or line drawings that are read into the computer using a scanner. They can then be labeled or described with text, and you can locate a specific illustration by searching for one or more words used in its label or description.

- You can maintain checking accounts so that you can ask questions like, "What checks have been written to Dr. Smart?"

RECORD MANAGEMENT AND DATABASE MANAGEMENT

Databases and database management are among the more complicated and important aspects of computer applications. As a result, users frequently misunderstand them, and advertisers misrepresent them. Although several programs for microcomputers are referred to as database management programs, this label is not always accurate. These programs fall into two distinct categories: record management programs and database management programs.

Record Management Programs

In the early days of business computing, separate programs were created for each application. For example, the payroll department would have a program that created and maintained a file containing names, addresses, and payroll information of employees. The personnel department would use a different program that maintained a separate file containing names, addresses, hiring dates, insurance policies, and vacation schedules. Whenever a new application was needed, a new program was written, and the data needed for that application was entered and maintained. The data in the payroll file could not be used by the personnel department's program. Each of the files the information was stored in could be used only by the program that created it. If an employee changed her name or left the firm, several files would have to be updated.

Record management programs (sometimes called file management or flat file database programs), like those integrated into The TWIN, Lotus 1-2-3, and Word-Perfect, store, maintain, and use data stored in single files like these early programs (Figure 5-1). If you use a record management program to store data on various aspects of a business, you must store the data for different applications in separate

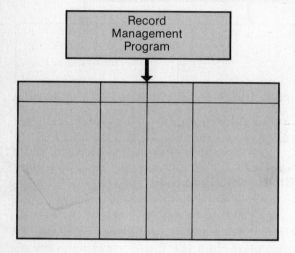

FIGURE 5-1
Record management
program

files. If you want to make changes, you must make them in each file when information is duplicated. Let's say you have one file for names, addresses, and phone numbers and another file for payroll. If a person's name occurs in both files, the name must be entered separately in each file. If the name must be changed or deleted later, it must be changed or deleted separately in each file.

Database Management Programs

As the amount of information being processed increases, the record management method of using separate files to store information becomes cumbersome because information must be extensively duplicated. An employee's name might appear in several different files, for example, payroll, vacation, expense accounts, and so on. There are a number of disadvantages to this duplication.

■ It increases the risk of errors in the information. Since a person's name would have to be entered more than once, any changes in status would have to be made in different files, perhaps by different people. Over time, the data's accuracy deteriorates. For example, changes might be made in some files and not in others, or some data might be entered correctly in one file and incorrectly in another.

- It increase the amount of data entry since some information must be entered more than once.
- BACKGROUND

The concept of a database, introduced in the early 1970s, eliminates these problems. The data is stored in such a way that there is no duplication in data. For example, a person's name can appear in the database only once, so a change must be made only once. **Database management programs** (also called database management systems, or DBMS), used to manage these databases, can do everything a record management program can do, but they can do much more. The main difference is they can use interrelated data stored in one or more files (Figure 5-2), eliminating the duplication of data and the need to enter updates more than once in different files.

FIGURE 5-2
Database management programs

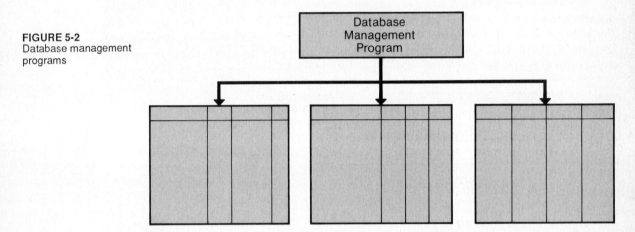

Record Management Programs versus Database Management Programs

Database management programs have a major advantage over record management programs since many applications require more than one file. For example, the accounting process requires separate files for the general ledger, accounts receivable, and accounts payable. A program that can work with more than one file eliminates the need for duplicating information in separate files, and reduces the task of updating the information. Because data is entered only once, the accuracy of information is improved.

Partly as a result of their power, database management programs are harder to learn and operate than record management programs. The application you plan for the program, not the advertiser's claims, should determine which type of program you use. Using a database management program simply to maintain a mailing list would not offer any advantage over doing the same task on a record management program. But trying to create a customized, full-featured accounting system using a record management program would be equally difficult, if not impossible.

RELATIONAL DATABASES

When you create a database, you can store the information in more than one file. This is called the physical storage of the information. Programs that update and manipulate the information in the database handle all aspects of the physical storage so that you do not have to. Although the physical storage is not important to you, the way you view the data, called its logical storage is important. Logical storage refers to the way the information in different files can be related.

ID	LASTNAME	FIRST	STREET	CITY	ST	ZIP	AREA	PHONE
101	Culman	Tina	100 Elm Street	New Haven	CT	10000	203	555-1000
102	Benjamin	Nancy	25 Oak Street	Cambridge	MA	20000	617	555-1001
103	Kendall	Liz	14 Lark Ave.	Chicago	IL	20000	312	555-1002
104	Hogan	Dennis	40 Main Street	Edgewater	NJ	30000	201	555-1003
105	Swabey	Daphne	168 Bridge Road	Beverly	MA	20000	617	555-1004
106	Sobel	Carol	45 Porter Ave.	Fairlawn	NJ	30000	201	555-1005
107	Anthony	William	900 Maple Road	Reading	MA	20000	617	555-1006
108	Poe	James	10 Preston Lane	Oakland	CA	40000	415	555-1007

FIGURE 5-3
Relational database

The logical arrangement of files is called the database model, or schema. Three typical models are currently in use: network, hierarchical, and relational. The one most often used to manage databases with microcomputers is the relational database. For that reason, we discuss only relational databases like dBASE III Plus.

A relational database consists of one or more tables, technically called relations. You see the information arranged as tables, not the way it is stored on the disk. A relational database table (Figure 5-3) contains rows and columns much like a spreadsheet.

- The columns are fields, and the labels at the top of each field are field names. Each column on the table has a fixed length.
- There is one or more rows of data, and each row is a record.

Since a database can contain more than one table, the tables can be linked to one another, as Figure 5-4 shows. This database contains two tables. The first table (Figure 5-4a) is used to store customer names and addresses, and the second (Figure 5-4b) is used to store any charges the customers make. When more than one table is used, they are linked using a common field that contains unique data, in this case, the customer's ID number. As you see later in this part, you manipulate the data in these tables with **query commands**, a language used to enter, update, and find information stored in the database.

ID	LASTNAME	FIRST	STREET	CITY	ST	ZIP	AREA	PHONE
101	Culman	Tina	100 Elm Street	New Haven	CT	10000	203	555-1000
102	Benjamin	Nancy	25 Oak Street	Cambridge	MA	20000	617	555-1001
103	Kendall	Liz	14 Lark Ave.	Chicago	IL	20000	312	555-1002
104	Hogan	Dennis	40 Main Street	Edgewater	NJ	30000	201	555-1003
105	Swabey	Daphne	168 Bridge Road	Beverly	MA	20000	617	555-1004
106	Sobel	Carol	45 Porter Ave.	Fairlawn	NJ	30000	201	555-1005
107	Anthony	William	900 Maple Road	Reading	MA	20000	617	555-1006
108	Poe	James	10 Preston Lane	Oakland	CA	40000	415	555-1007

(a) NAMELIST File

ID	DATE	AMOUNT
101	06/08/88	10.00
102	06/09/88	15.00
103	06/10/88	35.00
104	06/11/88	25.00
105	06/12/88	20.00
106	06/13/88	50.00
107	06/14/88	15.00
108	06/15/88	10.00

(b) AMOUNTS File

FIGURE 5-4
Linked database tables

DATABASES — A GUIDED TOUR

One of the most popular applications for databases is in accounting. Let's look briefly at the process of setting up and using a relational database management program for a simple accounting system. The system contains the two files shown in Figure 5-4; one to store customers' names, addresses, and phone numbers and the other to store customers' credit charges.

The file containing names and addresses, NAMELIST, contains the complete name, address, and phone number of each customer who has credit with the company. The file has nine fields: the customer's ID number, last name, first name, street, city, state, ZIP code, area code, and phone number.

The file containing customer charges, AMOUNTS, records credit sales as they are made. This file requires only three fields: the customer's ID number, which is the common field that links the two tables, the date, and the amount of the sale. Let's look closely at the makeup of these two files.

Step 1. Creating the Database

Every file created with a database management program is organized into fields and records. A record is a description of a person, thing, or activity. A field is one part of the description stored in the record. In this example, a record is either each customer or each customer charge. To describe a specific customer, you must decide what facts describe and differentiate this customer from all other customers. In the NAMELIST file, these facts, or fields, are the customer's ID number, first name, last name, address, and phone number. In the AMOUNTS file, the fields are the customer's ID, date of the charge, and amount. In these files, the fields are defined by specifying their names, lengths, and types of data to be entered.

Step 2. Entering Data

Once you define the database's files, you enter names and addresses, and then record credit charges. When a credit sale is made, it is recorded in the AMOUNTS file. The person recording the sale enters the customer's ID number, the date the sale is made, and the amount of the purchase. As sales are entered, the AMOUNTS file becomes a log of each transaction the company has with its credit customers.

Step 3. Updating the Files

Whenever a customer moves or changes their name, the files are updated to reflect the change. Since the person's name and address appear in only one file, NAMELIST, the same change does not have to be made to a number of files. To make changes of this kind, the necessary file is opened, query commands are used to locate the record, and the new data is entered in place of the old.

Step 4. Querying the Database

What if a customer calls about his or her account, and wants to know the date a purchase was made? Using the customer's ID number and the amount of the purchase, you can use the program's query language to locate the date of the purchase by asking the program to display the record from the AMOUNTS file for any charge to that customer's account for the specified amount.

Step 5. Joining Files

Although data is only entered once in each file, you can view all of the data in the database in different ways. For example, you can join the customer names in one file with the amounts they owe in another to create a new table. At the end of each month, the AMOUNTS file can be joined with the NAMELIST file to prepare a complete file from which reports and bills can be prepared. When the two files are joined, the customer's ID number, which appears in both files, is used as the identifying, or key, field.

Step 6. Printing Reports

Once the AMOUNTS and NAMELIST files are joined into a new table, reports using data from the two original files can be generated, in this case, a monthly report of amounts owed by state (Figure 5-5). The monthly report lists the customer's name, state, phone, and a record of credit purchases. It also shows subtotals and totals. The NAMELIST file supplies the address information, and the AMOUNTS file supplies the list of charges.

```
Page No.      1
11/03/87
                          AMOUNTS  DUE

FIRST NAME   LAST NAME    AREA CODE PHONE #    AMOUNT DUE


** Amounts due from state: CA
  James        Poe          415       555-1007      10.00
** Subtotal **
                                                    10.00


** Amounts due from state: CT
  Tina         Culman       203       555-1000      10.00
** Subtotal **
                                                    10.00


** Amounts due from state: FL
  Jose         Alverez      305       555-1010      61.00
** Subtotal **
                                                    61.00


** Amounts due from state: IL
  Liz          Kendall      312       555-1200      35.00
  John         Davis        312       555-1020      75.00
** Subtotal **
                                                   110.00


** Amounts due from state: MA
  Nancy        Benjamin     617       555-1212      15.00
  Daphne       Swabey       617       555-1004      30.00
  Robert       Fiske        617       555-1008      18.00
** Subtotal **
                                                    63.00


** Amounts due from state: NJ
  Dennis       Hogan        201       555-1003      25.00
  Carol        Sobel        201       555-1005      50.00
** Subtotal **
                                                    75.00


** Amounts due from state: TX
  Lars         Porsena      512       555-1009      43.00
** Subtotal **
                                                    43.00

*** Total ***
                                                   372.00
```

FIGURE 5-5
Printed reports

QUESTIONS

1. What is the difference between a record management program and a database management program?
2. What is the difference between a single file and a database?
3. What are two or three disadvantages to duplicating information when using a record management program?
4. Name the characteristics of a relational database.
5. What is the difference between physical storage and logical storage?
6. What are columns and rows known as when discussed in the context of a relational database table?
7. Explain the purpose of a key field.
8. When do you use a program's query language?

TOPIC 5-1
Getting to Know Your Program

In this topic, we introduce you to the following procedures:

- Installing the program
- Loading the program
- Understanding the screen display
- Executing commands
- Using on-line help
- Clearing database files from memory
- Quitting the program

BACKGROUND

Before you can use a database management program, you must turn on the computer and load the operating system (called **booting** the system). You then install the database management program so that it knows what kind of system you are running it on. After installing it, you load the program and use the menus and help screens as a guide when entering records and executing commands.

LOADING THE PROGRAM

The way you load a database management program like dBASE III Plus depends on whether you are loading it from a system with floppy disk drives or from a system where the program files have been copied to a hard disk drive.

Loading the Program from a Floppy Disk Drive System

The way you load an applications program on a computer system with two floppy disk drives depends on how your program disk has been set up. There are three basic variations of a program disk.

■ If your program disk does not contain the operating system files needed to load it, you must first load the operating system from the operating system program disk by booting the system. On the IBM PC, you insert the disk labeled MS-DOS or PC-DOS, and then turn on the computer. You then enter the date and time, and the system prompt, A>, appears. You remove the operating system disk, insert the applications program disk, and type the name you use to load the program. For example, to load dBASE III Plus, you insert the System disk #1 into drive A (the one on the left if your drives are side by side or the one on top if one drive is above the other), and then close the drive's door. You load the program by typing **DBASE** and then pressing **Return**. The dBASE III Plus program comes on two disks, so when you are prompted to insert System disk #2, you insert it into drive A, and then press **Return** to continue.

■ If the needed operating system files have already been copied to your program disk, the disk is **self-booting**. When you format a blank disk as a system disk and then copy the database management program's files to it, as you did in Part 2, you create a self-booting program disk. You load the program from this disk the same way you do from a non-self- booting disk, but you do not have to insert the DOS disk first and then replace it with the program disk when the 'A> prompt appears on the screen. You load both the operating system and the applications program from the same disk.

■ If your disk is self-booting and contains an AUTOEXEC.BAT file (see Part 2), the operating system and the program are automatically loaded when you boot the program. If your computer does not have a built-in clock, you have to enter only the date and time.

Loading the Program from a Hard Disk Drive System

To load an applications program from a hard disk drive, you first turn on the computer, and then, if necessary, enter the date and time. You then change the default drive and directory to the one containing the program's files if there is not a batch file to load the program in the root directory. For example, if the applications program's files are in a directory named DBASE, type **CD\DBASE**, and then press **Return**. (To see the name of the current default directory, change the prompt by typing **PROMPT PG**, and then press **Return**.) You then load the program by typing its abbreviated name; for example, to load dBASE III Plus, you type **DBASE**, and then press **Return**.

UNDERSTANDING THE SCREEN DISPLAY

When you load dBASE III Plus, the program's screen display appears (Figure 5-6). The screen display has the following elements:

■ The menu bar at the top of the screen contains a series of menus that can be pulled down by typing **ASSIST**, and then pressing **Return**. You can turn this menu off by pressing **Esc**.

■ The dot prompt is displayed on the action line when the program's menus are not displayed.

FIGURE 5-6
Opening screen

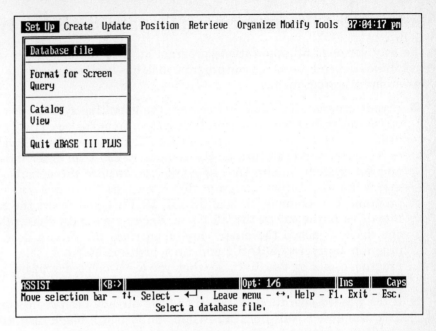

- The status bar displays the command in progress, the current default drive, the name of the current file, and the number of records. It also indicates if the **Caps Lock** and **Num Lock** keys are engaged or not.

- The navigation line, just below the status bar, displays messages listing the keys and commands you can use.

- The message line, the bottom line on the screen, displays messages when the program wants you to enter information. When the menu bar is displayed, this line briefly describes the highlighted menu choice.

EXECUTING COMMANDS

On a program like dBASE III Plus, you can execute all commands just by typing them from the dot prompt. Many commands are also listed on menus if you use the optional assist mode.

Typing Commands

The dot prompt is displayed when the menu is not. If the menu is displayed, press **Esc** to display the dot prompt. The dot prompt is like the A> or B> prompt when using the operating system. It indicates that dBASE is waiting for a command. You enter a command following the rules described in Table 5-1, and then press **Return** to execute it. If you make a typo while entering a command, press **Backspace** to delete characters, and then retype them correctly. If you incorrectly enter a command, the program displays an error message and often displays the prompt *Do you want some help? (Y/N)*. Press **Y** for help or **N** to return to the dot prompt.

The most frequently used commands are assigned to function keys. Table 5-2 describes these commands.

If you make a mistake when entering a command, and notice it only after you have pressed **Return**, you can return it to the dot prompt for editing by pressing ↑. This is a valuable command to know because many of the commands you type can be quite long. Each time you press ↑ a previous command is displayed. The program remembers not just the last command but the last twenty.

TABLE 5-1
Rules for Entering Commands

■ You can type commands in uppercase letters, lowercase letters, or any combination of both. For example, to quit the program, you can type **QUIT**, **quit**, or **Quit**.

■ Each command must begin with a command verb, for example, DISPLAY, SET, CLEAR, HELP.

■ Each command must follow the syntax required for the command. For example, to display help on the DISPLAY command, you type **HELP DISPLAY**, not **HELP ON DISPLAY**.

■ Commands can be as long as 254 characters (including spaces).

■ Words within a command can be separated by one or more blank spaces.

■ When typing longer commands, you must type only the first four characters. For example, typing **DISPLAY STRUCTURE** and **DISP STRU** give the same result.

■ dBASE III Plus automatically records your previous twenty commands so that you can easily repeat them. To scroll though these commands when the dot prompt is displayed, press ↑ until the command you want to repeat is displayed, and then press **Return** (or press ↓ to back up through the commands).

TABLE 5-2
Function Keys

Key	Command	Topic
F1	HELP	5-1
F2	ASSIST	5-1
F3	LIST	5-4
F4	DIR	5-12
F5	DISPLAY STRUCTURE	5-2
F6	DISPLAY STATUS	5-1
F7	DISPLAY MEMORY	5-12
F8	DISPLAY	5-4
F9	APPEND	5-3
F10	EDIT	5-5

Assist Mode

Using assist mode, you can execute many commands by making choices from a menu bar. To display the menu bar when the dot prompt is displayed, type **ASSIST**, and then press **Return**. One menu is always pulled down.

■ To pull down another menu, either press the first letter in its name, or press → or ← to highlight it. (Press **Home** or **End** to move the cursor to the first and last choices on the menu bar.)

■ To make a choice from a pulled-down menu, press ↓ or ↑ to move the highlight between choices. As you do so, the message line displays a brief description of the highlighted choice. When you have highlighted the desired choice, press **Return**.

■ To remove the menu bar from the screen and return to the dot prompt, press **Esc**.

HELP

dBASE III Plus provides extensive on-line help. You can obtain help through a menu, or display help information about a specific command as described in Table 5-3. (If you want help when the Assist menu is displayed, first press **Esc** to remove the menu.)

TABLE 5-3
Help Commands

Command	Description
HELP	Displays the Help Main menu (Figure 5-7). When the menu is displayed, you can use the commands described in Table 5-4 to display help on selected topics.
HELP <COMMAND>	Displays help on a specific command. For example, for help on the ASSIST command, type **HELP ASSIST**, and then press **Return.**

TABLE 5-4
Help Menu Commands

To	Press
Make selection from Help Main menu	↑ to highlight choice, **Return** (or press the number preceding the desired choice)
Display previous menu (if any)	**F10**
Display next screen (if any)	**PgDn**
Display previous screen (if any)	**PgUp**
Display help of specific command when the prompt reads *ENTER>*	Type command and press **Return.**
Return to dot prompt	**Esc**

FIGURE 5-7
Help main menu

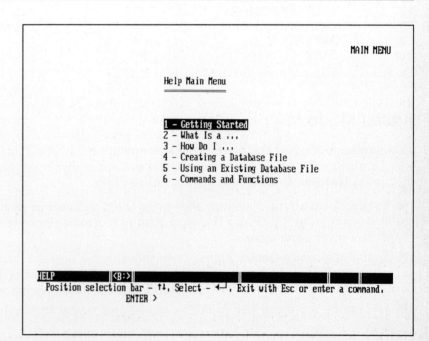

474   DATABASE MANAGEMENT APPLICATIONS

CLEARING OR QUITTING

When you work on a database program, the program opens files that you must close before quitting the program or working on another project. If you turn off or reboot the computer without quitting properly, files you have been working on may be damaged and data may be lost. Two commands close the open files, CLEAR ALL and QUIT. Table 5-5 describes them.

TABLE 5-5
Clearing or Quitting Commands

Command	Description
CLEAR ALL	Closes all open files and displays the dot prompt so that you can continue working
QUIT	Closes all open files and returns you to the operating system so that you can run another program or quit for the day

EXERCISE 124

Getting Acquainted with Your Program

In this exercise, you load and quit the dBASE III Plus program and operate its menus. To begin this exercise, the computer must be off.

Step 1. Load the Operating System. Before you can install or run the dBASE III Plus program, you must first load the operating system.

To load the operating system

Insert   the DOS disk into drive A, and then turn on the computer. If your computer does not have a built-in clock, you are asked to enter the date.

Type   the date in the format month/day/year (for example, 1/1/88), and then press **Return**. A prompt asks you to enter the time.

Type   the time in the format hour:minute (for example, 10:15), and then press **Return**.

Result. In a moment, the A> prompt is displayed.

Step 2. Install the Educational Version of dBASE III Plus. Before you use the dBASE III Plus program, you should install it to run on your computer. If you are using the full-featured version, we assume your disk has already been installed so go to Step 3 for instructions on loading the program. If you are using the educational version, insert the dBASE III Plus System Disk #1 into drive A.

- On a floppy disk system, insert the DOS disk into drive B.

- On a hard disk system, the dBASE program files are copied to a directory named \SAMPLER that the install program creates.

To install the dBASE program

Type   **INSTALL**, and then press Return.

Result. The Memory and Drive Selection menu is displayed (Figure 5-8) and the prompt reads *Type the letter corresponding to your computer's configuration:*. Press one of the letters A through D that best describes your system.

FIGURE 5-8
Install screen display

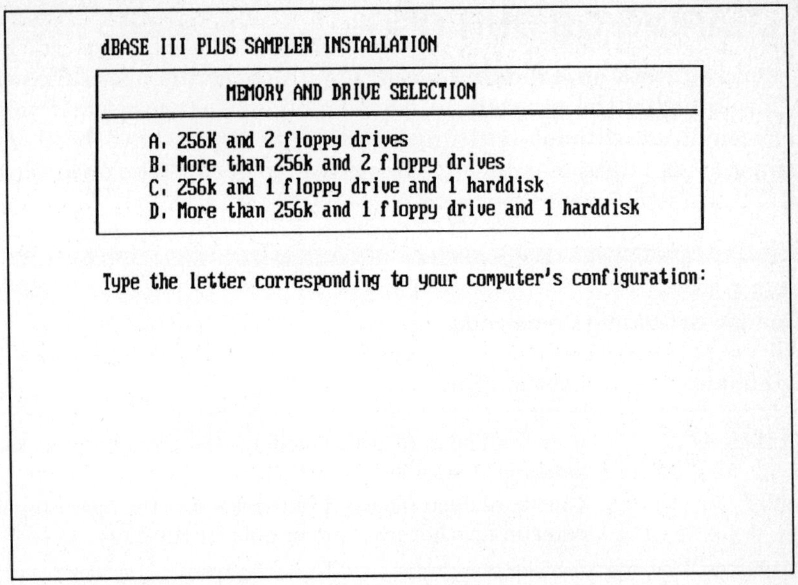

```
┌──────────────────────────────────────────────────────────────┐
│                                                                │
│      dBASE III PLUS SAMPLER INSTALLATION                       │
│      ┌──────────────────────────────────────────────┐         │
│      │            MEMORY AND DRIVE SELECTION         │         │
│      ├──────────────────────────────────────────────┤         │
│      │  A. 256K and 2 floppy drives                  │         │
│      │  B. More than 256k and 2 floppy drives        │         │
│      │  C. 256k and 1 floppy drive and 1 harddisk    │         │
│      │  D. More than 256k and 1 floppy drive and 1 harddisk │  │
│      └──────────────────────────────────────────────┘         │
│                                                                │
│      Type the letter corresponding to your computer's configuration: │
│                                                                │
│                                                                │
└──────────────────────────────────────────────────────────────┘
```

- On a floppy disk system, the prompt reads *Put Sampler disk 1 in drive A, and your Dos Disk in drive B (Remember to remove any write protect tabs from disk) Strike a key when ready.* The disks are already in the drives, so press the designated key to continue. The drives spin and in a moment the system A> prompt reappears and the prompt reads *Now reboot your computer with your Dos disk in drive A (CONTROL - ALT - DEL). Then place Sampler disk 1 in drive A and type DBASE.* Now, go to Step 3.

- On a hard disk system, the files are copied from the disk in drive A to a directory named SAMPLER on the disk in drive C. When the files are copied, the prompt reads *Place Sampler disk 2 in drive A. Strike a key when ready.* Remove System disk 1 from drive A, insert System disk 2, and press any key. The files from that disk are copied to drive C. When the files are copied, the prompt reads *Reboot your computer (CONTROL - ALT - DEL) and type CD \SAMPLER, then type DBASE.*

Step 3. Load dBASE III Plus. With the operating system on the screen, you can load dBASE III Plus by typing **DBASE**, and then pressing **Return**. Since you just installed the program, however, you must first reboot the computer so the program reads the configuration file created when you installed the program. (On a floppy disk system, begin by inserting the DOS disk into drive A). On an IBM PC or compatible computer, press **Ctrl-Alt-Del**, or turn off the computer for fifteen seconds, and then turn it back on. When the A> or C> prompt appears,

- On a floppy disk system, insert the dBASE III Plus System disk #1 into drive A, and insert a formatted data disk into drive B.

- On a hard disk system, type **CD\SAMPLER**, and then press **Return** to change to the directory that contains the dBASE program files.

To load dBASE III Plus

Type   **DBASE**, and then press **Return**.

Result. The drive spins as the program is loaded. In a few moments, the copyright screen appears. If you are using the educational version, the prompt reads *Press ↵ to assent to the license agreement and begin dBase III Plus.* Press **Return** or wait a few moments, and then the prompt reads *Insert Sampler Disk 2 in drive A and a Data*

Disk in drive B, and press ENTER or press Ctrl-C to abort. Insert System disk #2 into drive A, and then press **Return** to continue. In a moment, the dBASE screen appears with the menu bar at the top of the screen, and the Set Up menu is pulled down (Figure 5-6).

Step 4. Explore the Help Menu. You can get help on the program while using dBASE by just typing **HELP**. This displays the Help Main menu from which you can select topics you want help on. To begin, remove the menu bar from the top of the screen, and display the dot prompt.

To remove the menu bar

Press   **Esc** to display the dot prompt.

To display the help main menu

Type   **HELP**, and then press **Return**.

Result. The Help Main menu is displayed (Figure 5-7). To make choices from this menu, either press the number preceding the choice, or press ↓ to highlight the choice, and then press **Return**. After reviewing the help on a topic, press **F10** to return to the previous menu to make another selection (see Table 5-4). When you are finished, press **Esc** to return to the dot prompt.

Step 5. Explore Help on a Specific Command. If you want help on a specific command, you can get help on it without going through the Help Main menu. You just type **HELP**, the name of the command, and then press **Return**.

To display help on a specific command

Type   **HELP ASSIST**, and then press **Return**.

Result. Help on the ASSIST command is displayed, and the prompt reads *ENTER >*. Type **QUIT**, and then press **Return**. Help on the QUIT command is displayed. Press **F10** to return to the Help Main menu. Press **Esc** to return to the dot prompt.

Step 6. Explore Menus. If you are using the educational version, the menu bar was displayed when you first loaded the program. You then removed the menu bar to experiment with the help commands. Anytime you want to use the menu bar, just type **ASSIST**, and then press **Return**.

To display the menu bar

Type   **ASSIST**, and then press **Return**.

Result. The menu bar appears at the top of the screen. To pull down other menus to see the commands listed, either press the first letter in the menu's name, or press ← or → to move the highlight along the menu bar, and then press **Return**.

Step 7. Execute Commands. Let's now execute a command, first by using the menu bar and then by typing it in. The commands change the default drive to drive B and then display a list of files on drive A.

To execute a command with the menu bar

Press   **T** to pull down the Tools menu and highlight **Set drive**.
Press   **Return** to select **Set drive**.

Press	↓ if necessary to move the highlight over **B:**, and then press **Return**.
Press	↓ to move the highlight over **Directory**, and then press **Return** to display a submenu listing your computer's disk drives.
Press	↑ to move the highlight over **A:**, and then press **Return**.
Press	↓ to move the highlight over **.* All Files**, and then press **Return** to display a list of files on drive A.
Press	any key to return to the menu bar.

To execute commands by typing

| Press | **Esc** to remove the menu bar and display the dot prompt. |
| Type | **DIR A:*.***, and then press **Return**. |

Result. Both sets of commands have the same effect. But choosing commands from a menu is easier than remembering the commands, and typing is faster then pulling down menus. You can use both approaches as you work with the program. When you change the default drive, the current default drive is displayed on the status bar at the bottom of the screen.

Step 8. Execute a Command with a Function Key. Many commands are assigned to function keys so that you can execute them with a single keystroke. Here, press the function key that displays the program's status.

To display the program's status

| Press | **F6**. |

Result. A list of default settings is displayed, and the prompt reads *Press any key to continue*. Press any key, and the status of many commands and the function key assignments are displayed, and the dot prompt reappears.

Step 9. Make Calculations. Whenever the dot prompt is displayed, you can have dBASE make calculations for you. To begin the calculation, enter a question mark and then the formulas. You can use any of the following operators in formulas: + (addition), - (subtraction), / (division), * (multiplication), ^ or ** (exponentiation). You can also use a function that calculates the square root, SQRT(#) where # stands for the number you want to calculate the square root for.

To make calculations

Type	**?100/5**, and then press **Return**.
Type	**?100*2**, and then press **Return**.
Type	**?100-33**, and then press **Return**.
Type	**?10^2** (10 to the 2nd power), and then press **Return**.
Type	**?SQRT(100)**, and then press **Return**.

Result. The calculations are made, and then the dot prompt reappears on the screen. The answers are always displayed on the screen rounded to two decimal places or the number of decimal places you enter in one of the numbers. The program stores numbers with up to fifteen decimal places and uses those numbers in calculations. To clear the screen, type **CLEAR**, and then press **Return**. All the formulas and answers are cleared. You can execute this command whenever you want to clear unwanted data from the screen.

Step 10. Continue or Quit. You have now completed this exercise. You can either close all files and continue to the next exercise, or quit the program if you have finished.

To close all files

Press   **Esc** if necessary to remove the menu bar and return to the dot prompt.
Type   **CLEAR ALL**, and then press **Return**.

To quit the program

Type   **ASSIST**, and then press **Return** to display the menu bar.
Press   **S** (for Set Up) if necessary to pull down the Set Up menu.
Press   ↓ to highlight **Quit dBASE III PLUS**, and then press **Return**.

Result. If you quit the program, the operating system prompt reappears. Remove your disks, and then turn off the computer.

QUESTIONS

1. What three ways can you execute dBASE commands?
2. What purpose does assist mode serve?
3. To display the Help Main menu, what command would you enter?
4. To display help in assist mode, what command would you enter?
5. When you want to quit a dBASE session, what task must you perform before you turn off the computer?
6. How do you select a choice from a pull-down menu?
7. If you want to perform a calculation, what symbol precedes the formula?

TOPIC 5-2
Defining a Database File

In this topic, we introduce you to the following procedures:
- Organizing and planning a database
- Defining a database file
- Moving the cursor and editing field definitions

BACKGROUND

The first step in using a database management program is to define the database file you want to store data in.

THE ORGANIZATION OF A DATABASE

When you enter information into a database management program, it is stored in a file. The information you enter must be organized so that the program can easily manipulate it. To understand how a program manages information, you must first understand the five levels of organization used to store and manipulate data (Figure 5-9).

- When you enter information into a computer, you type it in from the keyboard. The first level of organization is, therefore, the alphanumeric *characters* you type, for example, numbers, and letters.
- You use one or more characters to enter *fields,* for example, a person's name. Fields can be names (Smith), numbers (100.10), names and numbers (100 Main Street), or formulas (100*3).
- Related fields are stored together as *records,* for example, a person's name, address, and phone number.
- Related records are stored together as *files,* for example, a mailing list.
- Related files are stored together as a *database,* a system of interrelated files that can be combined or from which information can be drawn.

FIGURE 5-9
Fields and records.

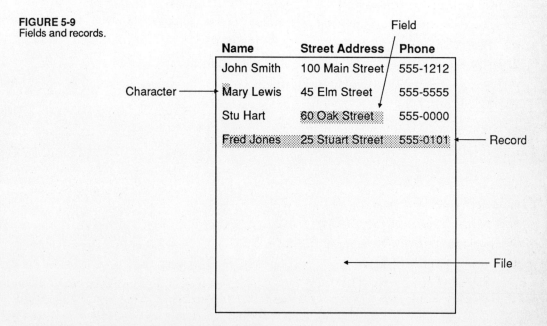

PLANNING YOUR DATABASE FILES

When you first create a record file, you must tell the program what information you are going to keep. In deciding what information you keep, you should spend a good deal of time thinking about what type of questions you wish to ask and have answered by the data. This, in turn, will tell you what data you need to keep.

As you compile a list of data you want to store, you can sketch it out specifying the fields each record is to contain, the maximum length of the data to be entered in each field, and the type of data each field will hold (Figure 5-10). While planning a record file, you must also consider the limitations of the program you are using. Programs differ in the types of fields they provide, the number of fields allowed per record, the length of fields, and the length of records.

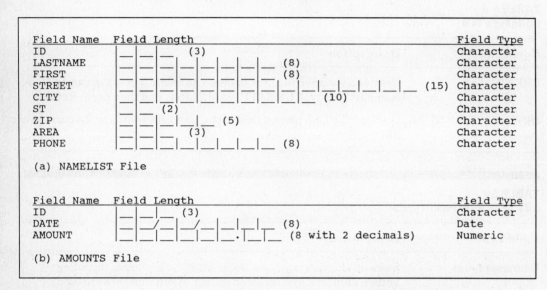

FIGURE 5-10
Planning a database file.

As you have seen, relational databases can be thought of as interrelated tables of information. Each table should have a field containing key attributes that uniquely identify the records in the table. The field containing these key attributes is used to link the files in the database. In the NAMELIST and AMOUNTS files, we have used the customers' ID numbers, but many other kinds of key attributes are often used.

- Social security numbers
- Vehicle license numbers
- Driver's license numbers
- Bank account numbers
- Dates and times
- Account numbers
- Employee serial numbers
- Purchase order numbers
- Telephone numbers
- Credit card numbers
- Policy numbers
- Membership numbers

DEFINING A FILE

When you define a file, you specify the fields it contains and provide information about each field. For example, you specify

- The names of the fields to be included in the file
- The type of data to be entered in each field
- The length of each field

The number of fields you set up depends on the amount of information you want to store. In some cases, you might divide certain basic information into more than one field so that you can manipulate it more easily. The fields you use to sort the file and find specific records are called key, or search, fields. For example, if you used only one field for both the persons' first and last names, and then entered names like John Smith, Betty Lewis, and Roger Wentworth, your file would be limited. You could not sort names based on the persons' last names. You also might not be able to find the record. To sort the persons' names, you set up two fields, one for the first name and one for the last name. The same is true of addresses. For example, if you do not enter ZIP codes in a separate field, you will not be able to sort the records by ZIP codes. Your decision on what fields to set up will be influenced by the field types provided by your program. Table 5-6 describes the commands you use to define a file.

TABLE 5-6
Defining a File

Command	Description
CREATE	Creates a specified file. For example, to create a new file named Namelist, you type **CREATE NAMELIST**, and then press **Return**.
DISPLAY STRUCTURE	Displays the field names, field types, and field widths of the current file.

TABLE 5-7
dBASE III Plus Field Types

Field Type	Description
Character fields	Store all characters you can enter from the keyboard, including letters, numbers, symbols, and spaces. When numbers are used, for example, ZIP codes, they are treated as text, not values. Numbers entered in these fields cannot be used in calculations.
Numeric fields	Store values, including numbers, signs, and decimals. There are two kinds of numeric fields, integers (numbers without decimal places) and decimals. Numbers entered in these fields can be used in calculations.
Logical fields	Sometimes called Boolean fields, are used to enter only true or false notations. On dBASE III Plus, you enter true as T, t, Y, or y and false as F, f, N, or n.
Date fields	Store dates, which you can display in several formats. (The default format is MM/DD/YY.) When dates are entered in this field type, they can usually be used in calculations. Dates can be added and subtracted, or numbers can be added to or subtracted from them. This allows you to get answers to questions like, "What is the average number of days between orders?"
Memo fields	Are used to enter descriptive text, much as you would enter notes to yourself in a notebook. They are similar to character fields, but they generally hold more text and are not used in some operations. Though all other fields are used for specific information, these fields are for general information. You can enter notes about any of the other fields in the record, for example, a note that a price or address is expected to change and the date this is expected to happen. To preserve memory, a memo field often has a variable field length. As you enter text, the amount of memory used increases.

Field Types

All programs allow you to store characters and numbers, but some also allow you to store dates, times, or comments. Some even allow you to create fields that calculate an answer based on the entries in other fields. Table 5-7 describes the field types that dBASE III Plus allows.

Field Names

When naming the fields, use unique field names. The same field name cannot be used twice in the same file. Typical field names might be FIRSTNAME, LASTNAME, STREET, CITY, STATE, ZIP, and PHONE. Table 5-8 describes the field name rules that dBASE III Plus observes.

TABLE 5-8
Field Name Rules

Must be between one and ten characters long.
Must start with a letter and contain only letters, numbers, and underscores.
Must not have blank spaces but you can substitute underscores. For example, you cannot
  enter the field name FIRST NAME but you can enter FIRST_NAME.

Field Lengths

When planning the file, you need to decide how many characters long each field has to be. Table 5-9 describes the field lengths that dBASE III Plus allows. Deciding field lengths ought not to be taken lightly. If you make the field too short, you will lose information. For instance, if you allowed only seven characters for the name, you could enter the name Smith but not the name Hamilton. But if you make the field too long, you waste memory and space on the disk used to store the file, limiting the number of fields in the record or the number of records in the file. Therefore, you need to balance the amount of information held with the space required to hold that information.

The length of the field specifies the number of characters allowed. If the field is numeric, you must specify the total number of digits in the number and the number of decimal places. The program needs to know this so that it can store the values entered in these fields in such a way that you can use it in calculations. When designating the length of numeric fields, include room for a minus sign, the total number of characters, and a decimal point. For example, if you specify the field is five characters long with two digits to the right of the decimal point, you can enter values from -9.99 to 99.99. You cannot enter numbers lower than -9.99 (for example, -10.00) and greater than 99.99 (for example, 100.00) because they contain six characters.

TABLE 5-9
dBASE III Plus Field Lengths

Field Type	Length (in characters)
Character fields	1–254
Numeric fields	1–19 (including 0–15 decimal places)
Logical fields	1 (set automatically)
Date fields	8 (set automatically)
Memo fields	1–5000 (set automatically)

MOVING THE CURSOR AND EDITING

Many dBASE commands are called full-screen commands. When you execute a full-screen command, a fill-in form is displayed on the screen. The spaces where you are to enter data are usually highlighted. Table 5-10 describes the commands to move the cursor between these spaces and edit the contents. Table 5-11 describes the commands to edit field definitions.

TABLE 5-10
Cursor Movement and Editing Commands

To	Press
Move cursor to next field or line	**Return**
Move cursor to next field or one word to right	**End** or **Ctrl-F**
Move cursor to previous field or one word to left	**Home** or **Ctrl-A**
Move cursor up one line or field	↑ or **Ctrl-E**
Move cursor down one line or field	↓ or **Ctrl-X**
Move cursor one character right	→ or **Ctrl-D**
Move cursor one character left	← or **Ctrl-S**
Delete character highlighted by cursor	**Del** or **Ctrl-G**
Exit and save (in full-screen operations)	**Ctrl-End** or **Ctrl-W**
Exit without saving changes	**Esc** or **Ctrl-Q**
Turn option menus on and off	**Ctrl-Home**
Turn insert mode on and off	**Ins** or **Ctrl-V**
Insert new line or field definition	**Ctrl-N**
Display previous record	**PgUp** or **Ctrl-R**
Display new record	**PgDn** or **Ctrl-C**
Zoom out (exit and save in full-screen operations)	**Ctrl-PgUp** or **Ctrl-W**
Zoom in (enter and edit memo fields)	**Ctrl-PgDn**
Delete word to right of cursor	**Ctrl-T**

TABLE 5-11
File Definition Editing Commands

To	Press
Delete contents of field containing cursor	**Ctrl-Y**
Insert field above one containing cursor	**Ctrl-N**
Exit field definition and save definition	**Ctrl-End**

EXERCISE 125
Defining a Data File for Names and Addresses

In this exercise, you define a file that stores names, addresses, and phone numbers. You then display, edit, and delete selected records. To begin this exercise, you must load the program as described in Exercise 124.

Before proceeding, review the following ways for getting out of trouble:

■ Press **F1** to display help.

- Press **Esc** to cancel commands and return to the dot prompt.
- Press **Backspace** to delete characters to the cursor's left if you make a mistake when entering commands or data.
- As you work on a file, your entries are automatically saved. If you make a serious mistake, for example, find yourself back at the system prompt, reload the program (see Topic 5-1), and then execute the USE NAMELIST command described in Exercise 127 to reopen the file.

Step 1. Open a New File. The dot prompt is used to enter commands that create and work with dBASE III files. Here, use the command that sets the default drive to B so that files are automatically saved on that drive. Then, use the command that creates a new file. If the menu is displayed, press **Esc** to display the Dot prompt.

To make B the default drive

Type   **SET DEFAULT TO B:**, and then press **Return**.

To create a new file named NAMELIST

Type   **CREATE NAMELIST**. (If you make a mistake, press **Backspace** to delete it, and then reenter it correctly.)

Press   **Return**.

Result. The drive spins, and in a moment, the screen used to define a file appears (Figure 5-11).

- In the upper right-hand corner, an indicator shows how many bytes of memory are available for your file.
- Below the bytes-remaining indicator is a help screen that lists the commands you can use to move the cursor, insert characters and fields, display help, delete words characters and fields, and either save and exit the defined file or abort the procedure.
- Across the center of the screen are two sets of four columns with headings used to define fields. The cursor is blinking in the first column labeled Field Name.
- The status bar at the bottom of the screen displays the current command (CREATE), the default drive, the name of the file you are creating, and the position of the cursor by field and record.

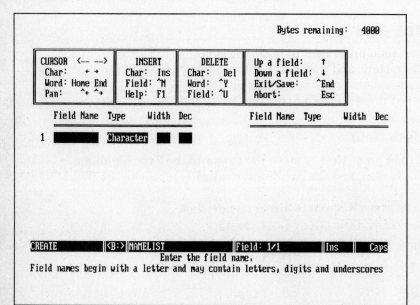

FIGURE 5-11
Create screen display

Step 2. Define a New Database File. Before you can enter data into a file, you must define it by specifying field names, types, and lengths. When you start, the cursor should be at the left of the column with the *Field Name* highlight. The number (1) at the far left indicates which field you are defining.

To enter field definitions, enter the field name, and then press **End** to move the cursor to the next description for the field. All field names are displayed in uppercase characters regardless of the case you use to enter them. When you press **Return** after entering the field width, a new blank field appears. If you make a mistake, you will have a chance to correct it in the next step.

To define the first field

Type   **ID**, and then press **End** to move the cursor to the *Type* highlight.

Press   **C** (for Character--the default field type), and the cursor automatically moves to the *Width* highlight.

Type   **3**, and then press **Return** to display a new field.

To define the second field

Type   **LASTNAME**, and then press **End** to move the cursor to the *Type* highlight.

Press   **C** (for Character), and the cursor automatically moves to the *Width* highlight.

Type   **8**, and then press **Return** to display a new field.

To define the third field

Type   **FIRST**, and then press **End** to move the cursor to the *Type* highlight.

Press   **C** (for Character), and the cursor automatically moves to the *Width* highlight.

Type   **8**, and then press **Return** to display a new field.

To define the fourth field

Type   **STREET**, and then press **End** to move the cursor to the *Type* highlight.

Press   **C** (for Character), and the cursor automatically moves to the *Width* highlight.

Type   **15**, and then press **Return** to display a new field.

To define the fifth field

Type   **CITY**, and then press **End** to move the cursor to the *Type* highlight.

Press   **C** (for Character), and the cursor automatically moves to the *Width* highlight.

Type   **10**, and then press **Return** to display a new field.

To define the sixth field

Type   **ST**, and then press **End** to move the cursor to the *Type* highlight.

Press   **C** (for Character), and the cursor automatically moves to the *Width* highlight.

Type   **2**, and then press **Return** to display a new field.

To define the seventh field

Type   **ZIP**, and then press **End** to move the cursor to the *Type* highlight.

Press   **C** (for Character), and the cursor automatically moves to the *Width* highlight.
Type   **5**, and then press **Return** to display a new field.

To define the eighth field

Type   **AREA**, and then press **End** to move the cursor to the *Type* highlight.
Press   **C** (for Character), and the cursor automatically moves to the *Width* highlight.
Type   **3**, and then press **Return** to display a new field.

To define the ninth field

Type   **PHONE**, and then press **End** to move the cursor to the *Type* highlight.
Press   **C** (for Character), and the cursor automatically moves to the *Width* highlight.
Type   **8**, and then press **Return** to display a new field.

Result. Your final results should match those in Figure 5-12.

Step 3. Edit File Definitions. Carefully check your entries against Figure 5-12. If you find any errors, move the cursor to the field name, type, or width, and type over the mistakes, or use the editing keys described in Table 5-10.

Step 4. Save the Definitions. When you have finished making corrections, save the file. *Be sure a formatted disk is in drive B and the drive's door is closed.*

To save the file

Press   **Ctrl-End,** and the prompt reads *Press ENTER to confirm. Any other key to resume.*
Press   **Return** to save the file definition on the disk.

Result. In a moment, the prompt reads *Input data records now? (Y/N).* Normally you could press **Y** and begin entering data, but let's look at the structure of the file first to be sure all the fields were defined correctly. Press **N**, and the dot prompt reappears. This dot prompt is used to enter commands to work with the file you have just defined.

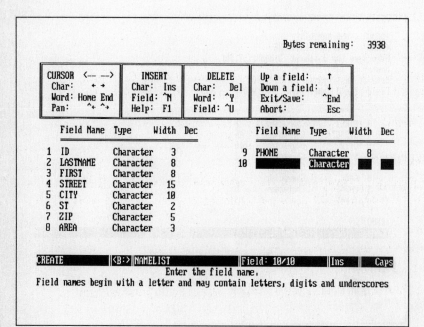

FIGURE 5-12
Defined NAMELIST
screen display

Step 5. List the File's Structure. Now that you have defined the file, let's look at its structure. Before listing the structure, toggle the printer on to print a copy for reference. After printing the structure, toggle the printer off again. Before proceeding, be sure the printer is on and has paper in it.

To toggle the printer on

Press   **Ctrl-P** (you do not see the effects until the next command).

To display a file's structure

Type   **LIST STRUCTURE**, and then press **Return**.

To toggle the printer off

Press   **Ctrl-P**.

Result. The information on the screen and printout gives you the number of records in the file, the date it was last updated, a description of each field, and the total width of all fields. Compare your printout with Figure 5-13 to be sure they match. If they don't match, type **USE NAMELIST**, and then press **Return**. Type **MODIFY STRUCTURE**, and then press **Return** to display the list of field definitions. Edit them as needed, and then press **Ctrl-End** to save the new definitions.

Step 6. Continue or Quit. You have now completed this exercise. Either close all open files and continue to the next exercise, or quit the program if you have finished.

To close all database files

Press   **Esc** if necessary to remove the menu bar and return to the dot prompt.
Type   **CLEAR ALL**, and then press **Return**.

To quit the program

Press   **Esc** if necessary to remove the menu bar and return to the dot prompt.
Type   **QUIT**, and then press **Return**.

FIGURE 5-13
NAMELIST structure

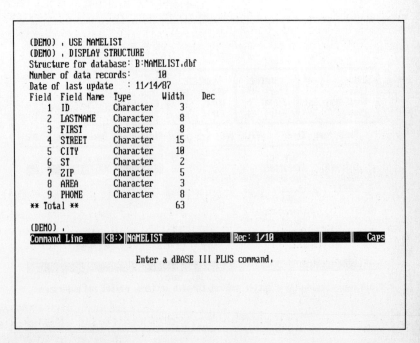

```
(DEMO) . USE NAMELIST
(DEMO) . DISPLAY STRUCTURE
Structure for database: B:NAMELIST.dbf
Number of data records:      10
Date of last update   : 11/14/87
Field  Field Name  Type      Width   Dec
   1   ID          Character    3
   2   LASTNAME    Character    8
   3   FIRST       Character    8
   4   STREET      Character   15
   5   CITY        Character   10
   6   ST          Character    2
   7   ZIP         Character    5
   8   AREA        Character    3
   9   PHONE       Character    8
** Total **                   63

(DEMO) .
Command Line    |<B:>|NAMELIST                    |Rec: 1/10      |        | Caps

             Enter a dBASE III PLUS command.
```

Result. If you quit the program, the operating system prompt reappears. Remove your disks, and then turn off the computer.

Defining a Data File for Amounts

In this exercise, you work in assist mode to define a database file that stores customer charges. To begin this exercise, you must load the program as described in Exercise 124.

Step 1. Open a New File. Before opening a new file, press **Esc** to display the dot prompt, set the default drive to B, and turn on assist mode. Then, open a new file using the assist mode's menus.

To make B the default drive

Type   **SET DEFAULT TO B:**, and then press **Return**.

To display the assist menus

Type   **ASSIST**, and then press **Return**.

To create a new file named AMOUNTS

Press   **C** (for Create) to pull down the Create menu.
Press   **Return** to select **Database file**.
Press   **Return** to select **B:**, and the prompt reads *Enter the name of the file:*.
Type   **AMOUNTS**, and then press **Return**.

Result. The drive spins, and in a moment, the screen used to define a file appears (Figure 5-11).

Step 2. Define a New Database File. In the NAMELIST file, all fields were defined as character fields. Here, you specify another character field but also add a date and numeric field. When you press **End** after entering the character field width, a new field appears. But when you specify a date field, the width is automatically entered, and a new field appears. When you specify a numeric field, press **End**, and you can set both the width and the number of decimal places. If you make a mistake, you will have a chance to correct it in the next step.

To define the first field

Type   **ID**, and then press **End** to move the cursor to the *Type* highlight.
Press   **C** (for Character), and the cursor automatically moves to the *Width* highlight.
Type   **3**, and then press **Return** to display a new field.

To define the second field

Type   **DATE**, and then press **End** to move the cursor to the *Type* highlight.
Press   **Spacebar** repeatedly to cycle through the available field types a few times.
Press   **Spacebar** until the field type displays *Date*.
Press   **End** and the width column automatically displays 8, and then a new field is displayed.

To define the third field

Type   **AMOUNT**, and then press **End** to move the cursor to the *Type* highlight.

Type   **N** (for Numeric), and the cursor automatically moves to the *Width*
        highlight.
Type   **6**, and then press **End** to move the cursor to the *Dec* highlight.
Type   **2**, and then press **Return**.

Result.   Your final results should match those in Figure 5-14.

Step 3. Edit File Definitions. Carefully check your entries against Figure 5-14. If you
find any errors, move the cursor to the field name, type, or width, and type over the
mistakes, or use the editing keys described in Table 5-10.

Step 4. Save the Definitions.   When you have finished making corrections, save the file.
Be sure a formatted disk is in drive B and the drive's door is closed.

To save the file

Press   **Ctrl-End**, and the prompt reads *Press ENTER to confirm. Any other key*
        to resume.
Press   **Return** to save the file definition on the disk.

Result.   In a moment, the prompt reads *Input data records now? (Y/N)*. Normally
you could press **Y**, and then begin entering data, but let's look at the structure of the
file first. Press **N**, and the menu reappears.

Step 5. List the File's Structure. Now that you have defined the database file, let's look
at its structure and print out a copy of it. Before proceeding, be sure the printer is on
and has paper in it.

To display and print the file's structure

Press   **T** to pull down the Tools menu.
Press   ↓ to move the highlight over **List structure**, and then press **Return**.
        The prompt reads *Direct the output to the printer? [Y/N]*.
Press   **Y**. When printing is completed, the prompt reads *Press any key to continue*
        work in ASSIST.

Result.   The information on the screen and printout gives you the number of records
in the file, the date it was last updated, a description of each field, and the total width

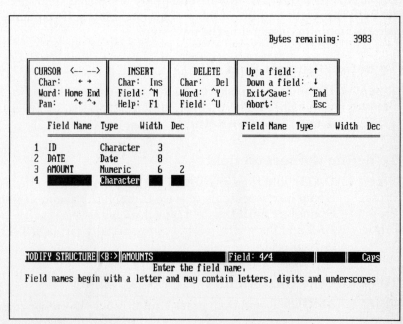

FIGURE 5-14
Defined amounts
screen display

of all fields. Compare your printout against Figure 5-14 to be sure they match. Press any key to return to the menu bar.

Step 6. Continue or Quit. You have now completed this exercise. Either close all open files and continue to the next exercise, or quit the program if you have finished.

To close all database files

Press   **Esc** if necessary to remove the menu bar and return to the dot prompt.
Type   **CLEAR ALL**, and then press **Return**.

To quit the program

Press   **Esc** if necessary to remove the menu bar and return to the dot prompt.
Type   **QUIT**, and then press **Return**.

Result. If you quit the program, the operating system prompt reappears. Remove your disks, and then turn off the computer.

QUESTIONS

1. Sketch out a database file you would use to maintain a file containing your friends' names, addresses, and telephone numbers. Assume you want to be able to sort the file by last name and ZIP code.

2. Briefly describe each of the following types of fields:

   a. Character

   b. Numeric

   c. Logical

   d. Date

   e. Memo

3. What length would you specify for a field into which the largest number you were going to enter was 100.00? 10.00? 1000.00?

4. Why not specify the maximum length available for each field so that you do not have to plan field lengths so carefully?

5. What information makes up a field? A record? A file?

6. Plan a database that you would use to catalog all of your record albums. List the field names you would use and indicate their type and length field. What do you think would be the best key attribute so that you could always find a specific song?

7. Why would you not be able to sort names based on last names if you entered both first and last names in one field?

TOPIC 5-3
Entering Records

In this topic, we introduce you to the following procedures:

- Opening files
- Entering records

BACKGROUND

Once you define a file, you can enter data into it. You can enter records in any order you want. The file can be sorted into any desired order after you enter the records. dBASE III Plus has several commands you can use to enter records into a file after it has been defined. The basic command is APPEND, but there are other commands (see Topic 5-6). When the field names are displayed, you can use the commands described in Table 5-12 to enter and edit records.

TABLE 5-12
Commands in Append Mode

To	Press
Move cursor left or right one character	← or →
Move cursor up or down one field	↑ or ↓
Display previous record (if any)	**PgUp**
Display next record (if any)	**PgDn**
Delete character	**Del**
Delete field	**Ctrl-Y**
Delete record	**Ctrl-U**
Toggle between insert and typeover modes	**Ins**
Return to dot prompt (with cursor in first field of new blank record)	**Return**
Return to dot prompt at any time	**Ctrl-End**
Enter data in memo field containing cursor	**Ctrl-PgDn**
Exit memo field and abandon changes	**Esc**
Exit memo field and save changes	**Ctrl-End**

EXERCISE 127

Entering Records in the NAMELIST File

In this exercise, you enter records using the APPEND command. To begin this exercise, you must load the program as described in Exercise 124.

Step 1. Open an Existing File. Before you can work with a dBASE III Plus file, you must retrieve it from the disk and load it into the computer's memory. But first set the default drive to B (the one containing the disk you used in Exercise 124). (If the menu is displayed, press **Esc** to display the dot prompt.)

To retrieve a file from the disk in drive B

Type   **SET DEFAULT TO B:**, and then press **Return**.
Type   **USE NAMELIST**, and then press **Return**.

Result. The disk spins as the file is loaded into the computer's memory, and then the dot prompt appears.

Step 2. Add Records. Now let's enter data into the file. Before doing so, turn on the help menu that lists commands you use to move the cursor and edit data while you enter records.

To turn on the help menu

Type   **SET MENU ON**, and then press **Return**.

To enter records into the file

Type   **APPEND**, and then press **Return**.

Result. The screen displays a help menu below which are the fields you enter data into (Figure 5-15). These are the field names you entered when you defined the file. Next to each field name are highlights indicating the field's length. The current field, the one you enter data into when you type, contains the cursor. To enter data into the file, refer to the following three steps and Figure 5-16.

1. Type in the data exactly as shown in Figure 5-16. Uppercase and lowercase letters are important because you will look for data, and the program is case sensitive. For example, if you enter Kendall, and later look for KENDALL, the program will not find it. If you make a mistake when making an entry, press **Backspace** to delete it, and then correctly reenter it.

2. After you complete a field entry, press **Return** to move the cursor to the beginning of the next field. If the number of characters you enter equals the field length, the computer beeps, and the cursor automatically moves to the next field. If the cursor does not move to the far left side of the new field, press ← to move it there before entering data.

3. When you enter date into the last field (PHONE), it fills the field. Then the computer beeps, a new blank record is automatically displayed, and the previous record is saved onto the disk.

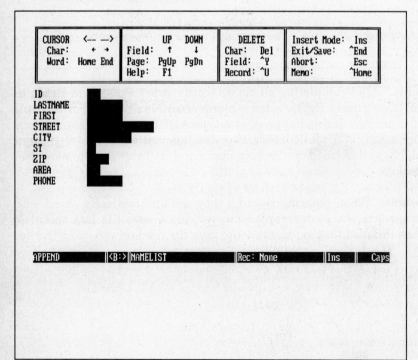

FIGURE 5-15
Entering NAMELIST records

FIGURE 5-16
Names and addresses
to be entered

```
Record 1:                                Record 2:
ID:           101                         ID:           102
LASTNAME:     Culman                      LASTNAME:     Benjamin
FIRST:        Tina                        FIRST:        Nancy
STREET:       100 Elm Street              STREET:       25 Oak Street
CITY:         New Haven                   CITY:         Cambridge
ST:           CT                          ST:           MA
ZIP:          10000                       ZIP:          20000
AREA:         203                         AREA:         617
PHONE:        555-1000                    PHONE:        555-1001

Record 3:                                Record 4:
ID:           103                         ID:           104
LASTNAME:     Kendall                     LASTNAME:     Hogan
FIRST:        Liz                         FIRST:        Dennis
STREET:       14 Lark Ave.                STREET:       40 Main Street
CITY:         Chicago                     CITY:         Edgewater
ST:           IL                          ST:           NJ
ZIP:          20000                       ZIP:          30000
AREA:         312                         AREA:         201
PHONE:        555-1002                    PHONE:        555-1003

Record 5:                                Record 6:
ID:           105                         ID:           106
LASTNAME:     Swabey                      LASTNAME:     Sobel
FIRST:        Daphne                      FIRST:        Carol
STREET:       168 Bridge Road             STREET:       45 Porter Ave.
CITY:         Beverly                     CITY:         Fairlawn
ST:           MA                          ST:           NJ
ZIP:          20000                       ZIP:          30000
AREA:         617                         AREA:         201
PHONE:        555-1004                    PHONE:        555-1005

Record 7:                                Record 8:
ID:           107                         ID:           108
LASTNAME:     Anthony                     LASTNAME:     Poe
FIRST:        William                     FIRST:        James
STREET:       900 Maple Road              STREET:       10 Preston Lane
CITY:         Reading                     CITY:         Oakland
ST:           MA                          ST:           CA
ZIP:          20000                       ZIP:          40000
AREA:         617                         AREA:         415
PHONE:        555-1006                    PHONE:        555-1007
```

Step 3. Edit the Records. After completing all eight records, press **PgUp** and **PgDn** to scroll through them. (Don't press **PgDn** when a blank record is displayed or you will be returned to the dot prompt. If this happens, just type **APPEND** and press **Return** to display the records again.) Carefully check your data against Figure 5-16. If there are mistakes, use the keys described on the help menu and in Table 5-10 to move the cursor and edit mistakes.

Step 4. Save the Records. When entering records, they are automatically saved onto the disk when you move to the next record. However, to be sure the last record is saved, when you have finished making corrections, save the file and return to the dot prompt.

To save the file

Press   **Ctrl-End**.

Result. The dot prompt reappears.

Step 5. Print Out the Records. Print out a list of the records so that you can check it more carefully. Before proceeding, be sure the printer is on and has paper in it.

To toggle the printer on

Press   **Ctrl-P.**

To display all records

Type   **DISPLAY ALL**, and then press **Return.**

To toggle the printer off

Press   **Ctrl-P.**

Result. The records you entered are displayed on the screen and printed on the printout. Carefully compare your printout against the data in Figure 5-16.

Step 6. Continue or Quit. You have now completed this exercise. Either close the open database file and continue to the next exercise, or quit the program if you have finished. (Press **Esc** if necessary to remove the menu bar and return to the dot prompt.)

To close all database files

Type   **CLEAR ALL**, and then press **Return.**

To quit the program

Type   **QUIT**, and then press **Return.**

Result. If you quit the program, the operating system prompt reappears. Remove your disks, and then turn off the computer.

EXERCISE 128
Entering Records in the AMOUNTS File

In this exercise, you enter records using menus in assist mode. To begin this exercise, you must load the program as described in Exercise 124.

Step 1. Open an Existing File. Before you can work with a dBASE III file, you must retrieve it from the disk and load it into the computer's memory. But first turn on the help menu, and set the default drive to B (the one containing the disk you used in Exercise 124). (If the menu is displayed, press **Esc** to display the dot prompt.)

To turn on the menu and make B the default drive

Type   **SET MENU ON**, and then press **Return.**
Type   **SET DEFAULT TO B:**, and then press **Return.**

To display the assist menu

Type   **ASSIST**, and then press **Return.**

To retrieve a file from the disk in drive B

Press   **S** if necessary to pull down the Set Up menu.

Press   **Return** to select **Database file**.
Press   **Return** to select **B:**.
Press   ↓ to move the highlight to **AMOUNTS.DBF**, and then press **Return**. The
         prompt reads *Is this file indexed? [Y/N]*.
Press   **N** (see Topic 5-8).

Result. The disk spins as the file is loaded into the computer's memory, and then
the menu reappears.

Step 2. Add Records. Now let's enter data into the file.

To enter records into the file

Press   **U** to pull down the Update menu.
Press   **Return** to select **Append**.

Result. The screen displays a blank record listing the three fields in the file. Next to
each field name are highlights indicating the field's length. The current field, the one
you enter data into when you type, contains the cursor. To enter data into the file,
refer to the following three steps and Figure 5-17.

1. Type in the data exactly as shown in Figure 5-17. You enter dates in the format
   MM/DD/YY. If you enter two digits for each part of the date, you do not have to
   enter the slashes. If you only enter one digit you do. For example, you can enter
   the date June 8, 1988, as 6/8/88 or as 060888. If you make a mistake when
   making an entry, press **Backspace** to delete it, and then correctly reenter it.

2. After you complete a field entry, press **Return** to move the cursor to the
   beginning of the next field. If the number of characters you enter equals the field
   length, the cursor automatically moves to the next field. If the cursor does not
   move to the far left side of the new field, press ← to move it there before entering
   data.

3. When you complete the first record, you normally press ↓ or **Return** after
   entering data in the last field (AMOUNT). This displays a new, blank record, and
   the previous record is saved onto the disk. If the data you enter fills the last field,
   as it does here, a new record is automatically displayed so you do not have to
   press these keys.

FIGURE 5-17
Amounts to be entered

Record 1:		Record 2:	
ID:	101	ID:	102
DATE:	06/08/88	DATE:	06/09/88
AMOUNT:	10.00	AMOUNT:	15.00
Record 3:		Record 4:	
ID:	103	ID:	104
DATE:	06/10/88	DATE:	06/11/88
AMOUNT:	35.00	AMOUNT:	25.00
Record 5:		Record 6:	
ID:	105	ID:	106
DATE:	06/12/88	DATE:	06/13/88
AMOUNT:	20.00	AMOUNT:	50.00
Record 7:		Record 8:	
ID:	107	ID:	108
DATE:	06/14/88	DATE:	06/15/88
AMOUNT:	15.00	AMOUNT:	10.00

Step 3. Edit the Records. After completing all eight records, press **PgUp** and **PgDn** to scroll through them. (Don't press **PgDn** when a blank record is displayed or you will be returned to the menu. If this happens, just highlight **Append** and press **Return** to display the records again.) Carefully check your data against Figure 5-17. If there are mistakes, use the keys described on the help menu and in Table 5-10 to move the cursor and edit mistakes.

Step 4. Save the Records. When you have finished making corrections, save the file.

To save the file

Press   **Ctrl-End**.

Result. The database file is saved onto the disk, and the menu reappears.

Step 5. Print Out the Records. Print out a list of the records so that you can check it more carefully. Before proceeding, be sure the printer is on and has paper in it.

To toggle the printer on

Press   **Esc** to remove the menu bar and return to the dot prompt.
Press   **Ctrl-P**.

To display all the records

Type   **DISPLAY ALL**, and then press **Return**.

To toggle the printer off

Press   **Ctrl-P**.

Result. The records you entered are displayed on the screen and printed on the printout. Carefully compare your printout against the data in Figure 5-17.

Step 6. Continue or Quit. You have now completed this exercise. Either close all open files and continue to the next exercise, or quit the program if you have finished. (Press **Esc** if necessary to remove the menu bar and return to the dot prompt.)

To close all database files

Type   **CLEAR ALL**, and then press **Return**.

To quit the program

Type   **QUIT**, and then press **Return**.

Result. If you quit the program, the operating system prompt reappears. Remove your disks, and then turn off the computer.

QUESTIONS

1. In what order do you enter records?
2. What command moves the cursor between fields?
3. When you enter data into the last field, what happens if the data fills the field? If it does not fill the field?

TOPIC 5-4
Displaying Records

In this topic, we introduce you to the following procedure:

■ Displaying records in a database file

BACKGROUND

Once data has been entered into a database file, you generally work with specific records. For example, you may want to look up the phone number of John Davis, change the number of baseballs in inventory, delete a specific record, or change the data in one or more fields. To do this, you use commands that display only a selected record on the screen, or you use designated keys to scroll through groups of records contained in the file, much as you would flip through the cards in an index card file. If the file has just been created, the records will appear in the order they were entered in. If the file has been sorted, they will appear in the order they were sorted into.

Many of the commands you use to display records move a record pointer within the file. This record pointer, which is not displayed, makes the file it points to the current record. Subsequent commands then start from, or apply to, the current record. For example, if you type **GOTO 5**, and then press **Return**, the record pointer moves to record 5. If you then type **BROWSE**, and then press **Return**, files are listed on the screen beginning with record 5.

Scrolling through a file to look at records one after another in the order they are stored or sorted can take a long time if the file has many records. Table 5-13 describes the dBASE III commands that display records.

TABLE 5-13
Commands That Display Records

Command	Description
DISPLAY	Displays specific records. For example, DISPLAY ALL displays all records, DISPLAY ALL STREET displays all entries in the field named STREET, and DISPLAY NEXT 5 STREET displays the contents of the STREET field in the next five records.
LIST	Displays specific records, but unlike DISPLAY, if the list is longer than the screen, the display does not pause when the screen is full. You can press **Ctrl-S** to stop and restart the scrolling for a large file.
BROWSE	Displays as many as seventeen records at a time on the screen. When in browse mode, you can press **Ctrl-Home** to display a menu of goto options (see Table 5-14).
GOTO	Specifies the record to go to when typed from the dot prompt before entering a BROWSE command. You can specify a specific record number or the options TOP or BOTTOM. For example, GOTO 5 displays record number 5, GOTO TOP displays the first record, and GOTO BOTTOM displays the last record when you then use the BROWSE command.
SKIP	Moves the record pointer ahead the specified number of records. For example, if you use the command GOTO TOP and then the command SKIP 5 when you specify the BROWSE command, it displays all records beginning with record 6.

TABLE 5-14
Browse Mode Commands

To	Press
Pan display right (if wider than screen)	Ctrl-→
Pan display left (if wider than screen)	Ctrl-←
Scroll database down	PgDn
Scroll database up	PgUp
Exit browse mode and save changes	Ctrl-End
Exit browse mode without saving changes to current record	Esc

EXERCISE 129

Displaying Records in the NAMELIST File

In this exercise, you display records in a database file. To begin this exercise, you must load the program as described in Exercise 124.

Step 1. Open an Existing File. First insert the disk you saved the NAMELIST file on into drive B. (If the menu is displayed, press **Esc** to display the dot prompt.)

To retrieve a file from the disk in drive B

Type **SET MENU ON**, and then press **Return**.
Type **SET DEFAULT TO B:**, and then press **Return**.
Type **USE NAMELIST**, and then press **Return**.

Result. The disk spins as the file is loaded into the computer's memory, and then the dot prompt appears.

Step 2. Use the LIST Command to List Records in the File. Now that you have entered records into the file, let's take a look at them.

To display a list of records in the file

Type **LIST**, and then press **Return**.

Result. A list of all the records is displayed, and the dot prompt reappears.

Step 3. Use the BROWSE Command to Display Records. The BROWSE command displays records just like the LIST command, but it displays seventeen records at a time.

To browse through records in the file

Type **GOTO TOP**, and then press **Return**.
Type **BROWSE**, and then press **Return**.

Result. A help menu and a list of all the records is displayed on the screen. When you are finished looking at them, press **Esc** to leave browse mode and return to the dot prompt. The reason you typed the GOTO TOP command is because the BROWSE command displays records beginning with the one to which the record pointer is pointing. The GOTO command moved this pointer to the first record.

Step 4. Display Records. dBASE III allows you to display specific records using the DISPLAY command. You can also display all records with the DISPLAY ALL command. This is like the LIST command, but if your database contains too many records to fit on the screen, it displays those that do fit and then pauses until you press a designated key to continue.

To display records by number

Press   **Esc** to return to the dot prompt. Type**DISPLAY RECORD 1,** and then press **Return.**

Type   **2,** and then press **Return.**

Type   **DISPLAY,** and then press **Return.**

Result. The first command displays record 1. The second command has the same effect but is in a slightly different form.

To display the next record

Type   **SKIP,** and then press **Return.** A message *Record No. 3* indicates you have skipped to record 3.

Type   **DISPLAY,** and then press **Return.**

Result. The SKIP command makes the program move the record pointer to the next record in the file. When you then use the DISPLAY command, the record to which the record pointer points is the one that is displayed.

To display the next three records

Type   **DISPLAY NEXT 3,** and then press **Return.**

To display the first record

Type   **GOTO TOP,** and then press **Return.**

Press   **F8** to automatically enter the DISPLAY command.

Result. The command displays the first record. The GOTO TOP command moved the record pointer to the first record in the file. Pressing **F8** displayed the record to which it was pointing.

To display the last record

Type   **GOTO BOTTOM,** and then press **Return.**

Press   **F8** to automatically enter the DISPLAY command.

Result. The command displays the last record.

Step 5. Display and Print All Records. Now display all records, and then print them. Before proceeding, be sure the printer is on and has paper in it.

To toggle the printer on

Press   **Ctrl-P.**

To display all records

Type   **DISPLAY ALL,** and then press **Return.**

To toggle the printer off

Press   **Ctrl-P**.

Result. The command displays and prints all the records. The result is identical to the LIST command you used earlier. If there were more records, the commands would have different results. LIST would scroll them all on the screen. DISPLAY ALL would display enough to fill the screen and then pause until you press a key to continue.

Step 6. Continue or Quit. You have now completed this exercise. Either close all open files and continue to the next exercise, or quit the program if you have finished. (Press **Esc** if necessary to remove the menu bar and return to the dot prompt.)

To close all database files

Type   **CLEAR ALL**, and then press **Return**.

To quit the program

Type   **QUIT**, and then press **Return**.

Result. If you quit the program, the operating system prompt reappears. Remove your disks, and then turn off the computer.

EXERCISE 130

Displaying Records in the AMOUNTS File

In this exercise, you use the Assist menu to display records in the AMOUNTS file. To begin this exercise, you must load the program as described in Exercise 124.

Step 1. Open an Existing File. First insert the disk you saved the AMOUNTS file on into drive B. (If the menu is displayed, press **Esc** to display the dot prompt.)

To turn on the menu and make B the default drive

Type   **SET MENU ON**, and then press **Return**.
Type   **SET DEFAULT TO B:**, and then press **Return**.

To display the assist menu

Type   **ASSIST**, and then press **Return**.

To retrieve a file from the disk in drive B

Press   **S** if necessary to pull down the Set Up menu.
Press   **Return** to select **Database file**.
Press   **Return** to select **B:**.
Press   → to move the highlight to **AMOUNTS.DBF**, and then press **Return**.
             The prompt reads *Is this file indexed? [Y/N]*.
Press   **N**.

Result. The disk spins as the file is loaded into the computer's memory, and then the menu reappears.

Step 2. Use the LIST Command to List Records in the File. Now that you have entered records into the file, let's take a look at them.

To display a list of records in the file

Press   **R** to pull down the Retrieve menu.

Press   **Return** to select **List**.

Press   **Return** to select **Execute the command**, and the prompt reads *Direct the output to the printer? [Y/N]*.

Press   **N**.

Result. A list of all the records is displayed. The dates are displayed in the format MM/DD/YY. Press any key to return to the menu.

Step 3. Use the BROWSE Command to Display Records. Here you use the BROWSE command to display the records in the file, but first you change the date format to ANSI format, which displays dates in the format DD.MM.YY; for example, October 10, 1988, is displayed as 10.12.88. Since the BROWSE command begins listing files at the current record, you first use the GOTO command to move the record pointer to the top of the file.

To change the date format

Press   **Esc** to remove the menu bar and return to the dot prompt.

Type   **SET DATE ANSI**, and then press **Return**.

Type   **ASSIST**, and then press **Return** to display the menu bar again.

To move the record pointer to the first record

Press   **P** to pull down the Position menu.

Press   ↓ to move the highlight to **Goto Record**, and then press **Return**.

Press   **Return** to select **TOP**.

To browse through records

Press   **U** to pull down the Update menu.

Press   ↑ to move the highlight to **Browse**, and then press **Return**.

Result. A list of all the records is displayed. The dates are now displayed in the new format. When you are finished looking at the records, press **Esc** to leave browse mode and return to the menu.

Step 4. Display a Single Record. The Retrieve menu lists the DISPLAY command, which you can use to display one or more records. Here, use the menu to display record 1. Before using this command, set the date format back to its original format.

To change the date format

Press   **Esc** to remove the menu bar and return to the dot prompt.

Type   **SET DATE AMERICAN**, and then press **Return**.

Type   **ASSIST**, and then press **Return** to display the menu bar again.

To display records by number

Press   **R** to pull down the Retrieve menu.

Press   ↓ if necessary to move the highlight to **Display**, and then press **Return**.

Press   ↓ to move the highlight to **Specify scope**, and then press **Return**.

Press   ↓ to move the highlight to **RECORD**, and then press **Return**. The prompt reads *Enter a numeric value:*.

Type   **1**, and then press **Return**. Press ↑ to move the highlight to **Execute the command**, and then press **Return**.

Result. The command displays record 1 and the date is restored to the format MM/DD/YY. The record pointer now points to this record, so it is the current record. Press any key to return to the menu.

Step 5. Display a Group of Records. After you have displayed a single record, the record pointer points to that record. The next command you execute begins with that record. Here, display the next three records beginning with the one to which the record pointer is pointing.

To display the next three records

Press   **R** to pull down the Retrieve menu.
Press   ↓ if necessary to move the highlight to **Display,** and then press **Return.**
Press   ↓ to move the highlight to **Specify scope,** and then press **Return.**
Press   ↓ to move the highlight to **NEXT,** and then press **Return.** The prompt reads *Enter a numeric value:*
Type   **3,** and then press **Return.**
Press   ↑ to move the highlight to **Execute the command,** and then press **Return.**

Result. The command displays the first three records. Press any key to return to the menu.

Step 6. Display All Records. For the final command, display all records.

To display all records

Press   **R** to pull down the Retrieve menu.
Press   ↓ to move the highlight to **Display,** and then press **Return.**
Press   ↓ to move the highlight to **Specify scope,** and then press **Return.**
Press   ↓ to move the highlight to **ALL,** and then press **Return.**
Press   ↑ to move the highlight to **Execute the command,** and then press **Return.**

Result. The command displays all the records. Press any key to return to the menu.

Step 7. Continue or Quit. You have now completed this exercise. Either close all open files and continue to the next exercise, or quit the program if you have finished. (Press **Esc** if necessary to remove the menu bar and return to the dot prompt.)

To close all database files

Type   **CLEAR ALL,** and then press **Return.**

To quit the program

Type   **QUIT,** and then press **Return.**

Result. If you quit the program, the operating system prompt reappears. Remove your disks, and then turn off the computer.

QUESTIONS

1. Why might you want to display specific records?
2. What is a record pointer?
3. If you want to display the first record, what command would you use?
4. What is the difference between the LIST and DISPLAY commands?

TOPIC 5-5
Using Criteria to Display Records

In this topic, we introduce you to the following procedures:

- Using relational operators
- Using logical operators

BACKGROUND

In Topic 5-4, we introduced you to several commands that display records so that you can edit or delete them. Those commands were useful in a small database, but when the number of records increases, it becomes harder to find the record you want with the DISPLAY, LIST, and BROWSE commands. Database management programs like dBASE III Plus also have commands that let you find one or more records by using a query language to specify criteria. Only those records that match the criteria are then displayed. You can also specify that only selected fields from the records be displayed. To find specific records, you use relational operators like those described in Table 5-15 and logical operators like those described in Table 5-16.

TABLE 5-15
Relational Operators

Operator	Description
	Finds all records greater than the criteria you specify. For example, AMOUNT>10.00 finds all records where the AMOUNT is more than 10.00; DATE>1/10/89 finds all records where the DATE is later than January 10, 1989; and NAME>JONES displays all records alphabetically after JONES.
<	Finds all records less than the criteria you specify. For example, AMOUNT<10.00 finds all records where the AMOUNT is less than 10.00; DATE<1/10/85 finds all records where the DATE is earlier than January 10, 1985; and NAME<JONES displays all records alphabetically before JONES.
=	Finds all records equal to the criteria you specify. For example, LASTNAME=JONES finds all records with JONES in the field named LASTNAME; AMOUNT=10.00 finds all records where the AMOUNT is 10.00; and DATE=1/10/89 finds all records where the DATE is January 10, 1989.
=	Finds all records greater than or equal to the criteria you specify. For example, LASTNAME>=JONES finds all records with JONES or any name alphabetically later in the field named LASTNAME; AMOUNT>=10.00 finds all records where the AMOUNT is 10.00 or more; and DATE>=1/10/89 finds all records where the DATE is January 10, 1989, or later.
<=	Finds all records less than or equal to the criteria you specify. For example, LASTNAME finds all records with JONES or any name alphabetically earlier in the field named LASTNAME; AMOUNT<=10.00 finds all records where the AMOUNT is 10.00 or less; and DATE<=1/10/89 finds all records where the DATE is January 10, 1989, or earlier.
<>	Finds all records not equal to the criteria you specify. For example, LASTNAME<>JONES finds all records except those with JONES in the LASTNAME field; and DATE<>1/10/88 finds all records not dated January 10, 1988.

TABLE 5-16
Logical Operators

Operator	Description
.AND.	Two or more conditions must be met. For example, AMOUNT=10.00.AND.NAME=JONES finds all records where the AMOUNT is 10.00 and the name is JONES.
.OR.	One or another condition must be met. For example, AMOUNT=10.00.OR.NAME=JONES finds all records where the AMOUNT is 10.00 or the name is JONES.
.NOT.	Condition must not be met. For example, AMOUNT=10.00.NOT.NAME=JONES finds all records where the AMOUNT is not 10.00 and the name is not JONES.

When using relational and logical operators to find records, you use them along with commands like DISPLAY. In dBASE III Plus, the commands to answer three typical questions would be written as follows:

■ What customers have credit with the company?

USE NAMELIST
DISPLAY ALL

In this query, the USE NAMELIST command tells the program what file you want the records selected from. The DISPLAY ALL command tells the program to display all fields for all records in the NAMELIST file.

■ What customers have a balance due greater than $25?

USE AMOUNTS
DISPLAY ID FOR AMOUNT>25

In this query, the file named AMOUNTS is opened, and the query is revised so that only the ID field is displayed. The criteria FOR AMOUNT>25 has added a condition to the command. This command will display the ID fields only for records of customers whose AMOUNT is more than $25.

■ What date was a charge made to ID number 101 in the amount of $15?

USE AMOUNTS
DISPLAY DATE FOR ID="101".AND.AMOUNT=15

In this query, the command specifies that the contents of the date field be displayed for records where the ID is equal to 101 *and* the amount is $15. The 101 is enclosed in quotation marks to indicate it is text, not a number that can be calculated.

EXERCISE 131
Using Criteria to Display Records in the NAMELIST File

In this exercise, you use relational and logical operators to find records in the NAMELIST file. To begin this exercise, you must load the program as described in Exercise 124.

Note. Many commands in this exercise are quite long. If you make a mistake and the command does not work, remember that you can press ↑ to return it to the dot command line for editing rather than retype the entire command.

Step 1. Open an Existing File. First insert the disk you saved the NAMELIST file on into drive B. (If you want to print out the results of these commands, press **Ctrl-P** to toggle the printer on.) (If the menu is displayed, press **Esc** to display the dot prompt.)

To retrieve a file from the disk in drive B

Type   **SET MENU ON**, and then press **Return**.
Type   **SET DEFAULT TO B:**, and then press **Return**.
Type   **USE NAMELIST**, and then press **Return**.

Result. The disk spins as the file is loaded into the computer's memory, and then the dot prompt appears.

Step 2. Display Records That Match a Single Criterion. You can look for a group of records that match specific criteria, for example, using a FOR clause to search for character strings like the state of MA. The character string must be enclosed in double quotations. When using this command, the case you use for characters is also important; if a field has been entered as MA, lowercase ma will not display any records.

To display a group of records

Type   **DISPLAY FOR ST="MA"**, and then press **Return**.

Result. The three records that match the criterion are displayed.

Step 3. Display One Field That Matches One Criterion. Now, display only one field name.

To display only one field

Type   **DISPLAY LASTNAME FOR ST="MA"**, and then press **Return**.

Result. The same three records are displayed but only the LASTNAME field.

Step 4. Display Selected Fields from Records That Match a Single Criterion. Now, display the information you would need to call all customers who live in Massachusetts.

To display a group of records

Type   **DISPLAY ID,LASTNAME,FIRST,AREA,PHONE FOR ST="MA"**, and then press **Return**.

Result. The three records matching the criterion are displayed. Only the specified fields are included. They were specified following the DISPLAY command by entering the field names separated by commas.

Step 5. Display Records That Match Two Criteria. What if you want to find the last name of the customers living in either Massachusetts or New Jersey?

To display records meeting two criteria

Type   **DISPLAY LASTNAME FOR ST="MA".OR.ST="NJ"**, and then press **Return**.

Result. The five records that match the criteria are displayed.

Step 6. Display Records That Are Greater Than. Now, display the ID, LASTNAME, and ST for all customers who live in Massachusetts and whose ID is greater than 108. (The quotation marks are entered around the ID number to indicate it is text.)

Type   **DISPLAY ID,LASTNAME,ST FOR ST="MA".AND.ID>"108"**, and then press **Return**.

To display records that are greater than

Result. Only one record matches the condition of living in MA and having an ID higher than 108.

Step 7. Continue to Experiment. Tables 5-15 and 5-16 list relational and logical operators. You might want to experiment with some of these before proceeding. If you make any mistakes, the program will respond with an error message and may ask if you want help. To try again, press **Esc** to return to the dot prompt.

Step 8. Continue or Quit. You have now completed this exercise. Either close all open files and continue to the next exercise, or quit the program if you have finished. (If you toggled the printer on to make a printout of the results of your commands, press **Ctrl-P** now to toggle the printer off. Also, press **Esc** if necessary to remove the menu bar and return to the dot prompt.)

To close all database files

Type   **CLEAR ALL**, and then press **Return**.

To quit the program

Type   **QUIT**, and then press **Return**.

Result. If you quit the program, the operating system prompt reappears. Remove your disks, and then turn off the computer.

EXERCISE 132

Using Criteria to Display Records in the AMOUNTS File

In this exercise, you use relational and logical operators to find records in the AMOUNTS file. To begin this exercise, you must load the program as described in Exercise 124.

Step 1. Open an Existing File. First insert the disk you saved the NAMELIST file on into drive B. (If you want to print out the results of these commands, press **Ctrl-P** to toggle the printer on.) (If the menu is displayed, press **Esc** to display the dot prompt.)

To turn on the menu and make B the default drive

Type   **SET DEFAULT TO B:**, and then press **Return**.

To display the assist menu

Type   **ASSIST**, and then press **Return**.

To retrieve a file from the disk in drive B

Press   **S** if necessary to pull down the Set Up menu.

Press	**Return** to select **Database file**.
Press	**Return** to select **B:**.
Press	↓ to move the highlight to **AMOUNTS.DBF**, and then press **Return**. The prompt reads *Is this file indexed? [Y/N]*.
Press	**N**.

Result. The disk spins as the file is loaded into the computer's memory, and then the menu reappears.

Step 2. Display Records That Match a Single Criterion. You can look for a group of records that match a specific criteria.

To display a group of records

Press	**R** to pull down the Retrieve menu.
Press	↓ to move the highlight to **Display**, and then press **Return**.
Press	↓ to move the highlight to **Build a search condition**, and then press **Return**.
Press	↓ to move the highlight to **AMOUNT**, and then press **Return**.
Press	**Return** to select **= Equal To**, and the prompt reads *Enter a numeric value:*.
Type	**50**, and then press **Return**.
Press	**Return** to select **No more conditions**.
Press	↑ to move the highlight to **Execute the command**, and then press **Return**.

Result. The one record matching the criterion is displayed. Press any key to return to the menu.

Step 3. Display Selected Fields from Records That Match One Criterion. Now repeat the previous command, but this time specify that only the ID and AMOUNT fields are to be displayed, and the criterion is all AMOUNTS equal to or greater than 30.

To display selected fields

Press	**R** if necessary to pull down the Retrieve menu.
Press	↓ if necessary to move the highlight to **Display**, and then press **Return**.
Press	↓ to move the cursor to **Construct a field list**, and then press **Return**.
Press	**Return** to select **ID**.
Press	↓ to move the highlight to **AMOUNT**, and then press **Return**.
Press	→ to return the highlight to the previous menu.
Press	↓ if necessary to move the highlight to **Build a search condition**, and then press **Return**.
Press	↓ to move the highlight to **AMOUNT**, and then press **Return**.
Press	↓ to move the highlight to **>= Greater Than or Equal To**, press **Return** and the prompt reads *Enter a numeric value:*.
Type	**30**, and then press **Return**.
Press	**Return** to select **No more conditions**.
Press	↑ to move the highlight to **Execute the command**, and then press **Return**.

Result. The ID and AMOUNT fields for the two records that match the criterion of amounts greater than or equal to 30 are displayed. Press any key to return to the menu.

Step 4. Display Records That Match Two Criteria. Now, find all records that have DATES after June 11, 1988, and AMOUNTS greater than 20.

To display records meeting two criteria

Press	**R** if necessary to pull down the Retrieve menu.
Press	↓ if necessary to move the highlight to **Display**, and then press **Return**.
Press	↓ to move the highlight to **Build a search condition**, and then press **Return**.
Press	↓ to move the highlight to **DATE**, and then press **Return**.
Press	↓ to move the highlight to **> Greater Than**, press **Return** and the prompt reads *Enter a date value:*.
Type	**06/11/88**.
Press	↓ to move the highlight to **Combine with .AND.**, and then press **Return**.
Press	↓ to move the highlight to **AMOUNT**, and then press **Return**.
Press	↓ to move the highlight to **> Greater Than**, and then press **Return**. The prompt reads *Enter a numeric value:*.
Type	**20**, and then press **Return**.
Press	**Return** to select **No more conditions**.
Press	↑ to move the highlight to **Execute the command**, and then press **Return**.

Result. The one record with a date later than June 11, 1988, and an amount greater than 20 is displayed. Press any key to return to the menu.

Step 5. Continue or Quit. You have now completed this exercise. Either close all open files and continue to the next exercise, or quit the program if you have finished. (If you toggled the printer on to make a printout of the results of your commands, press **Ctrl-P** now to toggle the printer off. Also, press **Esc** if necessary to remove the menu bar and return to the dot prompt.)

To close all database files

Type	**CLEAR ALL**, and then press **Return**.

To quit the program

Type	**QUIT**, and then press **Return**.

Result. If you quit the program, the operating system prompt reappears. Remove your disks, and then turn off the computer.

QUESTIONS

1. Assume you have a list of customers in the following file structure:

   Lastname:

   Firstname:

   Company:

   Phone:

   Last contact:

   Last sale:

   Items purchased:

How would you set up search criteria to find all customers named Jones? To find all to whom you made a last sale after January 1, 1985? To find all customers named Jones who bought a book?

2. If you had a field with part numbers 1000 through 9999, what wildcard would you use to display part numbers 1000, 2000, 3000, and so on? What wildcard would you use to display part numbers 1011, 1111, 1211, 1311, and so on?
3. What are relational operators?
4. What are logical operators?

TOPIC 5-6
Adding, Updating, and Deleting Records

In this topic, we introduce you to the following procedures:

- Adding records
- Editing and updating records
- Deleting records

BACKGROUND

When adding, updating, or deleting records in a database file, many of the commands affect the current record. The current record is identified by a record pointer within the file (see Topic 5-4).

ADDING RECORDS

When you want to add new records into a file, you display a blank record on the screen and type in a new record, just as you entered the initial records in the file. Unlike a card index file, where you would want to insert the card in the proper order, the database management program will generally add it to the end of the file or insert it in an a space where you have previously deleted a record. New records can be added one after another without worrying about the order they are added in or where they are inserted in the file. After they have been entered, they can be easily sorted into any desired order.

If you want to insert a record into a file at a specific point, some programs let you do so. You first display the record you want the new record to be inserted below, and then use the INSERT command to enter the new record. Inserting records takes more time than adding them to the file because the program must make room for them between already existing files. It is like trying to squeeze one more person into a crowded elevator—the new file has to elbow its way in. To make room for the new record, the file must be resorted by the program, and this takes time. Table 5-17 describes the commands used to add records to a file.

TABLE 5-17
Commands Used to Add Records

Command	Description
APPEND	Adds a new record at the end of a database file. When the field names are displayed, you can use the commands described in Table 5-12 to enter and edit records.
BROWSE	Displays a blank record when in browse mode when you go to the last record and press ↓ (see Topic 5-4).
INSERT	Adds a new record at the position of the current record.

UPDATING RECORDS

It is often necessary to update records in a database file; for example, when employees change addresses, their records must be updated.

To do this, you first use the command to find the specific record to be updated and display it on the screen. You then revise the contents of the appropriate fields. Table 5-18 describes the commands used to update records.

TABLE 5-18
Commands Used to Update Records

Command	Description
BROWSE	Displays as many as seventeen records at a time on the screen. When in browse mode, you can press **Ctrl-Home** to display a menu of goto options. This menu also displays the FREEZE command that specifies a single field to be edited. (You cannot edit memo fields while in browse mode.)
EDIT	Displays a record for editing. For example, the command EDIT RECORD 1 displays all fields in record 1.
REPLACE	Replaces the current contents of a specified field with new contents. For example, the command REPLACE RECORD 1 AMOUNTS WITH 20.00 replaces the existing number in the AMOUNTS field in record 1 with 20.00.
CHANGE	Displays specified fields for editing. For example, the command CHANGE ALL FIELD DATE displays all DATE fields one after another so that you can change the dates, and the command CHANGE RECORD 1 FIELD DATE displays the contents of the DATE field for record 1.

DELETING RECORDS

If an employee leaves the company, or a product is no longer manufactured, or an item is consumed, its record in a database file is no longer needed. These unwanted records should be deleted from the file. Some programs, like dBASE III Plus, do not immediately delete records from the disk when you specify that they be deleted. The deleted record is just marked with an electronic flag. Although these flagged records are ignored when other file operations are used, they can often be recovered if needed and if another record has not been added in their place. Usually, they can be permanently removed by a separate operation called packing. Table 5-19 describes the commands used to delete records.

TABLE 5-19
Commands Used to Delete Records

Command	Description
BROWSE	Marks a record for deletion when in browse mode (see Topic 5-4) by highlighting it and then pressing **Ctrl-U**.
DELETE	Marks files for deletion. For example, entering DELETE RECORD 5 at the dot prompt marks record 5 for deletion. Records marked for deletion are indicated with asterisks next to the record number when you use the LIST or DISPLAY commands. They are indicated with the message *Del* on the status bar when you use the BROWSE or EDIT commands and the record is highlighted or displayed full screen.
RECALL	Recalls marked files so that they are not deleted when the file is packed. For example, entering RECALL RECORD 5 at the dot prompt removes the mark from record 5.
PACK	Permanently removes all records marked for deletion.

EXERCISE 133

Updating the NAMELIST File

In this exercise, you add, edit, and delete records in the NAMELIST file. To begin this exercise, you must load the program as described in Exercise 124.

Step 1. Retrieve an Existing File. First insert the disk you saved the NAMELIST file on into drive B. (If the menu is displayed, press **Esc** to display the dot prompt.)

To retrieve a file from the disk in drive B

Type   **SET MENU ON**, and then press **Return**.
Type   **SET DEFAULT TO B:**, and then press **Return**.
Type   **USE NAMELIST**, and then press **Return**.

Result. The disk spins as the file is loaded into the computer's memory, and then the dot prompt appears.

Step 2. Append a Record to the End of the File. In Exercise 127, you added records to the database file with the APPEND command. You can use this same command to add new records to the end of the file. Use this command to add the record shown in Figure 5-18.

To add a record with the append command

Type   **APPEND**, and then press **Return**.

Result. A blank record appears on the screen, and the status bar indicates it is at the end of the file *(EOF)*. Enter the record shown in Figure 5-19. When you enter the last field of the record, a new blank record is displayed. Press **PgUp** to return to the record you just added. Check it against Figure 5-18. When you are finished, press **Ctrl-End** to save the file and return to the dot prompt.

Step 3. Insert a Record. You can also insert a record at a specific point in the file. Here you use the GOTO command to move the record pointer to record 5, and then use the

FIGURE 5-18
Record to Append to
the NAMELIST File

```
ID:           109
LASTNAME:     Fiske
FIRST:        Robert
STREET:       1500 Storybrook
CITY:         Boston
ST:           MA
ZIP:          02098
AREA:         617
PHONE:        555-1008
```

INSERT command to insert the new record shown in Figure 5-19 as record 6. All the following records move down one record number.

To move the record pointer to record 5

Type   **GOTO 5**, and then press **Return**.

To insert a new record

Type   **INSERT**, and then press **Return**.

Result. A blank record appears on the screen, and the status bar indicates it is record 6 of 9. Enter the record shown in Figure 5-19. When you enter the last field of the record, the dot prompt reappears. Type **EDIT**, and then press **Return** to return to the record you just added. Check it against Figure 5-19. When you are finished, press **Ctrl-End** to save the file and return to the dot prompt.

FIGURE 5-19
Record to Append to
the AMOUNTS File

```
ID:           110
LASTNAME:     Porsena
FIRST:        Lars
STREET:       110 Millbrook
CITY:         Austin
ST:           TX
ZIP:          50000
AREA:         512
PHONE:        555-1009
```

Step 4. Add a Record with the Browse Command. You used the BROWSE command in a previous exercise to display records, but you can also use this command to enter new records. Here, use it to enter the record shown in Figure 5-20.

To add a record with the BROWSE command

Type   **BROWSE**, and then press **Return**.
Press   **PgUp** to display all records.
Press   ↓ to move the highlight to the last record.
Press   ↓ one more time, and the prompt reads *Add new records? (Y/N)*.
Press   **Y** to display a blank record.

Result. A new blank record is displayed on the screen. Enter the record shown in Figure 5-20. If the data you enter does not fill a field, press **End** or **Return** after entering each field to move the cursor to the next field. When you enter the last field of the record, a new blank record is displayed. Press ↑ to return to the record you just

FIGURE 5-20
Record to Add to
NAMELIST File with
BROWSE command.

```
ID:          111
LASTNAME:    Alverez
FIRST:       Jose
STREET:      25 Stuart Road
CITY:        Miami
ST:          FL
ZIP:         60000
AREA:        305
PHONE:       555-1010
```

added. Check it against Figure 5-20. When you are finished, press **Ctrl-End** to save the file and return to the dot prompt.

Step 5. Edit a Record. To edit a record, you simply display the record, and then you edit it. Here you change an address and phone number for someone who has moved.

To edit a specific record

Type   **EDIT 3**, and then press **Return**.

Result. The record is displayed on the screen.

To change Kendall's address and phone number

Press   ↓ to move the cursor to the STREET field.
Press   **Ctrl-Y** to delete the field's contents.
Type   **26 Rosewood**, and then press ↓ to move to the PHONE field.
Press   ← to move the cursor to the leftmost character in the field.
Press   **Ctrl-Y** to delete the field's contents.
Type   **555-1200**, and then the next record is displayed.
Press   **PgUp** to return to the record you edited, and then check it.
Press   **Ctrl-End** to exit and save the change.

Result. To see the changes, type **BROWSE**, and then press **Return**. Press **PgUp** once to display all the records. The records you added with the APPEND and BROWSE commands are at the end of the file, but the one you added with the INSERT command is not. Move the highlight to it (ID 110), and the status bar indicates it is record 6 of 11. When you are finished, press **Esc** to return to the dot prompt.

Step 6. Flag a Record for Deletion. When records are no longer needed, you can delete them from the file. This is a two-step process, first you flag them, and then you delete them.

To delete a record

Type   **DELETE RECORD 8**, and then press **Return**.

Result. The prompt, *1 record deleted*, appears. But the record has not actually been deleted; it has just been flagged for deletion.

To display the records in the file

Type   **BROWSE**, and then press **Return**.
Press   **PgUp** to display all records

Result. Move the highlight to the record with ID 107, and the status bar reads *Rec:* *8/11.* The message *Del* on the status bar indicates the record has been flagged for deletion though it is still in the file. Press ↑ to highlight the record above. The *Del* indicator is not displayed because that record has not been flagged for deletion. Press ↓ to move the highlight back to the deleted record, and the *Del* indicator reappears. Press **Esc** to return to the dot prompt. Type **LIST**, and then press **Return**. The same record is flagged with an asterisk. Let's recall the record so that it is no longer flagged for deletion.

Step 7. Recall the Flagged Record. After flagging a record for deletion, you can recall it, which removes the flag.

To recall the flagged record

Type   **RECALL ALL**, and then press **Return**.

Result. The message *1 record recalled* indicates the record has been recalled. To see this, type **BROWSE**, and then press **Return**. Press **PgUp** to see all of the records. Move the cursor to the record with ID 107 and the record is no longer flagged for deletion on the status bar. Press **Ctrl-U** a few times. This toggles deletion on and off when in BROWSE. Be sure the record is not flagged before continuing.

Step 8. Flag a Record for Deletion and Then Delete it. Now let's actually delete the record. Press **Esc** to return to the dot prompt.

To delete the record from the file

Type   **DELETE RECORD 8**, and then press **Return**.
Type   **PACK**, and then press **Return**.

Result. The message *10 records copied* indicates the record has been deleted, and only ten of the original eleven records remain.

Step 9. List and Print Remaining Files. To confirm that the record has been deleted, list the file on the screen, and then make a printout.

To toggle the printer on

Press   **Ctrl-P.**

To list records

Type   **LIST**, and then press **Return**.

To toggle the printer off

Press   **Ctrl-P.**

Result. The old record 8 for ID 107 is no longer listed, and all the remaining records have been sequentially renumbered in the leftmost column.

Step 10. Continue or Quit. You have now completed this exercise. Either close all open files and continue to the next exercise, or quit the program if you have finished. (Press **Esc** if necessary to remove the menu bar and return to the dot prompt.)

To close all database files

Type   **CLEAR ALL**, and then press **Return**.

To quit the program

Type   **QUIT**, and then press **Return**.

Result. If you quit the program, the operating system prompt reappears. Remove your disks, and then turn off the computer.

EXERCISE 134

Updating the AMOUNTS File

In this exercise, you add, edit, and delete records in the AMOUNTS file. To begin this exercise, you must load the program as described in Exercise 124.

Step 1. Open an Existing File. First insert the disk you saved the NAMELIST file on into drive B. (If the menu is displayed, press **Esc** to display the dot prompt.)

To turn on the menu and make B the default drive

Type   **SET MENU ON**, and then press **Return**.
Type   **SET DEFAULT TO B:**, and then press **Return**.

To display the assist menu

Type   **ASSIST**, and then press **Return**.

To retrieve a file from the disk in drive B

Press   **S** if necessary to pull down the Set Up menu.
Press   **Return** to select **Database file**.
Press   **Return** to select **B:**.
Press   ↓ to move the highlight to **AMOUNTS.DBF**, and then press **Return**. The prompt reads *Is this file indexed? [Y/N].*
Press   **N**.

Result. The disk spins as the file is loaded into the computer's memory, and then the menu reappears.

Step 2. Edit a Record. You can use the CHANGE command to edit a specific record.

To edit a file

Press   **U** to pull down the Update menu.
Press   ↓ to move the highlight to **Edit**, and then press **Return**.
Press   **PgDn** four times to display the record with the ID 105.
Press   **End** four times until the cursor is in the AMOUNT field.
Press   **Ctrl-Y** to delete the contents of the field.
Type   **30.00** and the next record is displayed.
Press   **Ctrl-End** to save the file.

Result. The change is saved, and the menu reappears.

Step 3. Edit a Record with the REPLACE Command. You can replace the contents of any record with the REPLACE command. To do so, you must first make the record you want to change the current record.

FIGURE 5-21
Record to Append to
AMOUNTS file.

```
ID:         109
DATE:       06/16/88
AMOUNT:     18.00
```

To move the record pointer

Press   **P** to pull down the Position menu.

Press   ↓ to move the highlight to **Goto record**, and then press **Return**.

Press   ↓ to move the highlight to **RECORD**, and then press **Return**. The prompt reads *Enter a numeric value:*.

Type   **5**, and then press **Return** to move the record pointer to record 5.

To replace the contents of a field

Press   **U** to pull down the Update menu.

Press   ↓ to move the highlight to **Replace**, and then press **Return**.

Press   ↓ to move the highlight to **AMOUNT**, and then press **Return**. The prompt reads *Enter a number or a numeric expression:*.

Type   **30.00**, and then press **Return**.

Press   **Esc**, and then highlight **Execute the command** to select and press **Return**. Message reads *1 record replaced*.

Press   any key to return to the menu.

Result. The number replaces the previous entry in the AMOUNT field of record 5.

Step 4. Append a Record to the End of the File. First, add the record shown in Figure 5-21 with the APPEND command.

To enter records into the file

Press   **U** if necessary to pull down the Update menu.

Press   ↑ to move the highlight to **Append**, and then press **Return**.

Result. The screen displays a blank record listing the three fields in the file. Enter the record shown in Figure 5-21. When you enter the last field of the record, a new blank record is displayed. Press **PgUp** to return to the record you entered. Check it against Figure 5-21. When you are finished, press **Ctrl-End** to save the file and return to the menu.

Step 5. Add Records with the BROWSE Command. Now, add the two records shown in Figure 5-22 with the BROWSE command.

FIGURE 5-22
Record to add to
AMOUNTS file with
BROWSE command.

```
ID:         110
DATE:       06/17/88
AMOUNT:     43.00

ID:         111
DATE:       06/18/88
AMOUNT:     61.00
```

To enter records into the file

Press   **U** if necessary to pull down the Update menu.

Press   ↓ to move the highlight to **Browse**, and then press **Return**.

Press   ↓ to move the highlight past the last record, and the prompt reads *Add new records? (Y/N)*.

Press   **Y**.

Result.   A new blank record is displayed on the screen. Enter the two records shown in Figure 5-22. When you enter the last field of the second record, a new blank record is displayed. Press ↑ to return to the records you just added. Check them against Figure 5-22. When you are finished, press **Ctrl-End** to save the file and return to the menu.

Step 6. Delete a Record.   In the previous exercise, you deleted record 8. Here, you want to delete the same record, but in this file, it is not record 8. Because the menu does not have an INSERT command, you added new records at the end of the file with the BROWSE command. The addition of these records at the end of the file does not affect the numbers of the records above them. To be safe, delete the record using the BROWSE command so you are sure you are deleting the correct record.

To mark a record to be deleted

Press   **U** if necessary to pull down the Update menu.

Press   ↓ if necessary to move the highlight to **Browse**, and then press **Return**.

Press   ↑ to move the highlight to the record with the ID 107.

Press   **Ctrl-U** to mark it for deletion. (The status bar reads *Del.*)

To delete the record

Press   **Ctrl-End** to save the deletion mark and return to the Update menu.

Press   ↓ to move the highlight to **Pack**, and then press **Return**.

Result.   The message indicates the number of records that have been copied, and the record flagged for deletion is not one of them. Press any key to return to the menu and then press **Esc** to return to the dot prompt.

Step 7. List and Print Remaining Files.   To confirm that the record has been deleted, list the file on the screen, and then make a printout.

To toggle the printer on

Press   **Ctrl-P**.

To list records

Type   **LIST**, and then press **Return**.

To toggle the printer off

Press   **Ctrl-P**.

Result.   The old record 8 for ID 107 is no longer listed, and all the remaining records have been sequentially renumbered. The amount in record 5 has changed to 30.00.

Step 8. Continue or Quit. You have now completed this exercise. Either close all open files and continue to the next exercise, or quit the program if you have finished. (Press **Esc** if necessary to remove the menu bar and return to the dot prompt.)

To close all database files

Type   **CLEAR ALL**, and then press **Return**.

To quit the program

Type   **QUIT**, and then press **Return**.

Result. If you quit the program, the operating system prompt reappears. Remove your disks, and then turn off the computer.

QUESTIONS

1. What is the difference between inserting a record and adding one?
2. When you add new records to a file, where are they stored in the file on the disk?
3. Why does inserting a record take longer than adding one to the end of the file?
4. When you delete a record, what does the program do before permanently deleting the record?
5. How can you delete a record when in browse mode?

TOPIC 5-7
Joining Database Files

In this topic, we introduce you to the following procedure:

■ Joining database files

BACKGROUND

Since data in a relational database is stored independently from the way it is viewed, you can change your view of the data at any time. This is done by joining existing tables in different combinations. The result of joining two tables is always another table. In many respects, this is much like a cut-and-paste operation where rows or columns are cut from different tables and joined into a new table.

If you have two files with a common field, you can join them into a third table. The JOIN command constructs a new table by combining fields in one table with fields in another table provided both have the same value in a specified common field. For example, both your NAMELIST and AMOUNTS files contain a common ID field that can be used to join them into new tables. All records that fail to have the same value in the common field are deleted from the new table.

To work with more than one file, you must load them both into memory. To do so, dBASE III allows you to divide the computer's available memory into ten independent work areas. You specify the areas and make them current with the SELECT command.

You join tables so that you can combine information from them. For example, you may have a table that contains only customer names and addresses and another that contains the dates and amounts of customer charges, as shown in Figure 5-23. The table listing names and addresses (Figure 5-23a) can be joined to the table listing dates and amounts of charges (Figure 5-23b) to create a new table that contains all the customer information (Figure 5-23c). The two tables are joined on the common information in the ID field. A typical join command might be written as

```
SELECT 1
USE AMOUNTS
SELECT 2
USE NAMELIST
JOIN WITH AMOUNTS TO NEWFILE1 FOR ID=AMOUNTS—>ID
USE NEWFILE1
LIST
```

■ SELECT 1 selects memory area 1, and USE AMOUNTS opens the AMOUNTS file in that memory area.

■ SELECT 2 selects memory area 2, and USE NAMELIST opens the NAMELIST file in that memory area.

■ JOIN specifies that the NAMELIST file in the current memory area is to be joined with the AMOUNTS file, and the new file is to be named NEWFILE1. The FOR part of the command specifies that the common field is the ID field. When the JOIN command is executed, a new table is created. The JOIN command automatically deletes duplicate data.

ID	LASTNAME	FIRST	STREET	CITY	ST	ZIP	AREA	PHONE
101	Culman	Tina	100 Elm Street	New Haven	CT	10000	203	555-1000
102	Benjamin	Nancy	25 Oak Street	Cambridge	MA	20000	617	555-1001
103	Kendall	Liz	14 Lark Ave.	Chicago	IL	20000	312	555-1002
104	Hogan	Dennis	40 Main Street	Edgewater	NJ	30000	201	555-1003
105	Swabey	Daphne	168 Bridge Road	Beverly	MA	20000	617	555-1004
106	Sobel	Carol	45 Porter Ave.	Fairlawn	NJ	30000	201	555-1005
107	Anthony	William	900 Maple Road	Reading	MA	20000	617	555-1006
108	Poe	James	10 Preston Lane	Oakland	CA	40000	415	555-1007

(a) NAMELIST File

ID	DATE	AMOUNT
101	06/08/88	10.00
102	06/09/88	15.00
103	06/10/88	35.00
104	06/11/88	25.00
105	06/12/88	20.00
106	06/13/88	50.00
107	06/14/88	15.00
108	06/15/88	10.00

(b) AMOUNTS File

ID	LASTNAME	FIRST	STREET	CITY	ST	ZIP	AREA	PHONE	DATE	AMOUNTS
101	Culman	Tina	100 Elm Street	New Haven	CT	10000	203	555-1000	06/08/88	10.00
102	Benjamin	Nancy	25 Oak Street	Cambridge	MA	20000	617	555-1001	06/09/88	15.00
103	Kendall	Liz	14 Lark Ave.	Chicago	IL	20000	312	555-1002	06/10/88	35.00
104	Hogan	Dennis	40 Main Street	Edgewater	NJ	30000	201	555-1003	06/11/88	25.00
105	Swabey	Daphne	168 Bridge Road	Beverly	MA	20000	617	555-1004	06/12/88	20.00
106	Sobel	Carol	45 Porter Ave.	Fairlawn	NJ	30000	201	555-1005	06/13/88	50.00
107	Anthony	William	900 Maple Road	Reading	MA	20000	617	555-1006	06/14/88	15.00
108	Poe	James	10 Preston Lane	Oakland	CA	40000	415	555-1007	06/15/88	10.00

(c) NEWFILE1 File

FIGURE 5-23
Joining records

EXERCISE 135

Joining Files

In this exercise, you join the NAMELIST and AMOUNTS files to form two new files named NEWFILE1 and NEWFILE2. To begin this exercise, you must load the program as described in Exercise 124.

Step 1. Open the Files. You can select more than one area in memory to open database files in. Here, you open two memory areas, and then open the NAMELIST and AMOUNTS files in them. (If the menu is displayed, press **Esc** to display the dot prompt.)

To select memory areas and assign files to them

Type   **SELECT 1**, and then press **Return**.
Type   **USE AMOUNTS**, and then press **Return**.
Type   **SELECT 2**, and then press **Return**.
Type   **USE NAMELIST**, and then press **Return**.

Result. The drive spins, and both files are now open in memory.

Step 2. Join Complete Files. First, join all fields from both files so that you have a new file that contains all the data from each file.

To join the files into a new file

Type   **JOIN WITH AMOUNTS TO NEWFILE1 FOR ID=AMOUNTS—>ID**, and then press **Return**.

Result. The drive spins, and in a moment, the message reads *10 records joined*, and the dot prompt reappears.

Step 3. Display the New File. Use the BROWSE command to display the new file.

To display the new file

Type   **USE NEWFILE1**, and then press **Return**.
Type   **BROWSE**, and then press **Return**.

Result. The new file appears on the screen and looks just like the original NAMELIST file. But the two fields combined from the AMOUNTS file are at the right side of the screen. To pan the screen back and forth, press **Ctrl-→** a few times to pan the file to the left. The new database file now contains DATE and AMOUNT fields. Press **Ctrl-←** a few times to pan the file to the right. Press **Esc** to leave browse mode and return to the dot prompt.

Step 4. Join Selected Fields. When you join two files, you need not combine all the fields. You can specify that selected fields be combined to form a new table. For example, suppose you want to know the names and phone numbers of people who have outstanding charges so that you can call them.

To join the files into a new file

Type   **USE NAMELIST**, and then press **Return**.
Type   **JOIN WITH AMOUNTS TO NEWFILE2 FOR ID=AMOUNTS—>ID FIELDS FIRST,LASTNAME,AMOUNT,PHONE**, and then press **Return**.

To display the new file

Type   **USE NEWFILE2**, and then press **Return**.
Type   **BROWSE**, and then press **Return**.

Result. The new file contains the first and last names and phone numbers from NAMELIST and the amounts from AMOUNTS. Press **Esc** to leave browse mode and return to the dot prompt.

Step 5. Continue or Quit. You have now completed this exercise. Either close all open files and continue to the next exercise, or quit the program if you have finished. (Press **Esc** if necessary to remove the menu bar and return to the dot prompt.)

To close all database files

Type   **CLEAR ALL**, and then press **Return**.

To quit the program

Type   **QUIT**, and then press **Return**.

Result. If you quit the program, the operating system prompt reappears. Remove your disks, and then turn off the computer.

QUESTIONS

1. Explain what the JOIN command does.
2. When joining two existing tables, what conditions must be met?
3. Explain what the SELECT command does.

TOPIC 5-8
Sorting Records

In this topic, we introduce you to the following procedure:
■ Sorting database files

BACKGROUND

Sorting a file rearranges the records into a specified order. To sort a file, you first determine what information is to be arranged in order. For example, you can sort the file so that the names are arranged alphabetically, or you can sort it so that a given set of numbers is arranged in ascending or descending order. Since these values are stored in fields, you actually specify what field is to be reordered and in what order its data is to be sorted. When the file is sorted based on a specific field, all the records are rearranged, not just the fields. When you specify which field is to be used, you are designating it as the key. You can often specify more than one key—one primary key and one or more secondary keys.

■ The primary key is the field that is sorted first. If you are sorting a list of names in the original file (Figure 5-24a), the primary key will sort it so that all the names are in ascending alphabetical order (Figure 5-24b). Ideally, a primary key contains unique information, for example, a driver's license number, an employee number, or a social security number.

■ In some cases, a unique field does not exist or serve your purpose, for example, when you sort a file by last names, and more than one last name is spelled the same way. In these cases, a perfect sort is not achieved using just a primary key; a secondary key, such as the first name, must be used to break ties. In Figure 5-25(a), which was sorted using last names as the primary key, all the Poes are together, but Poe, James is listed above Poe, Adam. Secondary keys are used to break ties in the file after it has been sorted by the primary key (Figure 5-25b).

ID	LASTNAME	FIRST	ID	LASTNAME	FIRST
101	Culman	Tina	107	Anthony	William
102	Benjamin	Nancy	102	Benjamin	Nancy
103	Kendall	Liz	101	Culman	Tina
104	Hogan	Dennis	104	Hogan	Dennis
105	Swabey	Daphne	103	Kendall	Liz
106	Sobel	Carol	108	Poe	James
107	Anthony	William	109	Poe	Adam
108	Poe	James	110	Poe	Zachery
109	Poe	Adam	106	Sobel	Carol
110	Poe	Zachery	105	Swabey	Daphne
(a) Original File			(b) Sorted File		

FIGURE 5-24
Sorting a file on a primary key.

ID	LASTNAME	FIRST	ID	LASTNAME	FIRST
107	Anthony	William	107	Anthony	William
102	Benjamin	Nancy	102	Benjamin	Nancy
101	Culman	Tina	101	Culman	Tina
104	Hogan	Dennis	104	Hogan	Dennis
103	Kendall	Liz	103	Kendall	Liz
108	Poe	James	109	Poe	Adam
109	Poe	Adam	108	Poe	James
110	Poe	Zachery	110	Poe	Zachery
106	Sobel	Carol	106	Sobel	Carol
105	Swabey	Daphne	105	Swabey	Daphne
(a) File Sorted with Primary Key			(B) File Sorted with Secondary Key		

FIGURE 5-25
Sorting a file on a secondary key.

EXERCISE 136

Sorting the NEWFILE1 File

In this exercise, you sort the NEWFILE1 file you created in Exercise 135 by joining the original NAMELIST and AMOUNTS files. To begin this exercise, you must load the program as described in Exercise 124.

Step 1. Open an Existing File. First insert the disk you saved the NEWFILE1 file on into drive B. (If the menu is displayed, press **Esc** to display the dot prompt.)

To retrieve a file from the disk in drive B

Type   **SET MENU ON**, and then press **Return**.
Type   **SET DEFAULT TO B:**, and then press **Return**.
Type   **USE NEWFILE1**, and then press **Return**.

Result. The disk spins as the file is loaded into the computer's memory, and then the dot prompt appears.

Step 2. Sort a File. A file can be easily sorted on any field. Let's sort the file alphabetically by LASTNAME. When sorting files, you do not sort the original file; you create and name a new file that the sorted file is stored in.

To sort the file

Type   **SORT ON LASTNAME TO TEMP**, and then press **Return**.

Result. The drive spins as the file NAMELIST is written to a new file TEMP, where it is sorted alphabetically by LASTNAME. In a moment, the message *100% Sorted 10 Records sorted* appears along with the dot prompt.

To display the sorted file

Type   **USE TEMP**, and then press **Return**.
Type   **BROWSE**, and then press **Return**.

Result. The file is displayed in sorted order. All records are arranged by last name in ascending order. Press **Esc** to return to the dot prompt.

To display the original unsorted file

Type   **USE NEWFILE1**, and then press **Return**.
Type   **BROWSE**, and then press **Return**.

Result. The original file remains unchanged. Press **Esc** to return to the dot prompt.

Step 3. Continue or Quit. You have now completed this exercise. Either close all open files and continue to the next exercise, or quit the program if you have finished. (Press **Esc** if necessary to remove the menu bar and return to the dot prompt.)

To close all database files

Type   **CLEAR ALL**, and then press **Return**.

To quit the program

Type   **QUIT**, and then press **Return**.

Result. If you quit the program, the operating system prompt reappears. Remove your disks, and then turn off the computer.

QUESTIONS

1. Why might you want to sort a file?
2. What is the purpose of a primary key? A secondary key?
3. What is a tie in a sort?

TOPIC 5-9
Indexing Records

In this topic, we introduce you to the following procedure:
■ Indexing database files

BACKGROUND

Sorting is not always the best way to arrange a list for two reasons.
■ It can take a long time to sort an entire file if the list is long.
■ A file can be sorted in only one order at a time. For example, a name and address file used for mailings might be sorted by last name to produce a reference list. It would then be sorted by ZIP code for printing mailing labels because the post office gives reduced rates for mailings that are presorted by ZIP code. To maintain lists like these in more than one order, you would need separate files, each sorted differently.

To overcome these problems, some database management programs, including dBASE III Plus, have an index capability. To understand the difference between sorting and indexing, let's look at how a database management program finds a specific record without, and then with, an index.

Sequential Files

Records are physically stored in a file on the disk much like pages are organized in a book. When you sequentially search a file for a specific record, the program begins at the beginning of the file, and reads each record until it finds the one you want. If you create a file with many records, the data cannot all fit in the computer's memory at the same time. Much of it will be stored on one or more disks and read into memory as needed. When the program tries to sequentially find a file, it begins to read these records into memory in batches, looking for the record it wants. If it does not find the record, it replaces the first batch of records in memory with others from the disk and continues to look. Retrieving data from disks is a slow process compared to the speed of processing the records once they are in memory. It can take a long time just to find a specific record. If the program is also sorting the file into a specific order, it can go on for hours rearranging the records a few at a time.

Suppose your file has 10,000 records in it, and you want to find a specific record. Sequentially finding this record would be time consuming, especially if it were near the end of the file. As often as not, the program would have to read half the file, 5,000 records, before it found the record you wanted. Sequential file scans are fine if you always need to look at or process all the records in a file. But if you want to find only specific records, this method may not be satisfactory. The solution to this problem is to have the program index the file.

Indexed Files

Indexed files were developed to overcome the problems of using sequential files. The idea behind an indexed file is similar to the idea of an index at the back of a book. The index allows you to look up a term and go directly to where it is discussed. This is called direct access. Then you can sequentially search from there to find the exact place on the page. This combination of direct access and sequential search is called the index-sequential method.

As you enter records into a file, the program numbers them sequentially. These numbers represent the order in which they are physically stored in the file. This order is usually the one the records were entered in unless the entire file has been sorted.

To index a file, you select a field you want it indexed by. Ideally, this is a field that contains unique values. Once you specify the field, the program creates a shorter companion file for the index. The index usually contains the following:

- The actual contents of the field you are indexing the file by. The other data in the file is not used in the index because this would slow down a search operation. The field's contents are now organized in ascending order, and the record numbers are out of order. You need not index an entire file; instead, you can specify criteria in the command so that only certain records are indexed. This keeps the index short and speeds up the search process even more.

- Pointers, or index numbers, that give the physical location of where the records are stored in the file on the disk.

When you use an index to find a particular record, you specify the value to be looked for in the indexed field. The program first reads the index file and scans the records there. Since the index is generally much smaller than the file, this can be done quickly. When it finds a record that matches the search criteria you entered, it looks for its record number, or pointer, and goes directly to the place on the disk where that record is stored. The computer then starts reading data records from that point until it finds the record it is looking for or one that has a higher key. If it finds a higher key, it knows the record it is looking for does not exist.

Indexes allow you to keep a file in order by several keys without having to physically resort it each time or maintain duplicate files. For example, the original file can have two indexes, one sorting it by department and another by phone number.

Indexes do have a few drawbacks. Since they are automatically updated, making a small change in a field takes longer than it would without the index. Since you can have more than one index for each file, changes can take a long time. And indexes are like any other file; they take up disk storage space.

When working with indexes, keep the following points in mind:

- You can have more than one index per file. This allows you to maintain the file in different orders at the same time. For example, one index can be by name, another by amount owed, and a third on date of last purchase.

- Some programs allow you to specify more than one field in the index (multiple-field indexes), for example, only those records that meet a specified condition. An example might be to index names where the amount owed is overdue by more than sixty days.

- Some programs allow you to index large indexes so that they can be scanned faster. This breaks a search into two steps. The program uses the first index to find a record in the second index and, from there, finds its location in the file.

- Once you have created an index, some programs automatically maintain it. If you add, insert, or delete records in the file, these programs automatically update the index.

EXERCISE 137

Indexing the NEWFILE1 File

In this exercise, you index the NEWFILE1 file you created in Exercise 135 by joining the original NAMELIST and AMOUNTS files. To begin this exercise, you must load the program as described in Exercise 124.

Step 1. Open an Existing File. First insert the disk you saved the NEWFILE1 file on into drive B. (If the menu is displayed, press **Esc** to display the dot prompt.)

To retrieve a file from the disk in drive B

Type   **SET MENU ON**, and then press **Return**.
Type   **SET DEFAULT TO B:**, and then press **Return**.
Type   **USE NEWFILE1**, and then press **Return**.

Result. The disk spins as the file is loaded into the computer's memory, and then the dot prompt appears.

Step 2. Index a File. dBASE III Plus allows you to index a file, a fast and versatile way to arrange files in order. Indexing must also be done before you can use commands like FIND that locate specific records.

To index the file

Type   **INDEX ON LASTNAME TO LAST**, and then press **Return**.

Result. In a moment, the message reads *100% indexed 10 Records indexed*, and the dot prompt reappears.

To see the results

Type   **SET INDEX TO LAST**, and then press **Return**.
Type   **BROWSE**, and then press **Return**.

Result. The original file now appears in sorted order although the records in the file have not been physically sorted. To see this, first press **Esc** to return to the dot prompt.

To see the original file

Type   **CLEAR ALL**, and then press **Return**.
Type   **USE NEWFILE1**, and then press **Return**.
Type   **BROWSE**, and then press **Return**.

Result. The original file appears in its unsorted order. Press **Esc** to return to the dot prompt.

Step 3. Use Multiple Indexes. One of the advantages of indexes is that a file can be kept in more than one order. To do this, you create additional indexes. Let's create a new index based on the ST field and then look at the file using this new index and the LAST index created previously.

To create a second index

Type   **INDEX ON ST TO STATE**, and then press **Return**.

Result. In a moment, the message reads *100% indexed 10 Records indexed*, and the dot prompt reappears. Let's use the new index to view the file.

To see the results

Type   **SET INDEX TO STATE**, and then press **Return**.
Type   **BROWSE**, and then press **Return**.

Result. The file now appears sorted by state. Press **Esc** to return to the dot prompt. Let's look at the file indexed by last name. To do this, you first must specify the index.

To see the file indexed by LASTNAME

Type   **SET INDEX TO LAST**, and then press **Return**.
Type   **BROWSE**, and then press **Return**.

Result.   The file appears sorted by last name. Press **Esc** to return to the dot prompt.

Step 4. Update Indexes Automatically.   One of the advantages of indexes is that when you make changes to the file, they are automatically reflected in the indexes. Let's see how this works when you add a new record to the file. First you must make both indexes active.

To update indexes automatically

Type   **SET INDEX TO LAST,STATE**, and then press **Return**.
Type   **APPEND**, and then press **Return**.

Result.   A blank input form for record 8 appears. Enter the new record shown in Figure 5-26, press **PgUp** to review it, and then press **Ctrl-End** to save it and return to the dot prompt.

FIGURE 5-26
New record added to indexed file.

```
ID:                     112
LASTNAME:               Davis
FIRST:                  John
STREET:                 26 Alpine Road
CITY:                   Elmherst
ST:                     IL
ZIP:                    50000
AREA:                   312
PHONE:                  555-1020
DATE:                   06/19/88
AMOUNT:                 75.00
```

To display the physical file

Type   **USE NEWFILE1**, and then press **Return**.
Type   **BROWSE**, and then press **Return**.

Result.   All records appear in their original order as indicated by the record numbers (press **PgUp**, if necessary, to see them all). The new entry appears as record 11 at the end of the file. New records are always appended at the end of the file. Press **Esc** to return to the dot prompt.

To display the file indexed by LASTNAME

Type   **SET INDEX TO LAST**, and then press **Return**.
Type   **BROWSE**, and then press **Return**.

Result.   Press **PgUp** to display all records. The file appears sorted by last name with Davis in the correct position in the list. Press **Esc** to return to the dot prompt.

To display the file indexed by ST

Type   **SET INDEX TO STATE**, and then press **Return**.
Type   **BROWSE**, and then press **Return**.

Result. The file appears sorted by state with Davis's state, IL, listed in the correct position in the file. Press **Esc** to return to the dot prompt.

Step 5. Find a Specific Record. dBASE III Plus finds specific records using the FIND command. This command (like many others) works only on indexed files, and the index must be active. When using this command, be careful about uppercase and lowercase characters. If a field has been entered as Kendall, trying to find kendall or KENDALL will cause the program to display the message *No find*. The FIND command looks for the first characters you specify in the field. You can enter either a complete name or a partial name.

To display the record for Kendall

Type   **SET INDEX TO LAST**, and then press **Return**.
Type   **FIND Kendall**, and then press **Return**.
Type   **DISPLAY**, and then press **Return**.

To display the record for Davis

Type   **FIND Dav**, and then press **Return**.
Type   **DISPLAY**, and then press **Return**.

To display the next record as it appears in the index

Type   **SKIP**, and then press **Return**.
Type   **DISPLAY**, and then press **Return**.

To display the record with an amount of $25.00

Type   **FIND 25.00**, and then press **Return**.

Result. The program displays the message *No find*. This is because the program can find only records that have been indexed on the field you want to search. Let's see how this is done.

To display the record with an amount of $25.00

Type   **INDEX ON AMOUNT TO AMOUNT**, and then press **Return**.
Type   **SET INDEX TO AMOUNT**, and then press **Return**.
Type   **FIND 25.00**, and then press **Return**.
Type   **DISPLAY**, and then press **Return**.

Result. Now the record appears because you indexed the file on the field being searched and then used that index to locate the record with the FIND command.

Step 6. Print a Group of Records. You can display groups of records on the screen and send them to the printer for a hard copy at the same time. Before proceeding, make sure the printer is on and has paper in it.

To print a group of records

Type   **SET PRINT ON**, and then press **Return**.
Type   **DISPLAY FIRST,LASTNAME,AREA,PHONE FOR ST="MA"**, and then press **Return**.

Result. The three records matching the criteria are displayed on the screen and sent to the printer. To turn off the printer, type **SET PRINT OFF**, and then press **Return**.

Step 7. Continue or Quit. You have now completed this exercise. Either close all open files and continue to the next exercise, or quit the program if you have finished. (Press **Esc** if necessary to remove the menu bar and return to the dot prompt.)

To close all database files

Type   **CLEAR ALL**, and then press **Return**.

To quit the program

Type   **QUIT**, and then press **Return**.

Result. If you quit the program, the operating system prompt reappears. Remove your disks, and then turn off the computer.

QUESTIONS

1. What are two major advantages of using indexes? What is the primary disadvantage?
2. What is the difference between sorting and indexing a file?
3. Describe direct access.
4. Under what conditions can you use the FIND command, and what does it do?

TOPIC 5-10
Making Calculations

In this topic, we introduce you to the following procedure:
- Using functions to make calculations

BACKGROUND

dBASE III Plus has three functions you can use to calculate data stored in fields in database files. Table 5-20 describes these three functions.

TABLE 5-20
Statistical Functions

Function	Description
AVERAGE	Calculates the average in a specified numeric field
SUM	Calculates the total in a specified numeric field
COUNT	Counts the number of records that meet a specified criterion

EXERCISE 138

Calculating with Functions

In this exercise, you use functions to calculate fields in the NEWFILE1 file. To begin this exercise, you must load the program as described in Exercise 124.

Step 1. Open an Existing File. First insert the disk you saved the NEWFILE1 file on into drive B. (If the menu is displayed, press **Esc** to display the dot prompt.)

To retrieve a file from the disk in drive B

Type   **SET MENU ON**, and then press **Return**.
Type   **SET DEFAULT TO B:**, and then press **Return**.
Type   **USE NEWFILE1**, and then press **Return**.

Result. The disk spins as the file is loaded into the computer's memory, and then the dot prompt appears.

Step 2. Calculate Sums, Averages, and Counts. You can make calculations based on the records in the file.

To calculate a total for all records

Type   **SUM AMOUNT**, and then press **Return**.

Result. The total in the AMOUNT field of all records is 372.00.

To calculate an average for all records

Type   **AVERAGE AMOUNT**, and then press **Return**.

Result. The average in the AMOUNT field of all records is 33.82.

To calculate a total for selected records

Type   **SUM AMOUNT FOR ST="MA"**, and then press **Return**.

Result. The total in the AMOUNT field of the three records from Massachusetts is 63.00.

To calculate an average for selected records

Type   **AVERAGE AMOUNT FOR ST="MA"**, and then press **Return**.

Result. The average in the AMOUNT field of the three records from Massachusetts is 21.00.

To calculate a total for a specific record

Type   **SUM AMOUNT FOR LASTNAME="Davis"**, and then press **Return**.

Result. The sum for Davis is 75.00.

To count the AMOUNTS greater than 25

Type   **COUNT FOR AMOUNT>25**, and then press **Return**.

Result. Six records have amounts greater than 25.

Step 3. Continue or Quit. You have now completed this exercise. Either close all open files and continue to the next exercise, or quit the program if you have finished. (Press **Esc** if necessary to remove the menu bar and return to the dot prompt.)

To close all database files

Type   **CLEAR ALL**, and then press **Return**.

To quit the program

Type   **QUIT**, and then press **Return**.

Result. If you quit the program, the operating system prompt reappears. Remove your disks, and then turn off the computer.

QUESTIONS

1. What three calculations can you perform with dBASE III Plus?
2. What is the command for finding the average of all records where the amount for each record is stored in a field named TOTAL?
3. What is the command for displaying the total for a specific record for Smith?

TOPIC 5-11
Printing Reports

In this topic, we introduce you to the following procedure:

■ Printing reports

BACKGROUND

Most people in a business do not actually use the database file itself. Generally, they use reports created from part of the information stored in the file. The file might contain information about all aspects of the business. Reports are then designed to organize specific information needed by different people such as the sales manager, the president, or the finance department. Each report provides only the information needed by the person it is printed for. Reports consist of selected fields from selected records.

Reports are usually in tabular form, with information arranged in rows and columns. The typical report (Figure 5-27) contains the following information:

■ A heading that identifies the report.
■ A heading for each column.
■ The columns that contain data from selected fields.
■ Totals and subtotals (for groups of records), which can be printed by entering "report breaks" to indicate what records are to be included. Some programs allow you to have more than one level of break so that you can print subtotals within subtotals.

Reports are created in five basic steps and then printed.

1. Decide what fields are to be included in the report. A report does not have to print out all the data contained in a database file. Selected fields can be printed so that the report is customized for the use it is being put to. For example, you might have a file that contains names, addresses, and items purchased. When you print a report, you might want to list only the names and addresses of your customers.

2. Lay out the order the fields are printed in. Reports are arranged in rows and columns much like a table. But you can specify the order the columns are arranged in.

3. Sort or index the file so that it will print data in a desired order.

4. Specify the criteria, if any (see Topic 5-5). This allows you to print selected records and selected fields from those records.

5. Specify if there are to be totals or subtotals calculated for numeric fields. To do this, you specify the field that will be totaled. This field is not the field that contains the numbers to be totaled but any field that contains duplicate data. For example, in the report shown in Figure 5-27, the file contains a field named ST (for state) and a field named AMOUNT. To prepare a report that subtotaled amounts by state, it would be sorted or indexed so that all identical items are listed together, and then the ST field would be specified as the criterion for subtotals to generate the report shown. Some programs let you create subtotals at various levels.

Since it takes time to format a report, most programs, like dBASE III Plus, allow you to save the formats you create so that you can use them again. You assign each

```
Page No.      1
11/03/87
                              AMOUNTS DUE

    FIRST NAME   LAST NAME    AREA CODE PHONE #    AMOUNT DUE


    ** Amounts due from state: CA
      James        Poe           415       555-1007      10.00
    ** Subtotal **
                                                         10.00


    ** Amounts due from state: CT
      Tina         Culman        203       555-1000      10.00
    ** Subtotal **
                                                         10.00


    ** Amounts due from state: FL
      Jose         Alverez       305       555-1010      61.00
    ** Subtotal **
                                                         61.00


    ** Amounts due from state: IL
      Liz          Kendall       312       555-1200      35.00
      John         Davis         312       555-1020      75.00
    ** Subtotal **
                                                        110.00


    ** Amounts due from state: MA
      Nancy        Benjamin      617       555-1212      15.00
      Daphne       Swabey        617       555-1004      30.00
      Robert       Fiske         617       555-1008      18.00
    ** Subtotal **
                                                         63.00


    ** Amounts due from state: NJ
      Dennis       Hogan         201       555-1003      25.00
      Carol        Sobel         201       555-1005      50.00
    ** Subtotal **
                                                         75.00


    ** Amounts due from state: TX
      Lars         Porsena       512       555-1009      43.00
    ** Subtotal **
                                                         43.00
    *** Total ***
                                                        372.00
```

FIGURE 5-27
Typical report.

format a name, and it is saved on the disk where it can be retrieved the next time you need it.

When preparing a report with dBASE III Plus, you execute the CREATE REPORT command. If you later want to change the report format, you use the MODIFY REPORT command. When modifying a report, you can scroll the screen display with the commands described in Table 5-21.

TABLE 5-21
Modify Report Commands

To Scroll File Structure Display	Press
Up	Ctrl-→ or Ctrl-B
Down	Ctrl-← or Ctrl-Z

Printing Reports

In this exercise, you open the NEWFILE1 file you created in Exercise 135 by joining the NAMELIST and AMOUNTS files. You then create and print a variety of reports. To begin this exercise, you must load the program as described in Exercise 124.

Step 1. Open an Existing File. First insert the disk you saved the NEWFILE1 file on into drive B. (If the menu is displayed, press **Esc** to display the dot prompt.)

To retrieve a file from the disk in drive B

Type   **SET MENU ON**, and then press **Return**.
Type   **SET DEFAULT TO B:**, and then press **Return**.
Type   **USE NEWFILE1**, and then press **Return**.

Result. The disk spins as the file is loaded into the computer's memory, and then the dot prompt appears.

Step 2. Print a Report of All Records. Once you have created a database file, you can generate a variety of reports that display the information in the file on the screen or in a printout. These tables can include all fields and records or selected fields and records. Here, you display a report on the screen that contains only the first name, last name, area code, and phone number fields from all records. You then send the report to the printer.

To name the file the report format will be saved in

Type   **CREATE REPORT**, and then press **Return**. The prompt reads *Enter report file name:*.
Type   **PHONE**, and then press **Return**.

Result. The Options menu is displayed (Figure 5-28).

To add a heading and change a format

Press   **Return** to select **Page title**.
Type   **PHONE NUMBERS** in the page heading area.
Press   **Ctrl-End** to save the title.

To specify the first field and heading

Press   **C** to pull down the Columns menu.
Press   **Return** to select **Contents**.
Press   **F10** to display a list of field names.
Press   ↓ to move the highlight to **FIRST**, and then press **Return** two times.
Press   ↓ to move the highlight to **Heading**, and then press **Return**.
Type   **FIRST NAME**, and then press **Ctrl-End**.
Press   ↓ to move the highlight to **Width**, and then press **Return**.
Type   **11**, and then press **Return**.

To specify the second field and heading

Press   **PgDn** to display a new column form.
Press   **Return** to select **Contents**.
Press   **F10** to display a list of field names.

Press	↓ to move the highlight to **LASTNAME**, and then press **Return** two times.
Press	↓ to move the highlight to **Heading**, and then press **Return**.
Type	**LAST NAME**, and then press **Ctrl-End**.
Press	↓ to move the highlight to **Width**, and then press **Return**.
Type	**11**, and then press **Return**.

To specify the third field and heading

Press	**PgDn** to display a new column form.
Press	**Return** to select **Contents**.
Press	**F10** to display a list of field names.
Press	↓ to move the highlight to **AREA**, and then press **Return** two times.
Press	↓ to move the highlight to **Heading**, and then press **Return**.
Type	**AREA CODE**, and then press **Ctrl-End**.
Press	↓ to move the highlight to **Width**, and then press **Return**.
Type	**9**, and then press **Return**.

To specify the fourth field and heading

Press	**PgDn** to display a new column form.
Press	**Return** to select **Contents**.
Press	**F10** to display a list of field names.
Press	↓ to move the highlight to **PHONE**, and then press **Return** two times.
Press	↓ to move the highlight to **Heading**, and then press **Return**.
Type	**PHONE #**, and then press **Ctrl-End**.
Press	↓ to move the highlight to **Width**, and then press **Return**.
Type	**9**, and then press **Return**.

To save the report form

Press	**E** to pull down the Exit menu.
Press	**Return** to select **Save**.

Result. The drive spins, and the report form is saved onto the disk.

Step 3. Display the Report on the Screen. Now that you have defined the report format, you can use it to display the database file on the screen.

To display the report on the screen

Type	**USE NEWFILE1 INDEX LAST**, and then press **Return**.
Type	**REPORT FORM PHONE**, and then press **Return**.

Result. The report scrolls onto the screen. All eleven records are listed but only four of the original eight fields. The address, date, and amount information is not included. And the order of the fields is different from the way it appears in the file. First names are now listed before last names. The files are arranged by state, a field that has not been displayed. Let's change the order by creating a new index.

To change the order in which records appear in the report

Type	**INDEX ON AREA TO AREA**, and then press **Return**.
Type	**SET INDEX TO AREA**, and then press **Return**.
Type	**REPORT FORM PHONE**, and then press **Return**.

Result. The report scrolls onto the screen. The report is now in order by area code. After creating a report, you can change the way information in it is arranged by using a new index, as you did here.

To print the report

Type	**SET PRINT ON**, and then press **Return**.
Type	**REPORT FORM PHONE**, and then press **Return**.

Result. The report scrolls onto the screen and prints on the printer.

Step 4. Display Reports of Selected Records. Now, display reports of selected records.

To display records with MA in the ST field

Type	**SET PRINT OFF**, and then press **Return**.
Type	**REPORT FORM PHONE FOR ST="MA"**, and then press **Return**.

Result. The three records that meet the criterion are displayed on the screen.

To display records with amounts greater than 30

Type	**REPORT FORM PHONE FOR AMOUNT>30**, and then press **Return**.

Result. The five records that meet the criterion are displayed on the screen. Press **Return**, if necessary to return to the dot prompt.

Step 5. Print a Report with Subtotals. Now, let's prepare a report that prints subtotals for states.

To specify the name of the report format

Type	**CREATE REPORT AMOUNTS**, and then press **Return**.

Result. The Options menu is displayed (Figure 5-28).

To add a heading and change a format

Press	**Return** to select **Page title**.
Type	**AMOUNTS DUE** in the page heading area.
Press	**Ctrl-End** to save the title.

FIGURE 5-28
Report form screen

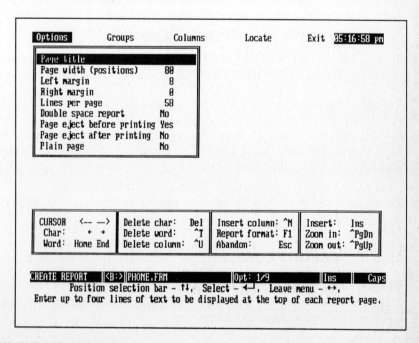

To specify the field to group subtotals on

Press	**G** to pull down the Groups menu.
Press	**Return** to select **Group on expression**.
Press	**F10** to display a list of field names.
Press	↓ to move the highlight to **ST**, and then press **Return** two times.
Press	↓ to move the highlight to **Group heading**, and then press **Return**.
Type	**AMOUNTS DUE FROM:**, and then press **Return**.

To specify the first field and heading

Press	**C** to pull down the Columns menu.
Press	**Return** to select **Contents**.
Press	**F10** to display a list of field names.
Press	↓ to move the highlight to **FIRST**, and then press **Return** two times.
Press	↓ to move the highlight to **Heading**, and then press **Return**.
Type	**FIRST NAME**, and then press **Ctrl-End**.
Press	↓ to move the highlight to **Width**, and then press **Return**.
Type	**11**, and then press **Return**.

To specify the second field and heading

Press	**PgDn** to display a new column form.
Press	**Return** to select **Contents**.
Press	**F10** to display a list of field names.
Press	↓ to move the highlight to **LASTNAME**, and then press **Return** two times.
Press	↓ to move the highlight to **Heading**, and then press **Return**.
Type	**LAST NAME**, and then press **Ctrl-End**.
Press	↓ to move the highlight to **Width**, and then press **Return**.
Type	**11**, and then press **Return**.

To specify the third field and heading

Press	**PgDn** to display a new column form.
Press	**Return** to select **Contents**.
Press	**F10** to display a list of field names.
Press	↓ to move the highlight to **AREA**, and then press **Return** two times.
Press	↓ to move the highlight to **Heading**, and then press **Return**.
Type	**AREA CODE**, and then press **Ctrl-End**.
Press	↓ to move the highlight to **Width**, and then press **Return**.
Type	**9**, and then press **Return**.

To specify the fourth field and heading

Press	**PgDn** to display a new column form.
Press	**Return** to select **Contents**.
Press	**F10** to display a list of field names.
Press	↓ to move the highlight to **PHONE**, and then press **Return** two times.
Press	↓ to move the highlight to **Heading**, and then press **Return**.
Type	**PHONE #**, and then press **Ctrl-End**.
Press	↓ to move the highlight to **Width**, and then press **Return**.
Type	**9**, and then press **Return**.

To specify the fifth field and heading

Press	**PgDn** to display a new column form.
Press	**Return** to select **Contents**.
Press	**F10** to display a list of field names.

Press	↓ to move the highlight to **AMOUNT**, and then press **Return** two times.
Press	↓ to move the highlight to **Heading**, and then press **Return**.
Type	**AMOUNT DUE**, and then press **Ctrl-End**.
Press	↓ to move the highlight to **Width**, and then press **Return**.
Type	**10**, and then press **Return**.

To save the report form

Press	**E** to pull down the Exit menu.
Press	**Return** to select **Save**.

Result. The drive spins, and the report form is saved onto the disk.

To display the report on the screen

Type	**USE NEWFILE1**, and then press **Return**.
Type	**SET INDEX TO STATE**, and then press **Return**.
Type	**REPORT FORM AMOUNTS**, and then press **Return**.

Result. The report scrolls onto the screen. All eleven records are listed but only four of the original eight fields. The address information is not included. And the order of the fields is different from the way it appears in the file. First names are now listed before last names.

To send the report to the printer

Type	**REPORT FORM AMOUNTS TO PRINT**, and then press **Return**.

Result. The selected records are printed on the printer along with subtotals. The command to print is different from the one you used last time. This form does not require that you set the printer to off when the command is completed. It is automatically turned off.

Step 6. Continue or Quit. You have now completed this exercise. Either close all open files and continue to the next exercise, or quit the program if you have finished. (Press **Esc** if necessary to remove the menu bar and return to the dot prompt.)

To close all database files

Type	**CLEAR ALL**, and then press **Return**.

To quit the program

Type	**QUIT**, and then press **Return**.

Result. If you quit the program, the operating system prompt reappears. Remove your disks, and then turn off the computer.

QUESTIONS

1. Define a report as opposed to a database file.
2. What information does a typical report contain?
3. What are the five basic steps to create reports?
4. If you had a database file with a field named ITEMS that contained item numbers and a field named AMOUNT that contained the number of each item in inventory, what field would you specify that subtotals be grouped on?
5. What command do you use to rearrange information in a report after you have created its format?

TOPIC 5-12
Restructuring the Database

In this topic, we introduce you to the following procedure:
- Modifying the structure of a database file

BACKGROUND

There are times when a database has to be changed after it has been created. Changes might include adding new fields or modifying the definition of existing ones. For example, what if one field contains ZIP codes, and the characteristics of ZIP codes change (as they recently did). The ZIP code field was initially five characters long. But the new ZIP code field might have to be ten characters long.

If a change like this is necessary, the file can be restructured. This is usually done by copying the file's contents to a temporary file while the original file is being restructured. When the restructuring is complete, the contents are copied from the temporary file back into the restructured file.

When restructuring files, keep the following points in mind:
- If the restructuring adds new fields, those fields are blank.
- You may not be able to make two changes at the same time, for example, the name of the field and the length of the field. If you do, the field may be left blank.
- If a numeric field is redefined as a character field, or other field type, it will be left blank.

EXERCISE 140

Modifying the NAMELIST File

In this exercise, you modify the structure of the NAMELIST file to increase the width of the ZIP code field. To begin this exercise, you must load the program as described in Exercise 124.

Step 1. Open an Existing File. First turn on the menu, set the default drive, and load the file into memory. (If the menu is displayed, press **Esc** to display the dot prompt.)

To retrieve a file from the disk in drive B

Type   **SET MENU ON**, and then press **Return**.
Type   **SET DEFAULT TO B:**, and then press **Return**.
Type   **USE NAMELIST**, and then press **Return**.

Result. The disk spins as the file is loaded into the computer's memory, and then the dot prompt appears.

Step 2. Modify the File's Structure. Now, use the command that displays the file's structure on the screen so that it can be modified.

To modify the files structure

Type   **MODIFY STRUCTURE**, and then press **Return**.

Result. The file's structure is displayed on the screen (Figure 5-29).

FIGURE 5-29
The file's structure

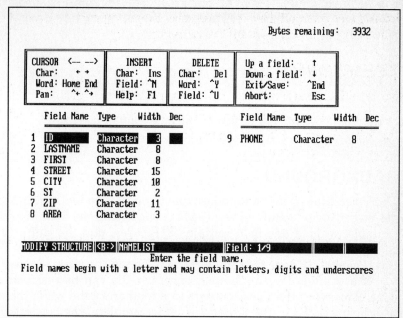

Bytes remaining: 3932

CURSOR <— —>	INSERT	DELETE	Up a field: ↑
Char: ← →	Char: Ins	Char: Del	Down a field: ↓
Word: Home End	Field: ^N	Word: ^Y	Exit/Save: ^End
Pan: ^← ^→	Help: F1	Field: ^U	Abort: Esc

	Field Name	Type	Width	Dec			Field Name	Type	Width	Dec
1	ID	Character	3			9	PHONE	Character	8	
2	LASTNAME	Character	8							
3	FIRST	Character	8							
4	STREET	Character	15							
5	CITY	Character	10							
6	ST	Character	2							
7	ZIP	Character	11							
8	AREA	Character	3							

MODIFY STRUCTURE <B:> NAMELIST   Field: 1/9

Enter the field name.
Field names begin with a letter and may contain letters, digits and underscores

To modify the structure of the ZIP field

Move   the highlight to the ZIP field.

Press   **End** two times to move the cursor to the *Width* highlight.

Type   **11**, and then press **Return**.

Press   **Ctrl-End** to save the change, and the prompt reads *Press ENTER to confirm. Any other key to resume.*

Press   **Return**, and in a few moments, the dot prompt reappears.

Result. Type **BROWSE**, and then press **Return** to display the records in the file (press **PgUp** if necessary to display them all). The ZIP field is now wider. Press **Esc** to leave browse mode and return to the dot prompt.

Step 3. Print Out the File's Structure. Make a printout that shows the new file structure. Before proceeding, be sure the printer is on and has paper in it.

To print the file's structure

Type   **SET PRINT ON**, and then press **Return**.

Type   **DISPLAY STRUCTURE**, and then press **Return**.

Type   **SET PRINT OFF**, and then press **Return**.

Result. The file's structure appears on the screen, and a copy is printed out. Notice how to ZIP field is now 11 characters wide.

Step 4. Continue or Quit. You have now completed this exercise. Either close all open files and continue to the next exercise, or quit the program if you have finished. (Press **Esc** if necessary to remove the menu bar and return to the dot prompt.)

To close all database files

Type   **CLEAR ALL**, and then press **Return**.

To quit the program

Type   **QUIT**, and then press **Return**.

Result. If you quit the program, the operating system prompt reappears. Remove your disks, and then turn off the computer.

QUESTIONS

1. How is a database restructured, and why is this done?
2. What happens if you restructure a file, and you add new fields?
3. What happens if you restructure a file, and you redefine a numeric field as another field type?

TOPIC 5-13
Writing Programs

In this topic, we introduce you to the following procedures:

- Displaying forms on the screen
- Creating menus to operate your own files

Up until now, you have entered commands one at a time. But dBASE III Plus allows you to write and save programs. This saves you time when you use the same commands over and over again and makes the program easier to operate for people with little or no experience. For example, you can write a program that displays menus that other users then make choices from so that they do not have to know the program's commands. You can also design and display forms on the screen so that users' can enter data more easily. You can also ensure that they enter the desired data, for example, amounts not larger or smaller than a given value.

WRITING, EDITING, AND RUNNING PROGRAMS

To write or edit a program, you execute the MODIFY COMMAND command, which puts the program into text edit mode. This mode is much like a word processing program. You can type and edit commands and then save them in their own file on the disk. For example, to write or edit a program named MENU, you type **MODIFY COMMAND MENU**. If you are writing the program file, the text edit screen appears blank. If the file already exists, it is displayed on the screen. You do not have to specify an extension for the file the program is stored in, but dBASE III Plus automatically adds the extension .PRG to all program files.

You can display the commands stored in a program file with the TYPE command. When using the TYPE command, you must specify the file's extension. For example, to display the contents of a program file named MENU, you type **TYPE MENU.PRG**, and then press **Return** to display the program on the screen.

After writing or editing a program, you execute it with the DO command. For example, to execute a program named MENU, you type **DO MENU**, and then press **Return**. The commands stored in the program file are then automatically executed.

EXERCISE 141

Writing a Screen Display Program

In this exercise, you write a program that displays a menu on the screen so that you can make choices to add records or browse through the records in the NAMELIST and AMOUNTS files. To begin this exercise, you must load the program as described in Exercise 124.

Step 1. Enter Text Edit Mode. To write a program, you first enter the program's text edit mode, and then specify the name of the file the program will be saved in. Here, let's specify that the program be stored in a file named MENU. (If the menu is displayed, press **Esc** to display the dot prompt.)

To enter text edit mode

Type   **MODIFY COMMAND MENU**, and then press **Return**.

Step 2. Enter the Menu Screen Display. Let's begin by writing that part of the program that displays a list of menu choices on the screen. Enter the commands shown in Figure 30. The first line beginning with an asterisk is a comment line. The asterisk tells dBASE not to execute what follows it when you run the program. The CLEAR command clears the screen before the menu is displayed. The SET BELL OFF command turns off the computer's speaker so that a beep does not sound when you enter a menu choice. The lines beginning with @ signs display text on the screen. The numbers following the @ sign specify the row and column the text begins in. The SAY command tells the program to display the text that follows on the screen in the specified position. The text to be displayed must be enclosed in double quotation marks as shown.

Result. When finished, your results should match those shown in Figure 30.

FIGURE 5-30
The menu choices

```
* MENU.PRG
CLEAR
SET BELL OFF
@ 2,33 SAY "MAIN MENU"
@ 4,25 SAY "1. ADD NAMES TO NAMELIST FILE"
@ 5,25 SAY "2. BROWSE NAMELIST FILE"
@ 6,25 SAY "3. ADD CREDITS TO AMOUNTS FILE"
@ 7,25 SAY "4. BROWSE AMOUNTS FILE"
@ 8,25 SAY "5. EXIT"
@ 10,25 SAY "ENTER CHOICE (1 - 4):"
```

Step 3. Save and Then Display the Program on the Screen. Now that you have written the program, save it and return to the dot prompt. Then display the contents of the program file on the screen.

To save the program

Press   **Ctrl-W.**

To display the program

Type   **TYPE MENU.PRG**, and then press **Return**.

Result. The program is displayed on the screen.

Step 4. Print the Program. Now, print the program so that you have a copy in case anything goes wrong.

To print the program

Type   **SET PRINT ON**, and then press **Return**.
Type   **TYPE MENU.PRG**, and then press **Return**.

Result. The program prints out. When finished printing, type **SET PRINT OFF**, and then press **Return**.

Step 5. Run the Program. Now, run the program and see what happens.

To run the program

Type   **DO MENU**, and then press **Return**.

Result. The menu is displayed on the screen, and the dot prompt reappears. You can't make choices from the menu yet because no commands have been added to the menu choices.

Step 6. Experiment with Memory Variables. When you have a menu you make choices from, the commands you use to execute the choice must know what choice you made. To accomplish this, you first store the choice you make into a memory variable, a buffer that can store any data you specify. Once data is stored in a memory variable, you can display it or retrieve it with another command. Here, experiment with a memory variable to see how data is stored in it and then displayed.

To create a memory variable

Type   **ANS=""** and then press **Return**.
Type   **STORE 2 TO ANS**, and then press **Return**.
Press   **F7** to display the status of the memory variables.

Result. The first command specified that a memory variable named ANS should be created and that it can store one character. The size of the storage area is specified by entering a single space between the double quotation marks. The second command stored the number 2 in the memory variable named ANS. The third command displayed the contents of the memory variable.

Step 7. Add the Menu Choices. Now, enter the commands shown boldfaced in Figure 5-31 that execute the choice you make from the menu.

To revise the MENU.PRG command file

Type   **MODIFY COMMAND MENU**, and then press **Return**.

Result. The program appears on the screen in edit mode so you can add to it. Enter the commands shown in Figure 5-31.
- The first command creates the memory variable ANS and specifies that it can store a single character.
- The second command tells the program to store any menu choice entered in row 10 on column 47 in the memory variable named ANS. The PICTURE "9" part of the command specifies that only a number from 0 to 9 can be stored in that memory variable.
- The READ command tells the program to read the number stored in the memory variable.

FIGURE 5-31
The menu commands

```
* MENU.PRG
CLEAR
SET BELL OFF
@ 2,33 SAY "MAIN MENU"
@ 4,25 SAY "1. ADD NAMES TO NAMELIST FILE"
@ 5,25 SAY "2. BROWSE NAMELIST FILE"
@ 6,25 SAY "3. ADD CREDITS TO AMOUNTS FILE"
@ 7,25 SAY "4. BROWSE AMOUNTS FILE"
@ 8,25 SAY "5. EXIT"
@ 10,25 SAY "ENTER CHOICE (1 - 4):"
ANS=" "
@ 10,47 GET ANS PICTURE "9"
READ
IF ANS="1"
    USE NAMELIST
    APPEND
    DO MENU
ELSE
    IF ANS="2"
        USE NAMELIST
        BROWSE
        DO MENU
    ELSE
        IF ANS="3"
            USE AMOUNTS
            APPEND
            DO MENU
        ELSE
            IF ANS="4"
                USE AMOUNTS
                BROWSE
                DO MENU
            ELSE
                IF ANS="5"
                    CLEAR
                    CANCEL
                ENDIF 5
            ENDIF 4
        ENDIF 3
    ENDIF 2
ENDIF 1
```

■ The commands beginning with IF tell the program what to do when you enter a menu choice. For example, if you type 1 to make a selection from the menu, the commands USE NAMELIST and APPEND are immediately executed. When you are finished adding records, the DO MENU command displays the menu again so that you can make another choice. Since you can make any one of five choices from the menu, the following ELSE and IF statements execute other commands.

■ The indents specify the level of nesting for the commands. Text edit mode has tab stops set every five characters. To indent a line, press **Tab**. These indents are important. The program executes a command and then looks to see if any commands are indented under it. If commands are indented, it executes those first before returning to commands at the same indent level.

When finished adding the commands, press **Ctrl-W** to save it and return to the dot prompt.

Step 8. Print the Program. After writing the program, make a printout for your records.

To print the program

Type   **SET PRINT ON**, and then press **Return.**

Type   **TYPE MENU.PRG**, and then press **Return**.

Result. The program prints out. When finished printing, type **SET PRINT OFF**, and then press **Return**.

Step 9. Run the Program. Now, run the program.

To run the program

Type   **DO MENU**, and then press **Return**.

Result. The menu appears as before, but now a highlight follows the make selection line. This is the position where your selection is entered.

Step 10. Make Selections from the Menu. The final test is to make a menu choice to see what happens.

To make selections from the menu

Type   **1** to display a new, blank record for the NAMELIST file.
Press   **Esc** to return to the menu.

Result. A blank record from the NAMELIST file should be displayed on the screen. Press **Esc** to cancel the command and return to the menu. Continue making choices, and then press **Esc** to return to the menu. When finished, select 5 for Exit to return to the dot prompt.

Step 11. Display the Files You Have Created. Now that you have completed all the exercises in this part, display the files you created.

To display the files you created

Type   **DIR *.***, and then press **Return**.

Result. A list of all the files you created in this part is displayed on the screen.

Step 12. Continue or Quit. You have now completed this exercise. Either close all open files, or quit the program if you have finished. (Press **Esc** if necessary to remove the menu bar and return to the dot prompt.)

To close all database files

Type   **CLEAR ALL**, and then press **Return**.

To quit the program

Type   **QUIT**, and then press **Return**.

Result. If you quit the program, the operating system prompt reappears. Remove your disks, and then turn off the computer.

QUESTIONS

1. What command do you execute to write or edit a program file?
2. What command do you execute to display the contents of a program file?
3. What command do you execute to run a program file?
4. What is a memory variable?

APPENDIX A
Software License Agreements

NOTE TO USERS OF THIS TEXT

Educational versions of WordPerfect, The Twin, and dBase III Plus are available either through purchase with this text or on a COURSE USE LICENSE to institutions adopting this text. For information on how to obtain a COURSE USE LICENSE, contact your local Prentice Hall representative or College Marketing (201-592-2000).

Information on the limitations of these software programs is contained in the Preface.

USE OF THESE SOFTWARE PROGRAMS IS CONDITIONAL UPON READING AND AC-CEPTANCE OF THE TERMS CONTAINED IN THE FOLLOWING LICENSES.

WordPerfect Educational Version Program License Agreement

WordPerfect Corporation and Prentice-Hall, Inc. provide this program and license its use for educational purposes only. You assume responsibility for the selection of the product to achieve your intended results, and for the installation, use, and results obtained from the program.

LICENSE

As license owner, you may:

a. use the program on a single machine.

b. copy the program into any machine-readable or printed form for back-up or modification purposes in support of your use of the program on a single machine.

c. transfer the program and license to another party if the other party agrees to accept the terms and conditions of this Agreement. If you transfer the program to another party, you must transfer all copies of the program, in either written, printed, or machine-readable form, at the same time to the same party or destroy any additional copies of the program in your possession; this includes all modifications and portions therein or elsewhere contained.

You must reproduce and include the copyright notice on any and all copies you create.

YOU MAY NOT USE, COPY, MODIFY, OR TRANSFER THE PROGRAM, OR ANY COPY, MODIFICATION IN WHOLE OR IN PART, EXCEPT AS EXPRESSLY PROVIDED FOR IN THIS LICENSE.

IF YOU TRANSFER POSSESSION OF ANY COPY OF THE PROGRAM TO ANOTHER PARTY, YOUR LICENSE IS TERMINATED.

This program is copyrighted and protected by the copyright laws of the United States. Any copying of this program unless authorized by WordPerfect Corporation and Prentice-Hall, Inc. is illegal and prohibited by law.

TERM

Your license is effective until terminated. You may terminate your license at any time by destroying the program, including all copies and modifications in any form. Your license will also terminate upon conditions and terms set forth elsewhere in this Agreement or if you fail to comply with any term or condition of this Agreement. You agree upon such a termination of your license to destroy the program and all copies in any form that you hold in your possession.

LIMITED WARRANTY

The Package, including the program, is provided "as is" without warranty of any kind, either expressed or implied, including, but not limited to the implied warranties of merchantability and fitness for a particular purpose. The entire risk as to the quality and performance of the program is with you. Should the program prove defective, you (and not WordPerfect Corporation or Prentice-Hall, Inc.) assume the entire cost of all necessary servicing, repair, or correction. Some states do not allow the exclusion of implied warranties so the above exclusion may not apply to you. This warranty gives you specific legal rights and you may also have other rights which vary from state to state.

WordPerfect Corporation and Prentice-Hall, Inc. do not warrant that the functions contained in this program will meet your requirements or that the operation of the program will be uninterrupted or error free.

However, WordPerfect Corporation and Prentice-Hall, Inc. warrant the diskettes on which the program is furnished, to be free from defects in materials and workmanship under normal use for a period of ninety (90) days from the date of delivery to you as evidenced by a copy of your receipt.

LIMITATIONS OF REMEDIES

WordPerfect Corporation and Prentice-Hall, Inc.'s entire liability and your exclusive remedy shall be:

1. The replacement of any diskette(s) or cassette(s) not meeting WordPerfect Corporation and Prentice-Hall, Inc.'s "LIMITED WARRANTY" and which is returned to Prentice-Hall, Inc. with a copy of your receipt or

2. If Prentice-Hall, Inc. is unable to deliver a replacement diskette(s) or cassette(s) which is free from defects in material or workmanship, you may terminate this agreement by returning the program and manual, and your money will be refunded.

IN NO EVENT WILL WORDPERFECT CORPORATION OF PRENTICE-HALL, INC. BE LIABLE TO YOU FOR ANY DAMAGES, INCLUDING ANY LOST PROFITS, LOST SAVINGS, OR OTHER INCIDENTAL OR CONSEQUENTIAL DAMAGES ARISING FROM THE USE OR INABILITY TO USE SUCH PROGRAM EVEN IF WORDPERFECT CORPORATION OR PRENTICE-HALL, INC. HAVE BEEN ADVISED OF THE POSSIBILITY OF SUCH DAMAGES, OR FOR ANY CLAIM BY ANY OTHER PARTY.

Some states do not allow limitation or exclusion of consequential damages so the above limitation or exclusion may not apply to you.

GENERAL

You may not sublicense, assign or transfer the license or the program except as expressly provided in this agreement. Any attempt otherwise to sublicense, assign or transfer any of the rights, duties or obligations hereunder is void.

This agreement will be governed by the laws of the State of New York.

Should you have any questions concerning this Agreement, you may contact Prentice-Hall, Inc. by writing to:

Prentice-Hall, Inc.
College Division
Englewood Cliffs, NJ 7632

YOU ACKNOWLEDGE THAT YOU HAVE READ THIS AGREEMENT, UNDER-STAND IT AND AGREE TO BE BOUND BY ITS TERMS AND CONDITIONS. You further agree that it is the complete and exclusive statement of the agreement between us which supersedes any proposal or prior agreement, oral or written, and relating to the subject matter of this agreement.

WordPerfect
Corporation
School Software Direct Order Form

Qualifying teachers, as well as college, university, and other post-secondary students, can now purchase Word-Perfect Corporation (WPCORP) software directly from WPCORP at a reduced price. To qualify, a participant must be teaching or currently enrolled as a full-time student, and must agree in writing not to resell or transfer any package purchased under this program.

If you satisfy these qualifying conditions and would like to purchase software directly from WPCORP under the School Software Program, complete the following six steps and sign at the bottom of the form.

Step 1. From the list below, select the appropriate software for your computer (please note that each student is limited to *one* package of WordPerfect) and mark an "x" in the corresponding box(es).

Product	Disk Size	Computer	Price*
❏ WordPerfect 4.2	5 1/4"	(IBM PC/XT/AT/Compatibles)	$125.00
❏ WordPerfect 4.2	3 1/2"	(IBM PC/XT/AT/Compatibles)	$125.00
❏ WordPerfect 1.1	5 1/4"	(Apple IIe/IIc)	$59.00
❏ WordPerfect 1.1	3 1/2"	(Apple IIe/IIc)	$59.00
❏ WordPerfect 1.1	3 1/2"	(Apple IIGS)	$59.00
❏ PlanPerfect 3.0	5 1/4"	(IBM PC/XT/AT/Compatibles)	$99.00
❏ PlanPerfect 3.0	3 1/2"	(IBM PC/XT/AT/Compatibles)	$99.00
❏ WordPerfect Library	5 1/4"	(IBM PC/XT/AT/Compatibles)	$59.00
❏ WordPerfect Library	3 1/2"	(IBM PC/XT/AT/Compatibles)	$59.00
❏ WordPerfect Executive	5 1/4"	(IBM PC/XT/AT/Compatibles)	$79.00
❏ WordPerfect Executive	3 1/2"	(IBM PC/XT/AT/Compatibles)	$79.00

Step 2. Make a photo-copy of your current Student ID or Faculty card *and* a photo-copy of some well known form of identification displaying your social security, such as your Driver License or Social Seurity Card. (WPCORP will hold this information strictly confidential and use it only to guard against duplicate purchase.) Your school ID must show current enrollment. If it does not show a date, you must send verification of current enrollment. If you have serious reservations about providing a social security number, call Educational Development ad (801) 227-7131 to establish clearance to purchase any of the above software produces at these special prices.

Step 3. Enter your social security number: __ __ __ - __ __ - __ __ __ __

Step 4. Enclose payment for the total cost of the package(s) ordered with personal check, money order, Visa, or MasterCard.
Account # _____
Expiration Date _____ ❏ VISA ❏ MasterCard
(Make check or money order payable to WordPerfect Corporation.)

Step 5. List your shipping address and the address of your local computer store (dealer) in the space provided:
Ship To _____ Your Dealer _____
_____ _____
_____ _____
Phone _____ Phone _____

Step 6. Enclose this signed and completed form, the photo-copies of your identification cards, and your signed check or money order (or Visa or MasterCard account number and expiration date) in an envelope and mail to School Software Program, WordPerfect Corporation, 288 West Center Street, Orem, UT 84057.

The information provided herein is correct and accurate, and I will abide by the restricting conditions outlined by WPCORP in this document. I understand that at its sole discretion, WPCORP may refuse any order for any reason.

Signature _____ Date _____

*Utah residents add 6.25% sales tax.

WordPerfect Corporation, 288 West Center Street, Orem, Utah 84057 (801) 225-5000

The TWIN Educational Version Program License Agreement

Mosaic Software, Inc. and Prentice-Hall, Inc. provide this program and license its use for educational purposes only. You assume responsibility for the selection of the product to achieve your intended results, and for the installation, use, and results obtained from the program.

LICENSE

As license owner, you may:

a. use the program on a single machine.

b. copy the program into any machine-readable or printed form for back-up or modification purposes in support of your use of the program on a single machine.

c. transfer the program and license to another party if the other party agrees to accept the terms and conditions of this Agreement. If you transfer the program to another party, you must transfer all copies of the program, in either written, printed, or machine-readable form, at the same time to the same party or destroy any additional copies of the program in your possession; this includes all modifications and portions therein or elsewhere contained.

You must reproduce and include the copyright notice on any and all copies you create.

YOU MAY NOT USE, COPY, MODIFY, OR TRANSFER THE PROGRAM, OR ANY COPY, MODIFICATION IN WHOLE OR IN PART, EXCEPT AS EXPRESSLY PROVIDED FOR IN THIS LICENSE.

IF YOU TRANSFER POSSESSION OF ANY COPY OF THE PROGRAM TO ANOTHER PARTY, YOUR LICENSE IS TERMINATED.

This program is copyrighted and protected by the copyright laws of the United States. Any copying of this program unless authorized by Mosaic Software, Inc. and Prentice-Hall, Inc. is illegal and prohibited by law.

TERM

Your license is effective until terminated. You may terminate your license at any time by destroying the program, including all copies and modifications in any form. Your license will also terminate upon conditions and terms set forth elsewhere in this Agreement or if you fail to comply with any term or condition of this Agreement. You agree upon such a termination of your license to destroy the program and all copies in any form that you hold in your possession.

LIMITED WARRANTY

The Package, including the program, is provided "as is" without warranty of any kind, either expressed or implied, including, but not limited to the implied warranties of merchantability and fitness for a particular purpose. The entire risk as to the quality and performance of the program is with you. Should the program prove defective, you (and not Mosaic Software, Inc. or Prentice-Hall, Inc.) assume the entire cost of all necessary servicing, repair, or correction. Some states do not allow the exclusion of implied warranties so the above exclusion may not apply to you. This warranty gives you specific legal rights and you may also have other rights which vary from state to state.

Mosaic Software, Inc. and Prentice-Hall, Inc. do not warrant that the functions contained in this program will meet your requirements or that the operation of the program will be uninterrupted or error free.

However, Mosaic Software, Inc. and Prentice-Hall, Inc. warrant the diskettes on which the program is furnished, to be free from defects in materials and workmanship under normal use for a period of ninety (90) days from the date of delivery to you as evidenced by a copy of your receipt.

LIMITATIONS OF REMEDIES

Mosaic Software, Inc. and Prentice-Hall, Inc.'s entire liability and your exclusive remedy shall be:

1. The replacement of any diskette(s) or cassette(s) not meeting Mosaic Software, Inc. and Prentice-Hall, Inc.'s "LIMITED WARRANTY" and which is returned to Prentice-Hall, Inc. with a copy of your receipt or

2. If Prentice-Hall, Inc. is unable to deliver a replacement diskette(s) or cassette(s) which is free from defects in material or workmanship, you may terminate this agreement by returning the program and manual, and your money will be refunded.

IN NO EVENT WILL MOSAIC SOFTWARE, INC. OF PRENTICE-HALL, INC. BE LIABLE TO YOU FOR ANY DAMAGES, INCLUDING ANY LOST PROFITS, LOST SAVINGS, OR OTHER INCIDENTAL OR CONSEQUENTIAL DAMAGES ARISING FROM THE USE OR INABILITY TO USE SUCH PROGRAM EVEN IF MOSAIC SOFTWARE, INC. OR PRENTICE-HALL, INC. HAVE BEEN ADVISED OF THE POSSIBILITY OF SUCH DAMAGES, OR FOR ANY CLAIM BY ANY OTHER PARTY.

Some states do not allow limitation or exclusion of consequential damages so the above limitation or exclusion may not apply to you.

GENERAL

You may not sublicense, assign or transfer the license or the program except as expressly provided in this agreement. Any attempt otherwise to sublicense, assign or transfer any of the rights, duties or obligations hereunder is void.

This agreement will be governed by the laws of the State of New York.

Should you have any questions concerning this Agreement, you may contact Prentice-Hall, Inc. by writing to:

Prentice-Hall, Inc.
College Division
Englewood Cliffs, NJ 7632

YOU ACKNOWLEDGE THAT YOU HAVE READ THIS AGREEMENT, UNDERSTAND IT AND AGREE TO BE BOUND BY ITS TERMS AND CONDITIONS. You further agree that it is the complete and exclusive statement of the agreement between us which supersedes any proposal or prior agreement, oral or written, and relating to the subject matter of this agreement.

You can use the subroutines or libraries provided in this software (modified or unmodified) in your or other software programs for your own use. However, you cannot sell, license, or distribute these subroutines or libraries themselves, nor the software program that contains these subroutines or libraries themselves, nor the software program that contains these subroutines or libraries to others. You can distribute portions of programs which exclude these subroutines or libraries, but may have provisions and are designed to work with these subroutines or libraries.

If you wish to to distribute programs, subroutines or libraries provided in this software package, you can do so upon written authorization from Mosaic Software, Inc.

dBase III Plus Educational Version Program License Agreement

Exhibit "A"

Important: Please read this page before using this dBASE III Plus program, a copy of which is being made available to you for use in conjunction with this Textbook pursuant to the terms of this Agreement for educational, training and/or demonstration purposes. By using the dBASE III Plus program, you show your agreement to the terms of this license.

EXCLUSION OF WARRANTIES AND LIMITATIONS OF LIABILITY

THE COPY OF THE dBASE III PLUS PROGRAM MADE AVAILABLE FOR USE WITH THIS TEXTBOOK IS A LIMITED FUNCTIONALITY VERSION OF dBASE III PLUS, AND IS INTENDED SOLELY FOR EDUCATIONAL, TRAINING, AND DEMONSTRATION PURPOSES. ACCORDINGLY, THIS COPY OF dBASE III PLUS IS PROVIDED "AS IS," WITHOUT WARRANTY OF ANY KIND FROM ASHTON-TATE OR PRENTICE-HALL, INC. ASHTON-TATE AND PRENTICE-HALL, INC. HEREBY DISCLAIM ALL WARRANTIES OF ANY KIND WITH RESPECT TO THIS LIMITED FUNCTIONALITY COPY OF dBASE III PLUS, INCLUDING WITHOUT LIMITATION THE IMPLIED WARRANTIES OF MERCHANTABILITY AND FITNESS FOR A PARTICULAR PURPOSE. NEITHER ASHTON-TATE NOR PRENTICE-HALL, INC. SHALL BE LIABLE UNDER ANY CIRCUMSTANCES FOR CONSEQUENTIAL, INCIDENTAL, SPECIAL OR EXEMPLARY DAMAGES ARISING OUT OF TH USE OF THIS LIMITED FUNCTIONALITY COPY OF dBASE III PLUS, EVEN IF ASHTON-TATE OF PRENTICE-HALL, INC. HAS BEEN APPRISED OF THE LIKELIHOOD OF SUCH DAMAGES OCCURRING. IN NO EVENT WILL ASHTON-TATE'S OR PRENTICE-HALL, INC.'S LIABILITY (WHETHER BASED ON AN ACTION OR CLAIM IN CONTRACT, TORT OR OTHERWISE) ARISING OUT OF THE USE OF THIS LIMITED FUNCTIONALITY COPY OF dBASE III PLUS EXCEED THE AMOUNT PAID FOR THIS TEXTBOOK. LIMITED USE SOFTWARE LICENSE AGREEMENT

DEFINITIONS

The term "Software" as used in this agreement means the Limited Use version of dBASE III Plus which is made available fur use in conjunction with this Textbook solely for educational, training and/or demonstration purposes. The term "Software Copies" means the actual copies of all or any portion of the Software, including backups, updates, merged or partial copies permitted hereunder.

PERMITTED USES

You may:

- Load into RAM and use the Software on a single terminal or a single workstation of a computer (or its replacement).
- Install the Software onto a permanent storage device (a hard disk drive).
- Make and maintain up to three back up copies provided they used only for back-up purposes, and you keep possession of the back-ups. In addition, all the information appearing on the original disk labels (including copyright notice) must be copied onto the back-up labels.

This license gives you certain limited rights to use the Software and Software Copies for educational, training and/or demonstration purposes. You do not become the owner of and Ashton-Tate retains title to, all the Software and Software Copies. In addition, you agree to use reasonable efforts to protect the Software from unauthorized use, reproduction, distribution or publication.

All rights not specifically granted in this license are reserved by Ashton-Tate.

USES NOT PERMITTED

You may not:

- Make copies of the Software, except as permitted above.
- Rent, lease, sublicense, time-share, lend or transfer the Software, Software Copies or your rights under this license except that transfers may be made with Ashton-Tate's prior written authorization.
- Alter, decompile, disassemble, or reverse-engineer the Software.
- Remove or obscure the Ashton-Tate copyright and trademark notices.

DURATION

This agreement is effective from the day you first use the Software. Your license continues for fifty years or until you return to Ashton-Tate the original disks and any back-up copies, whichever comes first.

If you breach this agreement, Ashton-Tate can terminate this license upon notifying you in writing. You will be required to return all Software Copies. Ashton-Tate can also enforce our other legal rights.

GENERAL

This agreement represents the entire understanding and agreement regarding the Software and Software Copies and supersedes any prior purchase order, communication, advertising or representation.

This license may only be modified in a written amendment signed by an authorized Ashton-Tate officer. If any provision of this agreement shall be unlawful, void, of for any reason unenforceable, it shall be deemed severable from, and shall in no way affect the validity or enforceability of the remaining provisions of this agreement. This agreement will be governed by California law.

NOTE TO STUDENTS: IN ORDER TO OBTAIN A COPY OF THIS PROGRAM FROM YOUR INSTRUCTOR YOU MUST INDICATE YOUR ACCEPTANCE OF THE CONDITIONS OF THE ABOVE LICENSE BY SIGNING BELOW AND RETURNING TO ASHTON-TATE.

"I have read and agree to be bound by the terms of this agreement.

_____

Signature/Name

"Return this agreement to: Legal Affairs Department, Ashton-Tate Corporation, 20101 Hamilton Avenue, Torrance, CA 90502-1319.

APPENDIX B
WordPerfect Quick Reference

Feature	Keystrokes	Feature	Keystrokes
Advance Line	Shift-F1	Generate	Alt-F5, 6
Advance Up/Down	Shift-F1	"Go" (Resume Printing)	Shift-F7, 4
Alignment Character	Shift-F8	Go to DOS	Ctrl-F1
Append Block (Block on)	Ctrl-F4	Hard Page	Ctrl-↵
Auto Hyphenation	Shift-F8, 5	Hard Return	↵
Auto Rewrite	Ctrl-F3	Hard Space	Home, Space Bar
Backspace	←	Headers or Footers	Alt- F8
Binding Width	Shift-F7, 3	Help	F3
Block	Alt-F4	Home	Home
Block, Cut/Copy (Block on)	Ctrl-F4	Hyphen	=
Block Protect (Block on)	Alt-F8	Hyphenation On/Off	Shift-F8, 5
Bold	F6	H-Zone	Shift-F8, 5
Cancel	F1	◆Indent	F4
Cancel Hyphenation	F1	◆Indent◆	Shift-F4
Cancel Print Job(s)	Shift-F7, 4	Index	Alt-F5
Case Conversion (Block on)	Shift-F3	Insert Printer Command	Ctrl-F8
Center	Shift-F6	Justification On/Off	Ctrl-F8
Center Page Top to Bottom	Alt-F8	Line Draw	Ctrl-F3
Change Directory	F5, ↵	Line Format	Shift-F8
Change Print Options	Shift-F7	Line Numbering	Ctrl-F8
Colors		Lines per Inch	Ctrl-F8
Column, Cut/Copy (Block on)		Lists Files	F5, ↵
Columns, Text	Alt-F7	List (Block on)	Alt-F5
Column Display	Alt-F7	Locked Documents	Ctrl-F5
Concordance	Alt-F5, 6, 5	Look	F5, ↵
Conditional End of Page	Alt-F8	Macro	Alt-F10
Copy	F5, ↵	Macro Def	Ctrl-F10
Create Directory	F5, =	◆Margin Release	Shift (Tab)
Ctrl/Alt Key Mapping	Ctrl-F3	Margins	Shift-F8
Date	Shift-F5	Mark Text	Alt-F5
Delete	Del	Math	Alt-F7
Delete (List Files)	F5, ↵	Merge	Ctrl-F9
Delete Directory (List Files)	F5, ↵	Merge Codes	Alt-F9
Delete to End of Line (EOL)	Ctrl-End	Merge E	Shift-F9
Delete to End of Page (EOP)	Ctrl-PgDn	Merge R	F9
Delete to Left Word Boundary	Home, ←	Minus Sign	Home, =
Delete to Right Word Boundary	Home, Del	Move	Ctrl-F4
Delete Word	Ctrl-←	Name Search	F5, ↵
Display All Print Jobs	Shift-F7, 4	New Number (Footnote)	Ctrl-F7
Display Printers and Fonts	Shift-F7, 4	New Page Number	Alt-F8
Document Comments	Ctrl-F5	Number of Copies	Shift-F7, 3
Document Conversion	Ctrl-F5	Outline	Alt-F5
Document Summary	Ctrl-F5	Overstrike	Shift-F1
DOS Text File	Ctrl-F5	Page Format	Alt-F8
Endnote	Ctrl-F7	Page Length	Alt-F8
Enter (or Return)	↵	Page Number Column Positions	Alt-F8
Escape	Esc	Page Number Position	Alt-F8
Exit	F7	Page (Print)	Shift-F7
Flush Right	Alt-F6	Paragraph Number	Alt-F5
Font	Ctrl-F8	Pitch	Ctrl-F8
Footnote	Ctrl-F7	Preview a Document	Shift-F7
Full Text (Print)	Shift-F7	Print	Shift-F7

Feature	Keystrokes
Print (List Files)	F5, ↵
Print a Document	Shift-F7, 4
Print Block (Block on)	Shift-F7
Print Format	Ctrl-F8
Printer Control	Shift-F7
Printer Number	Shift-F7, 3
Proportional Spacing	Ctrl-F8, 1
Rectangle,Cut/Copy (Block on)	Ctrl-F4
Redline	Alt-F5
Remove	Alt-F5, 6
Rename	F5, ↵
Replace	Alt-F2
Replace, Extended	Home, Alt-F2
Retrieve	Shift-F10
Retrieve (List Files)	F5, ↵
Retrieve Column (Move)	Ctrl-F4
Retrieve Rectangle (Move)	Ctrl-F4
Retrieve Text (Move)	Ctrl-F4
Reveal Codes	Alt-F3
Rewrite	Ctrl-F3, Ctrl-F3
Rush Print Job	Shift-F7, 4
Save	F10
Screen	Ctrl-F3
▶Search	F2
▶Search, Extended	Home, F2
◀Search	Shift-F2
◀Search, Extended	Home, Shift-F2
Select Print Options	Shift-F7, 4
Select Printers	Shift-F7, 4
Sheet Feeder Bin Number	Ctrl-F8
Shell	Ctrl-F1
Short Form Marking	Alt-F5
Soft Hyphen	Ctrl-=
Sort	Ctrl-F9
Sorting Sequences	Ctrl-F9
Spacing	Shift-F8
Spell	Ctrl-F2
Split Screen	Ctrl-F3, 1
Stop Printing	Shift-F7, 4
Strikeout (Block on)	Alt-F5
Super/Subscript	Shift-F1
Suppress Page Format	Alt-F8
Switch	Shift-F3

Features	Keystrokes
Tab	⇥
Tab Align	Ctrl-F6
Tab Ruler	Ctrl-F3, 1
Table of Authorities (Block on)	Alt-F5
Table of Contents (Block on)	Alt-F5
Tab Set	Shift-F8
Text In (List Files)	F5, ↵
Text In/Out	Ctrl-F5
Text Lines	Alt-F8, 4
Thesaurus	Alt-F1
Time	Shift-F5, 2
Top Margin	Alt-F8
Typeover	Ins
Type-thru	Shift-F7
Undelete	F1
Underline	F8
Underline Style	Ctrl-F8
Widow/Orphan	Alt-F8
Window	Ctrl-F3
Word Count	Ctrl-F2
Word Search	F5, ↵

Cursor Control

Go To	Ctrl-Home
Word Left	Ctrl-←
Word Right	Ctrl-→
Screen Left	Home, ←
Screen Right	Home, →
Screen Down	+ or Home, ↓
Screen Up	− or Home, ↑
Page Down	PgDn
Page Up	PgUp
Beginning of Text	Home, Home, ↑
End of Text	Home, Home, ↓
Beginning of Line (text)	Home, Home, ←
Beginning of Line (codes)	Home, Home, Home, ←
End of Line	Home, Home, →

APPENDIX C
The TWIN Spreadsheet Menu Commands

/ `Worksheet`

Global:	modify the entire worksheet
Format	specify how numbers subsequently entered will appear
Fixed	numbers have set number of decimals
Scientific	exponential notation
Currency	suffix numbers with $ symbol, and insert commas
,	commas and fixed decimal sign
General	clip trailing 0's after decimal
+/-	use +'s or -'s for horizontal bar chart
Percent	show values as percentages
Date	show Julian date number as date
1	show in DD-MMM-YY format
2	show in DD-MMM format
3	show in MMM-YY format
4	show in DD/MM/YY format
5	show in MM/YY format
Text	display formula instead of formula's value
Label-prefix	justify or align subsequently entered labels within cells
Left	all entries flush left, enters ' label prefix
Right	all entries flush right, enters " label prefix
Center	all entries flush center, enters ^ label prefix
Column-width	change width of columns whose width has not been changed
Recalculation	specify how the Spreadsheet will calculate
Natural	recalculate in order of dependency
Column	recalculate down columns
Row	recalculate by rows
Automatic	recalculate after every change to worksheet
Manual	recalculate only by F9, Calc, function key
Iteration	recalculate a set number of times
Protection	protect all cells, except unprotected ones, from changes
Enable	turn Protection on
Disable	turn Protection off after having enabled it
Hardware	select printer and other hardware default settings
Define-Colors	change the colors of various components of the Spreadsheet
Insert	insert extra rows or columns in the worksheet
Column	insert extra columns in the worksheet
Rows	insert extra rows in the worksheet
Delete	delete rows or columns from the current worksheet
Column	delete columns from the current worksheet
Rows	delete rows from the current worksheet
Column-width	change the width of a column
Set	change the column-width
Reset	return column-width to Global column-width
Erase	erase current worksheet from memory
Titles	lock display of columns or rows on screen
Both	lock display of both columns and rows
Horizontal	lock display of rows above cell marker
Vertical	lock display of columns above cell marker
Clear	unlock all titles
Window	split the screen into windows
Horizontal	split the screen horizontally
Vertical	split the screen vertically
Sync	scroll both windows at the same time
Unsync	scroll the windows separately
Clear	close the second window
Status	check the worksheet settings

/ `Range`

Format	specify will appear at the selected range
Fixed	numbers have set number of decimals

Scientific	exponential notation	
Currency	suffix numbers with $ symbol, and insert commas	
,	commas and fixed decimal sign	
General	clip trailing 0's after decimal	
+ / –	use +'s or –'s for horizontal bar chart	
Percent	show values as percentages	
Date	show Julian date number as date	
1	show in DD-MMM-YY format	
2	show in DD-MMM format	
3	show in MMM-YY format	
4	show in DD/MM/YY format	
5	show in MM/YY format	
Text	display formula instead of formula's value	
Reset	return display of number to Global/ setting	
Label-prefix	justify or align labels already entered within cells	
Left	all entries flush left, enters ' label prefix	
Right	all entries flush right, enters " label prefix	
Center	all entries flush center, enters ^ label prefix	
Erase	erase all entries at the range specified	
Name	use range names	
Create	make a name that will reference a range of the worksheet	
Delete	erase a range name already created	
Label	use label in adjacent cell as name for cell	
Reset	delete all current range names	
Table	enter into the worksheet a table of all range names	
Justify	justify labels to selected width	
Protect	to remove unprotection from cells	
Unprotect	unprotect a selected range of cells	
Input	cell marker can only go to unprotected cells	
/ Copy	copy a selected range to another part of the worksheet	

/ Move	move a selected range to another part of the worksheet	
File		
Retrieve	retrieve an existing file from disk	
Save	save the current worksheet to disk	
Combine	combine the current worksheet with another file	
Copy	replace incoming file's contents from current worksheet	
Add	copy values from incoming file and current worksheet	
Subtract	subtract values from incoming file and current worksheet	
Entire-File	for Copy, Add, and Subtract combine	
Named-Range	either the entire file or a named range of the file	
Xtract	save part of the current worksheet as a separate file	
Formulas	when Xtracting, save formulas and values	
Values	when Xtracting, save just values	
Erase	erase a file from the data directory	
Worksheet	erase data files with the .WKT, .WKS, and .WK1 extension	
Print	erase print files with the .PRN file extension	
Graph	erase slide files with .SLD file extension	
List	list files in the data directory by file extension	
Worksheet	list files with the .WKT, .WKS, and .WK1 extension	
Print	list print files with the .PRN file extension	
Graph	list slide files with .SLD file extension	
Import	bring into the Spreadsheet files in a variety of formats	
Text	transfer one line per cell in one column	
Numbers	read in one number (12.3) or (label ') per cell	
DIF	read Data Interchange format files	
Formulas	read in a formulas only print file	
CSV	read a Comma Separated Variable file	

Visicalc	read a Visicalc .VC file
Directory	change the pathname from the default in Hardware configuration
Translate	translate current worksheet into another file format
1-2-3	translate current file into a format 1-2-3 can read
DI F	translate current file into DIF format

/ Print

Printer	print a range of worksheet
File	store a range of the worksheet as a print file
Range	print only a certain section of the worksheet
Line	advance the page one line
Page	advance the page to bottom
Options	special print options
Header	print a message at top of each page
Footer	print message at bottom of each page
Margins	change the printer margins
Borders	print the same column or row on each page
Columns	print selected column on each page
Rows	print selected row on each page
Setup	send a special setup code to your printer
Grid	print the left and top bars that define the worksheet's current area
Page-length	change the page length
Other	to print in different formats
As-Displayed	print contents as they appear
Cell-formulas	print cell-formulas
Formatted	to print header and footer
Unformatted	to not print header, footer, and page breaks
Quit	return to Options menu
Clear	reset the printer settings to default
All	clear all settings to default
Range	clear range settings
Borders	clear border settings
Format	set setup string, page-length, and margins to default.

Align	move paper to top of page after adjusting manually
Go	start printing
Quit	return to READY mode

/ Graph

Type	define the type of graph display
A	Line
B	X-Y
C	vertical bar
D	horizontal bar
E	3-D bar
F	pie
G	3-D pie
H	pie-bar
X	define the numbers to use for the X values of an X-Y graph
1	define the first data range
2	define the second data range
3	define the third data range
4	define the fourth data range
5	define the fifth data range
6	define the sixth data range
7	define the seventh data range
8	define the eighth data range
Label	define X-axis and bar-top labels
X	data label range for X-axis
1	data label range for 1
2	data label range for 2
3	data label range for 3
4	data label range for 4
5	data label range for 5
6	data label range for 6
7	data label range for 7
8	data label range for 8
Options	specify titles, axes, and other graph attributes
First page	
Titles	Size **1–8**, color **1–8**, font **1–3**, justification **L**eft, **R**ight, **C**enter

Footnotes	Size **1–8**, color **1–8**, font **1–3**, justification **Left, Right, Center**	/ Data	
		Fill	fill a range
Second page		Table	compute a table of values with one input cell, one or more dependent formulas
X-axis label			
Y1-axis label			
Display (**Y/N**) *X*-axis, Y1-Axis, Y2-Axis frame, grids		**2**	data table with two input cells
X-axis	minimum and maximum values, Color **1–8**	Sort	sort records
		Query	manipulate data records matching given criteria
scale	**Linear, loGarithmic**		
Y1-Axis	minimum and maximum values, color **1–8**, scale **1–8**	Input	enter the range from which records are taken
Y2-Axis	minimum and maximum values, color **1–8**, scale **1–8**	Criterion	enter Criterion range, specifying which records to choose
Units between *X* labels		Output	enter range in which to place selected records
Tics between *X* labels			
Units between Y1 labels		Find	find records that match criteria
Tics between Y1 labels		Extract	place records that match the criteria in the Output range
Units between Y2 labels			
Tics between Y2 labels		Unique	list records that are unique
Units between Y2 labels		Delete	delete records that match criteria
Tics between Y2 labels		Reset	clear Input, Criterion, and Output ranges
Labels and legends size (**S/L**)			
Third page		Quit	return to READY mode
Legends colors **1–8**, Pattern **1–8**		Distribution	calculate a frequency distribution table
Highlight pie slice, **Y/N**			
Display data ranges in line chart at **Left** or **Right** Y-axis		/ Quit	leave Spreadsheet, return to DOS
Pie data range # or Value position # (select one only)			
Bars **Stacked** or **Clustered**			
Bar label range for pie/bar			
Subtitles (for pie/bar charts), pie: bar:			
View	display the graph on the screen		
Plot	plot the graph to a pen plotter		
Gprint	print the graph to a printer		
Name	create, use, or delete a name graph		
Use	retrieve named graph from memory		
Create	store named graph in memory		
Delete	delete named graph from memory		
Reset	erase all named graphs from memory		

APPENDIX D
dBase III Plus Quick Reference Guide

dBASE III PLUS FUNCTIONS

Function Name	Description
&	Macro substitution
ABS	Absolute Value
ASC	Character to ASCII Code Conversion
AT	Substring Search
BOF	Beginning-of-File
CDOW	Day of Week
CHR	ASCII Code to Character Conversion
CMONTH	Calendar Month
COL	Current Screen Column Position
CTOD	Character to Date Conversion
DATE	System Date
DAY	Day of Month
DBF	Name of Database File in USE
DELETED	Deleted Record
DISKSPACE	Free Space (bytes) on Disk
DOW	Day of Week
DTOC	Date to Character Conversion
EOF	End-of-File
ERROR	Number for ON ERROR Condition
EXP	Exponential (e^x)
FIELD	Names of Fields in Database File
FILE	File Existence
FKLABEL	Names of Function Keys
FKMAX	Maximum Number of Function Keys
FOUND	Result of Database File Search
GETENV	Operating System Environmental Variables
IIF	One Expression or Another
INKEY	Keypress during Program Execution
INT	Integer
ISALPHA	Evaluate for Letter
ISCOLOR	Evaluate for Color Mode
ISLOWER	Evaluate for Lower Case
ISUPPER	Evaluate for Upper Case
LEFT	Substring Selection from Left Side
LEN	Length of Character String
LOG	Logarithm
LOWER	Upper to Lower Case Conversion
LTRIM	Remove Leading Blanks
LUPDATE	Last Update of Database File
MAX	Determine Greater of Two Values
MESSAGE	ON ERROR Message String
MIN	Determine Smaller of Two Values
MOD	Modulus
MONTH	Month of Year
NDX	Names of Open Index Files
OS	Name of Operating System
PCOL	Printer Column Position
PROW	Printer Row Position
READKEY	Determine Full-screen Exiting Keypress
RECCOUNT	Number of Records in Database File
RECNO	Current Record Number
RECSIZE	Size of Record
REPLICATE	Repeat Character Expression
RIGHT	Substring Selection from Right Side
ROUND	Rounds Off
ROW	Current Screen Row Position
RTRIM	Remove Trailing Blanks
SPACE	Generates Blank Spaces
SQRT	Square Root
STR	Numeric to Character Conversion
STUFF	Replace Portion of String
SUBSTR	Substring Selection
TIME	System Time
TRANSFORM	Character/Number in PICTURE Format
TRIM	Remove Trailing Blanks
TYPE	Validates Expression
UPPER	Lower to Upper Case Conversion
VAL	Character to Numeric Conversion
VERSION	dBASE III PLUS Number
YEAR	Year

dBASE III PLUS COMMANDS

? <exp list>
    Displays an expression list on the next line.

?? <exp list>
    Displays an expression list on the current line.

@ <row,col> [SAY <exp> [PICTURE <clause>]] [GET <variable> [PICTURE <clause>] [RANGE <expN>,<expN>]]]/ [CLEAR]
    SAY displays user-formatted data on the CRT or printer. GET displays user-formatted data on the CRT for editing.

@ <row1, col1> [CLEAR] TO <row2, col2> [DOUBLE]
    Draws and erases boxes and lines.

ACCEPT [<prompt>] TO <memvar>
    Allows the entry of a character string into a memory variable.

APPEND [BLANK]
    Adds records to the end of a database file.

APPEND FROM <filename> [FOR <condition>] [TYPE] [<file type>]
    Adds records from other files to database files.

ASSIST
    The ASSISTANT. Menu driven; aids use of dBASE III PLUS commands.

AVERAGE <exp list> [<scope>] [WHILE <condition>] [FOR <condition>] [TO <memvar list>]
    Computes the arithmetic mean of numeric expressions.

BROWSE [FIELDS <field list>] [LOCK<expN>] [FREEZE<field>] [NOFOLLOW] [NOMENU] [WIDTH <expN>] [NOAPPEND]
    Menu assisted; edits using a full-screen window display of up to 17 records per screen.

CALL <module name> [WITH <expC>/ <memvar>]
    Executes a binary file (module) which has been placed in memory with the LOAD command.

CANCEL
    Abandons program execution and returns to dot prompt.

CHANGE [<scope>] [FIELDS <field list>] [WHILE <condition>] [FOR <condition>]
    Edits specified fields and records in a database.

CLEAR
    Erases the screen.

CLEAR ALL
    Closes all database files, index files, format files, and relations. It also releases all memory variables and SELECTs work area one.

CLEAR FIELDS
    Releases all FIELDS in the current work area from the SET FIELDS list.

CLEAR GETS
    Releases current GET variables from the READ access.

CLEAR MEMORY
    Erases current memory variables.

CLEAR TYPEAHEAD
    Empties the type-ahead buffer.

CLOSE ALL/ALTERNATE/DATABASES/ FORMAT/ INDEX/PROCEDURE
    Closes specified types of files.

CONTINUE
    Positions the record number to the next record meeting the condition specified in the LOCATE command.

COPY FILE <filename> TO <filename>
    Duplicates any kind of file.

COPY STRUCTURE TO <filename> [FIELDS <field list>]
    Duplicates the structure of the file in USE to new database file.

COPY TO <filename> [<scope>]
[**WHILE** <condition>] [**FIELDS** <field list>]
[**FOR** <condition>] [**TYPE**] [<file type>]
> Copies the database in USE to another
> database or to a specified file type.

COPY TO <new file> **STRUCTURE
EXTENDED**
> Copies the structure definition of the file
> in USE to a new database where the struc-
> ture of the original becomes the records in
> the new.

COUNT [<scope>] [**WHILE** <condition>]
[**FOR** <condition>] [**TO** <memvar>]
> Tallies the number of records specified by
> the scope and FOR/WHILE conditions.

CREATE <.dbf filename>
> Defines a structure for a new database file
> and adds the file to the directory.

CREATE <new file> **FROM** <structure
extended file>
> Creates a new database file from a file cre-
> ated by COPY STRUCTURE EXTENDED.

CREATE LABEL <.lbl filename>/?
> Menu driven; creates a label form file.

CREATE QUERY <.qry filename>/?
> Menu driven; creates a filter condition and
> stores it in a .qry file.

CREATE REPORT <.frm filename>/?
> Menu driven; creates a report form file.

CREATE SCREEN <.scr filename>/?
> Menu driven; creates a custom screen for-
> mat and stores it in a .scr file. It also gen-
> erates an .fmt file and has options for cre-
> ating and modifying the structure of a
> database file.

CREATE VIEW <.vue filename>/?
> Menu driven; creates a relation between
> files and establishes a working environ-
> ment.

CREATE VIEW <.vue filename> **FROM
ENVIRONMENT**
> Builds a view (.vue) file from the working
> environment.

DELETE [<scope>] [**WHILE** <condition>]
[**FOR** <condition>]
> Marks specified records for deletion.

DIR [<drive:>] [<path>\] [<skeleton>]
> Shows names of files on the specified disk
> drive.

DISPLAY [<scope>] [<exp list>]
[**WHILE** <condition>] [**FOR** <condition>]
[**OFF**] [**TO PRINT**]
> Displays records and fields from the active
> database.

DISPLAY HISTORY [**LAST** <expN>]
[**TO PRINT**]
> Displays the commands stored in the HIS-
> TORY mode in forward chronological
> order. Shows all lines unless LAST <n>
> is specified.

DISPLAY MEMORY [**TO PRINT**]
> Displays current memory variables.

DISPLAY STATUS [**TO PRINT**]
> Displays current information about active
> databases, index files, alternate files, and
> system parameters.

DISPLAY STRUCTURE [**TO PRINT**]
> Displays the structure of the database file
> in USE.

DO <.prg filename>/<procedure name>
[**WITH** <parameter list>]
> Causes a program or procedure to be exe-
> cuted, optionally passing parameters to
> the program.

DO CASE...CASE...[OTHERWISE]...ENDCASE
> Permits the execution of only one of sev-
> eral possible paths (CASEs), optionally
> including one alternative (OTHERWISE).
> DO CASE must terminate with an
> ENDCASE.

DO WHILE... <commands> **...ENDDO**
> Allows a structured loop in a program.
> LOOP skips all commands between it and
> ENDDO. DO WHILE must terminate with
> an ENDDO. EXIT escapes from the loop.

EDIT [<scope>] [**FIELDS** <list>]
[**WHILE** <condition>] [**FOR** <condition>]
> Permits changes to database field
> contents.

EJECT
> Sends a form feed to the printer.

ERASE <filename>/?
  Deletes the specified file from the directory.

EXIT
  Transfers control from within a DO WHILE...ENDDO construct to the statement following the ENDDO.

EXPORT TO <filename> **TYPE PFS**
  Builds PFS files from dBASE III PLUS files.

FIND <character string>/<n>
  Positions the record pointer to the first record with an index key that matches the specified character string. The character string does not have to be delimited.

GO or **GOTO BOTTOM/TOP** or <expN>
  Positions the record pointer directly to a specific record.

HELP [<keyword>]
  Menu-driven; explains dBASE III PLUS commands and functions.

IF...[ELSE]...ENDIF
  Allows conditional execution of commands in a program, optionally with an alternative path (ELSE). Each IF must terminate with an ENDIF.

IMPORT FROM <filename> **TYPE PFS**
  Creates dBASE III PLUS files from PFS files.

INDEX ON <keyexp> **TO** <.ndx filename> **[UNIQUE]**
  Causes the associated database to appear to be sorted according to a specified key.

INPUT [<prompt>] **TO** <memvar>
  Allows the entry of an expression into a memory variable.

INSERT [BLANK] [BEFORE]
  Puts a record into a specified position in a database file.

JOIN WITH <alias> **TO** <new file> **FOR** <condition> **[FIELDS** <field list>]
  Combines specified records and fields from two database files.

LABEL FORM <.lbl filename>/? [<scope>] **[SAMPLE] [WHILE** <condition>] **[FOR** <condition>] **[TO PRINT]** **[TO FILE** <filename>]
  Prints labels using the specified label form file.

LIST [OFF] [<scope>] [<exp list>] **[WHILE** <condition>] **[FOR** <condition>] **[TO PRINT]**
  Lists database records and fields.

LIST HISTORY [LAST <expN>] **[TO PRINT]**
  Displays the commands stored in the HISTORY MODE in forward chronological order. Shows all lines unless LAST <n> is specified.

LIST MEMORY [TO PRINT]
  Shows the name, type, and size of each memory variable.

LIST STATUS [TO PRINT]
  Shows information about the current dBASE III PLUS session.

LIST STRUCTURE [TO PRINT]
  Displays information about the active database.

LOAD <binary filename>[.<extension>]
  Places a binary file in memory where it can be executed with the CALL command.

LOCATE [<scope>] **[WHILE** <condition>] **[FOR** <condition>]
  Positions the record pointer to the first record that satisfies the specified conditions.

LOOP
  Transfers control from within a DO WHILE loop back to the DO WHILE statement.

MODIFY COMMAND <filename>
  Word processor; allows editing of ASCII text files, including program (.prg) files.

MODIFY LABEL <.lbl filename>/?
  Menu driven; creates and edits a label form file.

MODIFY QUERY <.qry filename>/?
  Same as CREATE counterpart, but "modifies" instead of "creates."

MODIFY REPORT <.frm filename>/?
Menu driven, creates and edits a report form file.

MODIFY SCREEN <.scr filename>/?
Same as CREATE counterpart, but "modifies" instead of "creates."

MODIFY STRUCTURE
Alters the structure of the database file in USE.

MODIFY VIEW <.vue filename>/?
Same as CREATE counterpart, but "modifies" instead of "creates."

NOTE/* <undelimited character string>
Inserts nonexecuting comments within a program file.

ON ERROR/ESCAPE/KEY
<dBASE command>
Executes the specified dBASE command when an error occurs, the **Esc** key is pressed, or any key is pressed.

PACK
Permanently removes database records marked for deletion.

PARAMETERS
Specifies memory variables that use information passed by the DO...WITH command.

PRIVATE [ALL[LIKE/EXCEPT <skeleton>]]/
[<memory variable list>]
Hides definitions of the specified memory variables from higher-level programs.

PROCEDURE <procedure name>
Identifies the beginning of each routine in a procedure file.

PUBLIC <memory variable list>
Makes memory variables global.

QUIT
Closes all files and exits dBASE III PLUS.

READ [SAVE]
Permits data entry to a GET field or variable.

RECALL [<scope>] [**WHILE** <condition>]
[**FOR** <condition>]
Reinstates records marked for deletion.

REINDEX
Rebuilds existing active index files.

RELEASE <memvar list>
[**ALL[LIKE/EXCEPT** <skeleton>]]
[**MODULE** <module name>]
Erases current memory variables or a LOADed module from memory.

RENAME <current filename> **TO**
<new filename>
Gives a new name to a file.

REPLACE [<scope>] <field> **WITH** <exp>
[,<field2> **WITH** <exp2>,...]
[**WHILE** <condition>] [**FOR** <condition>]
Changes contents of data fields to specified values.

REPORT FORM <.frm filename>/? [<scope>]
[**WHILE** <condition>] [**FOR** <condition>]
[**PLAIN**] [**HEADING** <expC>] [**NOEJECT**]
[**TO PRINT**] [**TO FILE** <filename>]
[**SUMMARY**]
Displays a tabular report of data.

RESTORE FROM <.mem filename>
[**ADDITIVE**]
Retrieves sets of saved memory variables from disk.

RESUME
Causes a SUSPENDed program to resume execution.

RETRY
Ends a command file and executes the same statement in the calling program.

RETURN [TO MASTER]
Ends a command file or procedure. It is the last executable line.

RUN <command>
Executes a program outside of dBASE III PLUS.

SAVE TO <.mem filename> [**ALL LIKE/
EXCEPT** <skeleton>]
Copies current memory variables to a memory file.

SEEK <expression>
Positions the record pointer to the first record with an index key that matches the specified expression.

SELECT \<work area/alias\>/?
Activates the specified work area.

SET
Menu driven; sets dBASE III PLUS control parameters.

SET ALTERNATE on/OFF
Sends/DOES NOT SEND output to a file.

SET ALTERNATE TO [\<filename\>]
Creates a file for saving output.

SET BELL ON/off
Bell RINGS/does not ring during data entry.

SET CARRY on/OFF
Writes/DOES NOT WRITE contents of the last record into the APPENDed record.

SET CATALOG ON/off
ADDS/does not add files to the open catalog.

SET CATALOG TO [\<.cat filename\>/?]
Creates a new catalog, opens an existing one, and closes an open catalog.

SET CENTURY on/OFF
Shows/DOES NOT SHOW the century in date displays

SET COLOR ON/OFF
Toggles between color and monochrome monitors.

SET COLOR TO [\<standard\>[,\<enhanced\>] [,\<border\>] [, \<background\>]]
Sets screen display attributes

SET CONFIRM on/OFF
Does not skip/SKIPS to the next field in the full-screen mode.

SET CONSOLE ON/off
SENDS/suspends all output to the screen.

SET DATE AMERICAN/ANSI/BRITISH/ ITALIAN/FRENCH/GERMAN
Determines the format for date expressions. DATE is normally set to AMERICAN.

SET DEBUG on/OFF
Sends/DOES NOT SEND the output of SET ECHO to the printer.

SET DECIMALS TO \<expN\>
Sets the minimum number of decimals displayed in the results of certain operations and functions.

SET DEFAULT TO \<drive\>
Specifies the default drive for file search.

SET DELETED on/OFF
Hides/PROCESSES records marked for deletion.

SET DELIMITERS on/OFF
Uses/DOES NOT USE specified entry delimiters.

SET DELIMITERS TO [\<character string\>] [DEFAULT]
Specifies the delimiters for full-screen field and variable displays.

SET DEVICE TO SCREEN/print
Sends the results of the @...SAY command to the SCREEN/printer.

SET DOHISTORY on/OFF
Determines whether or not command files are recorded in HISTORY.

SET ECHO on/OFF
Echoes/DOES NOT ECHO command lines to the screen or printer.

SET ESCAPE ON/off
STOPS/continues command file execution when **Esc** is pressed.

SET EXACT on/OFF
Requires/DOES NOT REQUIRE exact matches in character comparison.

SET FIELDS on/OFF
Respects/IGNORES specified field list.

SET FIELDS TO [\<field list\> ALL]
Determines which fields are accessible.

SET FILTER TO [FILE \<.qry filename\>/?] [\<condition\>]
Causes a database file to appear as if it contains only records that meet the specified condition.

SET FIXED on/OFF
Fixes/DOES NOT FIX the number of decimal places that will be displayed.

SET FORMAT TO [<.fmt filename>/?]
Opens a format file for data entry.

SET FUNCTION <exp> **TO** <exp C>
Sets function key values.

SET HEADING ON/off
Field names DISPLAY/do not display above the fields in LIST or DISPLAY.

SET HELP ON/off
PROMPTS/does not prompt the user for help when an error occurs.

SET HISTORY ON/off
Turns the command history feature on or off.

SET HISTORY TO <expN>
Specifies the number of executed commands to store in HISTORY. The default number of stored commands is 20.

SET INDEX TO [<.ndx file list>/?]
Opens the named INDEX files.

SET INTENSITY ON/off
USES/does not use the enhanced display.

SET MARGIN TO <expN>
Sets the left margin of the printer.

SET MEMOWIDTH TO <expN>
Adjusts the column width of memo field output. The default is 50.

SET MENUS ON/off
DISPLAYS/does not display a menu during full-screen commands.

SET MESSAGE TO <cstring>
Displays a user-defined message on the bottom line of the screen.

SET ORDER TO [<expN>]
Sets up any open index file as the controlling file without closing and reopening the files.

SET PATH TO [<path list>]
Specifies a path list for file search.

SET PRINT on/OFF
Sends/DOES NOT SEND output to the printer.

SET PRINTER TO <DOS device>
Redirects output to the specified device.

SET PROCEDURE TO [<procedure filename>]
Opens the named procedure file.

SET RELATION TO
[<key>/RECNO()/<expN> **INTO** <alias>]
Links two database files according to a key expression.

SET SAFETY ON/off
PROMPTS/does not prompt when a file is about to be overwritten.

SET STATUS ON/off
DISPLAYS/does not display the status line from the dot prompt.

SET STEP on/OFF
Halts/DOES NOT HALT program execution after each command is processed.

SET TALK ON/off
SENDS/does not send the results of command execution to the screen.

SET TITLE ON/off
PROMPTS/does not prompt for a catalog file title when a new file is added to a catalog.

SET TYPEAHEAD TO <expN>
Specifies the size of the type-ahead buffer. The default size is 20.

SET UNIQUE on/OFF
The first/ALL records with identical keys appear in an index file.

SET VIEW TO <.vue filename>/?
Opens a .vue file.

SKIP <expN>
Causes the current record pointer to be advanced or backed up relative to its current position.

SORT TO <new filename> **ON** <field> [/A]
[/C] [/D] [,<field2> [/A] [/C] [/D]...] [<scope>]
[**WHILE** <condition>] [**FOR** <condition>]
Creates an ordered copy of a database, arranged according to one or more of the data fields.

STORE <exp> **TO** <memvar list>
[,<memvar list>]
Stores an expression into one or more memory variables.

SUM [<scope>] [<exp list>] **TO**
[<memvar list>] [**WHILE** <condition>]
[**FOR** <condition>]

> Computes and displays the sum of an expression for database records specified in the scope.

SUSPEND

> Halts execution of the currently executing command file or procedure and presents the dot prompt. Continue execution with RESUME.

TEXT...ENDTEXT

> Displays a block of text data from a command file. TEXT must be terminated with ENDTEXT.

TOTAL ON <filename> **TO** <key> [<scope>]
[**FIELDS** <field list>] [**WHILE** <condition>]
[**FOR** <condition>]

> Creates a summary database of a presorted file, containing numeric TOTALs.

TYPE <filename> [**TO PRINT**]

> Displays the contents of a text file.

UPDATE ON <key field> **FROM** <alias>
REPLACE <field> **WITH** <exp> [,<field2>
WITH <exp2>...] [**RANDOM**]

> Allows batch modifications to a database file.

USE [<.dbf filename>/?] [**INDEX** <.ndx file
list>] [**ALIAS** <alias>]

> Specifies the database file to be used for all operations until another USE command is issued.

WAIT [<prompt>] [**TO** <memvar>]

> Suspends program processing until a key is pressed.

ZAP

> Removes all records from the active database file.

---
dBCODE
---

dBCODE accepts and transforms dBASE III source code to a form that can be read by dBRUN.

Command Line Formats

Help command: *dbc ?*
Interactive command: *dbc*
Process one file command: *dbc<filename>*
Options command: *dbc[– c <filename>*
                        – i <prefix>
                        – o <prefix>
                        – r <filename>
                        – s <prefix>
                        <filename>]

Options

Additional options are shown in brackets ([ ]).

– c <filename>

> Attaches your ASCII copyright statement to the beginning of each encoded file specified in the command.

– i <prefix>

> Generates an information file (.dbg).

– o <prefix>

> Indicates the destination drive or directory for your encoded files.

– r <filename>

> Specifies the response file, which contains a list of your application routines.

– s <prefix>

> Specifies the source drive or directory where your source code resides. The default extension is .src.

<filename>

> Names any files that you want processed before those indicated in the response file.

Requirements

DO WHILE, CASE, and IF/ELSE...ENDIF blocks of greater than 32K are not supported. Instead, use DO file. Do not replace command verbs or SET options with macros.

dBLINKER

dBLINKER links your application routines. It combines a set of files that have been processed by dBCODE into a single, functionally equivalent file. Linking results in increased execution speed and reduction in disk space required for your application.

Command Line Formats

Help screen: *dbl ?*
Interactive command: *dbl*
Options command: *dbl [– c < filename >*
– f < outfile >
– i[prefix]
– p – r < filename >
– s < prefix >
< filename >]

Options

Additional options are indicated in brackets ([ ]).

– c < filename >
Attaches your ASCII copyright header file to the beginning of your linked file.

– f < outfile >
Designates the name of the linked file (.prg).

– i < prefix >
Generates an information file (.map). The prefix is optional.

– p
Reads prefixes in the drive and directory specifications.

– r < filename >
Designates the response file that contains the list of your application routines.

– s < prefix >
Designates the source drive or directory for your encoded files. The default extension is .prg.

< filename >
Designates files you want processed before those indicated in the response file.

Requirements

The root file, or start-up program, must be the first file processed. Procedure files must not be linked; they must remain a distinct file on the disk.

dBRUN

dBRUN interprets and executes files encoded and/or linked by dBCODE and dBLINKER, respectively. It cannot interpret dBASE III source code.

NOTE: dBRUN ignores (without generating error messages) such commands as: ASSIST, HELP, full-screen SET, ECHO, DEBUG, STEP, and SUSPEND.

NETWORKING COMMANDS AND FEATURES

DISPLAY STATUS
Displays file lock and unlock status with periodic pauses.

DISPLAY USERS
Displays information about currently logged on users.

FLOCK()
Locks the current file in USE.

LIST STATUS
Same as DISPLAY STATUS except LIST STATUS does not pause periodically during output.

LOGOUT
Logs the user out of dBASE III PLUS and presents the login screen.

PROTECT
Calls the password protection utility.

RETRY
Returns to the line of the program that called it thereby providing a retry capability for locked files.

RLOCK()/LOCK()
Locks the record in use while sharing the rest of the file with other users.

SET ENCRYPTION ON/OFF
Avoids the deciphering overhead in cases where it is not needed.

SET EXCLUSIVE ON/OFF
Automatically locks files when USEd.

SET PRINTER TO
Directs the printer output to network or local device.

UNLOCK
Releases the user's file or record lock.

Index

A

Absolute cell references, 379–87
Access time, 39
Acoustic couplers, 47–48
Adding records, 510–19
Address, disk drive as, 83
Aligning text, 183–88
All points addressable, 26
Alphabetic keys, 17–18
Alt. *See* Alternate key
Alternate key, 19
American Standard Code for Information
    Interchange. *See* ASCII
APA. *See* All points addressable
Append mode, 492
Applications programs, 3–6
    installation of, 61–63
Arrow, 472–73
ASCII:
    characters and, 11
    codes and, 20, 27
    digital, 19
    text files and, 126–27
Assist mode, 473
Asterisk as wildcard, 93
AUTOEXEC.BAT file:
    database management applications and, 471
    WordPerfect and, 133
Automatically generated lists, 263–69
Automatic carriage return, 131
Automatic loading, batch files, 123
Autorepeat, 17
Auxiliary storage, 35

B

Backspace functions:
    destructive, 18
    WordPerfect and, 159
Backtab key, 19
Backup copies:
    COPY command and, 102
    of files, 42
Batch files, 122–26
Beeping of computer, 342
Binary system, 7–11
Binding widths, 196
Bins, paper, 34
Bit mapping, 26
Bits, 9–10

Blocks of text, 160–68
Boldface text, 189
Boolean fields, 482
Booting:
    cold or warm, 80
    databases, 470
    definition of, 80
    WordPerfect and, 132
Borders, 350–51
Boxes, drawing of, 233
BROWSE command, 498–503, 511–19
Buffers, 13
    WordPerfect and, 162
Built-in functions, 330–33
Bytes, 10–11

C

Calculations:
    converting formulas into, 342
    database management applications and, 532–33
    entering in columns, 256, 257, 263
Cancellation of command in progress, 136
Caps lock, 134, 140
Care of disks, 42–43
Carriage returns, 141
Case, changing of, 154
Cathode ray tubes, 23–24
CD-ROM disks, 41
Cell:
    erasing contents and, 343, 344
    hiding, 416, 417
    numeric value of labels and, 326
Cell references, 379–87
Centering of text, 183–84
Central processing unit, 11–12
Centronics interfaces, 14
CHANGE command, 511–19
Character, 10–11
    generator, 27
    images, 25–28
    optical recognition of, 19
    printers and, 28–29
    special, 238–41
Charts, 299
Checking of disk, 114
Chips, 68–69
CHKDSK command, 114–16
Cigarette smoke, 15
Circuit, integrated, 9
Circular references, 393, 394, 397

CLEAR ALL command, 475
Clearing, spreadsheet applications and, 313
Clipboard. *See* Buffers
Closed architecture, 15
Club, user, 67
Clusters, 114
Code:
    ASCII. *See* ASCII
    digital, 9
    setup, 351–52
Color displays, 24–25
Columns:
    branching macro, 439
    inserting and deleting, 344–45, 348
    newspaper-style, 241–45
    overlapping, 263
    parallel-style, 245–49
    resetting, 358
    sorting by keys, 275
    WordPerfect and, 161
Combining:
    boldface and underlining, 189
    of files 418–21
Command:
    append mode, 492
    BROWSE, 498–503, 511–19
    canceling of, 311
    CHANGE, 511–19
    CHKDSK, 114–16
    CLEAR ALL, 475
    combining of, 189
    CREATE, 482–85
    DEL, 111–13
    DISKCOMP, 107–8
    DISPLAY, 498–503
    EDIT, 511–19
    editing, 484
    entering of, 473
    ERASE, 111–13
    erase range, 367
    execution of, 57–61
        database management applications and, 472
        spreadsheet applications and, 310
    external operating system, 75–77
    formatting, 97–101
    function key. *See* Function keys
    GOTO, 498–503
    HELP, 474–79
    internal operating system. *See* Disk operating
        system
    LIST, 498–503
    menu, 310
    modify report, 535
    most frequently used, 472, 473
    operator input with macro, 439
    PACK, 512

printer, 350
processor and, 72
query, 467
QUIT, 475
range, 356
RECALL, 512
RENAME, 108–10
REPLACE, 511–19
SKIP, 498–503
TYPE, 126–27
typing, 58–60
    database management applications and, 472
    worksheet global, 367
Communications, 49
Comparing of disks, 107–8
Compatibility, 68
Compressed type, 351–52
Computers:
    beeping of, 342
    care of, 15
    customized, 14–15
    displays of, 26
    intelligent, 45
    portable, 24
Concordance, 269
Constants and variables, 329
Control key, 19
Control panel, 308
Copying:
    of data, 369–78
    DISKCOPY command and, 105
    ethics and, 66
    files and, 102
    from one model to another, 386
    line drawings and, 237
    spreadsheet applications and, 368–69
    wildcards and, 102
    WordPerfect and, 237
CP/M operating system, 73
CPU. *See* Central processing unit
CREATE command, 482–85
Criterion formulas, 450–52
CRT. *See* Cathode ray tubes
Ctrl. *See* Control key
Cursor:
    definition of, 18
    movement of:
        database management applications and, 484
        spreadsheet applications and, 309–10
    WordPerfect and, 150–51
Customized computer, 14–15

D

Data. *See also* Database management applications
    copying and, 369–78

disks for. *See* Disk
files and, 54–57
management of, 449–52
models and, 299
processing of, 5
sorting of, 275–82
tables for, 403–11
transfer rate of, 40
Database management applications, 463–527
  calculations and, 532–33
  criterion formulas in, 451–52
  defining file in, 480–92
  joining files in, 520–23
  records in:
    adding, updating, and deleting of, 451, 510–19
    criteria for, 504–10
    display of, 498–503
    entry of, 492–97
    indexing of, 526–31
    printing of, 534–44
    sorting of, 523–25
  restructuring of, 541–43
  spreadsheet applications and, 449–52
  writing programs for, 543–47
Data fill command, 321
Date and time functions, 411–15
dBASE, 471
dBASE III Plus field, 482–83
Decimal tabs, 204
Default drives, 83–85
Default settings, 132, 291–94
DEL command, 111–13
Deletion:
  of files, 111–13
  of records, 510–19
  of text, 153–54
Desktop computer. *See* Microcomputers
Desktop publishing:
  graphics and, 19
  programs for, 53
Destructive backspace, 18
Dictionaries, 176–77
Digital processing, 7–11
Digitizers, 20
DIR command. *See* Directory
Directional arrow keys, 18, 472–73
Directory:
  file, 86
  operating systems and, 98, 116–22
  WordPerfect and, 160
Disk. *See also* Disk operating system
  accidental erasure of, 79
  backup copy of, 78
  care for, 42–43
  CD-ROM, 41

checking, 114
comparing, 107
density of, 39
double-sided, 38–39
duplicating, 104–5
floppy, 35–39
formatting of, 97–99
full error message and, 148
high-density, 98
labeling of, 78
listing files on, 86–92
low-density, 98
optical, 41
self-booting, 78
  AUTOEXEC.BAT file and, 471
  WordPerfect and, 133
single-sided, 38–39
source, 77
space remaining on, 114–15
storage on, 114
system, 100
target, 77
unprotected, 66
worm, 42
write-protect notch and, 78–79
DISKCOMP command, 107–8
DISKCOPY command, 105
Disk drives, 35–39
  care of, 43
  hard, 12–13, 39, 42–43
Disk operating system, 71–127
  ASCII text files and, 126–27
  batch files and, 123–26
  checking disks and, 114–16
  comparing disks and, 107–8
  copying files and, 102–4
  default drives and, 83–85
  directories and, 116–22
  duplicating disks and, 104–5
  erasing files and, 110–13
  formatting disks and, 97–101
  listing files and, 86–92
  loading of, 80–83
  renaming files and, 108–10
  wildcards and, 93–97
DISPLAY command, 498–503
Displaying of records, 498–503
Display monitor, 23
  WordPerfect and, 291
Distribution devices, 44–50
  definition of, 3
Document:
  entering, saving, and printing of, 140–48
  retrieving and editing of, 149–60
Documentation, 67
Document-oriented programs, 141

Document screen, 133–34
Document view, 283
DOS. *See* Disk operating system
Downloading from mainframe, 298–99
Drawing of line, 233, 238
Drivers, 61–62
Drives:
   default, 83
   hard disk, 39
   WordPerfect and, 142
Dumb terminals, 45
Duplicating disks, 104–5

E

EDIT command, 511–19
Editing, 149–60
   database management applications and, 543
   models and, 343–48
   spreadsheet applications and, 343
   WordPerfect and, 149–54, 162, 168
   word processing and, 131
Electric current, 15
Electron beam, 21
Emphasizing text, 188–95
EMS 3.2. *See* Expanded Memory Specification
         Version 3.2
Emulation, 62–63
Entering, 140–48
   of document, 131, 140–43
   of records, 492
Enter key, 18
Envelope printing, 228–32
Environments, operating, 74–75
ERASE command, 111–13
Erasing:
   accidental, 111
      FORMAT command and, 98
      retrieval after, 111
   cell contents and, 344
   files and, 110–13
   range, 367
Ergonomics, 65
Error messages, 312
Esc. *See* Escape
Escape, 18
   WordPerfect and, 136
Expanded Memory Specification Version 3.2, 68
Expansion boards, 14–15
   color displays and, 25
External commands, 75–77
External storage devices, 35–43
   definition of, 3
Extraction of files, 418–21
Eye strain, 64–66

F

Facsimile, 49–50
F5 functions, 160
Fields, 482–83
   redefining of, 541
Files:
   ASCII. *See* ASCII
   backup copies of, 42
   batch, 122–26
   combining and extracting of, 418–21
   copying of, 102–4
   database:
      defining of, 480–92
      joining of, 520–23
   directory of, 86
   erasing of, 98, 110–13
   extracting of, 418–19
   listing of, 86–92
   lost, 114
   naming of, 142
   program, 54
   protection of, 42
   renaming of, 108–10
   saving of, 55–56, 319–26
   scattered, 114
   security of, 42
   sequential, 526
   types of, 56–57
   updating of, 468
Fill-in forms, 60–61
Financial analysis, 298
Fixed disks, 112–13, 39, 42
Fixed titles, 388–91
Flat file database programs, 466
Flat panel displays, 23–24
Floppy disks, 35–39
   care of, 43
Font, 33
Footers, 350–51
   WordPerfect and, 211–17
Footnotes, 270–74
Form, fill-in, 60–61
Format:
   document and, 131–32
   saving of, 126
   spreadsheet applications and, 360
   types of, 126
   WordPerfect and, 194–95
Formatting of disk, 97–101
Form letters, 218–27
Formulas:
   spreadsheet applications and, 303–2, 327–43
   WordPerfect and, 255–57, 263
Forward references, 393, 394, 397

Function, 327–43
    built-in, 330–33
    entering of, 333–41
    structure of, 302, 330
Function keys, 19, 58–60
    spreadsheet applications and, 311
    WordPerfect and, 134–35, 135

G

GB. *See* Gigabyte
Gigabyte, 11
GOTO command, 498–503
Goto key, 309
Graphics, 25–27
    input devices and, 19
    pad and, 20
    processing and, 6
    programs for, 51–52
    scanners and, 20
Graphs, 422–36
    development of data for, 299
Grid, 20, 25

H

Hard disk, 12–13, 39, 40
Hard hyphen, 148
Hardware, 2
Headers and footers, 211–17
    spreadsheet applications and, 350
Heat sensitive paper, 30
HELP commands:
    database management applications and, 474–79
    spreadsheet applications and, 313
Hidden characters/codes, 151–53
Hidden column, 354
Hiding cells or windows, 416, 417
Humidifier, 15
Hyphenation, 183–88
    hard/soft, 148

I

IBM Operating System, 2, 73. *See also* Disk
        operating system
Image digitizers, 20
Indenting paragraphs, 203–11
Index:
    database management applications and, 526–31
        WordPerfect and, 263–64,
Information processing, 3–6
Input devices, 17–22
    definition of, 3
Input/output manager, 72
Input range, 450

Insert mode, 151
Integrated circuit, 9
Integrated programs, 52–53
Intelligent computers, 45
Internal commands, 75
I/O manager. *See* Input/output manager

J

Joining:
    of database files, 520–23
    of text, 154
Justified text, 183, 188

K

KB. *See* Kilobytes
Keyboard, 17–19
    WordPerfect template and, 134–35
Keypad, numeric, 18
Keys, special, 311–12. *See also specific keys*
Kilobytes, 11

L

Labels:
    definition of, 299
    disk and, 78
    merge printing of, 228–32
    prefix characters and, 320
    spreadsheet applications and, 300, 319–26,
        357, 358, 359
Layout, page, 195–202
Learning disk for WordPerfect, 135
Letter-quality printers, 28–33
Letters, form, 218–27
Licensing, 66–67
Light, disk drive, 38
Light pens, 21
Line blocks, 161
Line drawing, 233, 237
Line patterns, 326
Line spacing, 197
Lines per inch, 196–97
Linking models, 419
List, generation of, 263–69
LIST command, 498–503
Listing files on disk, 86–92. *See also* Directory
Loading program, 100
    batch files and, 123
    DOS and, 80–83
    WordPerfect and, 132–39
Logical storage, 466–67
Lookup tables, 398–403
LPT1, 126

M

Macro:
  spreadsheet applications and, 437–44
  WordPerfect and, 249–53
Magnetic tape, 40
Main memory, 12
Margins:
  spreadsheet applications and, 350, 351
  WordPerfect and, 196
Marking/unmarking files, 148
Mathematics:
  spreadsheets and, 298
  WordPerfect and, 254–63
MB. *See* Megabytes
Megabytes, 11
Memory:
  clearing data from, 80
  definition of, 11, 12
  DOS and, 73
  graphics displays and, 26
  off switch and, 35
Menus, 58–60
  spreadsheet applications and, 310, 444–49
  WordPerfect and, 134–35
Merge printing:
  form letters and, 218–27
  labels and envelopes and, 228–32
Microcomputers, 3–70
  applications software for, 51–63
  distribution devices and, 44–51
  external storage devices and, 35–44
  information processing and applications
      programs and, 3–6
  input devices and, 17–22
  issues concerning, 65–70
  output devices and, 23–34
Microjustification, 183
Mixed references, 380–81
Mode indicators, 312
Model:
  database, 467
  spreadsheet applications and, 304
    changing appearance of, 355–67
    definition of, 299
    editing and reviewing of, 343–48
    linking of, 419
    printing of, 349–55
    saving of, 304
Modems, 13–14, 46–49
Monochrome screens, 24–25
Mouse, 21
MS–DOS. *See* Disk operating system
Multipage models, 352
Multiple-field indexes, 527
Multiuser systems, 45–46

N

N/A. 75
Name of file, 142
Network systems, 45–46
Newspaper-style columns, 241–45
Noise levels of printers, 34
Notch, write-protect, 37, 78–79
Numbering:
  of pages, 211–17
  of paragraphs, 284, 287
Numbers:
  processing of, 5
  spreadsheet applications and
      entering of, 301, 320–21
      formatting of, 360
  WordPerfect and, 140, 254–56, 257, 263
Numeric keypad, 18
  WordPerfect and, 150
Num lock key, 134

O

OCR. *See* Optical character recognition
On-line help, 57–58
On-line/off-line printers, 32
Open architecture, 15
Operating environments, 74–75
Operating systems. *See* Disk operating system
Operators:
  logical, 505
  relational, 504
  spreadsheet applications and, 327–29, 333
  WordPerfect and, 255–63
Optical character recognition, 19
Optical disks, 41
Order of precedence:
  spreadsheet applications and, 328
  WordPerfect and, 275–77
Outliners, 283–87
Output devices, 23–34
  definition of, 3
Output range, 450
Overriding of default settings, 291
Overtyping text, 151

P

PACK command, 512
Page:
  breaks and, 212
  layout changes and, 195–97
  length of:
      spreadsheet applications and, 352
      WordPerfect and, 197
  numbering of, 212

Page-oriented programs, 142
Paper, 30, 31, 33–34
Paragraph:
  definition of, 141
  numbering of, 284, 287
Parallel ports, 14
Passwords, 416, 417
Paths, 117–19
PC–DOS, 68. *See also* Disk operating system
Peripherals:
  connecting of, 15
  definition of, 2
Personal computer. *See* Microcomputers
Pin feed, 33
Piracy, 66
Pixels, 20, 22, 25
Portable computers, 24
Ports, 13–15
Power:
  failures of, 142
  portable computers and, 24
  processing and, 11
Primary memory, 12
PRINT command, 126–27. *See also* Printing
Printer, 28–34
  driver and, 62–63
  ports, 126
  spreadsheet and, 349, 350, 353
Printing:
  ASCII text files and, 126–27
  canceling of, 32
  documents and, 132, 140–48
  file names on screen and, 160
  form letters and, 218–27
  graphs and, 422–36
  labels and envelopes and, 228–32
  models and, 304, 349–55
  reports and, 534–40
Program:
  cost of, 68
  database management, 464–69
  definition of, 2
  desktop publishing, 53
  files for, 54
  graphics, 51–52
  installation of, 61–63
  integrated, 52–53
  licensing of, 66–67
  loading of, 100, 132–39
    spreadsheet applications and, 300
  quitting of, 313
  registration of, 67–68
  running of, 543
  self-booting, 133
  training and, 67
  updates of, 67–68

  utility, 53
  word processing. *See* Word processing
  writing of, 543–47
Prompts, 60–61
  answering of, 311
  system, 75, 80
  WordPerfect and, 134–36
Proofreading, 131
Protection:
  of cell, 415–16, 417
  of copy, 66
  of files, 42
  surge, 15

Q

Query commands, 467
Question mark as wildcard, 93
Quick reference card, 134–35
QUIT command, 475
Quitting of program:
  database management applications and, 475
  word processing and, 132, 136–37
  spreadsheet applications and, 305, 313
QWERTY keyboard, 17

R

RAM. *See* Random-access memory
Random-access memory, 12
Ranges, 355–56
Read-only memory, 12
Recalculation methods, 393–98
RECALL command, 512
Records:
  adding, updating, and deleting of, 492, 510–19
  definition of:
    database management applications and, 480
    WordPerfect and, 220–21
  displaying of:
    criteria for, 504–10
    database management and, 498–503
  entering of, 492–97
  management programs for, 466
  sorting of, 523–25
Rectangular blocks, 162
Redefining fields, 541
References:
  cell, 379–87
  circular, 393, 394, 397
Relative cell references, 379–87
RENAME command, 108–10
Renaming:
  of documents, 143
  of files, 108–10
Replace, search and, 168–76, 237

REPLACE command, 511–19
Reports, 534–40
Resaving documents, 143
Restructuring of database, 541–43
Retrieval:
    of documents, 149–60
    of files, 55–56
        accidental erasure and, 111
    of models, 343–48
Return key, 18
Ribbons, printer, 33
ROM. *See* Read-only memory
Rows and columns, 344–45, 348
RS-232-C ports. *See* Serial ports
Ruler, 204

S

Saving:
    files and, 319–26
    models and, 304
    WordPerfect and, 132, 140–48
Scanners, 19
Schema, 467
Screen:
    clearing of, 313
    color, 24–25
    database management applications and, 471–72
    display, 23–24
        spreadsheet applications and, 306–8
    monochrome, 24–25
Scrolling:
    off screen, 86
    spreadsheet applications and, 310
    WordPerfect and, 141, 150
Scroll lock, 310
Search and replace, 168–76
    graphics characters and, 237
Secondary storage, 35
Security:
    of files, 42
    spreadsheet applications and, 415–18
Self-booting disk, 78
    AUTOEXEC.BAT file and, 471
    WordPerfect and, 133
Sequential files, 526
Serial ports, 13–14
Setting, default, 291–96
Setup codes, 351–52
Site-licensing, 67
SKIP command, 498–503
Smoke, 15
Soft/hard hyphens and spaces, 148
Software:
    applications, 51–63
    definition of, 2

support for, 67
Sorting:
    data and, 275–82
    database files and, 523–25
    indexing and, 526–27
Soundproof enclosures for printers, 34
Source disks, 77
Spacebar, 18
    WordPerfect and, 160
Spaces, 140
    hard/soft, 148
Special characters, 238–41
Special keys, 311–12
Spell checker, 176–82
Spreadsheet applications, 297–462
    cell references and, 379–87
    combining and extracting files and, 418–21
    copying and moving data and, 369–78
    data management and, 449–62
    data tables and, 403–11
    date and time functions and, 411–15
    formulas and functions and, 327–43
    graphs and, 422–36
    labels and numbers and, 319–26
    lookup tables and, 398–403
    macros and, 437–44
    menus and, 444–49
    models and:
        changing appearance of, 355–67
        printing of, 349–55
        retrieving and editing of, 343–48
    protection and security in, 415–18
    recalculation methods and, 393–98
    windows and fixed titles in, 387–92
Statistical functions, 532
Status line, 134
Stop, tab, 203–11
Storage:
    buffer as, 13
    capacity, 11
    external, 35–44
    logical, 466–67
Strikeout, 189
Strings, 169
Subdirectories, 117
Subscripts and superscripts, 288–90
Support, software, 67
Surge protector, 15
Switches, printer, 34
System, definition of, 2

T

Table:
    of contents, 263–64, 269
    data, 403–11

lookup, 398–403
Tab stops, 203–11
Tape, write-protect, 78
Target disks, 77
Telecommunication, 46–47
Template, 299
Terabyte, 11
Terminals, dumb, 45
Text:
    aligning and hyphenating of, 183–88
    area, 134
    blocks of, 160–68
    emphasizing of, 188–95
    overtyping of, 151
Thesaurus, 176–82
Thimbles, 28
Time:
    access, 39
    spreadsheet applications and, 411–15
Title, fixed, 287–92
Toggle switch, 140
Toner, printer, 33
Tractor feed, 33
Training, 67
Transfer rate of data, 40
Transistor, 9
Tutorials, 67
Type, compressed, 351–52
TYPE command, 58–60, 126–27
Type-thru mode, 143
Typographical errors, 141

U

Underlined text, 189
Updates:
    program, 67–68
    of records, 511
User memory, 12
Utility programs, 53
    external and internal commands and, 75

V

Values:
    calculated, 342
    column width and, 357
    definition of, 299
    formatting, 359–60

Variables, 329
Vertical spacing calculations, 202
Virtual memory, 12–13
Voice input devices, 21–22
Volatile memory, 12

W

What-if analyses, 303, 404
Wildcards:
    COPY command and, 102
    definition of, 93
    erasing files with, 111
    WordPerfect and, 174
Winchester disk drives. *See* Hard disk
Windows, 387–88
    hiding, 416, 417
WordPerfect, 129–295. *See also* Word processing
Word processing, 129–295
    aligning and hyphenation and, 183–88
    automatic lists and, 263–69
    blocks of text and, 160–68
    columns and, 241–49
    default settings and, 291–96
    drawing lines and, 233–38
    emphasizing text and, 188–95
    entering, saving, and printing documents and, 140–48
    footnotes and, 270–74
    loading program and, 132–39
    macros and, 249–53
    math functions and, 254–63
    merge printing and, 218–32
    outline and, 283–87
    pages and, 211–17
        layout and, 195–202
    retrieving and editing documents and, 149–60
    search and replace and, 168–76
    sorting data and, 275–82
    special characters and, 238–41
    spell checker and, 176–82
    subscripts and superscripts and, 288–90
    tab stops and, 203–11
Word wrap, 141
Working area, 306–8
Workstation, 45
Worm disks, 42
Wrapping, automatic, 131
Write-protect notch, 37, 78–79
Writing program, 543–47